CADOGANguides

PORTUGAL

'Portugal's beautiful landscapes range from the simplicity of the Alentejo's vast arid space to the intricacy of the Minho's lush smallholdings.'

David J.J. Evans

Dedication

For Susan and in memory of John.

About the Guide

The **full-colour introduction** gives the author's overview of the region, together with suggested **itineraries** and a regional **'where to go' map** and **feature** to help you plan your trip.

Illuminating and entertaining **cultural chapters** on local history, art, architecture, food, wine, culture and everyday life give you a rich flavour of the country.

Planning Your Trip starts with the basics of when to go, getting there and getting around, coupled with other useful information, including a section for disabled travellers. The **Practical A–Z** deals with all the **essential information** and **contact details** that you may need while you are away.

The **regional chapters** are arranged in a loose touring order, with plenty of public transport and driving information. The author's top **'Don't Miss'** ✪ sights are highlighted at the start of each chapter.

A **language and pronunciation guide**, a **bibliography** and a comprehensive **index** can be found at the end of the book.

Although everything we list in this guide is **personally recommended**, our authors inevitably have their own favourite places to eat and stay. Whenever you see this **Author's Choice** ★ icon beside a listing, you will know that it is a little bit out of the ordinary.

Hotel Price Guide (*see also* p.67)

Luxury	€€€€€	€230 and over
Very expensive	€€€€	€150–230
Expensive	€€€	€100–150
Moderate	€€	€60–100
Inexpensive	€	under €60

Restaurant Price Guide (*see also* p.70)

Very expensive	€€€€	€45 and above
Expensive	€€€	€30–45
Moderate	€€	€20–30
Inexpensive	€	under €20

01 INTRODUCING PORTUGAL

Portugal is enchanting, if you give it the chance. Take your time, and let the land and its people work on you. It is a nation of few superlatives but many charms.

There are wonderful opportunities – even in the Algarve – for the curious traveller to get close to the country and its gentle attractions, and one of the country's main attractions is the Portuguese people. Do get into the villages: life is easiest to observe in tiny, thrilling, walled settlements, such as Monsaraz, Marvão, Monsanto and Óbidos. You may be stared at, but a smile is all it takes to break the ice – after which you might be invited home, to a kitchen with an open fire, for a cup of wine.

Portugal's astonishingly beautiful landscapes range from the simplicity of the Alentejo's vast arid space and strong, pure colours, to the intricacy of the Minho's lush, drowsy smallholdings. The provinces state their identities on every street corner and in every field: slim, delicate chimneys or no chimneys at all; dogs for herding goats, or wearing nail-studded collars to protect them from wolves; the smell of pine, or eucalyptus, or the sea. Brazen castles and uplifting cathedrals, a clutch of very good paintings, *azulejos* (tiles) everywhere, and a shower of gilt woodwork attest to Portugal's former wealth. But the Portuguese also have a love for the stuff of rural daily life: stirrups, firedogs and bellows take their place in most museums.

Portugal remains relatively inexpensive compared with the rest of Europe. If you want sophisticated pleasures, expect to pay a fair price for them, but some of the country's greatest pleasures aren't

Top: Albufeira coastline, The Algarve
Above: Faro Old Town, The Algarve

at all sophisticated, and you'll find some great bargains. Try at some point to stay in accommodation offered under the *Turismo de Habitação* scheme; staying in private homes offers a highly personal view of rural Portugal.

Above: Beach houses, Aveiro, The Beiras
Right: Mafra, Estremadura

Where to Go

The purpose of this guide is to ensure you have the best possible holiday in Portugal. It aims to enable you to find what you're looking for, and more besides: places to visit that you'll enthuse about to friends; accommodation you'll never want to leave; meals that will linger in your mind for years to come. Reviews are sharp and discerning, with a keen eye for value for money.

The following chapters offer practical details of getting to and around Portugal and all the useful things you need to know when you're there.

As for the provinces, the Minho is green and relatively densely populated, with grape vines climbing everything in sight. It is the home of the *Turismo de Habitação* scheme, whereby, guests stay for the most part, in grand country houses. The Minho's neighbour, Trás-os-Montes, has until recently been impossibly remote, with villagers living in medieval conditions. Motorways

*Top and above: Typical
Portuguese ceramic tiles*

and EU money have changed that, but when you're off the beaten track it still feels wild.

The upper reaches of the River Douro are dedicated to the production of port wine; near the mouth of the river, Porto is the country's second city, granitic, sloping and lively.

Getting off the beaten track isn't hard in Portugal, but eastern Beira Baixa is undeservedly neglected by most visitors. They tend to stick to coastal Beira Litoral or the mountainous Serra da Estrela in Beira Alta. Estremadura and the Ribatejo contain some very fine ecclesiastical buildings and come under the orbit of Lisbon, Portugal's delightful, beguiling capital, which can safely be recommended to anyone who enjoys urban life, and may well convert some who don't.

The Alentejo covers a great swathe of the country to the east and south of Lisbon, most of it vast flat plains of wheat with dazzling whitewashed settlements.

In places the sometimes wild Atlantic coast is quite deserted. The country's sand-fringed southernmost strip, the Algarve, attracts the most tourists; the large resorts still retain plenty of character, and the province's eastern and western portions remain fairly undeveloped.

Portugal is a country to savour, and it would be a pity to rush it. There's quite enough in any one or two provinces to satisfy a single visit to Portugal. If you are using public transport, travelling north or south on the west coast is fairly straightforward by either train or bus; the problems start when you head inland, and particularly if you want to travel up or down the eastern side of the country. The rail network here is at its least efficient and more often than not you'll have to rely on buses to get from A to B. If you are travelling on one of the various rail passes (p. 63), it can sometimes work out quicker to return to the west, make your way up or down the coast, and then cut across to the east again. Note that in the north there are no west–east lines at all above Porto, from where there is only one line, across to Bragança in the northeast of Portugal.

In theory, Portugal lends itself to exploration by train: some of the routes are among the most spectacular in Europe, and travelling at a sedate pace from town to town highlights the diversity of the Portuguese people and landscape. In practice, however, this demands patience and a lot of time and, occasionally, a skin thick enough to cope with inquisitive stares from the locals. Transport information for each town is included in the text.

Chapter Divisions

N

50 km
20 miles

SPAIN

08
THE MINHO
p.75
Braga

Bragança

09
TRÁS-OS-MONTES
AND THE
ALTO DOURO
p.123

Miranda
do Douro

Porto

10
PORTO
AND THE
DOURO LITORAL
p.171

DOURO
LITORAL

BEIRA ALTA

11
THE BEIRAS
p.203

Coimbra

ATLANTIC

OCEAN

BEIRA LITORAL

BEIRA BAIXA

12
ESTREMADURA
AND THE
RIBATEJO
p.267

SPAIN

ALTO ALENTEJO

13
LISBON
p.347

Évora

14
THE ALENTEJO
p.403

BAIXO ALENTEJO

15
THE ALGARVE
p.459
Faro

GOLFO DE CADIZ

Below: Port wine lodge, Vila Nova de Gaia
Right: Alfama district, Lisbon
Far right: Roman temple, Évora,
Below right: Castle, Monsaraz

Top Ten Places to Visit

Towns and cities

01 Lisbon – wander the higgledy-piggedly streets of The Alfama, have a leisurely meal in the Bairro Alto and view the world-class collection at the Gulbenkian Museum, *see* chapter 13.

02 Enjoy the sights of Portugal's second city – Porto. Explore its past and its present, and no visit would be complete without a trip to the port wine lodges of Vila Nova de Gaia, p.172.

03 Walk the cobbled streets of Évora, you will see arches, arcades, whitewashed palacios and Renaissance fountains, p.428.

04 Admire the ancient university city of Coimbra, p.241.

05 Tavira – the most beautiful town on the Algarve, with wonderful beaches nearby, p.474.

Walled villages

06 Explore the tiny, peaceful village of Sortelha, p.226.

07 Visit Monsanto, the most dramatic and astonishing of Portugal's hill settlements, p.238.

08 Wander the medieval streets of Monsaraz and enjoy expansive views of the Alentejo plains, p.440.

Other places

09 Take a walk in the magical Forest of Buçaco. You will come across pools and fountains, crosses and grottoes and tiny chapels hidden among the trees, p.257.

10 Marvel at the sublime Gothic interior of Batalha Abbey, p.275.

Places to Stay Near the Beach

If the sight of the sea sets your heart racing, Portugal offers a number of cultured towns and cities and undeveloped resorts with good beaches nearby.

Cultured towns and cities

• **Viana do Castelo** – an elegant fishing port at the wide mouth of the River Lima, p.99.

• **Aveiro** – less than half an hour away from good sand beaches, p.259.

• **Lisbon** – escape the hustle and bustle and explore the nearby beaches, located along the railway line linking Lisbon to Cascais, p.288

• **Lagos** – the lively harbour town overlooks the Baia de Lagos, p.508.

• **Faro** – a gentle town with interesting monuments and designer shops, just 9km from the beach, p.467.

Top: Aveiro
Above: Cliffs and beach near Lagos
Top right: Cabanas, just east of Tavira
Below right: Praça do Comércio, Baixa, Lisbon

Undeveloped resorts

- **Vila Nova de Milfontes** – this undeveloped and pretty port town is the most popular resort in the Alentejo, p.456.
- **Salema** – an old fishing village in a sheltered bay, with a happy mix of tourists and locals, p.513.
- **Tavira** – a centre for local artists and writers, with calm, gentle, endless sandy beaches nearby that are perfect for families, p.474.
- **Vila do Bispo** – serene little town with a sunny central square, the nearest beach is Praia do Castelejo, p.521.

Itinerary 1: The Classic Triangle Lisbon – Évora – Coimbra

This tour is known as the 'Classic Triangle', and with good reason. Take seven–nine days to complete this trip – Portugal's charm repays slow travel.

Days 1–3 Start with three days in **Lisbon**, with trips out to the **Serra da Arrábida**, or to **Sintra** and **Queluz**.

Days 4–6 You can easily see all of **Évora**'s high culture in a day, but meandering takes longer. Think about a trip to **Monsaraz**, too.

Days 7–9 Depart early for **Coimbra**, taking in **Estremoz**, **Marvão** or **Castelo de Vide** on the way. From Coimbra, travel back to Lisbon via **Batalha**, **Alcobaça** and **Óbidos**.

For a longer trip of 10–14 days, spend a couple of days off the beaten track in the **Beira Baixa** between Évora and Coimbra (you will need a car). If you can cope with the distance and have money for the *pousada*, Belmonte would be a great base.

Left: Palácio Nacional, Sintra
Below left: Palácio Nacional, Queluz
Right: Church of Bom Jesus
Below: Porto and the River Douro at dusk

Itinerary 2: Northern Portugal

For a meander through the rustic north of the country, follow as big a loop from Porto as you've got time for.

Days 1–4 Arrive in **Porto**, for some urban delights in the granite-trimmed city on the River Douro. Then spend a couple of days in a bucolic haze around **Ponte de Lima** or **Ponte da Barca**.

Days 4–5 Travel southeast, pausing in **Braga**, then on to **Pinhão**, which is at an elbow of the River Douro at the apex of port-wine country.

Days 6–7 From there, visit the **Parque Arqueológico do Vale Côa** for a prehistoric thrill.

If you want to keep moving and extend your trip, plan a tour of the low mountains that form the **Serra da Estrela** (you will need a car) before returning to Porto.

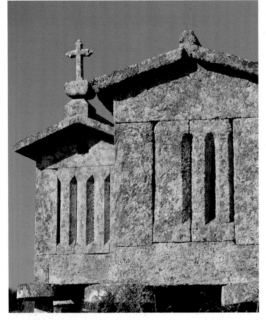

Above: Espigueiros,
Lindoso, The Minho

Curiosities

Portugal is delightfully quirky if you look in the right places. Keep an eye out for whimsical door knockers and weather vanes, and a smattering of thrilling oddities.

• Staircase at Bom Jesus do Monte – splendid Baroque staircase that climbs the thickly wooded hillslope, p.92.

• Celtiberian hill settlement at Citânia de Briteiros – 10km south of Braga, this thrilling site is thought to have been the last stronghold against the Romans, *c.* 6–19 BC, p.93.

• *Espigueiros* at Soajo – a fantastic group of *espigueiros* huddle on a granite threshing terrace, above the valley, just northwest of the town, p. 120.

• Prehistoric engravings in the Côa Valley – home to Europe's largest and most impressive concentration of prehistoric rock art, it's quite magical, p.154.

• *Menino Jesus da Cartolinha* in the cathedral at Miranda do Douro – this puppet-like figure is kept in a glass box to the right of the centre nave in the south transept, p.150.

• Lagoon at Aveiro – if you dislike swimming in the waves of the Atlantic, the blue lagoon offers a calm alternative, p.259.

• Caves at Mira d'Aire – a series of caves bristling with stalactites, p.287.

• Berlenga Islands – a diminutive archipelago of which Berlenga Grande is the largest and only accessible island, p.295.

• Westernmost point in Europe at Cabo da Roca – join the 70,000 other tourists who visit this rugged and spectacular place every year, p.312.

• Dinosaur footprints at Cabo Espichel – take a closer look at the dinosaur footprints and tailmarks at the end of Lagosteiros beach, below the church, p.333.

• Storks at Alcácer do Sal – majestic storks build basket nests on church roofs, particularly up by the Moorish castle, p.452.

Above: Alcobaça Abbey, Estramadura

Churches, Monasteries and Convents

Portugal's finest architecture is ecclesiastical, and its religious buildings remain repositories for dazzling gilded woodwork, serene sculpture and uproarious *azulejos*. The following towns and cities have many fine examples.

- The Minho: Braga, p.85; Tibães, p.94; Bravães, p.112.
- Douro Litoral: Porto, p.172.
- Beira Litoral: Coimbra, p.241; Aveiro, p.259.
- Estremadura: Batalha, p.273; Alcobaça, p.279; Mafra, p.298.
- Ribatejo: Tomar, p.340.
- Lisbon and Belém, *see* chapter 13.
- Alto Alentejo: Viana do Alentejo, p.439.
- Baixo Alentejo: Mértola, p.450.

Above: The hilltop town of Sintra is surrounded by woodland

Outstanding Natural Beauty

When the sun is shining and the wild flowers are in bloom, there's nowhere better in the world than some of Portugal's little-visited landscapes.

- The Minho: around Ponte da Barca, p.113; parts of Peneda-Gerês National Park, p.117.
- Trás-os-Montes: Mirandela to Tua train ride, p.127 (*also* p.63).
- Minho/Trás-os-Montes: road from Guimarães to Vila Pouca de Aguiar, p.79.
- Alto Douro: Régua to Vila Real train ride, p.127 (*also* p.63).
- Beira Alta: Sortelha, p.226.
- Beira Baixa: east of Castelo Branco, p.238.
- Estremadura: Serra de Sintra, p.302; Serra da Arrábida, p.331.
- Ribatejo: north of Constância, p.339.
- Baixo Alentejo and Algarve: along the River Guadiana, p.443 and p.480.
- Algarve: Serra de Monchique, p.504.

CONTENTS

Contents

History

02

Prehistory, the Romans, the Suevi and the Visigoths

When the Celts invaded the Peninsula in the first millennium BC, they mingled with the Iberians – who had been putting down roots since *c.* 8000 BC – and became **Celtiberians**. The Phoenicians came in search of metals, and by *c.* 800 BC were trading at Cadiz. Their empire passed to the Carthaginians, and later to the Romans, who occupied Hispania Ulterior (Andalusia) in 202 BC.

The Romans marched inland, where the fierce **Lusitanian** tribespeople of central Portugal waged a successful guerrilla war against them. The Lusitanians' leader, Viriatus, was fatally betrayed in 139 BC; so too was the Roman general Sertorius, who briefly championed the Lusitanian cause after 80 BC.

Rome never penetrated deeply north of the Tagus. South of the river, Julius Caesar founded Pax Julia (*c.* 60 BC), to bolster the port of Olissipo (Lisbon) and the towns of Ebora (Évora) and Myrtilis (Mértola). Roman *latifundias* established the pattern of landholding in the Alentejo; Roman roads were used until the Middle Ages, and their bridges are still in use today. They also introduced vines, olives, figs and almonds.

At the beginning of the 5th century AD, barbarian hordes entered the peninsula. The Romans enlisted the aid of the **Visigoths**, who disposed of all but the **Suevi**, or Swabians. The Suevi based themselves between the Rivers Minho and Douro, and were converted to Christianity by St Martin: their see of Braga incorporated Lamego, Viseu, Conimbriga and Idanha *c.* 569. The Swabian monarchy was suppressed by the Visigothic ruler, Leovigild, in 585.

The Moorish Occupation and the Christian Reconquest

The Moors were invited into Spain in 711, and nominally conquered the Peninsula within two years. They represented a salad of races – Arabs, Syrians, Persians, Jews, Berbers from Morocco, and Copts from Egypt, who had been Christian – all of whom preferred the sunny climate of the south. Christians rallied together in northern Portugal and Galicia.

In the middle of the 9th century, the Christians crept southwards: Portucale (Porto) was rebuilt in 868, and the region between the Rivers Minho, Douro and later Vouga became known as **Territorium Portugalense**. This territory was administered by successive generations of a ruling family, including Countess Mumadona (*c.* 931).

Ferdinand I, King of Castile, drove the Moors from Lamego (1057), from Viseu (1058) and from the city of Coimbra (1064). His successor, Alfonso VI, revived the metropolitan see of Braga – which reinforced the integrity of the province that was to become Portugal.

Alfonso's son-in-law, Henry of Burgundy, ruled the territory between the Rivers Minho and Douro from his capital at Guimarães. Later his widow, **Teresa**, governed Portugal as regent for their son, **Dom Afonso Henriques**.

When Alfonso VII, King of Galicia, invaded Teresa's lands, her barons united behind Dom Afonso Henriques. He defeated his mother at the battle of São Mamede in 1128, and the reign of the **first King of Portugal** had begun.

The House of Burgundy

Although the Pope did not recognize the kingdom of Portugal until 1179, the country had asserted its independence from other Iberian kingdoms. It was helped by the fact that none of its rivers were navigable across what was to become the Portuguese border, and the other Iberian kingdoms had no need of Portuguese ports.

Moorish chroniclers refer to **Dom Afonso Henriques** (1128/39–85) as 'the cursed of Allah': aided by internal strife among the Moors he crusaded southwards, capturing Santarém after the battle of Ourique in 1139, and Lisbon in 1147. But the reconquest was not completed for nearly 150 years. His son Dom Sancho I (1185–1211) continued the subjugation, but in 1191 was driven back north of the Tagus, except for a foothold in Évora. Dom Afonso III (1248–79) captured Faro.

His *Cortes* at Leiria in 1254 was the first at which the commons were represented. Structures of power were gradually taking shape. Large parts of the newly conquered lands had been granted to the military and monastic Orders to secure their defence and colonization. The Church fought hard to retain its independence: the bishops were so incensed at the Crown's meddling in the election of bishops that they declared the deposition of Dom Afonso III. The Portuguese Pope, John XXI, did very little to help.

Afonso's son, **Dom Dinis** (1279–1325), became one of the greatest Burgundian kings. He ruled with great foresight – earning Dante's praise in *Paradiso*. Dom Dinis strengthened the nation's defences by building or rebuilding most of her castles, and established the Order of Christ to take the place of the suppressed Knights Templar. Forests were planted, and the king authorized at least 40 fairs. Dom Dinis founded Portugal's first university, the General Studies, in Lisbon in 1290; he also required deeds and official documents to be written in the vernacular. In all this, he was assisted by his peacemaking queen, St Isabel.

The later Burgundian kings became embroiled in a series of Castilian marriage alliances: both Dom Pedro I (1357–67), who loved to dance to the sound of the trumpet, and his chivalrous heir, Dom Fernando (1367–83), followed this course. Dom Fernando obeyed his queen, Leonor, and married his heiress, Beatriz, to Juan, King of Castile: if this union produced no fruit, Juan would become King of Portugal.

When Dom Fernando died, Juan ordered the Portuguese townships to proclaim Beatriz queen. He received the backing of the entrenched nobility, who stood to benefit from Castilian-style government – but the spectre of absorption by Castile fired the towns and coastal regions in their support for a bastard son of Dom Pedro, João of Avis. In Lisbon he was 'accompanied by the common people as if he were dropping precious treasures for them all to grab', and in 1385 João was declared king (1385–1433).

Shortly afterwards he and his lieutenant, Nun' Álvares Pereira, defeated Juan at the battle of Aljubarrota: this secured the independence of Portugal for nearly 200 years. An Anglo-Portuguese alliance was cemented with the king's marriage to Philippa of Lancaster, sister of England's future Henry IV.

The House of Avis and the Age of Discoveries

Having made peace with Spain, Portugal turned her attention seawards. Fired by the desire for glory, piety and distraction, Dom João I took advantage of a civil war in the Maghrib to capture Ceuta in 1415. But it was his third son, **Henry the Navigator**, who did most to foster Portugal's maritime exploits. He set up a school of navigation at Sagres, and chanelled his funds into a succession of expeditions. These groped their way down the west coast of Africa; Gil Eanes rounded Cape Bojador in 1434. Madeira and the Azores were rediscovered, but were not colonized until 1445, during the reign of Henry's elder brother, the lawmaker Dom Duarte (1433–8).

Another brother, Dom Pedro, served as regent during the minority of Dom Duarte's heir, Dom Afonso V (1438–81). This riled the young king's half-uncle, the first Duke of Bragança, who fought and killed the regent in 1449.

Like his father and grandfather, Dom Afonso V fought in Morocco, storming to victory at the battle of Alcácer-Seguir in 1458. Also like his forebears, he strengthened the power of the *Cortes*, since expensive expeditions obliged the kings to woo the towns' resources.

His son, Dom João, negotiated peace with Castile. As king (João II, 1481–95) he beheaded the over-mighty Duke of Bragança, and received some 60,000 Jews fleeing persecution in Spain.

Overseas explorations were resumed. In 1487 **Bartolomeu Dias** rounded the Cape (of Good Hope) without seeing land, and Pêro de Covilhã was dispatched to India and Ethiopia. The Portuguese crown refused to finance Columbus' plan to find a westward route to the Indies: he took his idea to Ferdinand and Isabella of Spain, sailed in 1492, and discovered America. Now that Spain had a stake in the rest of the world, she and Portugal negotiated its partition. The **Treaty of Tordesillas** of 1493 allocated to Spain all lands west, and to Portugal all lands east, of a line running north to south 360 leagues west of the Cape Verde Islands. The Portuguese lands just happened to include Brazil, prompting suspicions that the Portuguese already knew of its existence.

The crown passed to Dom João II's impatient cousin, **Dom Manuel** (1495–1521), whose arms were so long that his hands dangled beside his knees. During his reign, Portugal's position in Morocco and the Congo was consolidated (the former partly because Portugal had begun importing wheat and looked to the wide Moroccan plains). Looking further afield, **Vasco da Gama** set sail in 1497, and returned two years later having discovered a sea route to India and its spices. Pedro Álvares Cabral was dispatched in that direction, but sailed too far west and discovered Brazil, in 1500. Portugal established an administrative capital at Goa, and set about destroying the Indian Ocean's complex web of trading links, to secure the supremacy of her own commerce. A crew sailing under a Spanish flag completed the first circumnavigation of the globe, though their Portuguese captain, Fernando de Magalhãis (Magellan) was killed en route.

The profits generated by the spice trade made Dom Manuel the wealthiest ruler in Europe – but Portugal's zenith was shortlived. The prospect of quick profit in Africa, India or Brazil lured the nation's entrepreneurs, leaving the home economy and agricultural productivity fatally weakened. Those of the merchant classes who stayed put were hit very badly by the royal monopoly, established in 1506. Nor was the new wealth invested productively. Portugal lost most of her banking and economic expertise in 1496, when the king expelled his Jewish subjects – a prerequisite for his marriage to Princess Isabel of Castile.

Dom João III (1521–57) and Charles V of Spain married each other's sisters (thus providing the basis for Philip II's claim to the Portuguese throne 50 years later). Portugal settled Brazil, and in 1557 was granted Macau to enable her to trade with Canton. But already the prices of spices in Europe were falling, and the mother country was drained of men, ships and money defending the lines of communication that held together her global empire.

In 1536 the New Christians – ostensibly converted Jews – braced themselves against the Inquisition, which established tribunals in Lisbon, Coimbra and Évora. The court grew larger and more slothful, and the countryside became alarmingly depopulated. The Jesuits were invited into Portugal, and were granted their own university at Évora. Other Jesuits did not stay long: St Francis Xavier was preaching in Japan in 1549.

Dom João III's heir became king while still in his mother's womb; his great uncle, Cardinal Henrique served as regent. **Dom Sebastian** (1557–78) was an odd fish, coupling a clear idea of his military calling with a childish impetuosity. The result was disastrous: he led an ill-prepared and clumsy expedition into Morocco, where 15,000 Portuguese were captured at the battle of **Alcácer-Quivir**. Dom Sebastian was killed (see 'Sebastianismo' box), and fewer than 100 escaped; the ransom payments beggared the nation. The elderly cardinal was proclaimed king (1578–80) but died shortly afterwards. In desperation he was replaced by António, Prior of Crato (1580), bastard nephew of Dom João III.

The Spanish Usurpation

Philip II of Spain saw his opportunity. Wealthy Portuguese supported his entry into their country because they wished to avoid the expense of protracted warfare; he may also have had the support of the Jesuits. In addition Portugal's weakening economy needed Spain's American silver. The new king (Philip I of Portugal, 1580–98) abided by his promises to preserve the autonomy of Portugal – although he strengthened those institutions which straddled the two countries, **the Jesuits and the Inquisition**. He closed the Portuguese ports to English and, later, Dutch

Sebastianismo

After the disastrous battle of Alcácer-Quivir in 1578, the body of Dom Sebastian could not be found. A whirlwind of rumours proclaimed the return of the king, and speculation gained momentum after Portugal was annexed to Spain in 1580. Dom Sebastian was cast as a hero who would throw off the Spanish yoke and restore the glory of the Portuguese: he became the focus of a Messianic cult which received a strong impetus from the New Christians – ostensibly converted Jews – who feared increased persecution under Spanish rule.

The upshot of this has lasted far beyond the four pretenders (youth, hermit, pastry cook and Italian) who popped up before 1600: in essence, *Sebastianismo* is akin to *saudade* (see p.41), and continues to revive in times of national despair. This occurred most forcefully when Prince Dom Miguel returned from Brazil in 1828, and possibly when Salazar – then Minister of Finance – turned around the budgetary deficit in 1928–9.

ships. Undeterred, the Dutch made their own way to the East, where they snatched the spice trade from the Portuguese.

His indolent son, Philip III (II) (1598–1621) had little contact with Portugal, and Philip IV (III) (1621–40) was distracted by the Catalan rebellion.

The Entrenchment of the House of Bragança

The Catalan rebellion gave the Portuguese a chance to rally around the Duke of Bragança, Dom João III's great-nephew. A group of nobles crowned him **King João IV** (1640–56) after overthrowing the Spanish authorities in Lisbon. Treaties were signed with the Dutch, who had occupied Brazil and had been attacking Portuguese shipping, and with the English, whose **Commonwealth Treaty** of 1654 set out privileges which held for nearly two centuries. At that time, approximately 14 per cent of Portugal's 1.5 million souls were either nobility or clergy, thus qualifying for the attendant financial privileges.

Dom Afonso VI (1656–67) was partly paralysed and partly stupid. Fighting against the Spanish dragged on until 1665: they made incursions to Olivença and Elvas in 1658, and to Évora in 1663.

Alarmed by Spain's peace with France, Portugal was desperate to strengthen its alliance with England. Thus **Catherine of Bragança**, Dom Afonso's sister, was married to King Charles II. Her massive dowry included two million cruzados, the right to trade with Portuguese colonies, and the cession of Tangier (Bombay was an afterthought). In return, England agreed to defend Portugal (and its overseas territories) 'as if it were England itself'. The king married Marie-Françoise of Savoy. Shortly afterwards he handed the government and his wife to his brother Dom Pedro.

Dom Pedro II (1667–83) convened a *Cortes* in 1698, the last time the consultative body was ever summoned: the discovery of gold at Mato Grosso in Brazil secured the king's financial independence (and stunted domestic manufacture; only the colonies generated wealth, which was spent on imported goods). In 1703 the **Methuen Treaty** implemented a defensive alliance with England and Holland; the subsequent commercial treaty generated favourable terms for Portuguese wine in Britain, and for British cloth in Portugal. The latter terms were the more significant, being the death sentence of the Portuguese textile trade. In the same year, Philip V invaded Portugal, but Spanish and French troops returned to Madrid in 1706.

The wealth created by Brazilian gold was compounded by that of **diamonds**, discovered there in 1728. Although the crown did not always receive its one-fifth share, **Dom João V** (1706–50) reaped an estimated 107 million cruzados over a period of 44 years. However, the money did little to benefit Portugal. The king modelled himself on Louis XIV of France, lavishing much of his fortune on ostentatious building projects – principally at Mafra – and the aggrandizement of his standing in the Catholic world. When he died, there was not enough money left in the royal treasury to pay for his funeral.

His featherbrained son, Dom José (1750–77), was entirely dominated by the tyrannical minister later entitled **Marquês de Pombal**. This 'hairy-hearted' autocrat was made chief minister shortly after the Lisbon earthquake of 1755. He destroyed his enemies, the Jesuits and the entrenched aristocracy, and implemented a policy of **state-aided capitalism** to reduce the foreign deficit and erode Portugal's stultifying network of privileges.

Some 71 manufacturing establishments were set up in 1769–78, but economic activity was over-regulated. The state took control of wine production in the Alto Douro, and Pombal reformed the education of the élite.

The benefits of Pombal's rule were temporary, limited, and overshadowed by the cruelty of his subjection. Pombal had no regrets: 'The prisons and the cells were the only means I found to tame this blind and ignorant nation.'

As soon as she acceded to the throne, **Dona Maria I** (1777–92) banished Pombal to his estates. Many of his trading ventures were scuppered, and political prisoners were released. When the queen went screaming mad at Queluz, her son Dom João (later João VI) governed.

The Napoleonic Wars

Napoleon put Portugal back on the European map – if only to decide how best to apportion the country. The French threatened to invade unless Portugal supported their naval blockade of Britain; Portugal refused to commit economic suicide, and a French army under **Junot** marched into Lisbon in 1807. The British had provided a fleet to whisk the royal family to Brazil, out of harm's way; they were to remain there until 1821. The British generals **Wellesley and Beresford** were left to secure the defence of Portugal. Twice the invaders were driven out. They returned, but recalled their final garrison in 1811, having been flummoxed by the Lines of Torres Vedras. The British, for their part, were granted free access to Brazilian ports – enabling them to trade without depending on Portugal as an intermediary. Thus the Portuguese lost a vital source of profit. Their commerce was wrecked and their treasury in debt.

Liberals versus Miguelites and the War of the Two Brothers

Dom João VI (1792–1826) remained in Brazil, and Beresford continued as marshal of the Portuguese army. When he temporarily left the country, an army-backed revolution took place in Porto. An unofficial *Cortes* was summoned, which devised a sweeping constitution: the *Cortes* was to be a single-chamber parliament elected by universal male suffrage; feudal and clerical rights were to be abolished.

The timid king returned from Brazil in 1821, and agreed to abide by this constitution, though it fettered his power – but his rambunctious queen, Dona Carlota Joaquina, and their younger son, **Dom Miguel**, refused. The latter became the focus of a rural anti-liberal movement.

When Dom João VI died in 1826, his eldest son and heir, **Dom Pedro IV** (1826–8), acceded to the throne. Things were not straightforward: he had already become Emperor of the newly independent Brazil, and was living there. His solution was to abdicate the throne of Portugal in favour of his young daughter, Dona Maria da Glória – on condition that she marry his brother Dom Miguel, and that Dom Miguel accept a **Constitutional Charter**. This was milder than the radical constitution of 1822, but more liberal than the traditional form of government.

The betrothal took place, but Dom Miguel (1828–34) reneged on the agreement. He was declared king with absolute powers, and there followed a purge of liberals.

His brother, Dom Pedro, returned from Brazil to **fight for the Portuguese throne**, a bloody task in which he was assisted by excellent generals and British support for the liberal cause. Dom Miguel finally capitulated at Évora Monte in 1834, and was exiled to Austria.

Liberalism

The state was not only war-weary but bankrupt. The liberals sought wealth by dissolving the country's monasteries and convents in 1834 – nearly a quarter of the cultivated land in Portugal changed hands.

Dom Pedro died soon after his victory, leaving the throne to his teenage daughter, **Dona Maria II** (1834–53). Governments came and went rather rapidly: some backed the Constitutional Charter of 1826; others supported the constitution of 1822. Neither was prepared to strike at the roots of the country's financial crisis: the unproductive economy, which relied on foreign investment and loans, and directionless governance. Governments became more stable after 1852, when the Duke of Saldanha introduced modifications to the charter, and a new electoral law had been applied.

During the brief reign of Dom Pedro V (1855–61), Fontes Pereira de Melo set up a **Ministry of Public Works**, to give Portugal the infrastructure necessary for economic growth. Roads and railways were built; agricultural production increased accordingly. However, Portugal's balance of payments took a drastic downturn: the country lacked industrial raw materials, skilled labour (in 1870 there were 150 qualified engineers in Portugal) and investment capital.

Nadir of the Monarchy

When **Dom Carlos** (1889–1908) acceded to the throne, he inherited a country bewildered by the succession of governments in power since 1871. Portugal had sunk into a mire of high unemployment, strikes and public demonstrations. In 1890, Portugal's hopes of gaining control of the territory linking her colonies of Angola and Mozambique were thwarted by an ultimatum from Britain. This rattled the belief that the British Alliance was a guarantee of security, and tipped Portugal into crisis.

The king was the butt of his nation's dishonour, and made matters worse by placing a dictator, João Franco, in charge of the government. Amid growing discontent, the king and his eldest son Prince Dom Luís Filipe were shot dead in Lisbon in 1908. The king was succeeded briefly by his younger son, Dom Manuel II (1908–10).

The monarchy was finally snuffed out in 1910, when the king fled to Britain in the face of a tentative uprising by Republican revolutionaries and their supporters in the navy. This freakish victory led to the proclamation of the Republic on 5 October 1910.

The Republic

The Republicans gained the support of the Church, the British, and rural Portugal – but were never democratic. They limited freedom of speech, and muzzled the press. Popular discontent was swelled by Portugal's (limited) involvement in the

First World War after 1916, on the side of the Allies. The war exaggerated the weaknesses of Portugal's economy, prompting a series of strikes.

In 1917 a military revolt gained popular support, and led to army major Sidónio Pais presiding over what some say was Europe's first recognizable fascist government. Pais's regime to some extent prepared the ground for later dictatorial rule by others, but his assassination after just a year in power ushered in seven years of chaos: there were 45 governments between 1910 and 1926. By 1923 the escudo had fallen to one-twentieth of the value it registered against the pound in 1917. Faced with this intolerable instability, the army overthrew the 'Democratic' regime in 1926.

The New State

Out of the morass emerged **Dr António de Oliveira Salazar**, an economics professor at Coimbra University, who was made Minister of Finance in 1928. With total control of revenue and expenditure, he turned a 330 million escudo deficit into a budgetary surplus – in his first year of office (and his regime continued to balance the budget until it was overthrown in 1974).

In 1932, Salazar became Prime Minister, an office he retained until 1968. His *Estado Novo* (New State) stressed nationalism, and Salazar secured the trappings of dictatorship: political parties, unions, and strikes were abolished; censorship was enforced; and the hated political police (the PIDE) thrived. Some 100,000 informers supplied the police with details of their friends, families or associates.

Portugal remained neutral during the Second World War, and in the postwar period, communications were extended and modernized. The construction of dams brought hydro-electric power. This enabled Portuguese industry to grow at a rate of nine per cent per year in the 1950s and 1960s.

The **colonies** ('overseas provinces') formed an integral part of the *Estado Novo*. Local independence movements in Angola (1961), Guinea-Bissau (1963) and Mozambique (1964) ushered in dirty wars that were to sap Portugal's meagre resources. By 1968, more than 100,000 Portuguese troops were fighting in Africa.

Democracy

The unpopularity of the wars in Africa, and discontent with the oppressive regime, crystallized into the Movement of the Armed Forces (**MFA**), which toppled the *Estado Novo* in a bloodless coup on 25 April 1974.

The **African territories** were granted their **independence**, and Portugal accommodated three-quarters of a million *retornados* from there. The revolution had a real effect on people's lives: the secret police were dispersed, censorship was lifted, industry, banks and insurance companies were **nationalized**, and nearly four million acres of land, especially the large *latifundias* of the Alentejo, was expropriated. Today much of this process has been reversed, as the government pushed through a series of privatization programmes in a rush to meet EU deadlines.

The country came close to civil war in November 1975, when a counter-coup attempted to prevent a communist takeover – but a crisis was averted. In 1976 a new constitution was drawn up, under which the Prime Minister and cabinet were responsible to the popularly elected President and to the Assembly of the Republic, which was elected by proportional representation.

The 1995 elections saw the end of a decade in power by the PSD. **Aníbal Cavaco Silva** was defeated as prime minister by the socialist mayor of Lisbon, **Jorge Sampaio**, and **António Guterres** of the PS party gained the largest number of seats in parliament – the first time in 25 years that president and prime minister had come from the same political party.

The Socialist administration continued its predecessor's modernization drive: flagship social measures such as the unprecedented guaranteed income support were coupled with privatization and budgetary cuts in other areas. Portugal was determined to be among the first EU member states to adopt a common currency; as financial markets absorbed the fact that it was on course to perform this near miracle, a virtuous circle ensued of falling budget deficits, inflation and interest rates. By the time the monetary union was formed in 1999, Portugal was enjoying its third year of economic growth above the EU average.

The reforms met with a mixed response from the Portuguese people, the poorest of whom felt the worst effects of the market-orientated politics. When the Socialists failed to win an absolute majority in parliament in the 1999 general election, which would have stiffened their resolve to tackle reforms in more intractable areas such as health and education, Guterres lost his stomach for the fight. The collapse in March 2000 of a century-old bridge over the River Douro was also seen as a symbol of how basic infrastructure had been neglected in the rush to prestige projects such as the 1998 Expo in Lisbon. Guterres resigned as prime minister in December 2001, after local elections produced a disastrous result for his party.

The PSD-led coalition that took office in May 2002 spent its first few months struggling to meet EU budget deficit restrictions, and failing to revive a fast-shrinking economy. Huge sums were nevertheless spent on renovating or building 10 stadiums for the 2004 European Cup finals, in the hope of profiting from the influx of visitors and promoting Portugal's image as a tourist destination.

In 2005 a legislative election was called in response to the political instability caused by the PSD-led coalition and their initial refusal to call an election following the departure of Prime Minister José Manuel Durão Barroso, who left office to assume the position of president of the European Commission. **José Socrates**, leader of the Socialist Party, was asked to form a new government on 24 February.

In January 2006 centre-right candidate **Aníbal Cavaco Silva** was elected president, and charged with assisting the prime minister in tackling the country's ecomonic plight, including unprecedented high unemployment. In January 2007, Portugal took over the rotating EU presidency for six months during which time Socrates arranged an EU–Africa summit for the first time in seven years.

Architecture
and the Arts

03

Architecture

Architecture is one of the few areas of artistic endeavour in which the Portuguese have made an international impact. **Álvaro Siza Vieira** continues to be popular in Spain; his best-known works in Portugal include the parish church in Marco de Canavezes, the Serralves Foundation in Porto (home to the Museum of Contemporary Art) and, in Lisbon, the national pavilion built for Expo 98, still standing in what is now the Parque das Nações. He also oversaw the rebuilding of the fire-ravaged Chiado district.

Pre-Roman

The earliest monuments in Portugal are the megalithic dolmens of the Alto Alentejo (4000–2000 BC). History then leaves a yawning gap until the Iron Age (800–200 BC) when the Celt-Iberians rooted themselves in hill camps: the Citânias of Briteiros and Sabroso are chock-full of the foundations of round houses, which had conical roofs. The contemporary *berrões*, crudely sculpted bulls and boars found throughout Trás-os-Montes, remain mysterious: they may have been the images of a fertility cult, funerary symbols, or territorial markers, or may have been invoked for the protection of flocks and herds. Rupestral art added spice to Celt-Iberian life – best seen at Foz Côa – while the *Colossus of Pedralva* (Museu de Martins Sarmento, Guimarães) is a more monumental creation.

Roman, Early Christian and Visigothic

The Romans set about building up the indigenous cities, particularly during the reign of Augustus: they constructed temples (Évora), baths and villas (Conimbriga, Milreu, Miróbriga and Pisões), amphitheatres, cryptoporticus (Machado de Castro Museum, Coimbra), and a shrine at Braga. Most Roman bridges are still in use, though their roads are not. The best **mosaics** are at Torres Novas, Conimbriga, Faro and Pisões.

Lisbon's first bishop was appointed in 357, and Braga's c. 400, but few traces remain of the Early Christians. The Visigoths have left us the Byzantine chapel of São Frutuoso (Braga), and two other buildings subsumed by later ages, the church of São Pedro de Balsemão (near Lamego) and the Sé at Idanha-a-Velha.

Romanesque

Few Moorish buildings survive – the Igreja Matriz at Mértola is an exception – but the Moors bequeathed to Portugal a legacy of whitewashed cuboid houses and shuttered balconies.

The nation of Portugal hatched when the Romanesque was at its prime: monks of Cluny and Cister brought the style from France to the Minho, which is peppered with out-of-the-way Romanesque churches. These granite buildings are decorated with simple capitals, columns, corbels and portal arches: foliage, fabulous animals and human figures ornament churches at Bravães and Longos Vales, while those of Monçao and Melgaço are less lively.

The thick walls and crenellations of Portugal's Romanesque cathedrals (those at Braga, Porto, Coimbra, Lisbon and Évora) attest to harsh times: their towers served as a refuge in case of invasion. Bragança's *Domus Municipalis* is a rare example of Romanesque civic architecture.

Gothic

The Abbey of Alcobaça (1178) is Portugal's earliest Gothic building, but the style didn't really catch on until the Franciscan and Dominican Orders established themselves during the reign of Dom Afonso III (1248–79). Then the Gothic took hold of Portugal until the second quarter of the 16th century, when it was dislodged by Renaissance sensibilities. The austerity of the mendicant Orders is reflected in sober façades with a rose window above the portal, and three naves divided by slim arches. Gothic capitals sprout realistic flora (grapevines and ivy).

Gothic architecture in Portugal found its supreme expression in the **monastery of Batalha**. Its progeny includes the Carmo Church in Lisbon, the Sé at Guarda, and the church of São Domingos at Guimarães. Gothic cloisters were added to many cathedrals and churches. There are few traces of Gothic civil architecture: the palaces are ruinous or restored beyond recognition, so it's more worthwhile to look at a humbler level, in parts of Castelo de Vide's *judiaria*.

Most of Portugal's castles are Gothic, with small balconies on the upper storeys of their towers. The castles at Estremoz and Beja are distinguished by their monumental keeps; elsewhere those of Bragança and Óbidos are the most impressive.

The intricate tombs of Dom Pedro I and Inês de Castro at Alcobaça represent Gothic sculpture at its most sublime. The double tomb of Dom João I and Philippa of Lancaster at Batalha created a vogue for monuments on which effigies of the couple rest side by side.

Beyond funerary monuments, fine Gothic sculpture exists in the shrouded *Cristo Morto* in Coimbra's Machado de Castro Museum, and in the Evangelists flanking the portals of the Sé at Évora and the Abbey at Batalha. Portuguese painting was practically non-existent until Nuno Gonçalves (died before 1492) arrived on the scene. His *Panels of St Vincent* (Museu de Arte Antiga, Lisbon) are outstanding as a group portrait and an illuminating historical document.

Manueline

The Manueline style is Portugal's own contribution to the world's architecture: its ebullient forms encapsulate the thrill of the Age of Discoveries, and its treatment of space belongs to generations of horizon-gazers. It developed out of the late Gothic, and reached its peak 1490–1521, during the reign of **Dom Manuel**, from whom it takes its name. This was Portugal's great age, when wealth from trade with the East generated numerous new artistic ventures, which attracted foreign craftsmen to Portugal.

The Manueline is a disparate style, with substyles derived from the Spanish Plateresque (finely detailed motifs in low relief), the Moorish revival called *mudéjar*, and a concoction of fantastic maritime motifs. Most Manueline work is found south of Tomar, for the court rarely ventured beyond Coimbra.

Boitac's breathtaking Jerónimos Monastery at Belém (Lisbon) is the finest Manueline building, while the window made for the Order of Christ at Tomar is strikingly forceful, and the Torre de Belém (Lisbon) an enchanting blend of Moorish and Manueline styles. The church of Jesus at Setúbal signals the early development of the Manueline style.

Flemish, Spanish, French and *mudéjar* craftsmen wielded the most influential chisels in Portugal. Manueline architecture required a feast of sculptural embellishment (Unfinished Chapels, Batalha), and thus serves as the finest showcase of Manueline sculpture: elsewhere the sculpture of the age is either late Gothic (the retable of the Sé Velha in Coimbra), early Renaissance, or *mudéjar*. *Mudéjar* craftsmen carved and painted wooden ceilings in the chapel of the National Palace at Sintra, in the Igreja Matriz at Caminha, and in the church of São Bento at Bragança. Like contemporary sculpture, the painting of the age followed the Renaissance style.

Renaissance

The Italian Renaissance came to Portugal via Flanders, with whom she had close trading links. Renaissance ornament arrived first: in architecture, full-blown Greco-Roman columns, pilasters and entablature were not embraced wholeheartedly until 1530 – when Portugal's wealth was just beginning to wane. The cathedrals of the new dioceses created by **Dom João III** – Leiria, Portalegre, and Miranda do Douro – take on a Renaissance austerity. Diogo de Torralva's cloister at the convent of Christ in Tomar is the supremely balanced work of the age. The Quinta da Bacalhôa and the Quinta das Torres, both at Azeitão, best represent the civil architecture of the period.

Nicolau Chanterène introduced the Renaissance to Portuguese sculpture: his career in Portugal began with the late Gothic west portal at Belém (Lisbon) and ended with the altarpiece in the Pena Palace at Sintra and the stunningly beautiful tomb now in Évora's municipal museum. His nominal successor, João de Ruão, pales by comparison.

Portuguese Renaissance painting adopts the realism, depth of perspective, and lively colours of Flemish work. Frei Carlos (Museu de Arte Antiga, Lisbon) himself was Flemish. Vasco Fernandes, called Grão Vasco (1475–1541; municipal museums of Viseu and Lamego), Gregório Lopes, Cristóvão de Figueiredo and the Master of Sardoal are the names to watch for.

The finest Portuguese work is to be found in the Setúbal Museum and the Museu de Arte Antiga in Lisbon; the Bruges school is well represented at the municipal museum in Évora.

Mannerism

The Portuguese Renaissance was snuffed out on the death of Dom João III in 1557. Mannerism's cold and frigid classicism set in, and did not thaw until *c.* 1710. The Spanish takeover in 1580 compounded the decline by dissipating the court and thus removing the focus of artistic patronage.

The newly arrived **Jesuits** did much to shape the ecclesiastical architecture of the period: true to the spirit of the Counter-Reformation, the pulpit was to be clearly visible from all parts of the church. Lisbon's church of São Vicente de Fora served as a prototype. The palace of the Marquês de Fronteira in Lisbon is the most complete example of 17th-century civil architecture.

At the end of the 16th century, stone sculpture gave way to wooden sculpture: initially, retables simply imitated their stony predecessors, but in the middle of the 17th century they acquired a style of their own – and niches were filled with sculpture (as in the sanctuary at Alcobaça). Josepha de Óbidos (1630–84) cast a rather dim light in the darkness of Portuguese painting. Having been sober, silverwork became richer (Sé, Porto). The craftsmen of India were set to work on traditionally formed Portuguese furniture, with giddy results. Arraiolos rugs were beginning to appear at the end of the 17th century.

Baroque

The discovery of gold and diamonds in Portugal's colony of Brazil brought a flood of wealth to a monarch who sought glorification through his monumental building works: **Dom João V**'s liberality attracted foreign craftsmen to Portugal, and the arts of Portugal were shaken from their stupor.

Eighteenth-century architecture was dominated by Italian influences. It took two different forms, reflecting the influence of Nasoni's dynamic work in and around Porto (active 1725–62; simple structures with complex surface ornaments), and of the Italian-trained Ludwig's monumental designs for the palace and monastery at Mafra, as well as his chancel at the Sé in Évora. Baroque architecture in Lisbon was cut short by the earthquake of 1755, which necessitated the economical, unadorned Pombaline style, named after the Marquês de Pombal. At that time the refreshing and much underrated André Soares was working in the north of the country (Casa do Raio, Braga). The rococo's brief flowering gave Portugal the delightful palace of Queluz.

The school of sculpture at Mafra secured an Italian bias to Portuguese Baroque sculpture, not only because Alessandro Giusti (1715–99) taught there, but through the influence of Italian sculptures imported to adorn the basilica itself.

The most exciting sculpture of the age was that architectural form called *talha* (carving) which the Portuguese used with peculiar enthusiasm. It was gilt with Brazilian gold leaf, producing a theatrical effect well suited to Baroque tastes: during its vogue in the 18th century, it spilled from the apse to frame pictures, pulpits and *azulejos* in the nave. In the late 17th century, the retable's concentric arches were ornamented by twisted chestnut columns aflutter with grapevines and phoenix birds (symbolizing the Eucharist and immortality respectively). Dom João V's Italian architects, sculptors and goldsmiths influenced the style, preferring canopies to arches, and adding festoons and volutes – dazzlingly employed in the church of São Francisco in Porto and the Convent of Jesus at Aveiro. The decorative appeal of gilt- or polychromed-wood imitations of Italian sculpture was soon appreciated.

Many Portuguese painters emigrated to Rome; palettes travelling in the other direction popularized trompe-l'oeil ceilings. Furniture bent over backwards to accommodate Baroque tastes, but then sobered under the influence of Queen Anne and Chippendale styles. Silverwork veered from Dom João's ostentatious pieces commissioned from Italy for the chapel of São João Baptista to the supreme

French craftsmanship of the Germains' work for Dom José (in the Museu de Arte Antiga and the Ajuda Palace, Lisbon).

The 19th and 20th Centuries

After a muted period of neoclassicism, Portugal settled into a mishmash of styles known as the '**Eclectic period**'. Architectural development was stunted by the dissolution of the religious orders in 1834, and the appropriation of their buildings by the state, which removed the need for any new commissions.

Machado de Castro (1731/2–1822; equestrian bronze in Lisbon's Praça do Comércio) is the only sculptor who approaches the talents of António Soares dos Reis (1847–89), who trained in Paris and Rome, imbuing a classical tradition with more than a dash of Romantic sentiment (Soares dos Reis Museum, Porto).

Romanticism arrived first in poetry and painting, the latter of which took its lead from foreign artists such as the Swiss Augusto Roquemont. Porto's Soares dos Reis Museum is the best place to see works by the late 19th-century painters Marques de Oliveira, Silva Porto, and their open-air colleagues José Malhoa, Carlos Reis, and José Júlio de Sousa Pinto. Columbano Bordalo Pinheiro, by contrast, was very much an *atelier* painter.

Twentieth-century Portugal appears to have been in rather too much of a muddle to produce much of artistic merit, other than paintings (Gulbenkian Museum of Modern Art, Lisbon) and literature. Jorge Barradas (1894–1971) was a particularly witty sculptor – a field now dominated by João Cutileiro (Évora's public garden and Lisbon's Campo Pequeno metro station).

One of Portugal's most celebrated 20th-century artists, Maria Helena Vieira da Silva, has a museum in Lisbon devoted to her (*see* p.366). Her large canvases, characterized by strong linear patterns and dark colours, owe something to the tradition of *azulejos*.

After a hiatus following the 1974 revolution, the 1980s saw a belated absorption of international trends by the tiny Portuguese art community. Among contemporary artists, Paul Rego (resident in Britain but maintaining a home in Cascais) and, from the next generation, Julião Sarmento, are probably the best known abroad, but their work pops up in public and private galleries in Lisbon and Porto. Rego's large figurative canvases featuring burly girls seem to tell stories with

Chimneys

You don't have to be Santa Claus to get a kick out of Portugal's chimneys. They were introduced into the country from south to north: the Algarve's pretty latticed flues hark back to Moorish times; but north of Coimbra, before the 20th century, only town houses and grand manors had chimneys. The discrepancy is rooted in climate and cooking habits: the northerners need to preserve heat in winter, and their stews generate less smoke than the southerners' grills.

In the Minho, some peasant houses still have a *trapeira* – a couple of wooden posts covered with tiles – or simply a hole in the ceiling with a removable cork bung. Smoke seeps through the thatched roofs of Trás-os-Montes, or a few tiles might be left loose. A large hearth is the nucleus of wealthier homes, but the vent itself is often very narrow. Further south, around Santarém, brick chimneys are kept apart from the framework of the house to reduce the risk of fire, while the chimneys of the Alentejo are broad oblongs. (Many of the Alentejo's church belltowers sport gleeful weathervanes – trumpeting angels and cherubs, and one skipping rat.)

a disturbing subtext, while the more abstract Sarmento works in a variety of media: sculpture, paint and video.

The Arts

Azulejos

Portugal's tiles are one of the most enjoyable and irrepressible facets of her artistic heritage. They are not peculiar to Portugal, but tiles in Portugal are used more extensively and for a greater variety of purpose than anywhere else. *Azulejos* date back to Moorish times; the term itself may be a corruption of two Arabic words, *azraq* (azure) and *zalayja* (a small polished stone).

In the late 15th century, tiles with geometric designs were imported into Portugal from Seville (National Palace at Sintra). To prevent their tin-glazed colours from blending with one another in the furnace, they were separated by rivulets filled with linseed oil, or by ridges in the clay paste.

In the 16th century, the Italians introduced the Majolica technique, by which the clay was covered with white enamel; this could then be painted directly. Andalusian craftsmen brought vitality to Portugal's *azulejos* when she was yoked to Spain 1580–1640, and it was during this period that the Portuguese developed their enthusiasm for *azulejos*.

Early 17th-century tiles were either solid blocks of dark blue or green arranged in simple geometric patterns, or more commonly *azulejos de tapete* (carpet tiles) (church of Marvila, Santarém). The latter imitate Moorish rugs, in yellow and blue. Tiled altar frontals were made to look like textiles, and in the second half of the century the first story-telling *azulejos* emerged. Both Portuguese and Dutch tiles of the period were exclusively blue and white, under the influence of Ming-dynasty porcelain imported into Europe.

The early 18th century saw the introduction of the Dutch-style independent *azulejo*, each of which contained one motif. These cost a fraction of the price of traditional tiles, and during their 40-year vogue a succession of flowers, ships, donkeys, castles and birds sprang up around the country. The same period saw the introduction of large tile panels depicting religious scenes, which mark the apogee of the *azulejo*. These were most perfectly integrated into their architectural settings by the grand master of tile design, António de Oliveira Bernardes (1684–1732) (Lóios Church in Évora, church of N.S. do Terço in Barcelos, Misericórdia in Viana do Castelo). He founded a school in Lisbon, where some of his disciples designed 'cutout' *azulejos*: the most amusing are human figures on staircase landings.

Baroque tiles teem with thick acanthus foliage, scrolls of stone, cherubs and urns sprouting frilled Dutch tulips. The 1730s saw the arrival of *azulejo* scenes depicting the pleasures of an idle life, after artists such as Watteau and Boucher. Tones of olive green and burgundy supplemented the blue and yellow, particularly in border garlands and swathes of vegetation.

The reconstruction of Lisbon after the earthquake of 1755 demanded a ready supply of *azulejos*: hasty production required a simplification of the style, which became delicate, decorative, classical and balanced. In the mid-19th century, the custom of decking the exterior of buildings with *azulejos* was introduced from Brazil. Tiles lent themselves to witty Art Nouveau designs, but fared less well with the rigid geometry of Art Deco in the 1930s. Competition from mosaics and marble signalled a lull in *azulejo* design, which was revived in the 1950s, and is still going strong.

Lisbon's excellent Museu de Azulejos provides an overview of the art, and the city's metro system provides an electrifying showcase of the contemporary use and design of *azulejos*. Check out Parque, Carnide and almost all stations on the new red line. Two are outstanding: Oriente, including *azulejo* panels by Iceland's Errö, Austria's Hundertwasser and several other leading foreign artists; and Olaias, by postmodernist architect Tomás Taveira.

Music

Portuguese music is little known and rarely heard abroad. Troubadours appeared in the late 13th century, but it was not until the mid-15th century that polyphony first cleared its throat. It ran out of breath in the mid-17th century, and is now enjoying a muted revival – keep an ear open for compositions by Manuel Cardoso and Estêvão Lopes Morago.

Mannerism brought a certain melancholy to the Portuguese keyboard, which was championed by António Carreira (1590–1650). Religious compositions dominated Portuguese music until the late 17th century. Dom João IV, who became king in 1640, required his ambassadors to send him every musical score they could find, which his court musicians were obliged to play. The king then marked the catalogue 'very good', 'good', or 'to Hell'. His music library was the largest in Europe, but both the good and the bad went to Hell in the earthquake of 1755.

Characteristically, Dom João V (1506–50) employed Domenico **Scarlatti** as his daughter's music teacher. Scarlatti was well impressed with José António Carlos de Seixas (1704–42), the greatest Portuguese composer of the age. The late 18th century spawned **João de Sousa Carvalho** (1720–98), who could air his compositions in the new São Carlos Opera House in Lisbon. João Domingos Bomtempo (1775–1842) composed a very fine Requiem Mass, but is better known for his sonatas.

The opera house was closed in 1910: music went into decline because it had been closely associated with the court. Luís de Freitas Brancone (1890–1955), a contemporary of Bártok, kindled the fire.

The São Carlos Opera House has been reopened. Its orchestra continues to improve, whereas the Gulbenkian orchestra (basically a chamber orchestra, with reinforcements for larger works) tends to rest on its laurels. A new orchestra has been formed in Porto, but does little to promote Portuguese musical talent – 95 per cent of the players are foreign. Among contemporary composers, France-based avant-gardist Emanuel Nunes is one of the better known.

Cinema

Like much of Portuguese culture, Portuguese cinema has been heavily influenced by France. To some that means intellectually challenging *pièces de résistance*; to

Fado

The musical equivalent of *saudade* (*see* p.41) is that melancholic, gut-wrenching song called *fado* (fate). The hard, untrained voice of the *fadista* is accompanied by a guitar: together they revel in tragedy, or assume a torpid resignation towards it.

Fado seems to have been born into the lowlife of Lisbon's Alfama district during the 1830s, and is still most at home there. It remains exclusively urban. Coimbra *fado* is quite different: more refined and sentimental, with a listless romantic yearning. The Coimbra guitar style is more chordal than its melodic Lisbon counterpart and has a slower tempo.

The words of the *fado* are not too important: *fadistas* often improvise. However, some *fados* tell the story of **Maria Severa**, a great *fadista*, whose mother was known as *A Barbuda* (the Bearded Lady). Maria let rip in Lisbon's Mouraria, next to the Alfama, where she conducted a stormy romance with a bull-fighting nobleman, the Conde de Vimioso. What the *fados* fail to mention is that Maria died at the age of 26, not from a broken heart but from a surfeit of roast pigeon and red wine.

For decades, Portugal's diva was **Amália Rodrigues**. Even she was banished from the airwaves during the initial confusion of the 1974 revolution, when it was illegal to broadcast *fado* on the radio – on the grounds that it encouraged listlessness and fatalism, and was therefore harmful to social progress. She made a comeback in the 1980s, and her death in 1999 prompted three days of official mourning. Today's *fado* star is **Mariza**, who has a bold contemporary image and is a favourite on the WOMAD world music circuit. Released in 2008, her latest album *Terra* includes the track 'Alfama', which pays homage to the Lisbon neighbourhood that has long been a nerve centre of the *fado* tradition.

others (including the mass of cinema-goers), turgid pretension.

For all this clash, one director who has won the admiration, if not love, of his compatriots is **Manoel de Oliveira**. In his nineties, the world's oldest active film-maker still churns out at least a film a year (often featuring Catherine Deneuve and John Malkovich like *O Convento* or his latest, *Um Filme Falado*), and has won several awards in Cannes. Among his best works are those set in his home city of Porto or in the Douro valley: the silent *Douro, Faina Fluvial* (1931) and children's tale *Aniki-Bóbó* (1942).

Other uncompromising directors include the late **João César Monteiro**, whose navel-gazing and nose-thumbing had some calling him a wayward genius, others a fraud; and, from the younger generation, **Teresa Vilaverde** (*Os Mutantes*) and **Pedro Costa** (*Ossos*), both of whom have portrayed the dark underside of society.

Maria de Medeiros' *Capitães de Abril* is an effective rendering of the wonderful story that is the 1974 revolution. **Joaquim Leitão** is another mainstream director.

Literature

The lyrical streak within the Portuguese has made them better poets than prose writers. **Fernão Lopes** (*c.* 1380–*c.* 1459) has been described as the father of Portuguese prose; he was commissioned to write the history of all the Portuguese kings, but only the last three survive – broad, balanced and colourful. Azurara succeeded him; through living in the household of Henry the Navigator, the aristocrat was well placed to write the *Chronicle of the Discovery of Guinea*.

The prolific playwright **Gil Vicente** (*c.* 1470–*c.* 1536) was a sort of Brueghel of the stage, who ranged from rollicking farce to solid character portrayal. Portugal's maritime exploits washed up **Luís de Camões** (1524–80), author of the great

Portuguese epic *Os Lusíadas* (*The Lusiads*). He served in Ceuta (where his right eye was removed), Goa and Macau, he was imprisoned, and he lost everything except his manuscript in a shipwreck. *The Lusiads* was published (1572) on his return to Portugal, where he died in genteel poverty. In closely structured but wonderfully fluid verse, Camões details Vasco da Gama's voyage to India, overlooked by a panoply of Olympian gods and goddesses. He interprets the greatness of the Portuguese people.

After Camões, the pens of Portugal ran dry until **Bocage** (1765–1805) exploded onto the scene, a debauched early Romantic subsequently exiled by Pombal's government. The Liberal **Almeida Garrett** (1799–1854) was the first of the true Romantics, whose *Travels in My Homeland* combines description of what crosses his path, with musings on what crosses his mind. His contemporary Alexandre Herculano (1810–77) used lucid prose to write the history of Portugal up to the reign of Dom Afonso III. He investigated social history, but ceased his project when accused of treason – for pooh-poohing Portugal's foundation myths. The realist novels of **Eça de Quieroz** (1845–1900) were highly admired by Zola. Eça and his generation, 'the Generation of 1870', aimed to effect a national regeneration; his concern with social reform is articulated in his highly enjoyable works, of which *The Maias* is the best known.

The great poet **Fernando Pessoa** (1888–1935) holds a special place in Portuguese hearts. Camões wrote at the beginning of the end of Portugal's empire, Pessoa at its eclipse, but both were concerned with the destiny of the Portuguese. Pessoa created what he called 'heteronyms', who served as vehicles for the poet to write outside his own personality.

Literature under Salazar was smothered by political censorship; one of the best-known works of protest is the *New Portuguese Letters* by Maria Teresa Horta, a feminist rallying cry which is sometimes obscure.

The best of the modern novels in translation is **José Saramago**'s *Balthasar and Blimunda*, a painstakingly researched, magical account of a flying machine and the construction of the Palace and Monastery of Mafra. Saramago won the 1998 Nobel Prize for literature, leapfrogging eternal candidate **Miguel Torga**, whose short stories are set in the harsh rural environment of Trás-os-Montes. Another writer sometimes mentioned as a possible Nobel candidate is novelist **António Lobo Antunes**. **Lídia Jorge**, who examines the impact of the colonial wars, made a splash in translation with *The Migrant Painter of Birds*.

The Portuguese

04

Better is the ass that carries me than the horse that throws me.

Portuguese proverb

The charm of the Portuguese is a compelling reason for travelling here. People tend to be gentle and friendly, while retaining great dignity. A genial pessimism pervades much of life, though often backed by quiet pride. The Portuguese are unerringly tolerant of foreigners, as George Borrow discovered in 1835: 'I said repeatedly that the Pope ... was the head minister of Satan here on earth ... I have been frequently surprised that I experienced no insult and ill-treatment from the people.'

Sometimes tolerance is occasioned by passivity. In 1726 Brockwell wrote: 'Be their Business ever so urgent, or the Rains ever so violent, they never hasten their Pace ... and seem to number each step they take.' But, as the receipts from Portuguese emigrants show, the Portuguese can be firm of purpose when they set their minds to it, and highly adaptable. The latter is not always apparent: there's a deep-rooted resistance to change. If you're travelling on a bus and open a window, someone will close it; if you get on the bus before anyone else and open a window, it will remain open throughout the journey – as the other passengers see it, the window has always been open, so it had better stay open. On the other hand, 'progress' is sometimes employed for its own sake, as the revamp of various historical buildings attests.

Traditionally, Portuguese women aged early, a fact which did not escape Brockwell's attention in 1726: 'No sooner are they in their Perfection than they suddenly decay ... Thirty once turn'd, they become as justly despicable, as before they were admirable.' Things have changed now. The average Portuguese woman may not be as *produzida* (dolled up) as her Spanish sister, but you only have to watch Portugal's increasingly brash television shows or go to a chic restaurant in one of the bigger towns to realize the growing importance of image in contemporary Portuguese society.

For the older generation, respectability is still very important. In small towns, the men appear never to remove their subfusc suits, whether they are playing dominoes in *tascas* or dawdling in town squares. They turn on their heels only to bestow the occasional, single handshake. Respectability also takes the form of courtesy: envelopes are commonly addressed to *excelentíssimo* (most excellent) so-and-so. It was Dom João V who first entitled his secretary of state 'Excellency'. The nobles were disgusted, but found it expedient to use that address for any chance acquaintance, and the custom caught on. Calling cards are distributed freely – the custom of turning down one corner may hark back to the days when they were proffered by the landed gentry in lieu of immediate payment: turning down the corner made them non-negotiable.

The picture today is more mixed. While business clothing remains conservative, Portuguese teenagers dress as scantily as anywhere else in southern Europe in summer, and topless sunbathing is widespread.

The more fanciful side of the Portuguese temperament may have been shaped at an early age: children are told the bizarre but tragic tale of *Carochinha* (Cockroach), an ugly insect who received numerous proposals of marriage after she discovered a crock of gold. The only sincere candidate was a mouse, who fell into boiling water and died. New Yorkers are not the only people with a fixation for cockroaches.

Horses and Bulls

The Greek armies were thrown into disarray by 50 Iberian horsemen brought to their country by Dionysius, the despot of Syracuse. Horses have long been important to the Portuguese: King Dom Duarte (1433–8) wrote the first serious treatise on classical equitation since the Greeks held forth on the subject, and thus incorporated the art of riding in the classical revival. This art lingers in Portugal: Lusitano horses are used to refresh the bloodlines of the Lipizzaners at the Spanish Riding School in Vienna. The Portuguese School of Equestrian Art is based in Lisbon, where riders in 18th-century dress (tricorn hats, patent-leather thigh boots, embroidered silk coats) prance about on Alter Real stallions, a strain of the Lusitano horse. The breed has maintained its purity due to the tradition of mounted bullfighting, which tests the skill of the rider and horse without killing the bull. The horse's delicate steps incite the bull to charge – the Iberian bull charges repeatedly, and turns in its own length to do so.

Saudade is a state of mind which lies at the heart of the Portuguese. There's no literal translation: 'longing' or 'yearning' come closest. It is a passive desire for something out of reach, either in the future or in the past. It pricks with an almost religious constancy.

The Church

Black is a popular colour for clothes in Portugal, and not because it's fashionable. Mourning is pervasive: the closer one's relationship to the dead, the longer one wears black. In rural areas or in the *bairros populares* in cities, the rule of thumb is still 7–10 years of mourning for a parent, 2–3 for an in-law. Many widows decide to stay in mourning for the rest of their lives. (Children's deaths are not formally mourned: they receive a Requiem Mass and no more.) Everyone needs a little colour in their lives, though, and bright underwear can be seen hanging from the nation's washing lines.

The Catholic Church inspires greater devotion from Portuguese women than Portuguese men, though on Sundays some village churches attract 90 per cent of the residents. In the village, religion is closely bound up with protection of the household, its animals, and its agriculture ('When there is food in the house, the Saints are left in peace', runs a proverb). The focus is on regional shrines and village pilgrimages – in which the priest serves as a kind of public functionary. Anticlericalism is fairly widespread, which may be evidence of the hiatus in people's minds between the local church and the national Church.

In his essay on Portuguese Catholicism, the poet Fernando Pessoa wrote 'Our true God-made-Manifest is ... a Catholic Cupid called the Child Jesus. So we pay no attention to the Virgin Mary, but only to Mother Mary.' Hence the two popular images, the pregnant Our Lady of 'O' (named, in part, from the seven antiphons in the Office of the days before Christmas, all of which begin with 'O') and the suckling Our Lady of the Milk. The Mother of Christ became a popular figure for devotion in the 13th century, which preached a more sentimental and direct relationship with God. By the end of the 15th century, over 1,000 of Portugal's churches, chapels and hermitages had been devoted to the Virgin. The cult of Our Lady of Fátima, which attracts ever greater numbers of pilgrims, is testimony to this, in spite of waning church congregations.

Wax ex-votos are an odd but touching feature of many churches. These limbs, heads, chests, breasts, stomachs, pigs, babies and hands are intended to attract divine cures for their respective ailments. They are heaped on altars in a promiscuous jumble, or hung from strings.

Attitudes Towards Spain

They would have us be Castilian men.
A lizard I would rather be
By the Holy Gospels verily.

So says Jorge, a player from Sardoal, in Gil Vicente's 16th-century *Tragicomédia Pastoril da Serra da Estrêla*. He echoes the sentiments of many of his compatriots. Portugal's only neighbour is more than five times bigger than she is, and the Portuguese maintain a wary dislike of the Spanish – or simply pretend Spain does not exist. There is a saying that from Spain come neither good winds nor good marriages: the east winds are sweltering in summer and piercing in winter, and a series of greedy dynastic marriage alliances made Spain the bogey of Portugal's history.

Yet the Portuguese used to call themselves Spanish – it was an umbrella term for the inhabitants of the Peninsula, and was phased out when Carlos II continued to call himself King of Spain even after Portugal regained her independence in 1640. As late as 1712, Portuguese delegates negotiating the Treaty of Utrecht insisted that the monarchy in Madrid be referred to as that of Castile, rather than Spain. The EU is forging trade and transport links between the two countries, and each year millions of Spaniards jaunt across the border to stock up on bath towels and bottle corks.

Old antipathies are never far from the surface, however. The recent influx – invasion, say some – of Spanish companies buying up Portuguese rivals has prompted accusations of double dealing. Portugal's normally diplomatic president felt moved to accuse the Spanish authorities of unfairly protecting their own companies. Even those Portuguese who have turned a profit selling shares to Spanish investors feel obliged to mollify anti-Spanish feeling; in mid-2002, prominent businessmen set up the Aljubarrota Foundation, aimed at highlighting the importance of the 1385 battle that secured Portugal's independence.

Attitudes Towards Britain

The next time you drink a cup of tea or eat a piece of toast, think of Catherine of Bragança. She popularized the former and is said to have introduced the latter to Britain – with good purpose: she held tea parties to keep an eye on her ladies-in-waiting, who were well within the orbit of her philandering husband, King Charles II. Portugal is Britain's oldest ally: the tie dates from the Treaty of Windsor in 1386, which is represented in the clasped hands of the effigies of Dom João I and his wife Philippa of Lancaster on their tomb in the Abbey of Batalha. The 600-year-old alliance was invoked most recently during the Gulf War; Portuguese ships transported British troops.

The Portuguese are fond of the British, and not just those that drink their port wine. But things have not always been rosy. In 1555, the prophet Nostradamus wrote, 'The great empire will be England ... the all-powerful for more than 300 years; the Portuguese will not be pleased with it' and the truth of his prediction lies in the shift in the relations between the two countries as Portugal's power declined. Britain became the protector of Portugal because her ports were useful, because of trade with her empire, and, most importantly, to offset the power of Spain. Portugal provided Catherine of Bragança with a mammoth dowry (finally settled in the reign of James II), and granted Britain terms of trade which proved so favourable to the British that Pombal severely curtailed them in the following century. When the French invaded in the early 18th century, the King of Portugal fled to Brazil in a British ship, and it was Wellington who expelled the aggressors.

Migrants

If you come to a village in the north of Portugal and spy a shriekingly incongruous house, built with urban materials and colourfully painted, it's likely to be a *casa de emigrante*. The Portuguese have been emigrating in a big way since the 18th century, when rural proverty drove thousands of men to Brazil. Emigration to France and West Germany, which had begun in the 1950s, surged ahead during the following decade, when young men journeyed abroad to escape conscription for the wars in Africa, and to earn relatively high salaries: by 1973 an estimated 800,000 Portuguese had left the country. Although many returned after the Revolution of 1974, remittances from hardworking emigrants remain one of the main props of the Portuguese economy.

Most emigrants come from the Minho and Trás-os-Montes, and they return in August, driving their flashy cars too fast and stuffing their breast pockets with crisp banknotes. Many houses remain half-built until the owner can afford to complete the project, which is intended to symbolize his escape from subsistence farming. If he runs into financial difficulties, the pretentious house reverts: the garage becomes a cowshed, the manicured garden becomes a threshing floor. Some labourers return to their previous professions – there are quite a few polyglot shepherds about the place. The tables have recently turned: Portugal now receives thousands more immigrants (mainly from Brazil and eastern Europe) a year than it sends out emigrants.

The Colonial Legacy

The Portuguese are fond of reminding visitors that their language ranks seventh in the world, in terms of numbers of people speaking it. This hangover from Portuguese colonial rule is still a cause for pride. But in a curious reversal of roles, the Portuguese spoken in Portugal is now being undermined by Brazilian Portuguese: Brazilian soap operas bring slang to their mother tongue.

Portugal fought long and expensive wars in Africa, and pulled out of the continent following the Revolution of 1974. The revolution also brought democracy to Portugal, and thus seems to have served as a kind of exorcism as regards people's attitude towards the empire. Indeed, Portuguese governments have been attempting to rekindle Portuguese influence in southern Africa, with a success that is limited mainly by Portugal's reduced economic clout. The former colonial power is trying, lately with Brazilian help, to give the Lisbon-based Community of Portuguese Speaking Countries a real existence, rather than just on paper. The community's newest member, East Timor, opted for Portuguese as an official language in a bid to keep it distinct from its neighbours, and Lisbon's effort to provide the country with school books and to train civil servants is something of a test case.

Portugal Today

Portuguese politics have stabilized after a muddled post-revolutionary decade (*see* **History**, 'Democracy', pp.27–8), but the instinct of the man in the *tasca* is still to send the whole business to the devil and leave someone else to sort it out. His passivity goes back a long way. The 18th and 19th centuries lacked a strong liberal tradition, so the population remained ignorant of the powers and limitations of democracy. In the absence of a middle class clamouring for a true parliamentary system, the landed élite dominated politics in Portugal. Salazar's aim to stunt the awakening of political consciousness compounded the situation. The revolution, with its street slogans and workplace confrontations, politicized sections of the population and left a legacy of party activism. Voting rates, although declining, have held up better than in Britain, but there is little participation in other manifestations of civil society.

Forty-eight years of dictatorship and two years of revolutionary chaos left a legacy of over-centralized economic structures, flimsy infrastructure, skeletal education, inadequate social welfare and housing. But things have changed enormously. Portugal joined the EU in 1986, and the Community has pumped billions of dollars into the country to help modernize the economy. Resources flooded into communications, transport, education and professional training. The tax and financial systems have been reformed, as have agrarian law and labour practices. Not all the money has been well spent, and there is great anxiety since the EU has switched funds to the new members in Eastern Europe.

Portugal has few natural resources. She labours under a chronic trade deficit, has yet to prove that state finances are on a sustainable footing, and the economy is heavily dependent on tourism and money sent back by emigrants working abroad – neither of which are dependable. Yet back in the late 1990s Portugal had the fastest-growing economy in Europe. There are three main industries: textiles, clothing and shoes (which face competition from Southeast Asia); wood pulp (from eucalyptus trees, which some ecologists denounce as too greedy for water, and harmful to neighbouring species); china and earthenware.

In 2005, Portugal suffered its worst drought in living memory, devastating agriculture and severely impacting on a host of planned financial projects. Furthermore, in contrast to the 1990s, Portugal has one of the lowest per capita GDPs in the European Union. On a more positive note, Portugal´s environmental awareness is growing, with the construction in 2007 of a €58 million solar power station in the Alentejo, which saves around 30,000 tonnes of the country's current carbon dioxide emissions.

Untypical 'Typical'

Tipico doesn't quite mean 'typical' in the sense of 'representative': it's more akin to 'quintessential', and ferreting out anything *típico* is a national pastime. Thus Coimbra University is described as a typical university, or Fernando Pessoa a typical poet. Restaurants advertise themselves as *típico* to suggest that they embody something peculiarly Portuguese. The cult of the *típico* was fostered by Salazar's nationalism, and the legacy remains.

Food and
Drink

05

The early 18th-century traveller Mrs Marianne Baillie noted that 'the courtly whisper of the highest bred *fidalgo*, loaded with garlic and oil, differed not at all from the breath of the humblest peasant'. Today garlic makes only muted appearances, and Portuguese cooking is not particularly oily, but the gist of her observation holds true: tastes are remarkably democratic, and the best food in Portugal is peasant fare. Fancy restaurants may have extensive wine lists, but for a good meal you'd be better off at an upmarket *tasca* (tavern) or a *restaurante típico* (*see* p.44). If in doubt, eat where the locals eat and choose the *prato do dia* (dish of the day).

Most Portuguese food is simple and heavy; it's well worth seeking out the more complicated dishes, as these are often the richest and most tasty (particularly the northern meat stews and the coastal fish stews). Regional dishes are the closest you're likely to get to Portuguese home cooking: the best-known are detailed below. These dishes rely on a narrow range of vegetables, and there are very few vegetable side dishes or salads – although meals often include a health-giving but unremarkable vegetable-based soup. Spices are little used, which is surprising given Portugal's role in the 16th-century spice trade. Vegetarians may strike it lucky in urban areas, but veggie-consciousness has a long way to go. Those who eat fish are well catered for. Vegans will find eating out almost impossible outside the main cities.

Portuguese Specialities

See also relevant chapters for further information on regional specialities.

Fish and Seafood

These together account for 40 per cent of Portugal's protein intake. Fish is usually grilled with lots of salt or boiled; if the latter, you'll be given separate flasks of oil and vinegar, or you could ask for a squeeze of lemon. Portugal is not merely a land of sardines: hake, whiting, *peixe espada* (scabbard fish, not swordfish), *carapaus* (horse mackerel), lampreys, and of course *bacalhau* (*see* opposite) are popular and widely available. One of the most enjoyable fish dishes is the *caldeirada*, a mixed fish stew, with potatoes and plenty of gravy. Be careful where you choose to order one, as you may end up with a mixture of trimmings. One of the simplest but most common shellfish dishes is *ameijoas à Bulhão Pato* – clams braised with garlic and fresh coriander. *Ameijoas* also pop up in the nearest thing Portugal has to a national dish: *carne de porco à alentejana* – pork meat with clams. It's a strangely delicious combination.

Lampreys are another great love – made familiar to English schoolchildren by Henry I (1100–35), who died of a surfeit of this eel-like fish. Abundant in the Rivers Minho, Lima, Cávado and Mondego, lampreys are caught in Lent, on their return to the river to spawn. They make a rich meal, commonly served in a stew with rice, wine and onions, called *arroz de lampreia*. Connoisseurs insist on the fish being cooked in its own blood. Less oily and more chewy is *arroz de polvo* (octopus rice). Popular wisdom dictates is that neither of these dishes should be eaten by a pregnant mother, or her baby will be born with weak bones or none at all.

Bacalhau

It seems perverse that a race whose shores are favoured by so many fish should adopt *bacalhau* as their national dish. This dried, salted codfish looks like ossified grey cardboard, and is cut with a saw before being soaked and cooked in one of (a reputed) 365 different ways. The first official *bacalhau* fleet set sail during the reign of Dom João I (1385–1433), and subsequent fleets made around 150 voyages to Newfoundland during the reign of Dom Manuel (1495-1521); now *bacalhau* is imported from Norway and Iceland.

We unfortunate foreigners are often incapable of appreciating the delights of *bacalhau*: it's only palatable when heavily disguised, as in *bacalhau com natas* ('with cream') or *bacalhau à Gomes de Sá*, supposedly named after an eponymous Porto *bacalhau* merchant who invented it. As with all *bacalhau* dishes, the fish is soaked first in water. In this case, it's also then soaked in milk for a couple of hours, before being lightly mashed with fried onions, boiled potatoes and eggs, and garlic. Oil is added and the mixture is baked, briefly. No Christmas would be complete without *bacalhau cozido com todos* (boiled with potatoes, onions, eggs and kale), eaten for dinner on the 24th. The fish, flaked and mixed with the other ingredients, traditionally reappears the next day as *roupa velha* – 'old clothes'.

Pork

The pork is excellent, particularly in the Alentejo (or Trás-os-Montes for smoked ham and pork sausages). In 1726 Brockwell wrote that Portuguese pork was the most delicious in Europe: 'their swine are small, short-legged, and generally black, their Bellies oft reaching to the Ground.' Of the many excellent cured hams, *pata negra* ('black foot') is the best. The best example is from Barrancos, on the Alentejo's Spanish border. Dishes in which bits of pig loom large include the fragrant *feijoada à trasmontana*. It's best to enjoy this bean stew with your eyes closed – the recipe calls for the ear, snout and trotter of a pig, as well as different kinds of sausages, cured ham, a little red pepper and an onion. Macbeth's witches may have had a hand in concocting *cozido à portuguesa*, a boiled medley of blood sausage, pork sausage, spiced sausage, ribs, vertebrae, pigs' ears and lips, kale, carrots, turnips and potatoes.

Pigs' body parts don't only appear in stews. *Salada de orelha* – a popular snack across the country – is what it says – 'ear salad'. Customers throng to restaurants in Mealhada, north of Coimbra, and Negrais, near Mafra, to eat the fatty flesh of roast suckling pigs – *leitão assado*. Massed ranks of them come out of huge ovens on large trays.

Less flagrant but equally authentic are the sausages, eaten grilled, fried, baked and boiled, for snacks, in sandwiches, or as the centre of a meal. *Chouriço* are the most common, filled with lean and fat pork meat, garlic and red-pepper paste. Usually about an inch (2cm) in diameter and 6 inches (15cm) in length, they are tied in a loop and slung over a wooden pole across the fireplace to be smoked. Variants include *linguiça*, *paio* and *salpicão*, the latter two spiced. In recent years, EU and national legislation has forced commercial producers to switch to sterile metal implements and mixing bowls, but at home, the smelly old wooden tools are still used.

Not all sausages are made of pork. The garlicky *alheira* and floury *farinheira* sausages were perfected by the New Christians, Jews expelled from Spain in the 15th century, who had ostensibly renounced their faith: the Inquisition sent inspectors to check that the 'converts' were eating pork. Smoked sausages were duly produced that tasted like pork – but were made with poultry or rabbit.

Other Meat

Portugal was one of only two EU countries to face a ban (long since lifted) on beef exports because of BSE, although the prevalence of the disease was a fraction of that experienced in Britain. If you're at all nervous on the subject, stick to beef that is clearly marked as coming from a regional denomination such as *alentejano* – it's organic by tradition and the only Portuguese beef that's really worth eating anyway.

Offal of all kinds, from tongue (*lingua*) and liver (*iscas*) to hooves (*māozinhos* – literally 'little hands') is common. The inhabitants of Porto are nicknamed *tripeiros* after, tradition has it, they generously donated all their meat to Henry the Navigator's expedition to Ceuta. It's more likely, though, that the name has its origins in the siege of the city in 1832–3. Portuenses love tripe, and drape it in extravagant folds from meathooks; most commonly, it's off-white and looks like a honeycombed sheet of rubber. Tripe is cooked in a rich stew, *tripas à moda do Porto*, which includes calves' trotters, sausage, butter beans, chicken, onions, carrots and cumin – the latter a relic of that spice trade. *Papos de sarrabulho* is another northern dish that might worry some diners. Eaten mainly in the Minho, often with tripe, it's a stew whose key ingredient is thickened blood, into which are thrown various organs, rice and onions.

Lamb (*borrego*) is usually excellent, particularly in the Alentejo, and kid (*cabrito*) is invariably a treat. It's especially flavourful in the inland Beiras, where the animals graze on wild herbs. Rabbit (*coelho*), often rather greasily fried, is common.

Snacks

For snacks, the Portuguese favour the *prego* (steak sandwich), *bifanas* (pork steak, braised with coriander and garlic), *rissóis* (deep-fried envelopes of meat or seafood), mince *croquetes* or *pastéis de bacalhau* (codfish croquettes). The quality of all of these varies enormously from restaurant to bar; they can be excellent, or chewy and greasy.

Desserts

The Portuguese have very sweet teeth. This may be one of the Moors' most persistent legacies, and has been kindled over the centuries by the kitchens of many convents – the nuns used to sell confections to supplement their income. Hence some of the more picturesque names: *barriga de freira* (nun's belly), *papos de anjo* (angel's breasts) and *toucinho do céu* (heavenly lard). All are made from egg yolks, sugar and almonds, with little else, except in the Algarve, where the stronger Moorish influence means a wider range of ingredients are used, such as figs, dates and carob.

Traditional cakes and pastries – usually eaten with coffee rather than as a dessert – include *pastéis de nata* (custard tarts), *pão-de-ló* (sponge cake) and *bolos de mel* (honey cakes).

Bread

Bread is one of the delights of Portugal, especially in the northern interior. In Trás-os-Montes, it takes on a mystical quality. They say 'O pão é sagrado' – 'Bread is sacred'. It sustains life, like the Communion wafer. For households it symbolizes the fellowship of eating together, and for the community it symbolizes fertility and a bond with the land, for 'In this land, those who do not work do not eat'. Dough, flour, grain and even the maize plant in the field are called pão. Traditionally, for a household to grow its own maize is symbolic of its independence.

In the villages around Bragança, the winter festas of the winter solstice, Christmas, New Year and Epiphany revolve around bread, piled into pyramids around wooden structures called charolos. The loaves are crafted into fancy shapes – stars, humans, animals – some of them plain bread, some of them baked with honey, eggs, and dried fruits. Each pyramid is topped with a jumble of delicacies. Having processed to the church, the charolos are blessed by the priest, and then auctioned off. Buying the bread is a source of great social prestige, not least because of the prophylactic qualities it is believed to have acquired. Prophylactic qualities or no, eating bread is one of the gastronomic delights of Trás-os-Montes. The maize bread called broa is popular both there and in the Minho. Its crust is hard on the roof of one's mouth, but the crumbly bread is delicious, and curiously rich. Sometimes villagers bake nuggets of pigfat into their bread, making it a meal in itself.

Other widely available regional breads include pão de Mafra and pão alentejana.

Cheese

Cheese is eaten both before and after a meal. In most restaurants your waiter will set on your table a queijo fresco – cottage cheese, delicious either plain or with salt and pepper – or a small sheep's cheese. At buffets in upmarket restaurants, at a private dinner or a formal occasion, more sophisticated cheeses from Serpa or the Serra de Estrela will probably be offered after dessert. They are invariably excellent, varying mainly in the type of milk from which they are made and in ripeness.

Portuguese Drinks

Water and Fruit Juices

With so many spas, Portugal produces a flood of bottled waters: the chalky Carvalhelhos is particularly distinctive. The waters of Monchique and Luso are especially good. Of the fizzy ones, Pedras is the most aggressive, Castelo rather gentler. In towns, fresh fruit juices and shakes are also widely available in snack bars, usually made on the spot.

Wine

See also regional chapters for further information on local wines.

The Portuguese have been drinking wine since Roman times. They regularly beat the French and Germans to the title of biggest consumers of alcohol per head, but very rarely get drunk. Wine is extremely cheap – from around €2 per litre – and makes a highly enjoyable communion with Portugal. Locally produced wine is regarded as therapeutic, so you may opt for the *vinho da casa* (house wine) – in the Minho this might arrive in a pottery jug with a couple of porcelain bowls to drink it from.

From the Minho, in the far north, comes **vinho verde** – one of the delights of Portugal. This 'green wine' is light (around 9 per cent alcohol) and slightly sparkling, with a slight acidity balanced by its fruitiness – enough to refresh the most parched of travellers. *Vinho verde* is best drunk very cool, as an apéritif or with shellfish or grilled fish. It's also great for picnics. The *'verde'* of *vinho verde* refers to the young age at which the wine is drunk – usually the summer after the grapes were picked – rather than to its colour. It's best to stick to the whites; red *vinho verde* accounts for about 60 per cent of production (most of it staying in the region), and, even though it is always drunk fridge cold it tastes like a mistake. (The reds are fermented in contact with their skins, pips and stalks, whereas the whites are not.) Monção's Alvarinho is the best of the cooperatives' *vinho verde* – though purists argue that it's not a true *vinho verde*. Alvarinho produced by the Palácio da Brejoeira will cost considerably more, if you can find it (wine made from single estates is the exception in Portugal). The best-selling *vinho verde* is the untypically sweet Gatão.

Portugal's most famous alcoholic product is **port wine** (*vinho do Porto*). Good port (*see* p.180) is like a liquid symphony playing upon the palate; anyone who thinks of it as a dark and sticky drink to send you to sleep after lunch is in for a surprise. The **Douro region**, from which the wine that forms the basis of the port, before it is fortified with *aguardente*, originates, has had some success in improving the quality of its table wines in recent years. Portugal's most expensive wine, Barca Velha, comes from the Alto Douro.

Dão wines – from an area comprising the southwest of Beira Alta, including Aguiar da Beira, Gouveia, Arganil, Mortágua, Tondela and parts of Viseu, mature into some of the country's most delicious: smooth, full-bodied and garnet-coloured. Fortunately, 90 per cent of the wine from this region is red, which is of a far superior quality to the white. Be wary of young wines, which can taste oddly tannic. The neighbouring **Bairrada** region also produces excellent reds from the native Baga grape.

In western Portugal, in both the Ribatejo and Estremadura, the quality of the wine produced is less impressive than its quantity. Most wines from these regions are red; look out for those of the **Serradayre** brand (literally 'Mountain Air'), a smooth, light, fruity wine. In the small Palmela region, fine reds are produced from the Periquita grape, another Portuguese native. Neighbouring Setúbal is famed for its Moscatel.

Inland, the Alentejo's cooperatives, particularly **Borba**, have made strides in improving the quality of their very drinkable reds. Famous labels include **Esporão**, which also produces wines from single Portuguese grape varieties.

Apéritifs, Liqueurs and Beer

White port is a good way to *abrir o apetite* – 'open' your appetite. The sickly *ginginha* cherry liqueur sold in picturesque little bars around Rossio in Lisbon is more likely to close it. Meals can be chased down with *aguardente*, at its best a brandy-like spirit distilled from wine, or clear **bagaceira**, a throat-burning firewater distilled from the leftovers of pressed grapes. If you want a good **brandy** at a fraction of the price of cognac, order an aged *Aguardente Velha* or an *Antiquíssima*.

Beer (*cerveja*) has been fast gaining ground over wine in recent years. The two main brands are **Sagres** and **Super Bock**. They are both inoffensive and slip down nicely. The *preta* ('black' – actually brown) beers produced by both majors are stronger, and not unlike a British brown ale.

Restaurant Generalities

Breakfast is usually a cup of coffee with a bread roll and butter, followed by another cup of coffee in the middle of the morning. Lunch begins about 12.30pm, and lasts until 2 or 2.30pm. After a mid-afternoon cup of coffee or tea, and/or a snack – *lanche* – dinner gets under way around 8pm; later if people are eating out.

Only very rarely do Portuguese restaurants have a cover charge, but the convention is that you pay for what you touch. It is normal for waiting staff to bring bread, butter, olives, spreads, cheeses or other appetizers. They are not (or not usually) trying to trick you into paying more than you bargained for. For the main course, helpings tend to be enormous, and many menus list the price of half-portions (*meia dose* – usually two-thirds of the full rate). If you lunch standing up in a snack bar, you may even be able to order a still cheaper mini-portion.

Portuguese restaurants are required by law to offer a tourist menu, comprising a main course with starter and/or dessert, water and coffee. Sometimes a glass of wine is included, too. This menu rarely offers very good value given the constraints involved. Set menus, sometimes available at lunchtime, are a different proposition. There is almost always a house wine, and it will invariably be drinkable, if nothing special. For restaurant price categories used in this guide and information on tipping, *see* p.70.

Menu Reader

Most of the restaurants listed in this book do not translate their menus; below is some essential vocabulary you need to translate them. For regional dishes, see the section on 'Portuguese Specialities' (pp.46–9). *See* **Language** (pp.525–7) for other useful Portuguese words and phrases.

Restaurant
ementa the menu
pequeno almoço breakfast
almoço lunch
jantar dinner
a conta the bill
O serviço está incluindo? Is service included?
a lista dos vinhos the wine list

Coffee and Tea
bica a small, black coffee
galão a tall glass of white coffee
Nescafé decaffeinated coffee
chá tea

Meat (*Carne*)
anho lamb
bife steak
cabrito kid
carneiro mutton
entrecosto rumpsteak
fiambre ham
fígado liver
leitão suckling pig
javali wild boar
veado deer
lingua tongue
lombo fillet
porco pork
rins kidneys
toucinho bacon

vaca beef
vitela veal

Poultry and Game (*Aves e Caça*)
frango chicken
galinha hen
peru turkey
perdiz partridge
coelho rabbit

Fish (*Peixe*)
atum tuna
bacalhau salt cod
carpa carp
cherne grouper
linguado sole
pargo bream
peixe-espada scabbard fish
pescada hake
robalo small bass
salmonete red mullet
cavala mackerel
sardinhas sardines
salmão salmon
truta trout

Shellfish (*Mariscos*)
amêijoas cockles
camarões shrimps
gambas prawns
lagosta rock lobster
lulas cuttlefish
polvo octopus

Vegetables (*Legumes*)
alho garlic
arroz rice
batatas potatoes
cebolas onions
cenouras carrots
cogumelos mushrooms
couve cabbage
couve-flor cauliflower

ervilhas peas
espinafres spinach
favas broad beans
feijão beans
pimentos peppers

Fruit (*Frutas*)
ameixas plums
ananás pineapple
figos figs
laranja orange
maçã apple
pêra pear
uvas grapes

Cooking (*Preparo*)
assado roasted
cozido boiled
estufado stewed
frito fried
fumado smoked
grelhado grilled
guisado stew
nas brasas braised
no espeto on the spit
no forno baked
mista mixed (e.g. salad)

Other
manteiga butter
queijo cheese
pão bread
gelo ice
pimenta pepper
sal salt
azeite olive oil
vinagre vinegar
cerveja beer
vinho tinto red wine
vinho branco white wine
vinho de mesa table wine
água water

Planning
Your Trip

06

Climate Guide

The following table gives average maximum daily temperatures (°C), average number of dry days, and average seawater temperatures (°C) in a selection of popular towns and cities in Portugal:

	January	April	July	October
Viana do Castelo	13/12/12	18/17/14	24/26/16	20/17/16
Bragança	8/14/–	16/19/–	28/27/–	18/20/–
Porto	13/14/12	18/18/14	25/26/16	21/18/16
Coimbra	14/15/–	21/22/–	29/28/–	24/19/–
Castelo Branco	11/20/–	19/22/–	30/30/–	21/23/–
Lisbon	14/16/13	19/21/14	28/30/16	22/22/17
Évora	12/17/–	19/20/–	30/30/–	22/22/–
Faro	15/22/14	20/24/16	29/31/21	23/25/18

Climate and When to Go

Portugal is a sunny country: even in the north, in December, you can reckon on 3½hrs of sunshine per day. In the south and northeast in July, visitors may fry in 12½hrs of sunshine per day (wearing a hat staves off headaches, and do bring a sunscreen or sunblock for the kids). The glare is high, so bring really good sunglasses. Winters are chilly in the north – you'll need a decent coat – but delightfully mild in the Algarve. Pack an umbrella and a raincoat if you intend to visit the Minho between October and May – it's the rain that keeps the province green. Spring and autumn are the best and most pleasant times to visit Portugal; if you can, aim for late April or early May (also coinciding with the wild roadside flowers and hotels' winter rates).

Festivals

Though more reserved than their Spanish neighbours, the Portuguese make the most of the many saint's days and other celebrations, many of them with deep pagan roots. Just about every town of any size has its annual summer festival, always with a fair and often with bullfights or a running of the bulls. Details of relevant festivals are given in the information for each town in the guide. The 'Calendar of Events' box (see pp.55–6) includes a selection of the most significant festivals.

Tourist Information

There are **tourist offices** throughout Portugal, operated by ICEP, the trade and tourism promotion agency and signposted as *Turismo*. These are distinct from, and more useful than, the municipal tourist information desks set up in various town halls. Generally, tourist offices try hard to be helpful: more often than not you'll find someone who speaks English. Some know up-to-date hotel prices, but they rarely have timetables for public transport. Opening times follow no set pattern, other than varying between winter and summer. Few tourist offices will open before 10, some close for lunch 12.30–2, and Saturday afternoon is a long shot.

Tourism officials have divided the country into regions: tourist offices may have

Portuguese National Tourist Offices

These offer potential visitors numerous maps, fact sheets, and glossy brochures depicting bikinis in various locations. The offices are to be found in:

UK: 22–25a Sackville Street, London W1X 2LY, **t** (020) 7494 1441.

Ireland: c/o Portuguese Embassy, Knocksinna House, Knocksinna, Foxrock, Dublin 18, **t** (1) 289 4416.

USA: 590 Fifth Avenue, 4th floor, New York, NY 10036, **t** (212) 354 4403, *tourism@ portugal.org*.

Canada: 60 Bloor Street West, Suite 1005, Toronto, Ontario M4W 3B8, **t** (416) 921 7376, *iceptor@idirect.com*.

Calendar of Events

January

Festa de São Sebastião in Vila de Feira, Aveiro, with processions.

February

Carnival in Portugal has been heavily influenced by its Brazilian offshoot; the Portuguese watch the celebrations in Rio live on TV. Carnival is at its most Portuguese in Ovar, Nazaré, Loulé and Portimão. The nearest carnival to Lisbon with any tradition is Torres Novas, with floats and giant papier-mâché figures.

March

Second Sunday in Lent *Senhor dos Passos* procession, in Lisbon's Graça neighbourhood, held since the 16th century, attended by prominent *lisboetas*.

Through to April the *Feira de Março* in Aveiro is the region's biggest trade fair with plenty of entertainment added on.

Holy Week (*Semana Santa*) marked in churches up and down the country, but at its most impressive (and solemn) in Braga's Holy Thursday *Ecce Homo* procession. Good Friday is a national public holiday; the following Monday is not. It is for the Spanish, who descend on Lisbon in huge numbers. Easter also kicks off the bullfighting season (to late September).

April

25 Anniversary of the 1974 Revolution, a national holiday; ceremonies and speeches mark the occasion.

May

First Sunday *Festa das Cruzes*, Monsanto, with religious celebrations, a fair and folk performances.

2–3 *Festas das Cruzes*, Barcelos – even bigger than the regular market.

12–13 Pilgrimage season opens in Fátima (monthly until the eve of 13 October).

Late in month *Queima das Fitas*, students in Coimbra burn faculty ribbons to mark the end of the academic year, and use the excuse for a huge street party; students in other towns follow suit.

June

First weekend *Festa de São Gonçalo*, Amarante – *romaria*, folk music, bullfights and fireworks, for a Catholic saint whose reputation has roots in pagan fertility cult.

One week in June (check dates with tourist office) beer festival in Silves.

Two weeks in June Troia film festival, the largest in the Lisbon region, in Setúbal.

12–13 *Festas Populares* start in Lisbon on the eve of *Dia de Santo António*, with groups from the older *bairros* squaring off in the *Marchas Populares*, after which the city parties all night, fed by grilled sardines and sangria. The next morning sees the saint's procession and a mass wedding for young locals paid for by the city council.

23–24 *Dia de São João* in Porto features a giant fireworks show then music and dancing around town, with strangers bopping each other with giant plastic hammers or waving giant leeks; the next morning there are boat races on the Douro.

28–29 *Dia de São Pedro* marks the end of the *Festas Populares*.

July

First weekend Jazz on a Summer's Day in Estoril, Portugal's oldest jazz festival, attracts big established names.

First Sunday, every four years (held 2007) *Festa dos Tabuleiros*, Tomar, in which young women process with trays on their heads piled high with loaves and flowers.

August

First week *Festival Sudoeste*, Portugal's largest music festival, at Zambujeira do Mar, two hours south of Lisbon, with three days of concerts and DJs and free camping and local transport.

First Sunday *Festas Gualterianas*, Guimarães, the annual summer festival of Portugal's first capital.

Early in the month the *Jazz em Agosto* festival features mainly experimental artists to the Gulbenkian's open-air auditorium in Lisbon.

Sunday after 15 *Festa de Santa Barbara*, the annual festival of Miranda do Douro in Trás-os-Montes, sees male dancers performing traditional dances, and emigrants gathering to see friends and family.

Middle of the month *Festas da Senhora da Boa Viagem* in the fishing town of Peniche, with processions on land and at sea as locals honouring the patron saints that keep their menfolk safe.

Friday nearest 20 *Festas de N. S. da Agonia*, Viana do Castelo, one of Portugal's most traditional festivals, featuring processions, folk music and dancing in regional costumes, bull-running and fireworks.

End of the month to middle of September
Festas de N.S. dos Remédios, Lamego, offers more of the same.

September

First weekend *Festa do Avante!* is a three-day festival organized by the communist party but cheap and eclectic enough (from *fado* to heavy metal) to attract thousands of apolitical Portuguese.

20–25 *Festas do Senhor da Piedade e Sao Mateus* in Elvas, on the Spanish border, are among the most traditional of Portuguese festivals, with processions, a fair and bullfights.

October

Last week of month/first week November
National Gastronomic Festival held at the trade fair grounds in Santarém is culinary Portugal in miniature.

November

1 *Dia dos Mortos*, families flock to cemeteries to leave candles and flowers on the graves of their loved ones.

11 *Festa de São Martinho* sees *magustos* or tastings to mark the opening of the first barrels of new wine, *água pé*, traditionally accompanied by roast chestnuts (already appearing on the streets).

11 National Horse Festival in Golegã, an hour north of Lisbon, with riding competitions, bullfights and plenty of food and drink.

December

24–25 Christmas – *Natal* – is marked above all by a dinner on Christmas Eve, traditionally *bacalhau* but increasingly turkey or other meat. Only the 25th is a national holiday.

26–6 Jan *Festa dos Rapazes* in villages around Bragança, up in Trás-os-Montes.

---

information and pamphlets about other towns in their regions, but not beyond. The exceptions are in Lisbon and Porto, where the tourist offices offer a gamut of brochures to entice the traveller.

On the Web

Portugal's official tourism website is *www.portugalinsite.com*, with information on accommodation, food, transport, sports and other special interests. Trade and tourism institute ICEP's *www.portugal.org* site is a good starting point for a general search. As well as information on geography, history, culture and weather, it contains a directory with links to North American tour operators' websites. The Lisbon tourist board has its own site: *www.atl-turismolisboa.pt*. For a quirky look at the capital by a local, see Lisbon pages *isboa.kpnqwest.pt/i/lisboa.html*. For those who are headed for the Algarve, *www.algarve-web.com/algarve* has maps, listings and background information.

For information (in Portuguese) on cultural events, mainly in Lisbon but also in Porto and some other towns, see *www.publico.pt* and click on *Guia do Lazer* (leisure guide). For comprehensive film listings, see *www.7arte.net* (films aren't dubbed).

See the 'Where to Stay' section below for some accommodation websites. The Portugal Hotel Guide on *www.maisturismo.pt/1/search.html* could also be handy.

Embassies and Consulates

UK: Rua São Bernardo 33, Lisbon, t (21) 392 4000; Avenida da Boa Vista 3072, Porto, t (22) 618 4789; Largo Francisco A. Maurício 7, 1st floor, Portimão, t (282) 417 800.
Ireland: Rua da Imprensa à Estrela 1, 4th floor, Lisbon, t (21) 392 9440.
USA: Avenida das Forças Armadas, Lisbon, t (21) 726 3300, *www.american-embassy.pt*.
Canada: Edifício Victória, Avenida Liberdade 196–200, 3rd floor, Lisbon, t (21) 316 4600.

Entry Formalities

There are no restrictions on visits by British, Irish and other EU passport holders. Holders of US and Canadian passports can enter Portugal for up to 60 days without a visa. These periods may be extended, before they expire, on application to the **Foreigners Registration Service**, Avenida António Augusto Aguiar 20, 1069–1118 Lisbon, t (21) 314 4053, *dir.lisboa@sef.pt*. In

Portuguese Embassies and Consulates Abroad

Embassies

UK: 11 Belgrave Square, London SW1X 8PP, **t** (020) 7235 5331/2/3/4 or 7325 0739, *london@portembassy.co.uk*

Ireland: Knocksinna House, Foxrock, Dublin 18, **t** (1) 289 4416 or 289 3375, *ptembassydublin@tinet.ie*

USA: 2125 Kalorama Road, NW Washington D.C. 20008, *www.portugalemb.org*. Consular Section **t** (202) 328 8610, 328 9025 or 328 8789, *embportwash@mindspring.com*

Canada: 645 Island Park Drive, Ottawa, Ontario K1Y OB8, Consular Section **t** (613) 729 0883, *www.embportugal-ottawa.org*

Consulates

www.portugalconsulate.org

UK: Silver City House, 62 Brompton Road, London SW3 1BJ, **t** (020) 7581 8722/3/4, *mail@cglon.dgaccp.pt*

Ireland: Knocksinna Mews, 7 Willow Park/Westminster Park, Foxrock, Dublin 18, **t** (1) 289 4416, 289 3375 or 289 6852, *vasco.pita@scdub.dgaccp.pt*, *luis-graça@dgaccp.pt*

USA: One Exeter Plaza, 7th Floor, Boston, MA 02116, **t** (617) 536 8740 or 536 9408, *mailcgbos@dgaccp.pt*;

The Legal Centre at One Riverfront Plaza, Main floor, Newark, NJ 07102, **t** (973) 643 4200 or 643 3900, *mail@cnew.dgaccp.pt*;

630 Fifth Avenue, Suite 801, New York, NY 10111, **t** (212) 246 4581 or 765 2957, *mail@cgnyk.dgaccp.pt*;

3298 Washington Street, San Francisco, CA 94115, **t** (415) 346 3400, *congenportugal@cgsfr.dgaccp.pt*

Canada: 2020 Rue de l'Université, suite 2425, Montreal, Québec H3A 2A5, **t** (514) 499 0359, *mail@cgmrl.dgaccp.pt*;

438 University Avenue, Suite 1400, Box 41, Toronto, Ontario M5G 2K8, **t** (416) 217 0966 or 217 0971;

904 Pender Place, 700 West Pender Street, Vancouver, B.C. V6C 3S3, **t** (604) 688 6514 or 685 7042, *mail@cnvan.dgaccp.pt*

practice, visitors are very unlikely to be challenged over how long they have been in the country.

Customs

Customs are usually polite and present few problems. It's forbidden to bring fresh meat into Portugal. There is no duty free for travel within the EU, and no limits to the amount of tobacco and alcohol that may be carried to and from Portugal and other member states (except for the three Scandinavian ones, which limit imports), so long as these are for personal use only.

From outside the EU, visitors aged 18 and over may bring in the following: 200 cigarettes or 100 cigarillos or 50 cigars or 250g of tobacco; 1 litre of spirits over 22% or 2 litres of spirits up to 22%; 2 litres of wine; 50g of perfume and 250ml of eau de toilette; 500g of coffee or 200g of coffee extract (if bought in a tax-free shop); 100g of tea or 40g of tea extract (if bought in a tax-free shop); further goods with a total value of up to €37.41.

Disabled Travellers

There are few special facilities for disabled travellers, though the Portuguese will always rush to aid anyone who has trouble getting around. There are parking spaces reserved for disabled people in the main cities and adapted WCs and wheelchair facilities at airports and main train stations. The **Portuguese National Tourist Office** produces some literature for the disabled, including a list of hotels with facilities. In Britain, contact **RADAR** (Royal Association For Disability and Rehabilitation) at Unit 12, City Forum, 250 City Road, London EC1V 8AF, **t** (020) 7250 3222, *www.radar.org.uk*. Their *Holidays and Travel Abroad: A Guide For Disabled People* is now out of print, but available through some bookshops. In the USA, a helpful organization is **Mobility International**, at PO Box 10767, Eugene, Oregon 97400, **t** (503) 343 1284, *www.miusa.org*. Also in the USA is **SATH** (Society for the Advancement of Travel for the Handicapped) at 347 Fifth Avenue, Suite 610, New York 10016, **t** (212) 447 7284, *www.sath.org*.

In Portugal itself, a useful association is the **ACAPO** (Association of the Blind and Partially Sighted of Portugal), Rua de S. José, 86, 1st floor, 1500 Lisbon, **t** (21) 342 2001, *www.portuguesealliance.com*.

There are facilities for the disabled at the following Olympic-sized **swimming pools**: Faro Sports Centre, Loulé Public Swimming Pool (both in the Algarve) and the Piscina Municipal do Areeiro in Lisbon.

Insurance and EHIC Cards

Portugal has a reciprocal health agreement with Britain. The **European Health Insurance Card** (EHIC) replaces the former E111 certificate. This entitles all UK residents to reduced-cost (sometimes free) health care. To get an EHIC, apply online at *www.ehic.org.uk* or pick up an application form from your local post office. The EHIC entitles you to free emergency medical treatment while visiting Portugal, on production of the form and your passport. Some charges are made for prescribed medicines and dental treatment. Keep all doctor's and pharmacy receipts. The British National Health Service will not reimburse medical expenses. Non EU citizens must carry private health insurance, but travel insurance is advisable for everyone, even if you have an EHIC.

Vaccinations

No vaccinations are currently required for visitors to Portugal from Britain, Ireland, the USA or Canada (although if you are coming from somewhere with a cholera epidemic you must be able to produce an International Certificate of Vaccination).

Geography

Portugal is a small country, as the 10 million Portuguese are fond of remarking. It covers 35,500 square miles (92,000 sq km). Three rivers serve as boundaries with Spain, but only one river, the Zêzere, originates in Portugal. The hummocky hills of the northwest are balanced by the high, rolling hills of the northeast. South of the latter rises Portugal's only true mountain range, the Serra da Estrela, which reaches 6,539ft

(1,993m). The rest of the country is fairly flat, though in places the plains ruck up into hills.

Flora and Fauna

For such a small country, Portugal has fair variation in topography and climate. This in turn means a wide range of flora and fauna, from maples and wolves in the far north to olives and flamingos in the south.

Traces of Portugal's primeval forest, including evergreen holm oaks (*Quercus ilex*) remain only in the less accessible mountain regions, including Peneda-Gerês, Portugal's only National Park (there are also, in decreasing order of protection, 12 Natural Parks, nine Natural Reserves and three Protected Landscapes). In the rest of the north of the country deciduous trees predominate, with conifers in the higher altitudes. In the south conifers and other evergreens predominate, with the Setúbal peninsula, particularly the Serra da Arrábida, the best example of the coastal pine forests.

Inland, cork oaks are dotted over much of the Alentejo. Their bark is periodically stripped for processing and turning into wine corks and the like; many argue this represents the only sustainable way of maintaining the region's ecology, which makes the advance of plastic stoppers and screw-tops all the more alarming for Portugal. Commercial forestry is increasingly dominated by the eucalyptus, beloved by pulp companies for its rapid growth, but seen by many as water-guzzling monsters. Portugal has one native species of palm, the trunkless dwarf palm (*Chamaerops humilis*) but many other types thrive in the south. A single specimen of the most common type, the Canary date-palm, can often be seen next to isolated farmhouses. The more exposed coastal areas of the south, such as the cliffs around Cabo da Roca, are notable for colourful succulents.

Portugal is a good place to see birds, being on the migration routes to Africa. Flamingos are abundant in the Tagus Estuary Natural Reserve, as are other wading species. The Serra de São Mamede Natural Park, with a micro-climate between the Mediterranean regions to the east and maritime air masses to the west, is a haven for golden eagles.

Further north, the woods of central and northern Portugal harbour roe deer, foxes and a few wolves. The number of wolves is much reduced, despite recent projects to breed and re-introduce them. (Rare species have full statutory protection in areas like Peneda-Gerês.) The Iberian lynx, Europe's only large cat, has all but disappeared in Portugal, although a lone animal sometimes sneaks across the border from Spain.

The lynx is one of those species whose habitat environmentalists warned would be irrevocably broken up by the creation of the huge Alqueva reservoir in the Alentejo, which began filling in 2002. Local farmers for decades dreamed of the giant dam on the Guadiana as this impoverished region's salvation. Gloomier observers, predicting rising soil salinity and the effects of the transfer of water from polluted rivers to cleaner ones, say it could be its ruin. Such mega-projects have proved lightning rods for increasingly confident ecological groups, who make expert use of a sympathetic press to make up for their continuing lack of mass appeal. Environmental awareness among the general public is slow in coming.

Wildlife across the country suffered from the unprecedented fires that raged during the summers of 2003 and 2005. During the latter, about 200,000 hectares (about 494,000 acres) burned, mainly in the central Coimbra region. Most forest fires in Portugal are the result of negligence rather than arson or natural causes; take care not to add to the danger.

As for natural threats to humans, keep a look out for scorpions and snakes when walking in the countryside. The latter in particular are common enough to be a real danger. As ever, they are generally more frightened of you than you are of them, but don't step on one. Since this may happen accidentally, it's best not to wear open sandals when walking. Also be on your guard near water, or when sitting down or leaning against anything. Wear long trousers (not least to keep ticks off your skin).

Maps

The tourist offices' most useful handouts are their maps. These vary from illegible photocopies to glossy productions that are the size of a desktop.

The **Automóvel Club de Portugal** produces by far the best road maps: one side represents the whole country, while the reverse depicts the north, the centre or the south of Portugal in fine detail.

Both **Michelin** and **Lascelles** produce acceptable maps, should you wish to buy one in advance.

Walkers should try their luck at the **Instituto Geográfico e Cadastral Geral**, Rua Artilharia Um, 107, 1099-052, Lisbon **t** (21) 381 9600, *igeo@igeo.pt*.

Money

Portugal adopted the **Euro** along with most of the rest of the European Union. The currency is made up of 100 cents (*céntimos* in Portuguese). Euros circulate in notes of 500, 100, 50, 20, 10 and 5. Coins are issued for €2 and €1, and 50, 20, 10, 5 and 2 cents, as well as 1 cent. Exchange rates vary from day to day, at the time of research it is €1.18 to the pound, or €0.76 to the dollar – which makes €1 worth about 84p or $1.30. Commissions are usually heavier at banks than at money-changers.

There are **banks** in every town, and most will change foreign currency or traveller's cheques. In Lisbon, most banks have branches in the Baixa. Most banks are open Mon–Fri 8.30–3. The rate of exchange varies between them, but not significantly. Some fancy hotels and travel agencies will cash traveller's cheques or exchange foreign currency, but the rates sting. The exchange counter at Lisbon airport is open constantly; at Santa Apolónia railway station, Lisbon, it's open every day 8.30am–8.30pm.

Portugal's **Multibanco** system of ATMs is one of the most ubiquitous in Europe, linked to the Cirrus network. Most also accept Visa, MasterCard and a dozen other types of card. Cash withdrawals are free for domestic transactions, so charge will vary according to the rapaciousness of your own bank.

Allow a couple of weeks for **wiring money from abroad**, and work through one of the major banks in Lisbon or Porto (Banco Espírito Santo, Banco Nacional Ultramarino,

Banco Pinto & Sotto Mayor, Banco Português do Atlântico, Banco Totta & Açores).

Credit cards – American Express, Diner's Club, Mastercard and Visa – will be useful for booking airline tickets, car hire, and peace of mind in case of emergency. They are accepted by virtually all of the upmarket hotels and restaurants. The further you get off the beaten track, however, the more redundant your plastic will become.

Getting There

By Air

Mainland Portugal has three international airports, Lisbon, Porto and Faro. If you book far enough ahead, especially with one of the no-frills airlines, flying often works out cheaper than overland transport plus ferries.

The country is not well served by flights from outside Europe, so if that's your situation you may have to fly to a European hub and then pick up another flight from there. Going via London means you have a good chance of connecting (perhaps via a different London airport) with a bargain flight, booked online.

From the UK and Ireland

Portugal is served by several no-frills carriers from the UK. **EasyJet** have flights from London Gatwick, Luton and Stanstead, and from several other UK airports to Faro, and from all London airports and Manchester to Lisbon. **Ryanair** fly to Porto and Faro from several UK airports, including Belfast in Northern Ireland and Aberdeen in Scotland. **Thomsonfly** have a regular service from Manchester to Lisbon and from London Gatwick and several other UK airports to Faro. **Monarch Airways** also flies from London Gatwick, Luton, Manchester and Birmingham to Faro. **BMI** flies from Birmingham, Cardiff and the East Midlands to Lisbon and Faro. See Airline Carriers (p. 61) for contact details.

From the USA and Canada

Direct flights from the USA to Portugal are fairly scarce. Portuguese airline **TAP** operates regular flights from Newark and Los Angeles to Lisbon while **Continental** have nonstop flights to the Portuguese capital from Newark. Continental operate flights to Lisbon from several other US airports, including Boston, San Diego and Los Angeles, but these incorporate one en route stop.

There are no direct flights from Canada to Portugal, most airlines stop in New York or London en route. **Air Transat** have inexpensive flights to various airports in the UK, from where you can catch a cheap no-frills airline to the Algarve, Lisbon or Porto (see above).

By Ferry

There are no direct passenger ferries operating between Britain and mainland Portugal. However, a ferry runs between Plymouth and Santander in northern Spain (see 'By Car', p.62). Ferry passengers without cars could take a train from Santander to Valladolid, from where there are connections to Lisbon and Porto.

By Train

From the UK

There are several daily services to Paris from the Eurostar Rail Terminal at St Pancras station, London (opened in 2008), via the Channel Tunnel, and then onwards to Coimbra and Lisbon via Irún (in Spain). Change at Pampilhosa for Porto. If you are heading for the Algarve, you have to change trains at Lisbon. Book online with **Eurostar** (www.eurostar.com) or **Rail Europe** (www.raileurope.co.uk) or via any major travel agent.

From Spain

There is a daily train service from Madrid's Chamartín station to Lisbon, which arrives in the early morning. The train has a choice of seats, couchettes or cabins with ensuite bathrooms. You can book directly from the Spanish **RENFE** website (www.renfe.es). There are regular direct trains from Seville to Lisbon, with connections en route for Porto and the Algarve.

Special tickets

EU citizens who have been resident for the past six months in the European country in which they wish to buy their ticket are eligible for the **InterRail** (www.interrail.com) pass (available from British Rail or any travel agent), which offers discounted train travel

Airline Carriers

UK and Ireland

British Airways, t 0845 773 3377, *www.british-airways.com*. Serves Lisbon, Porto and Faro with several flights daily from Heathrow. There is a BA reservation number in Portugal on t (808) 200 125.

TAP Air Portugal, Chapter House, 22 Chapter Street, London SW1P 4NP, t (020) 7630 0746 or 0845 601 0932, *www.tap-airportugal.pt*. More than matches BA flight for flight, with the advantage that it continues to serve Gatwick as well as Heathrow. In Ireland, **TAP** can be found at 11 North Frederick Street, Dublin 1, t (1) 874 6443. Its reservation number in Portugal is t (707) 205 700, while flight information can be had on t (808) 213 141. Sales offices in Lisbon are at the airport, t (808) 201 1483 and the main rail station, Gare do Oriente, t (21) 895 8310.

BMI, *www.bmibaby.com*.

Monarch, *www.monarch-airlines.com*.

Ryanair, *www.ryanair.com*.

Thomsonfly, *www.thomsonfly.com*.

USA and Canada

TAP, t (800) 221 7370, *www.tap-airportugal.com*. Has offices in New York (608 Fifth Street, 3rd Floor, New York, NY 10020, t (212) 969 5775), Boston (1 Exeter Plaza, Boston, MA 02116, t (617) 262 8585) and serves a large concentration of Portuguese emigrants in Newark (399 Market Street, Newark, New Jersey, NJ 07105, t (973) 344 4490), the only place from which TAP actually flies from Lisbon. There are no TAP offices in Canada; Canadian passengers should contact the US offices.

Continental Airlines, t (800) 231 0856, (800) 343 9195 (hearing impaired), Canada (800) 525 0280, *www.continental.com*. Direct flights from Newark to Lisbon.

Air Transat, *www.airtransat.com*.

throughout Europe with prices depending on which countries (or zones) you choose and the length of travel (from 16 days to one month). Check the website for up-to-date prices, but you can expect to pay around £230 for 16 days for one adult second-class ticket. Another pass, offered by **Intero Pass** (*www.eurodomino.com*), gives substantial discounts for travel over a number of consecutive days within one month. Eight days'

travel will cost approximately €125 for an adult second-class ticket.

The equivalent North American **Eurail** (*www.eurail.com*) pass can be purchased in the US, for 7, 15, 21, 30, 60 or 90 days: it too saves the hassle of buying numerous tickets, but cost-wise it will only pay for itself if you use it every day, everywhere. The Eurail pass is not valid in Great Britain, Morocco or Hungary, and supplements are payable on many express trains.

Rail Europe (*www.raileurope.com*) offers anyone under the age of 26 discounted (by 25–35%) tickets to a fixed destination. These are valid for two months, and allow travellers to stop off at any stations along the pre-planned route.

Tickets can be reserved via the respective websites or any reputable travel agency.

By Bus

From the UK

Eurolines, t (08705) 143 218, *www.eurolines.com*, offer services from Victoria coach station on Monday, Wednesday, Friday and Saturday nights to Lisbon (42½hrs), and to the Algarve on Mondays and Fridays only (45½hrs to Faro). Both services require a change of station plus a stopover in Paris of as much as six hours on the following morning. The direct service to Porto leaves on Saturday morning and takes 33hrs – change at Valladolid in Spain.

Tickets are available from any National Express agent, or by credit-card booking over the phone. An under-25 discount is available on the ticket to Porto. They also offer 15-day, 30-day and 60-day passes.

From Spain

Portugal's **Rede Expressos** runs daily services from Madrid to Lisbon, three a week from Seville to Lisbon, and daily buses from Seville to Faro.

By Car

More than 2,000km of main roads separate Lisbon from Calais. If you prefer a short Channel crossing and a long stint on the *autoroute*, take the ferry from Dover/

Folkestone to Calais/Boulogne, and continue to Paris, where you can join the toll *Autoroute de l'Aquitaine* to just beyond Bordeaux. Enter Spain at Hendaye, and drive to Portugal via Burgos and Salamanca. For a longer Channel crossing and less *autoroute*, take a night-time ferry from Portsmouth, and head south via Rennes, Nantes, and La Rochelle before joining the *autoroute*. If you want to take it comfortably, reckon on two overnight stops *en route*.

If you prefer to stay on dry land, **Eurotunnel Shuttle**, t (08705) 353 535, *www.eurotunnel.com*, transports cars through the Channel Tunnel on purpose-built carriers between the ports of Folkestone and Calais, for between £320 and £450. The UK terminal is off Junction 11a of the M20.

There are a couple of options for cutting down on driving times. A **Motorail** service operates between Paris and Madrid (daily all year round). Passengers and their cars travel on different trains. The car is loaded onto a train in the evening. Passengers take a train the following morning and arrive in Madrid the next day, when their cars are available for collection. For details, contact **Rail Europe**, t (0990) 300 003, or **French National Railroads**, Rockefeller Center, 610 Fifth Avenue, New York, NY 10020.

Alternatively, **Brittany Ferries**, Milbay Docks, Plymouth PL1 3EW, t (08705) 360 360, *www.brittany-ferries.com*, operate a twice-weekly 24-hour service from Plymouth to Santander in northern Spain. Costs for passengers are roughly the same as a charter flight to Portugal. There is a special rate for eight-day returns. Santander is approximately 800km from Porto, 960km from Lisbon, and 1,300km from Faro.

There are no longer any border controls between Spain and Portugal, except for one-off events such as the 2004 European Cup.

Getting Around

By Air

Portugal is such a small country that there should be no need to fly anywhere. If you're in a hurry, **TAP**'s 737s wing their way several times daily from Lisbon to Porto and Faro, and the airline's subsidiary, **LAR**, flies smaller aircraft less frequently to Vila Real, Chaves and Bragança. TAP's offices in Lisbon are at the airport, t (21) 841 6167, and the main rail station, Gare do Oriente, t (21) 895 8310. Calls to reservations, t (808) 205 700, from anywhere in the country cost the same as a local call.

Portugália also flies between Lisbon and Porto and Faro, sharing codes with TAP. Its offices in Lisbon are also located at the airport, t (21) 843 7000.

By Train

Travelling by train is inexpensive, cheaper than travelling by bus, and generally the routes are more picturesque. However, buses are usually faster: Portugal's rail network was cut back severely in 1990, and it's often necessary to travel via junctions or cities to get from A to B. Portugal's trains are nationalized, and are operated by **CP (Caminhos de Ferro Portugueses,** *www.cp.pt*). Their head office is in Lisbon, at Calçada do Duque 20, 1249–109 Lisbon, t (21) 321 5700. Information on train times and prices can be had between 7am and 11pm on t (800) 208 208. There's also a special 'tourist line', t (800) 296 296.

Most trains are designated *Regional* or *Inter-Regional* (*IR*): the former run shorter routes and stop at most stations along the way. *IR* trains make intermittent stops, while *Intercidades* (*IC*) trains stop only at major towns or junctions and *Alfa-Pendular* (Lisbon–Porto only) trains are faster still (the latter two usually require supplements and seat reservation fees to be paid at the time of buying your ticket, pushing the price up by as much as 60%).

Train timetables are generally available if you ask, and are usually posted on station walls. If you plan to travel a lot by train, it's worth asking in the Lisbon or Porto stations for a copy of **CP's official timetable** (*Guia Horário Oficial*), which has an introduction in English, costs some €1.50 (if it's available) and gives full details of routes and schedules throughout the country.

Tickets must be purchased at the railway station in advance, rather than on the train – otherwise you are fined. Allow time to queue for buying a ticket.

Discount tickets

Various discount schemes are available from major railway stations. CP sell *Bilhetes Turisticos* (railcards for tourists) valid for 7, 14 or 21 days. Travellers over the age of 65 can buy a *Cartão Dourado* for a nominal sum; this entitles them to 50% off the full fare, but may not be used 6.30–9.30am or 5–8pm. On frequent, designated *Dias Azuis* (Blue Days), usually Monday afternoon to Thursday, CP offers a 20–30% discount on all of their return fares.

There are also special fares (with 20–30% reductions) for groups of 10 or more (*Bilhetes de Grupo*), travelling for a minimum distance of 75km/47 miles (single journey) or 150km/94 miles (return journey). The group leader should arrange these fares at least four days in advance.

Families are eligible for the *Cartão de Família*, which entitles a married couple and at least one of their children under the age of 18 to discount travel on *Dias Verdes*. Young people aged 12–26 are eligible for the *Cartão Jovem*, which allows 30% discounts on journeys over 91km during limited periods. No discount is available on *Alfa* services. Children under 4 travel free if they do not occupy a seat, and from 4 to 11 pay half-fare.

Scenic routes

Four narrow-gauge railway lines are still open in the north, offering an opportunity to get close to country life: at each village, the train is stopped by a lady with a red flag; a sack of maize and a pitcher of wine are heaved aboard, a new pair of shoes is passed out the window, and the train goes on; periodically it hoots to alert villagers walking down the tracks or collecting their dried laundry from the railway sidings.

These lines are often undergoing repairs, shortened or closed, so it is best to check ahead before planning a trip.

The narrow-gauge routes run from Régua to Vila Real (**Corgo line**) and Tua to Mirandela (**Tua line**); both connect with the scenic Porto–Pocinho railway (**Douro line**; be sure to get a window seat, as the locals pull down the blinds!). There is a lovely journey from Livracao to Amarante (**Tâmega line**).

By Bus

Buses are a quick and painless way to get around the country – if you can find out where and when the correct bus departs. Tickets are cheaper than they would be in northern Europe, but they're no bargain. After privatization, the main national company is **Rede Nacional de Expressos (Renex)**, but there are now many private bus companies, causing some confusion. The main regional companies are mentioned below and in the text.

For Express travel, check that you're standing in the correct line before queueing to buy your ticket at the bus station. Most Express buses depart from a (fume-laden) central depot. On longer journeys, buses stop for a coffee break every couple of hours. Some of the private buses show films. Night-bus drivers have a habit of playing loud music for the duration of the journey.

For local buses, purchase your ticket on board. If you travel in the early morning or mid-afternoon, you'll probably have to scramble for a seat with the children who travel to and from school on local buses (some local bus timetables are devised especially to suit schoolchildren, so if you want to get somewhere out of the way those are the best times to try).

Coach tours

RN Tours serve as a travel agent and organize various regional and national coach tours. Some of the major regional bus company offices are located as follows:

Lisbon: Rede Expressos, Avenida Duque D'Ávila 12, **t** (21) 358 1460, *www.rede-expressos.pt* for online booking.

Algarve: Eva Transportes, Bus Terminal, Avenida da República, Faro, **t** (289) 899 760, *www.eva-bus.com*.

Alentejo: Rodoviário do Alentejo, Terminal Rodoviário, 7000 Évora, **t** (266) 769 410.

North: Rodoviário Entre Douro e Minho, Rua Dr. Alfredo Magalhães, Porto, **t** (222) 003 152.

Centre: Rodoviário do Tejo, Avenida Herois De Angola, Leiria, **t** (244) 811 507 or (808) 200 370.

Renex (*www.renex.pt*) **and Gray Line**, Avenida Praia da Vitoria, 12B, Lisbon, **t** (21) 352 2594, also offer a range of tours around the country.

By Car

The charms of Portugal are best appreciated by car, and if you're from the UK petrol is marginally cheaper, at around €1.45 per litre for unleaded, €1.30 for diesel. Be aware that petrol prices have soared in recent years – reaching an all-time high in mid-2008 – and are around 47.5 % higher than in 2004, when petrol retailing was taken out of government control in Portugal. Street parking is usually no problem, other than in the major cities of Lisbon and Porto.

Portugal's road network has improved enormously, with the motorway from Lisbon to the Algarve and a direct fast link to Madrid for the first time ever in the two countries' history. Over on the west coast, the newly extended A8 relieves some of the traffic from the main A1 north–south highway, and the network is still being expanded.

At the next level down, though, national roads often have only one lane in either direction and are clogged with lorries seeking to avoid tolls. Some secondary roads are riddled with potholes (not to mention flocks of sheep and figs laid out to dry). In spring, delightful roadside flowers are sufficient compensation for the slowest of roads.

It's difficult to anticipate the time a journey will take, because although traffic is rarely heavy, some roads – particularly in the Minho and parts of the Beiras – are almost entirely made up of hairpin bends. Some of these roads are more dangerous than they need be; before the current wave of motorway construction, a handful of pseudo-motorways were built – the IPs – that encourage drivers to accelerate while taking them careering round badly designed, steep curves that sometimes tilt crazily outwards. However bad the roads are, Portuguese drivers are worse. Portugal has one of the highest accident rates in Europe – most accidents occur not on the motorways but on lesser roads such as the Lisbon–Cascais Avenida Marginal, the N-125 in the Algarve, or on northern highways such as the IP-5

(known as the 'Road of Death'). Few people think twice before drinking and driving; most show a general disregard for basic rules of the road (such as overtaking on the outside only or signalling before a manoeuvre rather than after) and each other. The Minho and Trás-os-Montes are notorious in the summer months, when emigrants return to show off their flashy motors.

Foreign-registered cars may enter Portugal for up to six months if accompanied by a registration document and a green card proving limited-liability insurance. British and international driving licences are valid; the latter are available through the AA or the RAC, or any auto club in the USA.

Portugal uses the international road sign system. Drive on the right and overtake on the left; give way to cars approaching from the right. Drivers may overtake stationary trams on the right, when this does not endanger passengers. Seatbelts are obligatory outside built-up areas. Speed limits for cars are: 60kph (37mph) in built-up areas; 90kph (55mph) outside built-up areas; 120kph (75mph) on motorways.

Almost all the motorways are toll roads; all are quite a bit cheaper than in the rest of Europe. On entering a paying stretch of motorway, you pass an automatic booth where you press a button and take the proffered ticket; on leaving the road you pay at a manned booth. In both cases, avoid the Via Verde lane – that's for cars with the automatic electronic bank debit system. If you go through it when you shouldn't, your photograph is taken and they use your licence plate to track you down.

For more information on motoring in Portugal, contact the **Automóvel Clube de Portugal**, 24 Rua Rosa Araújo, Lisbon, **t** (21) 318 0202, *www.acp.pt*, which operates a breakdown service. On motorways, there are orange SOS phones at regular intervals.

Car hire

Car hire is comparatively cheap by European standards. In **Lisbon**, **Porto** and **Faro**, all the major firms are represented at the **airport**; Avis also has one at Porto's Campanhã rail station. In addition, in Lisbon you'll find:

Avis, Avenida Praia da Vitória 12C, Lisbon, reservations **t** (800) 201 002.

Europcar, Avenida António Augusto Aguiar 24, Lisbon, **t** (21) 353 5115.

Hertz, Rua Castilho 72, Lisbon, **t** (21) 381 2430.

The minimum age for hiring a car is usually 23, and customers must have held a full driving licence for at least one year.

By City Bus and Taxi

Lisbon, and possibly Porto, are the only towns where you are likely to require a bus (see 'Getting Around' sections in **Lisbon**, p.351, and **Porto**, pp.176–7); elsewhere in Portugal the attractions are within easy walking distance within the towns and cities. Both Lisbon and Porto have efficient, rapidly expanding metros.

Taxis are inexpensive enough to be used by many locals for getting their groceries home. The vehicles are black, with greeny-turquoise roofs. In Lisbon and Porto they are metered: there is a flat rate, plus additional charges for every 300m travelled (with surcharges at night and for heavy luggage) – even in Lisbon, journeys rarely cost more than €7–8. It is difficult to hail a cab from the street: you're much better off going to a taxi rank, or phoning for a radio taxi.

By Bicycle

Cycling is very much a minority pursuit in Portugal, although mountain biking is winning adherents. On the roads, the difference with neighbouring Spain – where jersey-clad over-achievers steam up hills on weekends – is stark, and Portuguese motorists seem outraged that as a cyclist you are even on the road. Most will give you a much narrower berth than you would like, and may even hoot at you just for obliging them to divert their course slightly.

Rising car ownership and use also mean that the kind of country roads that could be most pleasant to ride along are all too often full of local traffic, while remaining disconcertingly bumpy.

Yet, if you have a robust cycle and are willing to brave these hazards, large parts of Portugal are good cycling country. With some exceptions, the south is much flatter than the north; areas such as the Minho and Trás-os-Montes are almost exclusively composed of challenging hills.

If you just want to ride around your resort, you should have little problem finding somewhere to hire a bicycle or mountain bike. Your hotel or the local tourist office can point you in the right direction.

Getting your own bike to Portugal is straightforward. The scheduled airlines take them for free, as do ferries; with no-frills airlines you're likely to bump up against baggage allowance limits. If you're travelling overland, you can take your bike free or for a minimal charge on some French, Spanish and Portuguese trains (those displaying a bicycle symbol on the timetable).

For more information in the UK on cycling abroad, contact the **Cycling Touring Club**, Cotterell House, 69 Meadrow, Godalming GU7 3HS, **t** (01483) 417 217, *www.ctc.org.uk*.

Where to Stay

There are still a few bargains around, but prices for accommodation in 'undiscovered' Portugal have mostly caught up with the rest of Europe.

Hotels

Most hotels and *pensões* in Portugal are decent enough, and you are unlikely to have cause for complaint. Should you do so, hotels are obliged to provide an official complaints book (*Livro Oficial de Reclamações*). Hoteliers are not permitted to oblige guests to accept full board or half-board.

Accommodation is divided into a pretty bewildering range of categories, which are allocated according to facilities: hotels (one to five stars); apartment-hotels (two to four stars); *pousadas* (*see* below); *estalagems* (four and five stars); *albergarias* (four stars); *residencials* and *pensões* (one to four stars). The system is not very helpful, and there are plenty of anomalies. Three-star *residencials* are often more comfortable than one- or two-star hotels. The distinction between *estalagems* and *albergarias* is very slight: both are inns, and usually very pleasant. In general, *residencials* are incorporated within larger buildings, and include breakfast in the tariff (unlike some *pensões*).

Establishments are obliged to display prices in their lobbies and guest rooms. Unless listed or agreed otherwise, single occupancy of a double room is charged at the full rate less the cost of one breakfast. An extra bed installed in a double room will cost 30% of the room rate, though children under the age of eight are charged half that. Single rooms are usually charged at 60–75% of the rate for a double.

Hotel accommodation in this book is listed under five price categories (see p.67), which are intended as guidelines and nothing more: prices may vary in high and low season or during festivals; and rates vary within some hotels, such as when some rooms have a pretty view and others do not. Inflation is currently running at roughly 5% per annum, and establishments are free to raise their prices from year to year as they wish.

Pousadas

Pousadas are government-owned hotels, intended to make use of the best Portugal has to offer. Almost half of them are installed in monasteries, convents, castles or palaces. The rest are in places of outstanding historic or scenic interest. They vary from opulent to modestly comfortable: most of them are reviewed in the text. Pousadas can be memorable in their own right, and pousada holidays are popular – but their prices have risen steeply (see p.67). Their restaurants provide good, well-presented food, and are open to non-residents. All pousadas are very well signposted.

Pousadas can be booked direct, or through: **ENATUR**, Empresa Nacional de Turismo EP, 10-A Avenida Santa Joana a Princesa, 1749-090 Lisbon, **t** (21) 442 001, www.pousadas.pt.

Turismo de Habitação (Solares de Portugal)

The grand private homes of Portugal have shaken the dust from the tapestries bearing their coats of arms, wafted woodsmoke through their huge kitchens of rough-cut granite, and opened their spare bedrooms to paying guests – under the aegis of the Turismo de Habitação scheme. This enables visitors to stay in antique accommodation and receive a highly personal view of rural (or in some cases urban) life.

The name Turismo de Habitação has been changed to the more manageable Solares de Portugal (www.solaresdeportugal.pt), although in the text, as in the country, this scheme is still referred to as Turismo de Habitação. The character of the participating houses differs as much as their owners: baronial, baroque or bacchanal. Most are manor houses smacking of faded opulence. Some have ten rooms available, others two.

Under this scheme there are two other categories of property available – country estates and farms, and cottages and rustic houses.

Rooms in a number of rustic houses and farmhouses are also available under the **Turismo Rural** and **Agro Turismo** banners. In addition, clusters of traditional houses in some villages are available to rent individually, under the **Aldeias de Portugal** scheme, www.aldeiasdeportugal.pt. For the sake of clarity, all are listed in the text under Turismo de Habitação.

The highest concentration of Turismo de Habitação is in the Minho, where the central reservations office in Ponte de Lima handles bookings for some 60 homes. The owners may be there to offer an expansive welcome to the home their ancestors built centuries ago. Most hosts are charming, forthcoming, and not averse to a bit of company. How much you see of the master or mistress of the house depends upon the set-up: some enthuse in English or French at breakfast, in a dining room glinting with crested silver. Most hosts will provide dinner if requested in advance.

A few words of warning are in order. Although signposting has improved in recent years, it's best to ask for detailed directions from the local tourist office or the house itself. Most Portuguese antiques are heavy, and these can be oppressive. Sometimes visitors are intimidated by their museum-like surroundings; others feel they are invading their hosts' privacy. If you're planning a winter visit, check how well the house is heated. See below for the booking restrictions. That said, Turismo de Habitação offers an excellent opportunity for a unique experience of accommodation in Portugal – at very reasonable rates.

Rooms should be booked in advance. Reservations should be made either with the owners of the houses (who may not speak English) or with an agency representing them. Reservations for the majority of manor houses in Portugal can be made with: **TURIHAB** (Associação do Turismo de Habitação), Praça da República, 4990-062 Ponte de Lima, **t** (258) 931 750 or 742 827, *www.turihab.pt*. Other houses are represented by the **PRIVETUR** association, whose reservations are handled in London by Maria Teresa Coutinho, **t** (020) 7834 4364, *mari.t.coutinho@amserve.net*. **ANTER** (Associação Nacional de Turismo Espaço Rural) also represent some houses. Find them at Rua 24 de Julho 1–1D, 7000 Évora, **t** (266) 744 555, *www.ruraltourisminternational. org/Portugal*.

Some houses have no agency representing them. Information can be obtained from the Portuguese national tourist offices in the UK, Ireland, the USA or Canada (*see* p.54).

Resort Accommodation

Most of Portugal's resort accommodation has been built in the last 25 years and, with the exception of some upmarket 'tourist villages' in the Algarve, offers about as much atmosphere as an unpainted *azulejo*. Expect block bookings from package-tour operators: to get away from them, head for the west coast. The Algarve and Estoril coasts are the most expensive parts of Portugal, but they also have the greatest price variants between high and low seasons, so you can make substantial savings on accommodation by booking out of season.

Cheap Accommodation

Shoestring travellers can find their own kind of *Turismo de Habitação*: ask at local tourist offices for rooms to rent in people's houses, or look in windows for signs advertising *quartos*. You may end up with a scrupulously clean little room complete with a religious icon, a lace runner on the chest of drawers and home-made bread for breakfast.

Some of the cheaper *pensões* are a bit unsavoury: you can save money by asking for a room without a private shower room, but pack a pair of flip-flops to wear in the public one. It's advisable to ask to see a room before

Accommodation Prices and Categories

Hotels

Throughout this book, prices listed are for a double room with bath in high season.

luxury	€€€€€	€230 and over
very expensive	€€€€	€150–230
expensive	€€€	€100–150
moderate	€€	€60–100
inexpensive	€	under €60

Pousadas

The *pousadas* are divided into four categories according to style of property:

Charm – **C**
Historic – **H**
Historic Design – **HD**
Nature – **N**

High-season prices for a double room are as follows:

Level	1	2	3	4
Double room	€170	€230	€240	€312

These are rack rates, but there are usually promotions and discounts available.

Turismo de Habitação

Generally these properties are divided into three categories and where possible these categories are given in the text after the price (as per those listed for hotels above):

Casas Antigas – **CA**
– manor houses and stately homes
Quintas e Herdades – **QH**
– country estates and farms
Casas Rústicas – **CR**
– cottages and rustic houses

you commit yourself to renting it. You'll be asked to submit your passport and may have to pay a day in advance. Check whether breakfast is included in the room rate.

Youth Hostels

Portugal has 44 youth hostels (*Pousadas de Juventude*). You can reserve online at *www.pousadasjuventude.pt* (the website also has suggested itineraries and other useful information in English for budget travellers) or book through Central Reservations, Rua Lúcio de Azevedo 29, 1600-146 Lisboa, **t** (707) 203 030, *reservas@ movijovem.pt*. Guests must have a valid Youth Hostel Association **membership card**, which is available in the UK from YHA,

Trevelyan House, Dimple Road, Matlock, Derbyshire, DE4 3YH, t (01629) 592 600, www.yha.org.uk. In the USA, these can be obtained from the American Youth Hostels, Inc, PO Box 37613, Washington D.C. 20013-7613, t (202) 783 6161. In Portugal, they can be obtained from hostels or Movijovem at the same address as reservations.

Youth hostels carry an array of regulations: you can only check in from 5 or 6pm; 1 Oct–30 April you must book in advance; dormitories must be kept absolutely silent during the night. In short, unless you're travelling alone and really can't afford to spend more, you'd be better off finding a good *pensão*.

Camping

Camping is a low-key affair, and can work out remarkably cheap. Ask in bookshops for the *Roteiro Campista*, which offers a detailed listing of all campsites, some of which may be booked online at www.roteiro-campista.pt. Unofficial camping is OK if you're discreet, but don't try it in the Algarve.

Specialist Tour Operators

Dozens of general and specialist companies offer holidays in Portugal. Some of the more specialist companies are listed here. Not all of them are necessarily ABTA-bonded; we recommend you check before booking.

Abreu is one of the driving forces behind **The Association of Tour Operators to Portugal** (ATOP), www.atop.org, which groups together 17 US-based companies offering travel to the country.

In the UK

Alternative Travel Group, 69–71 Banbury Road, Oxford OX2 6PJ, t (01865) 315 678, www.atg-oxford.co.uk. Art and culture, manor house, *pousada* and walking holidays.

Cadogan Travel, 9/10 Portland Street, Southampton SO14 7EB, t (0238) 082 8331. Art-and-culture tours, city breaks, golf, tennis and walking holidays, wine tours and pilgrimages.

Caravela, t 08704 438 181, www.caravela.pt. TAP's tour arm, handling bookings for *pousadas* and *Turismo de Habitaçao*, as well as arranging various fly/drive options.

Destination Portugal, 37 Corn Street, Witney, Oxfordshire, t (01993) 773 269, www.destination portugal.com. An excellent agency which can accommodate virtually any needs, from flight only to pilgrimage, wine or *pousada* tours and national park hiking holidays.

Explore Worldwide, 1 Frederick Street, Aldershot, Hampshire GU11 1LQ, t (01252) 344 161, www.explore.co.uk. Hiking specialists who offer small group tours in the Gerês and the Douro.

Light Blue Travel, 1 Longview Terrace, Cambridge CB4 3JH, t (01223) 568 904, www.lightbluetravel.co.uk. Tennis and golf holidays at the prestigious Vale do Lobo resort in the Algarve.

Mundi Color, 276 Vauxhall Bridge Road, London SW1V 1BE, t (020) 7828 6021. Art-and-culture tours, pilgrimages, wine tours, tailor-made and *pousada* holidays, golf.

North Portugal Travel, Foxhill, Gambles Lane, Woodmancote, Cheltenham GL52 4PU, t (01242) 679 867. Art-and-culture tours, *pousada* holidays, pilgrimages, fishing, golf, tennis and walking holidays, self-catering accommodation.

Portugala Holidays, 94 Fortis Green, London N2 9EY, t (020) 8372 2237, www.portugala.com. Self-catering accommodation, pilgrimages, tailor-made and *pousada* holidays, as well as golf and walking holidays.

Portugal Walks, t 0871 711 3315, www.portugal walks.com. Guided and self-guided walks in Madeira, Algarve and elsewhere on the mainland. Accommodation arranged.

In the USA

Abreu Tours, 350 Fifth Street, Suite 2414, 24th Floor, New York, NY 10118, t (800) 223 1580 or (212) 760 3301, www.abreu-tours.com. A Portuguese-run agency with many years of experience.

Cycling Through the Centuries, PO Box 7535, Jupiter, FL 33458, t (800) 473 0610, www.cycling centuries.com. This operator organizes cycling holidays in the Alentejo, Minho and the Algarve.

Easy Rider Tours, PO Box 228, Newburyport, MA 01950, t (800) 488 8332 or (878) 463 6955, www.easyridertours.com. Also offers cycling holidays for all abilities, featuring manor house accommodation and excursions.

Practical A–Z

07

Crime

The vast majority of foreign visitors to Portugal will come and go without a hitch. The farther you are from other foreigners, the less likely you are to get hustled: in the Algarve, Lisbon and the Estoril coast, watch out for pickpocketing, theft from parked cars and dodgy timeshare and property deals.

Eating Out

Food is sacred to the Portuguese; they appreciate good quality and don't like to rush it (*see* **Food and Drink** (pp.45–52) for a detailed description of what's on offer). Service is rarely included in the bill. To calculate the tip, do as the Portuguese do and add 10%, rounded down. Give more only if the service is excellent; otherwise your waiter will start to believe all tourists are rich.

Electricity

The current is 220V, 50 cycles, which takes a continental two-pin plug. Some fancy hotels have adaptors – otherwise, bring your own.

Entertainment and Nightlife

If you want to escape from *bacalhau*, head for the cinema: films are cheap (€3.50–4) and only children's cartoons are ever dubbed. Foreign films are released at the same time as in their native country, which often means well before they open in the UK. Some cinemas have a 10-minute interval, during which half the audience head outside to light up a cigarette. If it's Portuguese cinema you're after, watch out for the films of Manoel de Oliveira, João Botelho and Paulo Rocha.

Discos and nightclubs are legion in tourist areas and student towns. If they're going to gamble, most Portuguese gamble on the lottery, but there are some casinos for hardened addicts. Ask at the local tourist office for details of music concerts, which are only frequent and varied in Lisbon and Porto (*see* pp.36–7).

Gay and Lesbian Travellers

The Portuguese are, on the whole, somewhat conservative in their attitudes, but their conservatism is offset by a native tolerance long remarked upon by travellers.

Parts of central Lisbon in particular are positively gay-friendly, especially the tiny Príncipe Real district, where many of the main gay and lesbian bars and clubs are found. Even in the supposedly mixed Bairro Alto, female *lisboetas* frequently wail there isn't a straight man to be had in the hipper bars.

The tourist authorities in Lisbon have been keen to promote the city's appeal to what is perceived to be a free-spending group, even producing a guide to what the city has to offer for gays and lesbians, available from local tourist offices.

Other useful contacts in the capital include **ILGA Portugal**, Rua de São Lazaro 88, **t** (21) 887 3918, *www.ilga.org* (community centre open Mon–Sat 5–9, *ilga-portugal@ilga.org*; helpline Mon–Thurs 9pm–midnight), **Centro Comunitário Gay e Lésbico de Lisboa**, Rua de São Lazaro 88, **t** (21) 887 3918, a community centre, and **Opus Gay**, Rua da Ilha Terceira 34, 2nd floor, **t** (21) 887 6116, *www.opusgayassociation.com*, *opusgayturismo@hotmail.com*, whose name is a naughty pun on that of Opus Dei, an ultra-conservative Catholic movement. Both organizations offer advice, information and counselling; the former also has a bar and cyber café and organizes regular social events; the latter offers legal help, a laundry service and tourist advice via email.

Rural areas, particularly the north, are more conservative, although as ever an

Restaurant Price Categories

Price of a full meal for one, without wine:

very expensive	€€€€	over €45
expensive	€€€	€30–45
moderate	€€	€20–30
inexpensive	€	below €20

exception must be made for towns with large concentrations of students, while in Porto the sophisticated local bourgeoisie has given rise to a fair sprinkling of bohos and others leading ostentatiously alternative lifestyles. Still, it's only in Lisbon that you're likely to see single-sex couples holding hands in the street, despite the generally greater physicality of Latin cultures. The increasing visibility of gays and lesbians in the capital has lately been brought into question by populist politicians, who say the country is in hock to an undefined gay 'lobby'. In general, though, that spirit of tolerance wins through.

Other websites that may prove to be useful are *www.portugalgay.pt* and *www.lesbicas.homepage.com*.

Health and Emergencies

To call the **police** (and/or **ambulance**) in an emergency, dial **t 112** throughout Portugal.

A fair proportion of doctors speak English, because they have been trained abroad. There is a **British Hospital** at Rua Saraiva de Carvalho 49, Lisbon, **t** (21) 395 5067.

Pharmacies (*farmácias*) are usually open Monday to Friday from sometime after 9 until 1 and 3–7, and Saturday mornings.

Don't swim where there are flags warning you not to. The tap water is safe to drink throughout the country, except possibly in the Algarve in high season. Delicious bottled water is available.

Media

Newspapers

The Portuguese are not great newspaper readers. The three top-selling dailies are all sports papers, devoted almost exclusively to football and just the three biggest clubs at that. Rivals *Público* and *Diário de Notícias* are the two serious daily papers, with opinion columns read and discussed by Lisbon's small chattering classes. Financial affairs are reliably covered by *Diário Económico* and *Jornal de Negócios*. The fact that Portugal has the lowest newspaper

National Holidays

In 1736 Dom Luís de Cunha estimated that there were only 122 working days in the Portuguese year, because of the number of religious festivals. Things have tightened up somewhat, but everything closes on the following important dates:

1 January (New Year's Day)
Shrove Tuesday
Good Friday
25 April (Liberation Day)
1 May (May Day)
Corpus Christi (late May/early June)
10 June (Camões Day)
15 August (Assumption)
5 October (Republic Day)
1 November (All Saints' Day)
1 December (Independence Day)
8 December (Immaculate Conception)
25 December (Christmas Day)

Every region, town and village also finds some excuse for at least one annual holiday.

readership of any EU country has its roots in Salazar's dictatorship, when the press was heavily censored. When the Revolution came, the newspapers were filled with turgid revolutionary propaganda. Thus were the most stalwart of readers turned off their daily or weekly paper.

Before the Revolution of 1974, most newspapers were owned by banks. When the banks were nationalized, the newspapers were tagged on too – which explained the high proportion of state-owned publications for some years, including the long-established Lisbon daily *Diário de Notícias*. *Expresso* is the leading privately owned weekly, while the highest circulation non-sports daily is *Jornal de Manhã*, an excessively worthy publication whose main commercial strength is a distribution system that enables it to have a handful of pages filled with local news for each region.

Most British newspapers and the *International Herald Tribune* are available in major tourist areas and cities. Some arrive in Lisbon the day of publication, but take a while to be distributed from there.

Newsweek and the European edition of *Time* arrive in Portugal a couple of days after publication. *The News* is Portugal's weekly English-language newspaper. It is published in the Algarve and is also available on the web at *www.the-news.net*

Television and Radio

Go into any cheap eating place of an evening and the patrons are bound to be transfixed in front of a soap opera or a football match. There are 6.5 million peak-time viewers in a population of 10 million. The two oldest TV channels are both state-run and state-funded. The arrival in the mid-1990s of first one, then a second independent TV station brought a breath of fresh air to programming from news to comedy, but the private channels are currently engaged in a crippling race to the bottom.

For 13 years the Roman Catholic church had the only non-state radio station, *Radio Renascença*. In 1988 this stranglehold was broken, and dozens of new private local stations have been licensed.

Opening Hours

Some **shops** open at 9, but most unlock their doors at 9.30 or even 10. If they close for lunch it will be from 1 to 3: the Portuguese do not take a siesta as such, but prefer long, slow, discursive lunches. On weekdays, shops usually close at 6.30 or 7, though shopping centres, where shops open up at 10 or even 11, stay open till midnight. Many smaller establishments close at 1pm on Saturday.

The majority of public **museums** are open Tues–Sun 10–12.30 and 2–6; these and the eccentrics are listed in the text. Some close for lunch. Admission charges for museums and archaeological sites are usually around €2.

All small **churches** are kept locked: the keys – giant or otherwise – are with the sacristans or caretakers, who are almost invariably old ladies living nearby, who shuffle over and are delighted to help.

Post Offices

Dom Manuel created Portugal's first postal system before 1520, which makes it one of the longest-running institutions in the country. Portugal's post offices or *correios* (*open Mon–Fri 8 or 9–12.30 and 2.30–6; main post offices are open at lunchtime and Sat morning*) are always a hub of activity, partly because they incorporate public telephones (*see* below). If you're buying stamps, be sure to stand in the correct queue.

Standard airmail (*por avião*) letters and postcards to EU countries cost €0.60, and to countries outside Europe €0.78. Reckon on mail taking 5–7 days to Britain, and 7–10 days to North America. There are no air letter-cards (aerogrammes) for postage abroad, though there are letter-cards for postage within Portugal. Post offices also handle telegrams. The poste restante system works well (letters should be marked '*Lista do Correios*', and will be held for the addressee at the designated post office; bring your passport when you collect letters, for which there is a small fee).

In Lisbon, the main post office is in the Restauradores (*open Mon–Fri 8am–9pm; Sat and Sun 9–6*), but poste restante goes to the Praça do Comércio.

Shopping

Leaving aside the hideous pottery cockerels, there are some good buys in Portugal – but if it's quality you want, you'll have to pay for it. **Food and drink** (see pp.45–52) are always a good bet; keep an eye out for single-quinta olive oils and vacuum-packed cured meats. Creative young Portuguese are trying hard to slough off the country's dowdy image, so you can pick up interesting **designer goods** at attractive prices – look out for Cutipol cutlery or items from the new 'mg' range of glass from Marinha Grande producers, or clothing by Portuguese designers such as Fátima Lopes or José António Tenente, both of whom have shops in Lisbon's Bairro Alto. **Recorded music** is another idea. There's *fado*, of course, but also groups such as Madredeus and singers Dulce Pontes or Maria João.

For more **traditional purchases**, there are gold and silver filigree (Lisbon and Porto), Arraiolos rugs (Arraiolos, Évora and elsewhere), leather goods (Porto), crystal (*see* Alcobaça p.282), embroidery and lacework from Madeira, embroidered bedspreads (Castelo Branco) and Vista Alegre porcelain. Less pricey alternatives include fun ceramic crockery (Coimbra), pottery figures (Barcelos), black pottery (Chaves, Viseu), basketwork (Lamego and elsewhere) and chunky-knit sweaters (Porto, Lisbon, Nazaré, Sagres).

Sports and Activities

The Portuguese are crazy about **soccer**, and tend to support one of three clubs: Porto, from Porto, which won the European Cup in 1987; or Sporting or Benfica from Lisbon (though the latter isn't what it was when Eusébio played for it). Since tiny Rosa Mota won the 1988 Olympic gold medal for marathon running, Portugal has produced a string of fine long-distance runners of both sexes, but it's far from being a spectator sport.

Water sports make a big splash in summer, but don't expect any infrastructure outside the Algarve and the Estoril coast. (Guincho, on the latter, is renowned for its wind- and kite-surfing.) Monstrous water parks have sprung up throughout the Algarve. Ask at the **Club Naval de Lisboa**, Pav. Náutico, Doca de Belém, **t** (21) 363 0061, for a calendar of sailing events.

Portugal is a great place for **golf**, as many Britons have discovered. The Algarve and the Estoril coast are carpeted with golf courses, and there is one course near Espinho, south of Porto: some of these have been reviewed in the text. Many resort hotels have tennis courts, but public courts are hard to come by.

You'll need a licence if you wish to **fish** (trout streams in the north) or **hunt** (wild boar, deer, quail, hare, partridges). Contact the **Direcção Geral das Florestas**, Avenida João Crisostomo 26–28, Lisbon, **t** (21) 312 4800, *info@dgf.min-agricultura.pt*, and register with the local town hall.

A little, rather tentative **skiing** takes place at Torre in the Serra da Estrela – but it's certainly not worth going out of your way for.

Telephones and Internet

There's no doubt that privatization, or rather the competition that went with it, has transformed Portugal's once creaking telephone system. It's now reliable and much cheaper both in absolute and relative terms. Public booths, still all run by **Portugal Telecom**, are common and most accept both coins and cards; the latter are sold by tobacconists and at many newspaper kiosks. For long, expensive international calls, you may want to call from a post office (hotels whack on a heavy surcharge), but there are also cards on sale specifically for international calls that you can use from any phone by dialling a toll-free number. To call the UK from Portugal, first dial **t** 00 44; for Ireland **t** 00 353; for the USA and Canada **t** 00 1 (cheap rate 9pm–9am). To phone Portugal from the UK, first dial **t** 00 351; from the USA dial **t** 011 351.

If you have a **mobile phone** but don't want to use your own SIM card, it's straightforward to buy a pre-paid English-language package, from any branch of The Phone House.

Internet cafés are surprisingly few and far between outside the more touristy areas, although they are becoming more common, especially in cities and larger towns. Where major facilities exist (e.g. in Lisbon) these are listed in the respective section. In general, expect to pay €1 for half an hour of surfing. You'll have to pay considerably more for the use of **computer terminals** in hotels. Some hotels may also allow guests to send e-mails even if you can't surf the web.

Toilets

All the places to stay listed in this book have western-style toilets rather than the squat variety, as in some Mediterranean countries. In a few of the cheap places you are requested to put used toilet paper in a bin.

Public facilities are uncommon other than at bus and train stations (bus stations in the marble towns of the Alto Alentejo sport marble urinals) but nobody will mind if you ask to use the toilets of a hotel or restaurant without being a customer.

Women and Children

Sexual harassment is nothing in Portugal compared with what it is in some Latin countries: in rural areas, single women travellers are a cause of amazement rather than anything else; in large towns and cities, infuriating men on the street hiss or cluck their approval. Steer clear of the areas around bus and train stations at night. For those interested in the feminist movement in Portugal, the **Comissão para a Igualdade** (Avenida da República 32, 1st floor, 1050 Lisbon) has links with feminist groups throughout the country. It also organizes conferences and meetings, encompassing every aspect of women's lives, and is active in social and legal reform.

Portugal is an excellent country in which to travel with small children because the Portuguese are entirely tolerant of them and their ways, though there are few separate amusements for kids. Portuguese babies are often wrapped in several blankets whatever the season.

The Minho

The northwestern province of Portugal tilts towards the ocean. The mountains in the east reach about 2,300ft (700m), lowering to a hilly central zone divided by broad valleys, covered – particularly in the north – with dense woods of oak and chestnut, and patches of eucalyptus and pine, at about 650ft (200m). The low coastal region is fringed with sand beaches, open to the winds and beaten by the wild waves of the Atlantic. At the height of summer the average seawater temperature remains cool – around 60°F (16°C). Not for nothing is this called the Costa Verde – the Green Coast is the wettest province of Portugal.

08

Don't miss

1 Vibrant local market
Barcelos **p.97**

2 A hiker's delight
Peneda-Gerês National Park **p.117**

3 Wander medieval streets
Guimarães **p.79**

4 Splendid Baroque staircase
Bom Jesus **p.92**

5 Lush, laconic countryside
Ponte da Barca **p.113**

See map overleaf

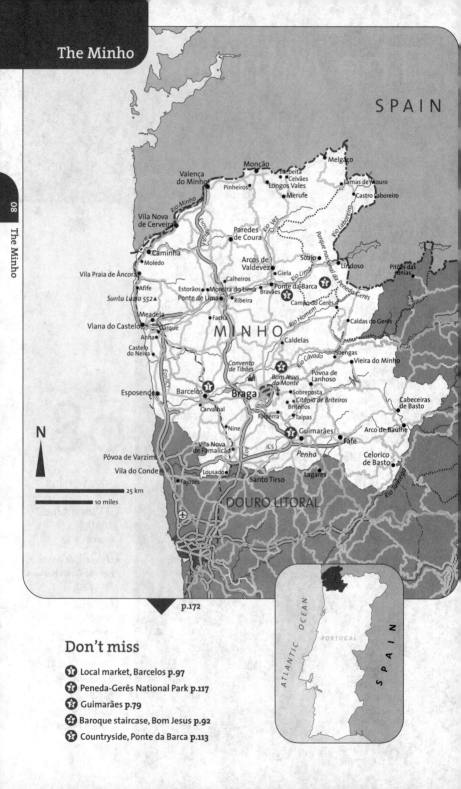

The Minho

SPAIN

Melgaço
Moncão
Barbeita
Ceivães
Valença
do Minho
Pinheiros
Longos Vales
Lamas de Mouro
Merufe
Castro Laboreiro

Vila Nova
de Cerveira

Paredes
de Coura

Rio Vez

Porque nacional do Peneda-Gerês

Rio Laboreiro

Caminha
Moledo

Arcos de
Valdevez
Sôajo
Lindoso
Pitões das
Júnias

Vila Praia de Âncora
Calheiros
Giela
Rio Lima

Afife
Estorãos
Moreira do Lima
Ponte da Barca
Santa Luzia 552
Ponte de Lima
Bravães
Ribeira
Campo do Gerês

Meadela
Facha

Viana do Castelo
Darque

M I N H O

Rio Homem
Caldas do Gerês

Anha
Castelo
do Neiva
Caldelas

Rio Cávado
Soengas
Vieira do Minho

Convento
de Tibães
Bom Jesus
do Monte
Póvoa de
Lanhoso

Esposende
Barcelos
Braga
Sobreposta
Citânia de Briteiros
Briteiros

Cabeceiras
de Basto

Carvalhal
Falperra
Taipas
Arco de Baúlhe

Nine
Guimarães
Fafe
Celorico
de Basto

Póvoa de Varzim
Vila Nova
de Famalicão
Penha

Vila do Conde
Lousado
Lagares

Fajozes
Santo Tirso

Rio Tâmega

N

25 km

10 miles

DOURO LITORAL

p.172

ATLANTIC OCEAN
PORTUGAL
SPAIN

Don't miss

1 Local market, Barcelos **p.97**

2 Peneda-Gerês National Park **p.117**

3 Guimarães **p.79**

4 Baroque staircase, Bom Jesus **p.92**

5 Countryside, Ponte da Barca **p.113**

Its high rainfall, temperate climate and relatively rich, granitic soil support intense agricultural development. The introduction of maize in the early 17th century heralded an agricultural breakthrough. Well suited to the climatic and geologic condition of the Minho, maize was much more productive than the wheat and rye it replaced. The by-products of maize – stalks, leaves, flowers and even the grain itself – were and are fed to cattle, reducing the need for pasture land. The unfailing maize crop ended periodic famines. The population expanded.

Typically, fields are used to cultivate fodder and legumes which were introduced in the 17th century but are still called *novidades* (novelties) – parsnips, beetroot and lupins. Bean plants grow up the maize stalks, providing one of the farmer's most important staple foods. Another nifty use of space was the introduction of climbing vines (*see* 'Vinho Verde', p.79). In the 19th century, many small-holders ditched their goats and planted small pinewoods on unprofitable hilltops, which now provide financial security in case of some extraordinary expense like hospitalization. It is said that, if a Minhoto puts a cow out to pasture in his own field, her dung falls in his neighbour's field. The Minho is a land of smallholdings which are themselves divided, because primogeniture is rare. The Minhotos are conservative as well as pious, devoted both to their landholdings and to the Virgin Mary, whose image is ensconced in little Romanesque churches.

The people's poverty leads the more dynamic among them to seek work abroad. When they return to the Minho, having made their fortunes, emigrants trumpet their changed status by building ostentatious houses known as *casas de emigrante* (*see* 'Migrants', p.43). The Minho is green and rustic, close knit and alive. Life happens as slowly as the dry stone walls which divide the fields. To many Portuguese, this is the most beautiful province. Cattle with huge, lyre-shaped horns pull carts with squealing wooden axles – or the untrustworthy beasts are led for walks on strings. There are vines everywhere, creeping up tree trunks, festooned on fences. In *tascas*, people drink purple wine from white porcelain bowls. On every summer weekend, some village or other will be celebrating its *festa* or *romaria*.

History

The Minho's system of smallholdings dates back to subjugation of the Celt-Iberians and Lusitanians by the Romans, who forced them to come down from their hilltop *castros* and settle the fertile valleys. Agriculture was organized under the auspices of the *villa*. Because the land was hummocky, each Roman settler was given a parcel of land comprising several discontinuous plots. The Minho calls itself the cradle of the nation because it comprised the

Getting around The Minho

By Car

The nooks and crannies of the Minho lend themselves to exploration by **car** or **on foot**: the manor houses in the *Turismo de Habitação* scheme around Ponte de Lima make a good base, because of their location at the heart of the province. Now Ponte de Lima is so easily accessible by **motorway**, from Porto airport, the Minho is becoming increasingly popular as a weekend destination. The **main roads** are well maintained, but beware the crazy driving of emigrants in flashy cars, who come, in the summertime, to visit the folks back home and take them for a spin. The road network is very limited within the Peneda-Gerês park.

By Train

The **railway network** covers major towns, but doesn't venture inland north of Braga. The **main line** from the south passes through Barcelos and Viana, then goes up the coast and beside the River Minho as far as Valença. Braga and Guimarães are both on **branch lines** (change at Nine and Lousado respectively). It's best to take a bus between Braga and Guimarães, as the train involves two changes.

By Bus

Express **buses** in the north of Portugal are adequate at best. Privatization has opened the way for 60-odd bus companies to operate, and much confusion. Timetables tend to be kept in people's heads: just keep asking.

---

patrimony of the first King of Portugal, Dom Afonso Henriques (1128–85). Having defeated his mother, Teresa, he established his capital at Guimarães. The see of Braga – which was established by the Suevi in the 5th century – reinforced the integrity of the region.

Turismo de Habitação (*Solares de Portugal*)

The Minho has the highest concentration of *Turismo de Habitação* (*see* pp.66–7), because of the large number of manor houses in the region, especially around Ponte de Lima: most date from the 18th century. The Portuguese Government, and more recently the EU, made large grants available to offset the cost of adapting these houses to the needs of tourists, in order to encourage tourism in the north of the country, and to preserve houses which the owners can no longer afford to maintain.

Generally the delights of sniffing the woodsmoke in a huge kitchen of rough-cut granite, of wandering through doorways hung with emblazoned tapestries, of peaceful terraces and wild flowers, far outweigh the hitches. Houses are much better signposted than they used to be, and owners are given lessons on what guests do and do not like. Some of the houses are oppressively heavy – the guide to individual houses around Viana do Castelo, Monção, Ponte de Lima and Ponte da Barca will help you avoid these. There are also whole villages that have been adapted to rental properties. For information on other houses or villages, visit *www.solaresdeportugal.pt* or *www.aldeiasdeportugal.pt* respectively. The simplest way to book is through the central system, **CENTER**, Praça da República, 4990-062 Ponte de Lima, **t** (258) 931 750, or visit *www.turihab.pt*.

Minho Specialities

The Minho is as green as its *caldo verde* **soup**, which is the province's most diffuse culinary export to the rest of the country. The soup takes its colour from shredded galega cabbage, like curly kale, which is stirred up with a warming blend of puréed potatoes, olive oil, and garlic. There will always be a slice of *chouriço* floating in the soup, and there ought to be an accompanying slice of maize bread.

Between October and December, the Minhotos slaughter the one or two **pigs** they have fattened through the year, and eat the spin-offs at least until March. Nothing is wasted, least of all the blood, some of which is used to make *chouriço de sangue* (blood sausages). Like rich black pudding, these are made of cooked pork, blood, bread, oil, wine and other seasonings. Blood comes into its own in *sarrabulhos* (blood stews) made with various organs, rice, onions and blood, and often accompanied by tripe. (The best onions in the Minho come from Barcelos.) The more inventive and frugal pork dishes are not generally available in restaurants or *tascas*.

Lampreys are another great love (*see* **Food and Drink**, 'Fish and Seafood', p.46), as is *bacalhau cozido com todos* (salt cod boiled with potatoes, onions, eggs and kale – *see* **Food and Drink**, '*Bacalhau*', p.47).

Vinho Verde

Vinho verde is one of the delights of Portugal (*see* p.50), produced only in the Minho. Climbing vines were introduced to the Minho in the 17th century, and they have never looked back. The idea was to use space most efficiently by growing other crops beneath the vines, and at the same time protect the grapes from frosts and the damp. So, rather than being pruned back to form low bushes, the vines creep up telegraph poles, oak trees, house walls. Some 60,000 Minhoto farmers sell their grapes to private wine firms, to be marketed under brand names, or to the 21 cooperatives. The more substantial producers have disciplined their runaways to grow along horizontal wires borne a couple of metres off the ground; they harvest the grapes by tractor. The smaller farmers grow vines at the side of their fields, and in September/October harvest them from rickety ladders.

The Southern Minho

Guimarães

 Guimarães   First capital of the Portuguese nation, **Guimarães** busies itself among gently sloping evergreen hills – dominated by the steeper Penha hill – and industrial environs. The superb municipal museum is buffered by a core of well-kept medieval streets, designated a UNESCO World Heritage Site. Afonso Henriques, the first King of Portugal, set eyes on many of the monuments. The town is a centre for linen production, and has been at least since a fair was established at Guimarães in 1258, in which year both linen cloth and household linen were for sale (as well as rabbit fur – by the piece or made-up – black or white feathers, red or green leather, pepper, horseshoes and Moorish slaves). The fair was kept merry by 'buffoons who put up their tents', for which they paid a fee of three shillings.

History

Afonso Henriques was born in Guimarães, and here he nurtured the embryonic nation. In 1096 Alfonso VI of Castile had bestowed the governance of the hereditary lands of Portucale and Coimbra, which lay between the Rivers Minho and Mondego, on his bastard daughter Teresa and her husband Henry, Duke of Burgundy. They

Getting to Guimarães

By **road**, Guimarães is 22km southeast of Braga and 53km northeast of Porto.

Guimarães is on a branch line: there are frequent direct **trains** from Porto, but from elsewhere you must change at Lousado. Frequent trains run from Lousado to Guimarães (1hr). From Braga, change at Lousado and Nine. João Ferreira das Neves, t (253) 513 132, run frequent **buses** from Porto (1hr). REDM has three or four daily express services from Porto (1hr) and a couple from Lisbon (5hrs) and Coimbra (2¼hrs).

reinforced the 150-year-old earth-and-wood castle built by a local noblewoman, Countess Mumadona, to protect herself and her foundation church of N.S. da Oliveira. Here Teresa bore a son, Afonso Henriques, and she administered the lands on his behalf when Henry died. A Coimbra document subscribed by Afonso Henriques may reveal something of his boyhood: it specifies that small boys were to be beaten till the blood came if they were caught trespassing or stealing from vineyards. There was no love lost between mother and son. She leant too much towards Castile, and the emergent nation united behind Afonso Henriques to defeat her at the battle of S. Mamede in 1128. Her tomb and Henry's are at Braga. Seven years later, Afonso Henriques refused to join other north Spanish princes in homage to Alfonso VII of Castile, choosing to swear and pay tribute to the papacy. He took the title Prince of Portugal, but the Pope did not recognize him as such until 1179, by which time he had moved the seat of government from Guimarães to Coimbra.

What to See

Castle
t (253) 412 273; open 9.30–12.30 and 2–5.30; adm

Dignified on a green hillock, the **castle** looks like a theatre backdrop. It was reconstructed by Count Henry c. 1100, and pillaged by 19th-century town councillors, who used the granite for paving stones. Now restored, the castle lacks atmosphere. Dom Afonso Henriques was baptized in the little Romanesque **church of São Miguel** (details as for castle) next door. Should his ghost choose to revisit the site, he will not come on horseback. A portcullis fell on his leg at the siege of Badajoz, fracturing the bone so badly that he could never ride again.

Ducal Palace
t (253) 412 273; open 9.30–12.30 and 2–5.30; free Sun am, adm all other times

A lawn links the castle and church to the **Ducal Palace**, a building loathed by purists. It was constructed in the early 15th century by Dom Afonso, bastard eldest son of the bastard Dom João I and first Duke of Bragança. He travelled in Europe on diplomatic missions, which explains why he and his French architect, Anton, built a Burgundian palace. Indeed, he is the first known emigrant to return to the Minho and build a pretentious home in an incongruous style. It was grossly restored as a presidential palace in 1933. Nevertheless, there are some good pieces in it, including medieval Persian carpets, numerous 18th-century Flemish tapestries, and two still lifes attributed to Josefa de Óbidos. The duke was assured a warm pate while sleeping: a panel at the head of his bed allowed heat through from the fireplace on the other side of the wall. Note that the building is under restoration and that only half of the interior is open to the public until 2010.

Largo da Oliveira

Medieval spirits waft around the **Largo da Oliveira**, dodging the children who play hide and seek around a mid-14th-century Gothic canopy or portico sheltering a stone cross, in front of the **church of N.S. da Oliveira** The shrine commemorates the miracle to which the church owes its name. In the early 14th century, an olive tree grew at São Torquato, several kilometres away. It provided oil for St Torquato's lamp. The tree was uprooted and transported to Guimarães to perform the same function for the altar of the church of N.S. da Oliveira. Not unreasonably, the tree died. It remained dead until 8 September 1342, when Pedro Esteves placed upon it a cross his brother had brought from Normandy. Three days later, the olive tree broke into leaf. (Perhaps inspired by this example, the Chapter of Guimarães wanted to transport the relics of St Torquato himself into town, because the saint would yield large profits in the guise of ex votos. They attempted to do so forcibly in 1501, 1597, 1637 and 1805. The parishioners of São Torquato love their saint, and are a tenacious lot.)

Church of N.S. da Oliveira
open 7.15–12 and 3.30–7.30

Museu de Alberto Sampaio

The conventual buildings of the collegiate church now house the outstanding **Museu de Alberto Sampaio**, centred on a rhythmic 13th-century Romanesque cloister, later extended. Monks and nuns rubbed shoulders within the wealthy institution after its foundation in the 10th century. Later the pope thought this unwise, and it reopened for men only. The museum is named after an ethnographer/sociologist.

Museu de Alberto Sampaio
t (253) 423 910; open summer 10–12.30 and 2–5.30; closed Mon; free Sun am, adm all other times

Upstairs the museum's treasures are astonishing. The highlight is a fabulous silver-gilt late 14th-century triptych altarpiece offered by Dom João to Santa Maria of Guimarães. Gaspar Estaço, writing in the 16th century, says it was made from Dom João's silver measuring weights; the older tradition is that it was booty from the travelling chapel of Juan I of Castile. The centre panel shows the Nativity, breathed on by cow heads, whizzed over by cherubs swinging censers, all covered by Gothic arches. Also displayed are a robe said to have been worn by Dom João at Aljubarrota, the heaviest processional cross in the country, weighing in at 48lb (22kg), a stunning silver-bound Bible, and a Spanish hand-painted leather altarfront. Do notice the head carved on the back of the lectern, with an aquiline nose and surely an evil glint in his eye.

Guimarães

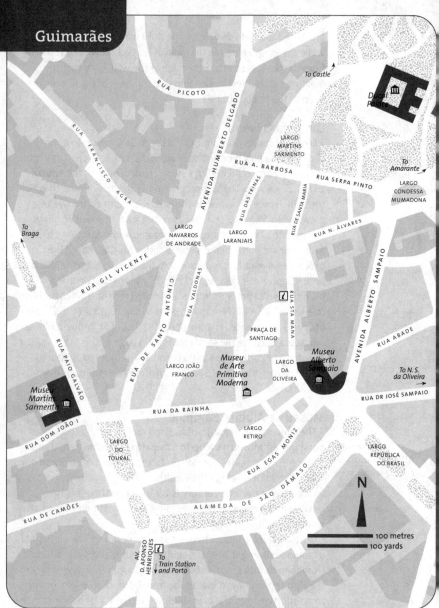

On the ground floor, beside the entrance to the museum, note the four sculpted saints' figures. St Bartholomew holds a card for folding linen, with a chained devil at his feet. In the ground-floor rooms, look at the unusual and delightful 18th-century polychromed wood *Flight from Egypt*. Compassionate and dynamic, it lacks only baby Jesus, who was stolen by a visitor to the museum. The open sarcophagus in the inner cloister was taken from a farm, where it was used as a watering trough.

Museu de Martins Sarmento

Museu de Martins
Sarmento
*Rua Paio Galváo,
t (253) 414 011; open
9.30–12 and 2–5; closed
Mon and hols; adm*

On the road into town from the bus station, the **Museu de Martins Sarmento** is named after the 19th-century archaeologist who conserved and continued the excavations at Citânia de Briteiros and at Sabroso. It is crowded with fragments from those Celtiberian sites, mostly ceramic and numismatic. The larger objects are more striking, displayed in and around the appropriated 14th-century cloister of the monastery of S. Domingos. The most forceful is the *Colossus of Pedralva*, an awesome and curiously unpublicized 3,000-year-old 10ft (3m) giant. Two headless Lusitanian warriors clasp their round shields in front of them.

Museu de Arte Primitiva Moderna

Museu de Arte
Primitiva
Moderna
*t (253) 414 186; open
9–12.30 and 2–5.30*

Located in the 14th-century Antigos Paços do Concelho, the current town hall, the **Museu de Arte Primitiva Moderna** is worth checking out for its diverse collection of some 300 works by self-taught artists, ranging from the depressingly feeble to the extremely accomplished.

ⓘ Guimarães ›
*Main: Alameda de São
Dâmaso 86, t (253) 518
790, www.cm-
guimaraes.pt*

*Branch office: Praça de
Santiago, t (253) 518 790*

Tourist Information and Services in Guimarães

There are two **tourist offices**: the main one is at Alameda de São Dâmaso and there's a more usefully located branch office in the Praça de Santiago. To get to the centre of town from the rail station, **t** (253) 412 351, walk up the Avenida Dom João IV; from the bus station, walk up the Avenida Conde Margaride.

A **cable car**, **t** (253) 515 085 *(April–Sept, Mon–Fri 11–7, Sat, Sun and hols 10–8; Aug every day 10–8)* makes the 10-minute journey to the religious sanctuary of Penha, a decent place for horse-riding and walking.

Festivals in Guimarães

On the first Sunday of August, the *Festas Gualterianas* (Festival of St Walter) coincides with the free fair held in his name, which was first held in 1452. The following night is a much more unusual affair: the *Marcha Gualteriana*, which does not take place every year, is a satiric rather than a devotional procession, based on medieval allegories.

Where to Stay in Guimarães

Expensive (€€€)
Hotel de Guimarães, Rua Eduardo M de Almeida, **t** (253) 424 800, *www.hotel-guimaraes.com*. Near the railway station and next to a major flyover, is a slick, modern, minimalist hotel, a little businessy, but reassuring. Ask for a room at the back, with double glazing and a wonderful view. Health club, indoor pool, spa and parking.

Moderate (€€)
★★★★Hotel do Toural, Largo do Toural, **t** (253) 517 184, *www.hoteltoural@com*. The entrance is in the Largo A.L. Carvalha. An elegant townhouse converted with contemporary style.
★★★Hotel Fundador, Avenida Dom Afonso Henriques 740, **t** (253) 422 640, *www.hotelfundador.com*. Tall and fairly standard – with stunning views.

Inexpensive (€)
★★★★Albergaria Palmeiras, Centro Commercial das Palmeiras, Rua Gil Vicente, **t** (253) 410 324. Part of a shopping mall complex, which can make access problematic. It's quiet, but some of the rooms are a bit small.

★★★**Residencial S. Mamede**, Rua de São Gonçalo 1, **t** (253) 513 092, *www.residencialsmamede.com*. Closer to the centre of town, and without the crucifixes, this place is simple, clean and a bit noisy. It tends to get booked up.

⭐ **Residencial das Trinas >**

Residencial das Trinas, Rua das Trinas 29, **t** (253) 517 358, *www.residencial trinas.com*. In the historic centre of town, it's a nice little place, and double-glazed to boot. The best budget option.

Casa de Retiros, Rua Francisco Agra 163, **t** (253) 511 515 – beyond the bus station, turn right and uphill. Provides no frills, as you would expect from pilgrim accommodation, and no pressure but for the 11.30pm curfew. Rooms or dormitory.

Pousadas

⭐ **Pousada de Santa Marinha >**

Pousada de Santa Marinha, 4810-011 Guimarães, **t** (253) 511 249, *www.pousadas.pt* (L2 H). Occupies a magnificent monastery on the Penha hillslope that has been sensitively and tastefully adapted. It was founded for the Augustinian Order in 1154 by Dona Mafalda, wife of Dom Afonso Henriques, and splendidly revamped in the 18th century. Some guest rooms used to be monks' cells – they remain small and simply furnished – others occupy a modern wing, with views of urban Guimarães. The drawing room is filled with antiques borrowed from Lisbon's Ajuda Palace, and the vaulted dining room is wonderful. Note the lively tiles depicting an indulgent lay life, dated 1747 and attributed to Policarpo de Oliveira Bernardes, lining the staircase.

Pousada de N.S. da Oliveira, 4801-910 Guimarães, **t** (253) 514 157, *www. pousadas.pt* (L1 C). Converted from a block of town houses to make just 16 guest rooms, overlooking a superb medieval square and adjacent to the fine town hall. Public rooms are delightfully furnished, like a grand but homely country inn and the rooms are

pleasant. The food is unremarkable. Bring ear plugs, as the nearby church bells ring enthusiastically. Good deals on the Internet.

Turismo de Habitação
Casa dos Pombais, Avenida de Londres, **t** (253) 412 917 (€€ CA). An 18th-century house opposite the bus station, with two rooms and a delightful garden.

Eating Out in Guimarães

Solar do Arco, Rua de Santa Maria 50, **t** (253) 513 072 (€€). Just up the road from the Pousada, occupying a town house and serving very good seafood. Try the monkfish. *Closed Sun.*

El Rei, Praça de São Tiago 20, **t** (253) 419 096 (€€). Nicely central, cosy and good value. *Closed Sun eve.*

Vira Bar, Largo Condessa do Juncal 27, **t** (253) 518 427 (€€). Consistently attracts favourable comments. It's a charming, bistro-esque place with trees at the back, specializing in grills. *Closed Sun.*

Dan José, **t** (253) 418 844 (€€). If you take the cable car to Penha, you could eat here. *Closed Mon.*

Valdonas, Rua Val de Donas 4, **t** (253) 511 411 (€€). The town's most talked about new restaurant sports fashionable minimalist décor within an evocative 17th-century house. The menu (including dishes such as monkfish rice) changes according to what produce is in season.

Mumadona, Rua Serpa Pinto 268, **t** (253) 414 971 (€). Serves good, solid fare. Child-friendly. *Closed Sun.*

Cozinha Regional, Praça de Santiago 16, **t** (253) 516 669 (€). Popular, with seating on the square.

Bar in Guimarães

Ultimatum Jazz Café, Rua Rei do Pegu. Regular live music.

Braga

Of all the cities in Portugal, Braga will get to heaven first: it seems that at one time every other building in Braga was a church or a seminary. The cathedral was the seat of the immensely powerful Primate of Portugal, and his palace is at the heart of Braga.

Because the cathedral is the only church that the casual visitor will wish to visit, it's best to wander around the centre of town in the early morning, before the bustle chases away the angels. For the town has grown into the largest city north of Porto, and industry has brought its quota of bland buildings (previously the only industries were connected with the Church – carving, organ-making, bell-making, candle-making, stitching and embroidering vestments).

Braga's museums house excellent works of art and craft. The one *palácio* open to the public is delightful. Exceptionally interesting sites surround the city.

History

Braga is well sited at the meeting of inland hills and fertile valleys ripe with orchards, market gardens, grasslands and vineyards. In 27 BC the Romans chose the spot to administer the newly conquered territory of Gallaecia, comprised of the Minho and Galicia. Five Roman roads converged on Bracara Augusta, which quickly became a centre for trade and industry: glass, ceramics and other Roman artefacts from Egypt, the Aegean and Germany have been found here, and local products were sold in towns 125 miles (200km) away.

Conquered by the Suevi in 409, Braga became the seat of a bishopric as well as the Suevi's capital until 585. They were cattle-men, farmers – who introduced the quadrangular plough into the region – and robbers. Braga was sacked by the Visigoths and formally incorporated into the Visigothic kingdom by Leovigild in 585 (though the 9th-century *Chronicle of Sebastianus* distinguishes the realm of the Goths from that of the Suevi as late as 701).

Braga's ecclesiastical dominance began with a coup, when at a council in 561 St Martin of Dume (an environ of Braga), also called St Martin of Braga, converted the Suevi to Christianity. The Hungarian saint's other major contribution to Portugal as we know it was his condemnation of pagan names for days of the week. He was a forceful man (his favourite author was Seneca) and now the days of the week are given numbers, Monday being *segunda-feira*, Tuesday *terça-feira*, and so on.

Braga was occupied by the Moors from *c.* 730 until they were driven out by Fernando I of Castile. The see was not restored until 1070, after which the bishops squabbled with those of Santiago.

Getting to Braga

By **road**, Braga is 53km northeast of Porto and 51km southwest of Viana do Castelo.

Braga is on a **rail** branch line. Passengers from Barcelos (frequent, 1hr), Viana do Castelo (frequent, 1¾hrs) and north of Viana must change trains at Nine. There are some direct trains from Porto, or you can change at Nine (frequent, 1½hrs). From Póvoa de Varzim, change at Vila Nova de Famalicão and at Nine (frequent, 1½hrs). From Guimarães, change at Lousado and Nine (frequent, 1¾hrs).

Buses are run by a confusing number of private companies including REDM, Rede Expressos and Rodonorte. They all operate out of the bus station on Avenida General Norton de Matos. Very infrequent buses arrive from Viana do Castelo (2hrs), Ponte da Barca (¾hr), Arcos de Valdevez (¾hr), Monção (1¼hrs), Melgaço (2¼hrs), Chaves (4hrs), Boticas (3¼hrs), and Montalegre (2¼hrs). There are six or seven daily buses to Coimbra (2½hrs), about a dozen to Porto (1hr), three or four to Bragança (4¼hrs) and six to Lisbon (5½hrs).

The pope adjudicated in favour of Braga's superiority. The Council of Trent awarded the see of Braga the right to its own liturgy.

In 1926 the military coup which facilitated Salazar's dictatorship was launched here.

Around the Town

At the centre of town, a **keep** tufted with green is all that remains of the fortress-palace of 1378. Nearby is the sprawling **Archbishop's Palace**, mixing styles from the 14th to the 18th centuries. It is now an important public library, with books and manuscripts creamed from 20 convents. Its open courtyard, the 18th-century Largo do Paço, contains a curious castellated fountain which is said to be a stylization of the heraldic symbols of Dom Rodrigo de Moura Teles, who commissioned it in 1723. The cathedral is almost opposite, entered across the courtyard and through the 18th-century cloister.

The Cathedral

The cathedral is a wonderful place to wander about. It dates from 1070, when the bishopric was restored. Ignore the absurd pinball trays of electric candles, and enjoy the veritable salad of Romanesque, Gothic, Renaissance and Baroque styles, of which the last mentioned is the most eye-catching, trumpeting itself in a magnificent pair of organs. These face one another as if in battle, gilt with a crècheful of cherubs, who no doubt delighted in the music of Carlos de Seixas: he was a pupil of Scarlatti. (Cherubs meet a less glorious fate by the font, where they appear to be eaten by lions.) During the Baroque period, the visual impact of organs was considered to be as important as their musical potential. Many Portuguese cathedrals contain multiple organs, simply for show: their close arrangement at Braga quashes any argument about intended antiphonal effects.

The east end of the cathedral was rebuilt in 1532, and contains a finely carved Manueline high altar retable. The building's

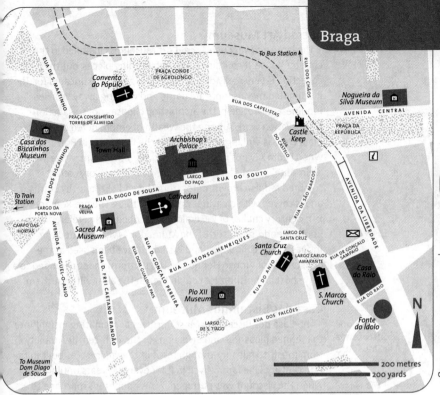

To Bus Station

Convento do Pópulo

PRAÇA CONDE DE AGROLONGO

RUA DOS CHÃOS

RUA DE S. MARTINHO

RUA DOS CAPELISTAS

Nogueira da Silva Museum

AVENIDA CENTRAL

PRAÇA CONSELHEIRO TORRES DE ALMEIDA

Archbishop's Palace

Castle Keep

PRAÇA DA REPÚBLICA

Casa dos Biscaínhos Museum

Town Hall

LARGO DO PAÇO

RUA DO SOUTO

RUA DE SÃO MARCOS

RUA DOS BISCAÍNHOS

RUA D. DIOGO DE SOUSA

Cathedral

AVENIDA DA LIBERDADE

To Train Station

LARGO DA PORTA NOVA

PRAÇA VELHA

CAMPO DAS HORTAS

Sacred Art Museum

LARGO DE SANTA CRUZ

RUA D. AFONSO HENRIQUES

Santa Cruz Church

LARGO CARLOS AMARANTE

RUA DE GONÇALO SAMPAIO

AVENIDA S. MIGUEL-O-ANJO

RUA D. FREI CAETANO BRANDÃO

RUA DOM GUALDIM PAIS

RUA D. GONÇALO PEREIRA

Casa do Raio

Pio XII Museum

RUA DO ANJO

S. Marcos Church

RUA DO RAIO

LARGO DE S. TIAGO

RUA DOS FALCÕES

Fonte do Idolo

N

To Museum Dom Diago de Sousa

200 metres
200 yards

lichenous main Romanesque façade was embellished with a Gothic porch *c.* 1500. This shelters a very interesting 12th-century portal whose two arches are carved with scenes of the *Chanson de Roland* and *Roman de Renart*, of Burgundian influence. The porch opens onto the attractive Rua D. Paio Mendes. The cathedral's frilly rooftops are the work of João de Castilho.

The several dependent Gothic chapels are well worth visiting, included in the price of the **Sacred Art Museum** ticket. The **Capela dos Reis** contains the tombs of the cathedral's founders, Dom Henry and Dona Teresa, parents of Dom Afonso Henriques, the first King of Portugal (*see* 'Guimarães', 'History', pp.79–80). Note the stonemason's elaborate mark on the ceiling – stonemasons were paid on the basis of piecework, and had to distinguish their own labour from other people's. In the **Capela da Gloria** the 14th-century tomb of Dom Gonçalo Pereira is very fine: it was commissioned during his lifetime. The figures on one side of the tomb are singing. The man with the keys also has access to the roof and to the *coro alto* or raised choir. Note the splendid breasts of the caryatids on the choir stalls.

Sacred Art Museum

Sacred Art Museum
t (253) 263 317; open 9–12 and 2–6; adm

The large and very rich **Sacred Art Museum** is installed in the chapter house. It contains some outstanding pieces, but the collection is very badly displayed and disgracefully uncared for. The illuminated manuscripts are damp and wasting away. Worried inquiries will not help: the archbishop chooses not to sanction conservation work. Among the wealth of embroidered cassocks, a plain cross is striking. It was used at the first Mass in Brazil, in 1500, when Pedro Álvares Cabral had discovered the country (*see* 'Belmonte', p.233). The Hispano-Arab cylindrical ivory coffer, coloured reddish brown, dates from the end of the 10th century and is carved with creatures on unlikely trees. The pre-Romanesque 11th-century chalice of S. Geraldo is inscribed with a reference to Count Mendo, grandson of the Mumadona who founded the monastery at Guimarães, and is said to have been used at the christening of Afonso Henriques. The platform shoes belonged to a very short archbishop. He couldn't reach the altar without them.

Casa dos Biscaínhos Museum

Casa dos Biscaínhos Museum
Rua dos Biscaínhos, t (253) 217 645; open 10–12.15 and 2–5.30; closed Mon and hols; adm

The **Casa dos Biscaínhos Museum** gives a fascinating insight into the refined pleasures and diversions of the 18th-century nobility, from music to falconry, though most of the *palácio* was built in the 17th century. One family lived in it for over 200 years until 1963, when the viscount was outraged by his daughter's marriage to a plebeian. He shot her horse, buried it in the garden, and sold the house to erase her from his memory.

At street level the ground floor is ribbed, to allow precious charges to exit their carriages at the foot of the staircase, which is designed as if it were outdoors. The vehicle would then drive through to the stable block incorporated in the main house, in the French style. The 18th-century gardens follow the Italian fashion: there is a winter house, and a fountain within trained hedges, for cooling the summers. The residents enjoyed the sound of water: the house is built around a fountain cloister, rare in civil architecture. *Azulejos* chronicle 18th-century life, with scenes of falcons and hunting and the priming of a gun. A painting depicts Braga in the 16th century, near the Portuguese copy of a roundbacked Chippendale chair. The Romantic Room includes a working music box and a perfumery for aromatic herbs. The Porcelain Room was formerly the Music Room, as the ceiling paintings show. There are collections of fans and jewellery, and temporary exhibitions downstairs.

Other Museums

Pio XII Museum
Largo de S. Tiago 47, t (253) 200 130, www.museupioxii.blog spot.com; open 9.30–12.30 and 2.30–6; closed Mon; adm

Lavishly housed in a former seminary since 2002, the **Pio XII Museum** is an umbrella for two museums. The **Pio XII Museum** proper is home to 10,000 religious artefacts, including some fine copes, crucifixes and Baroque woodcarving. Next door, the **Medina Museum** is a showpiece for the cheesy paintings of Henrique Medina, and is best avoided.

Museum Dom
Diogo de Sousa
*Rua dos Bombeiros
Voluntários, t (253) 273
706; open 10–12.15 and
2–5.30; closed Mon*

Museum Dom Diogo de Sousa

This excellent modern archaeological museum opened in 2007. The Museum Dom Diogo de Sousa displays the accumulated archaeological riches of the area with emphasis on the Roman settlement of Bracara Augusta.

Other Sights

At right angles to the façade of the Casa dos Biscaínhos is the very beautiful **Town Hall**, attributed to the Baroque André Soares da Silva, whose architecture has received less scholarly study than it deserves. Even more sumptuous is his elaborate **Casa do Raio**. The granite casements accompany a blue tiled front. Down some steps nearby, the **Fonte do Ídolo** is a Roman sanctuary carved into living granite. The small, simple shrine is dedicated to the God Tongo Nabiacus, as identified by an inscription, but it is not clear whether the carved male figure is the god or the donor, one Celicus. Unusually, there is a votive offering to the goddess Nabia in the same place. Doubtless the god and the goddess, who are symbolized by a carved hammer and dove respectively, are displeased by the stagnant pool beside their sanctuary.

Nogueira da
Silva Museum
*Avenida Central 61,
t (253) 275 391; open
10–12 and 2–5; closed
Sat morning, Sun, Mon
and hols*

The **Nogueira da Silva Museum** is one man's collection displayed in his home, financed by the monopoly on lottery tickets over most of Portugal during the dictatorship of his friend Salazar, whose sculpted head is among the tusks in the hallway (this is one of the few representations of him not destroyed during the Revolution of 1974). The taste is eclectic, like that of the more civilized crooks in a James Bond movie – from Louis XVI furniture, to a 15th-century Italian chest telling the story of Samson, to Adam chairs and imitation Chippendale, to neoclassical silver in the dining room, and cases of porcelain. The fountain from Tibães is at the bottom of the garden, purchased from the children of the late owner's maid. Under the colonnade are three heads awrithe with sea flowers, concocted by Jorge Barradas in 1969. (His figures at the Museu da Cidade, North Lisbon, are even more striking.) Nogueira da Silva enjoyed electric curtains in his ballroom, and financed the completion of the Baroque church tower opposite his residence.

Chapel of São
Frutuoso de
Montélios
*open 9–12 and 2–5;
key from a neighbour;
closed Mon*

The Environs of Braga

Just outside Braga off the road to Ponte de Lima stands the tiny Visigothic **Chapel of São Frutuoso de Montélios**. Built in the second half of the 7th century, it is one of the oldest Christian buildings in Portugal. The chapel is in the shape of a Greek cross, supported by columns topped with acanthus leaves. The exterior is a series of recessed arches, alternately pointed and round-topped. The columns' ornamentation and the triple arches are probably Visigothic, while the roofing and lateral chapels were contributed by the Moors in the 9th century.

The Hungarian St Frutuoso was Bishop of Braga from 650 to 665: the chapel was adjacent to the monastery he founded, which was destroyed to build the 18th-century church of São Francisco. St Frutuoso's relationship with his adopted country was stormy. He wrote to his friend the Bishop of Saragossa describing Portugal as 'An extremity of the west, an ignorant country where naught is heard but the sound of tempests'. The chapel's atmosphere is not as impressive as its antiquity: though dim and pagan, it does not reek.

(i) Braga ›
Praça da República,
t (253) 262 550,
www.cm.braga.pt

Tourist Information and Services in Braga

To find the **tourist office** from the railway station, head straight up the Rua Andrade Corvo, through the Porta Nova and past the cathedral. From the bus station, cross the Praça Alexandre Herculano and continue down the Rua dos Chãos, which leads into the Praça da República. The **post office** is in the Avenida da Liberdade, 300 yards from the tourist office. Municipal **internet** access is provided at Praça Conde de Agrolongo 177 (*open Mon–Fri 9–7.30, Sat 9–1*) and in the Parque da Ponte (*open Mon–Sat 9–12.30 and 1.30–5*). Also in the Parque da Ponte is an Olympic-sized **swimming pool**.

Shopping in Braga

If you want to take home something out of the ordinary, there are three promising **antique shops** in the Rua Dom Gualdim Pais, near the entrance to the cathedral, including Vilhena at number 6, **t** 918 790 505. Nothing is priced, so dress down, and keep your eyes peeled for old plates, pewter, wall sconces and such like.

Festivals in Braga

Easter Week ushers in a series of processions, for which the city is decorated with lights, flowers, and streetside altars. For the *Ecce Homo* procession on Easter Thursday night, hundreds of barefoot penitents carry torches and wand-like cressets, iron baskets holding pitched rope or coal, lighted and mounted on poles.

The Church Christianized the summer solstice by turning it into the Feast of St John the Baptist, here celebrated 18–24 June, culminating in the final two days with processions including that of King David and the shepherds, whose characters are the descendants of a medieval play (*auto*), folkloric groups, endless bands and *papier maché* giants. People give each other pots of sweet basil, and hit each other with squeaky plastic hammers. The city is adorned with images of the ascetic saint sporting fabulously rouged cheeks. Don't expect much sleep.

Where to Stay in Braga

For more-luxury hotels, *see* Bom Jesus (p.95).

Moderate (€€)
★★★★**Hotel Turismo**, Praçeta João XXI, **t** (253) 206 000, *www.hotelturismo braga.com*. A bit too large to be very personal, and although it's perfectly decent it feels more like a three-star hotel. The service is efficient, rooms have balconies overlooking a few trees (though some

of them face the city's noisy principal thoroughfare), and there's a swimming pool on the eighth floor, and a garage.

★★★★**Albergaria da Sé**, Rua D. Gonçalo Pereira 39–51, **t** (253) 214 502, *www.albergaria-da-se.com.pt*. Well located close to the Cathedral and good restaurants, offering simple rooms with wooden floors. There are no double beds, only twins. Do be sure to ask for a room on the third floor, with a view of rooftops; otherwise you'll be facing a wall.

Inexpensive (€)

★ Albergaria Senhora-a-Branca >

★★★★**Albergaria Senhora-a-Branca**, Largo da Senhora-a-Branca 58, **t** (253) 269 938, *www.albergariasrabranca.pt*. Housed in a town house in a little square filled with orange trees, this offers very good value accommodation. The public areas are dark, with dramatically lit fragments of 18th-century woodcarving and a good use of modern art. Bedrooms are comfortable if a little stark; rooms at the front can be a bit noisy, rooms at the back are smaller, and overlook a little garden. A garage is available.

★★★**Residencial do Central Comercio Avenida**, Avenida Central 27–37, **t** (253) 275 722. Entered through a shopping centre, basically OK. Don't make it your first choice, but if you do stay ask for a room overlooking the unexpectedly pretty little park. Satellite TV.

★★**Hotel João XXI**, Avenida João XXI 849, **t** (253) 215 178/9. Opposite the Hotel Turismo, fairly basic and feels rather youthful. Traffic can be very noisy, but ceilings are nice and high, and there's 24-hour internet access in the CyberSala.

★★**Residencial Avenida**, Avenida da Liberdade 738, **t** (253) 609 020, *www.residencialavenida.net*. Centrally located and family run, with no fancy trimmings and quite nice for it. Cheaper rooms, without en suite bathrooms, are available.

Residencial Dora, Largo Senhora-a-Branca 92–94, **t** (253) 200 180. Bright, fresh and very pleasant.

Pousada

★★★★**São Vicente Pousada**, Largo de Infias, **t** 902 011 932, *www. pousadas.pt* (L1 C). One of Portugal's newest *pousadas*. Located in a sumptuous late 19th-century palace complete with private chapel. Rooms are elegant and spacious and retain many original features.

Eating Out in Braga

Head for the little square called Campo das Hortas for a choice of four or five good restaurants that are pretty much next door to one another. You're unlikely to do badly in any of them.

Expensive (€€€)

Inácio, Campo das Hortas 4, **t** (253) 262 095. Rustic in look, and reputed to be the best restaurant in Braga. The *bacalhau* is good. *Closed Mon*.

Beijo de Frade, São Vicente Pousada, Largo de Infias, **t** 902 011 932. Master chef Beijo de Frade whips up traditional Minho culinary delights at Braga's newly opened *pousada*. Dishes include *bacalaoa la narcisa* (fried cod with onions and potato) and *arroz de pato* (duck with rice). The dining room is elegant, the service impeccable.

Moderate (€€)

Bem-me-quer, Campo das Hortas 6, **t** (253) 262 095. Like a restaurant in a New York brownstone, long, thin, and brick, with old photographs on the walls, it serves a range of very good fish and meat dishes. *Closed Wed evening*.

Anjo Verde, Largo da Praça Velha 21, **t** (253) 264 010. Excellent (and rare) vegetarian restaurant serving tasty dishes using local ingredients. Surroundings are bright and airy with original stone walls – and artwork.

O Alexandre, Campo das Hortas 10, **t** (253) 614 003. Traditional cuisine.

Closer to the cathedral, the restaurant at the **Albergaria da Sé** (*see above*), serves good, simple, nicely presented food. There's a covered area at the front that's open to the pavement. *Closed Sun*.

Inexpensive (€)

A Moçambicana, Rua Adrade Corvo 8, **t** (253) 262 260. Frequented by men in flat caps ignoring the TV and eating beefsteak cooked like it was in Mozambique.

A Ceia, Rua do Raio 331, **t** (253) 263 932. Buzzing, convivial and a great place to gorge. Arrive early to secure a table. *Closed Mon.*

Cafés and Bars in Braga

Café Astória, Praça da República 5, **t** 966 908 260. A large café with a fabulous moulded ceiling that serves coffee during the day and becomes a bar at night. On Friday and Saturday night the upper storeys become a disco bar – the three life-sized figures weirdly suspended are angels – with a wonderful terrace.

Other good bars include **Barbieri** on the Avenida Central, near the Congregados church, and **Populum**, at Campo da Vinho.

Around Braga

Caldelas

Spa
open 1 June–10 Oct

The typical early 20th-century **spa** of Caldelas lies 14km northeast of Braga, a rural niche sheltered by the spurs of the Serra do Gerês, with its complement of neogothic houses. The Romans took advantage of its medicinal qualities: Caldelas is particularly good for gastritis, colitis and other intestinal disorders, and certain dermatological complaints. Give or take a little global warming, the Romans must also have enjoyed the fresh clean air, which somehow stays pleasant even on sultry days.

Bom Jesus do Monte

 Baroque
staircase

In the 18th century it was deemed unseemly for pilgrims to ascend to their climax by dirt paths. The solution was the **Baroque staircase**, splendid at Bom Jesus. It climbs the thickly wooded hillslope in a series of terraced zigzags of white plaster, embellished with wall fountains representing the five senses and, higher, the three virtues, and with granite biblical figures who grow more and more rococo as one ascends. Some wear turbans and oriental cloaks. The eye is led up the tier of rich Christmas crackers to the twin-towered church at the top. Penitents climb on their knees, but the fainthearted succumb to the hydraulic funicular from near the base of the staircase. It has become acceptable to descend the stair by mountain bike.

The lower portion was begun by the Archbishop of Braga in 1723. Cruz Amarante added the upper portion some 60 years later, and the church itself was not completed till 1837. The church of Bom Jesus is of no special interest, and there is no sign of the late 15th-century sanctuary on which it was built. The church is surrounded by manicured gardens, tranquil except at weekends. Among the trees are snackbars and hotels, which can be reached by road.

Getting to Bom Jesus

Bom Jesus is 2km east of Braga. Frequent buses for Bom Jesus depart from outside the shopping centre in Braga's Avenida Central.

The mid-18th-century vogue for elaborately decorated façades was adopted with special vigour in the region of Braga. Should you wish to continue reeling, this is well illustrated by the rococo **church of Santa Maria Madalena** at **Falperra**, 5km south of Bom Jesus. Designed by André Soares da Silva in 1750, the windows and doors are awrithe with stylized granite vegetation, set against brilliant whitewash.

Citânia de Briteiros

Citânia de Briteiros
t (253) 415 969; open 9–12 and 1–5; adm

The site of **Citânia de Briteiros**, 10km southeast of Bom Jesus, is the largest and most thrilling of the fortified Celtiberian hill settlements in Portugal. It is thought to have been the last stronghold against the Romans, c. 26–19 BC. For 200 years the Celtiberians and their similarly ferocious neighbours the Lusitanians had kept the Romans south of the Serra da Estrela. In this they were helped by two brilliant commanders, Viriatus and Sertorius. Times were tough and the locals fought dirty: in *The Georgics*, Virgil extols the advantages of good sheep dogs – with guards like these, you need never fear 'the unpacified Iberians creeping up on you from behind.'

Strabo, writing his *Geographia c.* 20 BC, asserts 'Some authors affirm that ... the Celtiberians and their neighbours to the north offer sacrifices, on nights of the full moon, to a nameless god, in front of their houses, spending the whole night long with their families dancing, singing in chorus and feasting. The Lusitanians ... practise augury, by observing the entrails of prisoners.' Otherwise, they 'live simply, drink water and sleep on the bare earth ... two-thirds of the year they live on acorns, which they roast and grind to make bread. They also have beer. They lack wine but when they have it they drink it up, gathering for a family feast. When they assemble to drink they perform round dances to the flute or the horn, leaping in the air and crouching as they fall.'

Strabo's sources got it wrong about the nameless god: misled by the lack of temples, they overlooked the numerous Celtiberian gods venerated in rivers and woods, streams and rocky places. The Celtiberians may have left Citânia de Briteiros, but the spirits remain today. The granite walls of the 150 dwellings are now only a few blocks high; there's enough to divine the primitive urban plan, the water system, and to walk the footpaths. Two wonderful huts were reconstructed by Dr Martins Sarmento after he excavated the site in 1875. They come complete with conical thatched roofs and an unspoilt view. Some of the round huts have no entrances; perhaps they were silos entered by ladder. Downhill stands the most controversial structure, a trench flanked by the granite slabs. Now archaeologists consider this the bath house rather than the funerary chamber, marked no. 17 on the good site plan issued at the entrance.

Castro de Sabroso

Another hill settlement, Castro de Sabroso, is visible from Citânia de Briteiros. It's smaller, older, and better fortified. Unless you are especially interested, there is no need to see both sites. From Taipas, take the Santa Cristina de Longos road to Cancela. Turn right and follow the road to the hilltop *castro*.

Tibães

Convento de Tibães
t (253) 622 670,
www.geira.pt/
msmtibaes;
open summer 10–6.30;
winter 10–5.30; adm

Six km northwest of Braga, the **convento de Tibães** was once the greatest Benedictine monastery in the land and now seeps with picturesque decay. Extensive renovation has reclaimed some of the buildings from the encroaching ivy and removed some of the romance of the place, but it's still very impressive, and there's an opportunity to wander among the ruined outhouses.

Things were different in the 17th century, when Tibães was enormously wealthy and well-managed, buoyed by generous land grants in addition to its original 12th-century endowment. The abbey was virtually self-supporting – producing wheat, corn, rye, barley, oats, chestnuts, cork and wine as well as pigs, cattle and goats. The lands contained two linen mills: by 1668, textile production was booming, and a justice had to be appointed to adjudicate disputes relating to cloth manufacture. Two years later, probably because textile workers were female, a woman was appointed as justice. Carpenters, potters, tilers, blacksmiths – whose iron was one of the few imports – cobblers, millers, masons and tailors worked for the abbey. The Benedictines chose to show off their worldly wealth: in the late 17th century they decided to do away with all their old-fashioned Romanesque and Gothic architecture to make way for the Baroque. Hence nothing remains of the 12th-century foundation.

Church
open 9–12 and 2–5;
closed Mon and hols

Visitors seeking more than magnificent decay should head for the gilded glory of the **church**. André Soares' mid-18th-century retable is an excellent example of Portuguese rococo woodwork, influenced by engravings of rococo work in Augsburg, and by Nasoni's work in Porto. The garlanded columns are set on Oriental-looking pedestals, probably inspired by the fashion for Chinese art and ceramics. The stalls in the *coro alto* are very odd – draped figures emerge from the backs, beside caryatid partitions. They were brought to life in 1666–8, and along with the reliquary chapel

Where to Stay and Eat Around Braga

Caldelas

***Grande Hotel da Bela Vista, t** (253) 360 100, *www.hotelbelavista.com* (€€€). On the road to Amares, built on an elegant platform above the baths to which it is connected by a private elevator. Treat yourself to the Sea Salt Peeling treatment in the Health Club, and then enjoy the lovely rural panorama from the terrace.

Bom Jesus

Near the top of the staircase there are two four-star hotels owned by the same management. The first is far nicer than the second.

****Hotel do Elvador, t** (253) 603 400, *www.hoteisbomjesus.pt* (€€). Fabulous views, light, attractive bedrooms and a good restaurant. The only problem is that the beds are a bit small for two people. Tennis court.

****Hotel do Parque, t** (253) 603 470 (€€). Feels plastic and the colour scheme is offensive. Check out the murals in the reception area, worthy of any meditational sect, and the frilly chandeliers. Drinks are served in the covered courtyard, and the hotel shares its sister's restaurant.

Turismo de Habitação
Casa dos Lagos, Bom Jesus Estrada Nacional, t (253) 676 738, *www.home page.oninet.pt/331mde* (€€ CA). At the top of the road leading to Bom Jesus, it suffers slightly from the vibrations of road traffic. Still, the four apartments available to rent are quite pleasant and, mercifully, sparsely furnished. Each has fine views, two bedrooms, a sitting room, a nice little kitchen and a bath or shower room, and all have the use of the house's small oval pool and sun deck. The one room available in the main house is large, heavy and distinctively Portuguese.

at Alcobaça they mark the emergence of a new and particularly Portuguese style of woodcarving, which adopts a sculptural rather than an architectural form, to create the impression of continuous movement. There are good tiles of Joseph and his brethren in the huge chapter house. One cloister is paved with tombs, which relations etch with artificial flowers.

In 1834, when the religious orders were dissolved, Tibães was sold into private hands. The last owner left the property to her maid's children, who sold off the portable parts: the fountain can be seen at the Nogueira da Silva museum in Braga. The government purchased Tibães some years ago.

Barcelos

Barcelos is famous for its market, the largest and most illuminating in Portugal, and for its fantastical pottery. The town of about 17,500 souls spans the River Cávado, surrounded by deposits of clay, granite and kaolin. Pine trees cloak the gentle hills and open valleys of the outlying region, fertile land planted with maize, vineyards, beans and orchards. Having existed for centuries on agriculture and pottery, the town became a focus for the manufacture of industrial textiles in the first half of the 20th century. Kiln chimneys stretch upwards on the outskirts of town,

Getting to Barcelos

By **road**, Barcelos is 20km west of Braga, and 29km southeast of Viana.

Barcelos is directly connected with all the **railway stations** to the north: Viana (13 daily; ½hr or ¾hr); Afife (6 daily; 1¼hrs); Âncora-Praia (7 daily; 1hr); Moledo (5 daily; 1½hrs); Caminha (7 daily; 1½hrs); Cerveira (7 daily; 1¾hrs); Valença (8 daily; 2¾hrs). From Porto, there are 13 trains daily (1¼hrs). From Braga, change at Nine (14 daily; 1hr total). From Guimarães, change at Lousado (1hr), from which there are intermittent trains to Barcelos (¾hr).

Buses run frequently from Braga.

and barefoot children carry trays of pottery. Centred on the large, elegant Campo da República, Barcelos seems to save all its energy for Thursday, market day.

Barcelos is also responsible for the legend of the cock, which has been immortalized in the hideous pottery cockerel beloved by tourists. In the 14th century, a Galician pilgrim was saved from the gallows when he successfully challenged a roasted cock to crow on a judge's table. That cockerel still has a lot to answer for.

Barcelos makes a good day trip from Braga or Viana do Castelo: there's little choice of accommodation in the town, and finding a bed on a Thursday – market day – is virtually impossible.

Around the Town

The **Campo da República** is Barcelos' huge market square, centred on a beautifully proportioned fountain and surrounded by fine, low buildings. To the north, behind its plain front, the **Igreja do Terço**, or **das Beneditinas**, contains remarkable tiles of the life of St Benedict, created by António de Oliveira Bernardes (1684–1732), who presided over the great period of *azulejo* design. He made these panels in 1713, two years after his work on the Lóios chapel at Évora: the use of space and line is outstanding. One panel depicts three monks bending to lift a platform on which a small, winged, half-goat devil dances. The high dado of Baroque allegorical medallions illustrates contemporary dress. Perched between *azulejo* panels, the vigorous, gilt pulpit probably also dates from 1713. It displays the Hapsburg crowned double-headed eagle, which after the Spanish domination of 1580–1640 remained a popular motif in the art of Portugal. St Michael tops the canopy, attended by statues of children bearing emblems of the Benedictine Order. The ceiling of the church is panelled with the same saint's life.

Pottery Museum
Rua Cónego Joaquim Gaiolas, t (253) 824 741, www.museuolaria.org; open 10–5.30 Tues–Fri, 10–12.30 and 2–5.30 Saturday and Sunday; closed Mon and hols

The **Pottery Museum** is well worth a visit. It contains a rotating collection of 7,000 pieces from Portugal, Portuguese-speaking countries and elsewhere. At its best it's excellent, the evidence of a fabulous imagination at work. The shop sells good examples of locally-made pieces, and there are live demonstrations of working with clay and painting tiles. Children are encouraged to create their own works of art, and to return to the museum several days later to collect them.

Barcelos Pottery

Barcelos pottery was made famous by Rosa Ramalho (1888–1977), a local girl who had a way with clay and produced glazed green tabletop figures, especially Christ on the cross, wearing a crown of thorns. By the time she died she had spawned a number of popular potters, who create zany imaginary creatures with distorted features, doing unlikely things like trumpeting.

The more representational work is usually religious – whole Last Suppers are produced, and many devils – or simply whimsical, such as hedgehogs stuck with olives. Everything is hand painted in bright colours. It cannot be called beautiful, but it's unique and it has a certain naïve charm. A selection is on sale in the tourist office and the Museu de Olaria (Pottery Museum).

Two of the leading lights of Barcelos pottery were Ana Baraça and Mistério. Ana Baraça's hallmark is her figures' literally pinched faces. Deaf, gummy, and round, she worked among her family, eyes shining, laughing silently. Interviewed at the age of 91, she said the ideas just don't stop. She passed the baton to one of her sons and three of her grandchildren, who continue the tradition. Mistério produced devils and apostles. His grandmother started him as a potter when he was 12. (When it got too cold for her fingers to make pots, she made socks instead.) Mistério's ideas came to him in dreams. He worked in a shed, while his wife wielded a broom outside, sweeping the chickens around the courtyard. She and two of his children continue his work.

The attractively plain **Hospital da Misericórdia**, formerly a Capuchin convent, dominates the eastern side of the Campo. More splendid is the 18th-century **Igreja do Senhor da Cruz**, built in a corner of the Campo by João Antunes some 30 years after his Igreja da Santa Engrácia in Lisbon and following its centralized plan. The church's beautiful Baroque cupola dominates a garden of obelisks; it contains some very rich giltwork, right up to the tassled pelmets.

The other focus of interest is by the River Cávado, which is crossed by a 15th-century bridge. In the ruined **Ducal Palace** of the eighth Duke of Barcelos, first Duke of Bragança, grass cushions the miscellaneous remains of the **Archaeological Museum**. These include the 16th-century crucifix known as the Gentleman of the Cock, which depicts a man being hanged. The palace was struck by the 1755 earthquake. Nearby are the Gothic **Igreja Matriz**, and the pillory (*see* p.412), apparently draped with neck fetters.

Archaeological Museum
Rua Dr Miguel Fonseca, t (253) 809 600; open 9–6; closed hols

The Barcelos Market

 Barcelos market

Do plan to be in Barcelos for the Thursday market, which dates back to 1412 and fills the huge Campo da República with row after row of handbags, orange trees, sausage skins, witches' brooms, dog collars, sieves, lace, embroidered linen, carved yokes, cassettes by the tableful, bread by the vanful, fruit and vegetables by the crateful – or laid on a strip of hessian, the entire produce of one smallholding. Swarthy women hawk their wares, nimble and urgent, filigree earrings flapping. A woman in black arrives with a reed basket and a couple of live chickens or pigeons or rabbits, weighs them in her hands, haggles, pokes, and leaves with potatoes or bras or an umbrella. She fumbles in her ample breast for the cloth bag that holds her money. At lunchtime vendors drink wine from yogurt pots. Beggars lie on thoroughfares, displaying their disabilities. In winter, chestnuts roast. The market packs up around lunchtime, so get there early – it's humming from eight o'clock onwards.

Tourist Information and Services in Barcelos

(i) **Barcelos >**
Largo Dr José Novais 8, t (253) 811 882; open Mon–Fri 9–12.30 and 2.30–6, Sat and Sun 9–4

The **tourist office** occupies the Torre de Menagem, one of the seven towers of what was the city wall. It sells local craftwork; pottery cockerels simply fly off the shelves. From the **railway station**, t (253) 811 243, walk straight ahead, and diagonally across the Campo da República to the craft centre.

There are two **bus stations**: one is near the Campo in Avenida dos Combatantes da Grande Guerra and the RN depot is in the Avenida Dr Sidónio Pais.

Festival in Barcelos

The Campo da República is illuminated by innumerable lightbulbs for the **Festas das Cruzes** on 2 and 3 May. Featuring a 'Great Fair' and a carpet of flowers, the festival dates back to 1504, when a peasant who insisted on working on the Day of the Holy Cross saw a luminous, aromatic cross in the land he was digging. The church of Senhor da Cruz is decorated with coloured lightbulbs, until it resembles a giant cake.

Where to Stay in Barcelos

(★) **Quinta do Convento da Franqueira >**

Quinta do Convento da Franqueira, Carvalhal, t (253) 831 606, *www.quintadafranqueira.com* (€€€). Five km southwest of Barcelos, the lovingly restored 16th-century *quinta* has been in English ownership since 1965, and the Gallie family make excellent hosts. Surrounded by pine trees, cork oaks and eucalyptus, with a working vineyard and winery, and a spring-fed swimming pool. Four attractive bedrooms are available, and a studio apartment. *Open 1 May –30 Oct.*

★★★Hotel Bagoeira, Avenida Dr Sidónio Pais 49, t (253) 809 500, *www.bagoeira.com* (€€). This hotel has been revamped and sports modern rooms with wood panelling and shiny white paintwork to complement the delightful stone-clad restaurant (*see* below).

★★Residencial Arantes, Avenida da Liberdade 35, t (253) 811 326 (€). Overlooking the market square. Some of the rooms are cramped and fairly airless.

Eating Out in Barcelos

Bagoeira, Avenida Dr Sidónio Pais 49, t (253) 811 236/088 (€€). Facing the market square, Bagoeira is a respectable eatery, despite the predominance of striplights. Try the grilled meats.

Restaurante Arantes, Avenida da Liberdade 33, t (253) 811 645 (€€). This restaurant (below a hotel of the same name) has lots of character, with curing hams hanging from the ceiling and handy adjacent patisserie. Enjoy traditional Minho dishes such as marinated pork.

Restaurant Casa dos Arcos, Rua Duques de Bragança, t (253) 811 975 (€€). A family-run, entirely stone-built restaurant situated in the historic part of town. Despite feeling a little like a tourist trap, the seafood is very good and the prices are reasonable. *Closed Mon.*

Dom António, Rua Dom António Barroso 85, t (253) 812 285 (€€). Serves good food and specializes in wild boar. Being windowless, it tends to feel snug in the winter and airless in the summer.

The Minho Coast

The Minho's wonderful sand beaches are backed by low, coarse-grassed dunes, and are exposed to the winds and wild waves of the Atlantic. That makes them great for surfing and other sports, but bring a wetsuit – at the height of summer the average seawater temperature is around 60°F (16°C). If you feel like a reprieve from sunbathing, the beaches are great for walking.

Viana do Castelo

An elegant fishing port at the wide mouth of the River Lima, Viana do Castelo is backed by the woody Monte Santa Luzia, and overflown by seagulls. The town is more or less arranged on a grid pattern, but wanderers will come upon *palácios* and rococo churches as well as the delights of daily life. Discreetly dispersed among these is a good range of hotels, from which guests can make the most of the magnificent, sweeping beach and its big waves. Surf shops rub shoulders with more traditional establishments, and there's an air of holiday about the place.

Viana's fairly low-key fishing industry has been overtaken by the heavy industry on the opposite bank of the river estuary.

History

Viana served as the port for the north of Portugal until the late 17th century, when it was eclipsed by Porto. Cloth and cod were shipped from England to Viana (and, to a lesser extent, to Monção) from the 16th century, and bartered on the quayside for the red wine of the Minho – red portugal. Trading links were established with Brazil, Scandinavia and Russia, and Viana's merchants were said to rival those of Venice and Florence. Periodically the canny English and Scottish merchants forsook their Baroque town houses in Viana, loaded their Carolingian wigs and account books, and set off in flat-bottomed boats up the River Lima. The wine they bought did not travel well: it was frowned on in England. Large quantities were supplied to the British naval commissioners as 'beverage for the sailors'.

Political events then played into the merchants' hands. Colbert, Louis XIV's minister, implemented ultra-protectionist policies, forbidding the import of English cloth into France. Charles II retaliated by banning the import of French wine into England. Demand for red portugal drained the supplies, and the merchants in Portugal looked for new vineyards. They hit upon the Upper Douro – and it was easier to ship wine from the Upper Douro via Porto: Viana was never the same again.

Getting to Viana do Castelo

Trains run directly to Viana from Porto (13 daily; 1¾hrs), Barcelos (13 daily; ½hr or ¾hr), and intermittently from all stations north of Viana. From Guimarães, change at Lousado (intermittent; 1hr plus 1½hrs). From Braga, change at Nine (frequent; 1½hrs total).

REDM express **buses, t** (258) 825 047, run to Viana once or twice daily from Lisbon (6hrs), Coimbra (3hrs), Porto (1½hrs), Póvoa de Varzim (¾hr), Esposende (½hr). The same company also runs frequent stopping buses from Porto (1¾hrs) and from Póvoa de Varzim (1hr). Intermittent buses run down the coast from Monção.

Around the Town

Church of Santa Luzia
open summer 8–7; winter 8–5

Best start at the top: a cobbled road snakes up to Santa Luzia, and makes a pleasant walk. The hideous grey pilgrimage church of Santa Luzia, built in the early 20th century in neo-Byzantine style, has been likened to a bowl of sprouting tulips, but it offers a broad view of Viana and the rivermouth. Behind the *pousada*, **Citânia de Santa Luzia** is a Celtiberian settlement dating from the 3rd century BC (*see* 'Citânia de Briteiros', p.93); the 40 dwellings are razed to their stone foundations (closed for renovation at the time of research).

The Praça da República

The heart of Viana is the Praça da República, a satisfying mélange of 16th-century styles centred on a well-proportioned Renaissance fountain, built by João Lopes the Elder to suit the contemporary Italian taste for water falling from graduated basins. Behind it stand the three arches of the restored **Paços do Concelho** (the old town hall), which is at right angles to the extraordinary three-storeyed façade of the **Misericórdia House**. João Lopes' self-satisfied granite caryatids have borne their load since 1520, as they remained in place when the **Misericórdia** was rebuilt two centuries later. The *azulejos* in the nave were begun in 1720 by António de Oliveira Bernardes, whose work at Évora and Barcelos is so exceptional. Though grand, these biblical scenes lack the others' nobility – they were completed by António's son, Policarpo. Viana is fond of its folk traditions, and 12 fabulously bright traditional skirts are displayed at the **Museu do Traje**, where there's also a temporary exhibition space.

Museu do Traje
t (258) 809 377; open 10.30–12.30 and 3–6; closed Sun am and Mon; adm

Towards the River

Veering riverwards past the old town hall, the Rua Gago Coutinho passes the rococo chapel of the **Casa da Praça**, which is ornamented with granite shells. There's nothing of interest inside. Nearby, the castellated 15th-century **Sé Catedral** is fronted with horrid stone figures who see, hear, and speak no evil. The interior was burnt by a Napoleonic fire. It contains a fine model of a *caravela*, and a nice juxtaposition of angles at the staircase.

Moored in the docks opposite the Largo Vasco da Gama, the ship **Gil Eannes** was built in Viana's boatyard in 1955. From then until 1963 it served as a floating hospital for the cod-fishing fleets on the coast of Newfoundland and Greenland; it was also an ice-breaker, and supplier of provisions, including bait. Sold for scrap and rescued by the municipality in 1997, it now houses a little

Gil Eannes Museum
open Sat and Sun 9–12 and 2–7; adm

museum to illustrate its history and a bar.

At the mouth of the docks, the **Santiago da Barra Fort** is the 'castelo' in Viana do Castelo, but it's uninteresting. Philip II of Spain, at that time King of Portugal, ordered its construction in 1592. Every Friday there's a **market** next to the castle on the Campo do Castelo, which is good for clothes and pottery.

Inland

From the Praça da República, the Rua Cândido dos Reis leads past the gracious rococo façade of the town hall, formerly the **Palace of the Counts of Carreira**, to a hospice suffused with kindness and good humour, formerly the **convento de Sant'Ana**. There's an

Convento de Sant'Ana
closed to view at weekends

interesting collection of antique wheelchairs in the vestibule; and the chapel is delightful, its ceiling panelled with biblical scenes – Christ is in red – and the gilt retable bursting from the surrounding tiles. The convent was less quiet in former times. In the late 17th century, the nuns were meeting with their lovers in the small buildings on the grounds of the nunnery, which had been built to provide the sisters with somewhere to practise their cooking on days when they were permitted to leave the convent. In 1700 Pedro II ordered these cauldrons of vice to be torn down. Even as the love nests were being razed, the Sisters of Sant'Ana were selling contraband tobacco.

Museu Municipal
t (258) 820 377; open 9.30–12 and 2–5; closed Mon and hols; adm

From the Praça da Républica, the Rua Manuel Espregueira runs parallel with the river to the **Museu Municipal**. The museum is housed in a *palácio* built by Vilalobos in 1720, and auctioned 10 years later to a family who lived in it until 1922. The *palácio's* original *azulejos*, by Policarpo de Oliveira Bernardes, depict the continents personified, aboard unlikely chariots and smiled on by cherubs. The museum contains some good furniture, including a rare Indo-Portuguese table inlaid with ivory dots right down to its feet. Also displayed are a Spanish painting of a black magic ceremony and a picture of the Praça da República in the 19th century.

Ferry
departs from pier at Largo 5 de Outubro; May–Sept, until 7pm

A five-minute **ferry** shuttles passengers across the river to the **Praia do Cabedelo**, Viana's huge and wonderful curved beach backed by grassy dunes crossed by wooden walkways, just like Cape Cod. Infrequent TransCunha buses depart from the Largo 5 de Outubro. For a taxi, call **t** (258) 826 641. If you have a car, drive across the river. There's a shower by the car park, and a couple of cafés.

(i) **Viano do Castelo >**
Rua Hospital Velho,
t (258) 822 620

Railway station:
t (258) 824 402;
open 15 July–30 Sept

(★) **Estalagem Melo Alvim >>**

Services in Viano do Castelo

The railway station, t (258) 822 296, is near the centre of town – walk straight ahead down the Avenida dos Combatentes. The **bus station** is on the northeastern edge of town, at the end of the Rua da Bandeira. **Internet** access is available at the Post Office at Avenida Combatentes da Grande Guerra 66, t (258) 800 080, or at the Public Library in Rua Cândido dos Reis, t (258) 809 302.

Shopping in Viano do Castelo

If you like tat, be sure to visit **Bazar Económico** at Rua Manuel Espregueira 112. It's a feast of jaunty sailor desk ornaments, dolls in satin dresses, hair ornaments and religious ephemera.

Sports and Activities in Viano do Castelo

The municipal **swimming pool** is in the Avenida Capitão Gaspar de Castro, t (258) 809 365. **Surfing** equipment can be rented from Surf Clube de Viana, Centro Comercial 1 de Maio, t (258) 826 208. The tourist office distributes a free **walking** map with routes around the watermills near Montaria, but scant verbal description.

Festivals in Viano do Castelo

Viana's *romaria* is special: on the Friday nearest 20 August, the image of N.S. da Agonia is carried in procession from the church of the same name, along a route stencilled with coloured sawdust and draped with fishing nets, to the docks, where the boats are hung with flags. The image then goes for a short cruise. Drums announce everything. People camp by their coaches, make coffee on spirit lamps at 4am, play table football, wash in the river, and eat *farturas*, nasty fried sugared flour. Houseplants are put on doorsteps, anyone with gold to wear wears it. For the procession, each village provides a float illustrating the local speciality, be it winemaking, mending fishing nets, picking olives, making bread or killing the pig. The last float is the *caravela*, symbol of Viana.

After the *romaria* comes the only bullfight of the year. At the fort on Sunday evening, local costumes are displayed. The costumes of the farm women (*lavradeiras*) get very specific – one for going to church, one for going to the fields, one for collecting seaweed. The ladies of Viana itself wear flowery red headscarves and shawls, white blouses, and pleated red, black and yellow skirts. Traditionally, they keep their wealth in gold – medallions and necklaces of coins – and this Sunday evening is when all the heirlooms get displayed.

Where to Stay in Viano do Castelo

*****Estalagem Melo Alvim (Relais & Chateaux), Avenida Conde da Carreira 28, t (258) 808 200, www.meloalvimhouse.com (€€€). A fine example of what stylish restoration can do to a mansion of 1509 with later additions: it's tasteful, light and bright, it makes the most of unique features, such as the great granite staircase, while remaining thoroughly respectful. Each bedroom is different. The location is convenient, but it has its drawbacks: it can't offer views like the *pousada*'s, and it's next to the railway station, although not overly disturbed by trains. Parking is available. The restaurant, open to non-residents, is slightly less attractive; half-board is available for an extra €30. Duck with port wine sauce is a speciality.
**Hotel Viana Sol, Largo Vasco da Gama, t (258) 828 995 (€€). To the fore of the town, a popular hotel offering pleasant, sparingly

★ **Quinta do Paço d'Anha >>**

★ **Albergaria Margarida da Praça >**

furnished, though viewless bedrooms surrounding a fabulously retro atrium: with its smoked glass and spider plants, it feels like a pimp's palace. You can't help but feel Starsky and Hutch are about to burst in and bust you. Good facilities include an indoor swimming pool, sauna and a tennis court. Skip the restaurant.

Albergaria Margarida da Praça, Largo 5 de Outubro 58, **t** (258) 809 630, *www.margaridadapraca.com* (€€). It's appealingly simple and spacious, with clean lines, an unpolished granite floor, and views of the harbour. The restaurant is attractive but pricey.

★★★**Residencial Jardim**, Largo 5 de Outubro 68, **t** (258) 828 915 (€€). A reliable option overlooking the waterfront. Rooms are quite well equipped, if somewhat heavy, and the staff are helpful.

★★★**Residencial Viana Mar**, Avenida dos Combatentes da Grande Guerra 215, **t** (258) 828 962 (€). On Viana's principal street, this feels like someone's home. The ceilings are high and the rooms somewhat down-at-heel; the four at the back are best.

Pensão Alambique, Rua Manuel Espregueira 88, **t** (258) 823 894 (€). Basic but fine. Its prices shoot up in August.

Verde Minho, Rua do Anjinho 34-36, **t** (258) 822 386 (€). Located on an attractive cobbled street, this hotel has simple, spotless rooms.

Pousadas
Pousada de Santa Luzia, Monte de Santa Luzia, **t** (258) 828 891, *www.pousadas.pt* (L1 C). The hilltop *pousada* enjoys broad views of the church of the same name, hills, beaches, the town and its heavy industry. The solid building of 1918 has been refurbished in Art-Deco style, right down to the fittings. Bring flip-flops for walking to the swimming pool. The restaurant is well finished, with engraved glass candle-guards.
Pousada da Juventude Gil Eannes, Gil Eannes, waterfront area, **t** (258) 821 582 (€). One of the most unusual *hostals* you can find, located in the bowels of a grand old ship. It's not the

lap of luxury, but it's comfortable enough and certainly memorable.

Turismo de Habitação
Quinta do Paço d'Anha, Vila Nova de Anha, **t** (258) 322 459 or 917 059 538, *www.solaresdeportugal.pt* (€€€ QH). Five km southeast of Viana do Castelo, approached through vineyards which the owners' ancestors established in 1503. The farm buildings facing the Paço have been converted into three wonderfully rustic two-bedroom bungalows. Expect leather chests around a fireplace, a beamed ceiling above an open kitchen, and a supply of homegrown lemons if you're in season. Squeeze these over a drink and sit on the peaceful lawn behind the bungalows. Another dependent building has been converted into two apartments, sharing a covered patio and a small walled lawn. One has a single bedroom, the other has two, all attractively furnished and equipped with mod cons. Each year the Paço d'Anha produces 50,000 bottles of its own *vinho verde*. Part of the main house's colonnade is taken over by girls sticking labels on the delicious stuff. You can visit the vineyards.
Casa da Torre das Neves, Largo da Casa da Torre das Neves, 40, Vila de Punhe, **t** (93) 20 32 980, *www.casa torredasneves* (€€). Located 12km from Viana do Castelo, this is a classic Minho country house dating back to the late 16th century. Tastefully restored, the atmosphere is homey and welcoming with ancestral portraits, French windows leading out to the terrace and individually furnished bedrooms with antiques and the occasional four poster.
Casa do Ameal, Rua do Ameal 119, Meadela, **t** (258) 822 403 or 914 744 158, *www.solaresdeportugal.pt* (€€ CA). Off the main road from Viana to Ponte de Lima, offering seven cottagey bungalow apartments, each with its own entrance, in two blocks converted from outhouses. Early 20th-century prints, shaggy rugs in front of the log fireplace, patterned bedcovers, and well equipped, discreet kitchenettes characterize the viewless apartments, which come in various sizes. Two stone tables sheltered by a vine are

available for eating outside, and the guest dining room has a TV and card table. A good place if you're travelling with kids. The house itself was purchased in 1669 for 3,500 shillings, by forebears of the present residents.

Quinta do Vale do Monte, Lugar de Limão, Darque, **t** (258) 826 035 or 965 813 563, *www.quintavale monte.com* (€€). A burnt pink mansion of 1905, 6km from Viana, close enough to make restaurants and the beach easily accessible – and to ensure there are plenty of other houses in view. From Viana, cross the bridge, turn left for Barroselas and left again immediately. Rooms are pleasant if a little short on 'character' and Dona Rosa is eager to please. She makes the tomato and apricot jams served at breakfast, and the orange juice is home grown. A pergola leads down to a small vineyard. The two-bedroom bungalow, Adega Branca, is well worth considering if you have children – it opens onto the swimming pool.

Quinta de Monteverde, Sendim de Cima, Castelo do Neiva, **t** (258) 871 134, *www.quintamonteverde.com* (€€ CA). Seven km south of Viana, a squat 16th-century manor house with later additions; some rooms look towards the sandy beach just a mile (2km) away. The house was restored in 1998–2000. Dark furniture with scrolling woodwork comes as standard, and there's a pool.

Eating Out in Viano do Castelo

Costa Verde, Rua de Monserrate 411–413, **t** (258) 829 240 (€€€). Seafood is the speciality here. Serves good food in a bright and featureless restaurant on the northern edge of town towards Valença.

As da Quinta, Afif, **t** (258) 829 434 (€€). This village is around 8km north of Viana. Follow the signs to the restaurant where owner Luis will treat you royally. Dishes are excellently prepared and include a traditional bean casserole with prawns, and duck and pork dishes. The outside terrace is delightful on a sunny day.

O Pescador, Largo 5 de Outubro 28, **t** (258) 826 039 (€€). This seafood restaurant is reliably good with a wide range of catch-of-the-day choices. Family run and friendly, it is popular with locals so get here early to grab a table.

Os 3 Potes, Beco dos Fornos 9, **t** (258) 829 928 (€€). Near the Praça da República. Cosy and convivial, this is a safe bet, if a bit touristy. It's on the site of Viana's first public bakery. Sixteenth-century townspeople would bring their homegrown flour here, pay their fee, stick an emblem in their dough and bake their own bread. Gourds hang from the beamed ceiling, lampshades shed a gentle light, and the good food is subtly adapted to non-Portuguese palates. Folk dancers perform on Sat evenings (and Fri in August). *Reservations recommended. Closed Mon.*

Alambique, Rua Manuel Espregueira 92, **t** (258) 823 894 (€€). Decorated with agricultural implements, with the kitchen open to view at the back of the restaurant. The menu is small and ambitious. If you're skint, head for the bar counter.

Taverna do Valentim, Rua Mons. Daniel Machado 180, **t** (258) 827 505 (€€). Another popular place for seafood, and justifiably so. *Closed Sun.*

Cozinha das Malheiras, Rua Gago Coutinho 19, **t** (258) 823 680 (€€). If you fancy a break from fish, this place does a great *papas de sarabulho. Closed Tues.*

Getting to Vila Praia de Âncora and Moledo

There is one lunchtime and one evening express **bus** from Viano do Castelo to Vila Praia de Âncora (20mins), plus more frequent local buses.
For Moledo, **trains** from Porto (2¼hrs) pass through Barcelos (1hr) and Viana (¼hr).

Vila Praia de Âncora and Moledo

The railway follows the coast from Viana do Castelo to Moledo, passing through **Vila Praia de Âncora**, a small port at the mouth of the Âncora river, with a great beach that stretches a couple of kilometres, sheltered from northerly and southerly winds. The flat expanse of sand is fairly empty, except at weekends, and even then you only need to walk to get away from other people. Behind the beach, dry stone walls separate red-soiled fields into strips. If you prefer not to swim in big waves, head for the sheltered, reedy river estuary, or if you fancy a little fossicking, there are plenty of rock pools to the north of town.

Moledo, Portugal's most northerly Atlantic beach, celebrates its position at the mouth of the River Minho with a semi-ruined castle on a spit. Portuguese families come here on day trips, and the beach is easily accessible from the railway station.

ⓘ **Vila Praia de Âncora >**
Avenida Dr Ramos Pereira, **t** *(258) 911 384; open summer months*

ⓘ **Moledo >**
Open 15 July–30 Sept

Tourist Information in Vila Praia de Âncora and Moledo

In Vila Praia de Âncora the **tourist office** sells handicrafts and will arrange rooms in private houses.
In Moledo, the **tourist office** may be able to help you find a room.

Where to Stay and Eat in Vila Praia de Âncora

★★★**Hotel Meira**, Rua 5 de Outubro 56, Vila Praia de Âncora, **t** (258) 911 111, *www.portugalvirtual.pt/hotel.meira* (€€). One minute from the beach.
★★★★**Albergaria Quim Barreiros**, Avenida Dr Ramos Pereira 115, Vila Praia de Âncora, **t** (258) 959 100, *www.albergariaquimbarreiros.com* (€€). Plush accommodation overlooking the beach.

Casa da Torre, Lugar da Igreja, Âncora, **t** (258) 911 897, *www.casadatorre.eu*. Two kilometres south of Vila Praia de Âncora, this 18th-century building near the Âncora River and pine woods has a delightful house for rent (up to nine people, minimum one week), containing three double rooms and one single bedroom, sitting room with double sofa bed, dining room and fully equipped kitchen. There are three bikes available.
There's a lot of good fresh fish to be found in the local restaurants.

Sports in Vila Praia de Âncora and Moledo

If you want to hire surf equipment, you'll need to go 5km east of Caminha to do so: **Afluente**, Lugar da Sentinela, Lanhelas, **t** (258) 727 017, *www.angelfire.com/biz/afluente*.

Along the River Minho

Caminha

Caminha was once a mighty riverport, but in the 16th century intermittent border fighting inclined its shipping to Viana do Castelo, draining the small town of any significant revenue. Now Caminha is an unhurried minor frontier post, like a smaller version of Viana do Castelo. A busy road separates Pinhal Praia beach from the town.

The main square is centred on a fountain like Viana's, and dominated by a Renaissance clocktower on an 11th-century base. The carving of a woman who supports the sky decorates the portal of the **Misericórdia**. The **fire station** houses a small collection of antique hand-pulled fire engines, to your left as you look at the clocktower. The arch under the tower leads to a charming cobbled street and to a square with a fir tree and two double-decker birdboxes.

The **Igreja Matriz** is a fortress-church built in the 75 years after 1480. Pass beneath the Evangelists at the side door. The doors seem to have been made a little later than the rest of the church – though attractive, the figures are a clumsy interpretation of the Renaissance work brought to Coimbra by Frenchmen. The bossed wooden ceiling of the central nave is superbly carved, and represents some of the finest carpentry in the country. Its medallion faces may portray the commissioners of the building, or the craftsmen themselves, the principal of whom is believed to have been Francisco Munoz, from Tuy in Spain. On the outside of the church a stone gentleman points his arse at Spain.

Vila Nova de Cerveira

If you're passing through Cerveira, on the road from Caminha to Valença, the fortress-*pousada* is a great place to stop for a coffee. The village was named after its deer (*cervo*). The defence was built to stem river crossings, and probably dates from the 13th century, when Dom Sancho II granted the settlement to his wife as a wedding present.

Valença do Minho

Impregnable 17th-century fortress walls enclose the frontier town of Valença, built on a hill overlooking the River Minho. Now the old part of town caters to the invasion of gaudy Spanish tourists who come to buy bathmats and sackfuls of bottlecorks. They leave in the evening, and the cobbled streets are calm. Geraniums grow on wrought-iron balconies and granite casements. Moss seeps up the splendidly preserved polygonal

Getting to areas Along the River Minho

Caminha: there are eight **trains** a day from Porto (2½hrs) via Barcelos (1¼hrs) and Viana (½hr). There are also a couple of express **buses** a day from Viana (½hr) and Porto (2hrs).

Vila Nova de Cerveira: there are eight **trains** a day from Porto (2¾hrs) via Barcelos (1¾hrs), Viana (1hr) and Caminha (¼hr), plus two express **buses** from Porto (2½hrs).

Valença do Minho: there are a couple of express **buses** a day from Viana (1hr), Porto (3hrs) and Lisbon (7hrs), but just one from Braga (1hr), at 8am.

Monção: By **road**, Monção is 19km east of Valença and 39km north of Ponte da Barca. Express **buses** run twice daily from Lisbon (7¼hrs), three times from Coimbra (5hrs) and twice from Porto (3hrs). There are also stopping buses from Braga (1½hrs), Ponte da Barca (¾hr) and Arcos de Valdevez (¾hr). This bus continues through to Melgaço and S. Gregório. Auto-Viação do Minho, **t** (251) 652 917, runs infrequent buses from Porto (3hrs). The bus passes through Viana (1¼hrs), Âncora, Caminha (1hr), Cerveira and Valença (½hr).

Melgaço: Local company Salvador, **t** (253) 263 453, runs **buses** to Melgaço from Braga.

fosses, embankment, barbican and bastions. Valença has outgrown its battlements, and an uninteresting new town clamours below them. Stay here only if you can do it in luxury; otherwise, move on.

Idrisi, the Muslim geographer who completed his work in Sicily in 1154, wrote of the River Minho as 'a large, wide and deep river: the tide goes far up it, and vessels that go up it stop often because of the great number of villages and castles on its banks.' Valença was one of these stopovers, though at that time the settlement was called Contrasta, explained by a glance across the river to Tuy in Spain. The towns face each other like clenched fists. Dom Afonso V hoped to safeguard the loyalty of Valença by exempting two-thirds of the active male population from participating in raids on Spain. The Spaniards in the War of Restoration and the French in the Napoleonic War failed to take the town.

The **Roman milestone** in front of the church of S. Estêvão was originally near the River Minho jetty, marking the military road from Braga to Astorga.

The Environs of Valença do Minho

A little way east of town, the road to Monçao passes the lichenous granite of the Romanesque **Ganfei Monastery**, rebuilt for the Benedictines in the 18th century.

There are spectacular panoramic views from the **Monte do Faro**, 5km east of Valença. The ascent is fascinating because it gives an almost aerial view of several villages on the way. At the top, the view stretches down the valley of the River Minho to the ocean, and, on a clear day, as far as Pontevedra in Galicia. Some 22km south of Valença, the high village of **Paredes de Coura** makes a pleasant diversion.

Roughly halfway between Valença and Monção, the road passes the well-proportioned Romanesque **church of São Fins de Friestas**, which is all that remains of an early 11th-century Benedictine monastery. The real thrill is the cornice, carved with a collection of bizarre human and animal heads, whereas the portal is decorated with geometric shapes. The first foundation here dates from the 6th century. Subsequently the monks received wild boar in lieu of rent, but this could not sustain them for ever. By 1545 there were just three monks, and they were dissolute.

Monção

Monção is a charming, mellow little border town nudging the River Minho and centred on two squares ringed with Brazilian chestnuts (not true chestnuts: their fruit is inedible). At dusk an old man plays the accordion in the corner of his shop. An antique barber's chair, complete with a wrought-iron footrest and leather neckrest, awaits customers who can be shaved by a cut-throat razor, to the tunes of a harmonica played in an upstairs window. Monção is noted for its lampreys, rich little eels also found on the west coast of Ireland, and its Alvarinho wine.

A local lady named Deu-la-Deu showed her pluck in 1368 when she and her fellow townspeople were starving under siege by the Castilians. She grovelled about and found enough flour to make two buns. These she threw at the enemy, who left, disheartened by her show of plenty. The heroine and her buns stand gargantuan on Monção's blazon.

Behind its classical portal in the main square, the **Misericórdia** has a ceiling panelled with cherubs, and a floor paved with sepulchres. An alley to your left as you face the Misericórdia leads under an emblazoned arch to the Romanesque **Igreja Matriz**, which contains a cenotaph to Deu-la-Deu, erected by her great-great-grandson, and a Manueline chapel. Most of Dom Dinis' **fortress** of 1306 was destroyed when the now redundant railway line was built. The remains can be seen towards the riverbank, bushy with vegetation. The **spa** is not geared up for tourists. Baths with feet await benchfuls of quiet patients seeking help for rheumatism and bronchitis.

Around Monção

Five km south of Monção at Pinheiros, on the road to Arcos de Valdevez, the simple, balanced façade of the **Brejoeira Palace** (1806–34) was inspired by Lisbon's Ajuda palace. It's closed to the public but easily seen from the road.

In Longos Vales, 8km southeast of Monção on the road to Merufe, a mass of foul and fantastical faces glower from capitals at the back of the 12th-century Romanesque **church of S. João**. To see the round arches of the apse, and more weird creatures, ask for the key at the entrance of the driveway. Continuing a couple of km towards Merufe, take the turning marked Sta Tecla to see long views of the

Minho from the defunct **church of S. Caetano**, beside a Celtiberian site brightened by jonquils and converted by a cross.

The otherwise unremarkable **Ponte de Mouro**, between Barbeita and Ceivães, 8km east of Monção, was the bridge on which John of Gaunt, Duke of Lancaster, met João I on 1 November 1386. The latter had secured the independence of Portugal at the battle of Aljubarrota in the previous year. Together they planned the invasion of Castile. 'As further proof of friendship and a safeguard for these matters agreed upon,' writes the court historian Fernão Lopes, 'they then decreed and promised that the Duke would give his daughter, the Princess Philippa, to the King of Portugal to be his wife.' The wedding took place in Porto in 1387 (*see* **Porto and the Douro Litoral**, 'Dom João I and Philippa of Lancaster', pp.175–6). The couple were happily married: in the words of the same chronicler, 'God granted [Philippa of Lancaster] a husband to her taste.'

Melgaço

East of Monção, a pleasant road runs along the Minho river to Melgaço, past granite villages and opposite their equally humble Galician equivalents. This tiny town in vine land wakes from its sleep on market day, Friday. A wall circles the plain castle **keep** and its rocky outcrop, a frontier watchtower built by Afonso Henriques in 1170. Two viragos fought a memorable battle here in 1383. Inspired by a turncoat hussy – '*A Renegada*' – Castilians infested the castle, where they withstood siege by João I and the Duke of Lancaster. After seven weeks the renegade spotted Inês Negra among her besiegers, and suggested the two of them fight it out, hand to hand, winner take the castle. The renegade fled 'with signs of many punches on her snout', and the castle was Portugal's.

Taking the first left turn from the castle gateway, note the sharp-toothed wolf carved above the side door of the 13th-century Romanesque **Igreja Matriz** – the locals say it represents the Devil.

There's a border crossing into Galicia 9km east of Melgaço, at São Gregório.

(i) **Monção >**

Casa do Curro, Praça Deu-la-Deu, **t** *(251) 652 757, www.cm-moncao.pt*

Services in Monção

In Monção, the **bus station** is in front of the **old train station**. From there, the centre of town is straight ahead and to the right.

Festival in Monção

On 18 June, **Monção** celebrates Corpus Christi with a procession which dates back to the 16th century. It includes a blessed ox (*boi bento*), its horns varnished and decorated with flowers and ribbons, a symbol of plenty. A cart of herbs (*carro das ervas*), covered with greenery and filled with nervous or exhibitionist 'little angels', is followed by St George on horseback, wearing a long red cape and toting a sword. A lumbering dragon (*coca*) brings up the rear. After the procession, St George battles the dragon, symbol of evil. The dragon has never yet won.

Sports and Activities Along the River Minho

For rafting on the River Minho, contact **School of Atlantic Rafting**, *mop22459@mail.telepac.pt*.

Where to Stay and Eat Along the River Minho

Caminha

(i) **Valença do Minho >>**
Avenida de Espanha,
t *(251) 823 374*

(i) **Caminha >**
Rua Ricardo Joaquim de Sousa, **t** *(258) 921 952*

★★★★**Hotel Porta do Sol**, Avenida Dantas Carneiro, **t** (258) 722 340, *www.hotelportadosol.eu* (€€€). If you want somewhere comfortable and modern.

Casa de Esteiro, Rua Benemerito, Joaquim Rosas, **t** (258) 721 333, *www.manorhouses.com* (€€). A delightful 18th-century hunting lodge set in lush gardens. Has a friendly, homey feel. Self-catering apartments also available.

★★★**Pensão Galo d'Ouro Residencial**, Rua da Corredoura 15, **t** (258) 921 160 (€). Small, clean and friendly, off the main square, with a granite staircase, little iron balconies and lovely ceiling mouldings.

Residencial Arca Nova, Largo Sidónio Pais, **t** (258) 721 590 (€). Near the train station, it has lovely rooms.

Orbitur campsite, Mata do Camarido, **t** (258) 921 295.

(★) **Solar do Pescador >**

Solar do Pescador, Rua Visconde Sousa Rego 85, **t** (258) 922 794 (€€). An elegant little restaurant serving delicious fish, with *azulejos* on the walls, a wooden ceiling and a terracotta floor. *Open Nov–June; closed Sun night and Tues.*

Primavera, Praça Conselheiro Silva Torres 99, **t** (258) 921 306 (€€). On the corner of the main square, it has tables outside and a good selection of fish.

Vila Nova de Cerveria

★★★**Residencial Rainha de Gusmão**, Avenida Heróis do Ultramar, **t** (251) 796 227 (€). Nondescript rooms but clean if you get stuck.

Pousada

Pousada de D. Dinis, **t** (251) 795 601, *www.pousadas.pt* (L2 H). Drinks are served on the lawn beside ramparts fronting the river, and guests are cocooned with a chapel, a pillory, and the former town hall, each of which is edged with granite mottled by lichen. The four blocks of box-like guest rooms are decked with grandiose wooden furniture.

Valença do Minho

Casa da Eira, Laços Gondomil, **t** (251) 921 905, *www.casaeira.net* (€€). This low-rise building is a remodelled 18th-century farmhouse. Pleasant rooms, grassy lawns and a pool.

★★★**Hotel Lara Residencial**, Lugar de S. Sebastião, **t** (251) 824 348 (€€). Recently revamped bedrooms overlook the fortifications.

Pousada

Pousada de São Teotónio, **t** (251) 800 260, *www.pousadas.pt* (L1 C). A discreet building within the fortress walls, offering beautiful views of hilly fields towards the river and Tui beyond it. The service is good and the bedrooms are comfortable. The small restaurant serves very acceptable food, with a picture window to distract diners as they eat lamprey or wild rabbit.

Turismo de Habitação

Casa do Poço, Travessa da Gaviarra 4, **t** (251) 825 235, *www.casadopoco.fr.fm* (€€). Located next to the *pousada* in Valença do Minho, this is a real treat; stay here if you can. It's wonderfully elegant and furnished with a connoisseur's delicate antiques. Just one of the six bedrooms has a view, but there's a balcony from which all can enjoy it over a glass of wine. The director is French, and will cook with adequate notice. Good value.

There is a large choice of reasonable, family-friendly places to eat within the fortress walls.

Baluarte, Rua Apolinário da Fonseca, **t** (251) 824 042 (€€). Traditional food.

Sete á Sete, Rua Joôda Cunha, **t** (251) 652 577 (€€). Located around 1km out of town, a superb new restaurant serving traditional, deliciously prepared dishes.

Mané, Avenida Miguel Dantas (near the big roundabout), **t** (251) 823 402

(€€). For something rather better, go outside the town walls to Mané, which is above a café. *Closed Sun eve, Mon, Aug.*

Monção

★★★**Hotel Termas de Monção,** Av das Caldas, **t** (251) 640 110, *www.hotel termasdemoncao.com* (€€). A modern hotel with all the associated comforts, including an attractively landscaped outdoor pool. The friendly reception staff can organize sports and activities in the area.

★★**Residencial Esteves**, Rua General Pimenta de Castro, **t** (251) 652 386 (€). In front of the old railway station, comfortable and domestically furnished, with carved wooden furniture.

Cabral, Rua 1 de Dezembro, **t** (251) 651 775 (€€). Dine, in a pleasant stone-clad dining room, on well-prepared, typical local dishes.

Café Restaurant Central, **t** (251) 652 805 (€). One of a number of good little places to eat around the Praça Deu-la-Deu. *Closed Sun.*

Turismo de Habitação

★★★**Solar de Serrade**, Mazedo, **t** (251) 654 008, *www.solardeserrade.pt* (€€). A handsome 17th-century manor house with homey rooms furnished with antiques and rugs, plus several sumptuous suites.

Casa de Rodas, **t** (251) 652 105, *www.solaresdeportugal.pt* (€€ CA). Off the road from Monção to Arcos de Valdevez; contact the tourist office in Monção for directions. A driveway fenced with slabs of granite stretches through a pine forest towards the sprawling 16th-century house. Its reception rooms boast handpainted walls, and light but lordly furnishings. There are four cosy bedrooms fitted with new bathrooms, an old kitchen smelling of woodsmoke, and a comfortable apartment for four. Cabinets display pewter in the cavernous dining room. The owner, Maria Luisa Távora, speaks good English. The construction of a motorway nearby reduces Rodas' sublime peace but does not destroy it entirely.

Quinta da Calçada, **t** (251) 402 547 (€€ QH). A working farm in the village of São Julião just outside Monção; three rooms are available in the 18th-century house, which has good views. There is also a swimming pool.

Melgaço

Albergaria Boavista, Estrada Nacional 202, **t** (251) 416 464 (€). Reasonably comfortable accommodation, at the Peso spa 4km west of Melgaço. A convivial place, with a pool.

★**Residencial Miguel Pereira**, Rua da Calçada 5 (near the cinema), **t** (251) 402 212 (€). In Melgaço itself.

Restaurant Panorama, in the municipal market, **t** (251) 410 400 (€€). Serves surprisingly good food.

(i) **Melgaço** >>
Casa Castreja,
t *(251) 402 440,*
www.cm-melgaco.pt

Along the River Lima

Inland from Viana do Castelo, the terrain is flat between densely forested hills. Hay is stacked like pipecleaners. If you are driving, the route along the north bank of the River Lima is preferable to that along the south bank, because it keeps closer to the river's course.

The Romans believed that the Lima was Lethe, the River of Forgetfulness: its beauty would make anyone who crossed its banks forget his native country and his friends. Livy reports that having traversed most of Iberia, the soldiers of Proconsul Decimus Junius Brutus, who took office in 138 BC, refused to cross the 'Flumen Oblivionis'. Brutus grabbed the standard and crossed over with it by himself, persuading them to follow him.

Getting to areas Along the River Lima

There is one daily express **bus** to Ponte de Lima from Porto (2hrs), at 5pm, one from Braga (1½hrs), at 6.30pm, and even one from Lisbon (4hrs), at 1pm.

Bus company **Salvador, t** (253) 263 453, runs services from Braga to Ponte da Barca and Arcos de Valdevez.

Ponte de Lima

A long, low Roman bridge crosses the river 23km east of Viana do Castelo, at the point where it builds white sandbanks. Here stands the quaint and gracious middling-sized town of Ponte de Lima, centre of operations for *Turismo de Habitação* in the region and beyond.

It's a worthy destination in its own right; although there are no distinguished monuments, it's a good base for gentle walks. The bridge was built as part of the Roman road from Braga to Astorga, which was a favourite with pilgrims bound for Santiago de Compostela.

Around the Town

Off the principal road, at right angles to the river, the wide **Igreja Matriz** has been simply beautiful since the 15th century. Note the tracery on some of the ceilings. The **crenellated tower** at the waterfront is all that remains of the town's fortifications. The upper chamber was used as the town prison until 1966; prisoners used to lower buckets for pedestrians to donate cigarettes and money; and the strings have worn incisions in the stone window sill.

The narrow **Roman bridge** caterpillars across the Lima; the far side of the bridge was extended in the 14th century. Downstream stands a magnificent **avenue of plane trees**, excellent for lovers, cogitators, and photographing small children. It leads to the **convent of S. António**, which houses a small **museum** (note that both the convent and museum are closed indefinitely for extensive renovation).

Across the bridge, there's a garden, the **Jardims Tematicos**, laid out on different historical principles, containing a small but not wildly interesting **Museu Rural**. Since 1125, Ponte de Lima's fortnightly **Monday market** has been held on the sandbank. The bells of the church of Santo António de Torre Velho, on the opposite bank, used to ring to celebrate good business.

Museu Rural
open 2–6; closed Mon

Bravães

Travelling east of Ponte de Lima, the landscape changes as the dense, vinous hills start to close in on the river. The road to Ponte de Barca is a bit like Salome: exceptionally beautiful and always twisting – to the music of the River Lima. Twelve kilometres east of Ponte de Lima this road passes through the village of Bravães, whose superb little 11th-century Romanesque **Igreja Matriz** boasts one of the most elaborately carved Romanesque portals in Portugal: clinging quadrupeds, doves, birds of prey and tall figures standing on one another's heads come together in five arches. The pediment, supported by two stylized bull heads – thought to symbolize the death of Christ – depicts Christ flanked by St Peter and St Paul. The dark interior makes it hard to see the murals of St Sebastian, behind the font, and of the Virgin and Child.

Ponte da Barca

🟎 **Ponte da Barca**

The little town of **Ponte da Barca** has grown along the river, and is saturated by the lush countryside that surrounds it. The old part of town is delightfully drowsy. Here the riverbanks are low, with plenty of space to camp, and the water is great for swimming. An elegant mid-15th-century bridge employs the same thick arch/thin arch principle as at Ponte de Lima.

The bridge was the scene of the *baptizado à meia noite* (midnight baptism), which was practised until the early decades of the 19th century. If her previous child was stillborn, a pregnant woman would go to the bridge at midnight, raise a bucketful of water, and oblige the first male passer-by to dip his fingers into the water and make the sign of the cross on her bared belly. The local priest, it seems, looked the other way, though at a village in the Gerês mountains it was the priest himself who performed the baptism.

Twelve or fourteen trees constitute the **Jardim dos Poetas**, a garden ripe for merrymaking beside the river.

Arcos de Valdevez

Situated in a deep valley overlooked by granite pinnacles, the lovely little town of Arcos de Valdevez has moulded itself into an S-bend in the River Vez. The two parts of town are connected by an elegant, wide-arched bridge with oval portals. Just downstream of the bridge, a leafy island has been made into a public park.

Main roads separate the river from the pretty and labyrinthine centre of town, which focuses on a pillory square (*see* p.412). Set back from this, the odd Baroque **Igreja de N.S. da Lapa** was built by André Soares in 1767. It's an oval on the outside and an octagon indoors, with a low stone dome and a two-storey entrance porch topped by a weaving cornice.

ⓘ Ponte de Lima >
Praça de Marqués,
t (258) 942 335

ⓘ Arcos de Valdevez >
Avenida Marginal,
t (258) 516 001

ⓘ Ponte de Barca >
Largo da Misericórdia,
t (258) 452 899

★ Paço de Calheiros >>

Tourist Information and Services Along the River Lima

Ponte de Lima: the tourist office is located in a fortified building with excavations on display. The **bus station** is at the upstream end of the avenue of trees. Buses arrive frequently from Viana do Castelo and infrequently from Braga.

Ponte da Barca: Next door to the tourist office and upstairs, the headquarters of the **Peneda-Gerês National Park**'s development association, **t** (258) 452 250, *www.adere-pg.pt* (*open 9–12.30 and 2.30–6*), is a great source of information about all things relating to the Park, including an excellent series of walks, with notes in English. It also handles the rental of houses in the park, including Soajo and Lindoso (*see* p.120). A taxi to Lindoso will cost about €12.

Festival in Ponte de Lima

In Ponte de Lima, on the third weekend of September, the jolly **Feiras Novas** include fireworks, a funfair, a market for agricultural implements, and a religious procession (for which the children of the town are dressed as cherubs and carry anchors and fake palms; a bewigged gentleman bears the cross).

Sports and Activities Along the River Lima

The tourist office in Ponte de Lima has information about the **walking** route to Santiago de Compostela as well as numerous others in the area. If you like a short walk with a target in mind, try the panoramic Hermitage of Santo Ovídio (across the bridge and a half-hour walk off the road to Valença), or there's the Monte de Santa Maria Madalena (3km to the southeast, approached by a tortuous tarmac road). There's an 18-hole **golf course** nearby, at Feitosa, **t** (258) 743 414. For **horse-riding**, contact the Centro Equestre at the Quinta da Sobreira, Feitosa, **t** (258) 743 620. There's a **swimming pool** in Rua Dr Francisco Sá Carneiro, **t** (258) 900 412.

Where to Stay and Eat Along the River Lima

Ponte de Lima
★★★Hotel Império do Minho, Avenida dos Plátanos, **t** (258) 741 510 (€€). Simple, balconied rooms with a view of the avenue of trees, and the river beyond. There's a swimming pool at the back.

★★Pensão São João, Largo de São João, **t** (258) 941 288 (€). Basic but fine, if a little damp. A couple of rooms overlook the river and the low bank beyond. There's a restaurant on the ground floor.

Turismo de Habitação
The central booking office for *Turismo de Habitação* is in the Praça de Marquès, *info@center.pt*, *www.center.pt*. There are some 30 houses offering accommodation under this scheme in Ponte de Lima alone. The following is a selection.

Paço de Calheiros, Calheiros, **t** (258) 947 164 or 931 750, *www.pacode calheiros.eu* (€€€–€€ CA). Seven km north of Ponte de Lima is the quietly palatial flagship of the *Turismo de Habitação* scheme. Candelabra hang from chestnut ceilings, illuminating the family portraits and antiques, and many of the nine double guest rooms and nearby sitting rooms have fabulous views of the Lima valley. Outside, great magnolia trees shadow the raked gravel driveway, along which stretches the stable block, now converted into five apartments. There's a pool in the grounds and horses for riding. The charming young count is fluent and hospitable. The Calheiros landholding was granted by

Dom Dinis and confirmed by Dom Afonso IV in 1336. The present house was built at the end of the 17th century, since when it has not left the family. The count is elected mayor of the village that bears his name. His great-grandfather used to leave a barrel of wine at the manor gates for the villagers to help themselves.

★ **Casa da Lage** >

Casa da Lage, Arcos (S. Pedro), **t** (258) 731 417 or 931 750, *www.casa_da _lage.com* (€€ CA). Seven kilometres northwest of Ponte de Lima, this house offers 10 ensuite rooms. Arriving here feels like turning up at some fabulous place in Graham Greene's South America. A 17th-century classic.

Casa de Crasto, Ribeira, **t** (258) 941 156 or 931 750, *www.solaresdeportugal.pt* (€€ CA). It's not easy to relax in the dark and heavy Casa de Crasto on the southeastern edge of Ponte de Lima – it feels manorial and is built of dark wood from ceiling to floor. Parts of the 17th-century house were destroyed in 1896, by an owner looking for treasure. The five guest rooms have shower rooms; the comfortable furnishings may include an antique cot and a plant-filled alcove. A stepped garden incorporates tiny-stoned outbuildings and a well.

★ **Moinho de Estorãos** >>

★ **Casa das Pereiras** >

Casa das Pereiras, Largo das Pereiras, **t** (258) 942 939 or 931 750 (€€). In Ponte de Lima itself, surrounded by camellia trees, offering three splendid bedrooms and serving the best dinners in town on Fridays.

Casa do Arrabalde, Além da Ponte, Arcozelo, **t** (258) 742 442 or 931 750 (€€). A hundred yards from Ponte de Lima's Roman bridge and offering superb, if spartan, accommodation overlooking a few fruit trees, in a village. Not all bathrooms are en suite.

★ **Casa do Outeiro** >

Casa do Outeiro, Arcozelo, **t** (258) 941 206 or 931 750 (€€ CA). One kilometre east of Ponte de Lima, it offers a living slice of manorial life: the noble library smells of dried tea, religious paintings agonize on the walls, the family vine

(rather than tree) is stuck with photographs, and silver is displayed around the heavy dining room. Huge quantities of quince jelly (*marmalada*) are brewed in the kitchen. The house was restored in 1723, and has been owned by the same family since the early 18th century. In 1809 the invading French Marshal Soult established headquarters here.

Casa do Antepaço, Arcozelo, **t** (258) 941 702 or 931 750 (€€). The four newly timbered and decorated bedrooms – across the courtyard – are on the ground floor, and some have views up a fertile slope. The first-floor sitting room completes the family farmhouse style. Chicken pots are displayed in the open-plan kitchen.

Casa das Torres, Facha, **t** (258) 941 369 or 931 750, *www.casadastorres.com* (€€ CA). Ten kilometres south of Ponte de Lima. Beautiful it may be, and swimming pool it may have, but the apartment feels like a doghouse. The plain ground-floor rooms overlook the parking area and are kept in mothballs.

Moinho de Estorãos, Estorãos, **t** (258) 941 546 or 931 750, *www.solaresde portugal.pt* (€€ CR). Seven kilometres northwest of Ponte de Lima. It was a watermill, but the waterwheel decays beside a clear wide stream, by a willow tree and a little Roman bridge. The peace is interrupted only by the strangled quacks of waterside frogs. The miller's house is available for guests. Its simple furnishings are reminiscent of a mountain lodge. The double bedroom is very pleasant, and there are two fold-up single beds. The mill was built in the early 19th century; its 17th-century predecessor was on the opposite bank, and paid an annual rent of one chicken. Two nights minimum.

Quinta do Salgueirinho, Arcozelo, **t** (258) 941 206 (€€ CR). Owned by the same family as Casa do Outeiro. Pleasant and peaceful, the first-floor terrace overlooks a small orchard. It's

★ Carvalheira >>

★ Açude >>

★ Casa do Barreiro >

★ Escondidinho >>

★ Pensão Gomes >>

★ Os Poetas >>

furnished in a rustic style, though the carpetless ground floor is chilly, and the kitchen bare – nobody lives here permanently. Still, guests in the four double rooms and one single often comment on the housekeeper's hospitality. They share two bathrooms. Adjacent is the **Casa da Vinha**, a small self-contained unit, with a bathroom like a summer-house.

Casa do Barreiro, t (258) 948 137 or 931 750 (€€ CA). Still lived in by the family it was built for – in 1643. Not too grand; the spaces are gentle, and there's a stillness about the place. It smells of wood smoke and polish. Rooms are available in the main house and the outhouse, reached across the stunning ochre courtyard, which feels rather Mexican. Beg to taste the house's fabulous, grapey *vinho verde*.

Casa do Covas, Nelas, Moreira do Lima, t (258) 941 711 or 931 750, *www.solares deportugal.pt* (€ CR). Six km northwest of Ponte de Lima. The delight is its peaceful back garden, half of which is given over to wild flower beds, with vines trailing overhead, and silvery trees welling up to a ridge. There is an apartment that sleeps four, which is pleasant. It has a full kitchen and a games room opening onto the terrace. There are two double apartments, one of which is squashed and unornamented, the other generally unwelcoming.

Casa do Tamanqueiro, Estorãos, t (258) 941 916 or 931 750 (€). Seven km northwest of Ponte de Lima is a stone-walled, family-sized bungalow for the sole use of guests. The heart of the house is the kitchen, hung with onions, chillies and garlic, with a gun on the chimneypiece, a table that seats six, and four gas rings; the only oven is the ancient bread oven. Step over the weedy cement terrace at the back, and follow the pergola to the stream 100m away, overlooking the pine-covered slopes of a hill.

The first two restaurants below are outstanding, and are designed to cater for people who live or stay in the neighbourhood's manor houses.

Carvalheira, on the N202 at Arcozelo, t (258) 742 316 (€€€). Particularly recommended for its excellent steaks. *Closed Mon; reservations necessary.*

Açude, t (258) 944 158 (€€€). Take the first right across the new bridge. Less swish but no less delicious, this boat-like restaurant serves great fish.

Encanada, Passeio 25 de Abril, t (258) 941 189 (€€). Ponte de Lima is noted for its *sarrabulho*, rich minced meats and pig's blood. A reasonable place to eat it is this stone-floored restaurant, up some stairs on the corner of the Avenida Marginal, with a terrace overlooking the river. *Closed Thurs.*

Escondidinho, Rua do Rosário 5, t (258) 942 828 (€). If you want to eat with earthy locals, dine upstairs. Choose *feijoada* and, if people stare, just smile.

Ponte da Barca

Pensão Gomes, Rua Conselheiro Rocha Peixoto 13, t (258) 452 288 (€). The best budget place to stay, with views over the river and bridge. You can breakfast on the balcony to the soothing sound of babbling water.

Os Poetas, Jardim dos Poetas, t (258) 453 578 (€). Simple, but has fabulous views, cork and marble.

Residencial S. Fernando, Rua das Maceiras, t (258) 42 580 (€). If you're stuck.

There's a **campsite**, Entre-Ambos-os-Rios, t (258) 452 250, beside the river 11km upstream.

Turismo de Habitação

Casa Nobre do Correio-Mor, Rua Trás do Forno 1, t (258) 452 129, *www.laceme.pt.vu* (€€ CA). A 17th-century town house with four-posters, embroidered lampshades, Arraiolos rugs and a modern wing with a sauna, Turkish bath, games room and outdoor pool. *No parking.*

Quinta da Prova, Prova, t (258) 452 163, www.solaresdeportugal.pt (€€ QH). Set right on the riverbank at the edge of pretty woodland, the rooms at this *quinta* have divine views. The apartments are pleasant and spacious.
Cafe del Rio, t 933 959 509 (€€). Located beside the river, they offer trout and steaks here, but it's submerged when the river floods. It's a nice place for a drink, and if the weather's good the local talent pose outside in swimwear.
O Moinho, Largo do Corro, t (258) 452 035 (€€). At the end of town closest to Ponte de Lima. Simple, traditional cuisine. *Closed Tues.*

Arcos de Valdevez

★★★Pensão Ribeira, Largo dos Milagres, t (258) 515 174 (€). Modest but clean, on the riverside beside the bridge.
Residencial Tavares, Rua Padre Manuel José da Cunha Brito, t (258) 516 253 (€). Dull but functional.
Flôr do Minho, Largo da Valeta, t (258) 525 216 (€). A simpler option.

Peneda-Gerês National Park

Peneda-Gerês National Park

The **Peneda-Gerês National Park** is 173,000 acres (70,000ha) of natural reserve, named after the two mountain ranges it encompasses. Shaped like a horseshoe, it straddles the two provinces of the Minho and Trás-os-Montes, cushioning Spain on its northern edge. It's an excellent place for hiking, and driving can be rewarding, if your car will stand the roads. The park was established in 1971, as Portugal's contribution to International Conservation Year. It includes over a hundred villages, so sometimes it's not apparent that one is in a park at all.

Landscape

Both mountain ranges are dark grey granite, with small schistose strips, rising from tight gorges. A massive granite table mountain separates the Peneda valley from the Gerês valley, and a fissure in the granite produces thermal effects at the spa Caldas do Gerês. The rock is rounded rather than jagged, which makes it seem more friendly. The barren, biblical scree and weird fields of wind-sculpted boulders are not the crumbs of some giant explosion: they were prised from the bedrock by the freezing and thawing of water held within the rock.

A little glaciation has made dramatic scenery at the headwaters of the Rivers Vez, Homem and Couce-Coucelinho. The River Lima bisects the reserve from north to south, and the River Cávado forms its border in the south. Minor rivers cut deep, narrow valleys through the mountains, fed in winter by hundreds of streams – because granite is impervious – from which the goatherds drink. When it's very wet, there are little waterfalls.

Getting to Peneda-Gerês National Park

Various **bus** companies run services from Braga to Caldas do Gerês and Lindoso, or from Melgaça to Castro Laboreiro, at the Park's various entrances. The main ones are REDM, **t** (253) 616 097 and Salvador, **t** (253) 263 453.

Recently six major dams have been built, to provide hydroelectric power. Portuguese visitors, here as elsewhere, view the reservoirs with wonder and affection.

Flora and Fauna

There are spirits in the woods of Gerês: it's not surprising the Celts and Lusitanians worshipped them. The park's flora grows as it does because the land receives up to 2,800mm of rainfall annually, the highest in continental Portugal, and varies in altitude from 300ft (100m) to four peaks over 4,500ft (1,400m). The goatherds reckon that the climate is less predictable since Mt St Helena erupted. Mt St Helena or no, the climatic and altitudinal conditions allow a confusion of plant species, whose origins range from the Mediterranean and subtropical regions to Euro-Siberian and Alpine zones.

The cork oak (at Ermida), arbutus, Portugal laurel, Gerês fern, royal fern and bilberry can be found on the slopes of the warmer, more sheltered valleys. Woods of English oak (at Matança, Cabril and Beredo), with holly (at Ramiscal), can be found in places where the Atlantic makes itself felt, and at altitudes up to 2,500–3,000ft (800–1,000m). Higher still come Pyrenean oak and the flora of the Euro-Siberian zone, including the birch (near Mezio) and Scots pine (at Biduiça). Centennial yew trees prefer the high, humid sheltered valleys. Above here there is only scrubland.

Five plants are specific to the Gerês area, including the Gerês fern and the Gerês iris. But for the casual observer in spring, it is the carpets of irises and delicate yellow St John's wort which are most enchanting: the latter lend their colour to the Serra Amarela (the Yellow Mountains).

Over these soar occasional golden and booted eagles, as well as buzzards and goshawks. Eagle owls, tawny owls and scops owls elude most visitors. The wildlife of Gerês is thrilling but diminished: wild ponies and roebuck. Wolves are now thin on the ground – a more likely sight is a wolf/dog crossbreed, or a wolfskin on a villager's floor. There are lots of black caterpillars with silver linings, and butterflies after them. Sheep and goats need no introduction.

Black vipers arrive unannounced – there aren't many, but it's worth keeping an eye open. If you do see a snake, it is more likely to be a grass snake. Brown bears disappeared from here around 1650, Gerês mountain goats around 1890, and subsequently civet cats.

The park office produces very good glossy brochures to help visitors identify flora and fauna.

Settlement

Around 10,000 people live in the Peneda-Gerês park, walking the hills their prehistoric predecessors walked 5,000 years ago. Prehistoric man has left uninspiring dolmens at Castro Laboreiro, Mezio, Paradela, Cambeses, Pitões and Tourém, plus several now used as shepherds' shelters. Part of the Roman military road that linked Bracara Augusta (Braga) to Asturica Augusta (Astorga) in Spain passes along the River Homem, now on the southeast side of the Barragem de Vilarinho. Milestones are dotted about the place, at Bico da Jeira, Volta do Covo, Albergaria and Portela do Homem.

After the Romans came the Christian Church. The grassy ruined monastery of Santa Maria das Júnias is a 12th-century Romanesque foundation just next to the Campesinho Brook. It doubtless spawned the deserted village of Juriz, at Aldeia Velha de Pitões das Júnias, now surrounded by an oak forest.

In spring several village communities migrate from the valleys to the mountains. When the maize has been sown, the mountain people leave their granite huts: they move uphill in May, with their beef-cattle and newly born calves. (Bulls live in the mountains all year round.) Their summer quarters are some 1,000ft (300m) higher in altitude: here they will stay until October, cultivating rye and potatoes. In the valleys, they grow meadow grass as cattle-feed for winter. These traditional ways of life, however, are dying out, and as the younger generations move away village populations are ageing fast.

Caldas do Gerês

Caldas do Gerês has something of the parasol about it: a fashionable spa since the 18th century, it is duly primed with early 20th-century hotels. It's also a good place to stock up on herb teas – herbs grow wild in some of the surrounding woods. If you've been eating too much *pão-de-ló*, the spa, **t** (253) 391 113, is helpful for obesity – also goitre and diabetes.

Soajo

The tough, remote village of Soajo strikes a happy balance between a backwater and something more sophisticated. Its view of the Lima valley is slightly marred by *casas de emigrante*, which stand beside granite houses first established in the 12th and 13th centuries. A fantastic group of *espigueiros* huddle on a granite threshing terrace, above the valley, just northwest of the town. These coffers are built of granite slats and set on stilts, for storing winnowed grain out of the reach of rats. Topped with little granite crosses, they seem like strange pagan tabernacles. In town the pillory dates from the 17th century, and bears an image of the sun. If you like walking, the shepherds may be glad of a bit of company – they set out at 6am.

Lindoso

The very steep road from Soajo to Lindoso offers great views of the Lima valley, and passes a tall manmade waterfall. '*Lindo*' means 'beautiful' – here it's rugged beauty. The village is set in a dip between hills backed by the 4,600ft (1,400m) Outeiro Maior peak. Its lichen-encrusted border **castle** was built by Dom Afonso III, the resettler and administrator, some time before 1258, and reinforced by his son Dom Dinis. A line of low walls and battlements was built in the mid-16th century, and strengthened in 1640 for the War of Restoration. Downhill from the castle, chickens peck around a group of coffer-like *espigueiros*, on a threshing terrace overgrown with weeds.

Castro Laboreiro

Castro Laboreiro stands at an altitude of 3,120ft (950m), 20km southeast of Melgaço, at the tip of the Peneda-Gerês park, and its castle dominates the valley of the River Laboreiro, a small tributary of the River Lima. The little town is spoilt by a rash of *casas de emigrante*, which are sometimes hidden by mist. The air is cool even in summer. The tricky road to the ruined castle passes a granite rock shaped like a giant turtle, looking as if the unfortunate creature has been turned to stone by an angry god. There are some excellent **walks** nearby: it's simplest to follow the river, which is fine if you don't mind the slant.

Castro Laboreiro gives its name to a muscular breed of dog like a mastiff, used for herding sheep. They are not friendly dogs.

Getting Around the Park

The park has become much more user-friendly in recent years: at last there are decent walking maps for circular, waymarked trails of around 4½ miles (7km), with an estimated duration of 4½ hours – remember, it's hilly. There's also simple, rustic accommodation available throughout the park. Details of both are available from the park offices. What's more, it has all been done with sensitivity to the park's unique character.

The most helpful of several **park offices** are in Ponte da Barca (*see* p.114) and Braga, Quinta das Paretas, Avenida António Macedo, **t** (253) 203 480. Others are in Montalegre, **t** (276) 512 281, and Arcos de Valdevez, **t** (258) 515 338.

Entry to the park is free. Gates are at Lamas do Mouro (Melgaço), Mezio (Arcos de Valdevez), Leonte (Gerês), and Covelães (in Trás-os-Montes, west of Montalegre). All these are served by good asphalted roads.

Walking in Gerês can be sublime, set to the music of goatbells (and the occasional chainsaw). The air smells as air should. If you're serious about walking, buy a military map from *www.igeoe.pt*, or better still, hire a guide – the park office in Ponte da Barca can put you in touch with some excellent guides at very reasonable rates. It's best to walk on cart or goat tracks, furrowed with cleft hoofprints. If you're worried about getting lost, these tracks usually lead to a settlement of sorts, or at least to an asphalt road, from which you should be able to take bearings. Generally the villagers are extremely friendly and helpful. Many of the men have worked abroad, and speak French, or English with American accents. How much climbing you do depends upon where you go – for the most part there's nothing too strenuous.

For details of outdoor sports including **pony-trekking, canoeing, horse-riding and trekking**, contact TG

(i) Caldas do Gerês >>
*Av Manuel Ferreira da Costa, **t** (253) 391 133*

Trote-Gerês, **t** (253) 659 860, PlanAlto, **t** (253) 351 005, or AML, **t** (253) 391 779, *www.aguamontanha.com*.

Where to Stay Around the Peneda-Gerês National Park

Caldas do Gerês

There are many *pensões* and *residencials* both in Caldas and on the approach to it. Choose your view. Here is a selection:

Hotel Universal, Avenida Manuel Francisco da Costa, **t** (253) 391 141 (€€). A pleasant has-been, with a swimming pool.

★★★Hotel Aguas do Geres, Avenida Manuel Francisco Costa, **t** (253) 390 190, *www.aguasdogeres.pt* (€€). An elegant, handsome hotel with large comfortable rooms. Offers a range of spa packages. Full board available.

★★★Adelaide, Lugar de Arnasso, **t** (253) 390 020, *www.pensao adelaide.com.pt* (€). A large modern hotel that is excellent value, especially given the brand new swimming pool and pretty valley views.

Pousada
Pousada de São Bento, Cerdeirinhas, Soengas, **t** (253) 649 150 (L1 N). In the mountains above the Caniçada dam is a timber-beamed lodge, simply furnished and at its best when it has a roaring fire in the hearth. The sitting room and open dining area share picture windows, mesmerizing when mist is seeping up from below. The bedrooms are decorated in cuckoo-clock style, and they have tiny shuttered windows.

Soajo

Ten appealing rustic houses are available to visitors under the overall banner of *Turismo de Habitação*, *www.aldeiasdeportugal.pt*. With space for between two and eight people, they can be booked through the park office in Ponte da Barca. The price (€€) includes bedding and breakfast and 65lb (30kg) of firewood; a 50% deposit is payable when you book, and the other 50% when you collect the keys from the ADERE office in Soajo (*open Mon–Fri until 7pm, Sat until 1pm*). Check-in time is 2pm onwards.

Lindoso

Seven houses are available under the same scheme that operates at Soajo (*see* above). House keys are collected by arrangement with the owner.

Castro Laboreiro

Miradouro do Castelo, t (251) 465 469, *www.miradourodocastelo.com* (€€). This place has great views of the valley and a decent restaurant, plus riding stables.

Trás-os-Montes and the Alto Douro

Trás-os-Montes, behind-the-mountains – the name conjures up the fabulous realm of a campfire witch, not inappropriately. The province consists of a high plateau at 2,300ft (700m) that is hemmed in by 4,250ft (1,300m) mountains to the north and west; it divides into the wild, gritty terra fria *to the north of Murça or Mirandela, and the more moderate* terra quente *to the south. The southern hillslopes of the* terra quente *are planted with port wine vineyards, which are focused on the infernal gorge of the River Douro.*

09

Don't miss

⭐ **Heart of port wine country**
Pinhão **p.161**

② **Venerable oak trees**
Montezinho Park **p.145**

③ **12th-century castle**
Bragança **p.142**

④ **Observe Egyptian vultures**
Parque Natural do Douro Internacional **p.151**

⑤ **Prehistoric rock art**
Côa Valley **p.154**

See map overleaf

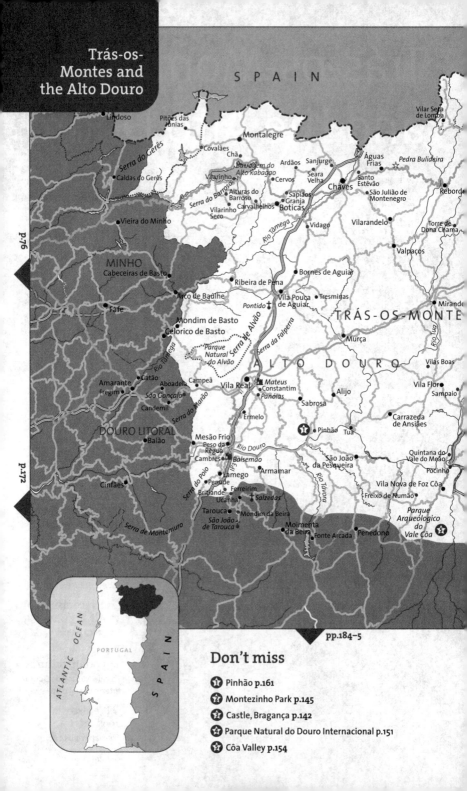

Trás-os-Montes and the Alto Douro

SPAIN

Lindoso
Pitões das Júnias
Montalegre
Covalães
Chã
Ardãos
Sanjurge
Águas Frias
Pedra Bulideira
Vilar Seco de Lomba
Caldas do Gerês
Serra do Gerês
Barragem do Alto Rabagão
Vilarinho
Cervos
Seara Velha
Santo Estêvão
Chaves
São Julião de Montenegro
Rebord
Serra do Barroso
Alturas do Barroso
Sapiãos
Granja
Boticas
Vilarinho Seco
Carvalhelhos
Vieira do Minho
Rio Tâmega
Vidago
Vilarandelo
Torre de Dona Chama
MINHO
Cabeceiras de Basto
Bornes de Aguiar
Valpaços
Fafe
Arco de Baúlhe
Ribeira de Pena
Vila Pouca de Aguiar
Tresminas
Pontido †
TRÁS-OS-MONTE
Mirand
Mondim de Basto
Celorico de Basto
Parque Natural do Alvão
Serra de Alvão
Serra da Falperra
Múrça
Vilas Boas
Rio Tua
A L T O   D O U R O
Amarante
Fregim
Gatão
São Gonçalo
Aboadela
Campeã
Vila Real
Mateus
Constantim
Panóias
Alijó
Sabrosa
Vila Flor
Sampaio
Candemil
Ermelo
Carrazeda de Ansiães
Serra do Marão
DOURO LITORAL
Baião
Mesão Frio
Peso da Régua
Cambres
Rio Douro
Bolsemão
Armamar
São João da Pesqueira
Pinhão
Tua
Quintana do Vale do Meão
Cinfães
Lamego
Penude
Ferreirim
Rio Távora
Pocinho
Serra do Poio
Britande
Ucanha
† *Salzedas*
Vila Nova de Foz Côa
Freixo de Numão
Tarouca
São João de Tarouca
Mondim da Beira
Moimenta da Beira
Penedono
Parque Arqueológico do Vale Côa
Serra de Montemuro
Fonte Arcada

p.76
p.172
pp.184–5

ATLANTIC OCEAN
PORTUGAL
SPAIN

Don't miss

The mountains of the west wring water from the Atlantic climate, generating Portugal's highest rainfall (3,000mm annually) and leaving a mere 600mm for the eastern plains. There, the climate is Continental, with the country's greatest annual variation in average temperature: Torre de Moncorvo averages 76°F (24.5°C) in summer and 42°F (5.5°C) in winter.

Where the soil is fairly rich in the *terra quente* of the south, it supports fruit trees – apple, pear, cherry and almond. Rye grows on the rolling plains of the *terra fria*, which are mottled with woodland in the hollows: poplar and willow and chestnut. Venerable oak and chestnut trees are found to the north, with some walnut. But it is the names of the scrub that most truly evoke the province – woadwaxen and spurgeflax, gum rockrose and gold and silver broom, wild thyme and rosemary (which, George Borrow reported, should be stuck in one's hat to guard against witches and the mischances of the road).

At weekends the *terra fria* is peppered with gunshot: villagers shoulder their shotguns and head for oak copses to shoot roebuck – the males' horns rarely have more than three spikes; or cultivated land to shoot red-footed, white-breasted partridges; or mixed woods and pastureland to shoot wild boars. Young boars have striped coats, alternating light and dark, which turn to a uniform ashen after the first year of life – when they have had time to reckon with the prospect of being shot. Village dogs wear collars spiked with long nails, which prevent their throats being ripped out by wolves. Wolves howl their way into the myth of Trás-os-Montes, enshrined on the jambs of Romanesque church portals, dreaded by children walking to school. As in the Peneda-Gerês park, most visitors' closest encounter with a wolf will be one crossbred with a dog – or the fur on a coat collar.

Trás-os-Montes is one of the poorest parts of Europe, but the excellent motorway from Porto to Bragança has made it far less isolated. In recent years Bragança and Chaves have grown and become more sophisticated; away from the conurbations, some villagers eke out a life only marginally less desperate than that of their medieval forebears. The province's area is more than twice that of the Minho, its population two-thirds the size. There is almost no industry in the province – its inhabitants depend upon their land and their animals.

In the villages the most common complaint is the lack of water in summer – feuds over water are the main cause for murder. Petty disputes can be settled by the village president, who is elected annually. He makes an announcement every Sunday after the church service which is attended by 90 per cent of the villagers, men on one side, women on the other.

In Trás-os-Montes the real monument is man and his life, struggling for sustenance and shelter against burning sun and biting cold. It's a distant, luminous land, and it offers a rare opportunity for travel in Europe.

History

A document of 1096 shows that Count Henry of Burgundy's jurisdiction extended into Trás-os-Montes, opening the way for it to be incorporated in the new nation of Portugal. Its population

Getting around Trás-os-Montes

The main **road** network of Trás-os-Montes is good. As in the Minho, the summer months are made more hazardous by the dangerous driving of returned emigrants in fancy cars.

The Corgo **railway** line from Regua to Vila Real and the Tua line to Mirandela make some of the most memorable journeys in Portugal, because the traveller gets so close to the land and people (*see* page 63). Trains of two wooden carriages ease their way through the granite landscape, clinging to hillsides, stopping at tiny stations when hailed by lone ladies with a red flag pinned to their batons. Sit next to a bag of kale or umbrellas, pass laundry drying on the railway cutting, and listen to the driver's sharp whistle as he alerts pedestrians ambling along the tracks.

The **bus** network is exasperating because services are infrequent, and there is no central office to provide details of all the small companies operating here. Timetables are usually kept in people's heads.

Tourist offices in the region are generally helpful and reliable and, in the end, all it takes is patience and determination.

was very sparse, so Dom Sancho I (1185–1211) attempted to attract settlers. Unlike other parts of the country, vast tracts were never handed over to nobles or military orders: new village societies were established which administered the land, facilities, herds and flocks collectively. Collectivism still exists: history has done little to change Trás-os-Montes.

Spanish troops invaded the province in 1762. Britain sent the 70-year-old Lord Tyrawley to command her trading ally's fleabitten army, but the Spanish Marquis of Sarria was undeterred. He entered Trás-os-Montes to free Portugal 'from the heavy shackles of Britannic dominion'. The army laid siege to Miranda do Douro, whose feeble garrison abandoned hope when their powder magazine exploded. The keys of Bragança were presented to the invaders as soon as they appeared. Chaves too was occupied. Finally a large number of peasants, reinforced by a few soldiers repulsed the troops attempting to cross the Douro near Torre de Moncorvo, and successfully held the mountain pass at Montalegre. Pitt sent 8,000 British soldiers to beef up the Portuguese army, and a truce was signed in November.

Trás-os-Montes was again in the limelight in 1809, when Soult headed the second French invasion. He entered from Galicia and occupied Chaves, before marching on Porto. The town was quickly recovered by Portuguese troops under Pinto da Fonseca.

Local Specialities

Trás-os-Montes celebrates with rich peasant stews and sausages; apart from some river trout, fish features less than in the coastal provinces. Chestnuts are sometimes served instead of potatoes, though very rarely in restaurants. The excellent dark runny **honey** is flavoured by heather.

The tasty *feijoada à Transmontana* will warm anyone's cockles. It's a **bean stew** with some interesting ingredients – the recipe calls for the ear, snout, and trotter of a pig, in addition to different kinds of

Witches

If you come to Trás-os-Montes and feel inexplicably ill, blame it on a spirit, or on someone casting the evil eye. Then seek the help of a white witch. The witch may be either male (*bruxo*) or female (*bruxa*). Witches accept no fees, so bring a sausage, a jar of olive oil or a sack of potatoes. In return for this small gift, you will be healed. Or your future will be laid bare. Or the reason for the failure of your business will be explained. Or you will be equipped with a love potion, to assuage any doubts about your spouse's infidelity. You may prefer a new-fangled witch. These inhabit towns and accept fees. They attract a different kind of clientele, employing 'folk' elements of the Catholic faith which parish priests will no longer sanction. (Catholicism came early to the north of Portugal, and some pre-Christian beliefs and practices crept into its orthodoxy. These practices were disowned by the Church in Portugal as recently as the 1960s – but their protagonists see no inconsistency between them and a creed that sanctions miracles and apparitions.)

sausages, cured ham, a little red pepper and an onion. *Cozido à Portuguesa* is a boiled mixture of blood sausage, pork sausage, spiced sausage, ribs, vertebrae, pigs' ears and lips, kale, carrots, turnips and potatoes.

Equally authentic are the **sausages**, which are not exclusive to Trás-os-Montes, but most at home here. They're eaten grilled, fried, baked and boiled, for snacks, in sandwiches, or as the centre of a meal. *Chouriço*, filled with lean and fat pork meat, garlic and red-pepper paste, are the most common. They are usually tied in a loop and slung over a wooden pole across the fireplace to be smoked. Variants on the basic model include *linguiça*, *paio*, and *salpicão*, the latter two being spiced.

The *alheira* sausage was created by a group called the New Christians, who were Jews expelled from Spain in the 15th century. They were supposed to have renounced their faith, and so the Inquisition regularly checked that these apparent 'converts' were eating pork. The New Christians duly produced smoked sausages that tasted of pork but were usually made with poultry such as turkey, or even sometimes rabbit.

There is more to a loaf of **bread** than meets the palate: in Trás-os-Montes, bread is believed to sustain life, like the Communion wafer. For each individual household bread epitomizes the fellowship of eating together, and for the wider community it symbolizes fertility and a bond with the land. Dough, flour, grain and even the maize plant in the field are all called *pão* (bread). For a household, growing its own maize is a traditional symbol of independence. Eating bread is one of the gastronomic treats of a visit to Trás-os-Montes. The maize bread called *broa* is as popular in this province as it is in the Minho. It has a hard crust, but the crumbly bread is tasty and curiously rich. On occasions the villagers bake nuggets of pigfat into their bread and this can make it a meal in itself. In the villages surrounding Bragança, the winter *festas* are centred on bread, which is traditionally piled into pyramids around wooden structures known as *charolos*. The loaves are moulded into different shapes, such as stars, humans or animals. Some of them are just plain bread, and others are baked with honey, eggs and dried fruits. Delicacies are then piled on top of each of the bread pyramids. After being taken to the church by procession, the *charolos* are first blessed by the priest and then auctioned off to the highest bidders. Purchasing the bread conveys great social prestige, partly because of the prophylactic qualities it is believed to have.

Red and rosé **wines** are produced over much of Trás-os-Montes, but it can't match the quality found elsewhere. Valpaços wines are heavy and dark, while the wine of Boticas and Carrazeda is lighter, more like the wines of the Minho.

Transmontane Houses

Traditional houses have been abandoned in many villages; their walls of uncemented granite blocks are collapsing. Occasionally you'll spot a house still inhabited by someone too old or too isolated to move. The better-off would live above, say, four oxen and a couple of pigs, whose heat ascended through wooden boards to the bedrooms above. Sometimes the family toilet would be a hole in the floorboards above the pigpen. Within, traditional houses are dark and still: doors, windows, and chimneys let heat escape. The kitchen is the heart of the home, where the fire burns and smooths the granite walls with soot. For cooking, a three-legged cauldron is placed over the fire, or in larger houses the cauldron will be suspended from an iron chain. Benches flank the fire, and above it hangs a pole slung with sausages changing from blue to brown in the woodsmoke. Even in the more modern houses you're likely to find traditional stores – of potatoes, maize, walnuts, apples, *marmalada* – rabbits are kept for special occasions, such as the return of an emigrant son. Barrels of wine and *aguardente* ensure that the blood will get pumping on winter mornings.

Masks

Many people believe that the spirits of the dead return to the land of the living, to safeguard the continuity of their *ideologia*. The spirits are selective about the time of year in which they choose to wreak their anarchic purpose; thus the safeguards to shoo them away are implemented during strictly delimited periods – particularly at the turn of the year. The idea is to use horrid masks to frighten off the malevolent spirits. The villagers create masks that are tangible nightmares: they hit at something deeply human. Usually they are made of wood, sometimes of leather, tin or cork. The best place to see these masks is in the Museu de Etnologia at Belém in Lisbon. However, the museum has no permanent display, so the masks may not be on show.

Berrões

Scattered around Trás-os-Montes are more than 200 crude granite sculptures of boars and bulls, usually about 5ft (1.5m) long. They are called *berrões*; they bristle with mystery and are hoofed with paganism, but the locals treat them with affection. The few that have been found *in situ* were within circular stone walls, which may have been sanctuaries. The older *berrões* probably date from before the birth of Christ, perhaps representing deities or divine manifestations, representations of the animals which accompanied the gods, or simply offerings to the gods. The inscriptions on other *berrões* can be dated to between the 1st and 3rd centuries AD, in which case they may represent the Lunones and the Tarboi, which were generally qualified as 'that which roars or moos under the ground'.

Masks are worn at the *Festa dos Rapazes*, celebrated in the villages around Bragança between the feast of St Estevão on 26 December and the feast of Epiphany on 6 January. Unmarried boys over the age of 16 signify their passage from youth to adulthood by dressing in masks and shaggy multicoloured suits draped with huge cowbells. They rampage through houses making grunting noises, terrorizing little boys and demanding sausages from women and wine from men. After the obligatory Mass, the whole village attends a *loas*, in which the young men declaim the events of the past year in the village.

Chaves and Around

Chaves

Chaves is a pleasant town of 14,000 souls, 10km from the Spanish border. Set in a fertile basin surrounded by low hills, it spans the River Tâmega, a tributary of the River Douro, and is bitten by cold easterly winds. Its isolated, 'top centre' location explain its name: '*chaves*' means 'keys', and this was a strategic key to the north of Portugal. Chaves can fill this rôle for the visitor today, serving as a useful base from which to explore the wild surrounding countryside. It's all the more attractive now it has an excellent hotel and easy access by road from Porto.

Despite its rumbustious history, Chaves today is remarkably calm, though drinking men tend to stress points by table-thumping. Fewer women wear black than elsewhere – either because the mineral water keeps everyone alive, or because they are not so strict in the observance. Spaniards hop across the border to shop, long-haired, green-eyed cats prowl about and mosquitoes whir beside the river.

Spa
t (276) 332 445

The **spa** generates water at a fairly stultifying 163°F (73°C) – these are reputedly the warmest sodium-bicarbonated waters in Europe. You will need to get a doctor's recommendation before

Getting to Chaves

By **road**, Chaves is 61km from Vila Real (1 hour), 130km from Braga (2¼ hours), and 100km from Bragança (1½ hours). Reckon on a good 2 hours from Porto.

The nearest **railway station** is at Vila Real. Rodonorte **buses**, on Rua do Sol, **t** (276) 333 491, run at least one bus daily, plus another 1 July–30 Sept, from Lisbon (7hrs), Coimbra (3½hrs), Santa Comba Dão (4½hrs), Viseu (2hrs), Lamego (2¼hrs), and Vidago (¼hr). There are more frequent services from Vila Real (1¼hrs), Porto (4¼hrs), Amarante (2¾hrs) and Vila Pouca de Aguiar (½hr).

Auto Viação do Tâmega, **t** (276) 332 351, have nine daily buses from Porto (2½hrs) and Vila Real (2¼hrs), as well as one from Bragança (3hrs). Another twice-daily service comes from Braga (3hrs), while there are some four a day from Lisbon (7hrs) via Coimbra (3½hrs).

Getting to Spain

On Thursday and Sunday an Internorte **bus** runs to Verín (1½hrs) and Orense (3hrs) in Spain.

---

you can let the ladies in white coats set to work on your liver troubles, rheumatism, metabolic disorders, intestinal complaints or hypertension.

Local Delicacies

One local delicacy is **octopus**, which is boiled and eaten for Chistmas lunch.

Chaves is justly famous for its delicious salty smoked **ham**, *presunto*, which is eaten raw in the same way as *prosciutto*. *Presunto* should be at least a year old. It's made by a simple but lengthy process: the leg of pork is kept in a paste of salt, paprika, wine and crushed garlic; it spends several weeks in a trough of salt, before the salt is scrubbed off and the pork is hung in the *fumeiro* (the smoking place: literally 'chimney'), for up to two months ending, traditionally, on the first Friday of May.

Hard **honey** is produced locally, and cafés advertise *pastéis de Chaves*, which are similar to Cornish pasties, filled with veal.

History

In AD 78, the Roman Emperor Flavius Vespasianus founded a burg where two highways crossed, by a thermal spring. He named it Aquae Flaviae. Hydatius, 5th-century Bishop of Chaves, compiled colourful annals of his time. The Visigoths, he lamented, showed no respect for virgins, whom they abducted (though often returned intact), or for the clergy, who were driven out indecently clothed, while churches were converted into stables and pigsties.

(Hydatius introduced a new system of chronology, which dated events from the beginning of the Era of Augustus in 38 BC. This, he believed, marked the start of the Roman pacification of the Peninsula. Formerly, chronologies began afresh with the reign of each emperor. In Rome, Dionysius Exiguus proposed another fixed point – the birth of Christ. AD caught on through the work of Bede and the chroniclers of the Carolingians, but the Era of Augustus continued in use in Portugal until 1422, when Dom João I changed it to AD.)

Chaves was destroyed and rebuilt once by the Suevi and twice by the Moors in 250 years. In the mid-13th century the castle was commanded by Portuguese loyal to Spain; and it fell to the Spanish General O'Reilly in the Peninsular War. It was briefly occupied by a monarchist faction rising against the new-born Republic in 1912.

Chaves Pottery

Chaves is renowned for its 'black' pottery, which is coloured like pewter or pencil lead. Burning brushwood subjects ordinary clay pots to a chemical reaction when they are placed in a pit and covered with soil and what looks like coal dust (thus starving them of oxygen). The plain, rounded pots are disinterred, black and heavy-looking. Many of them are made in the village of Nantes, and can be purchased from various shops such as Postigo on Rua do Sol; a pitcher costs about €15.

Around the Town

The town's **Roman bridge** was built across the Tâmega by the Emperor Trajan in AD 98 to 104 and is still well used. Cross the bridge to wander in the Madalena district, which has a villagey feel.

Chaves' historic streets are focused on the **Torre de Menagem,** a keep that was built by Dom Dinis in the 14th century on a low hill overlooking the river. Each block of the foundations is marked with a stonemason's hieroglyphic squiggle – stonemasons were paid by piecework, and this was how they distinguished their work from that of their colleagues. The keep's projecting machicolations were used for dropping molten lead, boiling oil and missiles.

Dom João I gave the keep to his Constable, Nun' Álvares Pereira, who in turn gave it to his daughter Beatriz when she married the king's bastard son, Dom Afonso, Count of Barcelos and future Duke of Bragança. He liked Chaves, and subsequently set up home in the keep.

The original protective walls were swallowed up by their 16th-century successors, built to reinforce Chaves for the War of Restoration. Catapult balls retrieved from the bottom of the river are piled at the base of the keep. The small **military museum** that is housed within the tower boasts some reproductions of ancient armour, but it's mostly dull 19th- and 20th-century stuff. The top of the building offers a fine view of patchwork fields and the river and the chance to orientate yourself if the maze of streets in Chaves has left you feeling bewildered.

Military museum
open Tues–Fri 9–12.30 and 2–5, Sat and Sun 2–5.30; closed Mon; adm

Museu da Região Flaviense and the Praça de Camões

Museu da Região
Flaviense and the
Praça de Camões
*open daily 9.30–12.30
and 3–6.30;
closed hols; adm*

Next to the keep, the **Museu da Região Flaviense** (archaeological and ethnographic museum) is interesting, but there's no feast for the aesthete. There are a number of post-Roman altars dedicated to Roman gods, including one to the nymphs. The most significant altar, lettered deep, refers to Chaves as a town in AD 78. A framed picture, enlarged from the back of a coin, depicts the Roman emperor who gave his name to the town. Roman terracotta pipes are displayed next to a 19th-century pipe in a splint, made in a nearby village. The similarity of the two types suggests unmodified production.

Up the stairs is a room of fascinating rupestral art, prehistoric figures carved on stone. To the left of the columned room is a 5ft (1.5m) phallus, a smaller statue representing the female sex, and the menhir of a warrior. Articles in the cases have been carbon-dated to 2700 BC. The room of ethnography houses an oxcart, and a triangular device for shaving strips of wood, to weave into baskets. There's also a shepherd's straw suit, formerly worn on the mountains when it rained.

Four granite cylinders intertwine to form the turreted **pillory** in the Praça de Camões, which is a pleasant space fronted by the museum and Chaves' two most notable churches.

The plain façade of the 17th-century **Misericórdia** has been enlivened by an external covered porch with wooden railings. The interior is chock-a-block with 18th-century *azulejos* of New Testament scenes.

The **Igreja Matriz** is at right angles to the Misericórdia. The doorway is all that remains of its romanesque beginnings: the church was reconstructed in the 16th century. It houses a fantastical organ decorated with latticework and a head that the Wizard of Oz would have liked to create for himself.

On the other side of town, the 17th-century **Fort of São Francisco** has been converted into a lovely hotel (*see* p.135).

In the 18th century, Dona Maria Ana of Austria, wife of Dom João V, commissioned the octagonal **Igreja da Madalena**, which stands on the far side of the Roman bridge. The interior is disappointing.

Prehistoric Boulders near Chaves

At Águas, 10km east of Chaves, a road leads north to **Pedra Bolideira**, a boulder the size of a small house which can be rocked with the nudge of a shoulder. The phenomenon was discovered by a shepherd, who discovered his horned sheep moving the great rock. The place became known to the wrong sort of people, who tried to blow up the boulder, for building materials. Their plan failed, and now Bolideira is a national monument.

At the village of Sanjurge, 3km northwest of Chaves, follow signs to **Outeiro Machado** or signs indicating 'Arte Rupestre'. Arriving at the dirt track, turn right, then fork left and fork left again. Leave your car at the 'platform' off to the right and walk a short way across the scrubland to the long humped granite boulder pockmarked with prehistoric signs, geometric shapes and symbols of axes. Like the Pedra Bolideira, the boulder came under threat from villagers with pickaxes convinced that it hid gold. They did little damage. The carvings in themselves are less remarkable than the magic of the place, peopled by spirits on the edge of revealing themselves: this is one of the weirdest places in Portugal. The land is hummocky and soft, the vegetation tough, and the site was once a lake, as indicated by the profusion of rounded stones.

(i) **Chaves >**
Terreiro da Cavalaria,
t *(276) 340 660,*
www.rt-atb.pt

★ **Forte de São Francisco Hotel >**

★ **Quinta de Santa Isabel >>**

Tourist Information in Chaves

The tourist office brochure reports: 'important agricultural centre, [Chaves] is known by its fairies', especially the *Feira dos Santos* held on 1 November, which sells farm and household equipment.

Where to Stay in Chaves

★★★★**Forte de São Francisco Hotel**, Forte São Francisco, t (276) 333 700, *www.forte-s-francisco-hoteis.pt* (€€€). Stylish and very welcome addition to Portugal's stable of luxury hotels. It occupies a 16th-century monastery within a 17th-century fortress at the centre of town, and its success lies in its elegant mix of ancient and modern and the owners' fine eye for design – sufficient to attract beautiful people from Lisbon and Porto, who give the place a much younger feel than most *pousadas*. Public rooms are spacious, well lit and not too monastic, and bedrooms are generous, though avoid the 'overflow' rooms in the former military hospital. The palm-fringed pool is large enough to swim rather than wallow, with views of the hills. The only minor drawback is the sound of the kitchen's extractor fan, from

10am to 7pm. Sauna, jacuzzi, tennis court. For the restaurant, see p.135.

★★★★**Hotel Aquae Flaviae**, Praça do Brasil, t (276) 309 000, *www.hoteis-arco.com* (€€). Slightly vast and primed for tour groups. Located next to the spa and the road from Braga, it lacks style but offers good views of the hills, a nice little swimming pool – covered with a polythene igloo in winter – and big beds.

★★★★**Albergaria Jaime**, Rua Joaquim José Delgado, t (276) 301 050, *www.albergariajaime.com.pt* (€). Clean and simple, overlooking the little park next to the spa.

★★**Hotel Trajano**, Travessa Cândido dos Reis, t (276) 301 640, *www.hotel trajano.com* (€). Pleasant rooms decorated in the Portuguese style. The staff are obliging and the terrace offers a good view of the old part of town.

★★★**Residencial Casadas Termas**, Rua do Tabolado, t (276) 333 280 or 190 (€; *but prices may be negotiable according to demand*). Friendly place with 12 decent rooms, a/c and small balconies. The street outside can get a little noisy. For cheap rooms, ask the manager about the annexe that is located around the corner.

Turismo de Habitação
Quinta de Santa Isabel, Santo Estêvão, t (276) 351 818 or 333 210, or 91 734

2434 (€€). Traditional manor house standing in an estate filled with pinewood and vineyards, 7km east of Chaves. The Sainted Queen Isabel is said to have spent the night here on the eve of her marriage to Dom Dinis – a good choice; the bedrooms are splendid, with four-poster beds.

★ **Quinta da Mata >**

Quinta da Mata, 5km southeast of Chaves on the road to Mirandela, **t** (276) 340 030 (€€ QH). Altogether a more grand, stone manor house dating from the 17th century, set in the Serra da Bruheira, with a pool, tennis courts and chapel. All five bedrooms are distinctively furnished and there is a terrace restaurant with lovely views.

★ **Kátia >>**

Quinta do Lombo, 3km from Chaves on the road to Mirandela, **t** (276) 321 404 (€). Typical Trás-os-Montes country house with granite walls. There are a number of rooms for eating: one for breakfast, one for lunch and one for dinner. The four bedrooms are pleasant and comfortable and the house has its own mini ethnographic museum, as well as a pool and a warm welcome.

Eating Out in Chaves

Expensive (€€€)

★ **Forte de São Francisco Hotel >**

Forte de São Francisco Hotel, Forte São Francisco, **t** (276) 333 700. The restaurant here is purpose-built and rather large, but the food and wine list are very good and the view of the pool is charming. Regional specialities include grilled steak, kid stew and boiled vegetables with pork sausage, veal, chicken and potatoes. There's also a **Taverna** (*closed Sun eve and Mon*) ceilinged with smoked hams, which makes a good option in winter.

★ **Restaurante Carvalho >**

Restaurante Carvalho, Largo das Caldas, **t** (276) 321 727. This has an excellent reputation for its tasty regional specialities. It's justly popular with smart-ish diners, who aren't too bothered that the staff are not always sufficiently attentive and the hard surfaces make for a bit of an echo. *Closed Thurs.*

Moderate (€€)

Verde Lirio, Canto do Rio, **t** (276) 321 616. Facing the old bridge occupying a superb location, with a large outside terrace. Has a menu of traditional local dishes with an emphasis on meat and fish.

Casa Costa, Rua do Tabolado, **t** (276) 323 568. Also offers al fresco dining, this time under a vine backing onto the river.

O Bernado, km 11, EN2, Vilelado Tâmega, **t** (276) 346 175. A sound choice for traditional cuisine with an attractive outside terrace.

Inexpensive (€)

Kátia, Rua do Sol 28–32, **t** (276) 324 446. Looks rather ordinary, but it's a friendly place and you may be in for a treat. One correspondent described the *arroz de marisco* – clams, mussels, shrimp, crab claws and rice – at €15 for two people, as 'the best meal I've ever eaten'. Roasted wild boar is served in portions big enough to satisfy a whole family of cave-dwellers. It tastes of gammon.

Jing Huá, Rua do Tabolado, **t** (276) 333 242. Promising Chinese restaurant with 10 little fixed-price daily menus for around €5.

Bars in Chaves

The **Cyber Bar** at the bottom of the Albergaria Jaime is the place to be – if you're young and want to be where the noise is. If not, head for the excellent **Adega Faustino**, Travessa do Olival, **t** (276) 322 142 (*closed Sun*), opposite the Hotel Trajano. It has the potential to be a great place – cobbled floor, huge wine vats, a wooden ceiling like the inside of a windmill, exhibitions by contemporary artists and good regional *petiscos* – if only it attracted more like-minded people. The bar at the **Forte de São Francisco Hotel** is very stylish, of course – the bar counter is backlit marble – but empty.

West of Chaves

The hills around Chaves have large, flesh-coloured bites taken out of them, which are clay mines. Clusters of pollarded chestnut trees grow interspersed with their uncut neighbours, waiting for their eventual transformation into woven baskets.

It took Marshal Soult and the second Napoleonic invasion two days to march from Chaves to Braga. From the fertile river plain the road climbs gently to Sapiãos, from which it rises a further 1,000ft (300m) to Cervos – the peaks here divide the tributaries of the River Tâmega and the River Cávado. Villages huddle together for warmth, growing potatoes and rye, separating the woods of pine and oak.

Vidago

Spa
open 1 June–15 Oct,
termasvidago@
unicer.pt

The southwesterly road from Chaves to Vila Real follows the course of the River Tâmega to the tranquil **spa** town of Vidago, which is sheltered and framed by tree-covered slopes. Portugal's most alkaline mineral water claims therapeutic qualities similar to those at Chaves; it also reckons to help asthma (when injected into the bloodstream – seek medical advice!). No doubt beneficial effects are claimed for the nine-hole golf course, too.

Capela da Granginha

This Romanesque chapel near Seara Velha is entered through an exceptionally interesting carved portal, depicting animals, plants and people. The face on the left is a devil's, with his tankard-handle ears, placed here so that the church-bound could leave their evil outside. The accompanying creatures look more like dragons than wolves. There's said to be a statue of a half-naked Venus buried outside the chapel – the priest thought it inappropriate. The chapel contains a T-shaped Roman altar excavated from the floor, and a very unusual baptismal font set in one wall which permitted the total immersion of an infant, rather than a token wetting.

Goldmines

The Romans mined this region for gold, particularly at Jales, Tresminas, and near the village of Ardãos, 6km west of Seara Velha and 18km west of Chaves. The gold partly explains the concentration of eight Roman forts in this area. A significant seam of gold was found at Jales in 1988. Curiously, there are often rainbows over the goldmines – so there's a true crock of gold at the end of the rainbow.

Around AD 75, 2,000 workers – probably slaves – daily laboured at Tresminas. Pliny describes the system of *ruina monticum* used here: a large amount of water was collected behind a dam; the sluice was opened, and water rushed out through ditches, over ore-bearing rocks which were thus smashed against one another. The loose rock was crushed in rectangular mortars, some of which have been incorporated in the walls of village buildings.

Boticas

Boticas is an airy little place, off the Chaves–Braga route, of 1,000 souls. It's half-rustic, half-townified, of no especial interest but for its restaurant and its odd wine. Boticas and the neighbouring village of Granja produce what is ironically called **Wine of the Dead** (*Vinho dos Mortos*), so named because the wine is buried and is believed to be life-giving. Local farmers buried their bottled wine to hide it from Marshal Soult and his thirsty troops. The French passed by, unaware of what lay fermenting beneath their feet.

After the French withdrawal, the locals tentatively dug up their bottles to celebrate. The wine had improved! Of course, this was a miracle – but, disappointingly, it has a scientific explanation: the wine benefits from fermenting at a constant temperature, protected from the light. You can buy it at Pingo do Mel in the Rua 5 de Outubro, and try asking in local bars. Actually it doesn't taste that special, just light and, shall we say, rather earthy.

The Serra do Barroso

West of Boticas, as far as the border with the Minho, lies the Serra do Barroso – generally abbreviated to Barroso – a very rewarding area for the wandering motorist keen on exploring rude villages lodged in the folds of the hills. Chaves is the most convenient base from which to explore. The hills reach more than 3,300ft (1,000m) above sea level, but this is not apparent because all the land is high, and there is nothing to contrast it with.

The villages of Barroso were brought together by a common need for defence, and the habits of the community die hard there. Each household owns its own sheep or oxen, but these are tended in one promiscuous flock either by the local shepherd, or by each householder in turn. Communal bakeries are now redundant, but meetings of the *homens bons* are still called to arbitrate disputes over water rights, uncultivated land, broken contracts and petty crime.

A curious ceremony of fetching the bride applied here at least until the middle of the 19th century: the groom and his relations went to the bride's house, to be asked, 'What seek you here?' 'A wife, honour and wealth', the suitor would reply, to which the traditional riposte was 'She has herded goats, has leapt hedges, and if she has spiked herself on one of them, and you want her as she is, so do I give her to you.' (The maidens of Barroso used to have to wear black stockings if they had been seduced.)

Shepherds used to wear straw suits to keep the rain off, looking like someone from *The Wizard of Oz*; now these odd garments are confined to ethnographic museums. The *capa de honras*, a heavy hooded cloak of brown blanket cloth, is still occasionally worn in the villages of the region.

Punishingly cold in winter, with occasional heavy snows, the soil is too poor to support cereal crops. Barroso is soaked with the highest rainfall in Portugal, which at least makes it suitable pastureland. This pastureland buffers the villages, divided by dry stone walls and oak woods. Indeed, so potent is the pasture that the villagers can drink the milk of the small Barroso oxen, unlike that of their cousins from Miranda.

This has not saved the breed from becoming prime movers in the favourite local 'sport' and source of community pride, the **Combate** or **Chega dos Bois**. It's a test of strength between two oxen, each destined only for this purpose. The beasts may weigh up to 2,200lb (1,000kg). The oxen are put face to face in a ring. They butt each other, they gore each other, they kick up clouds of dust, and eventually one of them runs away. He is the loser. The oxen used to be communally owned and fed by a village; now they are more likely to be owned by returned emigrants. There are no fixed dates for these spectacles, so there is no way to plan to see one, should you wish to.

Carvalhelhos

Seven kilometres west of Boticas, Carvalhelhos is dominated by its spring-water bottling factory, which spoils the view from the **Castro** a further 1km to the west. The iron-age fort is believed to be about 2,800 years old, and has tickled the curiosity of archaeologists because dwellings were built outside the fortified walls, which were restored to a height of 6½ft (2m) in the 19th century.

Montalegre

Montalegre is designated the capital of Barroso, a remote castle town of almost 2,000 souls lying north of the Braga–Chaves route, 46km from Chaves, that has been jolted into modernity by the construction and maintenance of hydroelectric dams nearby. So the name 'cheery hill' seems less appropriate now than it used to. Still, the café plays sacred music on Sundays. The tower of Dom Afonso's castle imitated the style of those built by his father Dom Dinis at the end of the 13th century.

Montalegre is 14km east of Covelães, one of the entry points to the Peneda-Gerês Park (*see* **The Minho**, p.117). The ruins of the monastery at Pitões das Júnias lie a further 10km to the northwest.

Where to Stay West of Chaves

ⓘ **Vidago** ›
Largo Miguel de Carvalho, t *(276) 907 470*

ⓘ **Montalegre** ››
Praça do Município, t *(276) 511 010*

ⓘ **Boticas**
Rua 5 de Outubro, t *(276) 410 200*

Vidago

★★★★Palace Hotel, Parque de Vidago, t (276) 990 900, *www.vidago palace.com*. The enormous pink Edwardian hotel is closed until mid-to late 2009 for extensive refurbishment. It is pleasantly grand. In the vast grounds you will encounter the pump room, along with the bandstand, the swimming pool, tennis courts, the lake and of course the park to wander in.

★★★Hotel do Parque, Avenida Teixeira de Sousa, t (276) 907 157 (€€). Decent though far less memorable alternative to the Palace Hotel.

★★★Pensão Primavera, Avenida Conde de Caria 2, t (276) 907 230 (€). A budget option.

★★Pensão Alameda, Rua Padre Adolfo Maglhães 2, t (276) 907 246 (€). More budget accommodation. *Closed Oct–Apr.*

Carvalhelhos

★★★★Estalagem de Carvalhelhos, t (276) 415 150, *www.carvalhelhos.pt* (€). There's no great atmosphere to the place but if you get stuck and need a room for the night you could try it.

Montalegre

★★★★Hotel Quality Inn, Rua do Avelar 2, t (276) 510 220, *www.choicehotels portugal.com* (€€). A former prison, now with a heated indoor swimming pool, Turkish bath and gym.

Casa Zé Maria, Rua Dr Victor Branco 10, t (276) 512 457 (€). A grand granite house with suitably rustic rooms boasting hardwood floors and high ceilings.

Residencial Fidalgo, Rua da Corujeira, t (276) 512 462 (€). Pleasant rooms and uplifting views over the valley. If you're here in the summer, trout from the River Cávado is very tasty – check that the fish hasn't been farmed.

The Northeast

Bragança

Bragança is a mellow place with quirky ways bred of its historic isolation. The name conjures something grand and romantic, but Charles II's consort, Catherine of Bragança, has left no trace. Bragança stands at the lordly height of 2,200ft (670m), beside the River Fervença, a small tributary of the River Sabor, and an amphitheatre of low mountains looms in the middle distance. Three roads converge at the cathedral square: from Chaves and Vila Real; from Spain, to the north; and from Bragança's own castle and citadel, which crown a hillock overlooking the rest of town. Ever since Portugal took its present boundaries, Bragança has been synonymous with isolation. But that is no longer the case: motorways now connect Bragança with Porto and Zamora (in Spain). In short, there's Bennetton in Bragança.

The people of Bragança are more full-bodied than their wine, which they sometimes mix with 7-Up. They favour long-haired Pekingese-type dogs, which are often called Poochie. Stray dogs (not called Poochie) stroll about. Men grow moustaches, and

Getting to Bragança

By **road**, Bragança is 100km from Chaves and 255km from Porto, 203km from Guarda and 248km from Viseu.

The **railway station** is now closed.

By **bus**, Rodonorte, **t** (273) 331 870, has an information office by the railway station on Avenida João da Cruz. Their timetabling is erratic, and it is best to check with them or the **tourist office** for the latest schedule. They have half a dozen daily services from Lisbon (12hrs), via Coimbra (9hrs), Porto (4½hrs), Viseu (6¼hrs), Régua (4¼hrs), Vila Real (3½hrs), Vila Pouca de Aguiar (3hrs), and Valpaços (1¾hrs). Buses shake, rattle and roll infrequently from Vidago.

Getting to Spain

Rodonorte also runs **buses** to Spain – which is only 34km away – including connecting services to Valladolid. There are also some occasional direct buses running to Valladolid and on to Madrid.

distraught women give their hair to the Church as a devotional offering, hoping to regain a husband's love.

The western approach to Bragança is dominated by new development: a mass of eight-storey buildings echoes the less attractive parts of the Algarve, only without the consolation of the beach. The town's population has soared to 37,000, boosted by country dwellers seeking employment, the university's 6,000 students and a big language school. A theatre is under construction, and a convent behind the cathedral is being converted into a cultural centre and library.

Bragança is better suited to the ethnographer than the art historian. Famous local son is the Abbot of Baçal (1865–1947), who devoted his life to writing 11 volumes on the ethnography of the region. He publicized the existence of the Marranos, Jews who fled the Spanish Inquisition under Ferdinand and Isabella.

History

Bragança started life as Brigantio, founded by Brigo IV, King of Spain, in 906 BC. Julius Caesar fortified it, building a stronghold at the convergence of Roman military highways. For 400 years the town was destroyed and rebuilt in the battles between Christians and Moors. It found its final resting place in 1130, when Fernão Mendes, brother-in-law of Afonso Henriques, rebuilt the town on the site of the village of Benquerença. Afonso IX of León attacked Bragança's newly built castle in 1199. By the late 14th century, the castellan's Castilian sympathies were sufficiently alarming for Dom João I to need to retrieve the town. In 1442 his bastard son, Prince Afonso, eighth Count of Barcelos, was created first Duke of Bragança.

The eighth duke came to the throne, albeit reluctantly, in 1640. The country united behind the man they made João IV, in order to oust Philip II of Spain. The House of Bragança ruled Portugal until the abolition of the monarchy in 1910. But the dynasts spent scant time in Bragança itself, preferring their seat at Vila Viçosa, in the Alentejo.

Around the Town

Bragança's 16th-century **cathedral** is unimpressive. It was a Jesuit college until Pombal expelled the Jesuits in 1759; five years later the diocese was moved here from Miranda. The sacristy is covered with scenes from the life of a skinny St Ignatius, and contains two hulking polychrome sculptures of him and of St Francis Xavier.

The Museu do Abade de Baçal

Museu do Abade de Baçal
t (273) 332 802,
www.ipmuseus.pt;
open Tues–Fri 10–5,
Sat–Sun 10–6; adm

From the cathedral, head up towards the castle along the Rua do Conselheiro Abilio Beça to the excellent **Museu do Abade de Baçal**. Featuring art, archaeology and ethnography, it occupies the 16th-century bishop's palace, an attractive building altered by the bishop of Miranda in 1737. No doubt the bishops would be surprised to see their garden hosting a couple of granite *berrões*.

One room is devoted to episcopal accoutrements. It includes a gold cage to stop wafers blowing away at open-air Masses; an *escrevaninha*, one compartment of which held sand, for 'blotting' wet ink; a deep silver bowl used by the bishop for washing priests' feet. Also in this room is a wonderful late 14th-century *Virgin and Child*, gilt and polychromed in the 17th century; and a strange barbed ivory image of Christ with sheep – he wears what they wear.

Another room houses writs issued by Dom Manuel to apportion justice and sanction construction around Bragança. The walls bear framed theses printed onto cloth, following a fashion instigated at the University of Salamanca whereby students would present their doctorates in this form to their home parishes. Such cloths were used within living memory to cover Communion chalices. Poles looking like billiard cues were given to members of the *câmara municipal* as symbols of authority. A stunning 900-year-old leather altarfront is displayed among them, decorated with coloured flowers.

The room of ethnography includes a fantastic iron cauldron, and two instruments of 19th-century popular justice: a head brace with a tongue depressor, used to stop a criminal talking; and what may be a woman's chastity belt.

Also notable are Abel Salazar's fluid paintings and Alberto de Sousa's watercolours of the pillories of the district of Bragança. An impressive collection of coins will interest numismatists. The palace's chapel now houses a small collection of magnificent embroidered vestments.

The Route to the Citadel

Bragança is endowed with a pious quota of churches, but sometimes it is difficult to locate their keys. From the museum, the first church on your right as you walk towards the citadel is the **church of S. Vicente**, with an irregular 17th-century façade – around the other side – beautiful in the evening sunlight. Dom Pedro the Cruel claimed to have clandestinely married Inês de Castro, c. 1354, and tradition says the service took place here (*see* p.281). The church is built on a 13th-century base and features a bizarre ceiling: a three-dimensional Christ is caught in the act of ascending, flying like Superman.

To the left of the citadel as you approach it is the **church of S. Bento**. People sit or stand beside its Renaissance granite doorway, sewing, gossiping, waiting for nothing in particular. The lovely *mudéjar* ceiling of the chancel is inlaid with wooden geometrical designs. This style marks the rebirth of Islamic techniques during the Manueline period.

Just downhill of the citadel stands the **pillory** (*see* p.412). For reasons unknown, the base of the shaft has been inserted through one of Bragança's *berrões*, a pig with a hollow in its snout, as if to skewer the unfortunate animal.

The main gate of the citadel is the Porta de Santo António, and beyond it the ogival Porta da Vila. The citadel is cluttered with peasant cottages – there used to be more of these, the place having provided safe accommodation for centuries, but they were razed in the late 1920s, in the interest of 'aesthetics' and 'hygiene'. The wall of the citadel incorporates the Poço do Rei, a well full of rubbish, periodically tidied by the Boy Scouts. The Centro d'Artesanato is here.

The Castle

Bragança castle

Fernão Mendes' 12th-century **castle** was reinforced by João I and Afonso V in the 30 years after 1409. The splendid, formidable schist and granite structure was a clenched fist affirming the king's independence from Castile and León, and his control of the surrounding regions. The battlements overlook rounded, interlacing hills, whose bleating sheep are well within earshot.

As well as having a defensive function, the tall, gracious Gothic tower was partly residential, as the wide upper-storey window indicates. The square Princess's Tower stands where the castle wall becomes the wall of the citadel. Now devoid of pale ladies with long blonde hair and conical hats, it must make do with the tale of Dona Leonor, unhappy wife of Dom Jaime, the fourth duke. Suspecting her of infidelity, he locked her in the tower until he murdered her in Vila Viçosa.

It's a great place for children, as there are plenty of nooks and crannies to explore, including the drawbridge, cistern and boringly sanitized dungeon. The doorways in the keep are about 5ft (1.5m), lit by kitsch electric candles. Having housed a regiment 1855–1928, the keep is now a **military museum**. The African weapons were assembled during the 1895 campaigns there. The most bizarre exhibit is the 'Replica of the trousers worn by Gungunhana during his detention in the Açores.' Gungunhana, King of the Vatuas, led many chiefs in their rebellion against the Portuguese in southern Mozambique in 1895. Mousinho de Albuquerque broke the back of the rebellion when he captured Gungunhana in his own kraal. The African leader was shipped off to the Azores, where he died. (Mousinho de Albuquerque was made tutor of the king's sons. He committed suicide in a Lisbon railway carriage in 1902.)

Military museum
open 9–12 and 2–5; closed Thurs and hols; adm

Within the Citadel

Beside the castle is the **church of Santa Maria**, built between 1701 and 1715, on the site of a Romanesque church. According to tradition, the patron's image was hidden in woods crawling with green lizards, to preserve it from the Moorish invaders. Hence the church is sometimes known as N.S. do Sardão (Our Lady of the Green Lizard). The ceiling of the nave is painted, possibly by the same artist who worked on the church of S. Bento.

The strange building next to the church is the **Domus Municipalis**, a very rare example of Romanesque civic architecture (because most public meetings took place within churches). It has five unequal sides; the upper storey's round-arched arcade sits on a lower storey of uninterrupted granite. This was the cistern, crucial to a citadel under siege. This importance is reflected in the building's other function: in medieval times it was the meeting place for the *homens bons* of the *vila*, who settled disputes over land rights and waterways. The Abbot of Baçal discovered Dom Sancho I's heraldic seal within the building, which suggests it was built in the first half of the 13th century.

The Back Streets

All the town's bread used to be baked in the **Rua Dos Fornos** (ovens), by a little bridge over the river. Old people now live in these bakeries, dark dwellings lit by small skylights and the candles that flank religious icons. They exaggerate past bread production to heroic proportions. Spanish Jews lived here when they fled the 16th-century Inquisition. The road leads into the **Rua das Moreirinhas**. Some say this was named by silk weavers to honour the mulberry tree which silkworms live off; others say the land was given to the Convent of Moreirola in Spain.

ⓘ **Bragança ›**
*Avenida Cidade de
Zamora (at the top),*
t *(273) 381 273,
www.cm-braganca.pt*

★ **Moinho do
Caniço ››**

Where to Stay in Bragança

★★★**Residencial São Roque**, Rua Miguel Torga, **t** (273) 381 481 (€). Stay here for the fabulous views. It occupies the seventh and eighth floors of a tower block; one side faces the castle, the other the mountains. Otherwise fairly basic.

★★★**Residencial Senhora da Ribeira**, Travessa do Hospital, **t** (273) 300 551 (€). Can't offer a view, but otherwise excellent value: limestone in the bathrooms, wood on the floors and air-conditioning everywhere.

★★★**Residencial Tulipa**, Rua Dr Francisco Felgueiras 8–10, **t** (273) 331 675, *tulipaturismo@iol.pt* (€). Provides simple, clean and standard rooms with stand-up balconies. You'll find better value elsewhere.

★★**Hotel Ibis**, Rotunda do Lavrador Transmontano, **t** (273) 302 520, *www.ibishotel.com* (€). Another place with great views of the mountains, but in the spanking-new, soulless part of town. The rooms are travelling salesman-esque.

Residencial Rucha, Rua Almirante Reis 42, **t** (273) 331 672 (€). Atmospheric place with a delightful owner. The budget rooms are clean and compact.

Pousada
Pousada de São Bartolomeu, Estrada de Turismo, **t** (273) 331 493, *www.pousadas.pt* (L1 C). A 20-minute walk from the centre of town, this tranquil *pousada* makes the most of its magnificent views across a wide ravine to the town and castle, and the surrounding hills and mountains beyond. The core dates from the 1959, and there is some good 1950s furniture about; another wing was built in 1996. These rooms are simple but very comfortable, thanks to the generous proportions and stunning views, with balconies from which to enjoy them. The circular pool is too small for a proper swim, but it's good for cooling off. Guests or visitors can dine on carpeted stone, enjoying very good food and panoramas.

Turismo de Habitação
Moinho do Caniço, Ponte de Castrelos, Castrelos, **t** (273) 323 577 or 933 224 503, *www.bragancanet.pt/moinho* (€€). Thirteen km west of Bragança, off the road to Chaves, there is a charming old watermill on the bank of the River Baceiro where you can fish for trout. This is truly a rural idyll, very green and quiet. The rooms are cosy and filled with rough wooden furniture.

Casa da Bica de Gondesende, Gondesende, **t** (273) 999 454 or 933 549 306, *www.bragancanet.pt/casadabica/* (€). Three kilometres closer to town, the same owner offers this four-bedroomed house to let. It's a traditional stone house in a village with a population of 25. Discomfort of this sort has its charms.

Eating Out in Bragança

Lá em Casa, Rua Marquês de Pombal 7, **t** (273) 322 111 (€€€). There's good cooking to be had at this popular and convivial restaurant. It offers some unusual fish dishes, but most people tend to go for the beef. One wall is bare stone, the chairs are pine, and hoots come from the family room at the back.

Solar Brangançano, Praça da Sé 34, **t** (273) 323 875 (€€). On the first floor of an 18th-century house opposite the cathedral is this attractive place: high ceilings, lace cloths, candlelight, chandeliers and hunter's guns on the walls. The flower-filled terraced garden is perfect for summer dining. Unfortunately the food isn't as distinguished as the setting, but prices are very reasonable. Choose game.

O Poté, Rua Alexandre Herculano 186, **t** (273) 333 710 (€€). This restaurant serves a good mix of traditional cuisine with more international choices. Game is the speciality. *Closed Sun.*

Restaurante Poças, Rua Combatentes da Grande Guerra, t (273) 331 428 or 331 216 (€). Attached to the *residencial* of the same name. The two-storey dining room is invariably packed. The staff are friendly, and the food is good.

Bar in Bragança

Within the castle walls, **Duque de Bragança**, Cidadela 92 (no telephone), has a few tables outside, which would be extremely atmospheric were it not for the cars parked nearby. *Open 2pm–3am, autumn and winter weekdays from 8pm.*

Around Bragança

Vinhais

The scenery on the road between Chaves and Bragança is magnificent – great green pastures and clusters of venerable chestnut trees, peppered with settlements whose slate roofs decay lackadaisically. Hillocks stand on hummocks around Vinhais, which lies 32km west of Bragança.

The quiet town of 2,000 people is strung out along 1km of the highway. It was settled in the 13th century, and was once a border post. At the extreme west end of Vinhais stands a long Baroque façade incorporating two churches. The lower part is the **convent of São Francisco**. The *vila velha* is at the other end of town, entered through a gateway, leading to the ruins of a 13th-century castle. Chickens, ducks, cats and dogs mooch harmoniously around the pillory.

Castro de Avelãs

Some 7km west of Bragança, off the road from Vinhais, stand the remains of the 12th-century Benedictine **monastery of Castro de Avelãs**, which was extinguished in 1543 – sufficiently long ago for the ghosts to have wandered elsewhere. The original church's triple apse is still intact, though redundant on one side. There is something disturbing about this brick structure composed of blind arcades, as if it was intended to silence something unpleasant. Although this is the sole example of the style in Portugal, it also occurs at Sahagún in León. A pair of remarkably masculine *berrões* sit atop the gate to the monastery, one with a flat head and bared teeth, the other decapitated. Both seem to be saddled.

Parque Natural de Montezinho

Montezinho Park occupies 185,000 hilly acres (75,000ha) in the extreme northeast of Portugal, covering the Montezinho and Coroa *serras*. Altitudes range from 1,435ft (438m) in the east, to 4,860ft (1,481m) in the Montezinho mountains, and down to sea level in the centre. Parts of the west and centre are evergreen, though the latter is rich in venerable oak and chestnut trees –

Montezinho Park

Getting to areas Around Bragança

which provide good shade for walkers. Modest hamlets are scattered among the gentle hills and narrow, steep-sided valleys; the east, with a lower rainfall, is more sparsely populated. Rivers and streams run from north to south, as does the road network.

There are some very fine walks – the River Sabor is particularly beautiful north of França, as is Vilar Seco de Lomba in the far west – although at present there are no walking maps available. You may be able to persuade the Park Office in Bragança to let you have a photocopy of a military map, or ask there about plans to waymark some routes.

Some villagers maintain whitewashed circular *pombals* (pigeon coops). Other signs of the traditional, communal ways of life are increasingly confined to ethnographic museums. You'll see traditional houses, certainly, but they're likely to be slightly gentrified and sandwiched between new ones.

Bragança, Vinhais and Gimonde (7km east of Bragança) are the points of entry to the park.

There are three mini ethnographic **museums** within the park, in the village halls of Babe, Caravela and Palácios respectively. They can only be visited by prior arrangement with the Park Office in Bragança (*see* above).

Rio de Onor

Some 22km northeast of Bragança, Rio de Onor is a slate-roofed hamlet within the Montezinho park. It straddles the border with Spain: a chain is slung between two stone blocks marked 'E' and 'P', but nobody takes much notice of it, and the nationalities have been intermarrying for years.

In 1953 the anthropologist António Jorge Dias published a study of Rio de Onor. He found one of western Europe's freak villages, organized on egalitarian collective principles, including the stipulation that no household could graze more than two cows and one calf on the communal meadows. Here were embodied the Germanic pastoral traditions of our ancestors, claimed the anthropologist. Other researchers arrived, documentaries were filmed. And then somebody noticed that the villagers' replies were verbatim quotes from the initial publication.

For all that, there is little apparently different between Rio de Onor and numerous other small villages in Trás-os-Montes.

Outeiro

Roughly 32km southeast of Bragança, the road to Miranda do Douro passes through the village of Outeiro. Its **church of Santo Cristo** was built in 1648, with a coupled portal surmounted by a rose window, itself surrounded by elaborate carvings.

Vimioso

Vimioso, 22km southeast of Outeiro, and just off the Miranda road, is dominated by its hard 17th-century **Igreja Matriz**. The towers support two gargoyles, nicknamed 'Thirst' and 'Hunger': they face, respectively, a water tank and a butcher's shop.

Algoso

It's not really worth travelling the 7km due south of Vimioso to the ruined castle of Algoso – set high between valleys and surrounded by boulders – but there's a nice legend attached to it. The castle is said to have been relocated after a plague of ants made life intolerable. Legend tells of Dom Soeiro, a lecherous 14th-century castellan who lusted after one of the villagers. She was about to be married; Soeiro refused to issue the marriage licence unless the bridegroom brought him two shirts made of nettles. The confounded gallant sought the aid of Aldonsa, a famous witch who lived in a marsh (where doubtless she fumed at not having been consulted about the ants). Aldonsa equipped the bridegroom with two tolerable nettle shirts, and had a word in the ear of King Pedro I, who flew into one of his tantrums, and ordered the execution of Soeiro.

There are fewer bends in the road from Vimioso to Miranda do Douro, and the land flattens out on the approach. Miranda is a very nice place to arrive at.

(i) **Vinhais >>**
Largo do Arrabalde,
t *(273) 770 309*

Tourist Information Around Bragança

The best source of information about **Montezinho Park** is the Park Office in Bragança, at Rua Cónego Albano Falcão, Lote 5, Apartado 90, Bragança, **t** (273) 381 444 or 234 (*open weekdays 9–12.30 and 2–5.30*). Otherwise there's an office in Vinhais, in the Rua Dr Álvaro Leite, Edifício de Casa do Povo, **t** (273) 771 416.

Where to Stay Around Bragança

Accommodation in the Montezinho Park area is limited, but there are a few options.

Vinhais

*Pensão Ribeirinha, Rua Nova 34, **t** (273) 771 490 (€). Nice, old rooms if you get stuck in Vinhais.

***Residencial Cidadela Transmontana, Rua dos Frades, **t** (273) 770 110 (€). An alternative if you need to stay in Vinhais.

Around Cova da Lua

Abrigo de Montanha, **t** (273) 999 414 (€€). Near Cova da Lua, and well signposted. Home to a young couple well used to the needs of walkers. Rooms are small and pleasant, and there's a pool. Dinner can be provided if requested in advance, though the huge dining room feels rather institutional.

Casa dos Marrões, t (273) 999 550, www.casadosmarroes.com (€€). At Vilarinho de Cova da Lua, there is a low-slung 18th-century farmhouse with wooden ceilings. Six rooms are available to guests. Dogs are not allowed.

Montezinho Village

There are two houses to let. Contact Antero Pires, t (218) 405 130 or (919) 860 500, or Donna Constância, t (273) 919 227.

Gondesende

Moinho do Caniço, t (273) 323 577, www.bragancanet.pt/moinho (€€). In an isolated spot on the bank of the River Baceiro, near Gondesende, this former watermill is deeply peaceful and attractively decorated in a rustic style.

Casa do Passal, t (273) 323 506, www.casadopassal.no.sapo.pt (€€). An intimate, snug stone house, sleeping only two.

Casa da Bica, t (273) 999 454, www.bragancanet.pt/casadabica (€). A stone house that can sleep up to eight – which is a bargain for €40 – but it's a little on the spartan side.

Varge

You'll find rooms above the Snack Bar O Careto, t (273) 919 112, or at França, above Café Turismo, t (273) 919 163.

Miranda do Douro

Miranda is one of the smallest 'cities' in Europe, but happily none of its 2,000 inhabitants produce memorabilia announcing the fact. It is located in the eastern corner of Trás-os-Montes, a hop, skip and a jump away from a barren gorge in which the River Douro has been dammed, forming the frontier with Spain; a road across the hydroelectric dam connects Miranda with distant Zamora.

Miranda is a sleepy town that has spilt outside the citadel's five parallel cobbled streets. The Rua da Castanilha is peppered with emblazoned *palácios*, the manifestations of former wealth. A gargoyle on one of these directs its bare buttocks towards Spain. This does not deter the many Spaniards in search of a bargain. Head for the cathedral, which contains some superb pieces.

History

In AD 716, Moors conquered the local Visigoths, and called the place Mir-Hândul. When the Moors were expelled in the late 11th century, the Castilians coveted Miranda, a gateway to Portugal. They occupied the town in the second half of the 14th century – until they were expelled by Dom João I – and in 1710, during the War of the Spanish Succession.

In 1762, the city was besieged by Franco-Spanish troops fighting the Seven Years' War. They fired a shell into the powder room of the castle, exploding the 23 tons of gunpowder stored there – which destroyed most of the castle, part of the town walls, and 400 inhabitants. The castle remains an ugly ruin, with a giant bite taken out of it. The blast left the cathedral unharmed; ironically the diocese was transferred to Bragança two years later. The locals comment bitterly, 'The sacristy is in Bragança, but the cathedral is

Getting to Miranda do Douro

By **road**, Miranda do Douro is 83km from Bragança. The nearest **railway station** is at Pocinho (two trains daily from Porto, 4¼hrs). The midday arrival at Pocinho connects with a bus to Miranda. A couple of **buses** run daily from Porto (5hrs) via Vila Real (3hrs) – it can be done as a day trip, if you get up early. Buses stop in the main square. Local bus company Santos, **t** (273) 432 667 has the most comprehensive service.

in Miranda.' The people of Bragança say, 'If ever you go to Miranda, see the cathedral and come home.'

More drama came during the Peninsular War: in 1813 Wellington was slung across the gorge in a 'kind of hammock' to inspect about 60,000 Anglo-Portuguese troops who had gathered within Portugal.

Miranda's isolation has left several unique legacies. In some of the surrounding villages, people speak Mirandês, a dialect developed directly from Latin, and the only such patois in Portugal. The ancient dance of the *pauliteiros* is still performed by young men, each dressed in a white flannel skirt covered by the tails of a long linen shirt with embroidered sleeves, a cloth jacket, and a hat decked with flowers. Some ethnographers reckon the dance derives from the Pyrrhic Dance, a war dance simulating the whirring of Hellenic hordes, but there is no place in this theory for the two sticks which each man carries, which suggest a sword dance of sorts. The best time to see the *pauliteiros* is at the *Festas de Santa Bárbara* on the Sunday after 15 August. Miranda has more practical ambassadors, too: its oxen are praised throughout Portugal for their aptitude for work and reproduction.

What to See

Terra de Miranda Museum
Praça Dom João III,
t (273) 431 164;
open summer Tues–Sat
10–12.30 and 2.30–5.45;
winter Tues–Sat 10–12.15
and 2–5.15, Sun
10–12.45; closed Mon
and hols

The very good **Terra de Miranda Museum** bubbles with intimate insights into people's lives since the start of the 20th century. The first room includes a small cage to constrain roving babies, a large plate for communal eating, a cork bucket to keep water hot overnight, irons like pincers for making Communion wafers, and a pepper horn. In the next room are displayed a cruciform iron for hanging a pig from the ceiling, a device for making rope from flax, and a wheat-chaff separator embedded with small sharp stones. On the landing upstairs local costumes are displayed on mannequins: one holds inflated pigs' bladders, used for hitting people on the head. In the first floor rooms, an Ancient Hebrew inscription on granite attests to the area's Jewish heritage.

Miranda's **cathedral** stands in that corner of the citadel nearest the dam.

In 1545, Pope Paul III created a diocese in Miranda. Miranda was unprepared. The bishop needed a cathedral, and construction began seven years later. The austere, windowed façade is the work of Gonçalo de Torralva, the Tomar architect; for the interior, Francisco

09 Trás-os-Montes and the Alto Douro | The Northeast: Miranda do Douro

Velázquez followed the design of Miguel de Arruda. Beneath reinforced rib vaulting, a stunning two-storey altarpiece depicts the elevation of the Virgin: on the lower level 12 wonderfully natural Apostles watch the Virgin rise gracefully on a cloud. The sacristy, to the left, contains an unusual collection of twelve 16th-century paintings personifying the months of the year. The cathedral's safe was in the sacristy – the only way in was through a wall vent 13ft (4m) from the floor. The chest of drawers decorated with Mannerist strapwork and fantastic masks may be of Spanish origin – otherwise it is one of the finest pieces of 16th-century Portuguese furniture. The cathedral's organ is beautiful, ornamented with leafy gold and a grim face to banish 17th-century devils.

To the right of the centre nave, in the south transept, a glass case shelters the rosy-cheeked *Menino Jesus da Cartolinha* (the child Jesus in a silk hat). The puppet-like figure is splendidly dressed. Rings jewel the stumps of his fingers, and he always wears a top hat. The locals make costumes for him: although created in the mid-19th century, he prefers the fashion of the mid-17th century, because he commemorates a boy who appeared in Miranda then. This diminutive hero rallied the occupants against the besieging Spanish, and vanished, leaving no doubt that he was the Menino Jesus.

The 16th-century **Bishop's Palace** stood behind the cathedral. It was destroyed by fire in 1706; the ruins include a fine arcade. Note the fountain.

The cathedral's terrace gives an impressive view of the sheer rock gorge and the dam, which was built 1956–60. A small **recreation ground** by the side of the lake offers a swimming pool and facilities for canoeing.

Just beyond the single-arched Roman bridge across the little River Fresno is the 18th-century **Fonte dos Canos**, in a sort of tabernacle, which incorporates five heads apparently in flames. There is a modest **Centro do Artesanato** around the corner from the museum. It sells bagpipes, woven garments, and finely carved *rocas* for hand spinning. Several shops sell high-quality Portuguese handicrafts, including Decorlar at 7A Rua Mouzinho de Albuquerque, which has some nice pieces of china and embroidery among a lot of ordinary stuff.

(i) Miranda do Douro >
Largo do Menino Jesus da Cartolinha,
t (273) 431 132

Where to Stay in Miranda

★★★★**Estalagem de Santa Catarina**, t (273) 431 005, *www.estalagemsanta catarina.pt* (€€€). Poised as if to take a running jump over the gorge, this quiet former *pousada* offers 12 decent marble-balconied bedrooms with stark views of the barrage and its lake. The light sitting room is attractive, set for chess and draughts or chequers, with plants, magazines, and an odd piece of wood. The dining room is lighter than some of its food. Tiled wild horses run across the walls.

★★Hotel Turismo, t (273) 438 030 (€). Next to the *estalagem*. Rooms are clean, modern and comfortable.

★ **Residencial Santa Cruz >**

★★Residencial Santa Cruz, Rua Abade de Bacale 61, t (273) 431 374 (€). In the old town, this place has character and is a good option for travellers on a budget. Breakfast included.

★★Pensão Vista Bela, Rua do Mercado 63, t (273) 431 054 (€). Budget accommodation with a view of the gorge.

iron pot. Here are three places where you can try it.

Capa d'Honras, Travessa do Castelo 1, t (273) 432 699 (€€). Elegant restaurant serving traditional, exquisitely prepared dishes.

Restaurante Buteko, Rua da Trindade 55, t (273) 431 231 (€). *Closed Sun*.

Restaurante Balbina, Travessa da Misericórdia 5, t (273) 432 394 (€). In the old town near the cathedral, offering a range of traditional local dishes.

Eating Out in Miranda

The favourite dish of the people of Miranda do Douro is *posta à Mirandesa*, which is a big, thick slice of tender beef or veal braised in a large

Festivals in Miranda

The dance of the *pauliteiros* (*see* above) is the highlight of the *Festas de Santa Bárbara*, which takes place on the Sunday after 15 August.

The Alto Douro

There is no clear boundary between Trás-os-Montes and the Alto Douro: the great river's tributaries penetrate deep into the *terra quente*. Further south, the hills of the Douro valley are terraced with port wine vineyards (*see* p.180).

🌀 **Parque Natural do Douro Internacional**

Covering the upper reaches of the River Douro in Portugal and Spain, the **Parque Natural do Douro Internacional** also includes the plateau of Miranda do Douro and the hills around Mogadouro. The steep escarpments of the Douro Valley are a sanctuary for black storks, golden eagles, griffon vultures and Egyptian vultures. The locals call Egyptian vultures 'messengers of the cuckoos', because it's one of the first of the migrants to arrive. It eats lizards, among other things.

Sendim

The road from Miranda to Mogadouro is pretty in parts, an easy drive because it's flat with long straight stretches. It passes pastureland and fields of cereals, uncultivated land, elms and the occasional ash supporting great storks' nests. At Sendim, the remains of frescoes decay in the 18th-century **Igreja do Senhor do Boamorte**. An *azulejo* panel reminds us that the church was built by Manoel Roanno who travelled on water for four years. More curious is the village's **Roman fountain** built like a dog kennel.

Getting to and around The Alto Douro

Sendim: local **buses** run infrequently from Miranda to Sendim; there is also one daily express from Vila Real, with Rodonorte, and another from Mirandela.

Mogadouro: Rodonorte runs fast buses from Vila Real and Mirandela. The local company is Santos, **t** (279) 342 537.

Freixo de Espada a Cinta: by **road**, Freixo is 90km from Miranda and 93km from Guarda. From Miranda do Douro, change **buses** at the Freixo railway station 14km north of town.

Vila Nova de Foz Côa: there are three express **buses** from Lisbon to Vila Nova de Foz Côa (7hrs). From Porto, take the **train** to Pocinho, then take the bus for the last 10 minutes of your trip.

Vila Flor: the local **bus** company is Santos, **t** (278) 512 254.

Mogadouro

There is little to see in the small town of Mogadouro, which lies 46km southwest of Miranda, once made wealthy by its silk industry. Dom Dinis built the **castle** in the 13th century; now it's ruined.

Freixo de Espada a Cinta

After a monotonous 32km, the flat road south of Mogadouro arrives at the foot of the Reboredo hills, at Freixo's railway station. Some 14km further south lies the town of Freixo de Espada a Cinta, surrounded by low hills and thousands of almond trees. Come in February or March, to see the blossom. It's within the Parque Natural do Douro Internacional, and only 4km west of the River Douro, which forms the border with Spain. The town's odd name, meaning 'ash tree of the girth-sword', is believed to refer to the sword Dom Dinis hung on an ash tree when he took a nap here.

History

Dom Afonso Henriques' charter of 1152 sought to encourage the growth of this important frontier post. To reinforce his wishes, the town was made a sanctuary for fugitives – provided they were neither fraudulent nor treasonable.

This was the birthplace of Jorge Álvares, the first Portuguese navigator to reach Japan (though the chronicler António Galvão claims this honour for António da Mota, in 1542). Álvares' descriptions of Japan were instrumental in luring thence his friend St Francis Xavier, who was fed up with living in the 'barbarous' Moluccas. The poet Guerra Junqueiro was born here, too. Both are commemorated by statues.

Dom Dinis rebuilt the town's defences. His plan included the almost windowless heptagonal **Torre de Galo** (Cockerel's Tower), which has outlasted other major constructions, including the keep. Dom Dinis did not complete the defences, so in 1342 the people of Freixo obtained permission from his successor, Dom Afonso IV, to use the church tithe to do so. Now it is a bell- and clocktower. From the first storey a spiral staircase leads to the top of the tower, with good views of the countryside.

Freixo's fine 16th-century **Igreja Matriz** stands just below the tower. There are good Manueline portals, but the real delight of the building is the proportions of the interior – a simplified, scaled-down version of the Jerónimos monastery at Belém, with three naves of equal height, separated by cylindrical columns. The retable is painted with 16 panels attributed to Grão-Vasco (*see* pp.210–11), including *The Annunciation* and *Judas' Kiss*.

Torre de Moncorvo

Torre de Moncorvo is located halfway up the leafy slope of the Serra do Reboredo, 26km west of Freixo station. Some say the town was named after an 11th-century *senhor*, Mendo Curvo, who lived in a tower; others say Mendo had a *corvo* (a crow). Maybe everyone is correct. Moncorvo's climate shows the greatest annual deviation in the country, averaging a fiery 76°F (24.5°C) in summer and 42°F (5.5°) in winter. Some of the largest deposits of iron in Europe, to the east of the town, brought a modest prosperity and spawned blacksmiths. Silk too was a moneyspinner. Now 3,000 souls live in Moncorvo, noted for its *amêndoas cobertas* (sugared almonds).

About 200 yards from the central square, the **Igreja Matriz** is the largest church in Trás-os-Montes, but its architecture is unremarkable. It was begun in 1544 and completed some 50 years later, a delay possibly caused by the distance from any stone quarries. In 1808 the church plate was hidden on top of the capitals, to escape discovery by French invaders. The church's most remarkable piece is the sumptuous sculpted retable, carved in the 17th century. The upper part shows scenes from the life of Christ, and the lower part depicts two Evangelists, the doubting of St Thomas, the Resurrection, and four church elders. Behind an attractive Renaissance portal, the 16th-century **Misericórdia** houses a fine granite pulpit.

The 7km drive to the top of the **Reboredo mountain** (2,950ft/900m) is excitingly leafy, winding up the forest road, with good views of the surrounding hills and plains.

Vila Flor

On the road between Torre de Moncorvo and Mirandela is to be found the small town of Vila Flor, which was named by Dom Dinis as he passed on his way to meet Isabel of Aragon, in the 13th century. He must have had bouquets on his mind: he called it 'Flower Town'.

Museu Doutora Berta Cabral
open 10–12.30 and 2–5.30; closed Tues

The only thing worth seeing here is the curious **Museu Doutora Berta Cabral**. The museum was founded in 1946, when three eminent locals donated the contents of their homes. Affectionately inserted among religious images, coins and an 18th-century writing desk are elderly typewriters, walking sticks, snake skins, sewing machines, a suite of zebra-hide furniture and the sculpture of a boar.

Parque Arqueológico do Vale Côa

⭐ Côa Valley

The **Côa Valley** is home to Europe's largest and most impressive concentration of prehistoric rock art. Until a museum is built, viewing the rock art requires planning, physical vigour and a dollop of imagination – but that makes it all the more thrilling. Come before the crowds do; it's quite magical.

In 1989, EDP, the Portuguese state electricity company, had big plans for the Côa river valley: it was to become the site of one of the country's largest hydroelectric power stations. The discovery of thousands of prehistoric engravings and paintings in the area due to be flooded created a six-year feud between the government and a battery of international archaeologists. In 1995, with the giant Côa Dam half-completed, the new socialist government bowed to worldwide pressure, and declared the valley a protected area. A national park was opened in 1996, and in 1998 UNESCO declared it a World Heritage Site.

Rock art has been found at 28 different open-air sites over roughly 80 square miles (200 sq. km), with around 1,200 individual motifs, particularly animals such as deer, goats and oryx, fish, and some human figures. Sixty to seventy per cent of the art was created by the hunter gatherers of the Upper Palaeolithic period, from 23,000 to 10,000 BC. But the place also inspired rock artists of the Neolithic, Copper and Iron Ages and their 18th- and 20th-century descendants. It's therefore possible to trace the dawn of humankind's urge to understand reality and abstract and stylize it, and to speculate on why precisely these rocks were used throughout the centuries. Were these places where the hunt was good? Or were these rocks portals to another dimension, as they were for North American Indians? Or were the pictures done for the fun of it?

One theory that has now fallen out of fashion is that by depicting animals the artists would have good fortune. Foz Côa has literally shed light on the art of the Upper Palaeolithic, which before this discovery was thought to have been confined to caves; it was therefore an art of darkness, the province of shamans and sorcerers. Now that seems far less likely.

The Côa Valley was formed 200 million years ago, creating vertical panels of extremely hard schist at right angles to the river. The rock art has been created in four ways: by pecking, scratching, scraping and fine-line incision. Be warned that some of the pictures are so faint they are difficult to discern no matter how carefully a guide points them out – but their antiquity and remoteness, the extremity of the climate and the fierce beauty of the landscape work together to make a visit extremely memorable.

Three sites may be visited. Visitor numbers are limited and group size is restricted to a maximum of eight; each visit involves a bone-rattling trip in a four-wheel-drive vehicle. When you arrive on site, you will have to clamber up and down the uneven surfaces of the riverbank. No umbrellas are allowed on site, so if you come in winter bring waterproofs. If you come in summer, remember that the schist takes in heat and reflects it back, raising the temperature by 10–15°F (5–10° C). If all this seems a nuisance, come back in 10 years' time and you'll probably be able to cruise around in air-conditioned splendour. In the meantime it's good to remember that not everywhere in the world is easy to get to. Note that there are no tours on Mondays. The sites are:

(1) **Canada do Inferno.** Depart from the Park Office in Vila Nova de Foz Côa. Departures 10–2.30 in winter and 9.15–10.30 in summer. Limit 50 visitors/day.
(2) **Ribeira de Piscos.** Depart from the Visitor Centre in Muxagata. Departures 10–2.30 in winter and 9.30–3 in summer. Limit 30 visitors/day.
(3) **Penascosa.** Depart from the Visitor Centre in Castelo Melhor. Departures 1–3.30 in winter and 2–5.30 in summer. Limit 30 visitors/day.

Ramos Pinto's Quinta da Ervamoira Museum
t (279) 759 229; open by prior arrangement; closed Mon

The port house **Ramos Pinto's Quinta da Ervamoira Museum** near Muxagata is dedicated to the geomorphology and ethnology of the region.

Tourist Information and Services in The Alto Douro

 Mogadouro >
Largo de Santo Cristo, t (279) 343 756

In **Mogadouro**, **buses** depart from the kiosk in the central gardens.

Visiting the **Côa Valley** is difficult and you need to be determined. Trips can only be undertaken with a guide, and must be booked through the **park office** at Av Gago Coutinho 19, 5150 Vila Nova de Foz Côa, **t** (279) 768 260/1, *www.ipa.min-cultura.pt/pavc (open 9–12.30 and 2–5.30; closed Mon and holidays)*. Each tour costs €6, to make them affordable to the locals,

and lasts a couple of hours. The **visitor centre** at the same address has a collection of books and literature *(opening hours as above)*.

Where to Stay and Eat in The Alto Douro

Sendim
Restaurante Gabriela, **t** (273) 459 180, Largo da Praça 28 (€€). Alice, the celebrity chef, cooks a wonderful *posta Mirandesa à Gabriela*, a veal steak braised over an open fire, with special sauce. The food tastes different in summer and winter,

★ Restaurante Gabriela >>

because she burns grape vines in the summer, and olive wood in the winter. Quail *cozido à transmontana* is also on the menu.

Mogadouro

★★★**Hotel Trindade Coelho**, Largo Trindade Coelho, **t** (279) 340 010, *www.hoteltrindadecoelho.com* (€; *price includes garage*). Roomy and rather good value.

★★★**Residencial Estrela do Norte**, Avenida de Espanha 63, **t** (279) 340 050 (€). Modern in style.

Pensão Russo, Rua 15 de Outubro 10, **t** (279) 342 134 (€). Budget accommodation.

① **Freixo de Espada a Cinta >**
Avenida do Emigrante,
t (279) 653 480

Freixo de Espada a Cinta

Casa do Conselheiro, Rua das Moreirinhas, **t** (279) 653 439, *albusquerqus@yahoo.com* (€€). Part of the Turismo Rural scheme. It's a 16th-century house in a cobbled street, with stone walls and a covered terrace at the back.

Hospedaria Santo António, in the square where the bus stops, **t** (279) 653 104 (€). Good if you're on a tight budget.

Restaurante Cinta de Ouro (€). Located on the southern route out of town, up the hill and on the left. It is rather good with a Spanish flavour to the cooking. Also offers attractive accommodation (€).

Torre de Moncorvo

★★★★**Residencial Brasília**, Avenida Luís Borges 19, **t** (279) 254 256 (€€). Has a children's playground.

Quinta das Aveleiras, **t** (279) 258 280, *www.quinta-das-aveleiras.com* (€€). Farmhouse with good views of tree-covered hillslopes from the pool. Furnishing is attractively simple, and there's a mini museum arranged around a wine press. Has tennis court.

Casa da Avó, Rua Manuel Seixas 12, **t** (279) 252 401 (€€). A 19th-century house in the old part of town with five rooms available under the Turismo Rural scheme. The façade is tiled, with a wrought-iron balcony, but the interior is rather fussy and frou-frou. *Closed Dec–Feb inclusive.*

Casa de Santa Cruz, Rua Cimo do Lugar 1, **t** (279) 928 060, *www.casadesantacruz.com* (€€). Twelve km northeast of Moncorvo, this dominates the village of Felgar. Dating from the 18th century, it looks better from the outside than the inside; bedrooms are not at all manorial, but the price reflects that. There's a small pool.

Restaurante Regional O Lagar, Rua Adriano Leandro 16, **t** (279) 252 828 (€€). A superb traditional restaurant with a homey rustic atmosphere located near the Igreja Matriz. Specializes in such carnivorous options as wild boar. *Closed Sun evening.*

Vila Nova de Foz Côa

Residencial Marina, Avenida Gago Coutinho 2/4, **t** (279) 762 112 (€). Nice and cosy, but if you're sharing a room make sure you know your room-mate well: the room's shower and toilet are around a corner, with no door.

Residencial Avenida, Avenida Gago Coutinho 8, **t** (279) 762 175 (€). In the same street as the Marina.

Restaurante Paleocoa, Cerca do Silvano, Lt 23, **t** (279) 765 166 (€). Offers some regional specialities.

Around Vila Flor

Quinta da Veiguinha, **t** (278) 511 089 (€€). In the village of Vilas Boas, 5km northwest of Vila Flor, this *quinta* has something of a Mexican feel to it, perhaps because of the covered terraces and the way it rambles up from the Tua River. Five rooms are available under the Agro Tourism scheme. Make sure you're hungry in time for breakfast: bread, cheese and sausages are made on site.

Quinta do Reboredo, near Vilas Boas, **t** (278) 516 872, *arqueiroverde@clix.pt* (€), isn't quite as comfortable, but the fields around it ensure it's quiet. There's a pool, as well as some horses, and it's possible to ride. There are a couple of cheap places to eat around the museum.

From Vila Real to Mirandela

Vila Real

Backed by a monolithic hill, and fronted by a steep gorge which plummets in a dramatic jumble of rock shelves to the small River Corgo, Vila Real is the largest town in Trás-os-Montes, with 16,000 souls. Founded in 1272 on an easily defended site, Vila Real became the administrative centre for the territory enclosed by the Rivers Tua, Teixeira and Douro, in the late Middle Ages. Scraps of this medieval heritage remain, swallowed up by emblazoned 18th-century *palácios*. There's an appealing pedestrian zone, but otherwise the place is fairly bland. The Solar de Mateus, just outside Vila Real, is certainly worth seeing.

Around the Town

The Avenida Carvalho Araújo is the centre of town. Here stands the **cathedral**, which is all that remains of the Dominican monastery of S. Domingos, constructed for Dom João I in 1427 and burnt to the ground some 400 years later. What's left is unexceptional, Gothic but for the chancel, which was altered in the 18th century.

Diogo Cão was born in one of the three 15th-century houses on the same street. He was the first navigator to reach the mouth of the Congo, where he erected a stone column in 1482, and visited the rich and powerful King Manicongo, who told him 'The kingdom of the Congo shall be like Portugal in Africa.' (Ten years later, news filtered back to Lisbon that the king and queen had been baptized as Christians, and had held a bonfire of ju-jus.)

Little more is known of the discoverer – probably because Dom João II ordered all records to be deposited in the Torre de Tombo in Lisbon, to guard the information, especially from the Castilians. The archives were destroyed by the earthquake of 1755.

On the other side of the Avenida, the Rua da Portela bifurcates where Roman-clad archangels flank St Peter on the top of the **Clérigos Church** (which is also called the Capela Nova). Its Italian Baroque style may be the work of the 18th-century master, Nicolau Nasoni, or of his disciple José de Figueiredo Seixas. The interior has recently been restored.

Parallel with the Rua da Portela runs the **Rua da Misericórdia**, a long, low-built road lined with 16th- and 17th-century houses, resembling a stretched-out London mews.

The Solar de Mateus

Solar de Mateus
*t (259) 323 121,
casa.mateus@utad.pt;
open June–Sept 9–7.30,
Oct, March–May 9–1
and 2–6, Nov–Feb 10–1
and 2–5; guided tours
only; adm*

For nearly two centuries travellers and historians were ignorant of the **Solar de Mateus**, 3km southeast of Vila Real on the Sabrosa

Getting to Vila Real

By **road**, Vila Real is 107km from Braga, 139km from Bragança and 108km from Porto. Five **trains** arrive daily from Porto; change at Régua (3¼hrs total) onto the narrow-gauge railway (*see* page 63).

Vila Real is the headquarters of Trás-os-Montes' leading **bus** company, Rodonorte, so it would be sensible to pick up any available timetables from their head office at 19 Rua D. Pedro de Castro, **t** (259) 323 234/5 or 322 247. Rodonorte has five daily services to Coimbra and Lisbon, seven to Chaves, eight to Braga and Guimarães, and two to Lamego and Viseu. There are two to Bragança and Mirandela. Rede Expressos has a further five to Lisbon, three to Coimbra, eight to Porto, four to Amarante, six to Lamego and Viseu, four to Faro, one each to Setúbal, Albufeira, Lagoa and Lagos. Auto-Vias do Tamega, **t** (259) 322 928, on Avenida Carvalho Araujo, have services to Porto via Amarante and Coimbra and Lisbon via Viseu and Lamego.

road; Rodonorte run a regular bus service from Vila Real. Now this sumptuous and fantastic palace is known world-wide because its image is on the labels of Sogrape's **Mateus Rosé**.

Mateus was completed by 1743, at the behest of António José Botelho Mourão. The architect is unknown; on stylistic grounds, it has been attributed to the (Italian) school of Nasoni, who had worked on the cathedral and the Clérigos Church in Porto, and who was to be the single most important influence on 18th-century architecture in the north of Portugal.

Mateus has a festive air about it: the eye never knows which part of the façade to focus on. Two wings create a deep forecourt enclosed by a carved granite balustrade – the building's effect depends upon the contrast of whitewash and granite. At the centre, a great double staircase diverges and converges beneath the family escutcheon. An obelisk tops every corner.

The chapel stands to the left of the palace, with a similar pediment but too high and too heavy to work very well. The art historian Angela Delaforce attributes the design of the chapel to Nasoni's disciple, José de Figueiredo Seixas. The square reflecting pool in front of the *solar* was added in the 1930s. In it lies the disturbing sculpture of a half-drowned naked lady by the contemporary Évora craftsman João Cutileiro.

Ten rooms and the library are open to the public. The interior retains the atmosphere of the late 18th century, when it was redecorated. Deeply coloured heavy silk hangings still drape the doors to keep the draughts out of a string of rooms with high wooden ceilings. The paintings include remarkably bad royal portraits, rural scenes, and seasonal vegetable heads juxtaposed with women's heads. The small museum includes two exquisite Sèvres vases, wonderful vestments, and one of the 250 copies of an 1817 edition of *The Lusiads*, printed in Paris at the expense of the heir to Mateus, displayed here with three of the original copperplates, by Fragonard and Gérard, which illustrated the work. A barn has been converted into a concert hall; keep an eye out for concerts.

Such is the theatricality of the place that it's difficult to stroll around the manicured terraces at the rear of the *solar* without imagining oneself in the 18th century, wearing long shoes with high wooden heels and a buckle or bow, and a wide-brimmed ostrich-feather hat. The darkness of the tunnel of trees trained together is perfect for flirtation, or adjusting one's wig.

The Sanctuary of Panóias

Sanctuary**of Panóias**
t (226) 179 385; open
9–12.30 and 2–5.00;
closed Mon and
Tues am; adm

The **Sanctuary of Panóias** is some 8km southeast of Vila Real. Take the Sabrosa road and after 7km follow the signs, through the village of Constantim. On weekdays, Rodonorte operates a single bus to the site from Vila Real; for the return, wait at the stop on the main road.

Three granite boulders are inscribed and carved with troughs. Four inscriptions were tooled at the beginning of the 3rd century, venerating Serapis, Moira, the Mysteries and the Dii Severi (Pluto and Proserpine). Another inscription mentions the sacrifice of animals: their innards were burnt in the larger cavities, and their blood was spilt into the smaller tanks. Other troughs were intended for believers' sacred amputations. Now the receptacles are full of rainwater and sheep impudently graze nearby. Bring your imagination with you.

ⓘ Vila Real >
Avenida Carvalho
Araújo 94, opposite the
cathedral, t (259) 322
819; open summer
weekdays 9.30–7,
weekends and holidays
9.30–12.30 and 2–6;
winter 9.30–12.30 and
2–6, closed Sun
and hols

Tourist Information and Services in Vila Real

An **Information and Visitors' Centre** for the **Parque Natural do Alvão** can be found in the Largo dos Freitas, t (259) 302 830, *www.icn.pt* (*open Mon–Fri 9–12.30 and 4–7.30, closed Sat and Sun*), behind the Town Hall at the bottom of the central Avenue. The Visitors' Centre has been thought out with much love, and labelled in English.

The **bus station, t** (259) 323 234, is next to the Hotel Cabanelas, on Rua Dom Pedro de Castro. From the **railway station,** head up the Rua Miguel Bombarda, and straight across three crossroads, to get to the main strip.

★ Pensão São
Domingos >>

Where to Stay in Vila Real

★★★★Estalagem Quinta do Paço, t (259) 340 790, *quinta.do.paco@ mail.telepac.pt* (€€). Located 3km out

of town in Arroios, just past the Solar de Mateus, is an 18th-century manor house. The interior is nice enough, but doesn't live up to the promise of the exterior. Bedrooms are in the Travel Inn style of historical décor.

★★★Hotel Miracorgo, Av 1 de Maio 76–78, t (259) 325 001, *www.hotel miracorgo.com* (€€). Large and a little conferency, with plenty of staff, and comfortable rooms giving dizzy views of the gorge below. There's a 25m indoor pool, and car parking is available.

★★Hotel Miraneve, Rua D. Pedro de Castro, t (259) 323 153/4, *reservas. miraneve@clix.pt* (€€). Plain and decent.

★★Pensão Tocaio, Avenida Carvalho Araújo 44, t (259) 323 106 (€). Centrally located, but dark even with the lights on. A stuffed boar lurks in the lobby. Rooms are clean if somewhat comfortless.

★Pensão São Domingos, Travessa de S. Domingos 33, t (259) 322 039 (€). Pleasantly atmospheric with uneven floorboards, a rooftop view, and stable-like wooden railings upstairs. The same family runs the neighbouring **Casa de Hóspedes Mondego** (**t** as above), which is less satisfactory.

Residencial Real, Rua Central 5, **t** (259) 325 879 (€). Above a popular café. It's perfectly decent; if you want quiet, choose a room at the back.

Residencial Encontro, Avenida Carvalho Araújo 78, **t** (259) 322 532 (€). A few doors down from the tourist office, rooms here are a bit claustrophobic, but clean and basically OK.

Turismo de Habitação

Casa Agrícola da Levada, Timpeira, **t** (259) 322 190, *www.solaresde portugal.pt* (€€). Part of an estate that still uses traditional farming methods to breed various species of game, including wild(ish) boar. They also produce their own delicious bread, honey, jam and sausages. The four rooms are comfortable, with stone walls.

Casa do Mineiro, Trás do Vale, Campeã, **t** (259) 979 720 (€). Only has two rooms, but is built entirely out of granite and occupies an exceptional site at the junction of the Marão and Alvão mountain ranges.

Casa da Cruz, Campeã, **t** (259) 979 422 or (917) 523 575, *casadacruz@mail. telepac.pt* (€). Another typical house from this region. Inside it has a warm feel with colourful rugs and granite chimneys – one looks to be made from dolmen.

Eating Out in Vila Real

Espadeiro, Avenida Almeida Lucena, **t** (259) 322 302 (€€). Reputed to be the best restaurant in Vila Real, with regional cooking and a fireplace. *Closed Wed.*

Terra de Montanha, Rua 31 de Janeiro 16–18A, **t** (259) 372 075 (€€). Regional specialities and a fine reputation. Plump for the fowl. *Closed Sun night.*

Churrasqueira Real, Rua Teixeira de Sousa 14, **t** (259) 322 078 (€). A superb restaurant serving up inexpensive grills. *Closed Sun.*

Nova Pompeia, Avenida Carvalho Araújo 82, **t** (259) 338 080/1 (€). Lacks atmosphere but is packed with locals at lunchtime. They know the food is good – try the tripe.

Around Vila Real

Parque Natural do Alvão

Portugal's smallest National Park occupies some 19,750 acres (8,000ha) on the western slopes of the Alvão mountain range, extending towards the Marão range. It includes the source of the Ôlo River and marks the transition from the humid coastal region to the drier interior. Traditionally, houses were constructed in granite and thatched with straw, or built of shale and roofed with slate. There are a few wolves about and some rare bats, but the real excitement is the Royal eagle, which nests around waterfalls. Numbers dropped when forests spread, myxomatosis rose and young men proved their manhood by clambering up to steal eggs.

In order to conserve the area, no footpaths are marked, but there are a couple of fairly gentle **walks** at the margins of the park. The first is a two-and-a-half hour circular walk from Agarez to Arnal, following cobbled paths and farm tracks. Arnal clusters at the foot of the tor, near the stream named after it, with a little waterfall

Getting to areas Around Vila Real

By **road**, Mondim de Basto is some 45km northwest of Vila Real. Murça is strung out along the main road to Mirandela and Bragança, 40km northeast of Vila Real. Alijo is 16 km south of Murça. In Pinhão, the **railway station** is in the centre of town. Trains from Porto run four or five times daily (3hrs); change at Peso da Régua.

and mill. There's a centre for the display of traditional crafts. The second walk is on minor roads from the village of Ermelo, to Fervença (now overbuilt with modern houses), Varzigueto and following the road through pine forests to Fisgas to see the waterfall, which is at its best in autumn.

For details of the **park office** in Vila Real, *see* p.159.

Mondim de Basto

The little town of Mondim de Basto makes a good base for hiking in the Alvão hills. The pine-covered **Monte Farinha**, to the east of town, makes a delightful and not too taxing two-hour climb: a road leads up to the peak, or there's a path up to the right just past Pedra Vedra, on the Cerva road out of town.

Murça

Murça is a little town set in a scoured, rolling landscape crossed by dry stone walls. The main square is the home of the most famous of Portugal's *berrões*, affectionately known as the **Porca de Murça**. The 5ft (1.5m) granite pig inhabits a plinth, impassive, like a hornless rhinoceros.

Alijo

Alijo is surrounded by burnt grasses, olive groves and vineyards. The only reason to visit the town is to stay at the friendly *pousada* (*see* p.162).

Pinhão

 Pinhão

The River Douro is most beautiful upstream of Régua, and the road from there to Pinhão runs along the riverbank, offering stunning views. On arrival, Pinhão feels like the heart of port country, and geographically that's what it is. The railway station is decorated with *azulejos* depicting scenes of the production and transport of the wines of the region and the names of the port houses are spelt out, Hollywood style, in giant letters on the vine-covered hillslopes. Pinhão is a quiet place dominated by the hills and the river, and a good one in which to commune with them. Walkers should be prepared for some steep hikes.

It's also home to a hotel that is a destination in itself, the **C.S. Vintage House Hotel** (*see* p.162). The hotel is home to a wine academy that organizes regular activities, courses and tours,

09

Trás-os-Montes and the Alto Douro | From Vila Real to Mirandela: Around Vila Real including a port wine tour. Special tutored tastings are also a regular feature, when wine-makers are invited to explore particular themes. It's also possible to book a 45-minute boat trip and visit to the **Quinta do Panascal**, which is a port wine lodge and vineyard belonging to Fonseca port. Mindful that wine isn't everyone's passion, the Academy also offers occasional tastings in single-quinta olive oil and wild mushrooms.

Quinta do Panascal
Valença do Douro,
t (254) 732 321; open
10–5.30; closed Sun

Where to Stay and Eat Around Vila Real

(i) **Mondim de Basto >**
Rua Comendador Alfredo Alves de Carvalho,
t (255) 381 479

Parque Natural do Alvão Information Centre, Lugar do Barrio,
t (255) 381 209; open 9–12.30 and 2–5.30; closed Sat and Sun

(★) **C.S. Vintage House Hotel >>**

(★) **Residencial Douro >>**

(i) **Alijo >**
t (259) 957 100

Mondim de Basto

Quinta do Fundo, Vilar de Viando, **t** (255) 381 291, *www.quintado fundo.com* (€€). A lovely spot just 2km from town, nestled among vineyards. Excellent facilities, including a pool and tennis court.

Casa do Barreiro de Cima, Parada de Atei, **t** (255) 386 491, *www.manor houses.com* (€€). Some 7 km north of town. Swish, and offers rooms under the Turismo Rural scheme.

Casa das Mouroas, Rua José Carvalho Camões, **t** (255) 381 394 or (966) 333 212 (€). Also offers rooms under the Turismo Rural scheme.

Residencial Carvalho (also called **O Sassego**), Avenida Dr Augusto de Brito, **t** (255) 381 057 (€). Plain rooms near the petrol station.

There are several places to eat, including **Transmontano, Ramso** and **Chasselik**, all located in the Avenida da Igreja.

Murça

Pensão Miradouro, Curvas de Murça, **t** (259) 512 461 (€). Offers plain rooms and a restaurant.

The *pastelaria* on the lower side of the main square sells exquisite pastries.

Alijo

Pousada
Pousada de Barão Forrester, t (259) 959 215, *www.pousadas.pt* (L1 C). Has the relaxed feel of a country club. The building is L-shaped, with comfortable rooms – some with balconies – and a tennis court and oval pool. The bar is well stocked with port, and there is a collection of engravings by Barão de

Forrester (*see* p.181) himself. The food is good but not exceptional.

Pinhão

C.S. Vintage House Hotel, Lugar da Ponte, **t** (254) 730 230, *www.csvintage house.com* (€€€€–€€€). Stretched along the riverfront, this is a splendid place that would combine well with a couple of nights in Porto for a long weekend break (without needing to hire a car) in May or Sept/Oct, when the heat isn't too fierce. With an 18th-century core and wisteria almost as old, it's elegantly decorated in an unashamedly British style. Public rooms are tasteful and have a certain langour about them. Each of the 43 rooms has a terrace or balcony, and each faces the river. Bedrooms are simple and airy, bathrooms very Czech and Speke. The **restaurant** is formal and the food and wine list are excellent, with a modern interpretation of traditional dishes, such as stewed partridge, and good to very good Douro wines. Light meals are served on the ivy-shaded waterfront terrace, which leads to a small swimming pool.

Residencial Douro, Largo da Estação, **t** (254) 732 404 (€€). This hotel offers some of the pleasures of Vintage House (*see* above) at a fraction of the cost. Choose an air-conditioned room facing the river, and enjoy spending hours with a book under the bougainvillaea on the terrace overlooking the water.

Residencial Ponto Grande, Rua António Manuel Saraiva 41–41A, **t** (254) 732 456 (€). An inferior option, with squashed little rooms and grumpy service.

Unusually, the choice for diners is limited to these places' restaurants.

Getting to Mirandela

By **road**, Mirandela is 54km distant from Chaves, 64km from Bragança, and 70km from Vila Real.

By **train**, 5 trains daily take 3½ hours to make the journey from Porto's São Bento station, via Tua. The journey from Tua to Mirandela can never take long enough – it is a truly spectacular ride.

Buses run twice daily from Chaves and Vila Real (via Murça). Cabanelas operate from behind the fire station on the Rua da República; Rodonorte buses from in front of the railway station.

Mirandela

For a town which lies at the centre of Trás-os-Montes' road network, Mirandela feels remarkably secluded. Sited beside the River Tua, it stands at the very edge of the *terra quente*: the wide river valley brims with peach and apple orchards, olive groves, and fields of rye.

There's not much to see in the airy streets of the town itself. A long **bridge** with 20 arches crosses the river; it was built in the 15th century on Roman foundations. The fine **Palace of the Távoras** dominates Mirandela. There is nothing interesting within the building, however, which is now the town hall.

The **Museu Municipal Armindo Teixeira Lopes** displays the painter's images of the town and other 20th-century Portuguese paintings and prints.

*Museu Municipal
Armindo Teixeira
Lopes
open Mon–Fri
10–12.30 and 2–6.30,
Sat 2–6.30; adm*

ⓘ *Mirandela >
Rua Afonso II,
t (278) 200 272*

Where to Stay in Mirandela

★★★**Grande Hotel Dom Dinis**, Avenida Nossa Senhora do Amparo, t (278) 260 100, *www.hoteis-arco.com* (€€). Cross the bridge to find this hotel which is fairly anonymous but with good facilities, large rooms and good views of the medieval bridge and river.

★★★**Residencial Globo**, Rua Cidade Orthez, t (278) 248 210 (€). Also near the centre of town.

★★**Residencial O Lagar**, 120 Rua da República, t (278) 262 712 (€). This is another central option.

★★**Pensão Mira Tua**, Rua da República 20, t (278) 200 140 (€). Located at the entrance to the old bridge. Includes breakfast.

Pensão Praia, Largo 1 de Janeiro 6, t (278) 262 497 (€). In a little square just off the main roundabout into Mirandela. Large, clean and dignified rooms have pretty lace curtains and bright white bedspreads. The proprietor is a kindly soul and the views over the lake make up for what little noise reaches the rooms from the roundabout.

Eating Out in Mirandela

Flor de Sal, Parque de José Gama, t (278) 203 063 (€€). Located near the town's new bridge, this restaurant is one of the more sophisticated options. Serves contemporary, exquisitely prepared dishes.

Lamego and Around

Peso da Régua

Some 25km south of Vila Real, Régua, as it's usually called, is the capital of the port wine country, being the nearest river port to Porto and the westernmost town in the Demarcated Region. Otherwise, the town is of little interest. Its principal worth to the visitor is as the nearest railway station to Lamego and as a luncheon venue for day trips by boat from Porto.

Lamego

The clean and handsome town of Lamego is set in hilly, fertile countryside, 9km south of Peso da Régua and the River Douro, surrounded by terraced vineyards and apple, pear and cherry orchards. The airy settlement of 11,000 souls sits aside the small River Balsemão, a tributary of the Douro. Two hills dominate the town, on one of which stands the castle, and on the other, which is wooded and, at 1,985ft (605m), slightly higher, the church of N.S. dos Remédios. The latter can keep an eye on the town, because the church's monumental staircase leads straight on from Lamego's central Avenida. Granite-and-whitewash Baroque *palácios* nudge one another, and in the streets men in flat caps wait for their stubble to grow.

Lamego will introduce visitors travelling up from the south to the rich and heavy breads of the north, which are imbued with a mystical significance. This highlights its role as a gateway to that wild, remote land beyond the mountains – though it was Lamego's position as a trading post between the east and west of the Peninsula that brought prosperity in the 15th century. Picnic on the local specialities – cured ham and sparkling wine.

The town had been the seat of a bishopric under the Suevi, and its episcopal status was restored in 1071. Lamego came into its own in the 16th century as a producer of velvet, satin and taffeta, with which it supplied the north of Portugal before the arrival of oriental silks. But the mainstay of the town's economy has always been its wines, described in the 16th century as 'the most excellent and most lasting ones to be found in the realm, as well as the most fragrant'. In the 18th century, Pombal built one of the first decent roads in the north of Portugal from Lamego to Régua, so that the wine could be shipped down-river to Porto. This is the wine from which port is made, but only a quarter of the crop is so honoured.

Getting to and around Peso da Régua and Lamego

Trains run fairly frequently to Peso da Régua from Porto (2¼hrs). They pass through Livração, where they can be joined by passengers from Amarante. From Bragança, change at Tua (from which, ¼hr). Three trains daily run from Vila Real (1hr). **Buses** arrive hourly from Lamego; the bus depot in Régua is next to the railway station.

Lamego is a 1½hr **drive** from Porto, via Amarante. The nearest **railway station** is at Régua; in front of it, buses to Lamego depart roughly hourly. Lamego is fairly well connected by the **bus** network, which includes infrequent daily Rodonorte buses, **t** (254) 63117, from Chaves (2¼hrs), and in the other direction Viseu (1½hrs), Coimbra (3¼hrs) and Lisbon (7hrs). It also runs two or three buses daily from Vila Real (¾hr).

Around the Town

Church of N.S. dos Remédios
open summer 7.30am –8pm; winter until 6

The 18th-century pilgrimage **church of N.S. dos Remédios** is an enticing destination. It's best approached as its architects intended, up the granite-and-whitewash double staircase which leads on from the Avenida Dr. Alfredo de Sousa. *Azulejos* and urns enliven the steps, which are fun to climb because it's such a tangible participation in the Baroque. (In the enjoyment of it all, take care not to be run over on the roads between flights of stairs.) Just below the church, the staircase culminates in the splendid **Court of the Kings**, circled by pillars and arches topped with theatrical granite gentlemen in sumptuous attire. The court is centred on an obelisk supported by four unfortunates traced with veins and spouting water from their mouths. The church's elaborate belltowers loom above, atop an unremarkable façade. Except for the portrait room, there's little to look at inside. The hill itself is peaceful and woody, so the road makes a nice walk down.

Raposeira Factory
t (254) 655 003

The road passes the **Raposeira Factory**, owned by Seagram, where the sparkling wine is made. The process is heavily mechanized, though the fizz is generated naturally by the second fermentation. An unusual part of the procedure involves the removal of sediment: it is allowed to sink to the cork-end of the inverted bottles; that end is then frozen, and the plastic-and-aluminium cork and ice are removed together.

The Cathedral

Cathedral
open 8–1 and 3–7

Back in town, the **cathedral** is at the heart of Lamego. Rebuilt in the 16th century and titivated in the 18th century, little remains of its Romanesque beginnings, except the base of the tower. A triple portal opens the façade, built 1508–15; devotees enter through arches ornamented with wild artichokes, pomegranates and other foliage, as well as babies, fantastical monsters, and even a fox munching a bird. Within, the ceiling painted in tapestry colours – sienna and grey-blues – canopies frescoes by Nasoni, who was clearly better at architectural than figurative painting, beautifully carved choir stalls, and a pair of organs dated 1753 (one helpfully provides spare parts for the other).

The real highlight is the silver frontal in the Capela do Sacramento – be sure to put the lights on. It was crafted 1758–68 by the master known by his initials MFG, a contemporary of Nasoni from Porto, to imitate both textile and embroidery. An elegant cloister stands to the left of the church.

Museu de Lamego

Museu de Lamego
Largo de Camões,
t (254) 612 008,
www.ipmuseus.pt;
open 10–12.30 and 2–5;
closed Mon and hols;
adm

The Bishop of Lamego did himself well: from 1775 to 1786 the wealthy Dom Manuel Vasconcelos Pereira rebuilt the episcopal palace, a fine building next to the cathedral. It now houses one of Portugal's best regional museums, the **Museu de Lamego**, with very good collections of paintings, tapestries and gilt woodwork.

In early 16th-century Brussels, huge rolls of vertical thread were slung in workshops and knotted with silk and wool, to produce wonderfully rich and lively tapestries, now exhibited in the museum. They include a series depicting the Oedipus story, and a panel vilifying profane music.

The five paintings by Vasco Fernandes (called Grão-Vasco; *see* p.210) are some of the most excellent ever produced in Portugal. They form part of a retable of 20 panels commissioned for the cathedral by Bishop Dom João de Madureira in 1506. (He was transferred from the Algarve in the – fulfilled – hope that he would mend his un-Christian ways, and his likeness is given to the central figure of the *Circumcision* panel.) The retable was dismantled while the cathedral was revamped in the 18th century; during the process 15 masterpieces were lost. The style of painting is Flemish, and Flanders has crept into the scenes in a more tangible form: the houses of the middle panel are clearly North European. The *Creation of the Animals* is quite unlike the other panels. It depicts God blessing his creatures, including a unicorn, and may belong to the School of Grão-Vasco, though the contract for the painting states that it is the master's own work.

The museum contains whole, richly gilt 17th-century chapels removed from the Chagas Convent; seeing them in isolation, it's easier to appreciate their artistic merits. Elsewhere, *azulejos* of the same date blossom with the exotica of Brazil. Finally, note the tomb of the Condessa de Barcelos, a big lady who died in the 13th century, and whose lasting memorial is decorated with scenes of pighunting.

Two Neighbourhoods

Castle
open from mid-
June–Sept 10–12 and
3–6, Oct–May Sun am
only; closed Mon

Lamego's unexceptional **castle** tops the hill to the north of town, reached via the Rua das Olarias behind the tourist office.

Surrounded by a huddle of stone houses, the fortification was heroically rescued in the 1970s by none other than the Boy Scouts, who removed 18 truckloads of trash from the place. They have now appropriated it, and are pleased to demonstrate knot-tying to anyone who might have come to look at the view of the town and hills.

It's much more interesting to wander round the **Bairro da Ponte**, a close-knit and archetypal Portuguese neighbourhood, on the southeastern edge of town, across the bridge on the way to Balsemão. There are some swimming places along the river. Here and in the neighbouring villages, look for *Fogos de Artifício* signs; the firework manufacturers add sparkle to the region's *festas* and *romarias*.

The Environs of Lamego

A good road runs northeast of Lamego, through variegated trees along the valley of the River Balsemão, which is white with rapids. After 3km the road peters out at the village of Balsemão.

Chapel of S. Pedro
open 10–12.30 and 2–6; closed Mon and Tues am, and the third weekend of each month

The **chapel of S. Pedro** is slightly set back from the road, up a steep bank. It's a jewel, behind a plain, reconstituted exterior, erected by the Suevi or Visigoths in the 7th century. A large proportion of the fascinating hotchpotch of later medieval additions was instigated by the 14th-century Bishop of Porto, Dom Afonso Pires, whose effigy is supported by two angels. Among the florid capitals and stonemasons' doodles is one of the *Termini Augustales*. In the 4th–5th centuries, these marked the corners of administrative units called *Civitates*, on which the episcopal dioceses were based. Balsemão makes an excellent walk, though most of the return is uphill.

Tourist Information and Services in Peso da Régua and Lamego

① Peso da Régua ›
Rua da Ferreirinha, t (254) 312 846

① Lamego ›
Avenida Visconde Guedes Teixeira, t (254) 612 005, douro.turismo @mail.telepac.pt; open weekdays 9.30–12.30 and 2–5.30, Sat 9.30–12.30, Sun 10–12.30 and 2–5

Peso da Régua: the tourist office can advise about visits to port wine lodges. The simplest one to reach is **Quinta de São Domingos, t** (254) 320 260 (open 9–7) where Quinta do Castelinho port is aged; turn left out of the railway station and it's a five-minute walk. For details of cruises on the river, contact **Douro Azul, t** (223) 402 500.

Lamego: the **bus station** is near the cathedral roundabout, from which the Avenida Visconde Guedes Teixeira

runs past the tourist office. The tourist office can arrange visits to **Sandeman's Quinta da Pacheca**, which is off the road between Régua and Lamego. Everything there is highly mechanized, and is really only of interest to specialists.

Festival in Lamego

Lamego gets its knees up and lets its hair down for the **Festas de N.S. dos Remédios**, a long-drawn-out affair lasting from the end of August to the middle of September, though the early days may feature nothing more spectacular than the mini-golf tournament. There are concerts of rock and classical music, displays of traditional costumes and dancing, a fair, an exhibition of painting, a night-time parade of local floats, and other events, all of which surround 8 September, the day of the religious procession. For this, coupled oxen pull heavy scenes from the life of the Virgin through the streets. Ordinarily, transport by oxen is considered undignified: these beasts participate only by papal dispensation. Kneeling penitents climb the steps to the pilgrimage church, no doubt grateful that they were not born in the 18th century, when sinners scourged themselves with leather thongs ending in balls of solid wax spiked with glass splinters.

(★) Pensão Solar da Sé >>

(★) Pensão Silva >>

Where to Stay in Lamego and Around

Peso da Régua

Hotel Régua Douro, Largo da Estação da CP, **t** (254) 320 700, *www.regua dourohotel.com* (€€). Together with views of the river, the Régua Douro offers all mod cons, complete with outdoor pool, Turkish baths and garage.

Residencial Columbano, Avenida Sacadura Cabral, **t** (254) 320 710 (€€). A couple of km out of town, with rooms overlooking the countryside. There is a pool and tennis courts.

Lamego

★★★★Albergaria do Cerrado, Lugar do Cerrado, **t** (254) 613 164 (€€). On the edge of town, on the road to Régua. Bright, fresh, and refined in its public parts, less characterful in the bedrooms. Cigar smoke reels around the bar. Only guests may dine; the food is OK. The private garage is locked at night.

Albergaria Solar dos Pachecos, Avenida Visconde Guedes Teixeira, **t** (254) 600 300 (€€). With a plum position on the central avenue, Lamego's upmarket option. The high-ceilinged rooms are nicely furnished and double glazed.

★★Hotel Parque, Parque N.S. dos Remédios, **t** (254) 609 140 (€€). At the top of Lamego's hill, next to the church. Apart from the church bells every 15 minutes and a woodpecker, it's a very peaceful place, overlooking trees and the hotel's own miniature garden. The staff are helpful and the building light, with decent bedrooms furnished with reproductions, and a too-large restaurant.

For the following three places, be warned that the cathedral bells chime every 15 minutes through the night.

★★★Residencial São Paulo, Avenida 5 de Outubro 22, **t** (254) 613 114 (€). Hygienic and favoured by Portuguese businessmen.

★★Pensão Solar da Sé, Largo da Sé, **t** (254) 612 060 (€). Across from the cathedral and good value: rooms, though small, may face the cathedral, the shower rooms are pleasant with very hot water, and the staff are cheerful. Leaving keys at the front desk might be risky, as it's often left unattended with the street door open.

★★Pensão Silva, Rua de Trás da Sé 26, **t** (254) 612 929 (€). Behind the cathedral and also good value. Once a private home, its bedrooms are impressively spacious and clean, with attractive wallpaper and Venetian blinds. The floorboards and screens to hide the sinks give the place an olde-worlde feel.

Residencial Solar Espirito Santo, Rua Alexandre Herculano, **t** (254) 655 060 (€). Backs onto the leafy main avenue; some rooms have balconies over-looking it and have been recently refurbished. Beware of the garage: the descent to it is too steep, and cars have been damaged.

Turismo de Habitação
Casa de Santo António de Britiande, Britiande, **t** (254) 699 346 (€€€ CA) Filled with valuable antiques, dating from the 12th to the 18th centuries. There is also a dazzling chapel containing panels of *azujelos* with an altar and ceiling in carved gilt. The rooms are airy and thoughtfully furnished.

**Casa dos
Varais >**

Casa dos Varais, Cambres, t (254) 313
251 (€€ CA). Burnt-pink, 18th-century
manor house magnificently situated
on a hillside with views over the River
Douro and vineyards. Worth staying
for the views alone.

Villa Hostilina, t (254) 612 394,
www.villahostilina.com (€€). A not-
very-rural member of the Rural
Tourism scheme, up a narrow road 20
yards beyond the Albergaria do
Cerrado. It's a 19th-century villa with
seven guest rooms, with big views
from the upper rooms and a
swimming pool. The house
incorporates a health club, Instituto
Kosmos.

Quinta do Terreiro, Lalim, t (254) 697
040/1, *www.geocities.com/
quintadoterreiro* (€€). In true feudal
style, 5km south of Lamego, this forms
one side of the village square, and
guests can watch the goings-on from
the terrace. And the feudal reso-
nances don't stop there: a servant
born in the *quinta* is entitled to land
on which to build a house, and one of
them is claiming his right. It's well
located for little wanders into the
hills, past ladies with hoes who stare
until you smile at them. The ten-
bedroomed guest wing is linked to
the main house by a glassed walkway;
in spite of the exposed stonework,
bedrooms are rather antiseptic, and
there's not much in the house that
could be called beautiful. Still, it's a
welcoming place and apparently well
run. There's a swimming pool, too.

Quinta da Timpeira, Penude, t (254)
612 811 or 614 126, *www.quinta
timpeira.com* (€€ CA). Three kilometres
south of Lamego, unusual for its
modernity – and hence its readiness
to admit daylight. It's a quiet place
surrounded by fruit trees, with good
views of the Serra de Meadas. Five
bedrooms are available, as well as a
swimming pool.

Quinta de Silvares, Lugar de Lapinha,
8km southeast of Armamar, t 934 262
584, *www.quintade silvares.com* (€€).
Quiet two-bedroom red-stone
farmhouse available to rent, with
views of fields and gentle hills. Make
sure you get good directions.

Casa da Santa Eufémia, Parada do
Bispo, t (254) 331 970, *www.qtast
eufemia.com* (€€). Converted granary
on a wine-producing and bottling
estate with three pleasant double
rooms available to guests. It's very
much a family affair.

Eating Out in Lamego and Around

Peso da Régua

Restaurant at the **Quinta de São
Domingos, t** (254) 320 100 (€€€).
Smart, and serves regional dishes.
Closed Mon.

O Malheiro, Rua dos Camilos 108,
t (254) 313 684 (€€). The food is good,
and the service friendly.

Muxima, Rua José Vasques Osório 30,
t (254) 313 344 (€€). Stone-walled,
offers *steak à Mirandesa. Closed Sun.*

Katekero, Largo 25 de Abril, t (254) 313
796 (€). Eat outdoors overlooking the
river at a plastic-chairs-and-paper-
tablecloth barbecue kind of place. If
you don't like the heat, go late – it's
open until 2am.

Cais de Baixo Bar, Av. João Franco,
t (254) 323 093. If you want to sit
outside and sip port in Peso da Régua,
directors' chairs await you here (*open
1pm–2am; closed Wed*).

Lamego

O Novo, Largo da Sé, t (254) 613 166
(€€). Can't miss it, located right in
front of the cathedral with a richly
tiled interior and a menu of
traditional reliably good dishes,
although you pay a premium for the
saintly position.

Trás da Sé, t (254) 614 075 (€€).
Opposite the side of the cathedral,
daubed with kids' paint and lined
with written plaudits from diners. The
food is memorable. *Closed Wed eve.*

Hong Fu, Rua da Santa Cruz, t (254) 615
638 (€). It's a source of some pride
among certain locals that Lamego has
a Chinese restaurant, and very
reasonable it is too.

O Lampião, Rua Direita 30, t (254) 612
550 (€). Chock-a-block at lunchtime –

no thanks to the dull décor. *Closed evenings and Sat.*

Churrasqueira Carvão, Rua Direita 50, t (254) 612 578 (€). The construction workers' favourite for barbecues. Think of those Diet Coke ads. *Closed Mon.*

O Combinado, Rua da Olaria 89, t (254) 612 902 (€). Up the street behind the tourist office. It's cosy, and the portions generous. *Closed Sun in winter.*

Porto and the Douro Litoral

Porto is such a magnet that the rest of the Douro Litoral seems to have been sapped of its energies. The province stretches along the coast from just south of Esposende to Espinho, and sweeps inland in a broad arc, beyond Amarante. The best way to see the Douro valley is by train from Porto. The railway joins the broad River Douro near Cinfães, some 50km inland, and follows a spectacular course. It's difficult to call the landscape 'beautiful', though many people do. Rather, it has a kind of brute force. Most Portuguese travellers take the scenery for granted, and pull down the window blinds to keep the sun out – try to pre-empt them by nabbing a window seat! The effect of this landscape is changeable: it can be heavy or light, depending on the sunshine – but it's impressive and memorable however you see it.

10

Don't miss

⭐ Contemporary art in Art Deco mansion
Fundação Serralves p.184

⭐ Overpowering giltwork
Church of São Francisco p.186

⭐ Riverfront restaurants
Ribeira **p.186**

⭐ Port wine lodges
Vila Nova de Gaia **p.188**

⭐ Stunning geometrics
Casa da Música **p.185**

See map overleaf

p.76

pp. 204–5

Don't miss

⭐ Fundação Serralves p.184

⭐ Church of São Francisco p.186

⭐ Riverfront restaurants, Ribeira **p.186**

⭐ Vila Nova de Gaia **p.188**

⭐ Casa da Música **p.185**

Porto

Cosmopolitan, polluted and higgledy-piggledy, Porto is Portugal's second city. It spreads itself and 265,000 souls over hill slopes descending to the granitic north bank of the River Douro; dull suburbs stretch to where the muddy river meets the Atlantic 5.5km away. Porto feels rooted in the late 19th century, in commerce and in granite-trimmed buildings – but in the past 10 years tastes have

Getting to Porto

Porto is a centre for communications in the north of Portugal; it's the obvious place to begin a fly/drive visit to explore that part of the country. The city is 67km from Aveiro, 53km from Braga, 254km from Bragança, 117km from Coimbra, 313km from Lisbon, 123km from Valença, and 70km from Viana do Castelo.

By Air

Francisco Sá Carneiro Airport is about 11km north. Bone-rattling buses 56 and 87 run from the airport to the Cordoaria, the square behind the Clérigos church. The journey takes 40 minutes to an hour in heavy traffic.

The **Aerobus** departs every 30 minutes from 7am–7pm from outside the Arrivals terminal, costing €4 (free for TAP passengers). It deposits passengers at well-known hotels and the Avenida dos Aliados.

By Rail

There are two **railway stations** in Porto. General train information can be obtained on **t** 808 208 208, *http://www.cp.pt*. Most trains creep across Eiffel's Dona Maria Pia Bridge to arrive at **Estação de Campanha**, **t** (22) 5519 1374, on the edge of the city. Change trains here for a 5-minute ride to the **Estação São Bento**, **t** (22) 2201 9517, at the heart of Porto (see p.185). Quick trains from Lisbon take about 3½hrs, via Coimbra (1½hrs); change at Entroncamento for Portalegre and Elvas, and from Castelo Branco, Covilhã and Guarda. Change at Lisbon (where you must cross the river by ferry to Barreiro) for the south of Portugal. Semi-frequent trains to Braga take 1½hrs (many require a change at Nine, 1¾hrs total), and to Guimarães 1¾hrs. There are three trains daily to Vila Real (change at Régua, 3¾hrs total), and two daily to Bragança (change at Tua – and Mirandela in the morning – 8½hrs minimum).

By Bus

Generally, buses to and from the north are based at **Praça Filipa de Lencastre**, opposite the Infante Sagres Hotel, just west of the Avenida dos Aliados. Most buses to and from the south are based at the **Garagem Atlântico** on Rua Alexandre Herculano, behind the Estação São Bento, from where all **RN** buses depart. There are also international buses to Spain and France. If you're leaving by bus, check your departure point with the tourist office. **Rede Expressos** buses run several times daily to Lisbon (3½hrs) via Coimbra (2hrs). Other routes include a frequent run to Leiria (3¼hrs) and infrequent services to Braga (40 mins) and Guarda (3hrs) via Viseu (2hrs). There are also eight or nine daily express departures for the Algarve.

become more sophisticated, with contemporary restaurants, bars and shops to match, and some exciting new architecture. Rarely more than three storeys high, Porto is a city of wrought-iron balconies and window shoppers, of newspapers in cafés, and of crazy drivers negotiating one-way streets.

The centre of town is the wide and pompous Avenida dos Aliados, at right angles to the river, sloping from the town hall and its clocktower down to the Praça da Liberdade. The straight streets to the east of the Avenida are dressed with boutiques and department stores, some of which have retained their early 20th-century fittings. The area to the west of the Avenida is more stately, as befits such weighty buildings as the law courts, the Hospital of Santo António, and the university. Small public gardens have sprung up here. From this core radiate the drab residential districts.

The guts of Porto lie south of the Praça da Liberdade, towards the river; this district has been declared a UNESCO World Heritage Site. Wide streets provide plenty of elbow room for the merchants' houses that line them. The downward slope briefly halts at the cathedral hillock, which sings to the tune of the speeding traffic

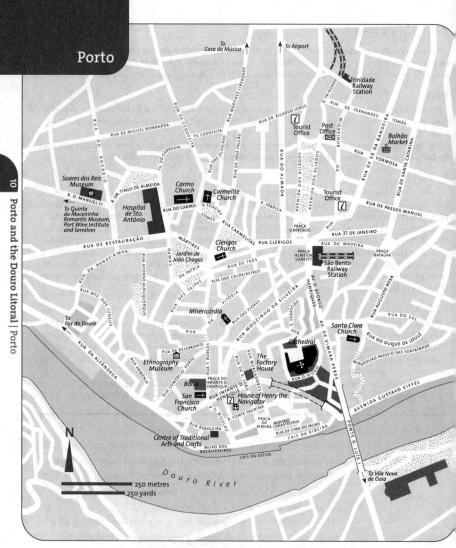

Porto

To Casa da Música
To Airport

Trinidade Railway Station

Tourist Office
Post Office

Bolhão Market

Soares dos Reis Museum

Carmo Church
Carmelite Church

Tourist Office

To Quinta da Maceirinha Romantic Museum, Port Wine Institute and Serralves

Hospital de Sto. António

Clérigos Church

São Bento Railway Station

Jardim de João Chagas

Misericórdia

Santa Clara Church

To Foz do Douro

Ethnography Museum

Cathedral

The Factory House

Bolsa

San Francisco Church

House of Henry the Navigator

Centre of Traditional Arts and Crafts

To Vila Nova de Gaia

N

250 metres
250 yards

Douro River

to-ing and fro-ing across the Douro on the upper level of the Ponte de Dom Luís. Clustered around the episcopal skirts, both roads and buildings narrow and darken. Among rickety homes kids chuck footballs at laundry aflap on lines, and slide down the steep streets in cardboard boxes. They arrive at the Ribeira, the area around the riverfront, where customs houses face the giant neon signs of the port wine lodges across the river. On summer evenings, a mass of restaurants and bars walled with honey-coloured stone spill out on to the streets around the cobbled Praça de Ribeira.

The Portuguese call the city Porto, prefaced by the definite article 'o', meaning 'the port'. The definite article has been incorporated in the anglicized version of the city's name, to give Porto.

History

The Romans' route from Lisbon to Braga crossed the River Douro near its mouth, at the Lusitanian settlement of Cale. As the ferry plied its way back and forth, it spawned the village of Portus on the opposite bank. The two were known as Portus-Cale. Briefly occupied by the Suevi and the Moors, Portus-Cale had a jerky start to life. Abandoned in the middle of the 8th century, resurrected by Vimara Peres in the late 9th century, it had its pride further jilted when Count Henry of Burgundy moved the capital of his feudal holding from Portucale to Braga. However, he took the name of the town for the province under his command, which, under his son Afonso Henriques, became the independent country of Portugal.

In 1111, Count Henry's widow, Dona Teresa, equipped the town with a cathedral. By 1208, the bishops of Porto had begun their struggle for jurisdictional control of their see: when Bishop Martinho refused to accord Dom Afonso II proper honours, the residents were scandalized, and forced the bishop to remain holed up in his palace for five months. The dispute with the Crown focused on the right to collect tolls and disembark merchandise. The Crown tried to safeguard its interests by establishing a royal borough, Gaia, on the riverbank opposite Porto, but the wrangling continued until 1253. Then, it was agreed that one-third of the ships sailing down the Douro and half those from abroad should unload at Gaia (which was formally christened Vila Nova de Gaia two years later). Suspicion of outside authority could not be waived, and manifested itself in the 14th century, when the burghers of Porto were privileged to forbid any nobleman to reside within the city walls. Though the privilege was repealed in the 16th century, subsequent *palácios* steered clear of the ancient city limits.

Dom João I and Philippa of Lancaster

The residents certainly knew how to make a new queen, and an English one at that, feel welcome. On Valentine's Day 1387, Porto hosted Dom João I's marriage to Philippa of Lancaster, a political match to seal the alliance between Portugal and Philippa's father, John of Gaunt, who had a claim to the throne of Castile.

The streets were strewn with herbs as the king and his bride rode forth, on horses blanketed with gold. The procession was announced by pipes and trumpets, and followed by singing noblewomen. After the ceremony in the cathedral, the couple feasted at the palace; the napkin- and cup-bearers were knights. Fernão Lopes (*c.* 1380 to after 1459) reports that 'When [the entertainments] were over everyone began to dance while the ladies stood around in a group, singing joyfully. Meanwhile the king went to his chamber: and after supper, in the evening, the archbishop [of Braga] and other prelates with many burning

Getting around Porto

Most of the points of interest in Porto are within **walking** distance if you don't mind the hills, so bring a pair of sneakers.

By Bus

The local bus network, **STCP**, has an office at Praça Almeida Garrett opposite the São Bento station, t (800) 200 166, *www.stcp.pt*. Based in the tourist office at Rua Clube Fenianos 25, t (800) 220 905, *www.porto turismo.pt*, the **Loj de Mobilidad** is an office dedicated to city transport. Both provide useful maps and timetables for day and night buses. Without these the local bus system is difficult to fathom because routes are not marked at bus stops. The most economical way of buying tickets is in advance from STCP, newsagents and kiosks and as a book of ten tickets (*caderneta*).

There are three categories (*módulos*) of fare, for short, medium and long journeys: the driver will indicate which is which. The central point for all local buses is the **Praça da Liberdade**. A trip on a bus costs €1.30, a one-day bus pass costs €3. A three-day pass valid for bus, tram and the **Aerobus** to the airport costs €6. **Passe Porto** for one or two days offers free transport and a variety of museum and discounts. These may be bought from tourist offices and various hotels (*www.portoturismo.pt*).

By Taxi

There are plenty of **taxis**, and they're inexpensive – the problem is getting one to stop, and to put the meter on. Drivers in Porto are in a hurry and take little notice of one another or of pedestrians; the result is hair-raising. There are taxi ranks outside the **Telephonaria** in the **Praça da Liberdade**, at the bottom of the **Avenida dos Aliados** and in some squares. Taxis add a fixed sum for crossing the Dom Luís I Bridge to Vila Nova de Gaia. If you think a taxi driver is ripping you off, call his bluff by asking for a receipt (*recibo*) with the taxi's number on it.

By Car

It's hard to find **parking** spaces in the city centre, and the one-way system is baffling. The easiest solution is to use a taxi, but there are numerous places to **hire cars** in Porto:

Auto Jardim, t (800) 200 613. Good-value rentals.

AVIS, at Ferro Campanhã railway station, t (800) 201 002, in town at Rua Guedes de Azevedo, 124, or at the airport.

Budget/AA Castanheira, t (808) 252 627. Unlimited mileage.

Europcar, Rua de Santa Catarina, 1158, t (22) 205 7737.

Hertz, Rua de Santa Catarina , 899, t (22) 205 2393 or (800) 238 238.

For car repairs and maps, contact the **Automovel Clube de Portugal**, t (219) 429 103, *www.acp.pt*.

By Metro and Tram

Five metro lines operate between 6am and 1.30am. **Line A (blue)** runs from Sr de Matosinhos to Trindade, **red line** runs from Póvoa de Varzim to Antas, **green line** runs from Trofa to Antas, **yellow line** runs from S João to Santo Ovidio. The most recent **purple line** runs from the Estádio do Dragão to the airport. The electronic **Andante** ticket covers all transport systems and can be bought from TIP vending machines in stations, TIP stores and kiosks and STCP outlets. Metro tickets can be bought for single or multiple trips covering the nine zones of the metro system, t (808) 200 444, *www.metro-porto.pt*. Dependent on the zones travelled through, a single trip costs €1.30–2.30, and 10 tickets cost €8–17.10.

The **tram** network is reduced to two routes: 1E to Foz from the Rua Nova de Alfandega, and 18 from the Praça Gomes Teixeira. A trip on a tram costs €0.50.

Boat Trips

If you'd like a fish's eye view of Porto, there's a wide choice of river cruises, lasting from 50 minutes to several days. They run throughout the year, with a reduced service in winter. If you've got time, a day trip to Régua is fun. Schedules are available from the tourist offices (*see* boat tours at *www.portoturismo.pt*). Via D'Ouro, t (22) 208 1935, *www.viadouro-cruzeiras.com*, uses renovated *barcos*. Others provide lunch or dinner; try *www.rotadodouro.pt*, *www.douroacima.pt*, Endouro, t (22) 208 4161. You can rent small boats, launches and fishing boats from Rentdouro, t (22) 476 9063. Guided expeditions in small boats are offered by Rotas de Agua, *www.rotasdeagua.com*.

Bus Trips

Bus tours with commentaries (hop on, hop off) are run by **Diana Tours**, Rua Delfim Lima 355, **t** (22) 716 0626 and (800) 203 983, *www.dianatours.pt*. Alternatively you can travel by a London cab for day or half-day tours through **RentaCab**, **t** (22) 200 1530, *www.rentacab.pt*. Both include a visit to a port lodge.

torches, blessed his bed... Then the king remained with his wife, and the others all went to their lodgings.' The bedding ceremony took place, incidentally, without papal dispensation for Dom João to break the oath of chastity he swore when he became Master of the Order of Aviz. Less than a week after the wedding, the king was at the head of an army, bound for Castile.

Henry the Navigator

The bedding ceremony was not held in vain. The couple's third son, Henry the Navigator, was born in Porto. It was on the Douro that he learnt his love of ships, a love that led him to found a School of Navigation at Sagres, and to devote his life to encouraging and financing Portugal's groping exploration down the west coast of Africa. At the age of 19 he commanded 20 war galleys to be built in Porto as part of the much larger fleet which set out to capture the North African trading post of Ceuta from the Moors in 1415. Azurara, a member of Henry's household, writes proudly that 'Men marvelled to behold' the galleys as they set out adorned with great standards and little flags, with tilts and canopies of rich stuffs, in the white, black and blue of the Infante, and bearing his device of garlands of holm oak overlaid with silver, surrounding the words 'Power to do well'.

The Inquisition made little headway in Porto: only one *auto-da-fé* took place, and that was in 1543.

Wellesley

In 1808, while Junot occupied Lisbon and the royal family had fled to Brazil from the first of three French invasions of Portugal, Porto arrested its French governor, and set up a provisional junta under the presidency of the bishop. By the end of June, central Portugal had freed itself of the invaders. Napoleon planned reconquest, and in 1809 Soult captured Porto. Within two months Sir Arthur Wellesley, later Duke of Wellington, marched north from Coimbra and relieved Porto in a brilliant surprise attack: the British had no boats, but found a barber who had rowed across the Douro during the night; they used his boat to locate three large barges, in which part of the army could cross the river. Battle ensued, and a flock of white hankies waving from windows in the lower part of town signalled the French retreat.

Dom Pedro

In the 1820s, Porto became a hotbed of revolt, attempting to force the Braganças to return from Brazil, and to remove Beresford from command of the Portuguese army. In 1820 Porto's revolt spread throughout the north of Portugal: the city's Military Council hoped to 'call upon a Cortes to organize a Constitution, the want of which is the origin of all our evils!' In 1828 Porto declared its loyalty to the constitutionalist Dom Pedro and his daughter Maria da Gloria; their absolutist brother and uncle respectively, Dom Miguel, had usurped the throne.

In 1831 the idealistic, epileptic Dom Pedro sailed from Brazil to the Azores, and in the following year made his way from there to Porto with 7,500 men. They entered the city in spite of Dom Miguel's garrison of 13,000, who retired only to besiege the newcomers. Cholera broke out and, we are told, 'for most people a slice of dog or cat was a great treat': troops kidnapped their officers' pets. In 1833 Dom Miguel's fleet was captured off Cape St Vincent. As his troops retreated from Porto, the river ran red – not with blood but with 27,000 pipes of port (each with a capacity of 522 litres) belonging to the Old Wine Company blown up at Vila Nova de Gaia.

Porto continued to support the liberal cause throughout the 19th century, electing the country's first Republican deputy in 1864.

The British in Porto

Fee, fie, fo, fum: the British have long been intimately entangled with Porto's economy and the history of port wine; equally, they have remained foreign.

The first British to come to Porto in large numbers were crusader-pirates en route for the Holy Land – 'plunderers, drunkards and rapists, men not seasoned with the honey of piety', according to Osbern. In 1147 they docked at Porto, where the bishop dosed them with wine and urged them not to be 'seduced by the desire to press on with your journey, for the praiseworthy thing is not to have been to Jerusalem, but to have lived a good life while on the way'. Thus he requested their assistance capturing Lisbon from the Moors – and promised them as much money as the royal treasury could afford. The brawlers were persuaded, and set sail for Lisbon, toting the bishop and his colleague João Peculiar, Archbishop of Braga, as security for their rewards.

British merchants took root in Porto in the 13th century, after the Christian conquest of Seville opened the route to the Mediterranean. They traded woollen cloth, cotton, corn and Newfoundland cod for oil, fruit and cash – Viana do Castelo was the base for the export of red portugal, the wine of the Minho. In 1353 the merchants of Lisbon and Porto made their own commercial treaty with Edward III. But it was the Commonwealth Treaty of 1654 which really sharpened the British commercial edge, codifying the Britons' right to appoint their own judge and to hold Protestant services in their houses, and setting a ceiling of 23 per cent on customs dues.

The viniculture in the Douro Litoral took off in the second half of the 17th century, when Colbert, Louis XIV's minister, forbade the import of English cloth into France; Charles II was suitably miffed, and imposed similar sanctions on the import of French wines into England. With bulging eyes, the British merchants in Portugal saw an opportunity, and bought up any wine they could – which was not enough, so they encouraged the cultivation of vineyards along the River Douro. Consequently the wine shippers – including the founders of Taylor Fladgate and Yeatman, Croft's and Warre's – gathered their quill pens and their fighting cocks and emigrated south from Viana to the port at the mouth of the Douro. Each year after the vintage the shippers travelled from Porto to Régua, an uncomfortable three-day journey which required 'sleeping on ye tables for reason of ye insects'. At Régua they tasted the growers' samples, and bought their wines.

Methuen and After

In 1703 the Methuen Treaty lowered the duty on Portuguese wines imported to Britain to a third less than that on French wines, to the despair of claret drinkers. Swift wrote:

> Be sometimes to your country true,
> Have once the public good in view.
> Bravely despise Champagne at Court,
> And choose to dine at home with Port.

While Britain was thirsty for Portuguese wine, Thomas Woodmass reported being told in Porto that 'there is much bad feeling against [the British], inasmuch as the principal trade of the country is in our hands, but that the treaties of commerce are in our favour'.

The British shippers pushed their luck. In 1727 they formed an association to regulate and improve their trade, and to keep down prices paid to the growers. Their high-handed behaviour was repellent to Pombal, who set about squashing them. In 1755, with barely time to straighten his wig after rebuilding an earthquake-torn Lisbon, Pombal decreed that the entire port-wine trade was to be controlled by a state monopoly company, from which all wine for export must be bought, at prices fixed by its officials.

The most permanent effect of the Alto Douro Wine Company was the delimitation of the Douro as the only area from which port wine could be exported. The British shippers uncorked their

Port

The nice thing about drinking port in Portugal is that you can leave behind its crustier connotations, whiskers and all. Good port is like a liquid symphony playing upon the palate: anyone who thinks of it as a dark and sticky drink to send you to sleep after Christmas lunch is in for a surprise.

Port is distinguished from other wines for two reasons: because the fermentation process is stopped with brandy; and because the climatic and soil conditions in which the vines grow are unique. Fermentation begins as soon as the grapes are pressed: the yeast on the grape skins acts on the natural grape sugar and transforms it into alcohol; the grape skins also provide colouring matter. After about two days, the grape juice or 'must' is run off into vats where pure grape brandy is added in the ratio of 80 per cent 'must' to 20 per cent brandy. This halts the fermentation process, leaving approximately half the natural grape sugar in the wine.

Port wine is born in the world's oldest **Demarcated Region**, established by Pombal, which runs along the River Douro from Barqueiros to the border with Spain at Barca d'Alva; its uneven edge covers the area north of the river as far as Vila Real and Murça, and south almost to Pinhel. The soil is a powdery, yellow schist, which retains such rainfall as there is, and the slabs of schist retain the heat of the daytime. The climate is extreme – they call it nine months of winter and three months of hell, sinking to 12°F (–11°C) and rising to an infernal 110°F (43°C) respectively.

The crop is harvested in the hard, merry weeks between 15 September and 15 October: the timing is crucial and depends on the weather, which is assessed by the farmers and the shippers who buy their grapes. Mountain villagers descend for the harvest, arriving at the *quintas* en masse to work from 7.30 in the morning to 7 at night. They earn relatively good money, and when they rest they drink wine. The women cut the grapes and sing, the men transport the basketfuls, bearing over 110lb (50kg) of fruit on their backs, steadied by a thong around the forehead.

Until 20 years ago, the men spent their evenings treading grapes in concrete troughs, arms interlinked, purple to their thighs – a custom quite familiar to the Romans. The advantage of this method is that the grape is crushed but not the pip, which releases unwanted tannin, but the problem with doing it by foot is that temperatures in the treading rooms get very high, inducing fermentation and hence volatile acidity. The alternative is the mechanized process called autovinification, by which grapes are crushed and fermented at a controlled temperature; now, 90 per cent of port is produced in this way. Advocates of mechanization say it makes no difference to the taste of the final product.

The finer wines are stored in the *quintas* scattered over the Douro valley, while lesser wines are kept at the equally scattered *adegas* in white concrete balloons called mummers. The cold temperatures of the winter cause the wine to clear and loose the slight cloudiness that follows fermentation. In March of the following year the wine is ready for transportation to the shippers' 'lodges', or warehouses, at Vila Nova de Gaia, opposite Porto at the mouth of the River Douro. Until 1987 port wasn't port unless it had matured at Gaia. It had to be matured there because that's where it had always matured, prior to being shipped abroad by British merchants, or transported within Portugal. Partly because of congestion in Gaia, port can now mature elsewhere, at the wineries in the Douro Litoral.

The wine that does make the journey is transported by road tankers. Previously, it was sent by railway, and before the damming of the Douro, by flat-bottomed, square-sailed *barcos rabelos*, piled with up to 60 pipes (a pipe is 522 litres). The only *barcos rabelos* still afloat are advertising devices moored at Vila Nova de Gaia.

The port wine lodges in Vila Nova de Gaia provide tours of their premises, with free tastings afterwards (*see* p.190). The Solar do Vinho in Porto and Lisbon, run by the Port Wine Institutes, sell a wide variety of port wines by the glass. The tourist office at Lamego (*see* p.167) can arrange visits to Sandeman's Quinta da Pacheca.

complaints, but continued to prosper once the laws relaxed. Pombal himself used Company certificates of quality to fob off wine produced on his estates outside Lisbon as port wine.

Exports to England doubled in the last two decades of the 18th century, and the sun shone on British merchants, who played whist and had little contact with the Portuguese. Wellington's officers were made honorary members of the port wine shippers' Factory. With the advent of constitutionalism during the remainder of the 19th century, the British became less insular, though they bathed at their own beach, now polluted, at Foz.

The most controversial of the British was J.J. Forrester, who arrived in Porto in 1831. He produced very detailed maps of the Douro and the vine district, and a monograph on *Oidium Tuckeri*, a disease which attacked the vines. For his services to wine the cartographer was made Barão de Forrester by the King of Portugal.

In 1844 Forrester changed tack, publishing *A Word or Two on Port Wine*: in it he accused shippers of encouraging farmers to adulterate the wine with sweeteners. He argued against the newly implemented practice of adding brandy to stop fermentation. Brandy is crucial to port as we know it: without it, port would have become a thin and bitter liquid. But Forrester is regarded as a hero for singlehandedly tackling the port wine establishments of Porto and London. He died in 1862 when his boat capsized on the Douro; the gold sovereigns in his money belt sunk him. Flags in Porto flew at half-mast.

Port sales boomed until the early decades of the 20th century, but did not recover after the Second World War. The market for port-and-lemon was as dry as summer in the Douro valley. With the exception of Sandeman's, the shippers considered 'advertising' a dirty word, and ignored its possibilities; port lost out to sherry, which was marketed as an apéritif to rival the American cocktail. Today port wine is Porto's fourth or fifth industry, and there are only about 900 British registered as resident north of Coimbra; but in Porto they remain disproportionately influential. They still play cricket, and some live within herbaceous borders – but if you want an enthusiastic account of the city and its river, there are few more willing sources.

East

Bolhão Market
open weekdays 7–5,
Sat 7–1

Surrounded by Porto's shopping district, to the east of the Avenida dos Aliados, the **Bolhão Market** is an attractive two-tiered semi-covered market. It's a good place to prepare for a picnic, but no longer the vital, screechingly competitive place it once was. The bakers sell marvellous bread as heavy as bread can be, cut into chunks with meat cleavers.

West

The Rua dos Clérigos leads uphill from the Praça da Liberdade to the elaborate granite façade of the **Clérigos Church**. Its garlands, festoons and spiral scrolls can be seen most clearly in the early morning sunlight. The architect, Nasoni (1691–1773), used these motifs in the frescoes he painted at the beginning of his career and later translated them into stone. Constructed between 1732 and 1749, its style draws heavily on the Italian Baroque of the previous century: Nasoni introduced the Baroque to the north of Portugal. His style suits Porto, and is very different from the contemporary Pombaline style in Lisbon. The church's audacious **granite tower** is a landmark, at 250ft (75m) still one of the highest in the country. A staircase spirals up to the top, which is a good place for getting oriented with Porto. Listen out for the carillon at noon and 6pm.

Clérigos Church
open Apr–Oct 9.30–1 and 2–7; Nov–Mar Mon–Sat 9–12 and 3.30–7.30, Sun 10–1 and 8.30–10.30

Granite tower
open Apr–Oct 9.30–1 and 2–7 (Aug 10–7); Nov–Mar 10–12 and 2–5; adm

Uphill, old men play chess in the palmy Praça Teixeira Gomes, fronted on one side by the enormous rectangular university. On the corner roughly opposite this stands the Carmo Church, a representative example of the Portuguese Baroque, built by Nasoni's disciple, José de Figueiredo Seixas, in the mid-18th century. The enormous *azulejo* panel was added in 1912. The Carmelite Church, next door, was completed in 1628 and subsequently turned into a barracks.

The Soares dos Reis Museum

Follow the Rua do Carmo around the side of the huge Hospital de Santo António into the Rua de D. Manuel II, where stands the **Soares dos Reis Museum**, which includes collections of 19th- and early 20th-century Portuguese painting and sculpture. It occupies the neoclassical Palace of the Carrancas, which was dogged by its own magnificence. Built in 1795, it housed the Jewish family of Moraes e Castro, whose nickname, Carranca, means 'frown' or 'gargoyle'. They were granted the monopoly of gold and silver thread for the north of Portugal, and thrived on church vestments and military uniforms. The wings of the palace were their workshops. Marshal Soult lived here for 44 days of the Peninsular War, in 1809. Sir Arthur Wellesley chased him out and then, with due aplomb, ate the dinner that had been prepared for the French.

Soares dos Reis Museum
Rua de D. Manuel II, t (22) 339 3770, www.ipmuseus.pt; open Tues 2–6, Wed–Sun 10–6; adm

The Carrancas' monopoly lapsed with the liberalization of industry and in 1861 they sold it to Dom Pedro V. He flattened the small farm at the rear of the palace and built a tennis court surrounded by a stadium for bicycle racing.

The last King of Portugal, Dom Manuel II, willed the palace to the charitable hospital of the Misericórdia. Salazar considered the hospital unworthy of such a distinguished setting and shooed it away with a token payment. The museum was installed in 1940, destroying most of the first floor's frescoes in the process.

The Collection

The museum takes its name from the sculptor **Soares dos Reis** (1847–89), and houses his collected works in marble. These feature *O Desterrado* (the exile), which was completed in a few, feverish months before Soares dos Reis left Rome at the age of 24, when the Portuguese government cut his study allowance. The collection also includes a mother and child of such humanity that a church rejected them.

Among the paintings are the refreshing works of Henrique Pousão, Silva Porto (1850–93) – one of the first naturalists to work outside the atelier and fiery paintings by Marquês de Oliveira. Other artists include Columbano and Sousa Pinto.

The dinner service made for the Bishop of Porto is outstanding among the china and ceramics. Much of the glass is Bohemian; the rarest local work is from Vista Alegre, before it became a porcelain factory.

Every museum claims its Indo-Portuguese chest is rare. This museum's chest is distinguished by its legs, which are mermaids with brass nipples.

Towards Foz

Follow the edge of the gardens of the Palácio de Cristal, named after a 19th-century building now replaced by a domed sports pavilion. Bear left down a cobbled lane to the **Quinta da Macieirinha Romantic Museum**. It's decorated and furnished in a style approved by the ghost of Carlos Alberto, abdicated King of Sardinia, who was briefly resident here in 1849. The museum provides an English guide.

Quinta da Macieirinha Romantic Museum
Rua de Entre Quintas 220, t (22) 605 7033; open Tues–Sat 10–12 and 2–5, Sun 2–5; closed Mon and hols; adm

The dressing room is a temple to facial hair, hung with portraits of the ex-king's bewhiskered relations. Carlos Alberto himself had ivory moustache and eyebrow brushes, a lice comb, and brilliantine for errant locks. He kept some clothes in the corridor outside, with a different drawer for each day of the week, opened in rotation, as his garments were rarely washed. Clearly he was a methodical man: his pocket watch too has seven faces, one for each day of the week. Concerts are still held in the ballroom, which was lit by gas chandeliers.

Solar do Vinho do Porto
t (22) 609 4749, www.ivp.pt; open Mon–Sat 2pm–midnight

The lower ground floor of the Quinta is the **Solar do Vinho do Porto**, a convivial, air-conditioned place to sample many and varied ports. Unlike its snooty sister in Lisbon, the atmosphere here is relaxed and friendly – and the wine is at home. Vintage ports are not available by the glass, because each bottle ought to be consumed on the day it is opened.

What to Eat

When Henry the Navigator was preparing his fleet for Ceuta, he requested the Portuenses to donate food to fuel the expedition. Tradition has it that the inhabitants of Porto were so generous that they kept only tripe for themselves – thus they are called *tripeiros*. It's more likely, though, that the name has its origins in the siege of the city in 1832–3. The Portuenses love tripe, and drape it in extravagant folds from meat hooks; most commonly, it's off-white and looks like a honeycombed sheet of rubber. Tripe is cooked in a rich stew, *tripas à moda do Porto*, which includes calves' trotters, sausage, butter beans, chicken, onions, carrots and cumin.

An Porto *bacalhau* (salt-cod) merchant is credited with inventing the dish named after him, *bacalhau à Gomes de Sá*. For foreigners, this is one of the most delicious forms the fish can take – as it's heavily disguised. The *bacalhau* is soaked in water, and then in milk for a couple of hours. Next, it's lightly mashed with fried onions, boiled potatoes and eggs, and garlic. Oil is added, and the mixture is baked, briefly.

Fundação Serralves

Bus no.78 takes about half an hour to get here from the centre of town. Alternatively catch it outside the Palácio de Cristal, or take buses nos.3, 19, 21 or 35. The Fundação Serralves is a wonderful institution incorporating a museum of contemporary art, large formal and informal gardens and a fabulous Art Deco mansion in the western part of the city. If gardens or contemporary art are of the slightest interest to you, it should be on your itinerary. Like the Parque das Nações in Lisbon, it's having a significant impact on the way Portuguese people think about their country. They come in droves: overall, 40 per cent of visitors are school children.

The Foundation was established in 1989, to 'stimulate the public's interest in contemporary art and the environment', through an ambitious and multi-disciplinary programme of events, using its various spaces, including an auditorium. Funding comes from 120 patrons, of which the government is one. Do consider becoming a Friend of the Foundation – it's a good way to support its aims, and beats taking home a hideous pottery cockerel.

★ **Fundação Serralves**
Rua D. João de Castro 210, t (22) 615 6500 or 808 200 543, www.serralves.pt; open Oct–Mar Tues–Sun 10–7, Thurs 10am–10pm; Apr–Sept Tues–Fri 10–7, Thurs 10am–10pm, Sat, Sun and hols 10–2; adm

The Museum

Designed by Álvaro Siza Vieira, the museum is a stunningly simple and flexible building that makes the most of natural light, clean lines and its setting. Each year it is used for three or four temporary exhibitions of works by artists from Portugal and abroad. In 2003 it hosted the country's first major exhibition of works by Francis Bacon. The museum's permanent collection includes works from the late 1960s to the present, some of them pretty weird. Check for details of temporary exhibitions.

The House

Casa Serralves was completed in 1940 as a residence for the second Conde de Vizela. Architecturally it's exceptionally interesting in its own right, and is used as an extension of the museum.

The Park

Using a 19th-century arboretum as its core, the gardens were designed by Jacques Gréber in the modernist style. Now maintained by nine gardeners, the design plays with light and shadow, and offers plenty of varied environments for wandering. Picnics are not allowed. Check out the Saturday evening jazz concerts in summer.

Foz do Douro

At the extreme west of Porto is the residential quarter of Foz, bordering the Atlantic. (Take bus no.1 from below the Igreja de S. Francisco.) The British had their bathing houses here; the 17th-century Castelo de Queijo (Fort of Cheese) takes its name from the rock on which it stands. It's more relaxed than central Porto, with a sand beach interspersed with rock pools. There are lots of places to eat fish and chips along the beachfront; inland Foz becomes rather upmarket, a place of boutiques.

North

Casa de Música
Avenida da Boavista
604, t (22) 012 0220,
www.casadamusica.com

Casa de Música, the city's latest combination of fabulous architecture and cutting-edge entertainment, opened in 2005 in a stunning geometric building. For a modest sum you can take a guided tour of the building (designed by Rem Koolhaas) or check out the website for the regular concerts of *fado*, classical music and jazz.

Towards the River

Estação de São Bento, the main railway station, is a good place from which to begin a visit to the lower and more historic part of Porto, a UNESCO world heritage site. Twenty thousand inky tiles depict scenes from Portugal's history, rendered in 1905–15.

Leading down from the Estação de São Bento, the Rua das Flores is lined with a jumble of 'typical' merchants' houses and their diverse wrought-iron balconies. At number 15, the Misericórdia offices contain a *Fons Vitae* painting, one of the finest Renaissance works in Portugal. The donor, Dom Manuel I, his third wife Dona Leonor and their eight children are arranged around a basin which collects the blood of the crucified Christ. One of the rear figures may be Dona Leonor, widow of Dom João II, sister of Dom Manuel, and founder of Portugal's charitable hospitals, the Misericórdias.

Misericórdia
t (22) 207 4710;
open weekdays 9–12.30
and 2–5.30; adm

The painter is unknown; scholars are even unable to agree on his or her nationality.

The Praça do Infante Dom Henrique

Doubling back into the Largo, the Rua Ferreira Borges falls steeply past the Bolsa, and, next to it, the church of São Francisco. The **Bolsa (Stock Exchange)** was built in the 1830s, incorporating a gross but very expensive pseudo-Moorish ballroom. The audience chamber contains a beautifully inlaid table.

Bolsa
t (22) 339 9000,
www.palaciodabolsa.pt;
open April–Oct 9–7,
Nov–Mar 9–1 and 2–6

⭐ **Church of São Francisco**
open 9–6

Immediately downhill, the fantastic and dazzling interior of the **church of São Francisco** is the country's most overpowering example of giltwork: the walls and ceiling are bathed in a relentless shower of golden foliage – acanthus, grapevine, and laurel – amid which crouch an assortment of golden cherubs. This is how the wealth of Brazil was spent. It is not the work of Midas, but of Miguel Francisco da Silva (active 1726 until after 1746), who showed little patience for the Gothic church restructured in the early decades of the 15th century: the rose window is one of the few interior indications of an earlier age. There is an early 18th-century tree of Jesse, with roots like seaweed, supporting 12 kings of Judah; a grim rendition of the decapitation of the martyrs of Morocco; and a good mid-16th-century painting of the baptism of Christ. Note the negro monk to the left of the chancel arch.

The Ribeira

Centre of Traditional Arts and Crafts (CRAT)
Rua da Reboleira 37,
t (22) 332 0201;
open Tues–Fri 10–12 and
1–6, weekends 1–7;
closed Mon and hols

 Ribeira

Across the road and slightly upstream of the church, the steep Rua da Alfândega runs from the Praça do Infante Dom Henrique towards the river. Henry the Navigator is supposed to have been born here in 1394. Downhill and off to the right, the **Centre of Traditional Arts and Crafts (CRAT)** showcases various crafts. It's worth dropping in, but you'll be hard pressed to find anything worth buying. Wooden toys are probably your best bet. The streets along the river here comprise the **Ribeira**, the most atmospheric district of Porto.

The Factory House

The Rua de S. João leads uphill from the Praça da Ribeira. Where it crosses with the Rua Infante Dom Henrique, previously known as the Rua Dos Ingleses, stands the inconspicuous headquarters of the British Association (of port wine shippers). **The Factory House** (Feitoria Inglesa) takes its name from the factors who belong to it. The building is closed to the public, but it's worth a visit if you can manage to contact a member. The British Consul John Whitehead designed the building like a Robert Adam town house in London; it was built 1786–90, with sash windows 'in the English taste'.

The entrance hall was used as a parking place for sedan chairs; the side benches were for bearers. (In the mid-18th century, English ships trading with the American colonies often docked at Porto and bartered a slave for a pipe of port. The English community liked slaves who spoke their language.) Upstairs the rooms are elegant, light and sober; a board on the balcony of the ballroom dictates 'Polka' or 'Mélange'. Outside the ballroom is a portrait of Lieutenant General Sir William Warre. Thereby hangs a tail: born in 1784, he was dismissed from the family firm for fastening the pigtail of one of the Portuguese staff to his desk with sealing wax, as he slept after lunch.

Diners enjoy their port unsullied by the odours of their meal. Keeping the same seating plan, they retire to the pudding room, where smoking is not permitted before 2pm. A multitude of jelly moulds clutters the kitchen: a memo of 1819 states that white port was used for culinary purposes, including wine jelly!

Sé Cathedral

At the top of the Rua de São João, turn right, go up through the narrow, chaotic streets to the imposing hilltop site dominating Porto's riverside. On it stands the **Sé Cathedral**. The Romanesque fortress church was founded by Dona Teresa, mother of Dom Afonso Henriques. Dom João I and Philippa of Lancaster were married here in 1387 but they would not recognize it now, as much of the 12th-century structure was 'done over' in the 18th century.

In the north transept, soft light illuminates a magnificent silver retable, created in two stages between 1632 and 1678. Manuel Teixeira and his son-in-law Manuel Guedes made a dozen reliefs depicting figures designed in the flat, elongated Mannerist style, trumpeted by silver cherubs. The second part was the altar front, commissioned of Pedro Francisco 'the Frenchman', who agreed to make it of 'low relief worked with flowers and in the foreign way', which is probably a reference to the swathes of acanthus foliage. In 1809 an ingenious sacristan protected the retable from Soult's troops by hiding it behind a wall of plaster.

Construction of the sober Gothic cloister began in 1385, the year of the battle of Aljubarrota; it now displays paintings on wood, tiles and vestments. From the cloister, a good staircase by Nasoni leads to an upper storey. There, the fine grain of the granite and the clean lines of the battlements give the place the feeling of a giant sandcastle. Rich 18th-century *azulejos* of the life of the Virgin and Ovid's *Metamorphoses* decorate the upper tier. Nasoni designed the porch on the city side of the cathedral, and, most successfully, the prominent Bishop's Palace abutting the cathedral.

Behind the cathedral, at Rua Dom Hugo 32, the **Guerra Junqueiro Museum** contains the poet's art collection, furniture and ceramics.

Sé Cathedral
t (22) 205 9028;
open Mon–Sat
8.45–12.30 and 2.30–7,
Nov–Mar closes at 6;
cloister open all year
Mon–Sat 9–12.30 and
April–Oct 2.30–6,
Nov–Mar 2.30–5.15,
closed Sun morning;
adm

Guerra Junqueiro Museum
t (22) 205 3644;
open Tues–Sat 10–12
and 2–5.30, Sun 2–5;
closed Mon and hols

From the cathedral, cross the main road approaching the upper level of the Ponte de Dom Luís I to the Rua Saraiva de Carvalho, off which stands the **church of Santa Clara**, which has remarkably ornate giltwork c. 1730. If you intend to visit it, do so before seeing the church of S. Francisco, which eclipses even this.

Vila Nova de Gaia

⭐ Port wine lodges

The suburb of Vila Nova de Gaia lies opposite Porto on the steep south bank of the River Douro, which is spanned on two levels by the Dom Luís I bridge, completed in 1886. It's dominated by the **port wine lodges** (*see* p.190), each of which spells out its name in giant neon letters. Until 1987, port could not be called 'port' unless it matured in Gaia. The area's narrow streets are a logistic nightmare for the road tankers that transport the wine from the Douro valley.

Buses nos.57 and 91 from Praça Almeida Garrett outside São Bento station will take you here. Taxis charge a small supplement for crossing the bridge. Otherwise, it's easy to walk across the upper level, and there is a fantastic view if you don't mind heights. There's a car park in some warehouses near the end of the esplanade. If you park elsewhere, beware of parking tickets.

Wander through the lanes at the top of the hill to see derelict wine lodges. Part of the hillslope above the lodges looks wonderfully forested. This has been the private garden of the **Conde de Campo Bello** for 620 years, complete with maize field, orchard, and the first camellias in Europe, brought from Japan in the mid-16th century. The Condêssa saw a UFO here in 1982.

The upper level of the Dom Luís I bridge leads to the **monastery of Serra do Pilar**, with a round 16th-century church and round cloister, enough to dizzy even the most level-headed monk. Here Wellington planned his crossing of the Douro, in 1809, and the buildings are still occupied by the military. Visitors are not welcomed, but there are great views of the city from the terrace.

ⓘ Porto >

Main municipal office: Rua Clube Fenianos 25, t (22) 339 3470, www.porto turismo.pt; open July–Sept 9–7; Oct–June Mon–Fri 9–5.30, Sat and Sun 9–4.30; city transport office, Loja de Mobilidad, located here

Services in Porto

Post Office

Main Post Office, Praça do General H. Delgado (*open Mon–Fri 8am–9pm, Sat 9–6*). Poste Restante, internet and international telephone facilities are available here. Should you wish to send a bottle of port home – perhaps because there is white port which is uncommon in both Britain and North America – you can buy bottle boxes and packing stuff in the GPO's package section (which is located at the far end of the 1st floor).

Telephones

There is a **Telephonaria** at Praça da Liberdade 62 (*open daily 8am–11pm*) and at the Telecom Office in Praça da Batalha. International phone cards can be bought from kiosks and newsagents.

Old Town: Rua Infante Dom Henrique 63, t (22) 200 9770

Praça Dom João I, t (22) 205 7514; open Mon–Fri 9–7.30, Sat–Sun 9.30–3.30, Aug Sat and Sun 9.30–7.30

ICEP tourist offices: Praça Dom João I 43, t (22) 205 7514, www.icep.pt; airport

Banks and Money-changers

As elsewhere in Portugal, banks are open Mon–Fri 8.30–3. You can change money at the airport and at most banks. In July and August, **Câmbios Bank** on Rua de Sá da Bandeira is open Mon–Fri 8.30–6, Sat 8.30–1. There are many **cashpoint** machines on Avenida dos Aliados, in Praça da Liberdade and in the large shopping areas.

The money-changing booths throughout the city charge lower commission rates than banks. Try **Portocâmbios** on Rua Rodrigues Sampaio 193, next to the Câmara Municipal (*closed Sat pm and Sun*) and **Intercontinental**, Rua Ramalho Ortigão near the main tourist office (*closed Sat pm and Sun*).

Internet

The cheapest access is **Portweb**, Praça General Humberto Delgado 291, t (22) 200 5922 (*open Mon–Sat 10am–2am, Sun 3pm–2am*). Beware queues. The **Portugal Telecom Office**, Praça da Liberdade 62 (*open Mon–Sat 10am–10pm, Sun 2–9pm*) has internet access using phonecards. For free access with long queues, go to the **Biblioteca Municipale Almeida Garrett**, Jardim do Palácio de Cristal (*open Mon–Sat 10–6*) or **Biblioteca Municipale**, Rua Dom João IV (*open Mon–Fri 9–7.30, Sat 10–6*).

Emergency Services

In case of emergency, dial t 112.

For the **Santo António Hospital**, Rua Vicente José Carvalho, t (22) 207 7500.

The **tourist police** are multilingual, t (22) 208 1833. Otherwise **police headquarters** is at Rua Augusto Rosa, off Praça da Batalha, t (22) 200 6821, 208 8518 or 205 5558.

Laundry

The laundry in the shopping mall opposite the Grande Hotel do Porto in the Rua Santa Catarina does service washes. If you have time, it's worth saving up your laundry to do it by hand in the municipal facility at the west end of the Rua da Reboleira, in the Ribeira. Although it's relatively new, the sight of steam rising from the ranks of troughs is thrilling and medieval. If you wish to cheat, there's a laundrette, and if the excitement has overwhelmed you there are showers and toilets.

Festival in Porto

When the Church Christianized the summer solstice celebration, some of the pagan rites remained: Porto's annual humdinger is the **Festas de S. João**, on the night of 23 June and the day of the 24th. The streets are filled with bonfires and religious images; people dance till dawn, sustained by roast kid and *vinho verde*. People hit one another over the head with squeaky plastic hammers, or leeks. There's a lot of noise about in the week before and after, so plan your visit with caution.

Shopping in Porto

Except on Sundays, nobody in Porto need ever be at a loss as to where to buy a bottle of **port**. It's sold all over the place. If you're going to tour one of the wine lodges, it makes sense to buy your bottles there, because you can sample the wares – unless it's a vintage port – and it's fun to see where it comes from.

Clothes are cheaper here than in Lisbon, and **handmade lace** is of very good quality, but not cheap. There is a long tradition of **gold filigree** workmanship in Porto and the Minho province: in the late 16th-century the goldsmiths of Porto successfully pleaded the nobility of their profession, which exempted them from guarding the city gates from travellers who were unfortunate enough to be afflicted with the bubonic plague. Keep an eye open for earrings and brooches.

In the main shopping district near and around the Avenida dos Aliados, **Rua de Cedofeita** is good for window shopping and shoe shopping: ladies' pumps are particularly abundant. Buy walking sticks at number 158 and antiques at A Vilarinha Lda, number 204. Rare books and book bindings are available at Rua das Flores 28.

⭐ **Hotel Infante
de Sagres >>**

You'll find Zara, Benetton *et al.* near the bottom of the **Rua de Santa Catarina**, which is the other great shoe shopping street. Nearby, E. Rodrigues Reis Lda, Rua de Passos Manuel, is entirely devoted to buttons. Livraria Britânica, Rua José Falcão 184, **t** (22) 332 3930, is a well-stocked English-language bookshop, but you can expect to pay about double the UK retail price.

Don't miss the fantastic 19th-century neogothic **bookshop** at Rua das Carmelitas 144, which runs uphill from the façade of the Clérigos church. Livraria Chadron (formerly Lello and Irmão) is full of Gothic arches, beneath a ceiling of wooden cartwheel shapes. A rounded double staircase reverses back upon itself, leading to an upper storey illuminated by stained-glass windows and hanging lamps like censers.

Sports in Porto

There's a swimming pool that is operated by **Clube Fluvial Portuense**, Rua Clube Fluvial Portuense 13, **t** (22) 205 4357, on the way to Foz do Douro. It's pretty basic, but in hot weather it does the trick.

Port Wine Lodges in Porto

The lodges in Vila Nova de Gaia are warehouses rather than cellars simply because Gaia is built on granite. The lodges organize excellent tours of their premises, vats, casks, bottles and all – just turn up and wait for an English-speaking group to assemble. The individual companies lay on a small-family-business spiel, though most have been bought out by multinationals. They allow visitors generous samples of the delicious stuff; cunning people crawl from one lodge to the next. It's a good idea to try dry white port, because the lodges serve them properly chilled. Most lodges are open weekdays 9 or 10–12 and 2–5.30, later in summer, when some are open on Sat: check at the tourist office and at

www.portoturismo.pt before setting out.

Barros, Rua D. Leonor de Freitas 180–2, **t** (22) 375 2320, www.porto-barros.pt. Does a very interesting tour.

Calém, Avenida Diogo Leite 26, **t** (22) 374 6660, *www.calem.pt*. A particularly attractive bar, and the only lodge that opens on Sundays.

Kopke, Rua Serpa Pinto 183, **t** (22) 375 2395, *www.kopkeports.com*. The oldest wine lodge, with another very interesting tour.

Noval. Doesn't offer a tour, only a tasting room.

Sandeman, Largo Miguel Bombarda 3, **t** (22) 374 0533, *www.sandeman.com*. Has an admission charge (as do Offley, Croft and Ferreira), but is said to be especially liberal with the samples.

Taylor's, Rua Choupelo 250. Has a marvellous restaurant (see 'Eating Out', p.193).

Where to Stay in Porto

Very Expensive (€€€€)

★★★★★Hotel Infante de Sagres, Praça D. Filipa de Lencastre 62, **t** (22) 339 8500, *www.hotelinfantesagres.pt*. Far and away the best hotel in Porto. Run by perfectionists and host to visiting dignitaries, it strikes an admirable balance between grandiose furnishings, friendly service, and luxury. Carved wood and wrought iron in the public rooms smack of 19th-century opulence, though in fact they date from the early 1950s. Centrally located and fairly quiet, the hotel has 80-odd bedrooms, each one unique. All rooms come with knockout film star bathrooms, and some display good contemporary art. The courtyard is a lovely antidote to the city, and there's a pink patio with showers, for sunbathing. The dining room is formal and businessy, providing quick but unhurried service. The menu is reminiscent of the era when the hotel was constructed: lobster bisque with Pernod, rack of lamb and sauces are a speciality. The bar is a gentlemanly cocoon; go for a cocktail (€9).

*****Sheraton Porto**, Rua Tenente Valadim 146, t (222) 040 4000, *www.starwoodhotels.com*. A luxurious hotel with acres of gleaming marble. The large, comfortable rooms have excellent facilities and there is a superb spa with several steam rooms and a large indoor pool.

****Pestana Porto Hotel**, Praça da Ribeira 1, t (22) 340 2300, *www. pestana.com*. A great place, largely thanks to its unsurpassed location in 11 converted houses (with double glazing) on the waterfront of the Ribeira, right where the action is; more than half the rooms overlook the river and Vila Nova de Gaia; if you also want a bathroom with a view, get one ending in 02. There's lots of unpolished granite and glass, slightly Art Deco furniture, wide beds and some odd-shaped rooms dictated by the layout of the buildings. In the restaurant (€€) the cuisine is Portuguese with a twist, and the prices are surprisingly reasonable. There's no high or low season, but if you want to sleep avoid the week before and after 24 June. Good value.

Expensive (€€€)
***Grande Hotel do Porto**, Rua de Santa Catarina 197, t (22) 207 6690, *www.grandehotelporto.com*. Nicely located in the city's main pedestrian shopping street, stately, spacious and chandeliered. It's popular with tour groups, and who can blame them? There's room for everyone in the vast breakfast room.

Moderate (€€)
****Tryp Porto Centro**, Rua das Doze Casas 17, t (22) 537 0014, *www.solmelia .com*. The former stuffy Hotel Castor has been taken over by the Sol Melia chain. The rooms are modern with light wood and attractive décor, while the Marques Restaurant serves traditional local cuisine. Facilities include a gym.

****Ipanema Park**, Rua de Serralves 124, t (22) 532 2100, *www.ipanema-park-hotel.pt*. It's too far to walk from the centre of town to this fairly standard hotel.

****Albergaria Miradouro**, Rua da Alegria 598, t (22) 537 0717, *alb.miradouro@net.vodafone.pt*, Cosy and comfortable, in 1950s style, and it has panoramic views of the city. *Parking space is limited.*

***Hotel da Bolsa**, Rua Ferreira Borges 101, t (22) 202 6768/69/70, *www.hoteldabolsa.com*. Just uphill from the Bolsa, small and well placed, with good rooms and no surprises. It can be a little noisy at night.

***Residencial dos Aliados**, Avenida dos Aliados, entrance: Rua Elisio de Melo 27, t (22) 200 4853/4, *www. residencialaliados.com*. Smack on the city's main strip, this well-used place has the proportions one would expect of an old building, particularly the high ceilings, and it provides internet access in the living room and air-conditioning in some of the bedrooms. Remember that the rooms with views will be noisy.

***Hotel International**, Rua do Almada 131, t (22) 200 5032, *www.hi-porto.com*. This atmospheric hotel has benefited from a revamp, with warm ochre paintwork and interesting artwork. Wi-Fi in the lobby.

Residencial Pão de Açúcar, Rua do Almada 262, t (22) 200 2425 or 201 1589, *www.residencialpaode acucar.com*. The broad balcony with rich views is the main attraction of high-rise Residencial Pão de Açúcar, but it's only available to the occupants of six rooms. Reserve one of them. Otherwise the place is well run, but not worthy of the hype it receives.

Hotel América, Rua de Santa Catarina 1018, t (22) 339 2930, *www.hotel-america.net*. A great choice if you want somewhere efficiently run, with mod cons, wooden floors, a winter garden, no decorative frills and its own garage. It does what it does very well, and it doesn't accept group bookings. It's a long walk to the Ribeira, though. One disabled room.

Hotel Boa Vista, Esplanada do Castelo 58, t (22) 532 0020, *www.hotelboavista. com*. If you're keen on sea air, it's worth considering staying out at Foz (*see* p.185). Relaxed, bright and spacious, with nicely fitted rooms and a fourth-floor pool. Rooms with views of the mouth of the river get booked up quickly. There's no low season.

Inexpensive (€)

****Pensão Século**, Rua de Santa Catarina 1256, **t** (22) 509 9120. A little way uphill and thus further from the action, this is good, if somewhat over gadgeted.

****Residencial Rex**, Praça da República 117, **t** (22) 207 4590. A fun place to stay, converted from a grandiose house and overlooking a garden square. The ceilings' stucco is amazing, and keeps guests' eyes off the grim carpets. Bedrooms are functional and spacious; one room has a round bed. *Parking is available.*

***Residencial Vera Cruz**, Rua Ramalho Ortigão 14, **t** (22) 332 3396. Centrally located and double-glazed, this place is curiously appealing and feels authentically Portuguese.

***Residencial Brasilia**, Rua Álvares Cabral 221, **t** (22) 200 6095 or 208 2981, *www.residencialbrasiliaporto. com*. A homely town house that doesn't feel like it's in the city at all. There's a garden, with rooms behind it. Rooms have air conditioning, and a garage is available at an extra €6 per day.

⭐ **Residencial Grande Hotel de Paris >**

 Residencial Grande Hotel de Paris, Rua da Fábrica 27–29, **t** (22) 207 3140, *www.ghparis.pt*. Just behind the Hotel Infante de Sagres, this offers some of the best value in the city. It's a curious building with more domes than the Soane Museum. Short on mod cons, it comes complete with cage lift, marble-topped furniture, a garden and plenty of quirk. Six rooms have spectacular views. *Book early.*

Pensão Residencial Belo Sonho, Rua de Passos Manuel 186, **t** (22) 200 3389. Clean, fresh and peaceful, and a good budget choice.

⭐ **Casa Mariazinha >>**

Pensão Astoria, Rua Arnaldo Gama 56, **t** (22) 200 8175. Despite its location to the west of the Avenida dos Aliados, this is a friendly and homely place, run by a small old lady.

Pensão Estoril, Rua de Cedofeita 193, **t** (22) 200 2751 or 200 5152. Feels like a boarding house. The rooms are a bit claustrophobic, with shower rooms carved out of them, but the great bonus is the lovely terrace at the back, with garden views. Lots of dogs wander about the place.

Pensão Cristal, Rua Galeria de Partis 48, **t** (22) 200 2100, *www.pensao cristal.com*. Near the Clérigos Tower, very straightforward and well run. Rooms have air conditioning.

Pensão Duas Nações, Praça Guilherme Gomes Fernandes 59, **t** (22) 208 1616/ 208 9621, *www.duasnacoes.com.pt*. A very decent place that provides internet access, a laundry service and rooms both with and without bathrooms.

Pensão Mondariz, Rua Cimo da Vila 139, **t** (22) 200 5600. Situated in the colourful district southeast of São Bento station, and run by a booming man who closely resembles Obelix out of the Asterix cartoon strip, down to the twinkle in his eye. Rooms are decent and large, and some have wonderful views over the city. Rooms with shared bath are cheaper.

Eating Out in Porto

The Ribeira is by far the most enjoyable area of Porto in which to eat, and provides a wide range of restaurants and bars.

Expensive (€€€)

Portucale, Rua da Alegria 598, **t** (22) 537 0717. At the top of the Albergaria Miradouro. Serves excellent food and has an intimate atmosphere, with stunning views of the city. The walls are hung with tapestries, the tables covered with fine linen and decorated with fresh flowers. The *cabrito á serrana* (kid in red wine) is a speciality. *Reservations recommended – ask for a table with a view.*

Casa Mariazinha, Rua de Belomonte 2–4, **t** (22) 200 9137, *casamariazinha @netcabo.pt*. Run by a husband-and-wife team, this is a unique and utterly wonderful place for a dinner you won't forget. It's tiny, romantic, around 450 years old and feels like a friend's house. One English fan makes his reservation first and then books his flight. The gourmet menu changes each day, and is complemented by an extensive wine list (only grape-based drinks and water are available). Take your time, and enjoy. *Evenings only.*

Don Tonho, Cais da Ribeira 13–15, **t** (22) 200 4307, *www.dtonho.com*. At the end of the Ribeira closest to the bridge, Don Tonho is emblematic of the new Portugal: confident, well designed, go-ahead and able to satisfy diners' exacting expectations. It's easy to recommend it to anyone – hence it attracts some tour groups, but they don't dominate. It makes the most of its great unpolished granite walls, with elegant table settings and attentive service. Try the sea bass baked in a sarcophagus of salt, followed by the coconut pudding.

O Escondidinho, Rua de Passos Manuel 144, **t** (22) 200 1079. A short walk away from the subsidiary tourist office in the Praça de S. João, this place has a good reputation, but can fall rather flat. It's mock baronial, and so hushed you can hear the tick of the cuckoo clock. Take granny for dinner. She will enjoy the informal, old-moneyed décor and clubby waiters. Steaks are good, as are the flambéed sole and the apple pie. *Closed Sun.*

Moderate (€€)

Chez Lapin, Rua dos Canastreiros 40–42, **t** (22) 200 6418. With its location on the waterfront, Chez Lapin would be full even if the food was bad. It's a bistro at heart, that spills onto the waterfront and maintains a sense of humour. A saxophone found at the bottom of the Douro exhibits itself on the wall. Prices are relatively high, but there aren't many complaints from people on holiday. Try the roasted octopus.

Abadia, Rua do Ateneu Comercial do Porto 22–24, **t** (22) 200 8757/8. Opposite the Rodonorte bus station, this bustling, noisy establishment seems more lively than the rest of the neighbourhood put together. Don't be put off by the touristy appearance, it's anything but, as the lack of

vegetables will testify. Try the entrecote. *Closed Sun.*

Tripeiro, Rua de Passos Manuel 191–195, **t** (22) 200 5886, *www.restaurantetripeiro.com*. If you want to try tripe, this is the place for it. Spread over three floors, it's fake rustic and a little too tour-groupy, but that helps make the strange food feel safe. *Closed Sun eve.*

Mercearia, Cais da Ribeira 32/33, **t** (22) 200 4389 or 208 9575. Offers an attractive interior – white linen, unpolished stone, sepia photographs of the Douro – good service and good food.

Alzira, Viela do Buraco 3, **t** (22) 200 5004. In an alley behind the riverfront, occupying a narrow, stone walled house. There's something very attractive about it, and the food and service are good.

Simbiose, Rua Infante Dom Henrique 133, **t** (22) 203 0398. Elegant restaurant with a candlelit dining room over-looking the river. The menu is traditional and there's a reasonably priced weekend buffet.

Romão, Praça Carlos Alberto 100, **t** (22) 200 5639. Informal restaurant serving familiar local dishes, such as roast kid and tripe.

Cozza Rio, Rua S. Francisco 8, **t** (22) 200 0712. Try the octopus with rice at this small, cosy place.

Farol da Boa Nova, Muro dos Bacalhoeiros 115, **t** (22) 200 6086. Good but not popular choice for eating cheaply on the waterfront. Standard menu, paper tablecloths.

Postigo do Carvão, Rua da Fonte Taurina 24/34, **t** (22) 200 4539, *postigo@oninet.pt*. Fun, youthful place that's not too touristy. With granite floors and walls, it contains three working street lamps and an open kitchen at the back. There's live music and the food is tasty. *Open 6pm–2am; closed Mon.*

Baroa Fladgate at Taylor's Wine Lodge, Rua Choupelo 250, Vila Nova de Gaia. The food is good, port is served and there are peacocks in the garden. There are great views from the car park.

⭐ Postigo do Carvão >>

Inexpensive (€)

Mar Norte, Rua Mousinho da Silveira 95, t (22) 208 3412. A big and popular Chinese restaurant specializing in the cuisine of Shanghai and the region to the north of it. With a wooden floor and coffered ceiling, it's popular with groups of students.

Casa Aleixo, Rua da Estação 216, t (22) 537 0462. Some 50 yards uphill from the Campanha railway station, this appeals to respectable locals in search of a 'typical' *tasca*. The setting is ordinary, the menu is ordinary, but the food is very good, and the half-portions large enough to immobilize most human beings.

Filha da Mãe Preta, Cais da Ribeira 39–41, t (22) 205 5515. One of the best-known restaurants among this energetic stretch of eateries. Serves excellent seafood dishes.

Al Forno, Rua Adro da Foz 4, t (22) 617 3549 or 616 4629. In Foz district, nestled near the main church is a small and popular Italian restaurant. The clientele is young and upwardly mobile.

Restaurant Arco Iris, Rua Candido Reis 65–76, Vila Nova de Gaia. A small neighbourhood restaurant with friendly staff.

Much of Porto's cheap, counter-top food is to be found in the streets around the university and behind the main tourist office. **Solar Moinho de Vento**, Largo do Moinho de Vento, is an unpretentious place that is usually filled with locals.

Cafés in Porto

There are several wonderful cafés to be found in Porto, but they're on the wane – one of the best known has unfortunately become a McDonalds. If you only have time to visit one, it should be the Majestic.

Majestic Café, Rua de Santa Catarina 112, t (22) 200 3887, *www.alvo.com/ majestic*. There's something Viennese about it – probably the cherubs and the hanging lamps. There are tables outside on the pedestrian street, but the whole point is to be inside, sipping your beer and eyeballing the vast wall mirrors and the surprising assortment of people reflected in

them. Omelettes and sandwiches are available. *Closed Sun.*

Il Café di Roma, Rua de Sá da Bandeira 75 (no telephone). Occupies part of the former Café Brasileira; elegant and Italianate.

If you're after a **snack**, many of the port houses in Vila Nova de Gaia do a good trade in riverfront cafés. If you've had enough of port, **The Fluvial Bar**, number 108 on the waterfront, in the green-and-white Art Deco building belonging to the Club Fluvial Portuense, serves sandwiches and beer.

Bars in Porto

Solar do Vinho do Porto, at the Museu Romantico, Rua de Entre Quintas 220, t (22) 609 4749, *www.ivp.pt*. Allows you views of the river after your cultural endeavours.

Max Café, Rua da Alfândega 114. In the Ribeira, there are so many bars for teenyboppers that it's a relief to find one which offers grown-ups dim lighting and cocktails on the waterfront.

Vino Logia, Rua São João 46, t (22) 205 2468, *www.vinologia.com*. Serves a staggering 150 varieties of port, produced by 35 different companies.

Downing Street, Praça da Ribeira 10. Offers a suave glass of port.

There are a number of good bars in Foz. You could try out the **Thirty One Bar** opposite the Jardim do Passeio Alegre, **Ourigo** and several others in the Rua do Padrão, **Oriental**, **Cafeina** and **Bull Bear**.

Nightclubs in Porto

Rock's, Rua Rei Ramiro 228. In Vila Nova de Gaia. Dance off the port, either in the cellars or on the terrace looking over the Douro.

Mare Alta, Alameda Basilio Teles/Rua do Ouro (Gás bus stop), moored at Ponte da Arrábia west, t (22) 609 1010. South American music.

Hard Club, Cais de Gaia 1158, t (22) 374 4755. A large club on the waterfront, which attracts international DJs.

Estado Novo, Rua Sousa Aroso 722, t (22) 928 5989. Slick nightclub with good mix of music.

The Douro Litoral

The Atlantic Coast

Porto is within easy striking distance of the beaches of what are marketed as the Costa Verde (the Green Coast) to the north, and the Costa da Prata (the Silver Coast) to the south. As far as the coasts go, there's little difference between the two: they share chilly water, fairly large waves when it's windy, and patchy development. Both are popular with the residents of the Minho and Trás-os-Montes. To the north of Porto, the main resorts are at Póvoa de Varzim and Viana do Castelo, and, to the south, Espinho, Aveiro, Figueira da Foz and Nazaré; with the exception of Viana and Aveiro, these offer few diversions other than sea and sun.

Póvoa de Varzim

Póvoa de Varzim is a brash resort 30km north of Porto. The beach, part sand, part pebble, is a mile (2km) wide and 5 miles (8km) long; it has incurred heavy development, butting out most of Póvoa's fishing fleet, but it's not unpleasant. The population of around 28,000 almost doubles in summer, when the mean temperature is 64°F (18°C), most of the increase being residents of the Minho and Trás-os-Montes. The fishermen keep themselves to themselves in the modest Bairro dos Pescadores. Eça de Quieroz, the brilliant and thoroughly enjoyable 19th-century novelist, was born here.

The **Museu Municipal de Etnografia e História** is large and covers topics such as fishing for *bacalhau*. It includes models of ships and nets, fishermen's clothes and domestic paraphernalia, equipment for collecting seaweed, and a cork life vest.

Museu Municipal de Etnografia e História
Rua Visconde de Azevedo; open 10–12.30 and 2.30–6; closed Mon and hols; adm

Vila do Conde

Vila do Conde is a once-grand boatbuilding harbour at the mouth of the Ave River. The bulk of the charming little town is set back from the wide sandy beach. Come before the developers set to work. Around 870 the settlement was fortified by a count, hence its name. Sold to the Monastery of Guimarães, and later assimilated into crown lands, the town boomed from fishing and trading under Dom João II and Dom Manuel I: in the 16th century, new money built the new town hall and parish church. The river silted up in the late 18th century, leaving Vila do Conde to a gracious retirement.

What to See

The heart of town is a huddle of interest. Do walk down the charming **Rua do Lidador**, at right angles to the waterfront.

Getting to and around The Douro Litoral

The **trains** from Porto's Estação da Trindade have been discontinued; Póvoa de Varzim is linked to Porto via metro line B. There is a standard and shuttle (the Expresso) service. There are two or three daily express **buses** from Porto and several local SCTP buses (*www.stcp.pt*). From the old railway station, turn right onto and walk along the Rua Almirante Reis to the Praça do Almada. Bear left there for the seafront.

STCP buses serve Vila do Conde from Porto. Espinho is on the main **rail** line from Porto Campanhã (¼hr), with several dozen trains daily. It is also served by **STCP buses**.

Impressive rather than beautiful, the late Gothic **Igreja Matriz** was finished *c.* 1514. João de Castilho crafted the rippling flamboyant Gothic portal: although it is more sober than his doorway of the Convento de Cristo at Tomar, on the tympanum the sculptor has seen fit to flank St John with a dragon on one side and a naked man on the other. The 17th-century belltower swamps the façade. Flying dragons face one another between each of the arches inside, by beautiful retables. The church now contains the **Museum of Sacred Art**, which houses the Processional Cross from the Chapel of Formariz. A surreal arm bearing a sword projects from the pillory nearby, begun in 1538, which is topped by what seems to be a lightning conductor – for divine wrath?

At the **Museu das Rendas de Bilros** (Bobbin Lace Museum) craftswomen demonstrate the art of *bilros*, a type of lace-work using numerous bobbins, pins and a kind of cushion to hold the pricked pattern. The art, which originated at Vila do Conde, requires a mind-boggling combination of finger movements. Splendid pieces are displayed – some are for sale.

The **convent of Santa Clara** is a prominent bastion in the grand style of the Bishop's Palace in Porto. The convent was founded in 1318, incompletely rebuilt in 1778, and made defunct 60 years later. Now it's a school, offering access to the finely sculpted tombs in the church. The inmates' water was supplied by an aqueduct which once had 999 arches, and looks two-dimensional.

Museum of Sacred Art
t (252) 631 424; open June–Sept 10–12 and 2–4, Oct–May 2–4

Museu das Rendas de Bilros
Rua de S Bento 70, t (252) 248 470, www.geira.pt/MRendas; open 9–12 and 2–6; closed Sat and Sun; adm

Convent of Santa Clara
open 9–12 and 2–5.30

Espinho

Planned on an unedifying grid, 16km south of Porto, the resort of Espinho manages to fill its white beach in the summer, but lacks entrepreneurial flair. The beach has receded 200 yards in the past hundred years, and is divided from most of the town by a railway line.

One of the world's two greatest **violin makers** works in Espinho. António Capela learnt the craft from his father, who made a violin for himself in 1924; then a neighbouring violinist brought an instrument to be repaired, lest he damage his own hands mending it, and the business was under way. António travels to Italy and

Germany to select Yugoslavian spruce or the more beautiful maple, the woods with the finest resonance. A large proportion of his creations are outstanding Stradivarius reproductions, which are used by musicians the world over. The strong-armed craftsman has a glint in his eye. He is continually paring, fining and polishing in his workroom, where he plays loud pop on the radio. He's assisted by his son, who made his first violin when he was 13. António is happy to speak French or Italian with musicologists.

Porto Golf Club

The golf club is on the coast a couple of kilometres south of town. It features a difficult 18-hole links course with narrow fairways parallel to one another. Most tourists who play here are Dutch: they feel at home with the flat land. Being so close to the sea has led to difficulties with irrigation, but these appear to be under control.

The north wind blows across the course, which is split by a road and includes a fair amount of sand. The rough is not very rough. The new clubhouse includes an uninspired TV room in which to dump children. Green fees are more expensive at the weekend.

Inland

The Church of Leça do Balio

Eight km north of Porto, and 2km south of the satellite town of Maia, stands the fortified Gothic church of Leça do Balio, which was founded as a monastery for men and women in 986, and in 1115, after the first crusade, became the headquarters of the Knights Hospitallers. In 1336 it was rebuilt by the head of the order, since when it has changed little, though it is not grand. The outside is wholly, fiercely crenellated, and the tower resembles a keep – more to emphasize its possession by a military order than for defensive purposes.

The most exciting object in the well-proportioned interior is the baptismal font, carved by Diogo Pires the Younger in 1514: the bowl is supported by toothy, menacing crocodiles with webbed feet and poised tails. Perhaps they drew inspiration from Azurara's chronicle, in which he described 'fish which have beaks three or four palmos [8in/20cm] in length ... and these beaks have teeth on either side, so close to one another that one cannot lay a finger between them... These fish are as great and sometimes greater than sharks'. The basin itself is decorated with pomegranates and maize-like massaroca fruits.

ⓘ Vila do Conde >
Rua 25 de Abril 103,
t (252) 248 473,
www.cm-vilado
conde.pt; open
Oct–Apr Mon–Fri 9–6,
Sat–Sun 2.30–5.30;
May–Sep Mon–Fri 9–6,
Sat–Sun 10–1 and
2.30–6

ⓘ Espinho >>
Rua 6 709, t (22) 733
5872; open June–Sept
Mon–Fri 9–9, Sat and
Sun 10–12 and 3–6;
Oct–May Mon–Fri
9.30–12.30 and 2–5.30,
Sat 9.30–12

ⓘ Póvoa de Varzim >
Avenida Mouzinho de
Albuquerque 166 (the
main road at right
angles to the ocean),
t (252) 298 120;
open 15 July–15 Sept
daily 9–9; 16 Sept–14
July Mon–Fri 9–1 and
2–7, Sat and Sun 9.30–1
and 2.30–6

Festival in Vila do Conde

In Vila do Conde the **Festival of Corpus Christi** is held in June every four years, most recently in 2009, and features fantastic carpets of flowers. The petals of roses, hydrangeas, carnations and other flowers are collected in sacks from the surrounding *quintas*. On the night before the festival, they are stencilled on 3km of roads – pink, green, yellow and red – along which the 35lb (16kg) silver monstrance processes.

Where to Stay in the Douro Litoral

Póvoa de Varzim

★★★Grande Hotel da Póvoa, Largo do Passeio Alegre 20, **t** (252) 615 464, *www.grandehoteldapovoa.com* (€€€–€€). Next to the casino, this obviously hopes to attract gamblers; it is ridiculously overpriced. Basic furnishings are enlivened with flowers and bowls of fruit; the first-floor sitting room is comfortable and relaxed, and some rooms have sea views from their small windows.

★★★★Hotel Sopete Vermar, Rua Imprensa Regional, **t** (252) 298 900, *www.novotel.com* (€€). On the coast road north of town, is this glitzy hotel, comfortable and neutral, trimmed with plants and spotlights. Some of the balconied rooms have sea views. Thatched umbrellas are pitched on the grassy poolside. The large, sunny dining room features seafood. *Disco on Fri and Sat.*

★★★Santo André Inn, Avenida Santo André, Aver-O-Mar, **t** (252) 615 666, *www.estalagemsantoandre.com* (€€). Located just 3km north of Póvoa. Directly across from a sandy beach, this modern hotel has good rooms and a restaurant with panoramic views.

Rua Paulo Barreto is recommended for cheap accommodation.

Vila do Conde

★★★Estalagem do Brasão, Avenida Dr João Canavarro 144, **t** (252) 642 016, *www.estalagemdobrasao.com* (€€). Family-managed *estalagem* offering comfortable rooms, good value and a local feel, 500 yards from the beach. Once it was a *palácio*. Now it has a discothéque. *Parking available.*

★★★Hotel de Santana, Monte de Sant'Ana-Azurara, **t** (252) 641 717, *www.santanahotel.net* (€€). Across the river. Modern rooms and facilities include a swimming pool and gym.

Espinho

★★★★Hotel Praia Golfe, Rua 6, **t** (22) 733 1000, *www.praiagolfe.com* (€€€). Near the casino, pleasant and sporty. Guests receive a 50% reduction on green fees at the Porto Golf Club 3km away – hence the tartan carpet in the restaurant. Some of the comfortable, neutral bedrooms have big sea views. Equally diverting is the very impressive health centre, which includes a heated indoor swimming pool, squash court, sauna, Turkish bath, gym, and massage room.

★★★Hotel-Apartamento Solverde, Rua 21 77, **t** (22) 731 3144 (€€). Part of the casino development at the nub of Espinho, providing space-effective apartments with well-equipped kitchens and curtained-off bedrooms. Bright tiles in the corridors give a beachside feel to the place. The hotel has access to two open-air saltwater swimming pools.

★★★La Fontaine Hotel, Rua Bombeiros Voluntarios 80, Esmoriz, **t** (25) 618 5482 (€€). A new hotel located 5km from Espinho. Has 31 double rooms, and 3 suites with Internet access and hydro-massage tub.

Turismo de Habitação

Quinta das Alfaias, Rua de António Azevedo dos Santos 515, Fajozes, **t** (252) 662 146 (€€). A large box-shaped building standing in its own estate. The garden is a maze of fruit trees, and is perfect for walks. The large bedrooms are individually furnished, some a bit heavily with too much dark wood. Otherwise, there's a high comfort factor.

Eating Out in The Douro Litoral

Póvoa de Varzim
There are a number of places to eat on the seafront, including **Belo Horizonte**, Rua Tenente Valadim 63 (€€), roughly opposite the fort, which serves very reasonable food. Boats are painted on the wall. **Estrela do Mar**, Rua Caetano de Oliveira 144 (€), is undecorated and popular with the locals, who are likely to stare inquisitively at any foreigners.

Vila do Conde
São Roque, Rua do Lidador 128, **t** (252) 631 184 (€€). Behind the São Roque church, this is quiet and popular with locals and Portuguese visitors alike. Choose either fish or pork.

Restaurante Ramon, Rua 5 de Outubro 176, **t** (252) 631 334 (€€). A warm and happy family *tasca* with its own-label wine. *Closed Tues.*

Le Villageois, Praça da República 94, **t** (252) 631 119 (€€). A tavern serving good food – try the whiting fillets with shrimp sauce. *Closed Mon.*

Caximar, Avenida Brasil, **t** (25) 264 2492 (€). Excellent seafood restaurant on the beach.

Espinho
Casa Marreta, Rua 2 1355, **t** (22) 734 0091 (€€). On the seafront try the *caldeirada* (fish stew) or the *cataplana* (sealed wok) *de tamboril*. Pots of fresh herbs ornament the tables.

A Varina, Rua 2 1269, **t** (22) 734 4630 (€). Nearby, but back from the seafront, featuring fillets of fish and rice-based dishes. The chairs are pine and the green walls weakly hung with fishing nets.

Amarante

Amarante is a town as beautiful as its name. Sited 56km east of Porto, it graciously bridges the River Tâmega, which is edged with willow trees and wooden balconies. These complement the lovely view across the 18th-century bridge to the brooding, disparate convent of São Gonçalo, with the church of São Domingos hovering behind.

The settlement is ancient. It was founded as Turdetanos in 360 BC, but changed its name to honour the Roman Governor Amarantus. Tradition claims that St Gonçalo built the first bridge across the Tâmega in the 13th century, to get to his hermitage on the other side. His bridge fell down in the floods of 1763, but his hermitage became a church and convent. The quaint but strong bridge that now stands was built in 1790. Several years later, in 1809, it was the scene of a heroic resistance by the people of Amarante, who staved off the French Marshal Soult's advance across the bridge for a full 14 days, but had their houses burnt in return.

The town feels somehow benign, despite the lack of pavements. The leafy park beside the river is inhabited by the occasional 4in (10cm) charcoal-black slug. A notice warns of polluted water, so

Getting to Amarante

There are five **trains** a day from Porto, and four from Livração.
Rodonorte runs a dozen **buses** every day from Porto.

swimming is not advisable. This does not deter the town's flock of
plump white geese, who motor up and down the river all day and
sleep on an island. For the past eight years they've been fed daily
by a man with no family and no job. He says he talks to them.
Amarante is famous for its egg-yolk-and-sugar sweets. The best
place to try them is Lailai, near the restaurant Zé de Calçada (*see*
p.202). Some of Amarante's accommodation offers very good value.

What to See

The **convento de São Gonçalo** was founded by Dom João III in
1540; it took 40 years to build. To the left of the Renaissance portal
stands an arcaded loggia with 17th-century figures. The cupola is
tiled with terracotta, beautiful against the church's mellow granite
body. Within, the finely symmetrical organ is supported by three
bearded and musclebound gentlemen, who have performed their
task since 1600. To the left of the altar lies the tomb of St Gonçalo,
believed to guarantee a quick marriage to anyone who touches it;
underestimating demand, the effigy was made in soft limestone.
Consequently the face and foot have been worn away. The cynical
will mutter about St Gonçalo reaching the parts other saints
cannot reach. The convent has two cloisters, the second of which
has been invaded on one side by the town hall.

Albano Sardoeira Museum
open 10–12.30 and 2–5.30

Upstairs, the **Albano Sardoeira Museum** of modern art is
overpowered by Amadeo de Sousa-Cardoso (1887–1918), the
greatest Portuguese artist of the 20th century. (His work has found
a more fitting home in Lisbon's Gulbenkian Museum of Modern
Art.) Born locally, he started his training as an architect, but
switched to painting because he loved colours and forms, hoping
to express in painting 'what he thought'. In 1906, he moved to Paris
and exhibited with Modigliani. He returned to Portugal in 1914, and
here he became a close friend of Robert and Sonia Delaunay. In the
final year of his life, Amadeo had to limit his painting as the paints
damaged his hands; he was killed by Spanish 'flu.

Amadeo's early, figurative work soon ceased to satisfy him; his
interest in shapes, colour and light led him to pure abstraction. He
later reintegrated figurative elements, painting images as if they
were shattered. On his return to Portugal, he became preoccupied
by his surroundings and reintroduced representation to his work.
His final paintings combine elements from all his periods, and are
lumbered with the generic term 'Cubo-photism'.

(i) **Amarante >**
t (255) 420 243,
www.cm-amarante.pt;
open Sept–June 9–12.30
and 2–5, July to mid-
Sept until 7.30

Tourist Information/ Services in Amarante

The **tourist office** is in the same building as the museum on the Alameda Teixeira de Pascoães. It produces an excellent guide to local walks (*Nature Guide Amarante*, €6) in English. If you need a detailed map for driving in the area, buy a **Forways map** from Tabacaria Havaneza, Rua 5 de Outubro.

The **railway station** is on Rua João Pinto Ribeiro. To reach the tourist office from the station, turn right outside and walk down to the bottom of the street. Turn left by the bridge and into the Alameda Teixeira de Pascoães.

Most **buses** stop in the Largo Conselheiro António Cândido; from there, walk along the Rua 31 de Janeiro to get to the Ponte de São Gonçalo.

Festival in Amarante

At the **Feast of S. Gonçalo** on the first weekend of June, the town commemorates the patron saint of marriages by baking little phallus-shaped cakes, offered by young men to young women. This is probably a hangover from a Roman fertility cult. (In her cookbook, Edite Vieira does not rise to the challenge: the recipe for *bolos de São Gonçalo* 'would demand elongated tins, but obviously any patty tins will do'.)

Where to Stay in Amarante

★★★Hotel Amaranto, Rua Acácio Lino, t (255) 410 840, *hotelamaranto@mail.telepac.pt* (€€). Clean and functional, with sophisticated equipment behind the reception desk and an enormous choice of lighting in guest rooms, which also have balconies. Staff in the hotel's restaurant are very keen to please; they speak English, and serve good food.

★★★Hotel Navarras, Rua António Carneiro, t (255) 431 036, *www.hotelnavarras.com* (€€). Has neat, clean rooms; corridor walls are fake granite. There's a nice rooftop swimming pool.

★Albergaria Dona Margaritta, Rua Cândido dos Reis 53, t (255) 432 110, *www.albergariadonamargaritta.panet.pt* (€). With 32 rooms, it's a pleasant size, decorated in grandish style. Ceilings are high, and there is a lovely view of the river. Breakfast is served on the trellised terrace.

Residencial Estoril, Rua 31 de Janeiro, t (255) 431 291 (€). The cheapest place – adequate though rather basic. Eat almond pastries on the shady terrace overlooking the river at the café near the Church of São Pedro.

Pousada
Pousada de São Gonçalo, t (255) 460 030, *www.pousadas.pt* (L1 N). Perched 2,750ft (850m) up the Serra do Marão, 20km from Amarante, off the main road east to Vila Real, this *pousada* takes advantage of stunning views of infertile hills. The *pousada* is provided with reproduction furniture, in rustic style.

Turismo de Habitação
Casa de Pascoães, São João de Gatão, t (255) 422 595 or 423 953, *www.manorhouses.com* (€€). A handsome house facing the Serra do Marão and next to the River Tâmega and a Roman bridge. Inside, the story continues, with elegant bedrooms often featuring four-poster beds and antique furniture. There's also a museum in which the belongings of the poet Teixeira de Pascoães are displayed.

Casa de Aboadela, Aboadela, t (255) 441 141 or (22) 9513 055 (€). Nine km from Amarante, in the beautiful village of Aboadela, with mountains on one side and impossibly green landscape on the other. The house has just four en suite rooms, but its simple style, exhilarating views and low price make it worth a stay.

Eating Out in Amarante

Zé da Calçada, Rua 31 de Janeiro, t (255) 426 814 (€€€). The upmarket place to eat, furnished like a drawing room, with round rugs for round tables, candlesticks, a fireplace and plates on the walls. The views are great and so is the wine list.

Triunfante, Rua Teixera de Vasconcelos, t (25) 543 7978 (€).

Cheap and cheerful restaurant, which serves hearty portions of local favourites such as rabbit stew and *bacalhau*.

Restaurante Amaranto, Murtos Madalena, t (255) 422 006 (€). Relatively large, wood-panelled place with giggly service.

Confeitara da Ponte, Rua 31 de Janeiro, no tel. Sublime cake shop by the bridge, with an outside terrace for sampling the goodies on the spot.

The Beiras

The Beiras occupy almost all the land between the Rivers Douro and Tagus. This vast territory is diverse, and separates into three provinces: Beira Alta (the Upper Beira), Beira Baixa (the Lower Beira) and Beira Litoral (the Coastal Beira).

11

Don't miss

⭐ **Ancient university city**
Coimbra **p.241**

⭐ **Magical forest**
Forest of Buçaco **p.257**

⭐ **Bizarre landscape**
Almeida **p.220**

⭐ **Massive views and pure air**
Parque Natural da Serra da Estrela **p.223**

⭐ **Dramatic hilltop village**
Monsanto **p.238**

See map overleaf

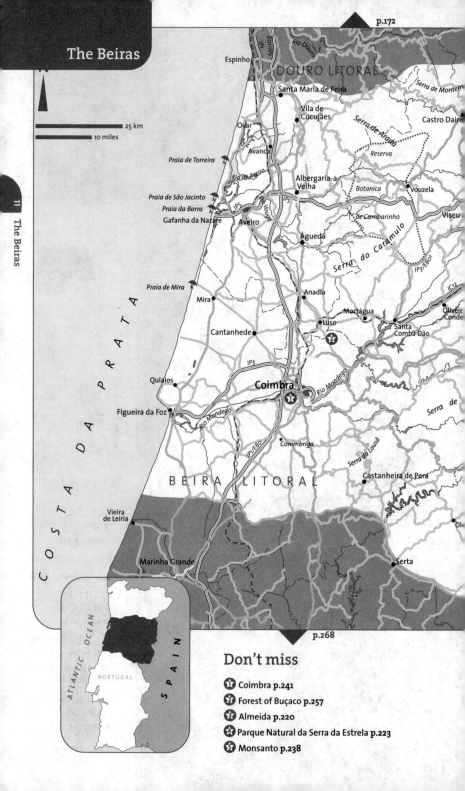

The Beiras

p.172

Espinho

DOURO LITORAL

Rio Douro

Serra de Montem

Santa Maria de Feira

Vila de
Cucujães

Castro Daire

Ovar

Serra de Arada

Avanca

Reserva

Praia de Torreira

Rio de Aveiro

Albergaria-a-
Velha

Botanica

Vouzela

Praia de São Jacinto

Praia da Barra

Gafanha da Nazaré

Aveiro

de Cambarinho

Viseu

Águeda

Serra do Caramulo

IP3/E801

Praia de Mira

Anadia

IC12

Mira

Mortágua

Oliveir
Conde

Luso

Cantanhede

Santa
Comba Dão

Quiaios

IP3

Coimbra

Rio Mondego

Figueira da Foz

Rio Mondego

Serra de

IP1/E80

Conímbriga

Serra da Lousã

Castanheira de Pera

BEIRA LITORAL

Vieira
de Leiria

Marinha Grande

Serta

Ole

p.268

Don't miss

⭐ Coimbra **p.241**

⭐ Forest of Buçaco **p.257**

⭐ Almeida **p.220**

⭐ Parque Natural da Serra da Estrela **p.223**

⭐ Monsanto **p.238**

25 km

10 miles

ATLANTIC OCEAN

PORTUGAL

SPAIN

COSTA DA PRATA

Tarouca

Vila Nova de Foz Côa

Rio Douro

Parque
Arqueológico
do
Vale Côa

Barragem
de Vilar

Serra da Lapa

Sernancelhe

Figueira de
Castelo Rodrigo

BEIRA ALTA

Serra da Marofa

Pinhel

Almeida

Fornos de
Algodres

Celorico
da Beira

RIBACÔA

Mangualde

Contenças de Baixo

Gouveia

Guarda

Estrela

Rio Mondego

Seia

Serra da

Manteigas

SPAIN

Parque Natural
da Serra da Estrela

Belmonte

Penhas da Saúde

Sortelha

Covilhã

Penamacor

Serra da Gardunha

Castelo Novo

Monsanto

BEIRA BAIXA

Serra do Muradal

Idanha-a-Nova

Castelo Branco

Getting around the Beira Alta

The **road** network is adequate, and most roads are good.

Pampilhosa serves as the Beiras' central **railway** junction, with connections to the east and on a north–south axis. A railway line runs from Guarda to Castelo Branco via Covilhã – otherwise, the inland Beiras are not well served by the rail network.

Similarly, the express **bus** network is much more comprehensive near the coast, with Coimbra serving as a staging-post for numerous north–south routes.

History

Before the Romans arrived in Portugal, Lusitanian tribespeople inhabited the *Montes Herminios*, which probably corresponds to the eastern slopes of the Serra da Estrela, in Beira Alta. Hannibal remarked that the people had always lived following their sheep on the mountains with no hope of reward for their perils and fatigues. So many people abandoned their difficult lives in these hills that the eastern Beiras became alarmingly depopulated, and in 1185, in the wake of Leonese aggression, Dom Sancho I launched a resettlement scheme which focused on the restoration of the ancient towns of Covilhã, Guarda and Idanha. Napoleon's forces entered the Beiras in 1807 under Junot, en route for Lisbon. In August 1810 Masséna led 66,000 troops into Portugal through the Beiras, occupying Guarda and Viseu, but their westward march was interrupted by Wellington at Buçaco.

Beira Alta

Beira Alta is a succession of small granite hills hemmed in by mountains, including the jagged Serra do Caramulo to the west and the massive Serra da Estrela, the highest mountain range in Portugal, to the southeast. Peaking at just under 6,500ft (2,000m), and being a mere 60 miles (100km) from the ocean, the Serra da Estrela receives an annual rainfall of up to 2,500mm. This nurtures a thick blanket of pine trees and supplies the region's rivers, including the Mondego – the only river that is Portuguese from its source to the sea – which run through flat-bottomed valleys from the northeast to the southwest. Rainfall diminishes farther inland, where the thin soil supports few crops.

Settlements are scattered, or grouped in small clusters, and traditionally employ the local granite. To the east the small-holdings support maize and pasture land, whereas to the west the local diet is more dependent on chestnuts, potatoes and rye bread. In his *Tragicomedia Pastoril da Serra da Estrela*, the dramatist Gil Vicente (*c.* 1470–*c.* 1536) writes of Lopo, a shepherd who breaks into song and dance 'in the manner of those of the mountains'. But these lapses are not frequent, and the people of Beira Alta seem more sombre and less friendly than those elsewhere. If you want to ingratiate yourself with the locals, try praising the excellent Serra cheese, made from goats' milk.

Very few tourists visit Beira Alta, because even in the large towns there are few monuments of note, and decent accommodation is sparse. But the strange, unpeopled landscapes will appeal to explorers, from the peculiar magnetism of the Serra da Estrela, to the barren lands pelted with boulders farther to the northeast.

Dão Wines

The southwest of Beira Alta – including Aguiar da Beira, Gouveia, Arganil, Mortágua, Tondela and parts of Viseu – has been demarcated as the Dão wine region, the second most productive in the country. It is named after a minor tributary of the Mondego. Dão reds mature into some of Portugal's best wines, smooth, full-bodied, and garnet-coloured (the young wines can taste oddly tannic). Most of the wine is red, which is of a far superior quality to the white.

The region is almost entirely granite, though the rock varies in hardness. The scattered plots of some 40,000 farmers are generally terraced, ideally at an altitude of 650–1,650ft (200–500m), though some vineyards are as high as 2,600ft (800m). The vintage usually begins in late September, at the end of the scorching, dry summer, and before the driving, snowy winter sets in. Most Dãos are matured and blended outside the region: by law, reds must be matured in the cask for a minimum of 18 months, though many remain there for two to four years. Though it is not indicated on the labels, the most balanced wines are produced in oak casks cut from the Forest of Buçaco or the Serra da Estrela. There is great consistency between the labels – if you like one, you'll like them all – because companies buy from the same suppliers. They are widely available and inexpensive.

Viseu

The capital of Beira Alta commands a plateau on the southern bank of the River Pavia, set at 1,650ft (500m) amid hills forested with Scotch pines, interspersed with gorse, ferns and vineyards. If the wealthy residents of 16th-century Viseu were to wander the town today, they would find much that is familiar. It was they who colonized the upper part of town around the cathedral, and many of their salubrious houses still stand, in wide streets; only the roofs look higgledy-piggledy. This antique part of town focuses on the lovely Praça da Sé, in which the visitor is sandwiched between the very dignified 18th-century façade of the Misericórdia and that of

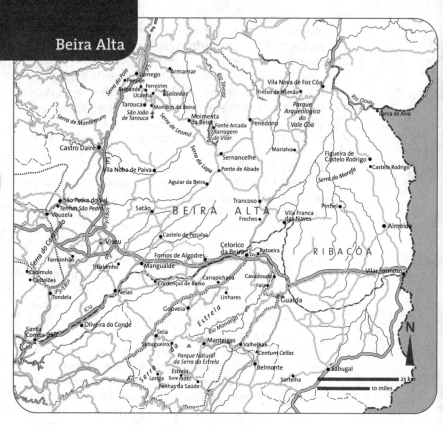

the once-Romanesque cathedral. To one side is the plain granite episcopal palace, which houses the Grão-Vasco museum. The modern heart of Viseu stands about 200 yards distant – as if out of respect – where it operates efficiently around the uncommonly leafy Praça da República.

History

The Romans chose this site for a military camp – the largest yet discovered in Portugal. Close to their roads to Conimbriga, Lamego and other towns, it also offered them relatively easy access to the coastal plain – via the valleys of the Rivers Mondego and Vouga, combined with the benefits of a large, fertile plateau.

Viseu was made the seat of a bishopric in the mid-6th century, after which the Suevi completely destroyed the Roman walls; Dom João I built new ones. Henry the Navigator was Duke of Viseu, and was thus able to milk the economic prosperity that came from trading the transhumant flocks of the Serra da Estrela. Today its importance as a commercial centre depends upon the production of Dão wines.

Getting to Viseu

By **road**, Viseu is 85km from Aveiro, 94km from Coimbra, 77km from Guarda, 127km from Porto, and 110km from Vila Real.

The **railway station**, along with all lines to Viseu, was closed at the end of 1990. From Lisbon, change at Nelas, where there is a direct bus connection to Viseu (min. 4½hrs total). From Porto, change at either Aveiro or Pampilhosa, followed by another change at either Sernada or Nelas respectively, connecting with buses (min. 3hrs total). If planning your route from Viseu, railway timetables are posted in the bus station, **t** (232) 426 685, so it's possible to work out the relevant connections.

Rede Expressos runs nine **buses** a day from Porto (2 hrs), nine from Coimbra (1½hrs) and 11 from Lisbon (4 hrs). They also serve Leiria (1½hrs, two daily), Lamego (3½hrs, five daily), Chaves (3¼hrs, two daily) and Guarda (1hr, seven daily).

The Cathedral

Cathedral
open daily 9–12 and 2–7

In the old part of town, all roads lead to the dirty-grey granite cathedral, which is located at the highest point in Viseu. Like most of Portugal's cathedrals, the building is a salad of styles: a mannerist façade, dated 1640 and niched with Evangelists, sits uncomfortably between two defensive Romanesque towers which are themselves topped with 18th-century minarets. The cavernous interior is a more elegant affair: 12th-century columns support the church's most interesting feature, the Manueline ceiling tracery representing ropes, which have been knotted loosely like pastry since 1513. Bishop Dom João de Melo tampered with the chancel in the late 17th century; now it is bathed in a yellow light, through which peer dark mermen painted on the ceiling – and the bishop, when he graces his rich throne of Brazilian jacaranda wood. A splendid 18th-century gilt retable glitters in replacement of Grão-Vasco's canvases, removed to the museum next door. A corridor decorated with 18th-century *azulejos* leads to the sacristy – if the door is locked, look through the keyhole at the wooden ceiling painted with exotic birds, whose extravagant plumage would no doubt be plucked by the cherubs, were they more nimble.

A staircase leads from the north transept, on the left of the church, to the *coro alto* and its delightfully carved choir stalls. These are ornamented by embryonic creatures and masklike faces, as well as a turtle, a whale and, most excitingly, a duck-billed platypus – evidence, to some, that the Portuguese discovered Australia around 250 years before Captain Cook. Lest the little creature's ego swell to continental proportions, it should be pointed out that its form may owe something to the description of a remora offered by the 15th-century chronicler, Azurara: 'another fish, no bigger than a mullet, which has upon the head a sort of crown by which it breathes, doing the office of gills'.

The *coro alto* opens on to the upper storey (*c.* 1730) of the formal, unmeditative cloister, of which the lower storey is interrupted by a late Romanesque/early Gothic portal, discovered in 1918. The upper cloister leads to the chapter house, which is remorselessly decorated with 18th-century *azulejos* depicting Herod's murder of the Innocents. Here is housed the **Cathedral Museum**. Note especially the two small 13th-century Limoges chests, of turquoise enamelled copper and gilt.

Cathedral Museum
adm

The Museu de Grão-Vasco

Museu de Grão-Vasco
t (232) 422 049; open Tues–Sun 9.30–12.30 and 2–5.30; closed Mon and hols; adm

The **Museu de Grão-Vasco** is installed in the bishop's palace, adjacent to the cathedral. During his lifetime, Vasco Fernandes, called Grão-Vasco (*c.* 1475–*c.* 1540), was the most outstanding painter in northern Portugal, rivalled only by Gaspar Vaz. Frei Carlos was working in Lisbon, and together they helped to introduce the Renaissance to Portuguese painting. Grão-Vasco's work in Viseu postdates the retable for the cathedral at Lamego, and shows a deeper, fuller style.

On the second floor of the museum, Grão-Vasco's monumental painting of St Peter portrays the apostle as a stern but human Renaissance bishop, with a Portuguese face; his painting of St Sebastian is set against the architecture and landscape of Flanders. The master was assisted by his pupils when painting the 14 zesty panels following the life of Christ, intended for the cathedral retable. Balthasar has travelled a long way to present his gift to the baby Jesus: at the adoration of the Magi, he is depicted wearing the feathers and pantaloons of an Indian wise man from newly discovered Brazil.

Around the Cathedral Square

Misericórdia
open Tues 2–6, Wed–Sun 10–6; adm, Sun free

The **Misericórdia** forms a third side of the cathedral square. Its well-proportioned granite and whitewash structure, with two towers, was designed by António da Costa and dates from 1775.

Casa-Museu de Almeida Moreira
t (232) 423 769; open daily 9–12.30 and 2–5.30

Head under the arch by the cathedral square and, when the road forks, bear left for the small **Casa-Museu de Almeida Moreira**, which contains unremarkable collections of furniture, ceramics and 19th-century paintings bequeathed by a former director of the Grão-Vasco Museum.

The Cava de Viriato

On the edge of town across the road from the old railway station is an octagonal enclosure dotted with trees: the embankments of the Cava de Viriato were thrown up by a Roman military legion after the campaign of Brutus Callaicus in 138 BC. There's not a great deal to see, except a statue of Viriatus, the Lusitanian guerrilla leader associated with the place on no decent evidence. (Viriatus roused the tribes of the Arevaci, the Belli and the Titti against the Romans, thus reviving the Celtiberian wars. Diodorus brings him to life by reporting Viriatus' warning to the citizens of the city of Tucci, who chopped and changed their allegiance between the Lusitanians and the Proconsul Servilianus some time after 141 BC. Viriatus told them of the middle-aged man who went bald because he had two wives: the younger wife plucked out his grey hairs to make him look younger, and the older wife plucked out his dark hairs to make him look as old as her. Thus Viriatus warned the fickle that they would be destroyed by both masters.)

(i) Viseu >

Avenida Calouste Gulbenkian, t (232) 420 950, turismo@ rtdaolafoes.com; open May–Oct Mon–Fri 9–12.30 and 2.30–6, Sat 10–12.30 and 2.30–5.30, Sun 9.30–12.30

Tourist Information and Services in Viseu

The **bus station** is on the busy Avenida Dr António José de Almeida. From here, turn right and walk uphill. To get to the Praça da República, bear left where the road veers to the right. From the Praça, take the Avenida 25 de Abril to the left of the Igreja dos Terceiros, and fork left for the **tourist office**.

Internet Access in Viseu

Instituto Portugues da Juventude (IPJ), Portal do Fontelo, **t** (232) 483 410 (*open Mon–Fri 9–6*). Free access for 30 minutes.

Festival in Viseu

During a drought in the 17th century, the millers of Vil de Moinhos, a village straddling the River Pavia just outside Viseu, were desperate for water to run their watermills – but the neighbouring farmers needed water for their crops. The two groups could not agree, so the matter went to arbitration. The millers prayed to **St John the Baptist**, and in honour of the favourable verdict they received from the judge, on 24 June, St John the Baptist's day, a hundred of them dress in parody of the nobility and process through the streets of Viseu on horseback. Called the *cavalhadas* (herd of horses) of Vildemoinhos, they are accompanied by drums, grotesque papier-mâché masks called *gigantones*, and various floats representing traditional local activities, such as sawing pine wood by hand.

Handicrafts in Viseu

Viseu is a good place to buy handicrafts, as the prices are lower than in other touristy towns. You may see people selling wickerwork by the roadside on the city outskirts. There are some shops located near Rua Direita.

Casa da Ribeira, Largo Nossa Senhora da Conceição. Local craftspersons' and artists' work is on sale, including ceramics, wickerwork, fabrics and wrought iron.

Sports and Activities in Viseu

Golfe Montebelo, Farminhão, west of Viseu, **t** (232) 856 464, *www.golfe montebelo.pt*. Eighteen-hole golf course and driving range.

Where to Stay in Viseu

★★★★**Hotel Grão Vasco**, Rua Gaspar Barreiros, **t** (232) 423 511, *www.hotel graovasco.pt* (€€). Doesn't really make the grade, in spite of its central location: it's outmoded and sleepy, more three-star than four, though the garden and pool are very appealing. Rooms are carpeted and there is free off-street parking. The restaurant serves local dishes such as roast leg of veal.

★★★**Hotel Moinho de Vento**, Rua Paulo Emilio 13, **t** (232) 426 049 or 424 116, *www.hmoinhodevento.pt* (€€). Across the Parque da Cidade from the tourist office, this more modern affair abounds with gadgets. The service is pleasant, and breakfast is a buffet. Surprisingly, the 'Don Quixote' bar is decorated in the style of an English pub.

★★★**Residencial Bela Vista**, Rua Alexandre Herculano 510, t (232) 422 026 (€). Near the cathedral and perfectly nice, though a little soulless. It has a private car park.

★★**Pensão Rossio Parque**, Rua Soar de Cima 55, next to the Jardim Major Teles, t (232) 422 085 (€). A splendid time warp back to bourgeois life in the 40s and 50s; glossy magazines would love it. A ewer and basin on a marble tabletop? That comes as standard – there's no sense of irony here. The restaurant has the same feel, but you'll eat better elsewhere. Come while you can.

★★**Hotel Avenida**, Avenida Alberto Sampaio 1, t (232) 423 432, *www.turism.net/avenida* (€). Has a slight William Morris feel. There's a caged lift, botanical prints, confidence with colours and a sense of beauty.

Residencial Dom Duarte, Rua de Alexandre Herculano 214, t (232) 421 980, *www.residencialdomduarte.pt* (€). For the less adventurous. Here some of the rooms have been done up. It's bright and quite OK, with heavy wooden furniture.

Turismo de Habitação
Quinta da Arroteia, Póvoa de Sobrinhos, 3km east of Viseu, t (232) 478 450 or (917) 378 598, *www. quintadarroteia.com* (€€). The delighfully simple interiors of this *quinta*, with its granite walls, solid wooden furniture, tiled floors and clean white linen, all add to its rustic feel.

Casa de Rebordinho, in Rebordinho, 6km south of Viseu, t (232) 461 258 (€€). A peaceful granite and whitewash manor house fronted by its staircase, set in a working farm. Ducks walk across the courtyard, and cows moo. It's furnished with white sofas around the fireplace, Arraiolos rugs on the terracotta floor, hunting prints and lots of flowers. Ground-floor bedrooms are bright and pretty, behind barred windows. Two of the four bedrooms do not have en suite bathrooms. The garden contains a Romanesque falcon house, and a 300-year-old rhododendron tree. Apart from breakfast, meals are not normally available.

Quinta de S. Caetano, Rua Poca das Feiticieras, Viseu, t (232) 423 984, *www.quintascaetano.com* (€€ CA). A distinguished manor house with a splendid chapel dating from 1638. Once the home of the Viscountess of St Caetano, it was the setting of contemporary novelist Augustina Bessa Luis' *Eugénia e Silvina*. The garden hosts a hundred-year-old Atlantic cedar and overlooks the Estrela mountains. All this added to the simple and elegant feel of the interior of the house, and the good regional food, makes for a comfortable stay.

Camping

Camping Moinhos do Dão, Tibaldinho, about 15km southeast of Viseu, t (232) 610 586, *www.moinhosdodao.nl*, (*camping €, room charges vary*). A campsite on the banks of the river Dão, on the farmland of a former watermill. Rooms are available in the mill house, log cabins, caravans or under canvas. Workshops and walks with a guide are organized. Wholesome food is on offer in the restaurant (€€), with vegetarian options, *open April–Oct*.

Eating Out in Viseu

Claustros da Sé, Rua Augusto Hilário 60–62, t (232) 426 452 (€€). Stylish restaurant and bar with a Brazilian cook who whips up all sorts of spicy and delicious dishes like rice, black beans and pork, and steak in a beer and mushroom sauce.

O Cortiço, Rua do Augusto Hilário 47, t (232) 423 853 (€€). Intimate and attractive, this granite-walled restaurant is just down from the statue of Dom Duarte. Offers good food from a traditional and varied Portuguese menu.

Casablanca, Avenida Emídio Navarro 70–72, t (232) 422 239 (€€). A menu of fresh seafood, served in an attractively tiled interior. *Closed Mon.*

Casa dos Queijos, Travessa das Escadinhas da Sé 7, t (232) 422 643 (€€). Excellently prepared dishes here from seafood to cheeses to wines –

and there's a shop downstairs to tempt you further.

Casa dos Queijos, Trav. Escadinhas da Sé, **t** (232) 422 643 (€). Translates as 'House of Cheese', the downstairs shop is packed with a delicious variety of local cheeses while upstairs a traditional restaurant serves tasty stews and similar.

Restaurante O Hilário, Rua Augusto Hilário 35, **t** (232) 436 587 (€). Good service and prices at this restaurant, with a variety of meat-based offerings.

A Caçarola, Travessa Major Teles 3, **t** (232) 421 007 (€). Bright and busy, particularly popular at lunchtime. The food is a bargain, but don't expect much atmosphere.

Bars and Clubs in Viseu

Galeria, in the Praça de Dom Duarte (no telephone). Stylish bar with regular live jazz. *Stays open until 2am.*

Day After, 1.5km north of town, **t** (232) 450 645. Big-time disco with international-calibre DJs, plus a restaurant.

Around Viseu

Termas de São Pedro do Sul

Spa
t *(232) 723 003 or 723 406, www.cm-spsul.pt*

It's refreshing to find a spa that has got its act together. The healing waters are channelled through an impressive modern complex on the bank of the River Vouga, and have spawned an array of accommodation, in an airy setting delightfully encroached on by pine trees.

The efficiently run spa treats over 10,600 patients throughout the year, for ailments including rheumatism, bronchitis, sinusitis and gout. Treatments normally last two to three weeks. Some doctors speak English, and, unlike other spas, the place does not feel like an asylum.

It was the Romans who first appreciated the waters here. They built baths at the time of Emperor Tiberius, but the plug has been pulled from their building complex, which lies in ruins beside its modern equivalent. In the 12th century Dom Afonso Henriques recuperated here from an injury received at Badajoz.

The Serra do Caramulo

West of Viseu, the Serra do Caramulo shields much of the inland Beiras from the coastal plain; its granite and precambrian schist support a thick cloak of Scotch pine, with rhododendrons and the occasional orchid. The otherwise undramatic range rises to a peak at Caramulinho, at 3,525ft (1,074m). It makes a pleasant drive, in spite of the condition of some of the roads. Keep an eye open for women wearing the *capucha*, a hooded black cape which makes them look like goblins, but is intended to stave off the cold and rain.

Caramulo itself perches at 2,600ft (800m), an altitude which led the village to be developed in the 1930s as a health resort for sufferers from tuberculosis. There are no special facilities, as one

Getting to areas Around Viseu

By **road**, Termas de São Pedro do Sul is 4km southwest of the town of São Pedro do Sul, itself some 22km northwest of Viseu. Caramulo is around 43km southwest of Viseu, depending on which route you take. Mangualde is halfway between Pampilhosa and Guarda by **rail** (*see* p.217).

may simply inhale the benefits – this may explain the local bidding, now used infrequently, 'that the blessing of the mountain may accompany you home'.

Museu do Caramulo
t (232) 861 270,
www.museu-caramulo.net; open
daily 10–6; closed
Easter, 24–25 Dec

This remote spot is an unlikely resting place for the excellent **Museu do Caramulo**, a miscellaneous collection of painting, sculpture, furniture, silver, archaeology and tapestry. The last category is represented by five early 16th-century Tournai tapestries depicting the first Portuguese in India, complete with weird animals and natives evidently based on garbled reports. There are works by Grão-Vasco and Frei Carlos; Picasso and Dalí presented minor pieces to the museum, and Queen Elizabeth II donated a painting by Sutherland.

A road leads uphill from Caramulo, past little granite houses, to the peak of **Caramulinho**. At 3,525ft (1075m), it offers huge 180° views of lesser heights, and is a gentle hour's walk away from town.

About 12km south of Caramulo, a thickly wooded mountainside provides the backdrop for bushy orange trees and a cluster of terracotta roofs, earning the village of **Castelões** the epithet 'the Sintra of the Beiras'. It's a good place for brief walks, as is the **Reserva Botánica de Loendros** at **Cambarinho**, 20km north of Caramulo, just past the village of Campia. In this hilly territory, the horizons are closer, and the land tickled by little streams. The best time to go is in May, when the rhododendrons flower, though their numbers have been depleted by forest fires.

The road veers northeast, and 14km later passes through the larger village of **Vouzela**, of which the only notable feature is the 13th-century **parish church**. Its gutter is supported by carvings of nightmarish human faces, as well as animals and angels, and the belltower is separate from the church.

Mangualde

Roughly 18km east of Viseu, the little town of Mangualde is surrounded by vineyards and orchards, especially crab-apple trees. Its most distinguished building stands on the extreme south side of town: the splendid **Palácio dos Condes de Anadia**.

Palácio dos Condes de Anadia
open Mon–Sat 2–6;
adm

The palace is distinguished by the rigid symmetry of its street façade – but each face of the building is different, including a loggia overlooking the courtyard. It was built in 1740, for the Count of Anadia. His descendants' nanny has clocked up 30 years of service, but her aprons have lost none of their starch as she proudly shows visitors around. She drops her voice in the marvellous kitchen glinting with copper pans, and conspiratorially swaps recipes.

There are some lovely handpainted ceilings, Sèvres statues, and various family portraits – the best are in the ballroom, an airy room lined with the most curious *azulejos* in Portugal. They depict a world of reversals: the sun and moon are within the ground, buildings are on clouds; a donkey flogs a man, horses ride men and joust; a man tends his baby while a woman totes a musket. The huge double staircase is lined with ladies and their massive hairdos hunting on horseback, and, on panels of the elements, winds puff out their cheeks almost until they pop.

Where to Stay Around Viseu

Termas de S. Pedro do Sul

★★★**Hotel Monte Rio**, Estrada da Lameira, Cruzamento c/a Vriante, Várzea, t (232) 720 040 or 720 050, *www.hotelmonterio.com.pt* (€€). Offers an 18-hole golf course, swimming pools, gardens, bedrooms with all mod cons, and, although the décor is a little dated, the place is comfortable and clean. Most of the rooms have wonderful panoramic views of the mountains around the river.

★★**Hotel Vouga**, Rua Mendes Frazao, Várzea, t (232) 723 063, *www.hotelvouga.com* (€€). Light and airy, with balconies overlooking the river.

Casa de Fataunços, Fataunços, Vouzela, t (232) 772 697, *www.termaspsul.com* (€€). Located just 3km away from the spa town, this beautiful 18th-century manor house offers great charm and comfort. All rooms have bathrooms, and facilities include a snooker room, table tennis, a pool and the house's own pretty gardens. Meals are available on request.

Caramulo

Hotel do Caramulo, Avenida Dr. Abel Lacerda, t (232) 860 100, *www.hotelcaramulo.com* (€€€). Sitting atop a hill, this slick hotel has impressive views over the Besteiros valley. The hotel's main focus is on its tip-top health facilities, from jacuzzis and a gym to treatment rooms and Turkish baths. The restaurant offers traditional Portuguese cooking, or there's a mix of tipples from the cocktail bar. Rooms are rather plain but offer more splendid views and a range of mod cons.

Pousada
Pousada de Sao Jerónimo, t (232) 861 291 (€€€). Looks like a suburban chalet, with a kidney-shaped swimming pool. The six bedrooms are attractively decorated and homey, with far views from their balconies, and polished granite bathrooms. The dining room takes advantage of the views; diners sit on rustic chairs talking across monastic candlesticks, eating rather plain meals.

Mangualde

★★★★**Casa D'Azurara**, Rua Nova 78, t (232) 612 010, *www.innsofportugal.com* (€€€). Recently restored, this 18th-century manor house was once the residence of the Earls of Mangualde. The décor is plush and comfortable inside the 15 large rooms, and there's a pretty garden. The gastronomic menu consists of traditional Beira Alta dishes.

Quinta da Boavista, Penalva do Castelo, t (232) 642 167 or 919 982 047/236, *www.toprural.com* (€€€). A fine *quinta* (the name means 'the estate with the beautiful view'), with a modest exterior hiding eight cosily decorated apartments. Resident staff look after your needs, and there are horses that guests may ride, and a pool.

Hotel Rural Mira Serra, Casal S. Sebastião, Abrunhosea-a-Vehla, Mangualde, **t** (232) 650 010, *www.miraserra.com* (€€€). Sitting 1,650ft (500m) up and looking out over the Serra da Estrela, this enchanting hideaway was built in 1927 as a health retreat. The hotel boasts its own microclimate, spa waters and landscaped gardens, and

a traditional menu is served in the restaurant from the wood oven, with a regional wine list.

Casa de Darei, Darei, **t** (232) 613 200, *www.casadedarei.pt* (€€). Stay in a medieval granite country house by the river Dão that is characterful but retains a simple sense of style. Several apartments accommodate 6–8 people and guests may use the canoes and boat for fishing from the private beach.

Guarda

The northeastern tip of the Serra da Estrela is host to the highest town in Portugal: Guarda stands at 3,465ft (1,056m), and on clear days it offers views stretching across the plains as far as the Spanish border. Dom Sancho I founded it here in 1199 for just that reason, and chose it to be the successor to the Visigothic episcopal seat of Egitânia. Its name and its ruined castle refer to Guarda's role as a frontier-guard; it became known as the city of the four F's: *Fria, Farta, Forte* and *Feia* – cold, well-supplied, strong and ugly. The second of these epithets refers to Guarda's fair, established in 1255. The success of the fair was so important to the welfare of the settlement that all those who came to it were exempt from civil or criminal liability for 30 days; their merchandise included linseed and iron, as well as wine, grain and livestock. Wellington used Guarda as a base for his operations in 1811–12.

The sloping town is charmless and unlovely because it feels bleak and exposed, and when it's cold, people are quite literally wrapped up in themselves. (Dozing beneath local wool blankets is like sleeping with a sheep.) There's little of interest about the place, but several good restaurants and a decent range of accommodation make it a good base from which to explore a wide area, particularly to the north and east.

Around the Town

The grim granite **cathedral** took 150 years to build. Construction began in 1390, under the direction of the sons of Mateus Fernandes, architect of Batalha, whose influence is seen in the flying buttresses and the clerestory. Boitac worked on the building 1504–17, shortly before it was completed *c.* 1540. The finished product is heavy, both inside and out, though the excellent gargoyles add a touch of wit – some of them have little legs sticking into the air. Lift each seat of the choir stalls to reveal a face with a different expression – grimacing, tipsy, angry, lecherous, smiling. Maybe this is a sardonic comment on the choristers.

Getting to Guarda

By **road**, Guarda is 140km from Aveiro, 193km from Bragança, 100km from Castelo Branco, 229km from Porto, and 77km from Viseu.

There are two **train** lines from Lisbon to Guarda, but only the more northerly route (6hrs total), via Coimbra-B (3¼hrs) and Pampilhosa (3hrs), is direct. The southerly route runs via Santarém (6½hrs), Castelo Branco (4hrs) and Covilhã, where you have to change (1¼hrs), and takes 7½hrs total. Both run four times daily. From Porto, Espinho and Aveiro, change at Pampilhosa. From Viseu, take the bus to Nelas (½hr), from where Guarda is 1¾hrs away.

Rede Expresso **buses**, t (271) 217 720, run with similar frequency, taking 6hrs from Lisbon, via Castelo Branco (2hrs) and Covilhã (¾hr). In some months, on some days of the week, buses run from Porto (4¼hrs) via Viseu (1¾hrs). Several other, regional, companies have regular services around the country.

Downhill and to the right, the façade of the **Misericórdia** exults in the Baroque of the 18th century, with an elegant granite and whitewash façade. It was built on the site of the old cathedral, which was considered to be too close to the town walls for safety. The façade faces the best-preserved of Guarda's ancient gates, known as the **Torre dos Ferreiros** (the Blacksmiths' Tower). Of the castle itself, little but the keep remains. One block downhill from the Misericórdia, the seminary dates from 1601 and now houses the well-displayed **Museu da Guarda** There's little worth seeing, except an adoration by two of the Magi attributed to the 16th-century master, Frei Carlos. Upstairs, ethnographic curiosities include clay models of traditional games, and a wooden sledge embedded with sharp stones, dragged to separate wheat from chaff.

Museu da Guarda
t (271) 213 460,
www.ipmuseus.pt;
open Tues–Sun 10–12.30
and 2–5.30; adm, free
entry Sun and national
hols until 2pm

Tourist Information and Services in Guarda

ⓘ **Guarda >**
Câmara Municipal,
Praça Luis de Camões;
t (271) 205 530;
open Mon–Sat 9–12.30
and 2–6.30, Oct–May
until 5.30

The extremely helpful regional **tourist office** has an abundance of information about the region and can help you plan walking and camping expeditions in the Serra da Estrela. Internet access is also available here (*see below*). The **railway station** is 5km out of town, but there are buses both ways every half-hour. The **bus station** is on Rua Dom Nuno Álvares Pereira, two roads downhill from the Hotel Turismo.

Internet Access in Guarda

Mediateca VIII Centernário, Praça Luís de Camões, t (271) 205 531 (*open Mon–Fri 9.30–12.30 and 2–5.30*). Free access.

Where to Stay in Guarda

★★★**Hotel Vanguarda**, Avenida Mendes do Carmo, t (213) 300 541, *www.imb-hotels.com* (€€). Newest hotel in town with excellent rooms, most with stunning panoramic views.

★★★**Hotel de Turismo**, Praça do Município, t (271) 223 366, *www. hturismoguarda.com.pt* (€€). By the lower end of the Jardim José de Lemos, this member of the Best Western chain is efficient and solid, though a little frayed and sombre. Frilled waitresses offer a very good charcoal grill. The price of rooms varies with view and equipment.

Residencial Santos, Rua Tenente Valadim 14, t (271) 205 400 (€). A very good place, housed in a converted mansion next to the Torre dos Ferreiros; it is nicely simple in a clean, modern way, with wooden floors, and showers rather than baths.

Pensao Residencia Filipe, Rua Vasco da Gama 9, **t** (271) 223 659 (€). Decent rooms, though some are a bit small, and centrally located.

Pensao Alianca, Rua Vasco da Gama 8a, **t** (271) 222 235 (€). Offers budget accommodation and a big smile. There's also a good cheap restaurant.

Turismo de Habitação
Quinta da Ponte, Faia, **t** (271) 926 126 (€€€). Well situated in the Serra da Estrela Park, by a Roman bridge over the River Mondego. The interior stays true to its 18th-century roots, with splendid marzipan-style decorations, combining comfort with a certain grandeur.

Solar de Alarcão, Rua Dom Miguel de Alarcao 25, **t** (271) 214 392 (€€). Just uphill from the cathedral in an interesting 17th-century granite house. Nice touches include the emblazoned door drape, the carved dark-wood canopies in the salon, and its own courtyard and loggia.

Quinta do Pinheiro, Cavadoude, **t** (271) 926 162, *www.quintadopinheiro.com* (€€). Located in the Mondego valley in the Serra da Estrela national park, a

few kilometres from Guarda, this enchanting 15th-century rural house was once a centre of cheese production. Accommodation is in the pretty granite buildings, with interiors decorated in a straightforward but traditional, comfortable style. There is a swimming pool for guests' use.

Eating Out in Guarda

Restaurante O Monteneve, Praça Luís de Camões 24, **t** (271) 212 799 (€€). Daily fish specials are the main offering here, with some meat dishes, served in a bright and modern setting. *Open Tues–Sun.*

O Ferrinho, Rua Francisco de Passos 23, **t** (271) 211 990 (€). At the top of the cathedral square, serving regional specialities such as cod dishes and spit-roast goat, plus good breakfasts and teas. *Closed Sun.*

Restaurante Belo Horizonte, Largo de S. Vicente 1, **t** (271) 211 454 (€). Not to be confused with the *residencial* of the same name, this is a typically Portuguese, family place that shyly serves enormous helpings of delicious regional specialities.

North of Guarda

The Ribacôa

The road north of Guarda follows the upper edge of the Parque Natural da Serra de Estrela, through the wide, gently sloping valley of the infant River Mondego. The route is more curvaceous than road maps indicate. North of Celorico da Beira the landscape becomes bare and severe, though stretches of the road are lined with poplars, and with ash and eucalyptus north of Freches.

Trancoso

Trancoso is sited on a hill spur at an altitude of 2,900ft (880m). Much of the town is contained within battlemented curtain walls, which were thrown up by Dom Dinis in the 13th century, so that the town could serve as a base from which to conquer the lands of the Ribacôa, the valley of the River Côa. Trancoso held a special place in Dom Dinis' heart: it was here that he married Isabel of Aragon in 1282. The town was draped with rich wall hangings and

Getting to The Ribacôa

By **road**, Transcoso is some 43km north of Guarda. Marialva is 17km northeast of Trancoso, and Pinhel some 36km east of Trancoso and 34km northeast of Guarda. Almeida is roughly 22km southeast of Pinhel.

Rede Expressos has a couple of **buses** to Transcoso from Guarda (1hr), more on Fridays; and one to Pinhel (½hr); local companies take up the slack. Pinhel is the necessary kicking-off point for Almeida if you're dependent on public transport.

branches of ash, but it was the carpet of rose petals that particularly delighted the 12-year-old bride. Dom Dinis presented her with Trancoso as a wedding gift.

The visionary cobbler known as Bandarra (1500–45) composed his *Trovas* in Trancoso. These popular verses were instrumental in creating the messianic cult of Sebastianism, which became widespread during the years of Spanish domination.

Trancoso is a good place to wander around. It's a time warp, a town of wrought-iron balconies and granite casements, where emblazoned *palácios* elbow tiny hovels. Only the web of electricity cables catches at modernity. To the north of the town, the formidable **castle** walls enclose a grassy oval space overlooked by the squat keep, which was also the work of the indefatigable Dom Dinis. In the centre of the walled town, a caged Manueline **pillory** stands in front of the **church of São Pedro**. Appropriately for St Peter, the weathervane is a lion.

Marialva

The ruined walled village of Marialva occupies a low hillslope overlooking its modern namesake and beyond to the plains of Beira Alta. The picturesque village is contained within the walls of a castle built by Dom Sancho I in 1200. Sprinkled with dark rubble and low boulders, the village retains its grandeur and its great poverty. The main reason for coming here is to stay in some of Portugal's most sophisticated accommodation, which has undoubtedly rescued the place from a slow death.

Pinhel

The attractive and isolated town of Pinhel lies between two tributaries of the River Côa. Dom Afonso Henriques wrested it from the Moors in 1179; subsequently, it has seen little action. Dom Dinis fortified the settlement in 1312, but much of the town wall was dismantled to build houses.

Two light-stone square castle towers remain, the more northerly with a discrete Manueline window and a Gothic gargoyle. Its twin was used as a prison until recently. The modest 14th-century Gothic **Castle Church of Santa Maria** is contemporary with its Ançâ-stone sculpture from the Coimbra School, attributed to Diogo Pires the Elder: the Holy Mothers are extravagantly draped in white robes. In

Museo Municipal
*Praça de Sacadura
Cabral; open weekdays
10–12 and 2–6*

the chancel, fourteen 15th-century paintings illustrate the life of the Virgin. The **Museo Municipal** is fairly humble, but the retable of 1537 is worth a look. It features a quartet of angels playing musical instruments.

Almeida

🏛 Almeida

The beautiful and unspoilt fortified village of **Almeida** is well worth a visit. The village is surrounded by a bizarre wilderness of plains pelted with boulders. Extraordinarily, the town is contained within star-shaped fortifications, a border fortress whose strength is second only to that of Elvas in the Alentejo.

Dom Sancho I conquered Almeida from the Moors in the 12th century. Such was its strategic importance that the site was refortified three times, by Dom Dinis, Dom Manuel, and Dom João VI. Almeida was captured by the Spanish in 1762, during the Seven Years' War, but later in that century it was rebuilt on a Vaubanesque plan – indeed Vauban himself is believed to have completed the works, which have a perimeter of 1½ miles (2.5km). The French took control of the stronghold twice: from the beginning of the Peninsular War until the Convention of Sintra; and in 1810, when Masséna managed to blow up the central magazine.

Castelo Rodrigo

The road north from Almeida passes olive trees and large vineyards, a dry landscape with distant horizons. Castelo Rodrigo lies 19km distant. This picturesque village mellows and decays beside the Serra da Marofa. The village is a clutch of small-windowed dwellings contained within the broken walls and fat towers of a smashed castle. The castle and its manorial residence were set on fire by indignant locals in the 16th century, disgusted at the traitorous behaviour of Cristóvão Moura, first Marquis of Castelo Rodrigo. He had been instrumental in securing the crown of Portugal for Philip II of Spain.

In the late 14th century, Castelo Rodrigo had sworn allegiance to Beatriz, Queen of Castile, and refused entry to Dom João I. He punished the settlement by decreeing that its coat of arms should always be displayed upside down.

Where to Stay in The Ribacôa

ⓘ Trancoso >
*Portas d'El Rei, **t** (271)
811 147, geral@cm-
trancoso.pt; open
Mon–Fri 9–12.30 and
2–5.30, Sat–Sun
10–12.30 and 2–5.30*

Trancoso

★★★★**Hotel Turismo de Trancoso**, Rua Prof Irene Avillez, **t** (271) 829 200, *www.hotel-trancoso.com* (€€€–€€). A luxurious hotel on the edge of town with grand spacious rooms and an elegant restaurant. Rates drop during the week and in winter.

Residencial Dom Dinis, Estrada de Lamego, **t** (271) 811 525, *www.domdinis. net* (€). Located centrally, behind the post office, with comfortable, stylish rooms.

Marialva

Turismo de Habitação

Casas do Côro, Marialva, t 917 552 020, *www.assec.pt/casa-do-coro* (€€€). An industrialist and his wife have developed six traditional granite houses here, some of which can be rented as a whole, others room by room. They have a very strong sense of design, with slate-floored bathrooms, impeccable bed linen, good works of art on paper and exposed granite walls. A large swimming pool, jacuzzi and deck are available to all guests. The housekeepers speak some English or French and traditional meals are available, preferably requested at the time of booking. The same concern runs an upmarket gift shop, Loja do Côro.

Almeida

Casa Pátio da Figueira, Rua Direita 48, t 919 469 170 or 914 697 803 (€€). Four double rooms in an elegant 18th-century town house, with a pool and charming gardens.

Pensão-Restaurante A Muralha, t (271) 574 357 (€). Decent rooms at a good price, just by the crossroads outside the fort, and a basic restaurant.

Residencial Morgado, Bairro de São Pedro, t (271) 574 412 (€). Clean and comfortable, also outside the fort.

Pousada

★★★Pousada da Senhora das Neves, t (271) 574 290, *www.pousadas.pt* (L1 C). A tinkling horsecart tours the town for guests at the *pousada*, which looks out incongruously from the highest part of the town. There's also a restaurant (€€€), serving fish and meat specialities.

Eating Out

Trancoso

Restaurante Área Benta, Rua dos Cavaleiros 30, t (271) 817 180 (€€€–€€). Traditional, well-executed dishes served in a classy modern setting. *Booking advised.*

O Museu, Largo de Santa Maria, t (271) 811 810 (€€). In the old town, within the castle walls, serving traditional Portuguese fare plus finer seafood dishes.

Northwest of Trancoso

From Trancoso, a leafy road leads northwest through the Serras da Lapa and de Leomil to Lamego and the Alto Douro (*see* pp.151–70).

Aguiar da Beira

Some 25km west of Trancoso, it's difficult to tell whether humans or animals live behind medieval doorways in the old part of Aguiar de Beira. Look for telltale straw. The town fountain is surmounted by a roofless granite chamber edged with stone benches, which probably dates from the late 13th century, and may have filled the same role as the 12th-century council chamber at Bragança.

Around the Barragem de Vilar

Twenty-nine km northwest of Trancoso, just southeast of the Barragem de Vilar, the village of **Sernancelhe** boasts a fine pillory topped with a cage, dated 1559. Nearby, the portal of the 13th-century Romanesque **Igreja Matriz** is flanked on either side by a niche containing three small sculptures, forming some of the finest Romanesque granite carving in the country. The four Evangelists, St Peter and St Paul wear togas. The portal itself features an arch of angels standing on top of one another. Within, there's not much to look at, except for a tomb depicting a lady on a dragon.

It's possible to swim in the sand-fringed **Barragem de Vilar**, a large man-made lake damming the River Távora, equidistant from Trancoso and Lamego. East of the lake, the village of **Fonte Arcada** worships in a Romanesque **Igreja Matriz**, which was restored in 1502. It contains good Flemish-style paintings of the Passion, and part of the construction appears to use living rock. Thirteen kilometres northeast of the Barragem, the photogenic triangular **castle** at **Penedono** is worthy of Macbeth: built on a rock outcrop, and mottled with lichen, its crenellated towers are like claws.

Around Tarouca

Nine km northwest of the Barragem de Vilar, a turning south of the main road at Mondim da Beira follows a little trout-filled river to the important monastery church at **São João de Tarouca**. It was the first Cistercian monastery in Portugal, founded in 1124, and has subsequently been filled with delightful oddities. A guide insists on reporting what century these date from; sometimes it's possible to escape from him. Among the vivid paintings from the School of Grão-Vasco is one attributed to the master himself, hung over the third altar to the right of the nave.

São João de
Tarouca
open Tues–Sun

Lift the seats of the choir stalls carved from Brazilian wood, to reveal the polished cheeks of the cherubs, against which weary choristers could prop their buttocks. In the chancel, excellent 18th-century *azulejos* narrate the story of the monastery's foundation, complete with a thunderbolt sent to indicate the desired site. The careful use of space and strong blue colouring are combined with a splendid attention to detail, right down to rabbits chomping leaves. Less contented animals appear on the granite tomb of Pedro, Count of Barcelos and illegitimate son of Dom Dinis. Dating from 1354, it depicts a wild boar hunt. Perhaps it was the excitement of the scene that led the gentleman on the front of the organ to wave his arms and open his mouth whenever the organ was played. Considerably less nimble is the whopping 14th-century granite statue of the Virgin, who weighs in at 2,200lb (1,000kg). In the sacristy, all 4,700 pictorial tiles are different.

One km east of Tarouca, a minor road runs north to the village of **Ucanha**, which is notable for its **fortified bridge**. The bridge itself is odd because it rises to a pointed peak, rather than being flat or humped. The stocky tower that defends it was built by the Abbot of Salzedas in 1465, probably to mark the entrance to the abbey's land, to serve as a customs post for taxes levied on produce, and to trumpet the wealth and importance of the abbey. The river at this point is shallow enough for women to do their laundry.

Small elder trees with dark, heavy leaves grow in the neighbourhood; the berries are harvested and the red dye exported.

Mosteiro de Santa Maria
open daily 10–12.30 and 2–6; guided visits only

The minor road continues to **Salzedas**, where the importance of the Cistercian **Mosteiro de Santa Maria** was superseded only by Alcobaça. It was built between 1168 and 1225, under the patronage of Teresa Afonso, widow of Egas Moniz and governess of the five children of Dom Afonso Henriques. The monastic buildings are ruined, but the church remains intact, though mercilessly 'modernized' in the 18th century. Today, the humble houses to the left of the monastery may be more interesting, with an alley right out of the Middle Ages, daub and all.

Returning to the main road to Lamego, a turning to the east just 4km north of Tarouca leads to Ferreirim, where the church of a Franciscan monastery contains panels attributed to Cristóvão de Figueiredo, Garcia Fernandes and Gregório Lopes. The road north to Lamego passes through vineyards and cultivated land, with isolated dwellings among rows of poplars and other trees.

Parque Natural da Serra da Estrela

✪ **Parque Natural da Serra da Estrela**

Stopping just short of 6,500ft (2,000m), the Serra da Estrela is the highest mountain range in Portugal, and forms a barrier across the centre of the country. They are old-fold mountains: the peaks are rounded and grassy, pelted with granite boulders, where deep, rocky glens split the gently sloping hillsides. There are deep glaciated valleys, with moraines as low as 2,300ft (700m), and glacial lakes. Snow lies on the heights from November to April, and being relatively near the Atlantic, the rainfall is as high as 2,500mm. The climate is not so much extreme as variable, shifting quickly from rain to sun, and following only a loose annual pattern. The lower slopes are blanketed with pine and dotted with chestnut trees, though forest fires are common, leaving bald wastelands. Pinaster and birch grow higher up. Heather and broom thrive above the tree line, sometimes level with the clouds. Thousands of crocuses and narcissi flower at the end of April, in shades from deep purple to almost white; the dwarf shrubs flower six weeks later, in the middle of June.

The invigorating, massive views and the pure air make the Serra da Estrela an excellent territory for walking. There's a magnificent walk of 3–3½ hours over easy ground from Penhas Douradas (a winding 20km west of Manteigas) up the gently sloping main ridge, to the summit of Torre, 6,540ft (1,993m).

Getting to and around the Serra da Estrela

Be careful if you are **driving** in the Serra: roads can be icy or wet, mist descends, and flimsy cars may get blown into the granite posts that line each road. The Gouveia to Manteigas road offers the most spectacular and impressive views in the mountains. From Guarda, the easiest way to approach the highest parts of the Serra is via Valhelhas, 20km southwest of the town. From Valhelhas, a road runs 17km west to Manteigas. Covilhã (Beira Baixa) is a good access point. The drive south from Guarda or east from Belmonte (Beira Baixa) to Sortelha is beautiful.

Public transport is a problem. Joalto/RBI, t (271) 221 515, have two **buses** a day on weekdays between Guarda and Manteigas. Buses run twice daily from Covilhã (Beira Baixa) to Seia and Manteigas, along the low route via Unhais da Serra, and there is a weekend bus service from Covilhã to Penhas da Saude. There are no bus services directly across the park, but services around its edges are frequent. There is also one express a day from Coimbra to Gouveia (2hrs) and three to Seia (2½hrs). The only access to Sortelha by public transport is by local bus, which runs twice daily from Sabugal.

Manteigas

The town of Manteigas is the most appealing in the Serra, nestled at the foot of sheer, pale hills, in the glaciated valley of the River Zêzere. The spa town takes pride in its appearance, with the town hall successfully offering incentives for homeowners to paint their houses white. Small frogs hop about the place at night. There are two springs at **Caldas de Manteigas spa**: the warm spring (107°F/42°C) and the holy spring (66°F/19°C). The waters help rheumatism, skin and respiratory problems. Two roads lead up into the hills: the forestry road is quicker, but scary. Both pass yew trees growing on the edge of the settlement.

Caldas de Manteigas spa
t (275) 980 300;
open 1 May–30 Oct

Ski Parque
t (275) 982 970,
www.skiparque.pt;
open Sun–Thurs 10–6,
Fri–Sat 10–1; adm exp

There is now a big dry-ski run 7.5km east of Manteigas, **Ski Parque**, on the N232; which serves as a stand-in when there's no snow. Gear is available to hire on-site.

Life in the Serra

All the clustered settlements in the Serra had established themselves by the 16th century, though the isolated hamlets put down their roots more recently. The people of the Serra are sheep farmers, but from April to September they sow rye – a hardy cereal which is well suited to poor soil, and can survive high summer and low winter temperatures – as well as potatoes and a few vegetables. But it is the ewes' milk, wool and lambs that their livelihoods depend on; this is the milk which makes *queijo da Serra*, the superb creamy hard cheese with an 18cm diameter. It takes 4–6 litres of milk to make a single kilo of cheese.

Cheese-making, of the local *queijo da serra* cheese, takes place between November and April; many farmers – or more usually their wives – perform each stage of the process, from preparing the milk and rennet to curdling, salting and curing. (*See* p.227 for a description of cheese fairs.) Industrialization is creeping in, however, and the farmers are up against strict production requirements from the EU, as well as competition from other

European cheeses. Many of them rent their properties – which are often just a single, windowless room walled with granite and schist – so there is little incentive to improve them. The thatch must be replaced every year, after the first rains.

Around the settlements, or in the hills, it's common to see the *Cão da Serra*, a breed of dog peculiar to the area. They're big, loping things rolling with heavy fur, equipped with collars that bristle with nails, to prevent wolves tearing out their throats.

Gouveia

The road from Manteigas to Gouveia affords dramatic views. About 2km east of the Pousada de S. Lourenço, it passes through a weirdly prehistoric landscape of sandy heather strewn with boulders. There's an indifferent collection of paintings in the **Abel Manta Museu de Art Moderna** only worth a look if you have time to kill.

Abel Manta Museu de Art Moderna
Rua Direita 45, t (238) 493 648; open Tues–Sun 9.30–12.30 and 2–6

Linhares

Fifteenth-century houses line narrow cobbled streets in the charming hilltop village of Linhares, some 20km northeast of Gouveia. In the days of the Visigoths the village was a bishopric. The medieval castle offers magnificent views of the plains below.

Seia

The little town of Seia stands 28km southwest of Gouveia. It offers little of great interest, other than being a good kicking-off point for exploring the Serra, and therefore furnished with some good hotels and eateries.

Sabugeiro

Eight km east of Seia, Sabugeiro stands, at 3,450ft (1,050m), just above the tree line, and is Portugal's highest village. The old part of the village lies off the main road, remote enough for the 700-odd residents to stare at foreign visitors and instruct their dogs not to growl. Wizened crones lope about the place, shooing chickens with bald necks. Stones keep slates on the roofs of houses and pine branches on top of chicken coops. There are plenty of shops selling Serra cheese, but Sabugueiro offers bargains of another sort, displayed beside the road: cowhide rugs, flecked with brown like the cattle of the Maasai, for €250. Perfect for loft living, and much cheaper than back home.

Torre

One of the most forceful parts of the Serra lies southeast of Sabugueiro, just before Torre, around the great rock-cut image of the Virgin, **N.S. da Boa Estrela** – there's something magnetic, almost cosmic, about the place. Torre, the highest point in Portugal at 6,540ft (1,993m), is huddled with corrugated iron huts, from which tentative skiers emerge. Just below the peak lie dams of drinking water, surrounded by rocks covered with electric-green lichen like some insecticide. The flat light illumines the birth of the River Zêzere, which becomes a tributary of the Tagus.

Sortelha

The tiny, peaceful village of Sortelha, roughly 40km south of Guarda and 33km northeast of Covilhã, is fixed in a landscape of granite boulders; the view from the castle bowls down to a tree-filled valley alive with the sound of running water, and beyond to mountains and plains.

The old village is contained within the castle walls and built only of granite: houses have been constructed around protruding boulders, and are roofed with lichenous terracotta. A mere dozen people live here permanently. One of them attends a moth-eaten donkey as it wanders home in the luminous evening light, with a bunch of bright grass strapped to its side. The other buildings within the castle walls are second homes, or spartan *Turismo de Habitação*, as most residents live in the more modern village.

The **castle** is excellently positioned for defence; Dom Sancho I chose the site in the 13th century, and took advantage of the rock formation when building its walls. Now ivy wells over the tower. A 16th-century **pillory** stands at the foot of the castle, and there is a **handicrafts shop** near its entrance. Although they know their prices, it's a good place to pick up the odd milking stool or spindle.

Sabugal

The extraordinary landscape between Sortelha and Sabugal has a strange beauty; 12km east, the early frontier town of Sabugal lies on a low hill overlooking the valley of the River Côa, surrounded by fertile plains.

The imposing early 14th-century **fortress** manages to be both strong and beautiful, but it was not always so: over the ages the high walls and oval ramparts were pillaged, that the locals might wall their kitchen gardens. Now the castle has had its dignity restored, complete with the unusual pentagonal keep. Its predecessor hosted a peace meeting between Dom Sancho II of Portugal and Fernando III of Castile.

Sports and Activities in the Serra da Estrela

Walking in the Parque Natural da Serra da Estrela, across some of Portugal's most rugged scenery and through some of her most isolated and traditional villages, is a hugely rewarding experience. Trails are easy to follow, and it's possible to spend anything from a day to a week in the park.

Manteigas is the best base for walking expeditions in the Serra. The village has a very helpful **park information office**, Rua 1 de Maio 2, t (275) 980 060, *pnse@icn.pt* (*open*

Mon–Fri 9–12.30 and 2–5.30), which sells hiking maps and provides other information about life in the Serra. They also organize guided walks and offer Internet access.

There are other **park offices** in Gouveia (Av. Bombeiros Voluntários 8, **t** (238) 492 411; *open Mon–Fri 9–12.30 and 2–5.30*) and Seia (Praça República 28, **t** (238) 310 440; *same opening hours*), and the regional tourist office in Guarda (*see* p.217) is also helpful.

Until recently, as elsewhere, there has been a lack of a decent walking map; three cheers, however, for the Serra da Estrela National Park, for producing a thorough, explicit, English-language book of walks (*Discovering the Region of the Serra de Estrela*) written by walkers, with maps included, for €5. It's available from the National Parks, Reserves and Nature Conservation Department, Serra da Estrela National Park, Manteigas, and should be available from all tourist offices in the park itself.

Skiers should head for Torre or Sabugueiro, where the Clube Nacional de Montanhismo, Rua Pedro Álvares Cabral 5, Covilhã, **t** (275) 323 364, *www.cnm.org.pt*, rents equipment. The season runs from January to March.

Paragliding is on offer from Linhares, at the Inatel Paragliding School, **t** (271) 776 590 or (218) 869 127, *www.inatel.pt*.

ⓘ **Manteigas >>**
Rua Dr Esteves de Carvalho, **t** *(275) 981 129, www.cm-manteigas.pt; open Tues–Fri 9.30–12 and 2–6, Sat until 8*

Festivals in the Serra da Estrela

Cheese Fairs, where you'll find *queijo da serra* cheese on sale, are held in the region between November and mid-April. They begin just before sunrise, at 7am, and usually end at 9am, and are held in Fornos de Algodres and Carrapichana fortnightly on Mondays, and in Celorico da Beira fortnightly on Fridays, in the marketplace. Fairs are also held at Carnival time: in Seia (Sat), Gouveia (Sun) and Manteigas (Tues).

Handicrafts in the Serra da Estrela

O Mundo Rural, Largo Dr Alípio de Melo, near the tourist office in Gouveia (*open Mon–Sat 10–12.30 and 2.30–6.30, Sun 10–3*). Ceramics, fabrics, food and wine at good prices.

Where to Stay in the Serra da Estrela

Manteigas

★★★★**Albergaria Berne**, Quinta de St. António, **t** (275) 981 351 (€). Modern complex, shiny and piney, with some rooms overlooking the pool. Rooms are simple and comfortable.

★★**Residencial Estrela**, Rua Dr. Sobral 5, **t** (275) 981 288 (€). Homely, with pumpkins ripening on the window sills. The bedrooms are basic but comfortable, and overlook the solar panels that heat the water, to a hill beyond. Gypsy scarves are draped over lamps in the restaurant, which offers stewed rump of veal, or a mixed *cozido serrano*.

Casa de São Roque, Rua de Santo Antonio 51, **t** (275) 981 125 (€). A charming older home with rooms furnished with antiques.

Pousada
Pousada de S. Lourenço, **t** (275) 982 450, *www.pousadas.pt* (L1 N). A winding 13km north of Manteigas, the *pousada* perches with a view of the town. It's a harmonious, mellow mountain lodge overlooking smooth, fanning wooded mountains. Double-glazed bedrooms are small and simple beneath wood-planked ceilings, the receptionists dress traditionally, like Gretel, and the comfortable restaurant serves good food (*caldo verde* with *chouriço* and corn bread, stewed veal with vegetables, rabbit and rice stew) at nicely laid tables ornamented by hairy chestnut husks.

Turismo de Habitação
Casa das Obras, Rua Teles de Vasconcelos, Manteigas, **t** (275) 981 155, *www.casadasobras.pt* (€€). Fine 18th-century manor house built for a local judge (and still in the same family). The grand old interiors are tastefully furnished with antiques and the six large rooms, with bathrooms, have great charm. There's a bar, a garden with a swimming pool

and private parking, and meals are available upon request.

Casa de S. Roque, Rua de Santo António 51, Manteigas, **t** (275) 981 125 (€). Cosily furnished with antiques. The best feature is the patio, where your breakfast will be served.

Camping

Parque de Campismo Rossio de Valhelhas, Valhelhas, **t** (271) 408 206, *jfvalhelhas@clix.pt* (€). Grassy municipal camping ground, about 15km east of Manteigas. *Open 1 May–30 Sept.*

Parque de Campismo Vale do Rossim, Vale do Rossim, **t** (238) 492 411 (€). Next to a reservoir, west of Manteigas. Hot showers, a restaurant and a shop are available. *Open 1 July–31 Aug.*

(i) **Gouveia >**
*Largo Dr Alipio de Melo, **t** (238) 492 185; open Mon–Sat 9–12.30 and 2–5.30*

Gouveia

★★★**Eurosol Goveia**, Av 1 de Maio, **t** (238) 491 010 (€€). A pleasant 3-star choice with 42 double rooms, 3 singles and 3 suites, all fully equipped with air conditioning, telephone, safe-deposit box, mini-bar and TV. The hotel's restaurant is recommended for its regional specialities.

Quintas das Cegonhas, Nabainhos, 6km from Gouveia, **t** (238) 745 886, *www.cegonhas.com* (€). Campsite on a restored farm with grassy terraces, pool, showers, bar and restaurant. Two basic apartments and two rooms are also available.

(i) **Seia >**
*Dr Afonso Costa, **t** (238) 317 762; open Mon–Fri 9–6, Sat–Sun 9–12.30 and 2–5*

(i) **Torre >>**
*shopping arcade, **t** (275) 314 551; open Fri–Tues 9.30–1 and 2–5.30*

 Casa Árabe >>

Seia

★★★★**Estalagem de Seia**, Avenida Dr Afonso Costa, **t** (238) 315 866 (€€–€). Occupies an 18th-century manor house on the town's main street, with a double granite staircase, carved furniture and shutters. There's a nice pool with a view. Not as luxurious as it sounds. *Winter is high season.*

★★★**Hotel Camelo**, Avenida 1 de Maio 16, **t** (238) 310 100, *www.camelo hotel.pt* (€). Located in the centre of Seia, most rooms share this hotel's marvellous view over the valley. A good three-star hotel rather geared for groups, but none the worse for it. It provides a pool, snooker, ping-pong, and very friendly service. Half the tennis court has been turned into a sandpit. *Winter is high season.* Restaurant *(see below)*.

★**Residencial Jardim**, Edificio Jardim 11, Av Luis Vaz de Camões, **t** (238) 311 414 (€). Modern and clean, some rooms have views of the surrounding valley.

Quinta das Mestras, Nogueira do Cravo, 4 km from Oliveira do Hospital, **t** (238) 602 988, *www.quintadas mestras.com* (€). Old granite country house in 7½ acres (3ha) of terraced olive groves and pines. The décor is simple: whitewash with pretty country-style patterns, wrought-iron beds and basket chairs. There are also two *cabanas* a short distance away from the main house.

Sabugeiro

Casas do Cruzeiro, Apartado 85, **t** (238) 315 872 or 312 825, *www.quintado crestelo.pt* (€€–€). Thirty-two more or less traditional houses or apartments in the old centre are available to rent from Casas do Cruzeiro, a reasonably well-organized set-up. All have a kitchenette, bathroom and fireplace; some have views, and prices vary accordingly. They're often block-booked by school groups.

Abrigo da Montanha, Largo Nossa Senhora da Fátima, **t** (238) 315 262 (€). Rooms with shower; breakfast included. Also has a standard restaurant.

Casa do Serrinho, Largo Nossa Senhora da Fátima, **t** (238) 314 304 (€). Across from the Abrigo da Montanha, at the top of the village, this house offers four rooms with a shared kitchen.

Penhas da Saude (near Torre)

Pousada da Juventude, **t** (275) 335 375, *penhas@movijovem.pt* (€). The road running southeast of Torre towards Covilhã passes through Penhas da Saude, which has this good youth hostel, which is open all year.

Sortelha

Various houses are available to rent, or there's *Turismo de Habitação*.

Casa da Cerca, Largo de Santo António, **t** (271) 388 113 (€€). A superb choice just off the main road. The rustic, yet comfortable rooms have wood floors and traditional furniture. Apartments are also available.

Casa Árabe, contact Raul Clara on **t** (271) 388 276 or 963 069 019 (€). The landlord of the bar **As Boas Vindas** – a great little place decorated with ceramics and tools – rents out a two-bedroom house complete with a four-poster almost as big as the room it's in. This is almost the only place in Portugal where you can see and use antique village furniture and ceramics of the highest order, far more beautiful than anything you'll find in Quinta this or Solar that. Unforgettable.

Casa do Vento Que Soa > Casa do Vento Que Soa, **t** (271) 388 182 (€). Three ancient houses within the castle walls are available to stay in, of which the dark granite one is the least uncomfortable. Entered by means of an unsupported external granite staircase, its many bedrooms are decently but rather sparsely furnished.

To rent one of the **Casas do Campanário** at the very top of the village, contact Luís Paulo on **t** (271) 388 198 or 388 638 or check at nearby Bar Campanário.

Turismo de Habitação

Casa do Pátio > Casa do Pátio, Sortelha, **t** (271) 388 113 (€). At the lower end of Sortelha village, outside the castle walls, is this delightful, cosily furnished wood and granite outbuilding of the Solar de N.S. da Conceição, with which it shares an informal courtyard, where local women stitch Arraiolos rugs. A small, well-stocked kitchen leads off the sitting room complete with sofabed, fireplace, woodburning stove and TV. Food and drink are provided; you pay for what you use. Upstairs is a bedroom with two single beds, and a shower room. The chic Viscondessa prattles in French, reserving the right of admission to an independent apartment (€€) on the ground floor of the main house. This includes both a double room and a triple room, with a great portico-type chimney in one corner of the dining room. It's cheapest to rent the house during the summer period from 1 June to 31 August, because of heating costs.

Sabugal

Residencial Sol-Rio, Avenida Infante D. Henrique 58, **t** (271) 753 197 (€). With views up to the castle and the river on the other side, this *residencial* is a small place offering nice little rooms, and good value. Meals are available in the attached restaurant.

Eating Out in the Serra da Estrela

Manteigas

Pensão e Restaurante Serradalto, Rua 1 de Maio, **t** (275) 981 151 (€€€). Offers marvellous valley views from your table, over traditional fare and decent inexpensive rooms.

Gouveia

Restaurante O Júlio, Travessa do Loureiro 11a, **t** (238) 498 016 (€€–€). Good-value, well-cooked traditional dishes.

Seia

Tempo de Sabores, at the Hotel Camelo (*see* p.228) (€€). Renowned for its gastronomic cooking and excellent Dão wine list. *Open daily 12–2.30 and 7.30–9.30, except Sun pm.*

Restaurante Borges, Travessa do Funchal 7, **t** (238) 313 010 (€€). Provides good-value food.

Restaurante Regional de Serra, Avenida dos Combatentes da Grande Guerra 14, **t** (238) 312 717 (€). This is the best place to eat: nothing fancy, and conversation will have to compete with the television, but the food's good and the prices are very reasonable.

Sortelha

Restaurante Dom Sancho I, Largo do Corro, **t** (271) 388 267 (€€). Just inside the village gate; serves very good food, particularly game, in an attractive, rustic setting. *Closed Tues.*

Alboroque >> Alboroque, Rua da Mesquita, **t** (271) 388 129 (€). Within the castle walls, this restaurant *típico* is all set for a medieval banquet, without the filth of the original or the kitsch of an imitation. The building is 500 years old, with treetrunk beams and granite walls, and a table made from a huge pair of bellows. At the bar, benches are draped with goatskins, and the walls are hung with gourds. The menu is brief but the food is very good. *Caldeirada de cabrito* is the obvious choice, or there's *bacalhau*, or chicken and French fries. Be sure to try the *javali* (wild boar) if it is on the menu at the time of your visit.

Beira Baixa

Beira Baixa, the southeastern or 'lower' Beira, is dominated by mountains in the north including part of the Serra da Estrela and, running parallel, the craggy grey granite Serra da Gardunha. Snowcapped in winter, the mountains are robed each spring in purple heather blossom, which withers to brown in the heat of summer, only to be relieved by the autumn rains. In the south, the mountains yield to vast plains of Alentejan proportions. Here the climate is scorching in summer, wet in spring, and moderate in winter, though frost is not uncommon.

In the mountains and hills, pines dominate the trees, oxen and goats the livestock, millet the cereals. But the cultivated area is small: although the rainfall is high, the level ground is poor. Great groves of cork oaks on the plains between Idanha-a-Nova and Castelo Branco were decimated by forest fires in the summer of 2003; other important cash crops include almonds, fruit trees and olive oil, of which Castelo Branco produces some of the best in Portugal. Wool and other textiles buoy the local economy. As in the Alentejo, houses in the south tend to be whitewashed, and the land is held in *latifundias*. The people are affable, tolerant and cordial – no more so than when they are eating superb roast kid, which is particularly aromatic here because the animals graze on wild herbs.

Beira Baixa contains some of the loveliest landscapes in Portugal, combined with places of peculiar magnetism. There are very few monuments of note, so the best thing to do is to drive and discover for yourself.

Covilhã

Built into a wooded hillslope on the southeastern edge of the Serra da Estrela, Covilhã is a surprisingly large town for such a remote and underpopulated region, with a population of 18,000 souls. The settlement overlooks flatlands to where hills converge in the distance. Its prosperity is dependent on textiles, especially wool, but Covilhã is being promoted as a base for walking in the Serra in summer, and for winter sports. The loiterers wear suits, and watch pine-trees truck through, as there's nothing much else to look at in town.

Museu de Lanifícios
*Rua Marquês de Avila
e Bolama, t (275) 319
700; open Tues–Sun
9.30–12 and 2.30–6;
adm*

The town's **Museu de Lanifícios** (Wool Museum) is, however, worth visiting. Covilhã is still a main centre of wool production and the museum is housed in the former Real Fábrica dos Panos (Royal Textile Factory), set up in 1763 by the Marquês de Pombal, and now a part of Covilhã's university.

History

Pêro de Covilhã was born here; of all the Portuguese discoverers, it would have been most interesting to accompany him. Since the

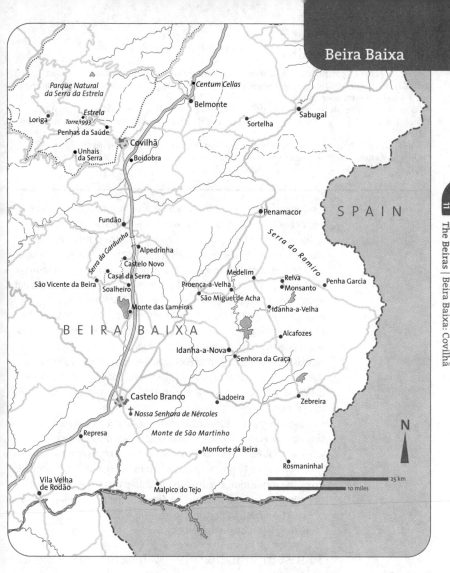

12th century, rumours had been circulating of the 'Lord of Lords and the Greatest Monarch under heaven', who received tribute from 72 kings, who lived in a palace of ebony and crystal, and who was accompanied by giant ants that dug for gold, and fish that squirted purple dye: they called him Prester John. Dom João II was looking for a Christian ally in Africa, so in 1487 he commissioned two men to locate this fabulous kingdom – Pêro de Covilhã, who spoke fluent Arabic, and Afonso de Paiva.

In Alexandria the pair disguised themselves as Arab merchants, and reached Cairo, where Afonso died. Pêro sailed to India, where he spent over a year in the western ports studying the pepper, ginger and gold markets. On his return to Cairo, he passed a

Getting around Covilhã

By **road**, Covilhã is 55km from Castelo Branco and 38km from Guarda. If you're driving, Covilhã is a difficult place to arrive in because one is never quite clear where it begins. If in doubt, keep going up and you'll know the centre when you see it.

Trains run four times daily from Lisbon (4½–6hrs), via Entroncamento (4½hrs), Santarém (4½hrs) and Castelo Branco (1¼hrs). From Porto, change at Entroncamento after 3hrs. Three trains run daily from Guarda (1¼hrs).

Rede Expressos **bus** routes are similar, t (275) 334 914, making infrequent daily journeys from Lisbon (5¼hrs), via Castelo Branco (1hr), and from Guarda (½hr). There are also four or five daily buses from Porto (4hrs), via Viseu (2hrs).

written report of his journey to Mestre Joseph, the cobbler of Lamego, one of Dom João II's two Jewish agents there, who in turn delivered it to the king. Doubtless it proved useful to Vasco da Gama a few years later. In Cairo Pêro was told that he would not be welcome in Portugal until he completed his original mission, so in 1490 he headed south. He arrived on the shores of Lake Tana, in what is now Ethiopia, and did indeed find a Coptic kingdom – but the Emperor Naod was not interested in an alliance, and would not allow foreigners to leave the country. Pêro was provided with a wife and an estate. He was still alive when Dom Rodrigo de Lima reached Ethiopia in 1521, though by then he was too weak to return to Portugal. The chronicler Ruy de Pina has the final word: 'Nothing is known of what he finally achieved, for he never came back from his travels.' His route is marked on a granite map in front of the town hall.

In the late 17th century English workers and looms were smuggled to Covilhã to teach the locals to card, spin and weave wool, so that Portugal could supply its own army uniforms. Dom João V was keen to promote the infant industry, but it was tripped up by the Inquisition, because many of the artisans were New Christians, converted Jews. British fears for their virtual monopoly of exports of cloth to Portugal were temporarily allayed, but ultimately the industry took root.

(i) **Covilhã >**
Avenida Frei Heitor Pinto, t (275) 319 560, turismo.estrela@mail.te lepac.pt; open Mon–Sat 9–12.30 and 2–5.30

Tourist Information in Covilhã

The tourist office – which seems to have a glossy leaflet for everything – and the booking office for bus tickets are both on the ground floor of the town hall, in the central square.

Internet Access

PostWeb, Rua Comendador Campos Melo 27. *Open Mon–Fri 9–7.30, Sat 9–1.*

Horse-riding

João de Deus Moniz Pereira, Esc. S. Silvestre 3, t (275) 323 201.

Where to Stay in Covilhã

Quinta do Sangrinhal, Estrada da Boidobra, t (275) 325 344 (€€). Two km from Covilhã, a restored, rustic granite house with extensive land. The décor is tasteful and comfortable; there is a pool, and meals are available on request.

★★★**Residencial Solneve**, Rua Visconde da Coriscada 126 (in the main square), t (275) 323 001 (€). Centrally located and recently refurbished. There's a public car park opposite. The restaurant has a separate entrance, and residents get 10% off their bill. Free Internet.

**Hotel Covilhã Parque, Avenida Frei Heitor Pinto, t (275) 329 320, *www. naturaimb.hotels.com* (€). A slick, modern hotel that overlooks the city and is conveniently located next to the tourist office. Ask for a top-floor room to take advantage of the views.

Hotel Santa Eufémia, Sitio da Palmatória, t (275) 313 308 (€). On the southern edge of town, this is sensibly furnished, with balcony views to the distant hills.

Pensão Central, Rua Nuno Álvares Pereira 14, t (275) 322 727 (€). Quiet and clean, despite exterior appearance. Rooms on the back have views.

Pensão Avenida, Avenida República 40, t (275) 322 140 (€). On one side of the Jardim Publico, a fun place brightened by paintings by the owner's son. Separate bathrooms.

Eating Out in Covilhã

Most of Covilhã's restaurants are affiliated to hotels (*see* above), but there are also a couple of eating places in the lively Rua das Flores, right in the midst of which there works an umbrella-mender.

Ovelhita, Largo da Infantaria XXI 19, t 912 509 659 (€€€). An elegant restaurant with tastefully restored decor. An excellent menu reflects the chef's flair for providing an innovative twist to traditional dishes. Popular with the smart business set.

Restaurante Montiel, Praça do Município 33–37, t (275) 322 088 (€€). This place is proud of its gastronomic regional dishes, which are good, if pricey. The service is friendly.

Restaurante Marisqueira A Traineira, Rua Peso da Lã 19, t (275) 314 253 (€€). A fake lobster and crab colonize the back room of this striplit fish restaurant located between the Rua Visconde da Coriscada and the Rua Marquês da Vila e Bolama, which fails to peel its prawns for the *arroz de marisco*; better skip the fish and try the *caldeirada de cabrito*.

Restaurante Tânia, Rua das Flores 23, t (275) 323 499 (€). In a back street downhill from the Solneve, a reasonable little *tasca* where some of the locals eat.

Belmonte

The village of Belmonte makes a worthwhile detour to the east of the Serra da Estrela. It is located 21km south of Guarda and 19km northeast of Covilhã, and overlooks the flat-bottomed, red-soiled valley of the River Zêzere. Some of its 3,000 souls inhabit rude granite houses, which sought protection from the now-ruined castle and the interesting little church of São Tiago. The *pousada* (*see* below) is a worthy destination in its own right.

History

Belmonte has been a stronghold for the *Marranos* for 400 years, housing a cluster of crypto-Jews descended from those forced to convert to Catholicism at the end of the 15th century, but who continued to practise their faith in secret. About 200 of the 4,000 village homes belong to direct descendants of *Marranos*: these people incorporate fragments of the Hebraic rituals in their Catholic observance, without knowing their original significance.

The charms of Belmonte were insufficient to detain Pedro Álvares Cabral, who left Belmonte and sailed west until, in 1500, he discovered Brazil. Brazil was all that the sailors could have wished: plump and vibrant naked ladies came to greet them. Pedro Vaz de Caminha, official clerk to the expedition, wrote that this seemingly perfect society lacked only knowledge of the true God. This the Portuguese could put to rights, encouraged by the fact that the natives were not circumcised and were therefore neither Mohammedans nor Jews. A Mass was arranged, which is commemorated by the people of Belmonte on 26 April each year. The Indians knelt beside the Portuguese and, in imitation of their guests, smilingly kissed the crosses that were handed to them.

The Town

The pillory square is shaded by *tilia* trees, a genus of lindens, whose leaves are different shades of light green and whose summer blossom can be dried and used to make tea. In the Rua Fonte da Rosa, the occupants of tiny windowed houses sit and crochet or bundle kindling wood.

Cabral's ancestors included Fernão Cabral, Giant of Beira, who went into battle with an iron mace weighing more than one *arroba* (33lb/15kg); his family had long been the castellans of Belmonte. The filmset **castle** was constructed in the 13th century, on granite, but a sober Manueline window is all that remains of the residence in which Pedro Álvares was born. On Christmas Eve young men doing military service dance around a flaming tree trunk beside the building, in a ritual similar to the St John's Eve festivities in the Minho and Porto. Jumping over the fire is seen as an effective means of counteracting the forces of evil that may attack during the following year.

In 1362 the same mellow stone was used to build the fascinating **church of São Tiago** opposite the castle. It has its own tiny belltower on a terrace formerly used as a graveyard, and its shadows cloak a painted 14th-century granite pietà. A side door connects with the pantheon of the Cabral family, though Pedro Álvares is entombed in Santarém. '*Cabra*' means 'she goat', so the Cabral family had few options when choosing their emblem: it's one goat on top of another, and can be seen on the wall of the second little church facing the castle.

The fascinating **Museu Judaico de Belmonte** provides a history of Judaism in the town and arranges visits to the historic synagogue.

Museu Judaico de Belmonte
Rua Portela 4,
t (275) 913 505;
open Tues–Sun
9.30-12.30 and 2–6

Centum Cellas

Two kilometres north of Belmonte, just off the road to Guarda, stands one of the oddest ruins in Portugal, at Centum Cellas. The three-storeyed granite structure is extraordinary because of its large number of windows: it has been classified as a temple or the *praetorium* of a camp, but rather unconvincingly. When the surrounding ground is excavated, the tower may prove to have belonged to a villa, possibly dating from the 2nd century, and preserved in isolation because of its use as a watchtower in the Middle Ages.

Where to Stay in Belmonte

ⓘ Belmonte ›
main town square,
t (275) 911 488

★★Hotel Belsol, t (275) 912 206, *www.hotelbelsol.com* (€€). On Quintado Rio, Estrada Nacional, with superb views of the mountains and the River Zêzere – and a pool. It's a significant distance (3km) out of town.

⭐ Pousada
Convento de
Belmonte ›

Pousada
Pousada Convento de Belmonte, 6250 Belmonte, **t** (275) 910 300, *www.pousadas.pt* (L2 H). One of the most enjoyable *pousadas* in Portugal. A stylish place – the pool is black – very well located for exploring a range of different and little-visited landscapes. Drive through the pretty part of town and continue on through the scuzzy part. The core of the *pousada* is a former monastic chapel and cloister built of rounded, honey-coloured granite boulders. To this have been added generously proportioned purpose-built bedrooms and dining rooms, with views down the hillside to the flat-bottomed valley. The interior decoration is exceptionally successful, using a lot of texture – linen, chenille, textured cement, sea grass – and subtle lighting which itself uses different textures. The Brazilian chef is excellent. Highly recommended.

The Serra da Gardunha

A mere blip compared with the Serra da Estrela, the Serra da Gardunha runs on a roughly northeast to southwest axis. Between the villages of Casal da Serra and Alpedrinha an infertile wedge of granite is sandwiched between fertile schists: the divide is sudden and apparent. Having peaked at 4,010ft (1,223m), the mountains quickly give way to gentle hills. The cherry trees around **Fundão** blossom at the end of March and bear fruit from the end of April through to June. A mouthful or two wouldn't go amiss, and they could be washed down with a draught of spring water from the roadside fountain southeast of the small town.

Alpedrinha

Twelve km southeast of Fundão, Alpedrinha is a charming, large and relatively affluent village strung out along the main road from Fundão to Castelo Branco, backed by a steep hillslope and looking down over a gentle one. Judging by the amazed looks from ladies carrying their greens, foreign visitors are rare in the higgledy-piggledy tangle of streets off the main road.

Castelo Novo

About 3km south of Alpedrinha, a turning to the right leads to Castelo Novo, a worthwhile detour if you're not in a hurry. The village is set in a basin of dark granite scree which looks so cursed to barrenness as to recall Camões' *Canção IX*, in Roy Campbell's translation:

There is a mountain, sterile, stark and dry,
Useless, abandoned, hideous, bare and bald,
From whose cursed precincts nature shrinks appalled ...

Castelo Novo is a wonderfully sleepy place: sometimes the most lively things there are the potatoes, sprouting.

Where to Stay and Eat in Alpedrinha

Casa da Comenda, Rua da Igreja, **t** (275) 567 161 (€€). Past the Igreja Matriz is an early 17th-century granite fortress house with elegant, cool rooms and a lovely garden.

Turismo de Habitação
Casa do Barreiro, Largo das Escolas, **t** (275) 567 120, *www.solaresde portugal.pt* (€€ CA). Provides lovely *Turismo de Habitação* at very reasonable rates. Surrounded by delightfully muddled gardens, the solid house was built in the early 20th

century in that late 19th-century style which topped its residences with little granite obelisks. Two sisters live here, both in their sixties and neither averse to a tipple. One of them speaks French. They prattle around the cool and airy interior, among homey antiques and colourful décor. Guest bedrooms look down the gentle hillslope to the plains beyond, and come with shower rooms – but one room is a dud.

★★★★**Estalagem S. Jorge**, Largo Da Misericórdia 5, **t** (275) 567 154 (€€). For meals, head here, where the service is courteous, the tables beautifully laid, and the food good. Rooms also available.

Castelo Branco

The prosperous capital of Beira Baixa occupies a low hill at the centre of flat lands, 18km from the Spanish border. The town has outlived the '*Castelo*' from which it takes its name: the castle is now ruined, and its place in the hearts of the 32,000 inhabitants has been taken by the surrounding technical colleges. Parts of Castelo Branco are laid out along wide, airy avenues, but it's a rather ordinary place with few traces of its ancient roots. However, the bishop's palace houses a worthwhile museum, and the celebrated palace gardens are filled with a fanciful array of little sculptures. Just outside the town lies a meadow hill with breathtaking views.

Castelo Branco marks the fusion of two Hispano-Roman *vilas*. The Templars built the castle early in the 13th century, and Dom Dinis, on a recce with his Queen Isabel, ordered the extension of the town walls. Being so close to the border, it was the scene of Spanish attacks in 1704 and 1762; in 1807, the French marched in, singing the *Marseillaise*. Junot commandeered the bishop's palace, and his troops pillaged the town before heading towards Lisbon.

What to See

Museu de Francisco Tavares Proença Júnior
Rua Frei Bartolomeu da Costa, **t** *(272) 344 277*, *www.ipmuseus.pt*; *open Tues–Sun 10–12.30 and 2–5.30*

The boringly regular façade of the **Palácio Episcopal** does little to enliven the northeastern edge of town. But the appearance is deceptive: it stands on the site of an earlier palace, built in 1596 as the winter residence of the Bishop of Guarda. His 18th-century successors revamped the building in the present manorial style, taking care to include a game park, now vanished.

The town's **Museu de Francisco Tavares Proença Júnior** is installed in the palace, which contains a good archaeological collection,

Getting to and around Castelo Branco

By **road**, Castelo Branco is 159km from Coimbra, 100km from Guarda, 80km from Portalegre and 262km from Lisbon. Three **trains** travel daily from Lisbon (4hrs) via Santarém (3hrs) and Entroncamento (2¼hrs). From Porto, change at Entroncamento after 3hrs. In the other direction, they run three times daily from Guarda (3hrs) via Covilhã (1¼hrs). Rede Expressos **buses**, **t** (272) 340 120, run half a dozen buses a day from Lisbon (2¼hrs), Guarda (2hrs) and Covilhã (1¼hrs), with three buses daily from Coimbra (2½hrs).

Castelo Branco is the only possible base for visiting Monsanto and Idanha-a-Velha by public transport.

from the Palaeolithic period on, and some rupestral art. The 16th-century Brussels tapestries were used in the last century as a pinboard for public notices, and until fairly recently the mounted 'canon ball' spewed random numbers, bingo-style, as a means of apportioning military service. Outstanding among the paintings are *St Anthony* by Francisco Henriques, *c.* 1510 – the Franciscan monk holds a red book on which sits a nonplussed baby Jesus – and a *Deposing of Christ in the Tomb* attributed to the early Renaissance master, Garcia Fernandes.

But the most interesting of the museum's collections are the *colchas*, linen bedspreads embroidered with large stitches of silk, like raffia, which have been the local speciality for 300 years. In the 18th century they formed part of the bridal trousseau, and used locally produced silk. This is the sort of thing that fantastical heroines in magic realist novels spend their lives working on, letting their imagination run away with them: the colours are bold yellows and greens, pinks and browns, in a style that might be called Persian Baroque. The motifs are doves, parrots, carnations, pomegranates, all of which are symbolic: a two-headed bird represents two souls in one body; two birds either side of a tree represent lovers; vegetables and trees represent the family. A workshop in the museum keeps the craft alive. Work can be commissioned: it's expensive stuff.

Bishop's Garden
open April–Sept daily 9–8, Oct–Mar daily 9–5; adm

The **Bishop's Garden** is a rare sight, planted with a host of profane little granite statues amid the boxed hedges and orange trees. This plethora of Baroque whimsy was the brainchild of Dom João de Mendonta, who saw the work completed in 1725, and who preferred to meditate in a rowboat on the water tank. The ladies and gentlemen are of little artistic merit, but this does not bother them. They are arranged thematically, including the zodiac, the seasons, the continents, and, most famously, the kings. A few were stolen by French troops in 1807: their memory is not well served by the flowerpots that have replaced them.

Some 200 yards nearer the centre of town, the **church of São Miguel** served as the cathedral of Castelo Branco 1771–1881, before the bishopric was extinguished. The 13th- or 14th-century building has been reconstructed several times, most notably in the 17th

(i) **Castelo Branco** >
Praça do Municipio,
t (272) 330 339,
www.cm-castel
branco.pt;
open Mon–Fri
9.30–7.30, Sat–Sun
9.30–1 and 2.30–6

Tourist Information/ Services in Castelo Branco

The **tourist office** is a short walk from the bus station (turn right), and the **railway station** is 500 yards to the south (walk up the wide Avenida Nun' Alvares). The **post office** is at Rua da Sé (*open Mon–Fri 8.30–6.30, Sat 9–12.30*), and has NetPost internet access.

Where to Stay and Eat in Castelo Branco

There isn't much choice in Castelo Branco. For very cheap rooms, ask the tourist office to point you to the area behind the Almeda.

Hotel Rainha Dona Amélia, Rua de Santiago 15, **t** (272) 326 315, *www.rainhadamelia.pt* (€€–€). Modern, centrally located Best Western hotel.

Tryp Colina do Castelo, Rua da Piscina, **t** (272) 341 637 (€). A corporate, modern hotel with large comfortable rooms and all mod cons.

★★★**Residencial Arraiana**, Avenida 1 de Maio 18, **t** (272) 341 634 (€). On the very long shopping street leading straight from the centre of town. Bare but decent, with showers, TV and mini-bar.

Pensão Impéio, Rua Prazeres 20, **t** (272) 341 720 (€). A budget *pensão*, near the post office.

Praça Velha, Largo Luís de Camões 17, **t** (272) 328 640 (€€). Enjoy the chic, designer interior within a restored former Knights Templar granary in the old town. Serves traditional cuisine with a modern twist.

Frei Papinhas, Rua dos Prazeres 31, **t** (272) 323 090 (€€). Grilled meats and local cheeses are the speciality here.

Restaurante Zé dos Cachopos, Rua Emilia Oliveira Pinto 13, **t** (272) 345 363 (€). Serves mainly meat dishes, and provides a pleasant atmosphere.

Café Restaurante Central, Rua Tavares Proença Júnior 14, **t** (272) 344 636 (€). Good-value servings.

century, which has left bits of Renaissance tracery. Really the only things worth looking at are the locally embroidered copes on show in the sacristy.

The Environs of Castelo Branco

Monte de São Martinho is a stunningly beautiful undiscovered mount of olives just southeast of town. It's an idyllic, enchanted place where the air really is sweet, the butterflies fly fast and meadow flowers nudge miniature irises. Cicadas and cuckoos announce themselves, oblivious to the enormous view towards Spain. It's best to walk the 2½–3 miles (4–5km); if you're driving, you'll need good suspension. Head for the chapel of N.S. de Mércoles. Continue straight. Take the track to the right past the last town road. The track splits into three; go left. Fork right. Fork right again. Fork left. To go up the hill, head left or right. Please respect it.

East of Castelo Branco

Monsanto

 Monsanto

Monsanto is the most dramatic and astonishing of Portugal's hill settlements; come here to know why the birds sing. Here there is

Getting to Monsanto and Idanha-a-Velha

If you're **driving** to Monsanto from Castelo Branco, choose the longer but much more beautiful route via Zebreira.

The only way to get to Monsanto by public transport is on the 7.10am **bus** from Castelo Branco, which, theoretically, returns late morning. However, the bus schedule seems to rely more on whim than timetabling, and it is best to check and double check with the bus station in Castelo Branco.

By far the easiest way to travel to and from Idanha-a-Velha is by car.

no ceiling on life – this is Monte Santo, Sacred Mount. It stands at 2,485ft (758m), some 50km northeast of Castelo Branco by the quickest route. The tiny community is camouflaged by its granite buildings and nourished by magnificent views in every direction, to hills and lakes and unregimented fields.

The site was first colonized by the Lusitanians, then by the Romans. Dom Sancho I ejected the Moors from the village in the 12th century. Gualdim Pais reconstructed the castle among still boulders above the village, atop the forbidding rock outcrop of almost volcanic harshness, and Dom Dinis further fortified Monsanto. Now the fortification is ruined; its grass is cropped by goats. In the village, life is intensified: it is difficult not to relish the crack of a carpet being flicked out of a window, or the shudders of a stick brush sweeping the street. There are few inhabitants under the age of 50, for there is little work here. Rabbit hutches are embedded in external staircases, chickens penned in on the dirt beneath overhanging boulders. Monsanto has been voted the most typical (read: quintessential) village in Portugal, so coaches of visitors come and go, assailed by an old woman drumming a square tambourine with her fingers. But Monsanto remains of itself, because there is nowhere for visitors to stay except the *pousada* and one café with rooms.

Idanha-a-Velha

The village of Idanha-a-Velha has been extraordinarily washed by history, and left alone. It occupies a flat, isolated site 48km northeast of Castelo Branco. It's a living village in the antique style; unlike Monsanto, few tourists come here, which makes a visit all the more rewarding.

History

It was once the Roman city of Igaeditânia, founded by Augustus in 16 BC: in that year Quintus Iallius gave a sun dial to the city. The soil here is fertile alluvium, and was once rich with gold – an altar discovered nearby was inscribed with a dedication to Iuppiter, in thanks for a find of some 90lb (40kg) of the stuff. Another reason for choosing the site was its proximity to the permanent Roman camp at Medelim, 6km to the north. The settlement became a *municipium* under Vespasian, but the only Roman public monument found so far is the base of a temple probably dedicated to Augustus, on which stands a ruined medieval tower built in the reign of Dom Dinis.

The Visigoths rebuilt Idanha in 534, and tradition has it that this was the birthplace of Wamba, whom they elected as king in 672. He is traditionally credited with having established the ecclesiastical divisions of the Peninsula, but showed little respect for the clergy themselves: he called them up for service in his army, in the wake of a Basque rebellion and an uprising in Gaul. The churchmen took violent revenge, conspiring with the nobles and capturing King Wamba. They shaved his head – as the mark of a slave rather than a grotesque tonsure – and deposed and banished him.

The settlement was destroyed by the Moors in the 8th century, and lay dormant until Dom Sancho I conceded it to the Templars. Much of its splendour is still to be unearthed: excavation is ongoing.

The Cathedral and Around

The Visigoths built a **cathedral** for their bishop in the 6th or 7th century, but the pure and simple edifice that now stands is the product of several reconstructions, the most drastic of which was in the 16th century. The horseshoe-shaped colonnade and the flagstones are original. Outside, and at a lower level than the cathedral, is a **baptismal basin**. (The unornamented side door was added much later, in the 16th century.) A little museum displays various ceramics, bones, and a terracotta statuette. Wander in the cemetery, composed of eerie Roman and Visigothic ruins which were abandoned, so they say, because of a century-long plague of ants.

ⓘ Monsanto ›
Rua Marquês da Gracioça, t (277) 314 642; open Sat–Sun 10–1 and 2–6

ⓘ Idanha-a-Velha
Rua do Castelo, t (277) 914 280; open daily 10–1 and 2–6; offers guided visits

Festival in Monsanto

In Monsanto, the **Festa das Cruzes** enlivens the first Sunday of May. It commemorates a legendary medieval siege of the stronghold, when the starving inhabitants threw their last calf at the attackers. So demoralizing was this show of plenty that the besiegers withdrew. Now girls and women process to the castle and throw from its walls a 'calf' made of roses and pitchers of flowers. The old women sing and dance with faceless rag dolls called *marafonas*, which are believed to give protection against thunder.

Where to Stay and Eat in Monsanto

Hotel Estalagem de Monsanto, Rua de Capela 3, *www.monsanto homestead.com* (€€). Ten rooms, all with private bathrooms, although just three of the rooms have a view. There is a bar and traditional meals are served in the restaurant.

Adega Tipica O Cruzeiro, Rua Fernando Namora 4, t (277) 314 528 (€). Two daily specials – ask for what is available. They also have a few rooms.

Café Monsantinho, Rua de Nossa Senhora do Castelo, t (277) 314 493 (€). Serves snacks and sandwiches.

Beira Litoral

Beira Litoral occupies the coastal plains from Espinho to Leiria, penetrating about 30km inland to the forested, granitic Serras of Arada, Caramulo and Buçaco. At the province's main city, Coimbra, it broadens to incorporate the Serra da Lousã, stopping short at the Serra da Estrela. The sand beaches are backed by low, sandy clay dunes which support little more than pine trees. The lower reaches of the Rivers Mondego and Vouga create waterlogged flatlands, the former supporting rice paddies and the latter salt pans. The main appeal of the province lies in specific monuments or features: the economy and landscape of the estuary of the River Vouga, the Forest of Buçaco, the art and architecture of Coimbra, the excavations at Roman Conimbriga, the Abbey of Batalha.

Coimbra

⭐ Coimbra   The noisy, lively university city of **Coimbra** focuses on a steep limestone hill on the north bank of the River Mondego, 40km inland, halfway between Lisbon and Porto.

Eight hundred and fifty years ago, Coimbra was the capital of Portugal. Subsequently, it received more than its fair share of the art and architecture of the 15th and 18th centuries, and its 103,000 residents play host to Portugal's oldest and most attractive university. But Coimbra does not relish its past glory. This has been eroded by nibbles and bites, most drastically under the Salazar regime, when featureless modern blocks replaced parts of the old town – which makes it difficult to follow Hans Christian Andersen's advice of 1866: 'Coimbra is a place where one should ... live with the students, fly out to the lovely open country around, give oneself up to solitude and let memory unroll pictures from legend and song, from the history of this place'. The city can be divided into upper and lower parts; the walls of the former have almost disappeared, but the steep access roads remain, leading up from the flat land at the foot of the hill.

The dominance of Coimbra's university in the fields of law and medicine has made the city into one of Portugal's think-tanks. Its most famous alumnus is the epic poet Camões, who may have been born in Coimbra, *c.* 1524, and who enjoyed his 'bright college years' learning Latin and Greek. There are a handful of outstanding buildings to see, as well as a couple of seductively domestic streets below the university, where music from Bach to Coldplay filters through from the fraternities and sororities called *repúblicas*. Coimbra has its own *fado*, a more sophisticated and intellectual version of the Lisbon lament. The guitar which accompanies it appears to be a descendant of the five-stringed lute introduced to Spain in the 9th century by Ziryab, who knew more than a

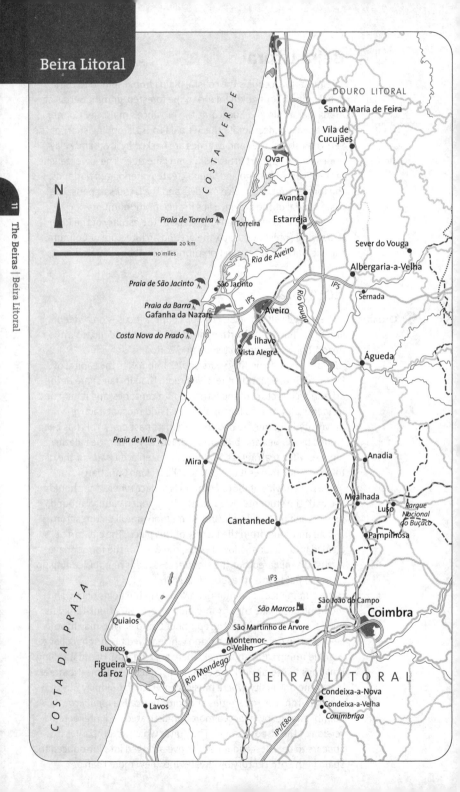

N

20 km
10 miles

DOURO LITORAL

Santa Maria de Feira

Vila de
Cucujães

Ovar

Avanca

Praia de Torreira
Torreira
Estarreja

Sever do Vouga

Ria de Aveiro

Albergaria-a-Velha

Praia de São Jacinto
São Jacinto

Sernada

Praia da Barra
Gafanha da Nazaré
Aveiro

Costa Nova do Prado

Ílhavo
Vista Alegre

Águeda

Praia de Mira

Mira
Anadia

Mealhada
Luso
*Parque
Nacional
do Buçaco*

Cantanhede
Pampilhosa

IP3

São Marcos
São João do Campo

Coimbra

São Martinho de Árvore

Quiaios

Montemor-
o-Velho

Buarcos

Figueira
da Foz
Rio Mondego
BEIRA LITORAL

Lavos

Condeixa-a-Nova
Condeixa-a-Velha
Conímbriga

Getting to Coimbra

By **road**, Coimbra is 60km from Aveiro, 159km from Guarda, 70km from Leiria, 120km from Porto, 94km from Viseu and 201km from Lisbon.

Coimbra is better served by public transport on a north–south rather than east–west axis. Frequent **trains** from Lisbon's Santa Apolónia and Oriente stations to Coimbra-B take a minimum of 2hrs, passing Santarém (1¾hrs). The quickest trains from Porto take 1½hrs (slow trains may have a change at Pampilhosa). Those that pass through Espinho take 1¼hrs, and Aveiro ½hr. Semifrequent trains run from Guarda (3½hrs) via Nelas (1½hrs, connecting with buses from Viseu).

Most **buses** run a couple of times a day from Faro (9¾hrs), Chaves (5½hrs), Lamego (3¼hrs), Viseu (1½hrs), Guarda (3hrs), Monção (5½hrs), Guimarães (3½hrs). The 3¼hr route from Castelo Branco connects with the Braga and Porto services.

Buses are much more frequent from Porto (1¼hrs), Lisbon (3hrs) and Leiria (1hr). International buses pass through Coimbra on their way from Lisbon to Paris

Getting around Coimbra

Everything within Coimbra is within **walking** distance, but the upper part of town is steep: it may be a good idea to take a taxi to the university, and walk your way down from there. The electrified buses run around the hill rather than up it – try the no.1 bus from Largo da Partagem and Coimbra-A train station. A visit to the Santa Clara-a-Nova convent may also warrant a taxi.

Connecting shuttle trains run between the two **railway stations**: Coimbra-B, the mainline terminal, and Coimbra-A, near the centre of town. Keep your wits about you as trains sometimes leave unannounced.

The **bus station** is on Avenida Fernão de Magalhães, just over a km from the old town centre. Two routes run from the bus station, one to Largo Dom Dinis and the stadium, the other to Praça da República and the hospital. Buy tickets from the SMTUC office, Largo do Mercado, **t** (239) 824 175, or at some kiosks or *tabacarias*, although it is possible to pay on board as well. **Driving** is not advised in Coimbra, due to lack of parking and traffic jams.

thousand songs (and is also credited with introducing toothpaste to Córdoba). One of the city's less welcome sounds is that of traffic, which tends to run close to the fairly abundant supply of accommodation for visitors.

History

The Romans knew Coimbra as Aeminium, which came into the orbit of their city at Conimbriga, 16km to the south. Conimbriga was abandoned, and in 872 the Moors were driven from the area. By linguistic debasement, Aeminium took the name of the settlement that had previously overshadowed it. The Moors were back in control 987–1064, and again in 1116, when a Moorish army stormed two of the castles erected to defend Coimbra: at Miranda de Beira, the garrison was slaughtered; at Santa Eulália, the governor, Diogo the Chicken, was true to his name, and surrendered. Coimbra itself came next. According to the *Chronicle* of the Goths, Ali, the Almoravid caliph, and his son Yasuf, brought an African army reinforced by Andalucians 'as numerous as the sands of the sea'. The city was sacked, and Countess Teresa sought refuge in the castle. Coimbra's defences lay in ruins until Dom Afonso Henriques built the castle of Leiria as his southern stronghold, in 1135.

He was crowned king in 1139, and transferred the nation's capital from Guimarães to Coimbra, which blossomed. Idrisi, the Muslim geographer who completed his work in Sicily in 1154, describes Coimbra as a flourishing city, whose inhabitants are 'the bravest of the Christians'. Its fertile fields were rich in vineyards and orchards of apples, cherries and plums, for 'the Mondego moves many mills and bathes many vineyards and gardens'.

Coimbra remained the capital during the reigns of Dom Afonso II, Dom Sancho II, and Dom Afonso III, who moved the main royal residence to Lisbon c. 1250. Portugal's university also migrated southwards, to Lisbon, after a couple of brief sojourns in Coimbra, but returned finally in 1537. With the university came the Jesuits – who were very influential here until 1772, when Pombal reformed the institution – and the Inquisition, which set up a base in Coimbra. In 1810, Masséna sacked the town, thereby venting some of his frustration at the outcome of the battle of Buçaco.

The Upper Town

The University

Coimbra is dominated by its lofty university, which rides the peak of the city.

In 1288 a trio of Portuguese ecclesiastics requested Pope Nicholas IV to confirm the creation of a university, which they had agreed with Dom Dinis to establish in Lisbon. The Church would finance the venture, as all the students were to become clergymen. Gradually, laymen infiltrated the place, and during the 14th century the university was transferred from Lisbon to Coimbra and back again several times. Standards were mediocre: serious scholars sharpened their quills and headed for Italy or France, particularly Paris. When Paris was split by religious differences in the early decades of the 16th century, Dom João III determined to lick Portugal's university into shape. In 1534 he appointed André de Resende to the faculty, whose searing inaugural speech, at a time 'when nearly the whole of Europe is being reborn', praised the care and patience other nations were devoting to their academic learning, and thundered '... we ought truly to feel ashamed of our gross ignorance and our slothfulness'. The king invited Erasmus to come and teach in Portugal, but the great humanist declined on the grounds of ill health. (In fact, Erasmus disliked the Portuguese as 'a race of Jews', and had criticized the efforts of the Portuguese crown to use its monopoly of the Oriental spice trade to maintain high prices in Europe.)

In 1537 the university was finally re-established at Coimbra, and a decade later the king founded the Royal College of Arts. He recruited a distinguished medley of international professors, only to be embarrassed when some of them were arrested by the Inquisition for precisely that free thinking that had recommended them to the king. In 1555 the College of Arts was handed to the Jesuits.

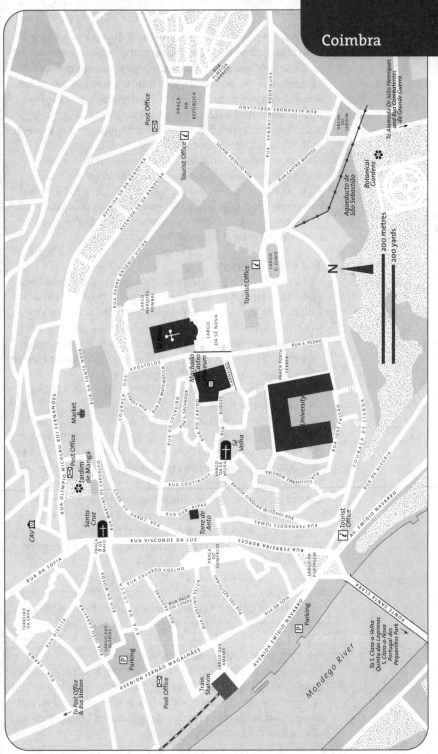

Post Office

PRAÇA DA REPÚBLICA

Tourist Office

RUA ALMEIDA GARRETT

RUA ALEXANDRE HERCULANO

RUA VENÂNCIO RODRIGUES

RUA OLIVEIRA MATOS

RUA CASTRO MATOSO

ARCOS DO JARDIM

To Alameda Dr Júlio Henriques and Rua Combatentes da Grande Guerra

Botanical Gardens

Aqueducto de São Sebastião

AVENIDA SÁ DA BANDEIRA

AVENIDA SÁ DA BANDEIRA

RUA PADRE ANTÓNIO VIEIRA

LARGO MARQUÊS POMBAL

Tourist Office

LARGO D. DINIS

N

200 metres
200 yards

Sé Nova

LARGO DA SÉ NOVA

RUA DA FONTE NOVA

COURAÇA DOS APÓSTOLOS

RUA FLORES

RUA DA MATEMÁTICA

Machado de Castro Museum

RUA BORGES CARNEIRO

RUA S. PEDRO

PRAÇA PORTA FÉRREA

University

RUA S. SALVADOR

RUA DO OUREIRO

RUA DO CABIDO

Sé Velha

RUA JOSÉ FALCÃO

COURAÇA DE LISBOA

Market

Post Office

Jardim de Manga

RUA OLÍMPIO NICOLAU RUI FERNANDES

RUA MARTINS DE CARVALHO

RUA CORPO DE DEUS

Santa Cruz

CAV

LARGO DA SÉ VELHA

RUA COUTINHOS

RUA SUB-RIPAS

Torre de Anto

RUA GUILHERME MOREIRA

RUA JOAQUIM ANTÓNIO AGUIAR

RUA DA ALEGRIA

PRAÇA 8 DE MAIO

RUA VISCONDE DA LUZ

RUA FERNANDES TOMÁS

Tourist Office

AV. EMÍDIO NAVARRO

RUA DA SOFIA

RUA DIREITA

TERREIRO DA ERVA

RUA JOÃO CABREIRA

RUA DA MOEDA

RUA DA LOUÇA

RUA EDUARDO COELHO

PRAÇA DO COMÉRCIO

RUA FERREIRA BORGES

LARGO DA PORTAGEM

RUA DO CARMO

LARGO DAS OLARIAS

RUA PADEIRA

RUA PAÇO DO CONDE

RUA ADELINO VEIGA

RUA DAS AZEITEIRAS

RUA DA SOTA

Parking

Parking

To Post Office & Bus Station

AVENIDA FERNÃO MAGALHÃES

LARGO DAS AMEIAS

Post Office

Train Station

AVENIDA EMÍDIO NAVARRO

PONTE SANTA CLARA

Mondego River

To S. Clara-a-Velha
Quinta das Lágrimas
S. Clara-a-Nova
Portugal dos Pequenitos Park

All was not rosy for the 1500 students. During the minority of Dom Manuel, João III's successor, the *Cortes* urged that the University of Coimbra 'be done away with as noxious to the kingdom, and the revenues be applied to the war [in Maghrib], and whomsoever wishes to learn, let him go to Salamanca or to Paris, and there will not be so many graduates in excess, or so many suits'. It was 200 years before Pombal attempted another shake-up at the university: he shooed away corrupt priests who sold doctorates, and added natural sciences to the curriculum. He swept away the castle to build afresh on the top of the hill, and established laboratories and the Botanical Gardens. In future, he determined, entry to the university was to be by examination only.

Coimbra remains Portugal's premier university, held in respect, affection and pride throughout the country.

The Old University

Its core is the Old University, a courtyard with buildings on three sides but open to the south, where a statue of Dom João III stands with his back to views of the River Mondego. The wide river valley winds down from the Lousã hills, fringed with willow, sedge and poplar, shallow enough to support sandbanks midstream. Since 1634, the Old University has been entered through the **Porta Férrea**, which replaced an earlier, fortified portal. The courtyard incorporates a royal palace donated by Dom João III in 1537, and subsequently much altered.

To the right of the entrance, a theatrical arched gallery, called the **Via Latina**, has engulfed a frontispiece by Cláudio Laprade, who carved figures symbolizing the academic faculties, *c.* 1700 – but his work was later remodelled as a monument to Dom José (1750–77). The door marked '*reitoria*' leads to the balcony of the **Sala dos Capelos**, which was formerly the throne room: students defend their doctoral theses under the uncomprehending gaze of various royal portraits, who would no doubt rather be looking at the wonderful view of the city offered by the catwalk, to be found off to one side.

The courtyard is dominated by its unattractive clock tower, in the northwestern corner, which has been calling the students to their lectures since 1733 and has consequently earned the undignified nickname of the '*cabra*' (the 'goat').

To the left of the clock tower is a relic of the former royal palace, a fine Manueline portal, probably by Marcos Pires, one of the stonemasons of Batalha, before 1522. Next to it, a door leads to the **Capela de São Miguel**, which was 'modernized' in both the 17th and 18th centuries, most notably with a blaster of an organ, dated 1733 and gilt with wafting shells and croissant shapes. Pews cushioned with leather anticipate lengthy sermons.

What to Eat

The Bairrada region, around Anadia and Mealhada just to the north of Coimbra, is renowned for its suckling pig roast in a brick oven (*leitão assado a moda da Bairrada*), served with its skin crispy and golden. The piglets should be between 1 and 1½ months old, and suckled on their own mother's milk.

Aveiro prides itself on its eel stew (*caldeirada de enguias a moda de Aveiro*), made with potatoes, stale bread, onions, and a little vinegar.

The Library

Press the doorbell under a monstrous national blazon to the left of the quadrangle for entry to the splendid library, the most famous of the university's buildings. The three adjacent rooms, built between 1717 and 1723, were a typically magnificent gift of that vivacious monarch, Dom João V. His portrait stands at one end, past a succession of shelves painted dark green, light green, and fleshy orange, each gilt with restrained ornament. Tapering columns support the galleries, above tables inlaid with ebony, rosewood and jacaranda.

(One of the most inventive characters of the 18th century must have hatched his ideas in these salubrious rooms, which are entirely unconducive to study. In the first half of the 18th century, Bartolomew Gusmpo invented a flying machine: it was a sort of fire balloon, which is said to have flown from the castle of St George in Lisbon to the Pato de Povo in the central square. If this is true, it was the first balloon ever to have carried a passenger. He was afraid that the Inquisition would accuse him of black magic, and became an expert on cyphers and how to crack them, before fleeing to Spain, whence he was pursued by his apocalyptic visions. His story is told by José Saramago in his novel, *Balthasar and Blimunda*.)

The Students

If you want to mingle among the students, they hang around the Praça da República; to witness student life at its most fervid, head for the Rua da Matemática. Students go bananas for a week in May called *Queima das Fitas*: fourth-years burn their narrow ribbons in chamber pots – each faculty is represented by a different colour – and exchange them for wider ribbons as befits final-year students.

Around the University

The **aqueducto de São Sebastião** terminates just below the Largo de Dom Dinis. The 21 arches of the water course run to the southeast of the university, past an entrance to Pombal's lovely **Botanical Gardens**, formally laid out on a circular plan. It's a treat to be surrounded by tall trees and birdsong, but don't come looking for grass.

Sé Nova
*t (239) 823 138;
open Tues–Fri 9–12
and 2–5.30*

The so-called **Sé Nova** (New Cathedral) stands to the northwest of the university, in the Largo da Sé Nova. It was begun in 1598 and took nearly the whole of the 17th century to complete, serving as a

Jesuit college until the abolition of the order, and shortly afterwards as the seat of the bishopric. The austere façade opens onto a chilly, sober interior. Flesh-coloured cherubs zip over the twin Baroque organs.

The Rua da Matemática and the Rua de S. Salvador are the two most interesting streets leading down fairly steeply from the Sé Nova and the university. Here small children sing to themselves, to the geraniums, and to the laundry, challenged only by caged songbirds. Impudent ferns sprout from the drainpipes. Many of the university *repúblicas* are here – look especially for the **República Bota-Abaixo**, at the bottom of the Rua de S. Salvador. It is decorated with a skull and crossbones, as well as various other large bones, pots and pans, and tin mugs are suspended by bits of string.

Museu Nacional Machado de Castro

Machado de Castro Museum
Largo Dr José Rodrigues, t (239) 823 727; open Tues–Sun 9.30–12.30 and 2.30–5; adm

The Rua Borges Carneiro leads downhill from the Largo da Sé Nova, past the **Machado de Castro Museum**. The excellent sculpture galleries will be closed until 2010, while the 16th-century bishop's palace that houses them is restored. An elegant loggia offers views of the river and lower part of the city.

Across the loggia and upstairs, one can trace the development of Coimbra's ceramics. It seems that the fanciful animals that poke their heads around the cups and plates that are on sale in the city today date back to the 17th century, when artists attempting to fashion animals they had never seen relied on travellers' rather inaccurate reports.

If you're short of time, it's best to walk straight through the several rooms of paintings to get to the 16th-century Portuguese and Flemish works. These include *A Assunção da Virgem*, from the school of the Master of Sardoal, in the first quarter of the century; the angels' robes are rather more beautiful than their faces. Contemporary with this work, but with a much less formal structure, are two panels from a retable by Quentin Metzys, *Ecce Homo* and *The Flagellation*.

Below the bishop's palace there is a two-storey hide-and-seek cryptoporticus; the lower storey is closed to the public. The Romans built these vaulted galleries as a foundation to give their forum an artificially high position: the cryptoporticus is an alternative to putting up an earthen platform. The forum itself was completely destroyed sometime between the Middle Ages and the 17th century, but, taken in conjunction with the cryptoporticus, it must have been one of the tallest buildings in Roman Portugal.

Sé Velha
Largo da Sé Velha, t (239) 825 273; open Sat–Thurs 10–12 and 2–6, Fri 10–12; adm for cloister

The Sé Velha

The Rua Borges Carneiro continues downhill past what is probably the finest Romanesque cathedral in Portugal, the **Sé**

Velha (Old Cathedral). It was built *c*. 1162, when Coimbra was the nation's capital, and is topped by a square tower, a blue and white fish-scale cupola, and an angel weathervane.

Tradition says that the building was converted from a mosque, which is quite plausible because the first governor of Coimbra, Dom Sisinando, was a Moor who converted to Christianity. His tomb, broken open by the French, lies in the chapter house. An Arabic inscription built into the outer wall of the nave appears to read 'Ahmed-ben-Ishmael built it strongly by order of ...' – but the layout of the cathedral is purely Christian.

The austerity of the battlemented western façade is broken by a recessed, round-arched window, which is almost the same size as the portal beneath it. The *Livro Preto* or *Black Book*, covering the period 1162–76, records that a certain Master Robert, a native of the Auverne, came four times from Lisbon to perfect his work on the eight shafts of this portico. Each time, he received four *morabitinos*, plus ten for his expenses, as well as bread, meat and wine for his four apprentices and food for his four asses.

The interior is grand and gigantic; it returned to its simplicity when the *azulejos* of 1508 were wrenched from the walls. Giant shells contain the holy water, so any devout sea nymphs will feel at home. But the retable is the eye-catching feature. Carved by two Flemings, Olivier de Gand and Jean d'Ypres, in 1508, it incorporates a high-relief panel of *The Assumption of the Virgin*, above the four Evangelists. The border of foliage contains figures of mermaids, hunters, a centaur, and a pig playing the bagpipes.

The Lower Town

The Church of Santa Cruz

Church of Santa Cruz
Praça 8 de Maio,
t (239) 822 941; open
Mon–Sat 9–12 and
2–5.30, Sun 4–6;
adm for cloister

The church of Santa Cruz is chock-full of goodies. It stands in the Praça 8 de Maio, at one end of Coimbra's main shopping street, the Rua Visconde da Luz. The church was founded by the clerics Dom Telo and Dom João Peculiar in 1131 as a priory of 12 Augustinian monks; São Teotónio, confessor of Afonso Henriques, was the first prior. The dilapidated building was reconstructed and enlarged by Dom Manuel from 1502 onwards. In 1539, Dom João III made the priors chancellors of the university in perpetuity, a rank they held until the Dissolution of 1834. From the plague of 1423 until it was forbidden in 1641, Santa Cruz was the destination of the eccentric Procession of the Nudes: penitents processed through the streets wearing only their shirts, engrossed in mutual flagellation.

The works of art within the church, mostly by foreign artists, are much more interesting than the body of the building. The façade has suffered from the rise of the street level and an 18th-century triumphal arch, but it was never beautiful. This western front is by Diogo de Castilho, with statues created by João de Ruão and Nicolau Chanterène: in 1524 Dom Manuel wrote from Évora ordering 100 gold cruzados to be paid to Diogo and to Master Nicolau for the statues, and two years later another letter granted Diogo the privilege of riding on a mule, 'seeing that he has no horse'.

The Interior

The polygonal **pulpit** is carved in Ançã stone, with a hydra-headed dragon at its base, and attributed to João de Roupo. His tutor wrote to Dom João III in 1522: 'All who see it, say that in Spain there is no piece of stone of better workmanship; for this 20,000 reis have been paid.' In 1520 the bodies of Dom Afonso Henriques, the first King of Portugal, who had died nearly 400 years previously, and his son Dom Sancho I, were disinterred from their graves in front of the old church, and reinstated in thoroughly ornamented anachronistic medieval-style **tombs** sculpted by Chanterène (to the left and right of the high altar), with the effigies in battle dress. The **sacristy**, of 1622, contains furniture of the same date, based on the simple architectural style of the previous century, and some excellent paintings, including a *St Vincent* attributed to García Fernandes.

Boitac's Chapter House squeaks with bats, who patently ignore the injunction of the Cloister of Silence, from which stairs lead to the *coro alto*, where a chain of reliefs at the top of the magnificent **choir stalls** depicts Portuguese vessels doing battle with those of the Turks sailing past rather Germanic cities. These suggest that Master Machim, who started work on the stalls in 1513, had come from northern Europe.

Jardim de Manga

Behind the church of Santa Cruz stands what seems to be a fanciful 20th-century bandstand: the central, circular platform is connected by buttresses to four satellites, and the whole set in a water tank choked by garbage. In fact it was completed in 1535, and its strange name, the **Jardim de Manga** (Garden of the Sleeve) hints at the origin of its design: according to tradition, Dom João III drew the plans for the building on his sleeve.

CAV (Centro de Artes Visuais) is the city's latest museum and exhibits contemporary photographic and video displays. The stark white building once served as a prison during the Inquisition.

Across the River

The second left turning across the river leads to the 14th-century Gothic convent church of **Santa Clara-a-Velha**, which was, until

CAV
Pátio da Inquição,
t *(239) 826 178;*
open Tues–Sun 2–7

Santa Clara-a-Velha
Rua das Parreiras,
t *(239) 801 160,*
www.santaclara avelha.drcc.pt;
open daily
1 Oct–30 Apr 10–5;
1 May–30 Sept 10–7

recently, one of the most bizarre sights in Portugal: flooded by the Mondego since the 17th century, the tops of the church's aisle arches protruded above the water level like Japanese bridges. The church reopened to the public in April 2009 after 12 years of restoration.

The Rua António Augusto Gonçalves runs several hundred yards from the front of the church to the 18th-century **Quinta das Lágrimas** where, according to tradition, Inês de Castro was murdered by order of Dom Afonso IV, who considered her unworthy of his son Pedro. When he became king, her demented lover compelled the nobility to pay homage to her exhumed corpse, claiming he had married her (*see* 'Alcobaça', p.281). The *quinta* is now a hotel (*see* 'Where to Stay', p.252), but it may be possible to see the **Fonte dos Amores**, the fountain made famous by Camões in *The Lusiads*: 'The nymphs of the Mondego were long to remember, with sobbing, that dark dispatch [of Inês]; and their tears became a spring of pure water, that remembrance might be eternal. The fountain marks the scene of her earlier happiness ...'

Children and their minders can get a kick out of **Portugal dos Pequenitos Park** which is entered near the church of Santa Clara-a-Velha: Portugal's monuments are represented in miniature, with pagodas and other exotics from the colonies, including African tribal spears, and bottles of locally brewed beer.

The Calçada Santa Isabel rises from the Rossio to the **convent of Santa Clara-a-Nova**, built 1649–77 as a successor to its inundated namesake. Most of it is now used as a barracks and the north wing houses a **military museum**. The tank standing outside does little for the building itself. Try to catch the afternoon sun, which shows fabulous 17th-century gilt woodwork in the convent **church** to its best advantage. Six panels depict the removal of the body of St Isabel from what threatened to become a watery grave in the church of Santa Clara-a-Velha, and its transference to a silver shrine here, in 1677; her clothes are displayed in the sacristy. The very large cloister was the gift of Dom João V, a man who loved nuns, though he preferred them to come from the convent at Odivelas.

Fonte dos Amores
gardens open daily 9–5; adm

Portugal dos Pequenitos Park
t (239) 441 225; open June–mid-Sept daily 9–8, mid-Sept–Feb daily 10–5, March–May 10–7; adm, children under 5 free

Military museum
open 10–12 and 2–5

Church
t (239) 441 674; open Tues–Sun 9–12 and 2–5; adm for cloister

The Beiras | Beira Litoral: Coimbra

ⓘ **Coimbra >**
Largo Dom Dinis, near the University, t (239) 832 591; open Mon–Fri 9–6, Sat–Sun 9–12.30 and 2–5.30

Praça da República, t (239) 833 202; open Mon–Fri 10–6.30, Sat–Sun 10–1 and 2.30–6.30

Services in Coimbra

The main **post office** is in Avenida Fernão de Magalhães 223, t (239) 850 700 (*open Mon–Fri 8.30–6.30*). There are two more centrally located branches, one in Rua Olímpio Nicolau Rui Fernandes (*open Mon–Fri 8.30–6.30, Sat 9–12.30*) and the other in Praça da República (*open Mon–Fri 9–6*).

Esp@ço Internet, Praça 8 de Maio 37 (*open Mon–Fri 10–8, Sat–Sun 10am–10pm*). Up to 30 minutes free internet access; this is a municipal outfit.

Casa Municipal da Cultura, Rua Pedro Monteiro, t (239) 702 630. Inside the public library; you must obtain a free library card in order to use the internet.

Festivals in Coimbra

Festa da Rainha Santa, around 4 July in even-numbered years is a festival

(★) Hotel Astória >>

(★) Casa Pombal >>

commemorating St Isabel: a procession with her statue from the Convento de Santa Clara-a-Nova to Igreja do Carmo and back. Folk music, dancing and fireworks; it coincides with the **Festa da Cidade** (Town Festival).

Shopping in Coimbra

Coimbra **pottery** is delightfully bright and whimsical, painted with unlikely animals and birds which flit through the foliage. Stylistic influences are jumbled: the Hispano-Arab tradition of the 15th century; 16th-century Moghul India and the Orient; and the influence of Delft, transmitted by 17th-century merchants trading with Flanders. The pottery is on sale throughout Coimbra, especially in the streets leading up to the cathedral from the lower part of town.

Sports and Activities in Coimbra

Horse-riding: Centro de Hípico de Coimbra, **t** (239) 837 695. For horse-riding in the Choupal National Forest.
Mountain-biking: Centro Velocipédico de Sangalhos, Rua da Sota 23, **t** (239) 824 646. Bike hire at €7.50 per day. *Open Mon–Fri 9–7.*

Where to Stay in Coimbra

Very Expensive (€€€€)
★★★★Quinta das Lágrimas, **t** (239) 802 380, *www.quintadaslagrimas.pt*. On the west side of the river, it claims to have been washed with the *lágrimas* (tears) of Inês de Castro just before she was stabbed to death in the 14th century. The pretty 18th-century manor house visible today fell into ruin and has been restored and expanded by Relais & Châteaux. Lacking the patina of age, it feels like a money-making business rather than a well of hospitality. Bedrooms in the ground-floor modern garden wing are

tight for space, and the interior decoration is rather peach and strays into the pseudo medieval. The restaurant does a good set-price dinner for €47.50, with wine for an extra €10. The site includes a pool, a pitch-and-put and a spa.

Expensive (€€€)
Hotel Astória, Avenida Emídio Navarro 21, **t** (239) 853 020, *www.almeida hotels.com*. Bang in the centre of town, overlooking the river and a noisy main road, this is a magnificent time warp from the late 1930s, like an ocean liner with high ceilings. The fixtures and fittings will make you drool. Skip the restaurant.

Inexpensive (€)
★★★Residencial Domus, Rua Adelino Veiga 62, **t** (239) 828 584, *www. residencialdomus.com*, offers very pleasant little rooms and there's a good feel to the place. Recommended.
★★★Residencial Moderna, Rua Adelino Veiga 49, **t** (239) 825 413, *www. residencialmoderna.com.pt*. Clean but a bit fusty, though the rooms with balconies and views of the old town are very nice.
★★Residencial Alentejana, Rua António Henriques Sco 1, **t** (239) 825 903, *www.residencialalentejana.com*. Removed from the centre of town, a clean and attractive bourgeois villa with high ceilings and air conditioning. Well worth considering despite the location.
★★Pensão Parque, Avenida Emídio Navarro 42, **t** (239) 829 202. Offers tall, well-finished bedrooms at bargain prices.
Casa Pombal, Rua das Flores 18, **t** (239) 835 175. Way up near the university is a fabulous little place run by a Dutch couple and something of a fixture with the world-travelling muesli-in-Kathmandu brigade. Rooms at the top have private bathrooms and good views, but they're a bit damp. Phone first to get directions from wherever you are; turn right from the top of the elevator, right downhill and then fork left.

Residencial Botânico, Bairro de São José 15, **t** (239) 714 824. With all the hallmarks of a good hotel, this represents the city's best value.

The Olives, Rue Manguinhas, Casal Sao Bras, Ansiao, *www.pureportugal holidays.com/ansiao.html*. Delightful 2-bed stone cottage, fully equipped with satellite TV and Internet. Long and short lets available.

Pensão Residencial Antunes, Rua Castro Matoso 8, **t** (239) 854 720. Close to bars and student life, a fairly basic rooming house which offers parking facilities.

Pensão Flôr de Coimbra, Rua do Poço 5, **t** (239) 823 865. Close to the railway station, monastically simple, with long hostel-like corridors and sloping wooden ceilings. The locally popular restaurant on the first floor serves cheap food, including vegetarian.

Eating Out in Coimbra

Moderate (€€)

Restaurante O Trovador, Largo da Sé Velha 15–17, **t** (239) 825 475. Next to the Sé Velha is this romantic and pleasantly unpretentious place with an *azulejo* dado and *fado* at 9pm. Try the kid or the sea bass. There's a balcony for drinkers who like *fado*. *Closed Sun*.

Zé Carioca, Avenida Sá da Bandeira 89, **t** (239) 835 450. Nothing to do with karaoke, this is a warm and welcoming Brazilian restaurant – a bit too brightly lit to be really intimate, but heading there. The food is delicious and justifiably popular. Live music every night, soft enough to talk across. *Closed Sun*.

Zé Manel, Beco do Forno 12, **t** (239) 823 790. Behind the Hotel Astória, irresistibly loaded with atmosphere, the walls are pinned with browning, curling poems, jokes, *fado* songs and compliments. The upmarket clientele squash in to eat enormous portions of very rich food. The soup is just like granny makes, the *feijoada* superb. A

separate staircase leads to an upper chamber, which is brighter and more intimate. *Closed Sat eve and Sun*.

Italia, Beco do Forno 12, **t** (239) 838 863. Excellent Italian restaurant on the riverfront with a superb choice of pizza and pasta dishes and a cosy *italiano* atmosphere.

Inexpensive (€)

Adega Paço do Conde, Rua Paço do Conde 1, **t** (239) 825 605. If you get lost in the back streets, follow a group of students off the Praça do Comércio to a covered courtyard with an open grill and a dining room to one side. The food is cheap and excellent. The chicken soup looks terrible but tastes wonderful, and the *Arroz de Marinheira* is simply magnificent.

Jardim da Manga, Rua Olímpio Nicolau Rui Fernandes, **t** (239) 829 156. Behind the church of Santa Cruz is a self-service cafeteria. *Closed Sat*.

Zé Neto, Rua das Azeiteiras 8–10, **t** (239) 826 786. Popular and noisy little place, serving vast portions. *Closed Sun*.

Cafés and Bars

Many of Coimbra's bars are in the Praça da República, including a café next to the tourist office, popular with students. Most are open until 4am.

Cartola Esplanada Bar, Praça da República. Good for people-watching.

Bar Diligencia, Rua Nova 30, **t** (239) 827 667. A pleasant and popular bar with regular live *fado* performances.

Quebra, Parque Verde do Mondego, **t** (239) 836 038. For jazz.

A Capella, Capela de Nossa Senhora de Victoria, Rua Corpo de Deus, **t** (239) 833 985. A former 14th-century chapel makes an evocative setting for nightly *fado* (9.30pm).

Santa Cruz, Praça 8 de Maio. Café in a splendid 17th-century construction adjacent to the church, complete with stained glass, ceiling tracery, and dragons tamed to hold lamps.

★ Adega Paço do Conde »

★ Zé Manel ›

Around Coimbra

Conimbriga

Portugal's most elaborate Roman site teems with wonderful mosaics and shrieking schoolchildren. The sprawling site occupies a plateau hemmed in by a V-shaped gorge, surrounded by wild rose bushes and low hills blanketed with umbrella pines and olive trees, girdled by a poorly preserved ceremonial wall. It's accompanied by an excellent museum, and a restaurant. Although there's plenty to · see, only about one-sixth of Conimbriga has been excavated; even the tribunal has not been located.

History

The name of Conimbriga separates into '*conim*', indicating a rocky outcrop or plateau, and '*briga*', the Celtic suffix denoting a defended site. Located midway along the Romans' Lisbon–Braga highway, it was first occupied by the Romans *c.* 200 BC, but fragments have been found dating back as far as 800–500 BC.

In 25 BC there was peace in Lusitania, and the Emperor Augustus determined to expand Conimbriga, to include an aqueduct, a forum with a temple, public baths, private housing and shops. It was Vespasian who made the town a monumental city, AD 69–79. The settlement flowered again in the 3rd century, blooming with those villas and mosaics that remain today. But the boom was short-lived: the Romans lost their grip in western Iberia, and *c.* AD 260–270 Franks and Almans crossed the Rhine and attacked the east of the Iberian peninsula. Although they did not reach as far as Lusitania, there was a general programme of fortifying the province. Conimbriga had to be protected, so a new defensive wall was built using materials wrenched from private houses, the baths, the amphitheatre and even the necropolis. To reduce time and cost, and to cut down on the policing of the walls, the residential part of the city was abandoned. Fear for the safety of the aqueduct led to the construction of a giant reservoir in one wing of the cryptoporticus of the forum.

The Swabians attacked Conimbriga in 465, seizing, among others, the wife and child of citizen Cantaber. They captured the city three years later and enslaved its populace – but Conimbriga was not deserted: its bishop attended the Council of Braga in 572. Shortly afterwards the settlement was abandoned in favour of a safer place also on the Lisbon-Braga highway, the Roman settlement of Aeminium. Through linguistic debasement, this became known as Coimbra. The preservation of Conimbriga depended on the departure of its residents.

Getting to Conimbriga

Sixteen km south of Coimbra, Conimbriga makes a good day trip. There are two **buses** at 9.05am and 9.35am on weekdays from the Avic Station on Rua Joao do Ruao (30mins), returning at 1pm or 6pm. On weekends, only the later buses operate. Otherwise, there are direct buses every half-hour to Condeixa-a-Nova, a 2km (½hr) uncomfortable walk from the site.

By **road**, the Serra do Buçaco is 27km north-northeast of Coimbra, and Luso some 3km downhill.

The Museum

Museum
t *(239) 944 100;*
open Mar–Sept
Tues–Sun 10–1 and 2–7,
Sept–Mar until 6pm;
adm

A good place to start, the **museum** brings the **site** to life, from needles, hoes, and nails to hairbands, rings, and clips. One whole case is devoted to health and hygiene. Note the maquette of the forum; the real one is not yet open to the public. The labyrinth mosaic, with the Minotaur at its centre, was either a game or a superstitious prophylactic, to bring good health to the family.

The site
open Mar–Sept daily
9–1 and 2–8, Sept–Mar
until 6pm; adm

Outside the City Walls

There are two main features outside the hastily constructed city walls. To the right (northeast) of the track leading to the excavations is the **House of the Fountains**, constructed during the first half of the 3rd century, on the site of a 1st-century house. The central peristyle of this family home is a pond jigsawed with flowerbeds, which tinkles with a mass of water jets. This design is very unusual, since normally Roman houses had an earthen courtyard in the middle, with only a small pool and flower garden; the Palace of Domitian in Rome is the only known parallel in a Roman town house. Amphoras built into the wall of another of the villa's pools were probably intended as a temporary home for the fish, while the pool they normally lived in was being cleaned. The villa's excellent tiles depict the four seasons, scenes from daily life such as stag hunting, and mythological happenings. They rely less on geometry than other tiles in Conimbriga, probably because they were created a couple of decades earlier.

To the other side of the track, the Roman shops, the two houses with well-preserved geometrical mosaics, and the poorly preserved baths, were disrupted by the hastily erected defensive wall.

Within the City Gates

Through the city gates stand the columns and half-columns of the **Villa of Cantaber**, which was one of the largest city residences in the western Roman world, dating from the 3rd century; the pampered residents had their own baths. On the far side of the villa, to the south, all that remains of the **Christian basilica** are the two semicircles of the baptismal font, and a tiny cruciform chapel whose shape suggests that it dates from the 6th century. When the city was abandoned, the consecrated area was employed as a cemetery.

The track continues past the villa of Cantaber and forks at the **Flavian Forum**. This was made up of two parts: the smooth expanse with the stumps of columns at its edges was the forum square, which was surrounded on three sides by covered porticoes. The upper part was the temple itself, built over a cryptoporticus to raise it to a dominant height.

A paved road ran from the forum to the **Thermae** (baths), past the **Insulae**. These shops, taverns, and storage rooms are now nondescript piles of rubble, but they were not always so dull: one of them produced the mind-boggling phallic vase displayed in the museum. The Augustan baths were at the terminus of the aqueduct; in Trajan's reign they were superseded by a much bigger complex, which is now reduced to large areas of flat stone, a staircase, a buttressed wall, and various sepulchral baths. The baths were supplied with water from one of two tanks fed by Conimbriga's aqueduct, which ran nearly 3,500 yards from Alcabideque. Parts of it are still standing, and the collecting basin at the source is still in use as a fountain, a laundry tub and a watering trough.

Montemór-o-Velho

Castle
*open Tues–Sun
10–12.30 and 2–5*

Set on a hill above the fertile plains of the River Mondego, the **castle** of Montemór-o-Velho looks impressive from the road; it dates from the 11th century, with 14th-century additions, and was built to protect Coimbra. In the early 13th century, Dom Sancho I bequeathed the castle to his daughters Dona Teresa and Dona Mafalda, much to the annoyance of their brother Dom Afonso II, who besieged them there. The pope intervened to calm the unhappy family, resolving that the castle should be administered by the Templars and the lordship of the town by Dona Teresa. There's little to look at within the castle walls, except the delicate twisted Manueline columns in the plain **church of Santa Maria de Alcáçova**, which was restored in 1510, or the skeleton of a 16th-century royal residence.

In the lower part of the village itself, beside a muddy little tributary of the Mondego, the modest 17th-century exterior of the **convento de Nossa Senhora dos Anjos** belies the older and more attractive interior, dating at least from the 14th century. It contains the tomb of Diogo de Azambuja, by the Manueline master Diogo Pires the Younger, *c.* 1518. On the sarcophagus, scenes allude to the trading of gold: Diogo helped to establish an important entrepôt for the metal.

Luso and Buçaco

Forest of Buçaco
May–Oct; adm for cars, walkers enter free of charge

The **Forest of Buçaco** (Bussaco) covers 260 acres (105ha) of the northern slopes of the Serra do Buçaco. It is a magical, deeply refreshing place – just give it time to work on you. Mossy paths, marked with botanical walks, ribbon between the venerable trees, winding through the sharp light past pools and fountains. Walkers can stumble on to crosses and peek into grottoes, which reveal tiny chapels hidden among the oaks and cork oaks. For peace of mind, collect a map from the tourist office in Luso, or from the Palace Hotel. Put it in your pocket, and get lost.

Spa
t (239) 930 597 or 930 615, www.termasdoluso. com; open May–Oct to day visitors, for massage, hydromassage, thermotherapy etc.

The airy **spa** town of **Luso** – jollier than most – is located some 3km downhill. The water tastes delicious – its high radioactive content is beneficial. If you're serious about a spa treatment, bring your reno-urinary disorders, hypertension, rheumatism, and/or your respiratory complaints.

History

It comes as no surprise that monks lived in this forest. The first were Benedictine hermits, in the 6th century. But it was not until the arrival of the Barefoot Carmelites in 1628 that Buçaco became famous: they walled the forest and planted an arboretum, which was enriched with unlikely species brought back by the Portuguese navigators. Now there are roughly 400 local and 300 exotic varieties, including Mexican cypresses – which look like cedars – and giant ferns, sequoias and ginkgo trees. Such were the qualities of the trees that in 1643 they came under papal protection: Urban VIII threatened to excommunicate anyone who damaged them. As with the trees, so with the monks. Their virtue had been kept intact by that pope's predecessor, Gregory XV, who forbade women to enter the precincts.

Things haven't always been this peaceful: in August 1810, a third French invading force of 66,000 men under Masséna entered the Beiras from Spain, occupying first Guarda and then Viseu. Wellington's guards held the main road to Coimbra, so the French attempted to get there by marching across the Buçaco hills. Wellington took up a position along the line of the ridge, and kept the majority of his 52,000 troops, half of them English, concealed behind it. Against advice, Masséna attacked up the steep slope, but his men were repeatedly thrown back. Eventually they were forced to work their way around the northern edge of the ridge, before turning on Coimbra. Wellington was able to withdraw undisturbed, to take up position at his Lines of Torres Vedras, north of Lisbon.

After the Dissolution of the religious houses, a scene-painter at the San Carlos Opera House designed a neo-Manueline summer palace for the royal family, completed in 1907, adjacent to what remains of the monastery, a small 17th-century church, with a cork-ceilinged cloister. The monarchy was extinguished in 1910, and the king's Swiss cook subsequently started to run the palace as a hotel.

ⓘ Luso >

*Rua Emídio Navarro,
t (231) 939 133,
jtlb@oninet.pt; open
June–Sept Mon–Fri 9–7;
Oct–May Mon–Fri
9.30–12.30 and 2–6;
all year Sat–Sun 10–1
and 3–5*

⭐ Palace Hotel
do Buçaco >

Tourist Information Around Coimbra

The **tourist office** in Luso has a plethora of information, including maps, accommodation, flora and site guides in English. Buses stop near here.

Where to Stay and Eat Around Coimbra

Buçaco

★★★★★Palace Hotel do Buçaco, Mata do Buçaco, t (231) 937 970, *www. almeidahotels.com* (€€€€€–€€€€). A thrillingly unique, fantastic, overpowering confection – but now somewhat frayed at the edges. Guests sway down the grandest of staircases for the sheer enjoyment of it, rub shoulders with suits of armour, settle in leather chairs beneath billiard-table lamps in the bar and peek at murals of lonely lute players. Bedrooms are nicely old-fashioned, with fine, highly polished furniture and huge bathtubs. It's tempting to cocoon oneself in the tall velvet curtains. The staff are efficient. In the restaurant (€€€), the chef's fortes are suckling pig, mutton and kid, and there's an excellent wine list. Beware that if you're staying here bus-loads will view it as a tourist attraction and peer through the windows. Alternatively, come for tea or a drink. The building gives a good indication of what Manueline architecture is not about – the decoration is superfluous, with no tension.

Luso

★★★Grande Hotel de Luso, Rua Dr. Cid de Oliveira 86, t (231) 937 937, *www.hoteluso.com* (€€). Connected to the spa is a large and well appointed hotel, with newly refurbished, neutral rooms and an Olympic-sized outdoor pool, as well as an indoor pool and sauna/steam room. Good value.

★★Pensão Central, Rua Emídio Navarro, t (231) 939 254, *www.pensaocentral.no.sapo.pt* (€). Has 16 cosy guestrooms and a restaurant.

Pensão Alegre, Rua Emídio Navarro, t (231) 930 256 (€). If you can't afford to stay in the Palace Hotel, Buçaco, this represents a budget version. Occupying the former villa of the Marquês da Graciosa, it's kitted out in mock baronial style. Shower rooms are fairly basic. Outdoor pool.

★★Pensão Astória, Rua Emídio Navarro, t (231) 939 182 (€). Ferns in the corridor and lacy curtains gentrify this airy *pensão* – opposite the Grande Hotel – with a pub attached.

Restaurante Cesteiro, Rua Monsenhor Mira, t (231) 939 360 (€€). On the edge of town near the railway station, very popular with families at the weekend. It lacks atmosphere, but the food is good and fresh: roast suckling pig (*leitão a bairrada*) or kid stew in wine (*chanfana*).

Restaurante Lourenços, Avenida Emídio Navarro, t (231) 939 474 (€). Comfortable atmosphere, with good traditional, well-cooked dishes.

Salão de Chá, near the Fonte de Sã João, t (231) 939 411 (€). Relaxed and civilized Art Deco tearoom.

Aveiro

Aveiro stands at the eastern edge of a grey, shallow *Ria* (estuary), which extends about 28 miles (45km) from Ovar to Mira, with a width of up to 6 miles (10km), and into which flows the River Vouga. The saltwater estuary was formed by the retreat of the sea and the subsequent formation of coastal sandbanks, which closed up to form a lagoon. Sediment accumulated, and the estuary is now shattered into dunes and meadows of reeds.

In the 16th century, the 14,000 inhabitants were buoyed to prosperity by salt, fishing and maritime trading. Over the next two centuries, the coastal sandbanks edged southwards until finally they closed up completely, leaving Aveiro high and dry. This combined with the fever-breeding marshes to reduce the population to about 3,500 in the second half of the 18th century. Aveiro's fortunes only revived when the sandbar was artificially, permanently breached in 1808, restoring the town's role as an important port.

Aveiro is less than half an hour away from good sand beaches, but the town is not a resort. It retains a kind of mellow dignity, with open streets and dragon's-tooth pavements, patterned with sea horses, ship's knots, seaweed boats and stylized crabs. Few buildings are more than two storeys, including fishermen's cottages in the streets around the Largo da Praça do Peixe and Art Nouveau villas, in the Rua do Dr Barbosa da Magalhães – though the fringe marred by horrid modern buildings. Three main canals lead in to town from the *Ria*. Just one building is outstanding, but the *Ria* gives plenty of scope for exploration, and if you dislike swimming in the waves of the Atlantic, the blue lagoon offers a calm alternative. There's a range of good places to stay in Aveiro, and a couple of worthwhile restaurants, although unhurried cafés are sparse.

Salt and Seaweed

Aveiro accommodates two antique industries: salt and seaweed. Brilliant little mounds of salt surround Aveiro in late summer, heaped between the grid of saltpans, before being transported in sober, heavy salt boats. Although it is probably much older, the salt industry dates back at least to AD 959, when Countess Mumadona Dias bequeathed her saltpans at Alvario, as it was known, to the monastery at Guimarães. Now refrigerated tankers bring cod to be salted and transformed into the ubiquitous *bacalhau*.

The estuary supplies a harvest of seaweed, which is used to fertilize Aveiro's crops, though the industry is being eaten away by artificial fertilizers. The green stuff is raked up from the shallow waters into dangerously low-slung, wide-bottomed *moliceiro* boats, which are punted when the wind is slack. The boats' high, curling prows are painted with matters of pride – crude horse riders, saints, women, even the poet Camões, in reds, blues, greens and yellows.

Getting to Aveiro

Aveiro's **railway station**, Avenida Dr Lourenço Peixinho, is served by frequent trains from Lisbon (2½hrs), Coimbra (¾hr) and Porto (¾hr). Rodonorte **buses, t** (234) 429 679, run infrequently from Lisbon (4hrs), via Leiria (2¼hrs). There is one express a day to Coimbra (¾hr).

It's possible to catch **ferries** from Aveiro to Torreira, and Forte da Barra to S. Jacinto, during June–Sept daily.

Getting around Aveiro

Most **buses** stop on the Avenida Dr Lourenço Peixinho; the railway station doubles as the bus terminal, at the top of the street. Buy tickets from kiosks or *tabacarias*, or from the bus drivers. The pastry shop near the station, Estação 90, Avenida Dr Lourenço Peixinho 352, also sells tickets. AV Aveirense run buses along the coast to the nearby **beaches**, which are good for surfing, every hour during the summer and nearly as frequently in winter. They go from the kiosk on Rua Clube dos Galitos, via Gafanha da Nazaré, to Costa Nova and back.

Aveira has a free **bike hire** scheme: look for the blue and white 'Parque BUGA' stands, where you can insert a 50 cent coin and take a bike to ride anywhere within the city. Return the bike to another stand and you'll get your coin back.

The Convent of Jesus

Museu de Aveiro
t (234) 423 297; open Tues–Sun 10–1 and 2–5.30; adm, free entry Sun 10–2

The **Museu de Aveiro**, Rua de Santa Joana Princesa – walk up the Rua Batalhão Caçadores from the Praça Humberto Delgado – is installed in the former Mosteiro de Jesus (Convent of Jesus), which was founded in 1465, and seven years later received the Infanta Joana, daughter of Dom Afonso V, into its starched folds. She was a remarkable woman of celebrated beauty, whose portrait sent Louis XI of France into a swoon, but who was only interested in one crown, the Crown of Thorns.

This she adopted as her personal device, embroidering it on church linen and having it stamped onto her silver. When her brother and father returned from the successful Tangier expedition of 1471, she abdicated her role managing the royal household and asked to enter a convent. At Aveiro she kneaded bread and made prickly hair shirts for the ascetic order, but grew dangerously ill from the diet of bread, herbs and water. She was forbidden to take full vows, to the delight of her father and brother. The latter became Dom João II, and attempted to marry his sister to Richard III of England. She claimed this was impossible, as that king was already dead, and was proved correct. The Infanta Joana was beatified in 1693.

The Church

The convent was revamped in the 18th century: between 1725 and 1729 António Gomes and José Correia transformed its **church** into a fantastic riot of gilt woodwork, with a vaulted chancel like a shower of gold and flesh-coloured cherubs flying up the altar columns. In 1699 Dom Pedro II commissioned the royal architect, João Antunes, to create a tomb to commemorate the beatification of the Princess Infanta Saint Joana. It was 12 years in the making, and its gorgeous Florentine marble inlay fills the lower choir. Two of the supports are phoenixes, symbolizing immortality. The church is lined with scenes from her life – part of which was spent in the low 15th-century cloister that magnifies the sky. In the 18th century, the walls and ceiling of the chestnut *coro alto* were painted with several saints, who rub shoulders with long-feathered birds, parasols, and bows and arrows; perhaps one of the nuns brought a taste for chinoiserie with her from Macau.

The Museum

The museum itself contains unremarkable stone sculpture from the Coimbra school, various Baroque polychromed statues, including a winged St Michael. There are ivory crucifixes and Vista Alegre porcelains, but the most eye-catching works are the primitive paintings. Note particularly the early 16th-century *Senhora da Madressilva*, named after the honeysuckle she holds; St John the Evangelist on a balcony, of the same date; and a portrait of Princess Joana from the third quarter of the 15th century. Cloaked by her red dreadlocks, her arresting face is rather modern.

Around the Convent

Around the corner in the Rua do Comandante Rocha e Cunha stands the **church of the monastery of São Domingos**, which serves as Aveiro's cathedral. It was founded in 1423, but subsequently remodelled. The only things worth looking at are the early 18th-century canvases depicting the life of St Dominic, over the choir stalls, and the 15th-century Cruz de São Domingos, a stone cross ornamented with scenes of the Passion, which used to stand outside the monastery but is now housed in the first chapel to the right of the entrance.

(i) **Aveiro >**
Rua João Mendonça 8, t (234) 423 680, www.rotadaluz.pt; open June–Sept daily 9–8, Oct–May Mon–Fri 9–7, Sat 9–1 and 2.30–5.30

Internet Access in Aveiro

Aveiro Digital, in the *Câmara Municipal* (town hall), t (234) 371 666, gab-tecnico@aveiro-digital.pt. Open Mon–Sat 10–8.

Sports and Activities in Aveiro

Boat Trips

The tourist office (*see* left) runs daily boat trips (mid-June to mid-Sept) to Costa Nova and back, from the Canal Centre in front of the tourist office.

Water Sports

Riactiva, Rua Banda da Amizade 32, t (234) 394 715, *www.riactiva.com*. They will arrange windsurfing, kitesurfing and kayaking.

Outr' Atitude, Edificio Cruzeiro, Rua Bento de Moura, t (234) 316 764. Rafting and mountain-climbing.

Horse-riding

Escola Equestre d'Aveiro, Quinta do Chão d'Agra, Vilarinho, t (234) 912 108, *www.escolaequestreaveiro.com*.

Where to Stay in Aveiro

Moderate (€€)
★★★★Hotel As Américas, Rua Eng. Von Haff 20, t (234) 384 640, *www.hotelasamericas.com*. A ten-minute walk from the centre of town, spacious but dull. The service is snappy, though, and they offer parking.

★★★Hotel Mercure Aveiro, Rua Luis Gomes de Carvalho 23, t (234) 404

400, *www.mercure.com*. Near the railway station, the former Paloma Blanca Hotel is installed in a lovely old 1930s mansion, though you wouldn't know that from within. It's very nicely done throughout, pretty and sturdy, with sports facilities including an indoor and an outdoor pool.

★★★**Best Western Hotel Imperial**, Rua Dr Nascimento Leitão, **t** (234) 380 150, *www.bestwestern.com*. Straight up from the central roundabout, large, neutral and efficient, monogrammed wherever possible. Saltpans are visible from the summer terrace. The restaurant caters for tour groups, offering fixed-price meals, or *à la carte* steaks, porks, veals, hake and eels.

★★★**Hotel Afonso V**, Rua D. Manuel das Neves 65, **t** (234) 425 191, *www. hoteisafonsov.com.pt*. Farther from the canals, but decent if you're stuck. Floral, stripey and everything is newish.

★★**Hotel Arcada**, Rua Viana do Castelo 4, **t** (234) 423 001, *www.hotelarcada. com*. You'd need a good reason to stay somewhere other than this friendly, efficient hotel. It's bang in the centre of town, double glazed and grander than its two stars suggest. The only drawback is that there's no parking.

Residencial Farol, Largo de Farol, Praia de Barra, **t** (234) 390 606, *www.residencialfarol.com*. Situated on the roundabout by the lighthouse, this has been jazzed up with strong colours and modern lighting, and geared to couples. The result is happy if you've come for the beach.

Inexpensive (€)
★★**Residencial Beira** Rua José Estevão 18, **t** (234) 424 297.

★★**Residencial Palmeira**, Rua da Palmeira 7, **t** (234) 422 521, *residencial.palmeira@netc.pt*. Close to Praça Humberto Delgado, solid and decent, with free Internet access.

Hospederia dos Arcos, Rua José Estevão 47, **t** (234) 383 130. Homey and spotless.

Eating Out in Aveiro

The Rua do Tenente Resende is full of restaurants. It leads into the Largo da Praça do Peixe, which is full of restaurants and bars that spill into the square.

Adega Tipica O Telheiro, Largo da Praça do Peixe 20, **t** (234) 429 473 (€€). Great atmosphere, whether you choose benches and paper tablecloths or chairs and linen. The lighting is a little harsh, and the €16.50 cover charge very steep. *Reservations are necessary.*

A Barca, Rua José Rabumba 5A, **t** (234) 426 024 (€€). Moneyed and elderly diners eat great fish in bistro style.

Mercado do Peixe, Largo da Praça do Peixe, **t** (234) 383 511 (€€). Fabulous seafood restaurant suitably located above the fish market. The décor is surprisingly sophisticated given the homey setting.

Sonatura, Rua Clube dos Galitos 6, **t** (234) 424 474 (€). Aveiro is lucky to have a self-service vegetarian restaurant, opposite the tourist office. It serves fairly complicated dishes, but can be beset by blandness (the malaise of Portuguese veggies). The fresh fruit juices cannot be faulted. *Open Mon–Fri 12–6.30.*

Around Aveiro

There are some good beaches around Aveiro, a memorable nature reserve and several forgettable towns that have come under the sway of the Aveiro lagoon or the sea itself. The inland towns have one or two places of interest to visit. The coastline bordering the Aveiro Lagoon is flat and backed by low grassy dunes, which offer meagre shelter from the Atlantic winds. The beaches are not really pretty, but if you're prepared to walk a little way from the access roads, you can sunbathe in splendid isolation. Infrastructure decreases southwards, and there's almost no development between Praia de Mira and Figueira da Foz. To the north, the coastline becomes increasingly developed as it approaches Espinho.

The São Jacinto Dunes Nature Reserve

Reserva Natural das Dunas de São Jacinto

t (234) 331 282 or 831 063, camarinha.aveiro-digital.net; open 9–12 and 2–5; prior booking essential; you can only enter between 9–9.30 and 2–2.30 for a maximum stay of 2½ hrs; closed Sun, Thurs and hols

Visitor Centre
open 9–12 and 2–5; closed Sun, Thurs and hols

Located on the strip of dunes that closes off the Aveiro lagoon to the north, the **Reserva Natural das Dunas de São Jacinto** covers 1,650 acres (666ha) of beaches, dunes, woodland and freshwater ponds. Keep your binoculars handy for resident lagoon birds and migrating sea birds. There's also a **Visitor Centre**.

Further south, São Jacinto itself is a humming little port on the *Ria*, with good swimming, and fun dockside cafés. The beaches are backed by woods as far as Torreira, a fishing village and resort with a direct ferry link to and from Aveiro. Oxen work on the beach, as at Praia de Mira.

At the mouth of the *Ria*, the beach at **Praia de Barra** is backed by ugly modern buildings and, to the rear, the blue lagoon. It tends to be pretty crowded, because it is served by bus from Aveiro.

Costa Nova, a couple of kilometres to the south, attracts an older crowd, and the sand seems whiter than at Barra. The beach houses are painted with red or green or blue vertical stripes.

With its wooden houses built on stilts and its rudimentary development, **Praia de Mira** is one of the most attractive options south of Aveiro, not least because teams of oxen are driven back and forth along the beach, from July to September, hauling in the fishing nets. Small tree trunks serve as rollers for launching the high-prowed fishing boats, and when the catch is landed it's auctioned on the beach.

Ovar

Some 34km north of Aveiro, Ovar marks the northern extent of the waterways. The village makes its living from the timber trade, now that it's landlocked. Decades ago, the dusty, hefty fishwives of the village penetrated as far as Lisbon to hawk their wares, walking barefoot with crates on their heads and training their voices to penetrate every nook and cranny. Their few surviving successors in the capital are still known as Ovarinhas, or Varinhas.

Museu de Ovar
Rua Heliodoro Salgado, t (256) 572 822 ; open Mon-Sat 9.30–12.30 and 2.30–5.30

The small, centrally located **Museu de Ovar** takes particular delight in its collection of pots. The village is renowned for its *pão-de-ló* (a sort of sponge-cake), and its carnival at the beginning of March, which is presided over by clowns with frizzy wigs, and humpty-dumpty suits.

Santa Maria da Feira

Nine kilometres northeast of Ovar, a Gothic castle looms over Santa Maria da Feira, a photogenic, right-angled bastion whose four towers are topped with a confection of cones. Built on the site

Getting to areas Around Aveiro

The peninsula between São Jacinto and Torreira is only accessible by **road** at its northern end, so drivers from Aveiro must follow the route via Estarreja. There is a **bus** link between Aveiro and São Jacinto, but it's much more fun to get there by **ferry**.

of a pagan sanctuary, the castle is best seen when swathed in moonlight. It took its present form in the mid-15th century, when four sizzling hearths warmed the vaulted main hall and musicians plucked lutes on the balcony.

Avanca

Museu Egas Moniz
Rua Dr Egas Moniz,
t (234) 884 518;
open Mon–Fri 9–12 and
2.30–4.30, Sat–Sun 2–5;
adm

At Avanca, 26km north of Aveiro, the **Museu Egas Moniz** is open to view, preserved and furnished in the jolly taste of Dr Egas Moniz, who studied at Coimbra and was awarded a Nobel Prize in 1949 for demonstrating the therapeutic value of removing bits of the brain in cases of mental disorder. He collected Vista Alegre porcelain, and paintings by his contemporaries José Malhoa and Guerra Junqueiro.

Ílhavo

Museu Municipal
Rua S. Francisco
Xavier, t (234) 365 024

According to legend, Ílhavo, 6km south of Aveiro, was founded by the Greeks, for it was a fishing port until landlocked by the accumulation of silt. Its **Museu Municipal** on the northern edge of the village, contains a collection of Vista Alegre porcelain, as well as models of fishing boats, a collection of shells, and models of the *moliceiros* that harvest seaweed.

Vista Alegre

Museum
t (234) 320 600,
centro.visitas.va@vaa.pt;
open Mon–Fri 9–6,
Sat–Sun 9–12.30 and
2–5

The beauty and delicacy of Vista Alegre porcelain are renowned throughout Portugal. The factory was founded in 1824, to produce both glass and ceramics, and is surrounded by a village of workers' cottages, a couple of km south of Ílhavo. The factory itself is cloaked in secrecy, but it is possible to visit the firm's **museum**, next to the porcelain factory, Fábrica de Porcelanas da Vista Alegre. Though uninformatively labelled, it shows how the porcelain evolved from the early attempts of 1824–32, which yielded only plain and lumpy earthenware. The founder of the factory dreamt of greater things, and went to collect samples of kaolin from Sèvres. Fortune favoured him, and in quarries near Ovar he discovered deposits of kaolin similar to that at Sèvres. He imported French craftsmen to train his workforce, and the way was set for the factory to produce anything from exquisite classic dinner services to Art Nouveau confections. The manufacture of glass was phased out.

It's worth looking in the adjacent **chapel of N.S da Penha** to see the tomb of its founder, Bishop Dom Manuel de Moura, one of the

Where to Stay Around Aveiro

★★★**Hotel Barra**, Avenida Fernandes Lavrador 18, Praia da Barra, **t** (234) 369 156, *www.hotelbarra.com* (€€). If you want to stay by the beach at Barra, 8km away from Aveiro, this comfortable hotel has two outdoor swimming pools and a disco bar but dated rooms.

★**Pensão Albertina**, Avenida Arrais Faustino, **t** (234) 838 306 (€). For less exalted living in Torreira itself, with 15 rooms.

Pousada
Pousada da Ria, Bico do Muranzel, Torreira, **t** (234) 860 180, *www.pousadas.pt* (L1 N). Located on the peninsula between Torreira and São Jacinto, on the banks of the Ria, this glassy place has a canopied verandah from where you can lazily watch the fishermen in their bright boats. Indeed, you'll find yourself surrounded on three sides by water – and if that's not enough, you also have a swimming pool to dabble in. The restaurant serves up specialities such as cockle pies and goat stewed in red wine.

Turismo de Habitação
Quinta do Paço da Ermida (near Ílhavo, 6km south of Aveiro), **t** (234) 322 496 (€€). Mitre-shaped windows indicate that the U-shaped *quinta* was a bishop's residence; now it belongs to a member of the family that founded the Vista Alegre porcelain factory. It's a working farm with attendant dogs and Siamese cats, much polished wood, a canopied terrace with crickets and camellias, marble-topped commodes, and big flower arrangements. The five quiet bedrooms are furnished with heavy, but not oppressive, furniture, and have elegant bathrooms. Breakfast is served in a dining room like a traditional billiard room. The lady of the house speaks English.

finest works carved by Cláudio Laprade, *c.* 1697. The bishop's effigy appears to be about to sneeze; in fact, he is gazing towards a low-relief carving of the Virgin Mary as he expires. The figure of Time waits impatiently with a shroud.

Figueira da Foz

'*Foz*' means 'mouth', and Figueira da Foz is a deep-sea fishing port at the mouth of the River Mondego, 40km west of Coimbra and 65km south of Aveiro. Since the beginning of this century, it has been one of northern Portugal's most popular and lively Portuguese family resorts. It also attracts a steady flow of Spaniards – all of whom combine to crowd even this very wide beach. The site has been occupied since Lusitanian times, but you wouldn't know it.

Museu Municipal do Dr. Santos Rocha

t (233) 402 840; open 16 Sept–31 May, Tues–Fri 9.30–5.15, Sat 2–7, closed Mon, Sun and hols; 1 June–15 Sept, Tues–Fri 9.30–5.15, Sun and hols 2–6.45, closed Mon; adm

The **Museu Municipal do Dr. Santos Rocha** on the Rua Calouste Gulbenkian is worth a look for the collections of archaeology, ceramics and coins, as well as numerous photographs of 19th-century bathing belles. Overlooking the river, four rooms of the 17th-century **Casa do Pato**, the palace of the bishops of Coimbra, are lined with Dutch tiles, each of which pictures a different

Getting to Figueira da Foz

There are three daily Rede Expressos **buses** to Foz from Lisbon (3hrs), one from Porto (4 hrs) and one from Coimbra; plus a plethora of regional companies.

horseman, landscape, or religious scene. They form part of a cache shipwrecked here in the 18th century.

The **casino** provides a centre for nightlife, but only gamblers may enter.

For Leiria, Batalha and Fátima, *see* pp.270–79.

Casino
Rua Bernardo Lopes,
t (233) 408 400;
open daily 3pm–3am

(i) **Figueira**
da Foz >
Avenida 25 de Abril,
t (233) 422 610,
www.figueiraturismo.
com; open June–Sept
daily 9am–midnight,
Oct–May Mon–Fri
9–12.30 and 2–5.30,
Sat–Sun 10–12.30 and
2.30–6.30

Tourist Information/ Services in Figueira da Foz

The **tourist office** is a veritable mine of information and is near the Grande Hotel. The **train station** and **bus station** are both east of the beach, on Avenida 25 de Abril.

Where to Stay in Figueira da Foz

***Hotel Costa de Prata II**, Rua Miguel Bombarda 50, **t** (233) 422 082, *www.costadeprata.com* (€€). Spruce, hygienic and well kitted out.
****Hotel Wellington**, Rua Dr Calado 23–27, **t** (233) 426 767/8, *www.sabirhoteis.pt* (€€). Well priced, but with smallish bedrooms.
****Pensão Residencial Moderna**, Praça 9 de Maio 61, **t** (233) 422 701 (€€). Elegant rooms with private bathroom. There is a garden to the rear and off-street parking.
***Pensão Central**, Rua Bernardo Lopes 36, **t** (233) 422 308, *www.pensaocentral.com* (€). A good bet, and very good value. The high-ceilinged rooms are homely and geraniums line the steps.
Residencial Aviz, Rua Dr Lopes Guimarães 16, **t** (233) 422 636 (€). Clean, if mildly old-fashioned, and very well priced. *Reservations essential.*

Turismo de Habitação
Casa da Azenha Velha, Caceira de Cima, **t** (233) 425 041 (€€). Nine km from Figueira da Foz, standing in its own estate. Geese are raised here. There are riding stables and a riding ring complete with obstacles for the keen equestrian. A fire burns in the large rustic fireplace in the sitting room, setting the tone for the farmhouse comfort.

Eating Out in Figueira da Foz

Restaurante Caçarola II, Rua Bernardo Lópes 85, **t** (233) 426 930 (€€€–€€). Very popular seafood restaurant; good-value dishes are on offer.
Restaurante Dory Negro, Largo Caras Direitas 16, Buarcos, **t** (233) 421 333 (€€). Bargain seafood dishes are to be had here; its shellfish, deep-sea fish and seafood stews are worth coming the distance for. *Open Wed–Mon.*
Pastelaria Restaurante Acrópole, Rua Bernardo Lopes 76, **t** (233) 428 948 (€). Omelettes and burgers in a no-fuss joint.

Bars in Figueira da Foz

Rolls Bar, Rua Poeta Acácio Antunes IE, **t** (233) 426 157.
Dom Copo, Rua de S. Lourenço 13, **t** (233) 426 817.
Perfumaria Bar, Rua Dr Calado, **t** (233) 426 442.

Estremadura and the Ribatejo

Estremadura is a swathe of rolling downland on Portugal's Atlantic coast, incorporating Lisbon in the south. The capital is bracketed by two ranges of hills, each totally different in character; to the southeast, the humped limestone Serra da Arrábida, with its panic of wild flowers; to the northwest, the mossy, craggy Serra de Sintra.

12

Don't miss

⭐ **Sublime Gothic interior**
Batalha Abbey **p.275**

⭐ **Celestial simplicity**
Mosteiro de Santa Maria de Alcobaça **p.280**

⭐ **Pretty walled village**
Óbidos **p.290**

⭐ **Teaming forests and tea**
Sintra **p.302**

⭐ **Beautiful limestone ridge**
Serra da Arrábida **p.331**

See map overleaf

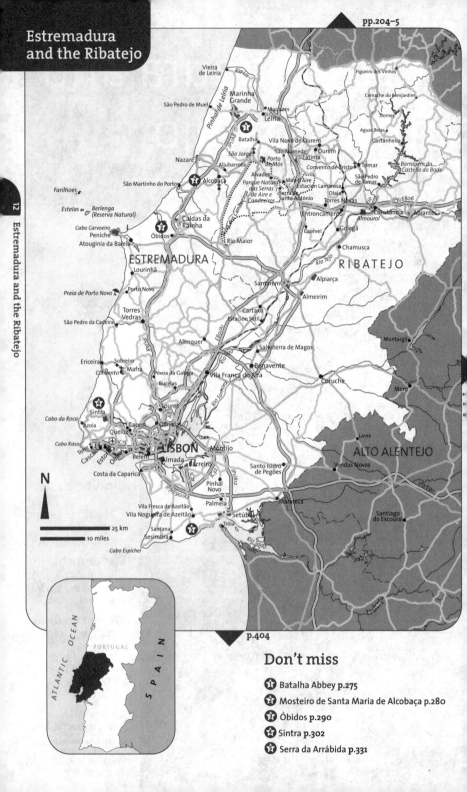

Estremadura
and the Ribatejo

pp.204–5

Vieira
de Leiria

Rio Lis

Figueiro dos Vinhos

Cernache do Bomjardim

São Pedro de Muel

Marinha
Grande

Marrazes

Leiria

Dornes

Aguas Belas

Castanheira

Batalha

Vila Nova de Ourem

São Jorge

São Mamede

Ourem

Fátima

Nazaré

Aljubarrota

Porto
de Mós

Convento de Cristo

Tomar

Barragem do
Castello do Bode

São Martinho do Porto

Alcobaça

Alvados

Parque Natural
das Serras
de Aire e
Candeeiros

Mira d'Aire

Serra de
Santo António

Estação Lamarosa

São Pedro
de Tomar

Farilhoes

Estelas

Berlenga
(Reserva Natural)

Olaia

Torres Novas

Constância

IP6/E806

Abrantes

Cabo Carvoeiro

Peniche

Atouguia da Baleia

Óbidos

Caldas da
Rainha

Rio Maior

Casével

Entroncamento

Almourol

Colega

Chamusca

ESTREMADURA

Lourinhã

Santarém

Rio Tejo

RIBATEJO

Alpiarça

Praia de Porto Novo

Porto Novo

Almeirim

São Pedro da Cadeira

Torres
Vedras

Cartaxo

Estação Setil

Montargil

Ericeira

Sobreiro

Convento

Mafra

Alenquer

Salvaterra de Magos

Moro

São Pedro da Cadeira

Póvoa da Galega

Bucelas

Vila Franca de Xira

Benavente

Coruche

Sintra

Cabo da Roca

Azoia

Loures

Quelua

Odivelas

LISBON

Cacém

Lavre

Cabo Raso

Torre

Cascais

Estoril

Oeiras

Belém

Almada

Barreiro

Montijo

Santo Isidro
de Pegões

Vendas Novas

ALTO ALENTEJO

Costa da Caparica

Pinhal
Novo

Vila Fresca de Azeitão

Palmela

Marateca

Santiago
do Escoural

Vila Nogueira de Azeitão

Setúbal

Santana

Tróia

Sesimbra

Rio Sado

N

25 km

10 miles

Cabo Espichel

ATLANTIC OCEAN

PORTUGAL

SPAIN

p.404

Don't miss

Getting around Northern Estremadura

By car

The road network is good, and incorporates a stretch of motorway from Lisbon to Setúbal. Be particularly careful driving on the Estrada Marginal from Cascais to Lisbon, which is infamous for its high accident rate.

By train

With the exception of suburban lines from Lisbon to Cascais and Sintra, the railway runs north–south from Lisbon to Óbidos, Caldas da Rainha, and Leiria (Beira Litoral) – thus avoiding Estremadura's principal monuments, and offering no route into the Ribatejo. There is no railway bridge across the Tagus, so southbound rail passengers must first take a ferry from Lisbon's Terreiro do Pato to Barreiro.

By bus

Most express buses departing from Lisbon head straight for Santarém (Ribatejo) or Setúbal, so the local bus network is particularly useful for getting around Estremadura. You'll need a car to get the most out of the Serra da Arrábida.

The province was named when it was the southernmost territory occupied by Christians (the Latin *'extrema Durii'* means 'farthest land from the Douro'). After the conquest of the Moors, much of the land in Estremadura was given to the Cistercians and to the canons of St Augustine. North of Sintra, ranks of trees and limestone walls separate orchards and olive groves, vineyards, fields of millet and wheat, and market gardens. Lone settlements straggle between clustered villages, where humble houses are built on two storeys, unlike those of the south. Lisbon exerts a magnetic pull on the economy and attitudes of Estremadura; farm produce is trucked to the capital; people's horizons are a little wider, their senses more canny. Those who live within the orbit of Lisbon are called *Saloios*, a name derived from the Arabic word *talliao*, the tribute paid by Moorish bakers in Lisbon. Perhaps because of the pull of Lisbon, Estremadura has little cultural integrity; there are some remarkable monuments – the palaces at Sintra and Mafra, the abbey at Alcobaça – but the towns, and the people, are rather colourless.

Rare in its lack of geographical boundaries, the Ribatejo straddles the River Tagus (Tejo in Portuguese), which is its main artery ('ribatejo' means 'Tagus riverbank'). The river's fecund alluvial plain is rich in pasture and cereals – rice and wheat grow where the soil is compact, millet and vines where the loam is light. Beyond the river's reach stretch yawning grasslands. Until the introduction of railways in the last century, the ports on the north bank of the Tagus were magnets for settlement. These now form the base of the industrial triangle of Torres Novas, Tomar and Abrantes, where textile, cellulose, paper, metallurgical and chemical factories loom. The province is fringed with oak woods. The Ribatejo is lacklustre; follow the example of the Tagus, and pass through it – but not before you have seen Tomar.

Wines of Estremadura

The *Oeste* (western) region is Portugal's most productive. Stretching northwest from the Tagus estuary as far as Caldas da Rainha, it makes reds and whites in equal quantity, including the dry yellow *vinho do ano* (wine of the year) of the Torres Vedras Cooperative. The light, cherry-coloured reds are more interesting, particularly the soft red of Óbidos. There are four small Demarcated Regions near Lisbon, all under threat from rising land and property prices. Indeed, the winery at Carcavelos is virtually extinct. This would have upset King Dom José, who was so proud of Carcavelos wines that in 1752 he sent some to the Chinese court. Wellington and his troops were more partial to the wine of Bucelas, which is produced by fermenting the grapes in open wood vats. This produces a light and slightly acidic wine, that gets very dry with age.

But the wine of Colares takes the prize; traditionally, Colares red is the finest and most distinctive in the country. The wine-makers have had plenty of time to perfect their technique – as long ago as 1255, a land grant made by King Dom Afonso III to Pedro Miguel and his wife Maria Estevão required them to plant vines. These peculiar vines are unmistakable: at Colares, dune sands cover the soil's clay base to a depth of 10–30ft (3–10m); the roots of the vine must be planted in clay, so a trench is dug, the roots are planted, and the trunk of the vine is covered with sand. Only the vine branches emerge; these are sheltered from the wind by cane and willow fences. Thus were they protected from the dreadful phylloxera epidemic which ravaged the vines of Portugal in the 1870s and 80s. The aromatic, full-flavoured red takes the colour of black cherries; the white is not in the same league.

For wines of the Ribatejo, *see* p.336.

What to Eat

Estremadura is renowned for its *atorda de marisco* – prawns, clams and cockles blended into mashed soaked bread, and topped with eggs.

Northern Estremadura

The charming walled settlement of Óbidos is a good base from which to explore the north of Estremadura province by car; if you're dependent on public transport, however, Leiria would be a better bet. From here you can easily reach Batalha, Alcobaça and the caves at Mira d'Aire.

Leiria and Around

Leiria

Set on the flat and fertile coastal plain, 70km southeast of Coimbra and 54km south of Figueira da Foz, at the southern extreme of the Beira Litoral, Leiria is tucked into an elbow of the River Lis. The green and pleasant town of 41,000 souls is built around a castle hillock, and hums with activity, forming a regional centre for small-scale heavy industry, including stonework, cement, steel and dyes. There are some good bars in the old part of town.

History

Dom Afonso Henriques built a castle at Leiria in 1135, to serve as his southern stronghold against the Moors, near the site of the

Getting to Leiria

By road, Leiria is 121km from Aveiro, 70km from Coimbra, 133km from Lisbon, 181km from Porto, and 162km from Viseu. **Trains, t** (244) 882 027, run infrequently from Lisbon (23/4hrs), via Caldas da Rainha (frequent, 1hr), and from Figueira da Foz (1hr). Avoid the train from Coimbra, which requires changing at both Alfarelos and Amieira. There are more than a dozen Rede Expressos **bus** services from Lisbon (2hrs), plus Rodoviário do Tejo services, **t** (244) 811 507, from Batalha (40mins), Lisbon (2hrs), Aveiro (21/4hrs) and Figueira da Foz (1hr). Buses run very infrequently from Braga (41/4hrs), Bragança (71/2hrs) and Chaves (71/4hrs) via Lamego (43/4hrs) and Viseu (3hrs).

Roman town of Collipo. The Moors sacked it two years later, killing 250 of the garrison. Small watchtowers were erected on nearby vantage points, which lit beacons in times of danger and launched horn-blowers into the countryside, shouting '*Mouros ha terra! As armas!*' Knights caught skiving this call to arms were punished with fines and the docking of their horses; lesser mortals had their beards cropped. Nevertheless, the castle had to be rebuilt for the third time in 1144. In 1254, Leiria hosted the country's first *Cortes* at which the Commons were represented. Leiria's paper manufacture encouraged local Jews to set up one of the Peninsula's first printing presses, in 1492.

Around the Town

Castelo

t (244) 813 982; open May–Sept Mon–Fri 9–6.30, Oct–April until 5.30; adm

Perched steep above Leiria, the **Castelo** looks best from a distance. The rigid keep of 1324 is ringed by a defensive wall. This is incorporated in Dom Dinis' palace, flanked by two crenellated towers and centred on a loggia overlooking the town. To the rear of the palace stands the plain roofless Church of N.S. da Penha, built by João I *c.* 1400. A museum, **Núcleo Museológic**, is located in the castle keep, with displays of replica weaponry from medieval times, and some items that have been found on-site.

Núcleo Museológic

open Tues–Sun 10–12 and 1–5

Cathedral

open Mon–Fri 10–7, weekends according to the time of mass

The road downhill opens onto the Largo da Sé, where the tall **cathedral** completed in the hundred years after 1559, provides the setting for sly glances and anguished prayer in Eta de Quieroz' novel, *The Sin of Father Amaro*. It stands at the edge of the sober and strait-laced old part of town.

Really the only curiosity in Leiria is the modern **Fonte Luminosa**, opposite the tourist office, an Adam and Eve-type sculpture that equips Adam with a semi-erection.

ⓘ Leiria ›

Jardim Luís de Camões, t (244) 848 770; open June–Sept daily 10–1 and 3–7, Oct–May daily 10–1 and 2–6

Tourist Information and Services in Leiria

The tourist office is at one corner of the municipal garden; the bus station is on the opposite side of the garden. The railway station is 4km northeast of town, with connecting buses.

Where to Stay in Leiria

★★★**Hotel Dom João III**, Avenida D. João III, **t** (244) 817 888, *www.best western.com* (€€€–€€). For service and comfort on the north side of town, towards Figueira da Foz, this hotel is exemplary and good value, though

⭐ Tromba Rija >>

little about it is Portuguese. It is also rather dated and provincial, but decent enough if you're into 70s smoked glass. It attracts a rare type of tailored and sun-glassed clientele, some of whose large-windowed bedrooms overlook the castle. The furnishings are substantial and thoughtful: even the shower nozzle has a massage setting. The cosseted restaurant (€€€) offers a large menu with a particularly good choice of soups and simply cooked meats.

★★★Hotel Eurosol Jardim, Rua D. José Alves Correia da Silva, **t** (244) 849 849, *www.eurosol.pt* (€€). On the southern edge of town towards Batalha. It is well run and the staff are extremely helpful, both of which make it popular with Portuguese business people. Rooms are OK. There's an outdoor pool. The restaurant with panoramic views tends to be empty. Parking available.

★★★Pensão Leiriense, Rua Afonso de Albuquerque 6, **t** (244) 823 054, *www.leiriense.net* (€). In a quiet street in the old part of town, this occupies what used to be a rather grand house. A fine place, though the beds aren't too comfortable.

★★★Residencial Dom Dinis, Travessa de Tomar 2, **t** (244) 815 342 (€). Across the bridge from the tourist office and provides pleasant rooms and a car park – you'll probably need a car to get up the steep road. Nice little rooms; it's best to choose a room facing away from the street to minimize noise.

Pousada da Juventude, Largo Câdido dos Reis 7D, **t** (244) 831 868, *leiria@movijovem.pt* (€). Located in a lovely old house, with a kitchen available for guests' use.

Pensão Berlenga, Rua Miguel Bombarda 13, **t** (244) 823 846 (€). Rooms are wood-panelled in this old house.

Eating Out in Leiria

There are several popular restaurants in the **Rua Dr Correia Mateus**, a pedestrianized street next to the newly developed Mercado, where a string of warm and lively restaurants offer large portions at low and moderate prices.

Tromba Rija, Rua Professores Portelas, Marrazes, **t** (244) 855 072, *www.trombarija.com* (€€€). Several kilometres from Leiria, offering home-style Portuguese cooking at its best. Square, cosy and wooden, its walls are pinned with the praises of happy gastronomes. There's no written menu. Do experiment with one of the more complicated dishes like *feijoada tromba rija*, or another of the daily specialities. It's a taxi ride away; if you're driving, cross the river heading for Figueira da Foz, take the second right to Marrazes, and the first left after the motorway bridge. *Closed Sun.*

Malagueta Afrodisíaca, Rua Gago Coutinho 17, **t** (244) 831 607 (€€). Highly unusual and utterly wonderful. It claims that everything on the menu is an aphrodisiac, including a large number of teas. Most of the food is Mexican, Indian or Brazilian. Strawberries are there, and margharitas. Try it and see.

O Manel, Rua Dr Correia Mateus 50, **t** (244) 832 132 (€€). An extensive choice of seafood.

A Toca, Rua Dr Correia Mateus 32, no tel (€€). A smart restaurant with an extensive menu that concentrates on meat and fish grills.

Restaurante Monte Carlo, Rua Dr. Correia Mateus 34, **t** (244) 825 406 (€). Probably one of the best budget restaurants: the portions are huge so the *meia dose* (half-portion) should satisfy even the greediest.

Bars

There are several good bars in town, including **Pátio das Cantigas**, Rua Fernão de Magalhães 8–10, **t** (244) 814 185 (*open until 2am*), and **Pharmácia**, Largo Candido dos Reis 1a, no tel, a popular Dutch-owned bar set inside an evocative 19th-century pharmacy. Three other bars spill into the Largo Cándido dos Reis.

Batalha

The great Abbey of Batalha, a UNESCO World Heritage site, stands in flat and verdant pinelands horribly close to the IC2, the old Lisbon–Porto highway, 11km south of Leiria. The effects of the pollution and vibrations have taken their toll. The Abbey has spawned a little town with some good places to stay.

History

When Dom Fernando I died in 1383, his venomous wife Leonor Teles assumed the position of regent, assisted by her lover Count Andeiro. The king had died without a son; his daughter Beatriz was married to the King of Castile, Juan I, who added the arms of Portugal to his standard, and ordered all Portuguese townships to proclaim Beatriz as queen. Those who feared absorption by Castile focused their hopes on one of Dom Fernando's illegitimate half-brothers, Dom João of Aviz, who 'was accompanied by the common people [of Lisbon] as if he were dropping precious treasures for them to grab', according to the chronicler Fernão Lopes.

Having consulted a visionary Castilian hermit, Dom João sought an audience with the queen, who sat doing needlework and wondered why Dom João was armed and 'not wearing gloves as the English do'. She soon found out: Dom João murdered her lover and forced her to flee for her life. He was proclaimed king at the palace window, but did not receive official backing until the *Cortes* met at Coimbra in 1385. Juan I of Castile set his sights on besieging Lisbon, which was held by the Portuguese forces together with the castles around the capital, and much of the Alentejo. As the Castilian forces advanced, they cut off the heads, or hands, or tongues of those Portuguese whom they captured.

On Tuesday, 14 August 1385, Nun' Álvares Pereira commanded the Portuguese army to take up a position at São Jorge on the Lisbon road. For this he used English terminology – the van, the rear, the right and left wings – which had been learnt from the English armies in the Hundred Years' War. On their left flank, the 6,500 Portuguese troops were supported by about 500 English crossbowmen, sent by Richard II. Together they dug shallow trenches, which were covered with brushwood. In the evening 30,000 Castilian troops came within range, travelling south. Juan I, being ill, rode a donkey, and forbade engagement with the Portuguese army, but his *hidalgos* were impetuous, and broke rank.

The battle of Aljubarrota was over quickly – the Castilian royal standard fell within an hour – but its effects were tremendous: it secured the independence of Portugal from Spanish domination until the dynasty of Aviz was brought to an end 200 years later. João of Aviz became Dom João I, the undisputed ruler of a united

Getting to and around Batalha

Six express **buses** daily ply the route between Lisbon (2hrs) and Batalha; there are three from Porto (3hrs). There are frequent buses to Leiria, Alcobaça and Fátima, from Largo 14 de Agosto.

kingdom. Many Portuguese nobles were killed, fighting for the Castilian king against the upstart bastard João. The latter's success heralded the reorganization of the nobility, elevating members of the bourgeoisie, artisans and the petty aristocracy. But it also had a more tangible legacy: before the battle João had vowed to build an abbey should he be victorious. Work on the Dominican Battle Abbey started three years later, in 1388, near the site of his victory.

The Abbey of Batalha

Abbey of Batalha
open daily April–Sept 9–6, Oct–Mar 9–5; adm, but free adm to church

The essential parts of the **Abbey of Batalha** were completed during the reign of João I under the architects Afonso Domingues and Ouguête. These include the church, the royal cloister, and the chapter house. The founder's chapel was concluded in 1434, the year after his death. His eldest son, Dom Duarte (1433–8) commissioned the same architects to build the octagonal 'Unfinished Chapels' as a pantheon for himself and his descendants. This work was continued by Dom Afonso V, who also built a second cloister according to plans by the Alentejan uncle and nephew, Martins Vasques and Fernão de Évora. But it was Dom Manuel who employed Mateus Fernandes and Boitac to alter the Gothic character of parts of the abbey, blending in exotic and extravagant ornament, until the king concentrated all his efforts on his own mausoleum at Belém. Dom João III constructed new dormitories and a cloister (destroyed 1811), a novitiate and an inn – but he stopped building c. 1550 as his attention wandered to Tomar.

Manuel Gandra, who was a geomancer of unorthodox views, offers an alternative explanation for this termination. He believes that the House of Aviz connected its emblem, the dove, with the symbol of the Holy Spirit, and intended Batalha as a temple of the Holy Spirit, with themselves at the head of the cult: the pious Dom João III ceased construction because he saw what his ancestors were up to.

The Exterior

The eye wanders over the exterior (once honey-coloured but now polluted), over the pinnacles, the flying buttresses and the tracery balustrades, for there is no focus of attention. Nor are there belltowers, because the Dominicans eschew belltowers. The western portal is very finely carved, with six columns either side of the doorway, on each of which stand modern copies of the 12 Apostles. Above them rises a series of arches niched with biblical kings and queens, the prophets and the angels. On the tympanum, the Creator is surrounded by the four Evangelists. The central octagon of the founder's chapel rises to the right. It all smacks of the English perpendicular style, and indeed Philippa of Lancaster, wife of Dom João I, may have had a hand in this – she could have imported English architects, during the reign of her cousin Richard II.

The Interior

Batalha Abbey, interior

The exterior belies the sublime interior: the effect is complicated and inexpressible, so thoroughly are the architects manipulating us. It refreshes wonderfully – the secret is in the harmony of the proportions and the purity of the style. The Gothic nave seems impossibly tall. Great plain piers separate the eight bays of the 80m nave from the aisles, which are tinted by modern stained glass. The tombstone of Mateus Fernandes (c. 1480–1515), who directed the building works during the Manueline period, lies just inside the western entrance.

The Founder's Chapel

To the right is the Capela do Fundador (founder's chapel), designed by Huguet, master of works from 1402 to 1438, and completed in 1434, after the death of João I. It centres on the tomb of João I and Philippa of Lancaster, whose effigies lie hand in hand beneath an exquisite octagonal lantern. He wears the insignia of the Order of the Garter, which was founded by Philippa's father, Edward III. The rear wall is lined with the tombs of their four younger sons. Dom Fernando's is farthest to the left; he was left as a hostage for the return of Ceuta to the Moors, following the capture of the Portuguese army by Sala-ben-Sala in 1437. Dom Fernando was put to work in the vizier's garden and stables at Fez, before being confined to a dungeon, where he died of dysentery after five years of captivity. His body was hung by the feet from the walls of Fez, from which awkward position his Portuguese companions cut out his heart and embalmed it. This was brought to Batalha, and the scant remains of his other parts followed 22 years later, in 1471. Henry the Navigator's tomb is second from the right. The face of his effigy is quite different to that portrayed in the panels of São Vicente (see 'Portuguese Painting', p.367).

The Cloisters

The nave opens onto the **Claustro Real**, built by Afonso Domingues, who was master of works from 1388 to 1402. Dom Manuel found it unsatisfying, and ordered Boitac to embellish the arches with marvellous thorny tracery, entwining crosses of the Order of Christ and armillary spheres, employing pearly columns and scaly artichokes (which prevented scurvy and were thus revered by the navigators). An arch opens onto the **Chapter House**, where the forceful unsupported vault provides a suitable setting for the Tomb of the Unknown Soldiers, one from Africa, and one from the Flanders front. The **refectory** is now a military museum and giftshop. At right angles to it stands the sober and elegant Gothic **Claustro de Dom Afonso V**.

The Unfinished Chapels

Dom Duarte, the pious eldest son of Dom João I and Philippa of Lancaster, attached a self-contained octagonal mausoleum to the east end of the abbey, the roofless Capelas Imperfeitas (Unfinished Chapels). Ouguête began work on the seven radial chapels *c.* 1435, but his design was profoundly altered by the imaginative genius of Mateus Fernandes, Dom Manuel's master of works, who intended to build an upper octagon, but was able only to begin construction on the forlorn stumps of its buttresses. The true legacy of Mateus Fernandes is the stunning western portal, created in 1509. It is 50ft (15m) high, and every inch of every arch is exciting: the stone is wrought to a fine filigree of thistles and ivy, chains and rope. At the base are stone snails! Double circles contain Dom Manuel's motto, which seems to read '*Tayas Erey*' or '*Taya Serey*', but which should be '*Tanaz serey*', the old Portuguese for 'I shall be tenacious': the 'y' is a pair of pincers, and the ivy around each word emphasizes the message. Dom Duarte died in 1438, and was entombed in a chapel opposite the entrance.

(i) **Batalha >**
next to abbey in Praça 25 de Abril, t (244) 765 180; open June–Sept 10–1 and 3–7, Aug 9am–10pm, Oct–May 10–1 and 2–6

 Pensão Gládius >

Where to Stay in Batalha

★★★**Pensão Residencial Batalha**, Largo da Igreja, **t** (244) 767 500, *www.hotel-batalha.com* (€). Friendly and attractive place.

★★**Pensão Gládius**, Praça Mouzinho de Albuquerque 7, **t** (244) 765 760 (€). Roughly opposite the south side of the Abbey, with geranium window boxes. Clean, simple and very good value. Portugal could do with more like it. There's no breakfast provided.

Pousada
Pousada do Mestre Afonso Domingues, Largo Mestre Afonso Domingues 6, **t** (244) 765 260/1 (€€). Built in 1985, the relaxed *pousada* stands near the Abbey (five rooms face it) – and near the busy main road. It's nice enough, but a place to pass through. The restaurant is more promising, with its dragon's-tooth floor and painted pebble-dash walls. Try the fried pork with turnip tops.

Turismo de Habitação
Quinta do Fidalgo, Avenida D. Nuno Álvares Pereira, **t** (244) 765 114, *quinta.do.fidalgo@teleweb.pt* (€€). The din of traffic doesn't really penetrate this hospitable *quinta*. A separate block of the house incorporates four guest rooms and a homey sitting room complete with reproduction furniture, a fireplace, card table and TV. Bedrooms are comfortably and substantially furnished, with luxurious marble bathrooms,

overlooking a sandy garden. There is also a suite with its own entrance.

 Casa do Outeiro >

Casa do Outeiro, Largo do Outeiro 4, t (244) 765 806, www.casado outeiro.com (€ CA). Slightly uphill from the centre of town, it offers very good value and a hint of Elle Decoration. The owner and his wife designed the building and furniture, and her paintings decorate the rooms. It's light and breezy, with a pool and garage, and views of the surrounding hills.

Eating Out in Batalha

Mestre Afonso, Largo Mestre Afonso Domingues 4, t (244) 765 601 (€). Specializes in shellfish.

Casa das Febras, Largo 14 de Agosto, t (244) 765 825 (€). A straightforward restaurant near the abbey serving traditional and well-prepared local specialties.

The Battleground of Aljubarrota

Four km south of Batalha (and 10km northeast of the village of Aljubarrota), the chapel of S. Jorge marks the battleground of Aljubarrota. The Spaniards were defeated in one hour, which was long enough for Nun' Álvares Pereira, the commander of the Portuguese troops, to get up a sweat; a jug of water stands in the porch of the chapel, to quench his ghost.

Nearby stands an iron statue of a baker's wife, who served her country by hitting Castilians with a baker's shovel. Beckford reports that after the battle the King of Castile scampered off and 'tore his hair and plucked off his beard by handfuls, and raved and ranted like a maniac – the details of this frantic pluckage are to be found in a letter from the Constable Nun' Álvarez Pereira to the Abbot of Alcobaça'.

Fátima

The Virgin Mary appeared six times at Fátima, 22km southeast of Leiria and 18km east of Batalha. The town has become one of the most important places of pilgrimage in the Catholic world. A giant neoclassical basilica flanked by colonnades overlooks a 37-acre (15ha) saucer-shaped tarmac esplanade, which penitants cross on their knees. It is of no architectural interest; Fátima is not for observers. An official notice puts it like this: 'If you come simply as a visitor, respect the pilgrims at prayer. This place has nothing to satisfy mere curiosity. What matters here is the heart.' Visitors are asked to cover their legs and shoulders. There are pilgrimages on the 12th/13th of each month; crowds reach 100,000 in May and October.

History

On 13 May 1917, three shepherd children saw the Virgin: Lúcia, Francisco and Jacinta, aged 10, 9 and 7. Only Lúcia could converse with her. The children were shown a vision of hell in which 'many

Getting to Fátima

Fátima is on the Entroncamento–Coimbra-B **train** route: from Lisbon's Santa Apolónia or Oriente stations, change at Entroncamento (from which Fátima is a mere ¼hr distant); trains from Coimbra-B take 1½hrs. Change there from Porto, Espinho and Aveiro.

Local **buses** run fairly frequently from Tomar and Leiria. Every day, 15 Rede Expressos buses make their way from Lisbon (2½hrs); four or more from Santarém (1¼hrs). A dozen buses run from Porto (2–3hrs); for Braga, there are two direct (4hrs), otherwise change in Coimbra (nine daily, 2hrs) or Porto. Just one bus makes the trip from Faro (7½hrs) in the opposite direction.

souls' were lost through 'sins of the flesh' and because they had 'no one to pray and make sacrifices for them'. The faithful were entreated to 'pray, pray a great deal and make many sacrifices', to 'pray the rosary every day to obtain peace for the world'. If her requests were heard, she promised 'the salvation of many souls, the conversion of Russia, and world peace'. Otherwise, a second war would engulf the world and Russia would 'spread her errors throughout the world, fomenting wars and persecutions against the Church. The good will be martyred, the Holy Father will have much to suffer, various nations will be annihilated ... But in the end, my Immaculate Heart will triumph. The Holy Father will consecrate Russia to me, it will be converted, and a period of peace will be given to the world.'

The Virgin subsequently appeared at the same place on the same day of the month until 13 October, when 70,000 pilgrims and sceptics witnessed the Miracle of the Sun: the sun danced in the sky and then zigzagged towards earth. The Virgin stated that 'the punishment for sin is war' and that 'men must cease to offend God and ask pardon for their sins'.

Pope Paul VI declared the occurrences at Fátima to be 'an affirmation of the Gospel'. Francisco died in 1919 and Jacinta in the following year; their tombs are in the basilica. In 1928 their cousin Lúcia entered the Carmelite convent at Pontevedra in Coimbra. She and Pope Paul VI attended the fiftieth anniversary of the apparitions, along with 1.5 million other pilgrims.

ⓘ Fátima >
Avenida D. José Alves Correia da Silva, t (249) 531 139; open June–Sept daily 10–1 and 3–7, Oct–May daily 2–6

Services in Fátima

The **railway station** is unfortunately 25km from the town, with few bus connections. The **bus station** is on Avenida D. José Alves Correia da Silva.

Where to Stay in Fátima

Among the large number of shops and stalls selling tacky mementos, there are many places to stay and eat in Fátima, but remember that they get heavily booked during the major pilgrimages. Reasonable options include the following.

★★★**Hotel Regina**, Rua Cónego Dr Manuel Formigão, **t** (249) 532 775, *www.hotelregina-fatima.com* (€).

★★★**Hotel Verbo Divino**, Praça Paulo VI, **t** (249) 532 043 (€).

Casa Poeira, Travessa Santo António, **t** (249) 531 419 (€).

Ourém Velha

On a high hill surrounded by plains and gentle valleys, 11km northeast of Fátima, 24km southeast of Leiria, 20km northwest of Tomar, and slightly southwest of the market town of Vila Nova de Ourém, the castle-palace of Ourém was rebuilt in the 15th century to satisfy the pretensions of Dom Afonso, son of the first Duke of Bragança, in a style clearly influenced by his travels in Italy. A random arrangement of Gothic windows open on to the courtyard, while balconies are supported by arched brickwork. The ornamental band of ceramic tiles on the north side of the Torre Solar may have been the work of *mudéjar* craftsmen.

Attached to the 15th-century Igreja Matriz, the **crypt of Dom Afonso** is a simple space which smacks of the synagogue at Tomar, completed in 1460.

Alcobaça and Around

Alcobaça

The dusty town of Alcobaça was spawned by one of Portugal's most impressive churches, the Mosteiro de Santa Maria de Alcobaça, a UNESCO World Heritage Site 20km south of Leiria at the confluence of the Rivers Alcoa and Baça. Fruitful, rolling fields surround the town with dwarfish trees, whose peaches are superb.

History

Dom Afonso Henriques founded the abbey as an offering of thanks for the capture of Santarém from the Moors. Building began in 1178, the year before Pope Alexander III recognized the new Christian nation of Portugal. The king chose the self-sufficient Cistercians, ever in search of lonely places, to colonize and develop the reconquered lands north of Lisbon; the abbey was granted vast estates, including 13 small towns and three seaports, over which the abbot held civil jurisdiction. He was entitled Lord of the Water and the Wind, because of the estates' many wind- and watermills. He was visitor to all the Benedictine abbeys in the country and was, for over 300 years, until the reign of Cardinal King Henry, the superior of the great military Order of Christ. The abbey yielded nothing to the king, except a pair of boots or shoes when he visited.

Before the Black Death reduced the number to eight, there are said to have been 999 monks. From the mid-13th century, the monks washed their hands of any farm work, to devote themselves to teaching. They founded the country's first public school in 1269,

Getting to Alcobaça

and provided books and money to help Dom Dinis to establish the University of Lisbon, which subsequently moved to Coimbra.

Decadence

Royal interference combined with inept and domineering abbots to foment decadence. But the agricultural activity of the monastery revived in the 18th century: the abbot was almost as dynamic as his cousin Pombal. He drained new land, planted olive groves, and founded an apiary which produced the clearest honey in Portugal. When questioned at the end of the century, the farmers and fruitgrowers of the district reported that it was 'our indulgent landlords and kind friends, the monks' who had taught them to cultivate with such care, to manure with such discernment and to spare their cattle from excessive labour, as Beckford reports.

He visited the abbey in 1794, just five years after Murphy had 'found the greatest temperance and decorum, blended with hospitality and cheerfulness'. Writing 40 years later, Beckford painted a different picture altogether:

... In came the Grand Priors hand in hand, all three together. 'To the kitchen,' said they in perfect unison, 'to the kitchen and that immediately.'

The kitchen was 'the most distinguished temple of gluttony in all Europe', loaded with every sort and size of river fish, heaps of game and venison, and 'pastry in vast abundance, which a numerous tribe of lay brothers and their attendants were rolling out and puffing up into an hundred different shapes, singing all the while as blithely as larks in a corn-field.'

Junot's soldiers pillaged the abbey in 1810, and the monks were expelled in 1834, when the religious orders were extinguished.

Mosteiro de Santa Maria de Alcobaça

② Mosteiro de
Santa Maria de
Alcobaça
Praça 25 de Abril,
t (262) 505 120; open
daily April–Sept 9–7,
Oct–Mar 9–5;
last adm 30mins before
closing; adm; service
Sun 11.30am

The celestial simplicity of the **Mosteiro de Santa Maria de Alcobaça** is awesome and calming. It is the largest church in the country, and its architecture heralds the emergence of the Gothic style in Portugal. But try to see it before Batalha (*see* p.274), which is more uplifting. The hybrid façade stretches over 720ft (220m). The plain wings, reconstructed in 1725, emanate from the original portal and rose window, but the structure has no fluidity, the eye does not travel. Statues of S. Bento and S. Bernardo were installed either side of the portal, statues of the Virtues flank the rose window, and the Virgin presides over all, between the towers.

The first abbot, Ranulph, was sent by St Bernard himself. He may have brought with him plans for the abbey: the interior is modelled on the Cistercian church at Clairval (1115), in Citeaux, Burgundy. At 350ft (106m), it is enormously long, and proportionally narrow, although the truncated pier shafts give breadth to the nave. The Cistercian canon prohibits decorations and statues; the interior has been thoroughly scrubbed in an attempt to restore the original austerity. Terracotta statues of the Kings of Portugal up to Dom José I are shelved in the 18th-century **Sala dos Reis**, to the left of the entrance, which also contains a bronze cauldron captured from the Spanish at Aljubarrota. The *azulejo* dado depicts the history of the monastery.

Tombs of Pedro and Inês

The unforgettable tombs of Dom Pedro and Inês de Castro stand in the transepts, foot to foot, as requested, so that on Judgement Day they will open their eyes and see one another. The story goes that, after the death of his wife, Prince Dom Pedro fell in love with her Spanish lady-in-waiting, Dona Inês de Castro. Fearful of her brothers' influence, leading nobles poisoned King Dom Afonso V's mind against her. He sanctioned her murder, unaware that the couple had married in secret at Bragança, to legitimize their children. Inês' 'heron-neck' was severed at Coimbra. When Dom Pedro succeeded to the throne two years later, in 1357, two of the three murderers were brought to him at Santarém, tied to an ox-yoke. He is reported to have ripped out their hearts and eaten them, before exhuming Inês' decomposing body and compelling the nobility to do homage to her, prior to her entombment here.

These 14th-century limestone sarcophagi embody the delicacy of Portuguese sculpture at its most magnificent and gracious. Each effigy is attended by six fairylike angels, and the sides of each tomb are entirely covered with reliefs representing biblical scenes, the supplication of various martyrs, and the Passion. A line of musicians play along the top of one side of Inês' tomb, and the dreadful Last Judgement is meted out at her feet, encompassing hell, purgatory and paradise. The figures supporting her tomb have the bodies of dogs and the grim faces of men, including Pedro Coelho, one of her murderers. The wheel of fortune stands still, at the head of Dom Pedro's tomb, bordered with scenes from the life of St Bartholomew. The tombs are inscribed '*Até ao fim do mundo*' ('until the end of the world'). Junot's soldiers damaged both monuments as they searched for treasure, pocketing Inês' nose in the process.

Abbey Buildings

A chapel off the south transept contains the tombs of Kings Dom Afonso II and Dom Afonso III, as well as a mutilated 17th-century terracotta tableau of the death of St Bernard incorporating some 30 figures and their complex hairdos. A pair of frothy, seaflower Manueline portals (*c.* 1520) lead off the Ambulatory behind the high altar, to the Sacristy, which contains pillaged reliquaries, or to the vestibule opposite.

The north aisle connects with the **cloister of Dom Dinis**, whose ground floor was built by Domingo Domingues 1308–11, making it the oldest Cistercian cloister in Portugal, and the model for those of Évora, Lisbon, Porto and Coimbra. The upper storey was added some 200 years later.

The monks performed their ablutions at the octagonal 14th-century lavabo, now primly restored and covered with plants. They ate in silence in the beautiful vaulted **refectory** opposite, while edifying passages from the Bible were read to them. A tributary of the River Alcoa runs through the mammoth 18th-century **kitchen**, adjacent to the refectory, that the monks might feed off fresh fish. Further down the cloister, a staircase leads to the **monks' dormitory**. (Until the 17th century, when cells were allowed, monks slept fully dressed in the dormitory in beds separated by low partitions – high partitions were forbidden by the Chapter's general.) By the staircase is the **parlatory**, where the prior gave audiences to the monks, and the square **chapter house**, where work was apportioned and friars elected their abbot.

Atlantis Crystal

Alcobaça is also the home of the Atlantis Crystal factory, on the bank of the River Alcoa. Unfortunately it is not open to the public, though the manufacturing process is fascinating. The full-lead crystal is made with 32 per cent red lead (lead oxide) – which gives it weight, brilliance, and a musical ring – mixed with iron-free Belgian sand, and potash. Each stage is worked by hand, from blowing the glass, and re-melting the sharp lip of goblets, to cutting with diamond saws and acid polishing. Atlantis export to Britain and North America, and have shops all over Portugal, including one to the north of town, on Rua Frei Fortunato (EN 8-5, signposted), which has a small **Museu da Atlantis** incorporating a little display and shop.

Museu da Atlantis
Casal da Areia, Cós,
t *(262) 540 200,*
www.atlantis-cristais-de-alcobaca.pt

Museu Nacional do Vinho
Olival Fechado, **t** *(262) 582 222; open May–Sept Tues–Fri 9–12.30 and 2–5.30, Sat–Sun 10–12.30 and 2–5.30; Oct–April Tues–Fri only; adm*

The 19th-century *adega* housing the **Museu Nacional do Vinho** is just over a kilometre away, on the road to Batalha. Devoted to the history of winemaking, the collection of buildings houses the paraphernalia of the trade, including giant vats and barrels that hold up to 23,000 litres. There are also reconstructions of a cooperage and an old tavern, and a small collection of carts. Naturally, you can also sample and buy wine.

Where to Stay in Alcobaça

ⓘ Alcobaça >
Praça 25 de Abril, t (262) 582 377; open June–Sept daily 10–1 and 3–7, Aug daily 9am–10pm, Oct–May daily 10–1 and 2–6

★★Hotel Santa Maria, Rua Dr Francisco Zagalo 20–22, **t** (262) 590 160, *hotel.santa.maria@mail. telepac.pt* (€). Well run and well appointed, offering some rooms with splendid views of the monastery. A little too geared towrds groups, and plastic chairs in the breakfast room don't start the day well.

★★Pensão Corações Unidos, Rua Frei António Brandão, **t** (262) 582 142 (€). Pleasant *pensão* with windows opening onto a walkway. Its restaurant (€), which is popular at lunchtime. English-speaking staff.

Parque Municipal de Campismo, Avenida Professor Vieira Natividade, **t** (262) 582 265 (€). Located 500 metres north of the bus station.

Turismo de Habitação
Challet Fonte Nova, Rua da Fonte Nova, **t** (262) 598 300, *www.challet*

fontenova.pt (€€€). Luxurious mansion of 1872, with six rooms available. It's light, gracious and a bit ritzy; the fruit of the interior decorator's art is much in evidence, including vast swathes of rich, ruched fleur-de-lys fabric so popular in the 1990s. Nobody lives in the house, so one doesn't have the sense one is intruding. There's also a well-designed contemporary house with four rooms furnished in the same style. Rates include drinks from the well-stocked bar.

Eating Out in Alcobaça

António Padeiro, Praça 25 de Abril, opposite the monastery, **t** (262) 582 295, *www.antoniopadeiro* (€€). This is the best place to eat.

O Telheiro, Rua da Lavadinha Quinta o Telheiro, **t** (262) 596 029 (€€). Superb restaurant that is well known in these parts. Dishes up superb and well-presented regional dishes.

West of Alcobaça

Nazaré

Some 34km southwest of Leiria and 11km northwest of Alcobaça, the fishing town and popular west-coast resort of Nazaré sits beside a wide, sweeping beach which terminates abruptly at a steep cliff. The first reference to fishing here dates from 1643, but the beach was not formed until the sea withdrew in the following century.

Nowadays tourists swell the filthy town, crowding the beach and staking it with tents. Nazaré's 9,000 souls claim Phoenician descent. Traditionally, women wore elaborate gold earrings, coloured headscarves, dark knitted shawls, pom-pom skirts. The men tend racks of splayed sardines and jack-fish drying in the sun on the promenade by the beach, where people walk around eating *tremoceiros* (lupin seeds), reminiscing about the days before the marina, when oxen lived on the sand and dragged boats ashore. The grid-patterned streets are filled with laundry, garbage and birdcages.

Funicular
summer daily 7am–1am; winter daily to 12am; adm

A **funicular** makes the 110m ascent to the district of Sítio on the promontory overlooking the town, where the 17th-century pilgrimage **church of N.S. da Nazaré** contains some good 18th-century Dutch tiles. The first church built on this site commemorated the miraculous rescue of Dom Fuas Roupinho, castellan of Porto de Mós: in 1182 the stag he was hunting along these cliffs leapt into the sea. His horse was about to follow, when he invoked the Virgin and she halted the beast. In September her image is taken in a procession down to the sea, to commemorate the miracle.

Pinhal de Leiria

North of Nazaré and west of Leiria grows a great pine forest. Dom Dinis planted trees on over 10,000 ha (110 sq km) of land, to produce wood for shipbuilding – Portuguese merchants increased their trade with English ports in the 13th century – and to halt encroaching sand dunes. The same trees were used to construct the first caravels. It's a lovely place for picnics, and has some good campsites; contact the tourist office in Leiria for more details.

São Pedro de Muel

From Leiria a straight road leads to São Pedro de Muel, a very quiet little place, with huge views of the coarse sandy beach stretching miles down the coast. But it doesn't feel like a welcoming place. The Atlantic wind is chill indeed.

São Martinho do Porto

Twelve km south of Nazaré and 18km southwest of Alcobaça, the smart little resort of São Martinho do Porto stands beside an amazing semicircular beach which is almost totally sheltered behind natural jetties. In the summer the sea is very calm and warm, and although the water isn't super-clean, it is a good place for children to swim. There are jet-skis and pedaloes for hire, and hang-gliding available on the beach; you can even dive for a red algae used in Chinese medicine.

Currently the resort has just about the right amount of development, though it may begin to suffer soon with the overspill from Nazaré. There are lots of apartments to rent, but very few rooms available, so your first stop might well be the tourist office. Don't come to São Martinho do Porto for the nightlife – not that the place is elderly, but it's not youthful either. Note that Salgado beach is nudist.

Tourist Information/ Services West of Alcobaça

Nazaré: the **bus station** is at Av. Vieira Guimarães, **t** (262) 551 172; the **railway station** is at Valado de Frades, in Largo da Estação, **t** (262) 577 331.

São Martinho do Porto: *quartos* are available from the **tourist office**. The **railway station** is located in the east of town, just 100 yards from the beach, on Largo 25 de Maio, **t** (262) 989 485. The **bus stop** is to be found on Rua Conde de Avelar.

Sports and Activities West of Alcobaça

Hang-gliding: Centro de Voo Livre do Oeste, São Martinho do Porto, t 96 607 48 82, www.voo.no.sapo.pt

Water sports: Clube Náutico de São Martinho do Porto, Rua Cândido dos Reis, São Martinho do Porto, t (262) 980 290, cnsmp@clix.pt. Canoe rental.

Where to Stay West of Alcobaça

Nazaré

There's a wide range of accommodation, and the prices are steep in August.

Albergaria Mar Bravo, Praça S. Oliveira 71, t (262) 569 160, www.marbravo.com (€€€). The view from the balconies of each room in this central *albergaria* takes in both town and beach.

★★★Hotel da Nazaré, Largo Afonso Zuquete, t (262) 569 030, hotelnazare@clix.pt (€€). Just off the esplanade, this incongruously modern hotel has a rooftop terrace and good views.

★★★Hotel Praia, Avenida Vieira Guimarães 39, t (262) 562 058/1423, www.hotelpraia.com (€€). Traditional inn with bathroom *azulejos*, plus modern new addition.

★★Pensão-Restaurante Ribamar, Rua Gomes Freire 9, t (262) 551 158, www.ribamar.pa-net.pt (€€). Situated on the waterfront.

★★★Pensão Central, Rua Monzinho de Albuquerque 83–85, t (262) 551 510 (€). Good value.

Camping Vale Paraíso, 2km north off the N242 road to Leiria, t (262) 561 800, www.valeparaiso.com (€). Well equipped, with bungalows (€€–€) for rent. *Open all year.*

Pinhal de Leiria

Parque de Campismo, Pedrógão, t (244) 695 403 (€). In the pine forest, and better equipped than many other campsites. At Pedrógão there is a huge sweep of white sand only 200 yards from the site – quite a popular hang-out in summer. *Open April–mid-Dec.*

São Pedro de Muel

There are lots of *quartos* available.

★★★Hotel Mar e Sol, only 100 yards from the beach at Avenida da Liberdade 1, t (244) 590 000, www.hotelmaresol.com (€€). Clean, fairly standard, with a good restaurant.

Residencial Verde Pinho, Rua das Saudades 15, t (244) 599 233 (€). Modest, surrounded by pine trees; the owner is helpful.

São Martinho do Porto

★★★★Albergaria São Pedro, Largo Vitorino Fróis, t (262) 985 020 (€€). Now rather worn. *Open all year.*

★★★Residencial Atlântica, Rua Miguel Bombarda 6, t (262) 980 151 (€€). Near the tourist office, about 30 yards from the beachfront. Small, neat, tiled, breezy rooms are kept fanatically clean. *Closed winter.*

Pensão Americana, Rua Dom J. Saldanha 2, t (262) 989 170 (€€–€). Basic, and the plumbing is dubious, but at these prices it's hard to complain, and service is friendly. *Closed in winter.*

Colina do Sol, Serra dos Mangues, 2km north on the EN8, t (262) 989 764, www.colinadosol.com (€). Well-equipped campsite.

Eating Out West of Alcobaça

Nazaré

The beach is lined by restaurants with plate-glass windows, which expose diners doing battle with their fishbones.

A Celeste, Av. República 54, t (262) 551 695 (€€€). One of the top restaurants here serving superb seafood specialities like swordfish in a mushroom and cream sauce and monkfish served on the spit. The *cataplana de marisco* (seafood stew) is truly memorable.

Beira-Mar, Avenida da República 40, t (262) 561 358 (€€). On the seafront, serving delicious seafood grills. *Closed Dec–Feb.*

(i) **São Pedro de Muel >>**

Praça Eng. José Lopes Vieira, t (244) 599 152; open 1 July–15 Sept

(i) **São Martinho do Porto >>**

Largo Vitorino Fróis, t (262) 989 110; open Mon–Fri 9–1 and 3–7, Sat–Sun 10–1 and 2–6, Oct–June closed Mon

(i) **Nazaré >**

Avenida da República 17, t (262) 561 194; open April–mid-June daily 10–1 and 3–7, late June until 8pm, July–Aug daily 10–10, Sept daily 10–7, other times daily 9.30–1 and 2.30–6

Pitéu, Largo das Caldeiras 8, **t** (262) 551 578 (€€–€). Recommended venue, like its nearby counterparts.

A Tasquinha, Rua Adrião Batalha 54, **t** (262) 551 945 (€). Very popular.

Brisa do Mar, Avenida Vieira Guimarães 10, **t** (262) 551 197 (€). Opposite the bus station, and mercifully ordinary.

São Pedro de Muel

Brisamar, Rua Dr Nicolau Bettencourt, **t** (244) 599 250, *brisamar@sapo.pt* (€€). A nice little restaurant, although the décor is rather bland, with a fish menu; the selection of Portuguese wines is also good.

São Martinho do Porto

Restaurant Carvalho (€€), located on the ground floor of the Residencial Atlântica, serves good food in a blue-and-white setting.

Restaurant Oceano, Avenida Marginal (€). Feels a bit more modern than most.

Ostra Bar, on the beach (€€–€). Decent fish.

East of Alcobaça

Parque Natural das Serras de Aire e Candeeiros

This natural park covers around 29,000 ha (96,000 acres) of a diverse limestone range, stretching south from Porto de Mós to Rio Maior, and east to Pedreira do Galinha. It's a landscape of olive groves, dry stone walls, pastures and breathtaking rocky peaks. The area is, however, best known for its spectacular underground cave systems. Leaflets on walking trails (*percursos pedestres*) and picnic areas (*parques de merendas*) are available from park offices.

Porto de Mós

Castle
open May–Sept Tues–Sun 10–12.30 and 2–6

Museu Municipal
Travessa de São Pedro, t (244) 499 615; open Tues–Sun 10–12.30 and 2–5.30

ⓘ **Porto de Mós**
Municipal Gardens, t (244) 491 323; open May–July and Sept Tues–Sun 10–1 and 3–7, Aug Mon–Sun same times, Oct–April Tues–Sun 10–1 and 2–6

On a limestone outcrop on the western slope of the Serra dos Candeeiros, 16km northeast of Alcobaça and 25km south of Leiria, the green-coned **castle** of Porto de Mós dominates the village below it. The fortress was rebuilt by Dom Afonso, son of the first Duke of Bragança, who transformed it into a fortified palace, adding a Renaissance patio and incorporating bits of Roman stonework in the defensive walls. It's not worth going out of your way to come here. The rocky gash to the left of the castle is called the Devil's Nostrils (*Ventas do Diabo*). A bizarre collection of odds and ends is found in the tiny **Museu Municipal**, underneath the town hall: dinosaur fossils, Neolithic fragments, traditional Portuguese costumes and bits of old *azulejos*.

Intrepretation Centres East of Alcobaça

Parque Natural das Serras de Aire e Candeeiros (PNSAC) Head Office, Rua Dr Augusto César da Silva Ferreira, Bairro do Matão, Rio Maior, **t** (243) 999 480/7, *pnsac@icn.pt*. Interpretation centre, for information on flora and fauna, mountain traditions and activities including speleology and outdoor pursuits.

Ecoteca das Serras de Aire e Candeeiros (Centro de Interpretação),

in the municipal gardens at Alameda D. Afonso Henriques, Porto de Mós, **t** (244) 491 904. Satellite interpretation centre, where information is also available. *Open Tues–Fri 9.30–12.30 and 2–6, Sat–Sun 2–6 only.*

Sports and Activities East of Alcobaça

For horse-riding, try the following: **Quinta da Ferraria**, Ribeira de São João, Rio Maior, **t** (243) 945 001, *www.quintadaferraria.com.*

Mira d'Aire

The smooth limestone hills of the Serra d'Aire give no indication of their spectacular bellies, a series of caves (*grutas*) bristling with stalactites.

Grutas – Mira d'Aire
EN 243,
t (244) 440 322,
www.grutasmiradaire.
com; open 9am–7pm;
adm

The largest and most accessible of the caves can be entered slightly uphill of the textile town of **Mira d'Aire**, 14km southeast of Porto de Mós. They were discovered in 1947 by a boy chasing a sparrow. Rough steps lead down through humid chambers whose roofs drip stone stakes and fragile tentacles, fantastically spotlit in shades of yellow and red. The batless chambers have picturesque names like Hell's Door, Jelly Fish and Church Organ. Around 65ft (20m) high, they are dizzying rather than claustrophobic. The visit lasts about an hour, ending beside the underground Black River, with coloured fountains. Then an elevator whisks visitors back through the mountain to the ticket office.

Other Caves

Grutas – Alvados and Santo António
t (244) 440 787,
www.grutasalvados.com,
www.grutassanto
antonio.com; open
May–Oct 10-5.30;
Nov–April 10-5; adm,
combined ticket
available

Grutas da Moeda
t (244) 704 302,
www.grutasmoeda.com

There are more, worthwhile caves near the hamlets of **Alvados and Santo António**, 15km southeast of Porto de Mós.

The **Grutas da Moeda** at São Mamede, 6km west of Fátima (*see* p.277) might be worth a visit if only because one of the underground chambers, the Cova da Moura (Moor's Pit), has been converted into a bar!

Caldas da Rainha

The spa town of Caldas da Rainha, 26km southwest of Alcobaça and 5km north of Óbidos, wallows beside clay deposits, which have made it a hive of pottery production. As she passed through her estates in a carriage, Queen Leonor, wife of Dom João II, noticed a man washing himself. Her eyes widened at this unusual occurrence; she was informed that the sulphuric waters he was bathing in had healing qualities, and, having noted the lack of any large hospital and baths for the poor of Lisbon, founded one here in 1485, at her own expense. A village was designed on the site, privileges were offered to settlers, and the hospital was equipped with linen sheets and feather beds.

Getting to Caldas da Rainha

Infrequent **trains** run from Lisbon (1¾hrs), while local trains arrive from Óbidos in less than 10 minutes. In the other direction, they come from Figueira da Foz (2½hrs), via Leiria (1¼hrs). Frequent Rodonorte Express **buses** follow a similar route, making the journey from Lisbon in 1½hrs, or from Coimbra in 2½hrs. There are numerous buses from Óbidos (20 minutes).

Dom João V came three times to take the waters, but William Beckford was unimpressed. On his excursion he noted: 'In my eyes the whole of this famous stewing-place wore a sickly unprepossessing aspect. Almost every third or fourth person you met was a quince-coloured apothecary – and every tenth or twelfth a rheumatic or palsied invalid, with his limbs all atwist and his mouth all awry, being conveyed to the baths in a chair.'

The pottery industry blossomed in the late 19th century, moulded by Rafael Bordalo Pinheiro, whose favourite creations included smiling wetnurses, open-handed farmers, sacristans, and John Bull. The tradition continues, kneading together wit and gross gaudiness. It's surprising what takes shape – even clay phalluses are sold in the daily market, discreetly bound in brown paper. Kiwi fruits and avocados grow unprotected in the environs, while chrysanthemums require a blanket of plastic tarpaulins.

Around the Town

Hospital Termal Rainha Dona Leonor
short walk from Praça da República in the largo of the same name, t *(262) 830 300/4, cdoc@chcrainha.min-saude.pt*

Before plunging in, curious visitors to the **spa – Hospital Termal Rainha Dona Leonor** – should stop at the reception desk, where the weak will be deterred by the all-pervasive stink of sulphur. If you don't want to take your clothes off, the nasal douche is worthwhile – but check that nobody is watching: water shoots up one nostril and out the other. Portugal will never smell the same again. Should you choose to go the whole hog, three 95°F (35°C) swimming pools await, in stone-walled rooms (with barrel-vaulted ceilings for people who swim on their backs). The spa hospital offers a whole gamut of intermediary treatments: note that you may have to pay for a whole day's regimen. Serious visitors should book an appointment with an English-speaking doctor for advice on a programme of treatment for rheumatism, traumatism, respiratory or female genital complaints, or detoxification.

As you exit the spa, take heart from the ceramic *bacalhau* at the top of a staircase to your right, and go round the back to the early Manueline **church of N.S. do Pópulo**. When this hospital chapel opened in 1496, anyone visiting on certain days of the year was granted a papal indulgence. Beaked, howling gargoyles relieve the heavy exteriors of the church and belltower, while the interior, merry with blue and yellow 17th-century *azulejos*, climaxes in an early 16th-century wooden triptych from the Lisbon school, fitted above the chancel arch. Lilies are painted on the door to the

Museu de José Malhoa
Dom Carlos I garden, off the Largo Rainha Dona Leonor in Parque Dom Carlos I, t (262) 831 984; open Tues–Sun 10–12.30 and 2–5; adm, free Sun 10–2

sacristy, which contains a very good pale and doleful *Virgin and Child* by Josefa de Óbidos. The ornate octagonal Gothic font is bunched with grapes.

The **Museu de José Malhoa** is named after Caldas's principal artist, who died in 1933. His chalks and early works are worth a look, and there is also work by other Portuguese artists of the 19th and 20th century such as Francisco Branco, Manuel Teixeira Lopes, Sousa Lopes, Silva Porto and Columbano Bordalo Pinheiro.

Museu de Cerâmica
at furthest tip of the park (close to the junction of Rua Rafael Bordalo Pinheiro and Avenida Visconde de Sacavém), Rua Dr Ilídio Amado, t (262) 840 280, mceramica@ipmuseus. pt; open Oct–May Tues–Sun 10–12.30 and 2–5; June–Sept Tues–Sun 10–7; adm, free Sun 10–2

Perhaps the most rewarding part of the museum is the basement, which is a sort of biblical Madame Tussaud's in pottery. Entered separately, it contains the masterwork of the caricaturist and potter Rafael Bordalo Pinheiro, begun in 1887: nine dramatic groups of detailed life size ceramic models of characters at the Passion, intended to replace clay figures in the chapels of Butaco. A colourful and ugly collection of reptilian, caricaturist and naturalist ceramics is also on show.

The **Museu de Cerâmica** contains some witty pieces by Rafael Bordalo Pinheiro, including Art Deco tiles of dragonflies and frogs.

Turning up the avenue, two sculptors' work is displayed in the **Atelier Museus João Fragoso e António Duarte**. Some pieces are very beautiful; others are wild, and accompanied by striking sketches. The **Art Centre** here contains artists' studios, and you can see collections of work by two well-known Portuguese sculptors, Leopoldo de Almeida and Barata Feio. Nearby, the **Faianças Artísticas Bordalo Pinheiro** factory manufactures fun glazed tableware in vegetal forms, 90 per cent of which is exported, including the bright cabbage leaf plates. It is not possible to tour the workshops; however, a small **Museu São Rafael** displays more of its imaginative, fantastical creations from the end of the 19th century to date.

Atelier Museus João Fragoso e António Duarte
Rua Dr Ilídio Amado, t (262) 840 540, centrodeartes@cm-caldas-rainha.pt; open July–Sept Mon–Fri 10–6, Sat–Sun 10–1 and 5–7, Oct–June Mon–Fri 10–6, Sat–Sun 9–1 and 2–5.30; adm, free Sun 10–2

Faianças Artísticas Bordalo Pinheiro
www.fabordalo pinheiro.pt

Museu São Rafael
Rua Rafael Bordalo Pinheiro 53, t (262) 839 384, museu@ fabordalo pinheiro; open Tues–Fri 9–1

ⓘ **Caldas da Rainha >**
Praça 25 de Abril, t (262) 839 700; open Mon–Fri 9–7, Sat–Sun 10–1 and 3–7

Tourist Information in Caldas da Rainha

To find the **tourist office** from the **railway station**, t (262) 831 067, follow the Avenida Independéncia Nacional as it veers right, following through to the Praça da República. To get there from the **bus station** turn left into the Rua Heróis da Grande Guerra, and take the second left into the Rua Almirante Cândido dos Reis. Free car parking near the hospital.

Where to Stay in Caldas da Rainha

Writing in 1726, Brockwell warned: 'For persons not admitted into the Hospital, here are the worst Accommodations in the Universe.' The situation has improved.

★★★Residencial Dona Leonor, Hemiciclo João Paulo II 9, t (262) 838 430 (€). Rather featureless, but solidly run and quiet.

★★Pensão Central, Largo Dr José Barbosa, t (262) 831 914 (€). The painter José Malhpo was born here. He has left no visible trace.

Turismo de Habitação
Quinta da Foz, Foz do Arelho, **t** (262) 979 369, *www.quinta-dafoz.com* (€€€). Just a few kilometres away on the Óbidos lagoon, a 16th-century manor house which is still in the original family's hands. The five rooms are furnished with antiques, and a small bottle of wine 'to help the sleep process'. Experienced horse-riders will appreciate the stables.
Casa dos Plátanos, Rua Rafael Bordalo Pinheiro 24, **t** (262) 841 810 (€€). Eight characterful rooms. Breakfast is included.

Eating Out in Caldas da Rainha

Restaurante-Bar Museu São Rafael, Rua Rafael Bordalo Pinheiro 53, **t** (262) 839 380 (€€). Near the ceramics museum; very smart.
Sabores D'Italia, Rua Engenheiro Duarte Pacheco, **t** (262) 845 599 (€€). This place has won awards for its home-made pizzas and pastas.
Tijuca, Rua de Camões 89, **t** (262) 824 255 (€). Good choice of dishes; near the spa.
A Lareira, Rua da Lareira, Alto do Nobre, **t** (262) 823 432 (€€€–€€). Traditional Portuguese menu served in a pine woodland; try the *perdiz à Lareira* – partridge with chestnuts, fruits and vegetables. *Closed Tues*.

Óbidos

'Eis aqui um vilão com cinturão de oiro'
('Behold, here is the town with a golden belt')
D. João V

 Óbidos

Óbidos is an outrageously pretty, albeit touristy, small town crowning a limestone ridge, 5km south of Caldas da Rainha. Most of its 5,000 souls are contained within the 13th- and 14th-century castle walls (the 'golden belt'); the five cobbled streets of white houses, some bordered with mauve or burnt yellow, are still deliciously domestic, awash with Siamese cats, laundry troughs and scrubbing boards, geraniums in urns flanking granite window casements, bougainvillea and wisteria. Homes are roofed with beautifully weathered, lichenous terracotta. Tourism has been relatively good for Óbidos; the streets are swept, the dust dampened, and the houses kept in good repair.

In 1148 Dom Afonso Henriques captured the castle from the Moors; he and his troops crept up on it disguised as cherry trees. Dom Dinis gave Óbidos to his queen, Isabel, as a wedding present, and it remained the property of the queens of Portugal until 1834. Josefa de Óbidos (1634–84), whose portraits were sought by fashionable ladies taking the waters at Caldas da Rainha, founded a painting school here. Her better works can be seen in Butaco, Coimbra, Évora and Cascais.

There are many small places to stay in Óbidos; those in despair of finding anywhere very cheap can console themselves with *ginjinha*, the local morello cherry liqueur, which tastes like celestial cough syrup.

Getting to Óbidos

Trains arrive infrequently from Lisbon (2hrs) and very infrequently from Figueira da Foz (1¾hrs). There are frequent trains from Leiria (1hr) and Caldas da Rainha (5mins). Local **buses** make the journey from Peniche (¾hr) and Caldas da Rainha (20mins). There are three direct buses to Lisbon every day.

Around the Town

Óbidos's main entrance gate is the zigzag **Porta da Vila** – scourge of cars' wing mirrors, a gossiping spot, and, since the 18th century, a tiled oratory, all rolled into one. At the opposite end of town, overlooking the flat basin of what was once the lagoon, the castle's high curtain walls with square and cylindrical towers are often used for a film set. The stronghold was built by Dom Dinis, substantially reconstructed in the third quarter of the 14th century, and altered by Dom Manuel. The 16th-century castellan's residence has been converted into a *pousada*.

Church of Santa Maria
open May–Sept daily 9.30–12.30 and 2.30–7, Oct–April same times until 5pm

Along the main street, the Manueline **pillory** bears a little granite shrimping net, symbol of Dona Leonor. The **church of Santa Maria**, in the pillory square, Rua Direita, was founded before the Portuguese monarchy, though the present church dates from the Renaissance. Walls of florid late 17th-century *azulejos* support a ceiling painted with 'Indian' masks and reddish cherubs hatched from ideas of Brazil. Here the 10-year-old king Dom Afonso V wed Dona Isabel, two years his junior, in 1444. The tomb of Dom João de Noroha, castellan of Óbidos, stands against the left wall of the church, a prototype Portuguese Renaissance vault (a decorated arch covering a sarcophagus panelled with a plaque, with either a group of biblical figures or a kneeling effigy of the deceased represented on the sarcophagus). Carved 1526–8, perhaps by Chanterène, the intimate relationship of the Ança-stone figures of the pietà, St John and Mary Magdalene, is detailed right down to the tear drops. João da Costa painted the panels over the high altar 1616–18; to the right are panels by Josefa de Óbidos, dated 1661.

Museu Municipal
Praça de Santa Maria, t (262) 955 010, c.m.obidos@mail. telepac.pt; open mid-Mar–mid-Nov Tues–Sun 10–1 and 2–6, mid-Nov–mid-Mar Tues–Sun 9.30–1 and 2–5.30; adm

To the right of the church, the **Museu Municipal** houses excruciating paintings from churches destroyed by the earthquake of 1755; among them are a portrait by Josefa de Óbidos (*sometimes on loan*), and double-sided panels still used in the Easter Week procession. There is a Peninsular War room, with guns. Monks spun the 16th-century *Roleta dos Irmãos* (Brothers' roulette) wheel to apportion their daily work, so doubt not: there really is a divine croupier.

Tourist Information/ Services in Óbidos

Buses stop beside the Porta da Vila, from which the Rua Direita leads to the astonishingly helpful **tourist office**. The **regional tourist office** is also in Óbidos. The tourist board produces a useful booklet in English, *Walking Tracks from the Sea to the Mountain*, with 10 routes, and details of *adegas* on wine routes.

The **railway station**, t (262) 959 186, is at the bottom of Óbidos's hill. Trains

ⓘ Óbidos >
*Rua Direita, t (262)
959 231; open May–Sept
Mon–Fri 9.30–7,
Sat–Sun 10–1 and 2–7,
Oct–April same times
until 6pm*

*Regional tourist office
(Região de Turismo do
Oeste): Rua Direita,
t (262) 955 060,
info@rt-oeste.pt*

**★ Pousada do
Castelo >>**

still run through although the station is unmanned. Buy your ticket on board – the tourist office has timetables.

Sports and Activities in Óbidos

Golf

The 'Oeste' tourist board, under which Óbidos falls, is keen to promote the area as a new golfing destination and many new courses have sprung up in recent years.
Golf da Praia d'El Rey, Vale de Janelas, t (262) 905 005, *www.praia-del-rey.com*. A few kilometres from town, this club lies right next to the beach, and is part of the nearby Golf and Country Club complex.

Horse-riding

Associação Hípica O Cavalo, Rua Principal, Casal do Pinheiro 1, Apartado 58, t 964 461 233.

Where to Stay in Óbidos

Note that cars cannot enter within the castle walls, so if you're staying there you'll need to park outside and carry your bags in.

Within the castle walls, several private houses make rooms available to guests. Ask at the tourist office for details.

Very Expensive (€€€€)
★★★★Hotel Real D'Óbidos, Rua D. João de Ornelas, t (262) 955 090, *www.hotelrealdobidos.com*. Slightly outside the castle walls, this is basically a comfortable hotel with a nice pool, wrecked by its attempt to become a medieval theme park. The staff wear mock-medieval tabards, Gregorian chants are broadcast in the garage, bedroom keys come on huge chains and fire extinguishers are cloaked with velour. Visit the toilet in the reception area: beside it is an iron bracket; from which hangs a mini-cauldron; in which is a toilet brush. Beware mosquitoes.

Expensive (€€€)
★★★★Estalagem do Convento, Rua Dom João de Ornelas, t (262) 959 214, *www.estalagemdoconvento.com*. Just outside the town walls, it used to be a modest nunnery. Decent, but not very memorable. Comfortable bedrooms are approached through an irregular courtyard set with tables. The popular arcaded dining room is decked in red and gold, serving international fare.

Moderate (€€)
★★★★Albergaria Rainha Santa Isabel, Rua Direita, t (262) 959 323, *www.arsio.com*. On the village's main street within the castle walls. Outmoded, but in good condition. The best rooms have balconies overlooking the practically carless cobbled main street, so guests can watch low-key life unravel. the clean rooms are simply but comfortably furnished, with attractive bathrooms, wood-panelling and *azulejos*. High season is August only.
★★★★Albergaria Josefa d'Óbidos, Rua Dom João de Ornelas, t (262) 959 228, *josefadobidos@iol.pt*. Closer to the town's main gate and preferable. Just outside the main entrance to the walled settlement, and built around a triangular courtyard, it's spacious, well appointed and doesn't try to be anything it isn't.

Inexpensive (€)
Hospedaria Louro, Casal da Canastra, t (262) 955 100, *www.hospedaria louro.com*. Outside the town walls, this new place has a pool and private parking. The rooms are comfortable and clean.
Óbido Sol, Rua Direita 40, t (262) 959 188. Private rooms to rent; this one has great views out over the hills.
Casa dos Castros, Rua Direita 41, t (262) 959 328. Another private house, with three old rooms to let.

Pousada
★★★★Pousada do Castelo, t (262) 955 080, *www.pousadas.pt* (L2 H). Installed in the castle, this excellent *pousada* occupies the castellan's residenceand is both comfortable and ancient. As castles go, it's very cosy, with just nine rooms: six doubles and three suites. It's very well maintained, with hand axes and a suit of armour to lend a touch of grandeur. Busy fabrics brighten

Alcaide >>

bedrooms with tiny deep-set windows – if you're in a turret room, you'll have an arrow-slit window rather than a view. Approached across the open battlements, the keep contains a cosy medieval maisonette. The restaurant is furnished like a provincial *quinta*. The food is very good: the pork on celeriac is scrumptious, and the lamb chops very fine. Try for a table at the Manueline windows, overlooking the courtyard topiary with shrubs like *My Fair Lady* hats. Reservations are necessary for summer lunches. Staff are attentive; one doesn't mind forsaking an elevator when there's a nice man to carry one's bags upstairs. Book well in advance.

★ Casa de São Thiago do Castelo >

Turismo de Habitação

Casa de São Thiago do Castelo, Largo de S. Thiago, **t** (262) 959 587 (€€). Several rooms are available here under the Turismo Rural scheme. Located close to the castle, it's a very attractive home, a bit of a warren, with its own courtyard and rooms furnished as if for friends. Car parking is available.

Casa do Rochedo, Rua Jogo da Bola, **t** (262) 959 120 (€€). If the prospect of a swimming pool appeals, try this house, which has six rooms.

Casa do Poço, Travessa da Rua Nova, **t** (262) 959 358 (€). Less costly option, downhill from the castle in the old Moorish quarter. With its tiny windows and internal courtyard, it feels like the real McCoy, albeit slightly claustrophobic.

Eating Out in Óbidos

There are restaurants in the *pousada* and the Estalagem do Convento (*see* p.292).

Alcaide, Rua Direita, **t** (262) 959 220 (€€). A lovely place with great views. Very good food is served in a room that is draped with ivy and red tablecloths. The proprietors' Azorean specialities include tuna steak in batter, and a pudding made with biscuits and powdered milk custard. The *ensopado de safio* (eel stew) is very rich, with plenty of gravy to soak into the bread. *Closed Wed.*

Vila Infanta, Largo do Senhor da Pedra, **t** (262) 959 757 (€€). Serves local specialities.

Casa do Poço, Travessa da Rua Nova, **t** (262) 959 358 (€€). Has a fun bar, dominated by a crane-like wine press built with a tree trunk. There are carvings around the fireplace, and *fado* on Saturday nights.

Petrarum Domus, Rua Direita, **t** (262) 959 620, www.petrarumdomus.com (€€). Expect good service and good food here, with its bare stone walls and limestone floor giving it an elegant rustic medieval look.

1 de Dezembro, Largo de S. Pedro, **t** (262) 959 298 (€€). Next to the town hall, this provides tables outdoors, but you pay for the privilege. *Closed Thurs.*

Bars

Cave do Vale, Largo do Chafariz Novo, **t** (262) 959 272. Cosy, mellow, antique, wood-and-stone little place is the best bar in town. The *ginjinha* is a must.

Lagar da Mouraria, Rua da Mouraria, **t** (262) 959 358. Built around an old wine press, with a sloping wooden ceiling and balcony and *fado* by candlelight.

Peniche and Around

Atouguia da Baleia

Fifteen km west of Óbidos, on the road from there to Peniche, the village of Atouguia da Baleia was once a port made wealthy by commerce. Its curious name – '*baleia*' means 'whale' – serves as a reminder that whales could be hunted off the coast of Portugal in

Getting to Peniche and Around

There is no **railway** service to Peniche. Semi-frequent Tejo **buses**, **t** (262) 782 133, run from Lisbon (2hrs), and infrequently from Porto (5½hrs), via Coimbra (3hrs), Leiria (2hrs) and Nazaré (1¼hrs).

· The **ferry** (45min) from Peniche runs to the Berlenga Islands from mid-May to mid-Sept, weather permitting, crossing twice daily during July and August (*departs 9.30am and 11.30am; returns 4.30pm and 6.30pm*; run by Viamar, **t** (262) 785 646), otherwise it runs once daily. Only 300 visitors are allowed to the islands per day, and therefore in summer tickets tend to sell out very quickly. Bear in mind that the crossing to the islands may be quite rough.

the 13th century. In 1245, the Abbey of Alcobaça collected the profits from whale oil in the ports which it controlled.

The village is now obscure, but well worth visiting to see the exceptional works of art in its early Gothic **church of São Leonardo**. Behind a plain and pockmarked 13th-century façade, the very good collection of paintings includes a stunning Renaissance representation of São Leonardo backed by a red cloth. Equally exciting is the 14th-century limestone low relief of the Nativity: the Virgin lies tucked in bed beneath a starched sheet, holding a little book in one hand and a flower in the other. The baby Jesus sits on her thighs, warmed by the breath of an ox and an ass, and watched over by angels. Joseph sits at the foot of the bed looking patriarchal. A petrified whalebone lurks in the corner of the church, one of several supposed to have been used to construct the roof.

Exquisite, florid Baroque marble inlay surrounds the retable of the **church of N.S. da Conceição** nearby, fronted by two massive bell-towers. The rough pillars beside the church are the remains of a bull stall, probably commissioned by Dom Pedro I in the 14th century – which would make this the earliest evidence for bullfighting in Portugal.

Peniche

As late as the mid-16th century, Peniche was an island in the Atlantic. Silt formed the narrow isthmus that now joins it to the mainland, flanked by gently sloping beaches; it has a perimeter of 5 miles (8km). The busy deep-sea fishing port and cannery centre hums around the harbour, to the left of the entrance to the fortifications. Peniche lies 22km west of Óbidos. Near the harbour, on the south face of the peninsula, the sprawling **Fortaleza** was constructed 1557–70, seeing action in 1589 when Norris landed with 12,000 troops in support of the Prior of Crato's claim to the Portuguese crown. The fortress served as a prison under both Pombal and the PIDE, Salazar's hated secret police; it now contains the **Museu de Peniche**, where you can peer at former cells, solitary chambers and the visitors' grille. There are also displays on local archaeology and the local lace-making, fishing and boat-building industries.

Fortaleza
open Tues–Sun 10.30–12.30 and 2–6

Museu de Peniche
t (262) 780 116; open Tues–Sun 10.30–12 and 2–5.30; adm

The peninsula is fringed with vertical rock cliffs battered by frothy waves and pierced by caverns. It's a breezy 3km walk eastwards to the Cabo Carvoeiro and the **chapel of N.S. dos Remédios**, which contains blue and white *azulejos* of the life of the Virgin attributed to the workshop of António de Oliveira Bernardes, *c.* 1711–20. The Berlenga islands are visible on a clear day.

The Berlenga Islands

With a circumference of 4km, Berlenga Grande is the largest and only accessible island of a diminutive archipelago about 12km offshore. It is treeless, craggy and magical, and has been declared a **National Bird Reserve**, accommodating fleets of seagulls and eiders, as well as rabbits and a cluster of fishermen. The island is granite, with a preponderance of feldspar. These wonderfully clear waters once harboured pirates. They made life too difficult for those Jeronymite friars who eschewed their brothers at grand Belém and came here in 1513 to assist the survivors of shipwrecks; the monastery was demolished, and a rust-coloured fortress was built on an islet approached by a skinny causeway. In 1666 a garrison of 20 men wounded half of the 1000-strong Spanish assault force unsuccessfully attempting to kidnap and ransom the bride of Dom Afonso VI. She was resting on the island on her way from her father's duchy of Nemours.

A few huts huddle around the small sandy beach near the ferry dock, from which rowboats can be hired to explore the weird rock caves. Paths across the island are marked with stones, to ensure the birds' privacy. The fortress has been converted into an unforgettable pensão. There's a **campsite** above the dock (*open May–Sept; contact the tourist office at Peniche for information*), as well as a little bar-restaurant and a shop for basic supplies.

Tourist Information in Peniche and Around

ℹ **Peniche >**
Rua Alexandre Herculano, **t** *(262) 785 934, turismo cmp@iol.pt; open July–Aug daily 9am–8pm; rest of year daily 10–1 and 2–5*

Peniche's **tourist office** is to be found on the waterfront between the two bridges.

The **Reserve Headquarters** for the Berlenga Islands is at Porto da Areia Norte, Estrada Marginal, Peniche, **t** (262) 787 910.

Sports and Activities in Peniche and Around

Kite Surfing

Kite Center, t (919) 424 952, *www. penichekitecenter.com*. Located on the beach near the dunes; equipment to rent, as well as courses available.

Boat Trips

Atraente, Rua das Traineiras 6, **t** (262) 781 661 or 962 766 621. Sailing and fishing trips.

Golf

Botado Golf Club, Praia da Consolação, **t** (262) 757 700. This course incorporates sand dunes from the nearby beach and several stretches of water. Close by is the monstrous-looking Atlântico Golf Hotel: multi-storey and orange.

Horse-riding

Campus Hípico, São Bernardino, **t** 933 343 204, *ww.campushipico.com*.

Lace-making

In Portugal Peniche is famous for lace, and you can watch lace-workers at the following:

Escola de Rendas, in the same building as the tourist office. *Open Mon–Fri 9.30–12.30 and 2–5.30.*

Redibilrosa, Rua Marechal Gomes Freire Andrade 57. *Open Mon–Fri 9–12.30 and 2–5.30.*

Multi-activity

Novas Aventuras, Rua da Alegria 60, **t** (262) 086 354 or 919 736 764, *www.novasaventuras.pt.* Sailing, horse-riding, paintball, speedball, rafting, canoeing, go-karting and general outdoor fun are among the offerings here.

Scuba-diving

Berlenga-Sub, Largo da Ribeira 24, **t** (262) 784 104 or 966 781 701, *berlengasub@oninet.pt.*

Mergulhão, Urbanização Fonte do Rosário, lote 10, **t** (262) 785 795 or 966 008 487.

Surfing

Baleal Surf Camp, Rua dos Amigos do Baleal 2, Ferrel, **t** (262) 769 270, *www.balealsurfcamp.com.* Offers surfing packages that include lodgings.

Peniche Surf Camp, Rua do Gualdino 4, **t** 962 336 295. A range of courses.

Where to Stay and Eat in Peniche and Around

Atouguia da Baleia

Casa do Castelo, opposite the church, **t** (262) 750 647, *www.turihab.pt*

(€€ CA). This tumble of pretty 17th-century buildings spring out from a ruined 12th-century Moorish castle, a short distance from Peniche. Rooms are very tastefully decorated to relaxing themes. At breakfast, orange juice is freshly squeezed from trees in the garden. There is a three night minimum stay.

Peniche

★★★Hotel Praia Norte, Avenida Monsenhor Bastos, **t** (262) 780 500, *www.hotelpraianorte.com* (€€). A whitewashed, three-storey concrete block overlooking its swimming pool. There are restaurants along the Avenida do Mar, and fish is cooked outside near the docks.

Residencial Rima Vier, Rua Castilho 6, **t** (262) 789 459 (€). One of the better of several *pensões* in the central area.

Estelas, Rua Arquitecto Paulin Montês 21, **t** (262) 782 435 (€). Large seafood menu, and some meat dishes.

Marisqueira Cortiçais, Porto d'Areia Sul, **t** (262) 787 262 (€). Overlooking the beach and locally popular, with good seafood.

Mira Mar, Avenida do Mar 42, **t** (262) 781 666 (€). Seafood of course; but with lots of choice.

Berlenga Islands

Pavilhão Mar e Sol, **t** (262) 750 331 (€€). The only civilized place to stay, although the restaurant is known for being pricey.

Torres Vedras and the Coast

Torres Vedras

On the bank of the minor River Sizandro at the southwestern edge of the rippling Serra de Montejunto, the town of Torres Vedras stands at the centre of a wine-producing region (the white is refreshing and light).

Torres Vedras was a royal residence from the mid-13th century to the early 16th century, and gave its name to Wellington's lines of

Getting to Torres Vedras

By **road**, Torres Vedras is 34km south of Óbidos and 33km north of Mafra.

Museu Municipal
t *(261) 310 485;*
open Tues–Sun; adm

defence for Lisbon early in the Peninsular War (*see* p.353). The Praça 25 de Abril contains a **memorial** to those who died and a 16th century monastery, the Convento da Graça, which contains the **Museu Municipal**, with models showing Wellington's defences.

In the Largo de S. Pedro, at the centre of town, winged dragons enliven the Manueline portal of the **church of S. Pedro**, which was rebuilt in the 16th century. Within, 18th-century *azulejos* depict birds in the sky and everyday life with palm trees, and a tomb contains the remains of João Lopes Perestrelo, who accompanied da Gama on his voyages to India. Behind the church, a Gothic pavilioned fountain, the **Chafariz dos Canos**, dates from 1561.

On a gentle hill on the edge of town, Dom Dinis' **castle** of 1288 was rebuilt for the last time in the 17th century, before being ruined by the earthquake of 1755. Today it is dry and unatmospheric, but for the hairy yellow flowers and geckos in the sun.

Tomatoes and green beans are grown for export, and timber is transported from here, still dripping with sap. The local *pastéis de feijpo* are a treat: made with boiled white beans and almonds; they have the consistency of hard honey, but are not too sweet.

The Lines of Torres Vedras

Torres Vedras is best known to students of British history. In 1809, Wellington planned to save Portugal from the French by concentrating on the defence of the capital. Reckoning a year in advance, he intended to turn 500 square miles into an impregnable fortress, by constructing chains of mutually reinforcing redoubts, each of which would crown a prominent feature of the landscape. The 152 forts were built secretly: Masséna was unaware of their existence until his advance guard sighted them four days before his arrival, and even the British minister in Lisbon and most of the staff officers in the British army appear to have been kept in the dark. For a whole year, 18 engineers directed 5,000–7,000 local peasants to construct the polygonal redoubts with 13ft (4m) thick parapets. Masséna was flummoxed; he dallied, waiting for a false move by Wellington, but retreated on 14 November 1810 – a retreat that ended at Toulouse in April 1814.

The British Historical Society of Portugal publishes a pamphlet, *The Lines of Torres Vedras*, which gives details of three day-long walks between various redoubts. Most of these outworks are made up of trenches and walls. The simplest to locate is at Torres Vedras itself.

ⓘ **Torres Vedras** >
*Rua 9 de Abril, **t** (261)
310 483, www.cm-
tvedras.pt*

Where to Stay and Eat in Torres Vedras and the Coast

Torres Vedras

★★Hotel Império Jardim, Praça 25 de Abril, **t** (261) 314 232, *info@imperio-online.com* (€€). The exterior looks like it's come straight from Toytown, but it is central, clean and functional. Give the restaurant a miss.

Casal do Gil de Cima, Monte Redondo, **t** (261) 911 184, *www.casaldogil.i8.com* (€). Rural *casa* that is spacious, clean and with friendly hosts; it's also well-placed for travel to Lisbon.

O Lampião, Rua João Carlos Alves, Turcifal, **t** (261) 951 142 (€€). Very good traditional dishes, including mountain kid and roast duck. *Closed Sat evening and Sun.*

O Barracão, Largo Fernando Vicente – Paúl, **t** (261) 324 908 (€€). A rustic surrounding; try their cod with cream or grilled octopus. *Closed Mon.*

Porto Novo

★★★Hotel Golf Mar, **t** (261) 980 800, *www.hotelgolfmar.com* (€€€–€€). The unexceptional interior of the hotel is eclipsed by its views over the beach and the ocean – the balconies allow a great feeling of freedom – and by its swimming pools: saltwater outdoors, Olympic-size indoors. With a 9-hole golf course and two hard tennis courts, the hotel is popular with conferences. The cavernous restaurant offers a limited choice of rather ordinary food.

Casal dos Patos, Areia Branca, **t** (261) 413 768, *www.casaldospatos.online.pt* (€). A German-owned small hotel with just five rooms, plus a cottage that sleeps four. Located 12km north of Porto Novo on the coastal road.

Convento de Santo António
*t (261) 314 120,
conv.varatojo@mail.tele
pac.pt*

The Environs of Torres Vedras

The 15th-century Franciscan **convento de Santo António** 3km west of Torres Vedras in the hamlet of Varatojo, contains marvellous 18th-century *azulejo* panels, some of which depict a hell where sinners' eyes are pierced with nails. There is a beautiful, rather domestic Gothic cloister; the rest of the interior has been modernized over the centuries.

Porto Novo

The road to Porto Novo beach, 16km northwest of Torres Vedras, passes a working **windmill** with bucket sails. Maize is jogged through a hole in the top grindstone, to be powdered by its quick rotation. The bow-shaped beach is enclosed by dramatic grey granite cliffs and pummelled by a strong wind.

Mafra and Around

Mafra

The small, nondescript town of Mafra, 39km northwest of Lisbon, snuggles around its huge 18th-century palace and monastery. Before the construction of the edifice, the settlement was a mere village of 100 houses gathered around a castle which no longer exists, near a hill which was dynamited on the instructions of Dom João V.

Getting to Mafra

Mafrense, **t** (261) 816 159, **buses** leave Campo Grande bus station in Lisbon at regular intervals (1¾ hrs) and also Sintra (¾ hr).

History

In 1711, three years after his marriage to Dona Maria-Ana of Austria, the childless King Dom João V pledged to build a monastery should he be favoured with an heir. Dona Maria Bárbara, later Queen of Spain, was born before the end of the year, and the first stone of the palace and monastery was laid in November 1717. It was intended to rival the Escorial and St Peter's in Rome, to express the splendour of the nation and its monarch. The basilica was dedicated at an eight-hour ceremony in 1730 (desperate to relieve himself, the archbishop nearly passed out), but the final works were not completed until 1735.

The statistics are boggling. The project cost over 48 million *cruzados*, sufficient to hasten Portugal's economic decline. At the peak of construction, it sapped the energies of 45,000 muddy and flea-ridden civilians, who were marshalled by 7,000 soldiers. Their absence from the productive workforce paralysed the country's economy. Some 1,270 oxen and 7,000 small carts shifted the materials needed to build the 880 halls and rooms, and the 4,500 doors and windows. The construction plan was drawn up by a team in Rome co-ordinated by the Marquis of Fontes. Ludwig of Ratisbon (1670–1752), a German trained in Rome, engineered the building and oversaw its construction. The master carpenters, builders and masons were Italian.

Having soaked up the wealth that poured into Portugal from newly discovered deposits of Brazilian gold, Mafra never really caught on as a royal or courtly residence. The blackening south turret, to the right of the façade, was for the king and the north turret, to the left, was for the queen. Dom João V was accompanied by a fleet of lackeys on his night-time forays northwards; on his arrival at the queen's chamber, her ladies-in-waiting retired behind an arras, until the king was ready to make his way southwards.

A distinguished School of Sculpture functioned here from 1753 to 1770, under the auspices of Alessandro Giusti, who had come to Portugal from Italy to assemble the chapel of St John the Baptist in Lisbon's church of São Roque. Machado de Castro was one of the school's progeny. In the early 19th century, sweet, bewildered Dom João VI wandered the palace carrying two small boxes in his pocket, one for snuff, and one for grilled chickens' legs. These he gnawed. He retired here to escape the venom of his boundless, bumptious, scheming wife, Carlota Joaquina, who complained, among other things, that he was placing too much confidence in his hairdresser. The king fled to Brazil at the insistence of the British, rather than become a puppet of the French invaders. He was accompanied by his wife and most of the furniture from Mafra, which never returned. In 1807, Junot billeted troops in the monastery, which was occupied by Wellington's men shortly afterwards. Parts of the buildings have been in military hands since the mid-19th century.

The Town

Palace and monastery
open 10–5; closed Tues and holidays; adm

Visitors to the **palace and monastery** enter the building where the queen entered, in the middle of the left half of its façade. The vast façade faces west, its flat expanse centring on the basilica topped by high belltowers; the monastery is focused on a square courtyard behind the church, incorporating a refectory, chapter house, kitchen, cells for 280 brothers, and library.

The Basilica and Belltowers

The porch of the basilica houses wonderfully fluid Carrara marble statues of the founders of various religious orders, with curly marble hair, carved by several sculptors in Italy in the style of Bernini. The beautiful proportions of the basilica's interior are complemented by the harmonious paving and panelling of soft yellow, pink, blue, grey, red and black marble. It's a curiously sober memorial to an ostentatious monarch. The arts and crafts of the basilica were imported, right down to the copes, canopies and 3,000 walnut panels for the sacristy cupboards and choir stalls. The six organs are almost identical with one another; they were constructed 1792–1807, to replace four earlier organs notable for their ugliness, built by a diminutive Irish monk named Egan.

The belltowers boast the world's largest assemblage of bells, 57 in each tower, 48 of which make up the carillons created in Liège and Antwerp in 1730. The largest carillon bell weighs 10 tonnes, the smallest 65lb (30kg). Before these were electrified, the carillonneur would shed around 5lb (2–3kg) per concert, for which he wore gloves with separate finger sheaths. Now the carillonneur depresses a pedal or a wooden peg – but few people have the skill. **Concerts** are given 4–5pm on Sundays from May to October.

The Palace and Monastery

The palace is kitted out with dull imperial-style furniture dating from the middle of the 19th century, spanning the reigns of the last four kings of Portugal. Only the whimsical pieces are worthy of attention: the skittle table in the games room, at which monarchs spun tops through the spreadeagled legs of small cherubs; the bathroom's merry bird murals; and the deer horn chandelier, chairs, sofas and wall-mounts in the dining room, made from beasts stalked in the palace's walled hunting ground. The elegant rococo **library** is the longest room in the building, in whose ivory light 30,000 volumes ruminate. The chequered marble floor is conducive to slippered pacing.

Maquettes from the School of Sculpture are displayed in corridors leading to the monastery. The monks' pharmacy is brought to life by a giant syringe – for giving enemas – displayed on a table and the infirmary is *à la* Florence Nightingale, with open cells and shuttered beds, from which insane monks could admire the only *azulejos* at Mafra. Sane monks were kept in simple cells, where they could whip themselves and wear millstone necklaces. The delousing booths offered rare luxury: they were made of Brazilian angelin wood rather than Portuguese pine, because it did not splinter.

Sobreiro

A sculptor has created a **miniature village** for children, at Sobreiro, 3km west of Mafra. Kids shriek about the place, delighting to find artisans at work, several windmills, boats bubbling on a trough of water, and a 'typical' (kitsch) kitchen selling hot bread. The rustic **bar** marked '*adega*' is hung with cowbells, hoe tops and bay leaves, flanked by wine barrels, and floored with crazy paving. Salami-style *chouriço* and red wine go down well here. The **restaurant** (€€) is dim and quaint. Avoid summer weekends.

Ericeira

Eleven kilometres west of Mafra, the whitewashed Atlantic fishing village of Ericeira has escaped overdevelopment as a resort, although its exposure to the full force of the Atlantic has fostered a thriving international surfing scene.

The cult of Sebastianism leapt to life at Ericeira in 1584, when a hermit proclaimed himself to be the headstrong young monarch killed at Alcácer-Quivir in 1578. The impostor addressed himself as '*infeliz Sebastião*' (unhappy Sebastian), selected a queen, whom he crowned with a diadem pilfered from an image of the Virgin in a nearby church, and collected an 'army' of 1,000 peasants armed with pitchforks. He was hanged and quartered in 1585. It was from Ericeira that the royal family sailed into exile, on 5 October 1910.

The Praça da República is at the centre of town, surrounded by ugly cuboid houses. From there the Rua Dr Eduardo Burnay leads down to the stubby sand beach. A prettier and less crowded beach lies around a headland to the north, a 25-minute walk away. (Minibuses serve local beaches in summer.)

Where to Stay in Mafra and Around

Mafra

★★Hotel Castelão, Avenida 25 de Abril, t (261) 816 050, *www.hotelcastelao. com* (€€). Opposite the palace and not bad value, but nothing special. Its plush restaurant specializes in fish cooked with rice, but the bass is a delicious alternative.

ⓘ **Ericeira >**
Rua Dr Edouardo Burnay 33a, t (261) 863 122

Ericeira

★★★★Hotel Vila Galé, t (261) 860 200, *www.vilagale.pt* (€€€). This long-established hotel is owned by a nationwide chain. There are four swimming pools (two of which are for children). Bedrooms are decent and smell of the sea, with nice wide balconies. The impersonal **restaurant** offers a no-frills fixed-price dinner.

★★Hotel Pedro Pescador, Rua Dr Eduardo Burnay 22, t (261) 864 302, *hotel.pedro@teleweb.pt* (€€). The best rooms are on the top storey, overlooking rooftops, with brightly painted wood furniture. The regimented restaurant is laid for couples. *Open 1 May–9 Oct.*

Hotel Vilazul, Calcada da Baleia 10, t (261) 860 000, *www.hotelvilazul.com* (€€). Smart and comfortable hotel with a terrace commanding sweeping panoramic views.

Pensão Fortunato, Rua Dr Edouardo Burnay 7, t (261) 862 829, *www.pensaofortunato.com* (€). Decent, clean and colourless little place.

Eating Out in Mafra and Around

Mafra

Restaurante Primavera (€). Across the road from the palace, it serves decent food and rents decent rooms.

If you have a car, consider driving to the village of **Negrais**, famed for its roast suckling pig. There are several restaurants offering the speciality; drink the local bubbly with it.

Ericeira

Restaurante Poço, t (261) 860 000 (€€). Below Hotel Vilazul. Offers good food outside, amid trellis vines and sheltered by plastic covering. *Closed Wed.*

Toca do Caboz, Rua Fonte do Cabo (€€). Savour the *açorda de mariscos* which is particularly good here.

Mar da Areia, Rua Fonte do Cabo, t (261) 862 222 (€€). On the first floor of an ordinary house. Typical, with grilled fresh fish the speciality.

West of Lisbon

There are several places of interest lying within easy reach of Lisbon, including the Serra de Sintra, the Estoril coast and Cabo da Roca, the westernmost point in Europe.

The Serra de Sintra

Sintra

⭐ **Sintra**

On the eastern slope of the Serra de Sintra, 28km northwest of Lisbon, the town of Sintra and its 16,000 souls are swathed by teeming, rich green forests of pine, oak and fern. It makes an easy day trip from Lisbon; once here, walking is the only proper way to relish its woods.

Getting to and around Sintra

Frequent **trains** make the ¾hr trip to Sintra from Lisbon's Rossio station, via Queluz; local **buses** run from Mafra and Cascais (½hr).

Walking in Sintra is wonderful, if you don't mind hills. There is no walking map. If you're fit, you may reach the Moorish Castle in an hour – but rushing saps the enjoyment. From there, intrepid walkers could get to Pena in 45 minutes. Monserrate is a comfortable 40 minutes from the centre of town.

By **taxi**, expect to pay €20 per taxi for a one-hour return trip to one monument. To cover the Moorish Castle and the Pena Palace will take two hours and €50. A tour around the town and then to the Pena Palace by **horse carriage** will cost €90.

An occasional **bus** leaves the Praça da República to visit the Pena Palace, the Capuchos Convent and Cabo da Roca. Check with the tourist office for details.

Sintra has been discovered by goats, monks, and the British, who are particularly fond of it. The place has a peculiar magnetism: the Romans knew the Sintra range as Mons Lunae (the Hills of the Moon), and in the 16th century the Jeronymite monastery of N.S. da Penha was built to cover an entrance to the Underworld, so they say. In the summer months of the early years of the 15th century, Dom João I, his English bride and his court took up residence in the National Palace, at the centre of town. Subsequent kings followed his lead, until Dom Ferdinand built the Pena Palace, on a hilltop high above. This ravishing neogothic confection contrasts with a ruined Moorish castle on a nearby peak, floodlit at night, as if suspended in the sky.

Eerie sea mists seep into Sintra's mossy walls and cool the town in summer. Dogs howl across the hollows. Visitors have been inspired to hymn these wonders: in 1529 the Portuguese playwright Gil Vicente hailed Sintra as 'A garden of the earthly paradise / Sent here by Solomon'. Byron lauded it in the opening two stanzas of *Childe Harold*: 'Lo! Cintra's glorious Eden intervenes, / in variegated maze of mount and glen'. Its 'horrid crags' delighted him; later in 1809 he wrote to his mother from Gibraltar claiming the village of Sintra to be 'perhaps the most delightful in Europe … It unites in itself all the wildness of the Western Highlands with the verdure of the south of France' (neither of which he had visited). Even the Spaniards have a saying: 'To see the world and yet leave Sintra out / Is, verily, to go blindfold about.'

Above all, Sintra appeals to Romantics, and its July **music festival** has adopted a Romantic theme (concerts are performed in the palaces of Sintra – including Seteais – and Queluz). The only reason that visitors might not enjoy the place is that there are too many other people doing just that. In the Praça da República, tour buses are packed together like slices of bread. There's a good range of accommodation, but it usually fills by lunchtime in high season. The town is famous for its *queijadas*, pleasantly sweet cheese cupcakes wrapped in thin pastry. Their secret recipe is protected by two rivals, one of whom is the curate.

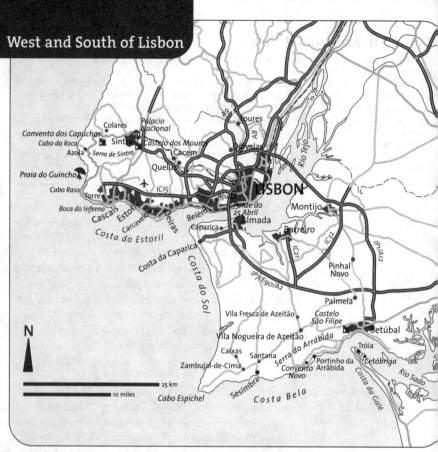

The National Palace

Sintra has grown up around the grey royal summer palace, an irregular assemblage topped with two conical chimneys. A **National Palace** has existed on this site since the reign of Dom Dinis. The core of what stands today was inhabited by Dom João I (1357–1433) and his English queen, Philippa of Lancaster; it hosted brilliant court balls and dancing and literary tournaments. Philip the Good, Duke of Burgundy, was received here in 1429, when he came to ask to marry the princess Dona Isabel. The duke brought his painter Jan van Eyck in train. When Dom João III took up residence, his courtiers' Latin, Greek and Hebrew conversations whispered around the palace. In the early 16th century, Dom Manuel made drastic alterations to everything except the proportions of the place. Dom Afonso VI had plenty of time to contemplate these. Childless, he resigned the government of the country in 1667 in favour of his brother Dom Pedro, to ensure the

National Palace
open 10–5.30; closed Wed and hols; adm

succession, and was subsequently incarcerated here for nine years, without a single lowlife, cockfighting friend to keep him company.

Extra buildings were added after the earthquake of 1755. The National Palace is still used for entertaining foreign dignitaries.

The muddled exterior indicates the palace's gradual evolution. The chimneys are like Kentish oast houses – bottles of champagne, said Hans Christian Andersen – as are the chimneys of various European monasteries. The distinguishing feature here is that there are two of them. The **kitchen** is the first room shown to visitors. Disappointingly bereft of bats, the chimneys would nevertheless accommodate several roasting wild boar.

The **Sala dos Árabes** follows, zigzagged with green, blue and white tin-glaze *mudéjar azulejos*, fabricated in Seville using the *corda sêca* technique and imported by Dom Manuel *c.* 1503, which makes them some of the oldest in the country.

Rooms with Painted Walls and Ceilings

The **chapel**'s rare tile carpet was probably executed by Moorish craftsmen in the 15th century. Painted doves flit every which way over the walls, representing the Holy Spirit and teasing Dom Afonso VI with their freedom; he died of an apopleptic stroke while hearing Mass from the side balcony, in 1683. Perhaps the late 15th-century Sevillian tile floor of his bedroom was worn away by pacing.

Dom Manuel shrewdly reinforced the nobility's novel perception of themselves as a court circle by ordering the coats of arms of 72 families to be painted on the ceiling of the **Sala dos Brasões**. Pombal erased the Távora escutcheon, having executed the marquis by breaking his bones for allegedly attempting to assassinate King Dom José I. The national arms of Portugal at the top is an 18th-century addition, incorporating the dragon crest of the Bragança dynasty, a motif mirrored in the high dado of 18th-century *azulejo* hunting scenes.

Formerly the royal audience chamber, the **Magpie Room** is one of the oldest rooms in the palace; each of the 136 ceiling triangles is painted with a magpie holding a rose in its claws, and clasping a scroll marked '*Por bem*' ('gladly' or 'willingly') in its beak: legend claims that Dom João I proffered a rose to a lady of the court when his wife wasn't looking. A magpie stole the rose, drawing attention to the infidelity. The king excused himself by saying '*Por bem*'. There is a more rational explanation: the bird sports the livery colours of the House of Avis – black, blue and white; and the rose could symbolize the House of Lancaster.

The larger and grander **Swan Room** is roofed with octagons of painted swans, each in a different position and each with a gold collar. They may commemorate a wedding present from Philip the Good, or may have been painted when Dona Isabel was to have married her cousin Henry V of England, whose mother's crest was a white swan. The boars' heads on the tables are soup tureens.

The **Archaeological Museum** of fragments in brightly lit cases is situated above the tourist office. The **Museu Ferreira de Castro**, a small museum of memorabilia donated by the writer Ferreira de Castro (1898–1974) may be fascinating to those familiar with his work. The rest should walk on by.

The Environs of Sintra

The Moorish Castle

The road leading westwards out of Sintra passes the **Estalagem dos Cavaleiros**, where Byron stayed in 1809, now boarded up and covered in graffiti, though knights still charge across the signpost. A sharp turning to the left leads to a leafy road, which climbs up to the Pena Palace. Travellers should turn left again to get to the

Moorish Castle
open daily, summer
10–6 and winter 10–5;
adm

Moorish Castle, whose fortifications run along the spine between two pinnacles (1,490ft/454m above sea level), within sight of the Pena Palace – and that was just the point. Finding the ruin too ruined for his Romantic taste, Dom Ferdinand II ordered the castle to be partially rebuilt. It hovers above Sintra, pelted with boulders which seem to be styrofoam, comprising five towers and a keep. The ruined Romanesque church within the enclosure may once have been a mosque. On a clear day, it's worth coming here for the views: southeast to Lisbon and the Serra da Arrábida, southwest to Cabo da Roca, and north to Peniche and the Berlenga islands. A steep path descends into town, emerging between the convento da Trindade and the church of Santa Maria.

The Pena Palace

Pena Palace
guided tours 10–5;
open until 6.30 in
summer; closed Mon;
adm

The zigzag road continues uphill to the **Pena Palace**, a fantastic hilltop confection, begun in 1840, which expresses Dom Ferdinand II's capricious Gothic longings. He and his cousins Albert and Leopold hailed from the obscure state of Saxe Coburg-Gotha. Each married the queen of an empire: Portugal, Britain and Belgium. If he produced a son, the Portuguese consort became king. Ferdinand complied – Dona Maria II had 11 children, the last of which killed her – and became the artist king, a philanthropist tall enough, so they said, to light his cigar from the gas lamps of Lisbon. Ferdinand commissioned Baron von Eschwege – whose statue stands in armour on a peak near the palace – to build it, 30 years before Ludwig of Bavaria let rip.

The exterior is a bonanza of crenellations, minarets, embellished windows and pillarbox turrets. A spreadeagled stone Triton supports a bay window, his legs becoming fishtails, his head sprouting tree roots, unconcerned that the palace's dome imitates that of the Jerónimos Monastery at Belém. It's difficult not to join the delighted children who make ghost noises beneath the portcullis. The best time to bring them here is during a thunderstorm, when the elements are lashing.

At the core of the palace stand the **cloister and chapel** of a 16th-century Jeronymite monastery, otherwise destroyed by the earthquake of 1755. The earthquake provided the patchwork of *azulejos* which wall the cloister. The chapel's superb alabaster retable depicts a variety of dramatic scenes centring on the dead Christ in the arms of angels. It was carved by Chanterène 1529–32, shortly after his work at Óbidos and before he moved to Évora, and resembles a piece of silverwork, tumultuous and delicate. The stained-glass windows are modern.

Visitors are shown through an interminable succession of rooms maintained – right down to the monarch's tooth mug – as they were when the royal family last resided here, in 1910. The frequence of the rose motif is explained by Dom Ferdinand's allegiance to the Rosicrucians, an offshoot of the Masons. Note the furniture designed by Eiffel in a boatlike reception room, the queen's silver hot-water bottle by her bedside, and the grass she stuck in her bed's headboard to dispel bad weather on Palm Sunday, 1910. Dom Ferdinand designed the china in the tea room, and made the engravings. Ceiling holes in the ballroom removed cigar smoke. A room decorated with canvases of naked ladies known to the king has recently been opened to the public – one of them is the queen, but nobody knows which. Be sure to see the kitchens, loaded with copper pans marked F.P.P., for Ferdinand Palácio da Pena, which are rather elaborate considering Dom Ferdinand's favourite foods were quince jam and chocolate.

The artless **grounds** form a splendid natural arboretum, filled with acacias, huge redwoods, and camellia trees. There are two valleys of those strangely prehistoric fern trees native to Australia and New Zealand, some of them 3m tall. The valleys are duplicated because when his queen died, Dom Ferdinand II took a mistress, a feisty German opera singer whom he created Condessa d'Edla. He bequeathed everything to her, rather than to his son, the king. This was intolerable, so the State confiscated her inheritance and fobbed her off with a chalet in the grounds of Pena, where she dabbled in her own garden.

The Convento dos Capuchos

The first left turning off the road descending from Pena leads 4km west of Sintra through the beautiful upper slopes of the Serra, near its peak at Peninha (1,600ft/490m), coming to a right-hand

Convento dos Capuchos
open daily, summer 10–7, winter 10–6; adm

turning to the **Convento dos Capuchos**. From 1560, 12 hermits lived in cork-lined cells hollowed from the mountain's rock, sheltered by bursting green vegetation, beneath the grandeur of the sky. With its pure light, the place has retained the force of their spirituality. Writing in 1726, Brockwell shrieked that the hermits were 'living by Theft, Rapine and Murder, of those unhappy Wretches, who are unfortunately Shipwreck'd on that Coast'.

Visitors are dwarfed by the surrounding granite boulders, and then made gigantic by the monks' cells, whose narrow doors are 1m high and insulated with weirdly insect-like cork bark.

Parque and Palácio de Monserrate

Parque and Palácio de Monserrate
t (21) 923 73 00, www.parquesde sintra.pt, high season 1 Apr–30 Sept; park open daily, 9.30–8, last entry 7; palace 10–1 and 2–6.30; adm

On the road to Colares 2km west of Sintra, a 40-minute walk from the centre of town, the **Palácio de Monserrate** is a bastard Moorish extravaganza well worth visiting. Flanked by round towers and roofed in rusty orange, the building was put up for London textile merchant Sir Francis Cook by James Knowles Sr. A thousand men worked on it daily 1858–63; at the end of their labours, Cook furnished it with 'contemporary' Indian furniture, and resided here in April and November. (William Beckford had sublet the Gothic house that previously stood on this site, 1794–1808, adding an English landscape garden – no doubt appetizing to the flock of sheep he had shipped in from Fonthill. In 1809 Byron dropped in, beginning the fashion for visiting the place.)

In the 1850s, the painter William Stockdale created a botanic garden. About a third of the plants came from Australasia, and many were from Mexico. Himalayan rhododendrons were planted here in 1860, just 10 years after they arrived at London's Kew Gardens. Parts of the garden were named after countries – Mexico, Australia, Japan – and parts after mythologies. In 1870 'Thomas of Ercildoune' published a dreadful 300-page poem about Monserrate: 'A blaze of Rhododendrons all around, / Flooding with colour all the enchanted ground'. By 1923 there were a thousand different species growing here. The site was sold to the Portuguese state in 1949 and neglected until an EU grant made possible the employ of three landscape architects and three gardeners. The place is now watched over by a private group called the Friends of Monserrate, **t** (21) 330 7100, whose members include many prominent expats and dignitaries and business owners.

Note that the gardens are on hill slopes, so be cautious if you find walking difficult. There's a picnic site behind the Visitors' Centre.

Quinta da Regaleira

Quinta da Regaleira
t (21) 910 6656, www.regaleira.pt; open Jan, Nov and Dec 10–5.30, Feb, Mar and Oct 10.30–6.30, Apr–Sept 10.30–7.30; adm

A few minutes' walk along the road to Monserrate, **Quinta da Regaleira** is a neo-Manueline mansion built in the early 20th century with grotto-filled gardens. It's a dull, kitsch place and not really worth the entrance fee. Especially avoid the interminable hundred-minute tour (*times vary throughout the year*) which costs €10, twice the entrance fee otherwise. The gardens are worth a wander, however.

Toy Museum

Toy Museum
Rua Visconde de Monserrate,
t *(21) 910 6016;*
open Tues–Sun 10–6;
adm

Toy museums can offer great insight into culture – as well as the shock of seeing the likes of one's own toys promoted to museum status. The substantial collection in the **Toy Museum** was in large part collected by João Arbués Moreira, and is housed in a former fire station. He wasn't too interested in animals or mechanicals, but there's a lot of good stuff. A shame then that the display is so squashed, and that extraordinary items like the toy Mercedes containing Hitler are rather lost in the throng. If you've never seen Barbie as an American Airlines Stewardess, now's your opportunity.

Museu de Arte Moderna

Museum of Modern Art
t *(21) 924 8179;*
open Tues–Sun 10–6;
adm

Splendidly housed in Sintra's magnificent former casino of 1924 in the Estefânia district beyond the railway station, the **Museum of Modern Art**, has at its core the collection assembled by financier José Berardo and Francisco Capelo. Their intention was to create an overview of art in the second half of the 20th century, using representative pieces. That makes it instructive, and although the pieces are not of the highest order it's extremely worthwhile. Much of the collection is kept in store at the Cultural Centre in Belém, Lisbon, and it rotates; also keep an eye on the temporary exhibitions. Regular guided tours 11am Thursday. The museum building, which was built in the 1920s, is next to Sintra's brand-new cultural centre, which regularly hosts shows by leading Portuguese and foreign performers.

Archaeological Museum

Archaeological Museum
open Tues–Fri 9–6;
closed Mon, Sat and Sun; adm

In the village of Odrinhas, 11km from Sintra, this little **Archaeological Museum** on the site of a Roman villa was inaugurated in 1955, but has a predecessor dating back to the 16th century. The museum houses bits of the villa's structure, a polychrome mosaic, an imposing Palaeo-Christian monument, the remains of a late-medieval necropolis, and the country's largest collection (*c.* 300) of Roman and Visigoth inscribed monoliths.

Tourist Information in Sintra

ⓘ **Sintra** ›
Main tourist office:
Praça da República 23,
t *(21) 923 1157*

The main **tourist office** is near the National Palace, with a smaller office in the railway station. From the **bus station** and **railway station**, follow the V-shaped Alameda de Volta do Duche into town.

Where to Stay in Sintra

Very Expensive–Expensive (€€€€–€€€)
★★★★★Hotel Palácio de Seteais, Rua de Barbosa Bocage 8 (1km west of Sintra on the road to Colares), **t** (21) 923 3200, *www.tivolipalaciosetais.com*. Delightfully grand and whimsical, this comprises twin blocks joined by a

triumphal arch, which were built in 1787 for a Dutch diplomat, and later purchased by the fifth Marquis of Marialva. 'Seteais' means 'seven sighs', which commemorates the Portuguese reaction to the lenient terms imposed on the French by the Convention of Sintra, which was signed here by Wellington in 1808. The furniture combines antiques with good reproductions, set among the murals of the main drawing room, the music room and the card room. Bedrooms number 2, 3 and 4 are also hand-painted. Grandfather clocks chime in the corridors, rivalling the springtime nightingales that sing in trees around the topiary at the rear of the building, which overlooks plains to the sea. Weekends are pretty solidly booked with honeymooners. However, parts of the hotel are teetering on the edge of being tatty; the place needs an injection of cash. And the service is not top-notch. Casual visitors are not encouraged. Go for tea or a cocktail. The restaurant is elegant but overpriced, serving rather disappointing food.

Expensive (€€€)

*****Lawrence's Hotel, Rua Consigliéri Pedroso, 38–40, Vila de Sintra, t (21) 910 5500, lawrences_hotel@iol.pt. Lawrence's opened in or around 1764, and therefore claims to be the oldest hotel in the Iberian Peninsula. Lord Byron stayed here in 1809. More recently the place fell into ruin until purchased and restored by a Dutch couple, who re-opened it in 1999. The décor is what might be called 'charming': rather floral and English, but tasteful throughout, and the place feels relatively homey. Avoid the rooms on the roadside – there's too much traffic, and it's too close. The classically elegant little restaurant (open 12.30–2.30 and 7.30–9.45) is excellent, and well worth a visit in its own right. The food is nouvelle and international, using local ingredients.

****Hotel Tivoli Sintra, Praça da República, t (21) 923 7200 (off the main square). Very comfortable and efficient modern hotel whose covered balconies offer lovely views of the wooded hillslope opposite. The staff are helpful and punctual. The good restaurant lacks atmosphere, and the waiters hover, but try the delicate marinated swordfish appetizer and you'll forgive anything.

Moderate (€€)

***Residencial Sintra, Travessa dos Avelares 12, t (21) 923 0738. Between Sintra and São Pedro, a big old place with lumpy beds and gas heating, run by a multi-lingual German. It could get spooky in winter.

Pensão Nova Sintra, Largo Afonso de Albuquerque 25, t (21) 923 0220, www.novasintra.com. A carefully tended pensão that feels more like an estalagem. Rooms are spick and span, but pricey for what you get. The huge terrace offers good views of the Moorish castle.

Inexpensive (€)

**Casa de Hospedes Adelaide, Avenida Guilherme Gomes Fernandes 11, t (21) 923 0873. Downhill from the building with the Gothic tower, towards the railway station. Managed by a very affable ex-commandant of police, it's homey, and some rooms have good views.

Casa Miradouro, Rua Sotto Mayor 55, t (219) 235 900, www.casa-mira douro.com. Stylish house thanks to the charming Swiss owner, with antiques, wrought-iron bedsteads and magnificent rooms.

Pensão Económica, Pátio Olivença, Avenida Heliodoro Salgado 6, t (21) 923 0229. A nice place in spite of the pre-fab feel, and a good option if your budget is limited.

Monte da Lua, t (21) 924 1029. Opposite the train station is one of the best-value and friendliest hotels in the town, with some good views from the rooms at the back.

Turismo de Habitação

Quinta da Capela, Estrada de Monserrate, t (21) 929 0170 (€€€). Further along the road to Colares, this was built by the Duc de Cadaval in the 16th century. Behind the weathered, time-tested farmhouse exterior lies a surprisingly elegant and gracious interior, with carefully

★ Quinta da Capela >>

chosen, simple furniture and cool colours. The owner is not resident, so the house lacks knick-knacks. Breakfast is the only meal available in the marble dining room, but a kitchen is provided for guests' use. There is a basement sauna and fitness room, at extra cost. The peaceful walled garden overlooks Monserrate to Pena beyond it. A chapel within the grounds is lined with biblical *azulejos*; other out-buildings have been converted into two self-catering guest cottages, one accommodating three people and the other four.

★ **Quinta de São Thiago** >

Quinta de São Thiago, Estrada de Monserrate, t (21) 923 2923 (€€). A couple of kilometres west of Sintra, a turning off the road to Colares leads down a long, very steep, bumpy road to a whitewashed, early 16th-century villa surrounded by trees, made splendid and cosy by an English family. Much of the furniture is antique, with vases of flowers, hunting prints, worked leather chairs, silver-framed family photos, and collections of banister knobs and Madonnas. Candelabra branch on the breakfast table. There are 10 double guestrooms, whose occupants may use the swimming pool and tennis court. Meals will be provided on request, for a minimum of six people.

Quinta das Sequóias, Estrada de Monserrate, t (21) 923 0342 or 924 3821, *www.quintadasequoias.com* (€€). On the road to Colares stands this less pricey converted manor house which nestles in the hills, with great views over Pena Palace and the coast. The large dining room was once the kitchen, complete with wooden oven. The tasteful rooms are quietly understated.

Eating Out in Sintra

Expensive (€€€)

Most of the fancy restaurants are in São Pedro, a couple of kilometres south of Sintra.

Solar S. Pedro, Praça D. Fernando II 12, t (21) 923 1860. French restaurant with smoochy music and red light. Steaks are a speciality. Waiters are numerous but not urgent, and the kitchen is open to view. *Closed Wed.*

Orixás, Avenida Adriano Júlio Coelho 7, t (21) 923 3505. For excellent Brazilian food in exotic surroundings (and live music at the weekend), near the Modern Art Museum.

Moderate (€€)

Cantinho de S. Pedro, Praça Dom Fernando II 18, t (21) 923 0267. This rustic establishment is one of the best, with bare brick walls, hanging plants and good French food. The fillets of sole with Gruyère sauce are very good. *Closed Mon, Thurs evenings, and Sept.*

Restaurante Regional, Travessa do Municipio 2, next to the Town Hall, t (21) 923 4444, *www.restaurante-regional-sintra.pt.* Cheerful atmosphere, mainly attributable to the bright-eyed waiters. There is an open kitchen, so you can be entertained by the chef's dramas. The regional food section on the menu is worth a try.

Caffee Hockell, Praça da República 12–14, t (21) 923 5710. Good pasta, pizza and salads in the square in front of the tourist office. There's a smart black-and-white interior, but most people prefer to eat outside.

Tulhas, t (21) 923 2378. Down the street to the right of the tourist office. This friendly place is a good bet – the inexpensive fish dishes are especially good; the delicious *bacalhau com natas* is a good introduction to Portugal's favourite fish, as it's disguised with cream and nutmeg. *Closed Wed.*

Café Paris, Praça da República 32, t (21) 923 2375. Prices are prominently displayed, possibly because clients complain they've been overcharged. Be warned.

Tacho Real, Rua da Ferraria 4, Vila Velha, t (21) 923 5277. Elegant and rather smarter than its clientele. The interior is full of character, better suited to dinner than lunch, and the menu is French/Portuguese. Try the veal. Books are available for children, which is a nice touch. *Closed Wed.*

Inexpensive (€)

Restaurant Alcobaça, Rua das Padarias 7, 9 and 11, t (21) 923 1651. A little way up a popular alley, Restaurant Alcobaça offers a good daily menu for €10, making it more popular than the staff are able to cope with.

Adega das Caves, Rua da Pendoa 2–10, **t** (21) 9230 848. Cosy, bistro-style, tourist-friendly.

Xentra, Rua Consiglieri Pedroso 2A, **t** (21) 9241 759. Occupies a carefully lit stone-walled basement just up from the tourist office. Snacks are available as well as more substantial fare (until 10pm), and there's a nice bar (until 2am). It's a relief to find somewhere in this part of Sintra that's unapologetically modern.

Around Sintra

Cabo da Roca

The westernmost point of Europe focuses the mind on the horizon. Every year more than 70,000 tourists come to this rugged and spectacular place 16km west of Sintra, where no plant grows over 4in (10cm) tall. Some of these visitors are North Americans pining for home. Others are Europeans trying to get away from it. Many pay for certificates to say they've been here. There are several beautiful beaches in coves just north of Cabo da Roca, such as **Adraga** and **Ursa**, both within (long) hiking distance of the bus route between Cascais and Sintra.

Colares

A very beautiful avenue threads its way through lush and leafy land west of Sintra, arriving 6km later at the village of Colares. Picturesquely sited on a spur of the Serra, it's a quiet place decked with purple camellias, revelling in pines, cypresses and chestnut trees. It was here that the Romans worshipped the sun and moon. The village square is lined with 17th- and 18th-century houses. Be warned that driving through Colares' narrow and steep streets could age even the most fearless a good few years.

Downhill, in Varzea de Colares, the main road curves off to the right across a stream; follow it and you'll end up at **Praia das Maças** and **Praia Grande**, two lovely open beaches served by a plethora of good fish restaurants.

Guincho

Rolling Atlantic waves crash against Guincho's two gently sloping sand bays; international windsurfing championships are held here, 9km south of Cabo do Roca and 10km north of Cascais. Free of pollution, inaccessible by public transport, and overlooked by just two buildings, both hotels, Guincho is a welcome relief from the rest of the Estoril coast farther south. The problem is that the undertow is extremely treacherous, strong enough to drown even the most confident swimmers.

Getting to areas Around Sintra

Direct local **buses** run to Cabo da Roca from Cascais. From Sintra, take a bus heading for Cascais, from in front of the railway station – a pretty ride past windmills and *quintas*. Get off at Azoia and walk the 4km.

Where to Stay and Eat Around Sintra

Cabo da Roca

Moinho Dom Quixote, Estrada do Cabo da Roca, **t** (21) 929 2523 (€€). One of the most spectacularly sited bars/restaurants in this part of Portugal, down a lane to the left after you turn off the main road towards Cabo da Roca. Interlinked esplanades decorated with *azulejos* command views of the hills and the Atlantic coast. On winter days the old windmill makes for a cosy haven. Mexican food and the Brazilian *caipirinhas* (a rum-lime concoction) are the specialities. *Open daily noon to 2am*.

Colares

★★★**Motel das Arribas**, Praia Grande, **t** (21) 929 2145 (€€). This motel is perfectly respectable and very clean.

Casa do Celiero, Pe da Serra, **t** (21) 928 0151, *www.portugalpainting.com* (€€). This rambling farmhouse just outside Colares is English owned and has spacious gardens, a swimming pool and nearby hiking trails. There is also a self-contained cottage to rent. It is a popular venue for painting holidays.

Guincho

★★★★★**Fortaleza do Guincho**, **t** (21) 487 0491, *www.guinchotel.pt* (€€€). Built on the site of a 17th-century fortress, with a bricked-up well in the glassed courtyard, brick ceilings in the halls, and a wide stone staircase. Crested tureens ornament the baronial dining room, and the living room is welcoming, with an excellent view of the Atlantic. There's something daunting about the bedrooms, but, guests may hide under very fine bed linen.

★★★★★**Estalagem Muchaxo**, **t** (21) 487 0221, *www.muchaxo.com* (€€). Just across the jagged rock outcrop, the low-key but very expensive restaurant here serves superb seafood – particularly the shrimps, the grilled bass, and the *caldeirada*. Leave room for dessert. With its beach views, the restaurant is decorated like a grotto: chunks of treetrunks, boughs and branches embellish walls of rough stone-chippings. The *estalagem* itself is ornamented in the same style.

The Estoril Coast

From Lisbon to Cascais, the south-facing coast has been been glutted by suburban sprawl, and developed as a series of resorts, though now the settlements virtually merge into one another. In summer, the sand beaches are packed with gasping Lisboêtas and basking tourists.

Estoril

Three km east of Cascais and 26km west of Lisbon, Estoril is marketed as the seaside haunt of fading European aristocrats, who oil themselves on the fine sand beach and enjoy one another to the sound of silver cocktail shakers. Anyone wishing to observe this species will be disappointed; if they are here at all, their villas are patrolled by Alsatians which froth behind flimsy fences, tormented by small boys.

Getting to the Estoril Coast

Part of the reason for the popularity of the Estoril coast is the excellent public transport link with Lisbon: electric **trains** depart from the Cais do Sodre approximately every 10 minutes, stopping at stations including Oeiras, Estoril, and usually Monte Estoril, en route for Cascais, ½hr away.

Estoril is a soulless place arrayed around a casino and its gaudy garden, which leads to the crowded beach now almost too polluted to swim at. The garden is dotted with date palms, and enshrines a bust of Fausto Figueiredo, 'patron saint' of Estoril, who founded the casino and brought the railway.

Estoril has assimilated Monte Estoril, located slightly to the west. Monte Estoril was the first resort to be developed on this coastline, and it has its own railway station. There are no real 'sights' of interest in Estoril, and most of the good restaurants and boutiques are to be found in Cascais (*see* p.318), which is a couple of kilometres along the coast to the west. If you have plenty of money, however, Estoril offers some appealing accommodation (*see* p.315).

ⓘ **Estoril >**
at coastal end of public garden, Arcadas do Parque,
t *(21) 466 3813*

Tourist Information in Estoril

Estoril's **tourist office** is at the coastal end of the public garden, Arcadas do Parque. The **train station** is on the beach front.

Golf

With its mild climate, the Estoril coast has long been popular for winter golf. The golf courses are now being supplemented by a variety of other facilities.

Estoril Golf Club, Avenida da República, **t** (21) 468 0176, *www.golfe.de*. One km inland from Estoril, this long-established club offers 27 holes designed by McKenzie Ross, dividing into a par-69 18-hole course – with good variety, excellent greens, and improved tees – and a 9-hole course for beginners. The longer course is fairly short and narrow, but sporty; prospective players must produce evidence of an official handicap, and it's members-only at weekends; the 9-hole course is always open to non-members. The 9th hole is played over a road. The walk uphill to the 16th is fairly strenuous, and no electric carts are available, so if you prefer to take it easy, you could play the flat 10 holes

and then 8 holes of the beginners' course. Canaries fly around the clubhouse's relaxed reception area, which leads to the trophy-lined sitting room. Meals are available, as are a small swimming pool, changing rooms, caddies, clubs for hire and overnight storage for clubs. Daily rates are available, or visitors can join for five weekdays.

Estoril Sol Golf Course, Estrada da Lagoa Azul, Linhó, **t** (21) 924 0331. A further 5km inland, this par-31 course is prettier. Clubs and trolleys can be hired; squash courts.

Tennis and Multi-activity

Cascais Country Club, Quinta da Bicuda, Torre, **t** (21) 486 9301 (4km west of Cascais). A private tennis club, surrounded by pine woods, geared up to residents or long-term visitors. Half the six clay courts are floodlit. Members have access to a pretty horseshoe-shaped pool, changing rooms with showers, a restaurant and bar, tennis coaching, and an osteopath. Family membership includes children under 21, and is available for 1 month or 6 months.

Clube de Ténis do Estoril, Avenida Conde de Barcelona, **t** (21) 466 2770. Just off the Lisbon–Cascais motorway, it has 14 clay courts and four fast ones, almost all with lighting. There's also a swimming pool and a sauna. Make the most of weekdays here; it's extremely busy at weekends.

Centro Hípico de Bicuda, Quinta da Bicuda, Torre, **t** (21) 484 3233. Three km west of Cascais is an ivy-clad farmhouse whose outbuildings have been converted into six basic little self-catering apartments, including one in the dove cote. Don't expect great style: the appeal of the place lies in the small swimming pool and quiet garden. The *quinta* incorporates a riding school, which is particularly suitable for children. Meals are served at the poolside bar or in the attractive restaurant (€€).

Quinta da Marinha, **t** (21) 486 9084, *www.quintadamarinha.com*. Five km west of Cascais, 1km inland from the coast road. Attractive and sensibly designed, this provides facilities for horse-riding, tennis and swimming as well as golf, so non-golfers and children can enjoy themselves too. The layout is compact, though the 200 horse stables and small race track are about 1km away. Three of the six tennis courts are floodlit. Guests stay in wood-and-stone villas tastefully decorated in soft colours. You may find duck on your menu in the restaurant (€€€€): know that it will be fresh, as the *quinta* runs a thriving duck farm. Robert Trent Jones designed the *quinta*'s long par-71 course several years ago; the greens are very good but the fairways are not. It's a beautiful course, though, and the 14th is played over a ravine. A halfway house is available for snacks, separate from the amicable clubhouse, and there are guards to hurry along dawdlers. Players must bring a handicap certificate. There are only six electric carts. Green fees for members rise at weekends; non-members pay 50% extra. Clubs can be rented.

Where to Stay in Estoril

Very Expensive (€€€€)
★★★★★**Palácio Estoril Hotel & Golf**, Parque do Estoril, **t** (21) 468 0400, *www.palacioestorilhotel.com*. Grand and elegant, backing onto the Estoril Park, the Palácio was purpose-built in 1930; once gilt with ex-monarchs, the hotel no longer feels exclusive. Public rooms are gracious, human, and light, flanked by tall arched windows opening onto the lawn and thermally heated swimming pool. A cosy piano bar overflows into the marble chequered hall, where bikinis rub shoulders with silk bodices. Two hundred bedrooms and suites are furnished with attractive reproduction furniture, and pampered by 24-hour room service, but only the duplex suites are air-conditioned. A poolside buffet operates in summer, while the dining-room menu includes club sandwiches or stewed quails with dried fruit. Room rates include free golf at the Estoril Golf Club, and there are six tennis courts beside the hotel, half of them floodlit. With an independent entrance, the hotel's restaurant is excellent (*see* p.316).

Expensive (€€€)
★★★★★**Hotel Inglaterra**, Rua do Porto 1, **t** (214) 684 461, *www.hotelinglaterra.com*. A sumptuous early 20th-century building houses this recently revamped hotel. It has large, comfortable and stylish rooms, several terraces with sink-into wicker chairs and a large landscaped swimming pool area.

★★★★**Hotel Atlântico**, Estrada Marginal 7–7A, **t** (21) 468 0270, *hotel.atlantico@mail.telepac.pt*. On the coast just east of Monte Estoril railway station, the Atlântico overlooks the sea, but is separated from it by a railway line and the hotel's swimming pool. The decent rooms are decorated on a nautical theme; guests read the *Daily Star*, prefer to eat Mixed Grill Americaine, and drink a lot of tea, slowly.

★★★★**Apart-Hotel Estoril Eden**, Avenida Sabóia, **t** (21) 466 7600, *www.hotelestorileden.pt*. Next to Monte Estoril railway station. Attractive and new, it is mostly comprised of studio-suites, with Habitat-style furniture, and beds that pull down from the wall. A chic clientele frequents the disco-bar and the swimming pools, and the small supermarket. The sea view is lovely, but noisy should you open a balcony door.

****Amazónia Lennox Estoril, Rua Eng. Álvaro Pedro de Sousa 5, **t** (21) 468 0424, *www.amazoniahoteis.com*. Parallel with the casino, two blocks towards Cascais, is a comfortable, pleasantly furnished hotel, offering small, homey guestrooms named after golf courses, an obliging staff, and a friendly atmosphere fostered by the free coffee and afternoon tea. The restaurant serves roast beef and Yorkshire pudding. Guests receive a discount at Quinta da Marinha golf course.

Moderate (€€)

***Hotel Alvorada, Rua de Lisboa 3, **t** (21) 468 0070, *www.hotelalvorada-estoril.com*. Opposite the casino. Competent but overpriced, functional but drab, with a roof terrace. The door locks are confusing, so check twice that your room is secure.

***Hotel Lido, Rua do Alentejo 12, **t** (21) 468 4098, *www.hotellido.pt*. Three blocks west of the casino and uphill. Pleasant, ordinary, and equipped with a swimming pool, though the restaurant's menu is small and unimaginative. The winter rates are particularly good.

Inexpensive (€)

***Pensão Continental, Rua Joaquim Santos 2, **t** (21) 468 0050. At the inland end of the grid of streets to the east of the park. Funky, and offers high ceilings with mouldings, and sanatorium-style bathrooms.

Residencial Parsi, Rua Alfonso Sanchez 8, **t** (21) 484 5744. Scruffy but reasonably clean, and the cheapest option in town.

Orbitur campsite, **t** (21) 487 0450. In Areia, 6km away behind the Praia do Guincho 'beach'.

Eating Out in Estoril

Expensive (€€€)

Four Seasons Restaurant-Grill, Palácio Estoril Hotel & Golf, Parque do Estoril, **t** (21) 468 0400. Rich, heavy and intimate. Many dishes are prepared at the tableside – the beefsteak *Palácio* leaps to life amid brandy flames, with onions, parsley, and a red wine sauce. Menus, uniforms, linen, china and glasses are changed with the seasons. *Reservations recommended*.

Mandarin, in the Estoril Casino, **t** (21) 466 7270. Has a view of the fountains in the garden, is decorated with a calming elegance and is believed by many to be the finest Chinese restaurant in the region. It's undoubtedly the most expensive around. The divine *dim sum* are an option for those watching their wallet, but even then one can easily get carried away.

The English Bar, Estrada Marginal, **t** (21) 468 0413. Next to Monte Estoril railway station. Don't shy away from the name: it serves very good food, particularly seafood, in sober, wooden surroundings, with pewter ornaments and leather chairs and menus. The waiters know their job well. Sea or stone bass are available; the meat dishes range widely, from *bœuf bourguignon* to shish kebab. Note that this restaurant is also (and confusingly) known as Cimas.

La Villa, Praia do Tamariz, **t** (21) 468 0033. Arguably the best restaurant in town, enjoying an ace location on the seafront. Serves up delicious and unusual seafood dishes, such as cod with coriander in a Spanish gazpacho-style sauce.

Moderate (€€)

Frolic, Avenida Clotilde, **t** (21) 468 1219. Overlooking the Estoril Garden, by the Palácio Estoril Hotel & Golf, the pink and white marble interior, with wicker chairs and a mirrored bar, make this café a suitable place to eat a doughnut, a soufflé, or a Godiva golfball.

Entertainment and Nightlife in Estoril

The cavernous **casino** complex, *www.casino-estoril.pt*, is supposed to be the lifeblood of Estoril, but the lobby is the only part worth checking out, as it's an important venue for exhibiting contemporary Portuguese art, and regularly hosts midweek free concerts by big Portuguese names. At 10.15pm diners in the giant restaurant (€€€) swallow the last grilled medallion of black grouper, banks of lights dim, ferns are spotlit on the black walls, and a husky voice introduces a troupe of three strolling musicians, who palpitate the ladies and issue red roses. After 45 minutes, ballet and acrobatics take the stage. It is possible to watch the floorshow without buying dinner, at a price. In the gaming rooms, communication is by taps and gestures; zones of the baccarat tables are labelled in Japanese – but not on behalf of the international clientele. The Portuguese generate 90% of the business. Many of them wear glasses, and smoke cigarettes which burn faster in the strong air conditioning. The dice game of French bank is popular, as well as roulette amd blackjack. Humourless croupiers dispense their kind of drug. Around 250 slot machines fill a separate room. There is a small cover charge.

Forte Velho, Estrada Marginal, t (21) 468 1337. On the edge of Estoril towards Lisbon is a 17th-century castle, but you wouldn't know that from the dark and smoochy interior, where the music hots up at midnight. *Open 10pm–3.30am.*

Oeiras

In the mid-18th century, people mumbled that the road running 17km west of Lisbon, to Oeiras, was the only decent thoroughfare in the country – because Pombal passed along it to get to his country *quinta*; the omnipotent minister was Count of Oeiras before being dubbed Marquis of Pombal. More recently, the village has been inundated by the Lisbon sprawl.

Pombal's Palace stands just inland of the railway bridge, and now serves as an overflow for the Gulbenkian Foundation; visitors may wander around the garden. The building's design is attributed to the Hungarian architect Carlos Mardel, who clearly built to last: the palace was spared by the 1755 earthquake, which the king considered providential. Without a hint of irony, the plain façade is ornamented with a dozen Carrera marble busts of Roman emperors. Excellent profane and allegorical *azulejos* ornament various minor façades, terraces and staircases.

On a rock jetty facing south, the very well preserved 16th-century **fort of S. Julião da Barra** was designed in the Italian style by Leonardo Torreano, in a broad V-shape with wide esplanades, constructed over almost a century from 1556. Showing no qualms about implementing his policies in his own back yard, Pombal incarcerated 124 Jesuits here in 1759 (45 survived), beginning the fort's long service as a prison. It now provides temporary accommodation to military VIPs.

The circular **Bugio Fort** was built 1586–*c*. 1640 on an islet 2.5km off-shore, to protect the mouth of the Tagus.

Cascais

Cascais is a fishing village turned commuter settlement and sophisticated resort, arranged around three small bays with sand beaches backed by rocks, 1km west of Monte Estoril, shielded from northerly winds by the Serra de Sintra. The mix works very well: in the Rua Frederico Arouca, calloused fishermen squelch past Charles Jourdan shoe shops. Cascais is still incredibly unspoiled given its proximity to the capital and the ease of travel. Even at the height of summer there's still room to roll over on the beaches. They're about as crowded as Estoril's, but they are supposedly less polluted. If you do swim, keep your head above water. There is a shortage of inexpensive accommodation.

The **church of N.S. da Assunção** stands in a leafy square towards the western edge of town. Its nave is lined with shadowy paintings by Josefa de Óbidos, while busy *azulejos* dated 1748 depict a conference in the clouds. José Malhoa painted the ceiling. The coast road continues westwards past the **Museum of the Counts of Castro Guimarães** which occupies the late 19th-century home of a family who died heirless in 1927. It retains enough furniture to keep its dignity, but lacks those personal effects which might invade someone's privacy. There is a good portrait by Columbano among the silver ewers and samovars, Indo-Portuguese embroidered shawls, and an early 18th-century Indo-Portuguese chest with legs carved like fetishes. A George O'Neil once lived here, which would explain the ceiling decorated with three-leaf clovers. Wide sandy paths wind around the house's garden, which is planted with small-leafed trees and called the **Parque do Marechal Cermona**.

Museum of the Counts of Castro Guimarães
t (21) 482 5407; open winter 11–5, summer 10–6; closed Mon; adm

The fishermen's daily catch is auctioned at the **fish market** (between the Praia da Ribeira and the Praia da Rainha beaches, beside a landbound anchor positioned like a great bow about to launch its arrow). From 5 or 6pm, when the fishermen return, the auctioneer starts high and reduces the price of each plastic crate of fish until a bidder grunts loud enough to stop him.

Just west of Cascais, the sea has pounded its way up through a cliff to make a hole known as **Boca do Inferno** (Hell's Mouth).

Bookshop in Cascais

There's a good bookshop with a decent stock of French and English books plus a pile of old *National Geographic*s near the train station: **Livraria Galileu**, Avenida Valbom 24A, t (21) 486 6014.

(★) **Hotel Albatroz >>**

Where to Stay in Cascais

★★★★★**Hotel Albatroz**, Rua Frederico Arouca 100, t (21) 484 7380, *www.albatrozhotels.com* (€€€€€). Sited on a rocky promontory which rises above two popular beaches, this is the country's most elegant seaside

(i) Cascais >
*Rua Visconde da Luz
14, t (21) 486 8204,
www.estorilsintra.com;
open 15 July–15 Sept
9–8, rest of year 9–7*

hotel and a real treat. It incorporates a 19th-century ducal palace, with fabulous views of the lively Cascais harbour and the coastline stretching east towards Lisbon. The oval swimming pool and sun terrace overlook the ocean, backed by 37 guest rooms and their balconies. (If you want a toilet with a view, choose room 101.) The interior decoration is warm and tasteful without being fussy. A covered terrace juts out from the nautical bar, like the prow of a boat. The marble and wood restaurant, sided with picture windows overlooking the coastline, serves very good, and occasionally inventive, food: fish may be served with a turnip sauce, or lamb with walnuts. If you're not able to stay overnight, at least drink a bottle of wine on the terrace at sunset. Reservations recommended. The hotel also owns a villa nearby (*see below*).

★★★★★**Estalagem de Farol Design Hotel**, Avenida Rei Humberto II de Itália 7, t (21) 4823 490, *www.faroldesignhotel.arth-hotels.com* (€€€€€). On a rocky promontory on the edge of town near the lighthouse is an extraordinary place where design rules. Everything in the lobby is black, white or red and such folly as to be fun. Bedrooms are more obviously appealing, going for a clean, loft look with wooden floors, lots of texture and muted colour. Baths provide hydro-massage, if you weary of the pool. There's a buffet brunch on the first and third Sunday of each month, but the food is unexceptional.

★★★★★**Villa Albatroz**, Rua Fernandes Tomás 1, t (21) 4863 410, *www.albatroz hotels.com* (€€€€). Overlooking the esplanade and beachfront. Prices are almost as high as the hotel, but try as it might it can't be as nice, and the trying gives it a slightly pretentious feel.

★★★★★**Hotel Cascais Miragem**, Av. Marginal 8554, t (21) 006 0600, *www.cascaismirage.com* (€€€€). The newest and splashiest hotel in town. Overlooking the sea, each floor is distinctly designed with an exciting colour scheme and décor. Infinity pool and free shuttle into town are appealing extras.

★★★★**Vila Galé Village Cascais**, Rua Frei Nicolau de Oliveira-Parque da Gandarinha, t (21) 790 7610, *www.vilagale.pt* (€€€€). Big resort-style hotel complex with circular pools, indifferent service and the noise of the coast road. Rooms have a kitchenette behind a curtain.

★★★**Hotel Baía**, Avenida Marginal, t (21) 483 1033, *www.hotelbaia.com* (€€€). Very well positioned overlooking the bay and its fishermen, this provides practical, no-nonsense bedrooms with balconies and a summertime bar on the roof. Corridors are linoleum, elevators unpredictable, and the staff rather serious. The restaurant offers 'monk on the spit'.

★★★**Residencial Solar de Dom Carlos**, Rua Latino Coelho 8, t (21) 482 8115, *www.solardomcarlos.com* (€€). King Dom Carlos's summer palace has fallen on hard times: rooms here are bright and sparse rather than grand. Slivers of cherubs may flake from the murals onto your bread roll at breakfast.

Turismo de Habitação
Casa da Pérgola, Avenida Valbom 13, t (21) 484 0040, *www.pergola house.com* (€€). Located off the seaward roundabout, this spruce, elegant, colourful and welcoming, late 19th-century *casa* offers a white marble hall and 12 rooms furnished with antique and reproduction Portuguese furniture (heavy, but not oppressively so) and paintings of saints. Garage parking is available.

Eating Out in Cascais

You won't be short of somewhere to eat: there are some 25 restaurants in the shopping centre next to the railway station. There are also a number of restaurants and bars at the marina, which has a permanent feel of loafers, expensive sunglasses and brunch.

O Retiro João Padeiro, Rua Visconde da Luz 12, t (21) 483 0232 (€€€). In the town centre, on the main street at right angles to the waterfront, it feels seasoned by time: floors are dragon's-tooth, chairs are leather, and leather panels line the walls. Confident in its specialities of shellfish and fried sole, the restaurant offers veal and pork as the only concessions to meat eaters; the fish tends to be undercooked, though. The efficient waiters can spot a large tipper before he or she sits down.

O Pescador, Rua das Flores 10-B, **t** (21) 483 2054, *www.restaurante pescador.com* (€€€). Stands out among several restaurants behind the fish market. Prickly brown blowfish and strings of garlic overhang tables where courteous waiters serve paella and good sole, the house specialities.

Chequers, Largo Luis de Camões 6, **t** (21) 483 0926 (€€€). Painted red, green and pink, behind restaurant João Padeiro. Serves good steaks. The ground-floor bar is decorated with film stars and is a nice place for a beer.

Furnas do Guincho, Estrada da Guincho, **t** (21) 869 243 (€€€). Located about 1km out of town on the road to Guincho, this superb and elegant seafood restaurant has appropriate ocean views.

Jardim Visconde da Luz, **t** (21) 484 7410 (€€). They take seafood seriously at smart green Visconde da Luz, in the garden of the same name, and the service is good. Fish and shellfish are priced by the kilo. *Closed Tues*.

Restaurante Bangkok, Rua da Belavista 6, **t** (21) 484 7600 (€€). Run by a long-time resident of the Portuguese colony Macau, this town house has been turned into a veritable Thai palace, full of nooks for romantic dining. It has fantastic food, superbly presented, and excellent service.

Sawasdee, Beco Esconso, **t** (21) 484 7967 (€€). Up an alley from the Largo Camões, Sawasdee is a nicely appointed Thai restaurant; the Thai chefs and careful Thai staff give it a welcome ring of authenticity. It's not a lunchtime place – go for dinner. There's live music Thurs–Sat.

Bar Esplanada Santa Marta, Avenida Rei Humberto II de Itália, **t** (21) 482 1986 (€€). A shack at the edge of the marina. You can eat fresh fish outdoors under cover overlooking a tiny beach. *Open until 10pm. Closed Mon*.

Jardim dos Frangos, Av. Com. da Grande Guerra 66 (€). The tall chimney sends up smoke signals from a host of chickens being grilled simply and deliciously. Finger-licking good, though the flies are a bit of a nightmare if you sit outside.

D. Pedro I, Beco dos Inválidos 4, **t** (21) 483 3734 (€). Up a flight of stairs next to the fire station. The house wine is rough, the food solid, especially the ribs. The clientele varies from old men and their crumbs to Portuguese families on holiday.

Nightclub

Coconuts, Avenida Rei Humberto II de Itália 7, **t** (21) 484 4109, *www.nuts-club.com*. On the western edge of town, Coconuts bar is a nightlife institution.

Queluz

Five km northwest of Lisbon, off the road to Sintra, and 12km northeast of Oeiras, the nondescript market town of Queluz is buoyed by Portugal's most elegant royal palace. This charming rococo summer retreat, a sort of intimate Versailles, was built 1758–94; although the garden façade and the garden staircase are the only features of especial architectural interest, the palace gives a lucid insight into the diversions of aristocratic life in the late 18th century.

Getting to Queluz

Queluz is a mere ¼hr **train** ride from Lisbon's Rossio station, or ½hr from Sintra in the opposite direction. From the **railway station**, walk downhill to the arches. Cross the road and continue (almost) straight, until you see the palace. The entrance is to the left.

History

The town takes its name from the Arabic 'Qu'al-Luz' (valley of the almond tree). The palace began life as a small hunting lodge set in rolling parkland, which was granted to the second son of successive monarchs in 1654. In 1747 Prince Dom Pedro, second son of Dom João V, ordered Queluz to be converted into a summer residence (there are still no chimneys). Barracks intended for the Royal Guard were constructed opposite.

Two architects worked on the core of the palace. Mateus Vicente de Oliveira was succeeded by Jean-Baptiste Robillon, a disciple of the French goldsmith Thomas Germain, when Prince Dom Pedro married his niece, the future Queen Dona Maria I. She was incarcerated here when she went insane; she walked in the garden with her white hair streaming in the wind, and saw her father's ghost, 'a calcined mass of cinder'. In 1794 the royal family's Ajuda Palace in Lisbon was destroyed by fire, and Queluz came to life as their permanent residence. It was then that Queluz became stamped with the spirit of that rambunctious poison dwarf, Carlota Joaquina, the Spanish wife of Dom João VI.

William Beckford was brought here by the young Marquis of Marialva. He came across the regent's wife amid the garden's odiferous thickets, 'seated in the oriental fashion on a rich velvet carpet spread on the grass ... surrounded by thirty or forty young women, every one far superior in loveliness of feature and fascination of smile to their august mistress.' The queen enquired after 'the fat waddling monks of Alcobaça', before insisting that Beckford race the marquis and two Indian girls. The Englishman won, which prompted the queen to, 'see whether he can dance a bolero', which Beckford performed 'in a delirium of romantic delight.'

She was fantastically ugly and extremely short, measuring only 4ft 6in (137cm). At Queluz she entwined her dirty hair with pearls and diamonds, and wrapped her body in an old green cloth coat with gold lace frogs, and a split skirt. Outdoors she sported a man's cocked hat. Alternately sniping at her husband and plotting for her favourite son, Dom Miguel, Carlota Joaquina found time to convert one salon into a cocoon-hung house for silk-worms. The royal family fled to Brazil to escape the French invasion. When she returned, as queen, in 1821, Carlota Joaquina was said to be excessively religious. She dressed in a filthy printed cotton gown, equipped with two enormous pockets stuffed with a collection of rotting religious relics.

Queluz is now painted a warm shade of pink. One wing accommodates visiting dignitaries. The palace's paraphernalia followed the royal family to Brazil, and remained there; the thoughtfully restored buildings are furnished with pieces in the Dona Maria I, Dom José and imperial styles.

The Royal Palace

Royal Palace
open every day except Tues and hols, 10–5; adm

The **Royal Palace**'s mirror-lined **Throne Room** opens on to the **Music Room**, where, in the mid-18th century, the queen and her four daughters performed concerts. The queen sang out of tune at the top of her voice. Only she and her brood were equipped with chairs; when overcome with fatigue, courtiers knelt at the back of the room – though the French ambassador preferred to lie on the floor of an antechamber. (The Count de Saint Priest blamed the palace's lack of chairs for the old servants' swollen legs.) The music room is still used for concerts: the acoustics of its curved wooden walls are so good that the window-doors are opened to prevent them being shattered by certain pitches. Beckford considered Dona Maria I's chamber orchestra to be one of the finest in Europe. He heard them play in the **chapel**, in which Dona Maria and her sisters painted the four panels against the walls beneath the cupola.

This is a fashionable place to get married; at weekends, couples are scrambled into matrimony every 45 minutes. The apartments of the Princess of Brazil lead through to the smoking room and dining room – an anachronism, since meals were served wherever the monarch wished, until the 19th century. Hot chocolate, a drink the Spaniards brought from South America, was served in the pot whose handle and spout are at right angles.

Oranges fall from *azulejo* trees in a pretty **corridor**, running to the **Ambassador's Room**, on the ceiling of which Bernardi painted the royal family attending a concert. **Dona Carlota's bedroom** was a square room made to look round, decorated with scenes from *Don Quixote*. Castrati feast on the walls of the **Picnic Room**.

The Grounds

The English lead statues in the **formal garden** used to be painted in flesh colours – perhaps it was their charms which prompted Dona Carlota Joaquina to plunge her legs into the fountains. The palace and formal garden are brilliantly linked to the park by a staircase and cascade of water. At the foot of the staircase, the wall blanketed with puce bougainvillea was frescoed, in 1772, with a scene of blind man's buff. The maze has vanished too, and Dom Miguel's menagerie roars no more. Dom Pedro III grew hot-house pineapples here; his sons kept birds in crystal cages. The Jamor stream runs through the grounds; by means of locks, it could be flooded to fill its canal lined with *azulejo* scenes of river and sea ports, that the royal family might go boating.

ⓘ Queluz >
*Palácio Nacional de
Queluz, t (21) 435 0039*

Where to Stay and Eat in Queluz

Pousada
Pousada Dona Maria I, t (21) 435 6158/72, *www.pousadas.pt* (L2 H). In a palace annexe formerly used by the Royal Guard of the Court is the only decent place to stay in Queluz. The town's proximity to major tourist centres means that's no great drawback, but this is the nearest *pousada* to Lisbon. It has a total of 24 luxurious rooms, two palatial suites, and a unique feature: a renovated former royal theatre.

Cozinha Velha, t (21) 435 0232 (€€€€). The palace's grand kitchen has been converted into a distinguished restaurant, which attempts to rekindle the sensuous pleasures of Queluz. Oozing refinement, pineapples ornament a long butcher's table beneath the central chimney and high stone arches, between niches filled with copper. But the expense of eating here exceeds the quality of the cooking. The menu is large; the sole is a speciality.

South of Lisbon

Costa da Caparica

Catering almost exclusively to *lisboetas*, Caparica, which is on the west coast of the peninsula to the south of Lisbon, offers 5 miles (8km) of sand beaches and coves, which are served by a narrow-gauge railway. Each of the railway's 20 stops has a different character: beaches close to the terminus attract families; at the time of research, no. 9 is gay, and no. 17 is nudist. The little town provides accommodation and restaurants to suit the gamut.

Where to Stay in Caparica

★★★★Hotel Costa da Caparica, Avenida General Humberto Delgado 47, t (21) 291 8900, *www.costcaparica hotel.com* (€€). Spacious and comfortable modern rooms with air-conditioning and private balcony in Caparica's largest hotel, dominating the main promenade.

★★Hotel Praia do Sol, Rua dos Pescadores 12, t (21) 290 0012, *www.hotelpraiadosol-caparica.com* (€€). Offers the best value middle-bracket accommodation. It's friendly, efficient and comfortable, with a view of the sea if you crick your neck.

Pensão Pátio Alentejano, Rua Prof. Salazar de Sousa, t (21) 290 0044 (€). At the north end of Caparica, to your right if you look at the sea, is a villa converted into a *pensão*. The bedrooms have character but tend to be dark, and some overlook the covered courtyard restaurant. This serves large portions of good food, especially *arroz tamboril*.

Eating Out in Caparica

Manie's, Avenida General Humberto Delgado 7E, t (21) 290 3398 (€€). Decked with pans and strings of onions. Seafood cooked with rice is the speciality.

O Barbas, Praia da Vila 26, t (21) 290 0163 (€€). On the beachfront, there is a Copacabana spin-off, which provides tasty grilled sardines.

Cabana do Pescador, Praia do Pescador, t (21) 296 2152 (€€). Down the coast, at train stop no. 12, is one of the consistently best restaurants in the area, serving a nice stretch of beach.

Carolina do Aires, Avenida General Humberto Delgado, t (21) 290 0124 (€€–€). A welcoming restaurant conveniently located near the beach, with a large terrace. Serves reliably good traditional dishes.

Getting to Caparica

Every 15 minutes, **ferries** run the enjoyable 10-minute route from the Praça do Comércio's Terminal Fluvial to Cacilhas. There, the **bus station** is next to the ferry dock; take a bus signed 'Caparica'. The more frequent of these take ¾hr (past the Cristo Rei and a corral of disused washing machines).

The narrow-gauge **railway** operates June–Sept. During those months, buses from Cacilhas stop at the railway's terminus. Out of season, follow the Rua dos Pescadores from Caparica's Praça da Liberdade to the beach. The direct bus from Lisbon's Praça de Espanha is a quicker but less interesting route to Caparica.

Tróia and the Setúbal Peninsula

The Setúbal Peninsula comprises the delightful, unspoilt southern half of the peninsula formed by the estuaries of the River Tagus in the north and the River Sado in the south. Rising to around 1,650ft (500m) in the stunning limestone Serra da Arrábida that skirts its southern shore, it is totally different in character from the sprawling industrial suburbs to the north. Both the eastern towns and Sesimbra are built in the wake of castles, between which shady roads wind through olive groves. The resort of Tróia is a short ferry ride across the river estuary from Setúbal.

Tróia

Tróia was first settled by the Phoenicians, and served as the Roman fishing port of Cetóbriga from the 1st century AD until it was destroyed by an earthquake in 412. The numerous fish-salting tanks discovered here and at other ports on the Sado estuary are evidence of the preserved fish and *garum* (a blend of fish, oysters, roe and crabs) industries, whose produce was exported in locally manufactured amphorae.

Cetóbriga

Cetóbriga
*t (265) 494 318;
open daily*

The Roman ruins of **Cetóbriga** – take the N253-1 – are on the landward side of the Tróia promontory, a couple of kilometres from the ferry point to and from Setúbal – but they are unlovely, and not worth a large diversion. At the entrance to the ruins, there is a cemetery that looks like an underground boiler room, and a graveyard. The marble tongues on gravestones mark kneeling spots. The dignitaries' crematorium remains fairly intact, complete with the wall niches where their 4th-century ashes were kept. The path forks: ruins surface along 2km of the left-hand fork, for part of the site remains unexcavated.

Setúbal

The prosperous town and port of Setúbal occupies a curve of the wide mouth of the River Sado, backed by low hills which rise to a

Getting to and around Tróia and the Setúbal Peninsula

A **road** runs along a narrow promontory at the mouth of the River Sado to the resort of Tróia. For **ferries** to Setúbal, *see* below.

A **drive** around the Setúbal Peninsula is an easy day trip from Lisbon, with Setúbal 48km away, and Sesimbra 40km – cross the Ponte 25 de Abril. **Trains** run roughly hourly from Barreiro (ferry from Lisbon's Terreiro do Paço, ½hr) to Palmela and Setúbal (¾hr), but it's much easier to take the frequent TST **bus**, t (265) 525 051, from the Praça de Espanha, which takes an hour to get to Setúbal. Local buses run eight or nine buses daily from Setúbal to Palmela and Sesimbra, from which two buses daily travel to the Cabo Espichel.

Ferries run to Tróia every 45 minutes, taking 20 minutes. The car ferry embarks from the Doca do Comércio (€6 for car plus driver), the harbour furthest upstream, roughly parallel with the tourist office, and the people ferry embarks near the Doca de Recreio, slightly downstream.

single peak in the northeast. The town is home to the sardine canning, cement, and long-established salt industries – in 1640, Setúbal salt paid for Portugal's peace treaty with the Dutch.

Other than the church of Jesus, the Municipal Museum, and the old fishermen's cottages surrounding the Largo António Correia, Setúbal is a charmless place (although the crowd of young, resident foreign-language teachers swear it has hidden appeal). Its main use is as a gateway to the Arrábida peninsula, though the smart pedestrian precinct is a good place to buy shoes. The town has a dark underbelly: drugs are a problem, and the Order of Mother Theresa of Calcutta has a home for homeless children. The nuns wear white saris and welcome visitors.

History

When the Roman town of Cetóbriga (*see* p.324) was destroyed by an earthquake at the beginning of the 5th century, Setúbal was constructed on the opposite side of the river mouth, on a site allegedly selected by Túbal, grandson of Noah. The town was in ruins when Dom Afonso Henriques reconquered it from the Moors in the first half of the 12th century, and he ordered it to be repopulated by the inhabitants of Palmela. Two centuries later, the construction of the *Cerca Velha* or old town wall was financed by the country's first conveyancing tax, under Dom Afonso IV. In 1458 a fleet sailed from Setúbal to Morocco with 25,000 men under Dom Afonso V, successfully capturing Alcâcer-Seguir. His successor, Dom João II, lived in Setúbal for several years, and it was here that he fatally stabbed the Duke of Viseu in 1484. Philip II of Spain ordered the enlargement of the castle in 1590, to the designs of the Italian Felipe Terzi, with bastions suited to the new developments in cannon.

The Church of Jesus

The Church of Jesus in the Praça Miguel Bombarda (along the Avenida 5 de Outubro from the bus or train stations) is the early

Bocage

The poet Bocage (1765–1805) was born in the Rua Edmond Bartissol, and lived here until he was 15. He exploded the petrified traditions of the neoclassical period, setting the tone for revolutionary Romantic poets to come: Beckford described him as 'perhaps the most original poet ever created by God', with a fabulous wit and an ungovernable character.

Much of his work contained erotic passages, earning him censorship and military exile abroad, under Pombal. He died at the age of 39, but not before issuing this warning: '... I stained / Sanctity! Impious folk, if you believe me, / Tear up my verse! Believe eternal life!'

work of Diogo Boitac, Languedoc-born architect of the Jerónimos monastery at Belém and originator of the Manueline style. Founded in 1494 by Justa Rodrigues Pereira, Dom Manuel's wetnurse, the church and convent are grounded in the late Gothic style, with Manueline additions – most strikingly, the twisted pillars and spiral ribs which writhe around the interior, formed from faintly polychrome Arrábida marble, which contrive to alter the chancel from a square at its base to an octagon at its top. The nave's dado of 18th-century *azulejos* depicts the life of the Virgin. At a late stage in the construction, Dom Manuel, who was financing the project, required a vaulted nave, causing the architect to alter his plans and add buttresses to sustain the new structure.

The Municipal Museum

Municipal Museum
Rua do Balneário Dr Paulo Borba,
t *(265) 524 772;*
open Tues–Sun 9–12 and 2–5; closed Mon and hols

The church's *coro alto* is now incorporated in the **Municipal Museum** and hosts the 2ft (60cm) mummy of Dom João II's illegitimate granddaughter.

The museum's star attractions are 14 canvases, painted in Lisbon probably at the studio of Gregório Lopes, *c.* 1520–30. These are some of the most compassionate and inspiring paintings in the country. They constituted a retable presented to the Church of Jesus by Dona Leonor, mother of Dom Manuel – who may be portrayed as St Veronica, offering Christ a piece of cloth as he carries the cross – and hung in three rows: at the top, five scenes of the Passion; below, five scenes of the infancy of Christ; and two saints either side of the altar.

There are indications that the paintings are rooted in the theology of the New Christians, those Jews forced by Dom Manuel to convert to Christianity. At Calvary, the Virgin Mary faints in St John's arms, a depiction of human weakness which the Council of Trent labelled heretical. Her figure was painted over, only to be discovered by X-ray in 1939. Wary of the stink, a haloed figure holds his nose while Christ's body is lowered from the cross; thus the painter cocks a snook at ideas of the incorruptibility of the flesh – only the soul is resurrected. On another canvas, the tomb remains closed. Painted at the time of Portugal's Discoveries, one of the

Magi is Indian. Note too the coal brazier which warms the crib – similar stoves are still used in the Alentejo.

The museum also has a remarkable collection of ecclesiastical gold and silver, including a 15th-century Gothic processional cross in crystal and gilt.

Museum of Archaeology and Ethnography
open Tues–Sat 9–12.30 and 2–5.30

House and Chapel of the Holy Ghost
open Mon–Sat 9–12.30 and 2–5.30; closed Sun and hols

Museum of Labour
Tues–Sat 9.30–6; closed Sun, Mon and hols

The Museum of Archaeology and Ethnography

At the end of the garden strip farthest from the castle is the large and very well-displayed **Museum of Archaeology and Ethnography**. Exhibits include prehistoric rupestral art, excavated pots, fishpots, ex votos, ploughs and looms.

Other Sights

Among other sights in town are the **House and Chapel of the Holy Ghost** and the **Museum of Labour**. A major port and manufacturing centre, Setúbal is one of few towns in Portugal with a deep-rooted labour movement.

Palmela

Five km north of Setúbal and 39km southeast of Lisbon, Palmela is a clean town of 14,000 souls on the edge of the Serra do Louro, occupying gentle slopes around a castellated hill of 780ft (238m).

The first King of Portugal, Dom Afonso Henriques, captured Palmela from the Moors in the mid-12th century, after a surprise attack on the King of Badajoz, 'just as in May, the bull in rut will leap out on the careless passer-by with the blind fury of a jealous lover', as Camões puts it. The knight-monks of Santiago were installed in the castle monastery in 1194, transferring to Mértola in 1239 and returning here in 1423, under the auspices of Dom João I.

Unless you've come to stay or eat in the *pousada* (*see* p.329), which now occupies the monastery, Palmela's only exceptional feature is the view from the castle, which the young Southey, writing in 1796, described as the most beautiful he had beheld.

The Castle Monastery

The castle, which was built on Roman foundations, was repaired and enlarged by successive kings until the construction of the bastioned wall in the 17th century. The middle series of walls, surrounding the garrison, the monastery and the church of Sant'Iago, dates from the 15th century. The castle was ruined by the earthquake of 1755, but the views of the massive, dry, reddish hills to the east and west, and the sea to the south, are more than adequate compensation for the visitor, as the wind whistles around the battlements. The view to the southeast is said to stretch to Beja, on a clear day.

One of the more interesting late 15th-century visitors to the castle was Bemoi, formerly Regent of Senegal, where he favoured Portuguese merchants in return for a supply of battle horses; additional military help was to be granted if he converted to Christianity. Thus Bemoi and 25 followers were transported to Portugal. Housed at Palmela, they were given splendid clothes and dined off silver plate. They were received by the king at Setúbal, where they prostrated themselves and made as if to sprinkle dust on their heads. Clearly this endeared Bemoi to Dom João II, who became his godfather at the christening three weeks after his arrival. But there was no happy ending: godson or no, on the return journey Bemoi was executed by the captain of the fleet.

The unquiet ghost of Dom Garcia de Menses, Bishop of Évora and speaker of elegant Latin, tinkles in the cistern. Betrayed by his mistress's brother, his role in the Duke of Viseu's plot to assassinate the king became known to Dom João II, who stabbed the duke to death in 1484 and, unwilling to spill the blood of an ecclesiastic, incarcerated the bishop in the dry cistern, where he was poisoned and found dead with a book in his hand.

The only notable feature in the monastery's 15th-century **church of Santiago** is the funerary urn of Dom Jorge de Lencastre, son of Dom João II and last Master of S. Tiago, built of red Arrábida marble in 1551.

Tourist Information in the Setúbal Peninsula

The main **tourist office** for the Setúbal Peninsula region is at Travessa Frei Gaspar, between two banks off the Avenida Luísa Tódi, where a disconcerting glass floor hovers above the remains of a Roman settlement. It's well worth picking up a copy of their exemplary plan view of the Blue Coast, covering the area from Caparica to Sines.

Boat Trips

Several companies offer boat trips with dolphin-watching:

Vertigem Azul, Avenida Luísa Tódi 375, t (265) 238 000, *www.vertigem azul.com*. Its people know the dolphins and their routes, and the boats only take about 20 people. Dolphin-watching can also be combined with jeep tours of the Serra da Arrábida.

Mil Andanças, Avenida Luisa Todi 121 t (265) 532 996, *www.mil-andancas.pt*.

A well-respected local outfit running regular dolphin-spotting river tours.

Where to Stay in Tróia and the Setúbal Peninsula

Tróia

High-rise hotels look across the river estuary to the port of Setúbal. New holiday villas and golf clubs continue to spring up along the edge of the lagoon. If you've come to Tróia for the **beach**, the seaward side of the promontory is less polluted and more empty.

Setúbal

★★★★**Hotel Bonfim**, Avenida Alexandre Herculano 58, t (265) 550 700 (€€). Cosmopolitan and comfortable.

★★★★**Esperança Centro Hotel**, Avenida Luísa Tódi 220, t (265) 521 780, *www.esperancacentrohotel.com* (€€). Crisp, clean, modern, friendly and definitely preferable to its rival, the Hotel Bonfim. Located on the garden

ⓘ **Setúbal >**
Main tourist office for region: Travessa Frei Gaspar 10, t (265) 539 120, www.costa-azul.rts.pt

Second tourist office: Praça de Quebedo, t (265) 534 222

ⓘ **Tróia >>**
Complexo Turistico de Tróia, t (265) 494 312

strip running parallel with the river, near the shopping district. The windows are small, which reduces the noise of traffic, as does the welcome double-glazing.

Albergaria Solaris, Praça Marquês de Pombal 12, **t** (265) 541 770 (€€). Cosy hotel, located right in the historical centre, with 38 air-conditioned rooms with private facilities.

★★★★Residencial Setubalense, Rua Major Afonso Pala 17, **t** (265) 525 790 (€). In an attractive pedestrian street, this is a very decent little place with air conditioning, though the lack of parking may be a problem.

★★★★Residencial Bocage, Rua de S. Cristovão 14, **t** (265) 543 080 (€). In a quiet street behind the Esperança, small and welcoming, making it pleasant for a short stay.

Pensão Mar e Sol, Avenida Luísa Tódi 606, **t** (265) 534 603, *www.resmaresol. com* (€). Another decent option situated on the town's main road.

Pousada
Pousada de São Filipe, **t** (265) 550 070, *www.pousadas.pt* (L2 H). Setúbal's castle is surmounted by the delightful *pousada*, overlooking the mouth of the River Sado from about 300 yards above the town. Visitors approach through a wide-stepped tunnel, passing grilles over wells and a chapel whose interior is covered with *azulejo* scenes of the life of São Filipe, created by Policarpo de Oliveira Bernardes in 1736, six years after his work on the church of São Lourenço at Almancil outside Faro. The *pousada*'s public rooms are intimate and convivial, while some cool guest-rooms offer very good views and careful attention to detail. The more historic rooms are small and internal, but they feel real and rather splendid. Summertime diners are served under dirty awnings on the terrace. Steak and local fish are of high quality but limited selection.

Turismo de Habitação
Quinta do Patrício, Encosta de S. Filipe, Setúbal, **t** (265) 233 817, *www.quintado patricio.com* (€€€). Take a sharp right on the road up to the castle. Decorated in a fresh, bright

style, with good modern pictures, flowery sofas and Arraiolos rugs. The two double guestrooms in the main house share a bathroom; if you're feeling more adventurous, the adjacent windmill has been converted into a guest apartment. The garden of cypress trees overlooks Setúbal and the Sado, with a small swimming pool. Double rooms vary in price.

Palmela

Pousada
Pousada Castelo de Palmela, **t** (21) 235 1226, *www.pousadas.pt* (L2 H). Within the castle battlements, the *pousada* occupies the 15th-century monastery of the Order of Santiago. It is grand and splendid. You can breakfast in the glassed cloister, pass by the civilized and intimate little bar, drift down great, simple corridors to your silent, polished room. There you can sit on the window seat and mildly regret that the very big view includes so much development. Before thinking about lunch in the *pousada*'s good restaurant, which offers excellent shellfish cooked with herbs. A light Arrábida marble lavabo, dated 1711 and decorated with the scallop shells and pilgrim staff of St James, stands outside it.

Eating Out in Setúbal

Leo de Petisco, Rua da Cordoaria 31, **t** (265) 228 340 (€€€). Among the more typical restaurants, one of the classier options, with good service and large portions of fish and other local produce. *Closed Sun*.

Restaurante Bocage, Rua do Concelho 1/Rua Marquesa do Falal 12, **t** (265) 525 513 (€€–€). Traditional, rather formal and well-staffed restaurant in the Praça do Bocage.

Alegria da Fonte Nova, Praça Machado dos Santos 9, **t** (265) 239 449 (€). A budget option: a *casa de pasto* or traditional snack bar.

Bar

Baco, Praça Marquês de Pombal 48, is an arty little stone-walled bar with a predominantly young clientele.

⭐ Pousada de São Filipe >

West of Palmela

Vila Fresca de Azeitão

Quinta de
Bacalhôa
*t (21) 218 0011; open
9–5 except Sun and
hols; adm*

Lording it over the village of Vila Fresca de Azeitão, 8km west of Palmela, the **Quinta de Bacalhôa** dates from the last quarter of the 15th century, blending Florentine Renaissance loggias with Moorish-looking melon domes. The gardens contain very fine *azulejos*, produced by Moorish techniques but, in part, representing Western design.

In the early 16th century, Bacalhôa was purchased by Afonso de Albuquerque, Viceroy of India; now it is the seat of Mrs Herbert Scoville of Connecticut, who rescued the house and grounds from ruin. Even her valiant efforts are helpless against the pollution and traffic vibrations which are destroying Bacalhôa's *azulejos*. The labyrinthine clipped box hedges are hemmed in by 16th-century tiles depicting the rape of Europa, overlooked by the garden loggia, itself panelled with 17th-century *azulejos* of muscular men with turquoise hair and watery vessels, representing the rivers of Portugal and the world. Beside the water tank which served to irrigate the orchards and shrubs, a pyramid-topped pavilion is walled with geometrical tiles in the Moorish style, incorporating the earliest dated tile panel in Portugal – unhappy Suzanna being mauled by a couple of Moorish-looking elders, of 1565.

S. Simão Arte
*86 Rua Almirante Reis
(at the rear of the
Quinta de Bacalhôa),
t (21) 218 3135,
www.saosimaoarte.com*

The whole process of hand-made **tile production** can be viewed nearby at **S. Simão Arte**. A 2 x 1ft (60 x 30cm) panel costs around €8. Commissions, done from photographs, take about two weeks.

Vila Nogueira de Azeitão

Two km to the west of the Quinta de Bacalhôa, the charming little town of Vila Nogueira de Azeitão takes its name from the Moors' *az-zaytuna* (the place of the green olives). It hosts several grand buildings, including the remains of a Dominican monastery, and the plain **Távora Palace of the Dukes of Aveiro**, dated 1520–3 and said to be Portugal's first purely Renaissance building. In 1758 the duke was extracted from this palace and executed by having his bones broken, accused by the Marquis of Pombal of being accomplice to the ambush and attempted assassination of King José. The Távora escutcheon was subsequently erased from the ceiling of the royal palace at Sintra.

José Maria da
Fonseca Winery
*t (21) 219 8940,
www.jmf.pt; open
Mon–Thurs 9–12 and
2–5, Fri 9–12 and 2–3*

Roughly opposite the *palácio*, visitors can tour the **José Maria da Fonseca Winery** visiting its cement igloos and mahogany and oak casks, as well as all the sophisticated machinery which takes the romance out of winemaking. It's an interesting excursion for the layman, with a collection of *azulejos* to boot. Fonseca is one of Portugal's largest wine exporters, using Portuguese native varieties of grape as the backbone of all their wines. The Old Winery, in the

Where to Stay in Vila Nogueira de Azeitão

> ⭐ Estalagem da Quinta das Torres >

****Estalagem da Quinta das Torres, Vila Nogueira de Azeitão, **t** (21) 218 0001, *www.quintadastorres.net* (€€). Across the road from Fonseca's winery is a 16th-century baronial mansion with square towers at each corner. Beside it, an odd columned pavilion with a cupola forms an island in the large water tank. Within the *estalagem*, the sympathetic decoration includes candelabra and gun cabinets in the hall, and china ornaments in the 11 high-ceilinged guest bedrooms. The huge suite is particularly good value: frothy bunches of material are attached to the wall above the twin brass beds, whose incumbents are asked to wait three minutes for hot water in the bathroom. In the gallery, two large, imported *azulejo* panels, dated 1570 and 1578, illustrate scenes from the *Aeneid*: the burning of Troy and the death of Dido. Tapestries hang in the dining room, which serves simple, solid dishes, accompanied by Fonseca wines.

centre of Vila Nogueira de Azeitão, produces a rich dessert wine, Moscatel de Setúbal, made with grapes bought from farmers on the Setúbal peninsula. Fonseca's best-known brand is smooth, ruby-coloured Periquita, sold in the winery alongside other Fonseca products. (**João Pires**, the Setúbal peninsula's other winery, is based in Pinhal Novo, 12km north of Setúbal, and markets Lancers brand and own-label Mateus Rosé-style wines.)

Azeitão is noted for its creamy derivative of Serra cheese, best scooped from its skin.

The Serra da Arrábida

> ✪ Serra da Arrábida

The enchanted, invigorating **Serra da Arrábida** is an isolated mass of limestone on the south side of the Setúbal peninsula, running parallel to the coast for about 22 miles (35km) west from Palmela. The rounded, whale-backed mountain rises to no more than 1,650ft (500m), from which it falls in steep scrub-covered cliffs to the sea. Weathering has pitted and flaked the rock, which is strangely beautiful as it lies exposed between pockets of red soil tightly carpeted with Mediterranean vegetation. Over a thousand species of plant have been recorded here, the most common of which are myrtle, aloe, cistus and arbutus. In late March or April the land is awash with wild flowers – Spanish bluebells and coral-pink peonies grow in the shade of dense forests of Lusitanian oak, beside the road leading down to the little village of Portinho da Arrábida. The range is fringed with sandy coves, whose limestone cliffs add a touch of the exotic. The more accessible beaches get quite crowded in season – if you want seclusion, you'll have to brave a steep descent. Try the **Praia dos Coelhos**, to the west of the Praia de Galapos. Another popular beach is **Praia da Figueirinha**, which attracts volleyball players and dragonflies.

The Arabic word *ar-rabat* signifies a fortified hermitage, so there is a precedent for the warren of small cells, a church, and dependent buildings of the Capuchin **Convento Novo** nestled into the slope of the Serra, just below the upper road running through the range, almost at its highest point. Would-be visitors should ask the tourist office in Setúbal for a key to the gates of the monastery – it's worth the effort.

There is something wonderfully simple about the place, as if it has taken the spirit of the hills and blessed it. Sometimes mist accentuates the solitude of the monastery, obscuring the ocean view and wrapping the beautiful hills which surround it. The statue of Frei Martinho near the entrance embodies the philosophy of the Order: his eyes are closed (to the outside world); his lips are closed (in silence); in one hand he holds a candle (of good deeds); in the other he holds a whip (to purge himself); he has two hearts, one locked (to the outside world), the other open (to God).

The monastery was founded by the first Duke of Aveiro for St Peter of Alcantara in 1542. The generous but worldly ducal family endowed the Convento Novo with porcelain crockery, which the monks broke, charmingly, and embedded fragments in some of the walls, with shells. This appears to have been the monks' sole indulgence. When he did things he ought not to have done, a brother banished himself to windowless cell number 11, where he slept with a log pillow on a cork bed until sufficiently purged. Perhaps the voluptuous and hirsute mannequin of Mary Magdalene, lying in a cage, served as example of the temptations others have borne.

The last monk died *c.* 1850; today the Convento belongs to the Duke of Palmela, who makes it available to members of the Unification Church (the Moonies) and their vociferous chihuahuas. The nine pillarbox Stations of the Cross, slightly to the west, are the chapels of the Convento Velho.

Sesimbra

On the southern side of the Serra da Arrábida, 40km south of Lisbon, the medium-sized town of Sesimbra wells up around a turquoise bay bracketed by limestone hills, overlooked by a hilltop castle. The edge of the town has been turned into a resort, development is increasing, and the beach (where you can go topless) gets crowded, but the rickety whitewashed back streets resemble a small-scale Greek island resort. Fish are auctioned beside the pretty harbour, at descending prices, and seagulls drop starfish on roads bordered by red-hot pokers.

The five-towered **castle** 800ft (240m) above sea level is a mere shell, empty but for the town cemetery: it's better seen from a distance. Constructed with the help of Frankish crusaders, it was granted shortly afterwards, in 1236, to the Order of Santiago. Sesimbra's **Santiago Fort** projects on to the beach, outshining the sandcastles around it. Built during the War of Restoration, as a bastion against the Spanish as well as the Algerian pirates, it was designed by a remarkable Fleming called Ciermans (Cosmander in Portuguese). Jesuit, mathematician, engineer and colonel, his combination of skills was so attractive to Philip IV of Spain that he kidnapped Cosmander and compelled him to use his knowledge to assist the Spanish in the siege of Olivença, in 1648. The unhappy genius was shot during the assault, and his fort at Sesimbra suffered the indignity of serving as a bathing hut for three of the four legitimate children of Dom João V.

The town's 15th-century Misericórdia, several blocks inland from the fort, contains a painting of *Nossa Senhora da Misericórdia* attributed to Gregório Lopes. The two foremost kneeling figures have been variously identified as Dom Manuel and Pope Leo X, or Dom João III and Pope Paul III.

Cabo Espichel

West of Sesimbra, the hills gradually fall away as they approach the southwestern tip of the Setúbal peninsula, whose steep cliffs are 15km from Sesimbra. There are stone-walled fields of beans and maize, marble quarries, and, on the flat Cabo Espichel promontory, a lighthouse and the **church of N.S. do Cabo**. Built in 1701, it contains embroidered, photographed, and painted ex votos, as well as the image of the Virgin found by a fisherman guided by its incandescence. Dogs and cats wander into the church at will.

Two long arcaded wings of pilgrims' lodgings project forward from the church, derelict but for two inhabitants. It's a quiet place, with an eerie magic about its deserted calm. Heed the warnings about the strong winds when approaching the edge of the cliffs.

Plate-sized **dinosaur footprints and tailmarks** have been found in fossilized mud at the end of Lagosteiros beach, below the church.

ⓘ **Sesimbra >>**
Largo da Marinha,
t *(21) 223 5743*

Where to Stay and Eat in the Serra da Arrábida

Praia do Portinho da Arrábida

Beira-Mar, t (21) 218 0544 (€€). Overlooking the water, this does a good *cataplana*. In high season, it's best to park your car before the descent.

Sesimbra

For cheap accommodation, ask the tourist office about rooms in private houses.

★★★★**Sana Park Sesimbra Hotel,** Avenida 25 de Abril, **t** (21) 228 9000, *www.sanahotels.com* (€€€). Makes the most of its beachfront location, with great views from the rooms' balconies, a rooftop pool, health club and all mod cons.

Estalagem dos
Zimbros >>

★★★★Hotel do Mar, Rua General Humberto Delgado 10, **t** (21) 228 8300, *www.hoteldomar.pt* (€€€). Slightly to the west of town, this private, relaxed hotel sprawls along the other end of the beach, with good facilities. From the sea it looks like an ocean liner. The restaurant has very pleasant outdoor tables. Some balconies overlook the garden and circular swimming pool too. Bedrooms are cosy, bathrooms squashed. An aviary chirps merrily at one end of the reception area.

★★Pensão Espadarte, Avenida 25 de Abril 10–11, **t** (21) 223 3189 (€€). On the promenade in town, this offers both dilapidated old rooms and attractively plain newer rooms, all of which are cramped.

★★★Residencial Naútico, Avenida dos Combatentes 19, **t** (21) 223 3233, *www.residencialnautico.com* (€). Offers attractive, no-frills rooms, some of which have balconies.

Turismo de Habitação
Quinta dos Medos, Lugar de Fornos, Caixas, **t** (21) 268 3142 (€€). An unpretentious house sitting in its own estate.

★★★★Estalagem dos Zimbros, Facho da Azóia, **t** (21) 268 4954 or 268 4967, *www.estalagemzimbros.com* (€€). In an isolated spot beside the road from Sesimbra to Cabo Espichel, this *estalagem* is slightly magical. The wind sings, there are stencils on the walls, and the views are vast. It's a pity that the restaurant tries to be so formal, though.

Tony Bar Marisqueira, Largo dos Bombaldes 19/20, **t** (21) 223 3199, *www.sabemais.pt/restaurantetonybar* (€€€). Centrally located, paved with dragon's teeth and walled with stone, serving good but pricey shellfish.

O Farol, Largo da Marinha 5, **t** (21) 223 3356 (€€). Good choice for lobster. It's quite a smart place with attentive service, and the fish is delicious.

The Ribatejo

Until the introduction of railways in the last century, the ports on the north bank of the River Tagus (Tejo) were magnets for settlement. These now form the base of the industrial triangle of Torres Novas, Tomar and Abrantes, where textile, cellulose, paper, metallurgical and chemical factories loom.

History

In 1147, the chaplain to Hervey de Glanvill, a knight waylaid en route for the Second Crusade, wrote of local pride in the fecundity of the Tagus, which was said to be two parts water and one part marvellously flavoursome fish. To the south of the river, the land was potent enough to produce two crops from a single seeding. Later British visitors to the Ribatejo were less reflective: in the second half of the 14th century, Dom Fernando I was so eager to get rid of the riotous English troops sent to assist him in his struggle against Juan of Aragon that he gave them horses and packed them off in the direction of Castile. The knights turned back, entered the Ribatejo and continued to rob, rape and pillage as before. The chronicler Fernão Lopes was shocked by the waste of it all: 'when such-and-such a man felt like eating a cow's tongue, he

Getting to and around The Ribatejo

Major **roads** run through the Ribatejo region on a north–south axis, parallel with the River Tagus (Tejo). The major north–south **railway** line runs through the province, with a junction at Entroncamento for connections from the east.

Northbound express **bus** services tend to peter out beyond Torres Novas.

killed the cow, cut out its tongue, and left the cow to rot.' With time, 'people began to punish this as discreetly as they could, and killed many of [the English] with poisoned bread and in other unobtrusive ways ...'

Camões spent his orphaned childhood in the Ribatejo, nourished not on mother's milk but on that of 'a wild beast', which may have been a cow or a mare, in both of which the Ribatejo abounds. For this is the centre of Portugal's horse- and bull-breeding industry.

Horses used to be necessary for the defence of the realm, and nobody was more aware of this than the king. In 1492 the country's roads were so pitted that anyone wishing to travel in comfort rode a mule, which was smoother than a carriage and more sedate than a horse. So many mares were mated with asses that Dom João II feared the lack of horses threatened the nation's ability to defend itself; he passed a law banishing saddle mules from the kingdom. The clergy let out a shrill objection – and were permitted to keep their mules. But the wily king then passed a decree which forbade every blacksmith to shoe a saddle mule, on pain of death!

Horses remain an important part of the Ribatejan economy: the Vale de Santarém hosts the national stud farm, and the country's largest annual horse fair attracts a cross section of traders, riders and breeders to Golegã, 31km northwest of Santarém, in mid-November.

Santarém

Built above the west bank of the Tagus 78km northeast of Lisbon, the bustling capital of the Ribatejo was once important for its strategic location; now Santarém's 26,000 souls are preoccupied with the flat pasturelands which surround the town. Although it lacks exceptional monuments, there are some attractive streets in the old part of town – and it's only 45 minutes from Lisbon airport. Santarém is a centre for bullfighting – note the witty bull pavement mosaics.

History

Dom Afonso Henriques was so delighted to capture Santarém from the Moors in 1147, 'by the labour of myself and of my body, and

Wines of the Ribatejo

Pombal prohibited the production of wine in the Ribatejo, to boost yields from wheat. The vines have crept back with a vengeance: output from the Ribatejo is second only to the Oeste region of Estremadura, but the quality is less impressive than the quantity. Most of the wines are red; one of the better brands is **Serradayre** (literally 'Mountain Air'), producing a smooth, light, fruity wine.

Bulls of the Ribatejo

The Ribatejan bulls make a great impression. They graze the plains; those fortunates which remain uncastrated stoke the powerful tossing muscle which rises between their shoulderblades. They are herded by *campinos* – wild, bow-legged men who wear woolly chaps, and, traditionally, a green stocking cap with a tassel, white blouson shirt, scarlet waistcoat, green cummerbund and black velvet knee-breeches. Before the main bullfights at the July and October fairs, bulls are driven, Pamplona-style, through the streets of Vila Franca de Xira, the Mecca of Portuguese bull fighting. (Should you be unlucky enough to get trapped, remember that bulls are only flummoxed by immobility.)

the vigilant subtlety both of myself and of my men', that he founded the Abbey of Alcobaça.

The settlement takes its name from Santa Iria (Irene), whose martyred body was flung in the River Nabão in 653, floated downstream, and made miraculous appearances here during the reign of Dom Dinis. Having erected a stone memorial to the saint, the king died at Santarém in 1325.

The plethora of wild boar attracted a succession of hunting monarchs to Santarém, whose royal palace in turn acted as a magnet for the *Cortes*, which met here occasionally in the 13th and 14th centuries, and fairly frequently in the 15th century. In 1491 Prince Dom Afonso, son of Dom João II, was fatally trampled by his horse while racing along the banks of the Tagus.

Having abandoned hope of breaking through the Lines of Torres Vedras before the onset of winter, Masséna dallied here from November 1810 to March of the following year. When they failed to capture Lisbon, the Miguelites made their last stand at Santarém in 1833–4.

Around the Town

There are many churches in Santarém, but only a couple worth looking inside.

A grandiose Jesuit seminary of 1676 occupies the site of the former royal palace, in the Praça Sá da Bandeira (named after the liberal party leader born here in 1795). The Rua Serpa Pinto leads to the 16th-century **Marvila Church** whose beautifully proportioned interior lurks behind a snakey Manueline portal. Early 17th-century blue and white carpet *azulejos* line the walls, topped by a row of geometric tiles. The square marble pulpit contains fiery preachers by means of a balustrade.

Marvila Church
*open Tues–Sun
9–12.30 and 2–5,
Sat–Sun until 6.30*

Past this church and round to the right, the church of N.S. da Graça was built 1380–1420, for the canons regular of St Augustine.

Getting to Santarém

Santarém is well served by links with the north and east of the country, and with Lisbon. Semi-frequent **trains** run from Barreiro, across the river from Lisbon (1½hrs) and from Tomar (¾hr). Many services require passengers to change at Entroncamento. Semi-frequent trains also run from Guarda (6hrs), via Covilhã (5hrs), Castelo Branco (3¼hrs) and Abrantes (1½hrs); from Porto (3½hrs), via Aveiro (2½hrs) and Coimbra-B (1¾hrs). Avoid the infrequent service from Elvas (Portalegre) if you can, as it usually requires at least two changes. Train station **t** (243) 333 180, *www.cp.pt*.

Frequent Rede Expressos **buses** take 1¼hrs from Lisbon. Very infrequent express buses run from Faro (7hrs), or from Vila Real de Santo António via Faro from 1 July to 15 Sept. Otherwise, bus connections are fairly local: Fátima (1hr), Tomar (1¼hrs), Abrantes (1½hrs). Bus station **t** (243) 333 200.

The portal's tracery is similar to that of Batalha, and harmonizes with the excellent rose window above it, which was carved from a single stone. Within, the three scrubbed and elegant Gothic naves contain tombs of the Menses family, the most impressive being that of Dom Pedro de Menses, whose grandfather founded the church, and who was governor of Ceuta for 22 years until 1437. Effigies of him and his wife hold hands atop the large tomb supported by eight lions, with carved canopies at their heads and leafy pedestals at their feet. If his effigy is anything to go by, Dom Pedro sported the ultimate rounded haircut. One of the Menses women married Pedro Álvares Cabral (*see* 'Belmonte', p.233), who discovered Brazil and is entombed here.

Town Museum
open Tues–Sun
9.30–12.30 and 2–5.30

Back on the Rua Serpa Pinto, the defunct Romanesque-turned-Gothic church of São João de Alporão now contains the jumbled **Town Museum**. From the outside, the double walls of the chancel are pierced by plain square-headed windows, which are transformed into attractive round-headed openings within. Among the display, the ostentatiously elaborate, scoured tomb of Duarte de Menses steals the show. According to the inscription, he was governor of Alcácer-Seguir and, with 500 troops, successfully defended the town against 10,000 Moors. In 1464 he extricated King Dom Afonso V from a Moorish ambush, but was hacked to death in the process. A cabinet in the museum displays the contents of his sarcophagus: one tooth. Surely he had been fighting hard.

Rising 72ft (22m) opposite the church, the 15th-century **Torre das Cabaças** was built on the orders of Manuel I. He was so disgusted by the resulting edifice that he demanded eight pots should be placed on high for all to see, symbolizing the empty-headedness of the unfortunates involved in its creation.

ⓘ Santarém ›
Rua de Capelo Ivens
63, **t** *(243) 304 437,*
turismo@cm-
santarem.pt

Tourist Information/ Services in Santarém

To get to the **tourist office** from the **bus station**, **t** (243) 333 200, cross the Avenida M. Sá da Bandeira and continue straight ahead. The **railway station**, **t** (243) 333 180, is roughly

1.5km downhill and east of town, to which it is connected by a local bus.

Festivals in Santarém

Santarém hosts Portugal's premier **agricultural fair** in June, a **flower festival** in October called *lusoflora* and a massive national **gastronomic festival** (Festival Nacional de Gastronomia), **t** (243) 330 330, in the last week of October and the first week of November. For this, visitors wander from ex-stable to ex-stable, sampling every region's traditional dishes. Each day a different region takes over the central restaurant and equips it with a folk group.

Where to Stay in Santarém

★★★★Santarem Hotel, Avenida Madre Andaluz, **t** (243) 309 500, *www. santaremhotel.net* (€€€). A good four-star hotel with all mod cons and some good views of the Tagus.

Casa da Pedra, Rua das Pedras Negras 16, Póvoa da Isenta, **t** (243) 769 754 (€€). In the middle of a game reserve and so offers hunting and riding. Built of natural stone, it's welcoming and has a family atmosphere. The fine food includes home-made bread and sausages.

★★★Hotel Alfageme, Av. Bernardo Santareno 38, **t** (243) 377 240, *www.hotelalfageme.com* (€€). A pleasant place. Good value.

(★) Taberna do Quinzena >>

★★Residencial Vitoria, Rua 2 Visconde de Santarém 21, 19, **t** (243) 309 130 (€). A friendly place. Some rooms have balconies, some have sitting areas, and others have neither but are a decent size.

Turismo de Habitação

Casa da Alcáçova, Largo da Alcáçova 3, Portas do Sol, **t** (243) 304 030, *www.alcacova.com* (€€€€–€€€). Within the castle walls is a treat: a delightful 17th-century manor house with eight rooms, generously furnished. Prices vary from room to room.

Eating Out in Santarém

There's a good choice of restaurants. Two of the best are:

O Mal Cozinhado, Campo da Feira, **t** (243) 323 584 (€€). *Closed Sun*. Taberna do Quinzena, Rua Pedro Santarém, **t** (243) 322 804, *www.quinzena.com* (€€). A proper tavern complete with bullfighting pictures. During the week it tends to fill quickly. There's just one dish of the day – otherwise it's grilled meat, and excellent it is too. *Closed Sat from 8pm, and Sun.*

Torres Novas and Along the River Tagus

Torres Novas

Torres Novas is an industrial town on the hilly bank of the little River Almonda, 39km north of Santarém and 23km south of Tomar; there are no monuments of note within Torres Novas, but 3km south of town, near Caveira, there are thrilling mosaics at a ruined Roman villa.

The original, 1st-century Vila Cardílio was successively remodelled up to the 4th century. Its peristyle is clearly discernible, but little remains above ground. The joy of the otherwise unatmospheric place lies in the figurative and geometric mosaics, which are kept under sand to retain their shades of rust and grey. The sand is swept away to reveal the wealth of the mosaics gradually – a bird becomes a hand, a single face is paired with another. One panel incorporates the words 'May Cardilius and Avita live happily in [their villa] at Torre'.

Getting to Torres Novas and Along the River Tagus

There are daily express **buses** from Lisbon, plus local ones from Tomar and Santarém, serving Torres Novas and towns on the Tagus river.

By **road**, the **castle at Almourol** is invisible from the south bank. Drivers should cross at the railway bridge, go straight ahead, then left, from where the castle is signposted. **Trains** daily leave Tomar for Entroncamento connecting with trains to Almourol. Check timetables carefully to ensure your connections work out and verify departure times for trains leaving Almourol. It's quite a walk from the railway station to the castle. From Lisbon, there are a dozen reasonable connections during the day, again changing at Entroncamento (1½hrs total).

Aside from local **buses**, there are 11 Rede Expressos services a day from Lisbon (2½hrs) to Abrantes.

Back in the Lapas district of Torres Novas, the provenance of smooth, cellar-like caves (key from house 1 in Rua P) has flummoxed historians. The grotto outside is more sinister: dead frogs rotate in a small black pool edged with primroses. At the highest point in town, wild flowers grow within the castle walls, built in 1373–6. They overlook a factory yard piled with wood, which is burnt to make steam used in the manufacture of *aguardente*.

Almourol

Like something from a child's dream, the fantastic **island castle** of Almourol crowns a rocky little island in the middle of the Tagus, 22km south of Tomar and 15km east of Torres Novas. Built on Roman foundations, the diamond-shaped, battlemented bastion and its 10 towers were constructed by Gualdim Pais, Master of the Order of Templars, in 1171. The setting is ideal for aspiring princesses, who should make a special effort to visit when the river is glassy and the moon is full. This will help to compensate for the castle's lack of romantic history, it was left high and dry as the Moors were pushed southwards and there was less need to defend this stretch of the Tagus. If you're lucky, you may find someone to row you to and from the bamboo-fringed island.

Constância

Eighteen km east of Torres Novas and 12km west of Abrantes, the town of Constância occupies an amphitheatre at the confluence of the Rivers Zêzere and Tagus. Camões was holed up in the Casa dos Arcos – now an uninteresting shell – in 1548–50, following his ill-starred affair with Catarina de Ataíde. The restored, hilltop **Igreja Matriz** of 1636 has a nice cockerel weathervane and a bright ceiling painted by José Malhoa, depicting N.S. da Boa Viagem soaring skywards.

Abrantes

The faintly charming small town of Abrantes stands dominant above the north bank of the Tagus, 26km east of Torres Novas and 72km west of Castelo de Vide. In 1807, Junot and 30,000 troops

Where to Stay in Torres Novas and Along the River Tagus

★★Residencial dos Cavaleiros, Praça 5 de Outubro, Torres Novas, t (249) 819 370 (€€). Smooth, newish, well fitted and hung with original art.

Quinta de Santa Bárbara, off the road to Abrantes from Constância, t (249) 739 214, *www.quinta-santabarbara.com* (€€). Surrounded by lovely countryside and offers quite grand rooms.

Residencial Casa João Chagas, Rua João Chagas, Constância, t (249) 739 405 *www.constancia.info* (€). Provides good, clean rooms along with smiley service.

Turismo de Habitação

Quinta Horta do Avô, Soudos village, Vila Nova do Paço, t (249) 791 116 (€€€€–€€€). A 20-minute drive north-northeast from Torres Novas. The long white *quinta* offers farmhouse-style guestrooms, with rugs and the occasional guitar, overlooking a jumbled garden, where flowers spill out of urns, amid lemon trees, white cobblestones and lilies, with a swimming pool. The one apartment is equipped with two single beds and a loft for a third bed.

O Palácio, Rua Francisco da Costa Falcão 1, t (249) 739 224 (€€€€–€€€). Built around a terracotta courtyard on the riverbank at Constância, right opposite a monstrous paper factory, signposted. It offers a warm welcome, and attractive rooms furnished with light antiques and reproductions.

captured the town (and subsequently requisitioned boots), for which Napoleon entitled him Duc d'Abrantes.

The castle walls enclose the squat **keep** of 1303, which offers distant views of the Ribatejo, and the **church of Santa Maria do Castelo**, reconstructed in 1433 and now housing the **Museu de Dom Lopo de Almeida**. Of the several tombs, the most elaborate is that of Dom João de Almeida (1445–1512), being beautifully carved and well proportioned, though there is no effigy. The **chancel** houses a collection of 16th-century Sevillian tiles, archaeological fragments, and sculptures including a fascinating late 15th-century Ança-stone Eternal Father, seated and deeply sad, holding the crucified Christ.

The **Misericórdia** houses six 16th-century panels depicting the life of Christ from the Annunciation to Calvary, attributed to Gregório Lopes.

Museu de Dom Lopo de Almeida
open Tues–Sun 10–6

Tomar

Sited on the banks of the River Nabão 62km northeast of Santarém, 23km northeast of Torres Novas and 45km southwest of Leiria, Tomar and its 20,000 souls are dominated by the wooded hill on which stands the Templar's Convento de Cristo, which is one of the country's five most significant buildings.

Clean, rickety cobbled streets run parallel through the old part of town, where there are spurts of geraniums. A main road bisects the centre of town, passing a wooden water wheel on the near side of the old bridge across the river, and failing to disturb the fish that mass at its far side. There are several good places to stay in Tomar, suited to different budgets, and some enjoyable restaurants.

Getting to Tomar

Direct **trains** run frequently from Lisbon (2hrs). There are frequent local **buses** to Fátima and Batalha and infrequent express buses from Lisbon (2hrs) via Santarém (1hr).

History

The Order of the Knights Templar was founded during the First Crusade, in 1118, by King Baldwin I, to keep open the pilgrim routes to the Holy Land. Free from all authority except the pope's, they built their first castle in Portugal at Soure, south of Coimbra, in 1128, on land donated by Dona Teresa. The Templars played a key role in assisting Dom Afonso Henriques fight the Moors, and were granted ecclesiastical superiority over Santarém when it was taken in 1147. This the Grand Master, Dom Gualdim Pais, renounced in 1150, in favour of a territory roughly 50km to the north. He built a church and began a castle on the banks of the River Nabão, before abandoning the site in favour of a more secure location nearby, on the levelled knuckle of two hills. The second castle, now ruinous, dates from 1160. Two years later, a church, the Charola, was constructed slightly to the west, within the fortified enclosure.

The Templars requested castles and land in return for their services, and so became immensely rich and powerful. (They provided the ransom money for Louis IX of France.) In the early 14th century, Pope Clement V considered them a threat to his authority, and ordered the suppression of the Templars. Jacques de Molay, the last Grand Master of the Templars in Paris, was arrested on charges of blasphemy and sodomy in 1307 – but it was rumoured that he managed to send part of his treasure to Portugal. He was a rich man: he is said to have arrived in Paris with 150,000 gold florins and 10 horse-loads of silver.

Dom Dinis dissolved the Portuguese Order of the Templars in 1314. However, he recognized their usefulness to the Crown, and shortly afterwards founded the Order of Christ, which became the Templars' spiritual and worldly successor, as the king intended. Initially, the headquarters of the new order was at Castro Marim, in the east of the Algarve, but this shifted to Tomar in 1356. Henry the Navigator presided over its most distinguished era; exempted from the Grand Mastership because its vow of poverty was inconsistent with his worldly interests, he was Governor of the Order of Christ 1418–60. Under his aegis, the white sails of the discoverers' caravels bore the order's emblem, the red Cross of Christ.

When Dom João III became Grand Master, he reformed the order into a monastic brotherhood – necessitating the construction of living quarters – and in 1551 swept the Mastership of Portugal's three religious orders into the custody of the Crown. At that time the Order of Christ controlled 21 towns or villages. It declined from

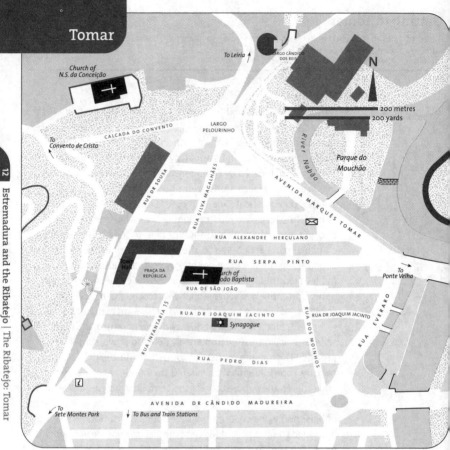

Tomar

the end of the 16th century, and was extinguished together with the other religious orders in 1834.

The Convento de Cristo

The mystical tenets of the Templars are never more apparent than in their architecture: the outer walls of the **Convento de Cristo** are a mirror image of a stellar constellation, with the Charola taking Orion's position.

Convento de Cristo
open daily June–Sept
9–6; Oct–May
9.15–12.30 and 2–5; adm

The Templars' 12th-century keep (*closed to the public*) stands beside the entrance to the *convento*, with crenellations adapted for crossbows, and next to it a triangular cistern whose orientation is said to indicate the location of hidden gold. An inscription records, with exaggeration, that in 1190 'came the King of Morocco, leading 400,000 horsemen and 500,000 foot and besieged this castle for six days', but God was on the side of the Templars. The Praça de Armas (terrace) between the keep and the church overlooks the original entrance to the fortifications (topped by granite eggs – either alchemists' eggs or ostrich eggs, which were traded by merchants on the west African coast): a row of plane trees marks the course of a road that led under the terrace and into the stables.

The Charola

The bell-like Charola, begun in 1162, was the Templars' church, which they entered through a portal – now marked by a plaque – where horsemen were blessed. The original church was a 16-sided polygon, based on the design of the Temple of the Dome of the Rock in Jerusalem. João de Castilho's splendid portal of 1515 uses the light carving of his native Spanish Plateresque style. (He worked at Belém too, and his work was pleasing to the king, for when he died in 1553 his daughter received a pension of 20,000 *reis*.) Within the Charola, a circular aisle surrounds a two-storeyed octagon containing the high altar. The early 16th-century panels attributed to Jorge Afonso, hang in the aisle.

Henry the Navigator built a chapel on the eastern side of the Charola, and dedicated it to St Thomas à Becket. Dom Manuel considered this addition insufficient for the size and wealth of the order, so he broke through the west side of the building and commissioned Diogo de Arruda to construct (1510–14) a *coro alto* above the chapter house. The floor of the latter is peculiarly high, as if something had been hidden beneath it.

The Cloisters and the Chapter House Window

A passage from the nave follows through to the Claustro do Cemitério (cemetery cloister) and the Claustro da Lavagem (cloister of ablutions), with tanks once full of water. The opposite side of the nave leads to the upper storey of the supremely balanced and ordered Claustro Principal. This magnificent High Renaissance work was commissioned by Dom João III, mostly built 1557–62, and hides much of his father's chapter house. Ironically, the architect of the cloister was Diogo de Torralva, who bricked over one of the elaborate windows his father-in-law had masterminded.

The Claustro Principal overlooks the famous Manueline chapter house window, which is much more forceful than would appear from photographs. The window is flanked by two coral-encrusted masts woven with seaweed, writhing with octopus tendrils and bobbing with cork-buoyed ropes, all of which rests on the roots of a tree borne by the sculpture of an old man, believed to represent its anonymous creator. The garter around the right buttress may refer to the Order of the Garter presented to Dom Manuel by the English King Henry VII. The 'ox's eye' above the window allowed the rays of the setting sun to penetrate the rotunda.

A short walk downhill from the Convento, the road passes the exquisite church of **N.S. da Conceição**, a Renaissance gem whose austere exterior belies the beautifully proportioned interior flooded with yellow light. It was built c. 1530–40, on the initiative of Frei António of Lisbon. Do note the tendinous spiral staircase.

N.S. da Conceição
open summer
10–12.30 and 2–6;
winter 9–12.30 and 2–5

Central Tomar

Back in the Praça da República, the **church of S. João Baptista** is overshadowed by its imposing tower, with a square base and octagonal top. Both church and tower were reconstructed for Dom Manuel in the late 15th century, being completed in 1510. The lively ornament around the north door – boars, dogs, snails and wild asses – is more curious than the western portal's sober motifs of acorns, grapes and armillary spheres.

Within, six excellent panels by Gregório Lopes hang in the side aisles, ill lit (which is ironic for an artist so concerned with the play of light) but rightly kept in the church for which they were painted 1538–9. Pupil and son-in-law of Jorge Afonso, Gregório Lopes is the most sensuous of Portugal's early 16th-century painters, richly detailing clothes, ornaments and particularly the work of goldsmiths. There's more cross-fertilization in the church's ornate limestone pulpit, which is decorated like a piece of contemporary silverware. Its three main faces bear the shield, sphere and cross of Christ respectively. The sacristan, who closets himself away with an electric waffle iron, making communion wafers, has the key to the baptistry, where hangs the fine early 16th-century *Baptism of Christ* triptych, possibly influenced by Quentin Metzys of Antwerp. On the right-hand panel, Christ is tempted by a horned devil.

The Templars sought wisdom in the ancient traditions of Judaism, so it comes as no surprise to find a small Gothic **synagogue** at no.73 Rua Dr Joaquim Jacinto (in the next street along, to your left as you face the Convento), dating from the mid-15th century. Eight inverted pottery jars have been embedded high in the corners of the square chamber, to improve its acoustics. Various stone inscriptions are displayed. The hot baths that were discovered under the floor of house no.77 in the same road are open to view.

Church of Santa Maria do Olival
open Mon–Fri 10–5 and Sat–Sun 10–6

Cross either bridge and take the first right, into the Rua de Santa Iria, to get to the **church of Santa Maria do Olival**. The lower part of its detached belltower is all that remains of the church and castle, initially constructed by Dom Gualdim Pais. His drastically scrubbed tomb is housed inside the church, which was altered by Dom Manuel and Dom João III. The polychrome **N.S. da Anunciação** of 1525 resembles Meryl Streep. Across the road, the private **Museu de Fosforos** will kindle the delight of many a pyromaniac.

Museu de Fosforos
open 10–5

Sete Montes Park

Tomar is fortunate to have the rambling, untamed Sete Montes park near the centre of town. It's a wonderfully peaceful place which formerly belonged to the Convento, and can be entered opposite the tourist office.

ⓘ Tomar ›

Avenida Dr Cândido Madureira, t (249) 322 427; open 10–1 and 2–6, April–Sept 10–8

Regional tourist office: Rua Serpa Pinto 1, t (249) 329 000; open Mon–Fri 9.30–12 and 2–6

Tourist Information/ Services in Tomar

The **tourist office** occupies a building constructed in 1930, in the style of a 16th-century mansion. The **railway station**, Várzea Grande, t (249) 312 815, is next to the **bus station**, t (249) 312 738; to get to the tourist office, cross the dirt park, continue straight ahead, and turn left at the Avenida Dr Cândido Madureira.

★ Chico Elias ››

Festival in Tomar

The *Festa dos Tabuleiros* is a harvest festival with a Portuguese twist to it. It's held every four years. On the first Sunday in July, 400–500 white-clad 'virgins' (who have been getting younger over the years) carry headdresses as tall as themselves. The headdresses are bread loaves stuck on a cylindrical bamboo frame, decorated with red, yellow and purple paper flowers and leaves, as well as wheat stalks. On the following day a cartload of bread and a cartload of wine are given to 50 poor families.

★ Calça Perra ››

Where to Stay in Tomar

★★★★Hotel dos Templários, Largo Cândido dos Reis 1, t (249) 310 100, *www.hoteldostemplarios.pt* (€€€). Located at a bend in the river, large, swanky and very nice too. It's geared for conferences, so there are all mod cons – indoor and outdoor pool, health club and big beds. All rooms have balconies; some have a view of the Convento. The restaurant's menu is international, as might be expected.

★ Estalagem Santa Iria ›

Estalagem Santa Iria, Parque do Mouchão, t (249) 313 326, *www.estalagemsantairia.com* (€€). A well-run place in a park on a manmade island with a wooden water wheel. It feels like an inn, and has just 13 rooms, some of which overlook the river and the flash hotel the other side of it. Best to eat elsewhere.

★ Residencial Cavaleiros de Cristo ›

★★★Residencial Cavaleiros de Cristo, Rua Alexandre Herculano 7, t (249) 321 203 or 321 067, *www.cavaleiros decristo.pt* (€€–€). Offers sober, tasteful, comfortable rooms and good value. It would suit anyone.

★★★Pensão União, Rua Serpa Pinto 94 (1st and 2nd floors; near the church of São João Baptista), t (249) 323 161 (€). A good little place, with wonky high ceilings, a nice light breakfast room, and a courtyard at the back.
★★★Residencial Luanda, Av. Marquês de Tomar 15, t (249) 323 200, *wwwresidencialluanda.com* (€). Offers clean, decent little bedrooms with pretty views but noisy traffic.
★★Residencial Luz, Rua Serpa Pinto 144, t (249) 312 317, *www.residencialluz.com* (€). Well located, but really very basic.

Eating Out in Tomar

Chico Elias, Rua Principal 70, Algarvias, t (249) 311 067 (€€€). For excellent home cooking, saunter off a couple of km southwest of town on the uphill road (113) to Torres Novas, a 15–20-minute walk away. Sit at benchlike tables beside a fireplace, beneath rough wood chandeliers, and try the *bacalhau* roasted with pork. *Closed Tues and Sunday evening; closed second half of July and first two weeks of Sept.*
Calça Perra, Rua Pedro Dias 59, t (249) 321 616 (€€). The quick lunch at Luso-Brazilian Calça Perra offers wonderful value. Be sure to choose the mango ice cream – it's fabulous. Prices rise in the evening, but it's still a very good place: first-floor, wooden floors, veranda.
A Bela Vista, Junto a Ponte Velha 6, t (249) 312 870 (€€). Across the old bridge, mauve bunches of wisteria cling to the rambling building, though the interior is disappointingly bright, and the menu not well stocked, though popular with children. *Closed Mon dinner and Tues.*
Piri Piri, Rua dos Moinhos 54, t (249) 313 415 (€€). Concrete floors, and offers some elaborate but bland dishes in large portions. At lunchtime in the market, chicken is barbecued with no nonsense, and eaten at benches, under corrugated iron. *Closed Sun dinner and Mon.*
Jardim, Rua Silva Magalhães 39, t (249) 312 034 (€€). May not look anything special, but the food's good. *Open daily July–August; closed Sat Sept–May.*
Salsinha Verde, Praça da República 19, t (249) 323 229 (€€). Select something from the basic menu.

Where to Stay Along the River Zêzere

These two establishments offer quiet accommodation on the forested banks of the dammed River Zêzere, which flows to the east of Tomar.

★★★★Estalagem Lago Azul, Estrada Nacional 348, in Castanheira , **t** (249) 361 445, *www.estalagemlagoazul.com* (€€€). Overlooking the aptly named Blue Lake, 28km east-northeast of Tomar, this peaceful place provides an unheated swimming pool, catamaran facilities, a hard tennis court, and a shrubby garden which faces mottled hills across the water, with bald patches caused by forest fires. The bedrooms are furnished like fancy offices, with lively wallpaper. The restaurant serves a selection of rather plain food, and dry dessert cakes.

★★★★Estalagem Vale da Ursa, Estrada Nacional 238, Cernache do Bonjardim, **t** (274) 802 981, *www.hotelvale daursa.com* (€€€). Very peaceful, situated on the north bank of the river where it is crossed by the road from Águas Belas to Cernache do Bonjardim. It sits among pine-covered hills on the sandy edge of a reservoir, which holds some of Lisbon's drinking water, 27km northeast of Tomar. If you ask in advance, the RN Express bus from Lisbon to Cernache do Bonjardim may stop near the *estalagem*. If not, the English-speaking management can arrange transport from Cernache. Everything feels new, from the polished granite lobby to the spacious, gadgety bedrooms and the marble bathrooms. It's also one of the very few hotels in Portugal designed to be accessible to wheelchairs – all credit to Sr Mariano. Try the restaurant's *achega*, a kind of black bass fished from the lake.

Along the River Zêzere

There are some enjoyable **walks** around the Estalagem Vale da Ursa (*see* 'Where to Stay', above) – the village of Dornes is a good target (it's a couple of kilometres west of the bridge), with an earth-coloured pentagonal tower that was built by the Templars. Keep an eye out for José Alberto, the last canoe-maker on the River Zêzere; he's usually happy to demonstrate how a boat is built, in exchange for a donation. Don't be disappointed by the absence of bears around the Estalagem Vale da Ursa (an 'ursa' is a female bear); partridges and rabbits are more in line.

Lisbon

Lisbon is a city of shambolic pomp and straitened circumstance. It blankets a series of hills at the southern edge of the Estremadura plateau, on the north bank of the Tagus. At Lisbon, 6 miles (10km) from the river's mouth, the Tagus broadens into an inland sea, the Mar de Palha (the Sea of Straw). The steep hills make Lisbon a narcissistic city – because there are so many vantage points from which to admire its loveliness. There is no skyline to speak of: the buildings seem to well up from one foundation, behind the docks and waterfronts. They are brilliant white or sorry grey, or, since the 19th century, washed with mellow shades of burnt pink, eau-de-nil and ochre. Still relatively cheap by comparison with other European cities, Lisbon's delightful atmosphere, beaches within easy reach, good food and buzzing nightlife have made it increasingly popular for weekend breaks.

13
Don't miss

⭐ **Portugal's most significant building**
Jerónimos Monastery, Belém **p.379**

⭐ **World-class collection**
Gulbenkian Museum **p.370**

⭐ **Restaurant-filled streets**
Bairro Alto **p.361**

⭐ **Higgledy-piggledy quarter**
Alfama **p.357**

⭐ **Quirky and unique museum**
Museu do Azulejo **p.360**

See map overleaf

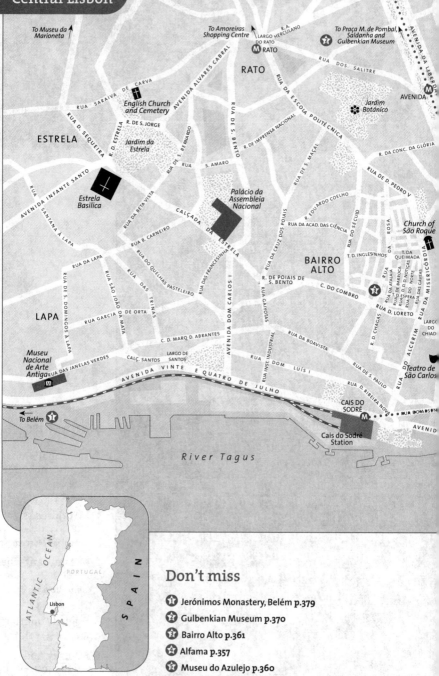

To Museu da
Marioneta

To Amoreiras
Shopping Centre

To Praça M. de Pombal,
Saldanha and
Gulbenkian Museum

LARGO
DO RATO

R. A
HERCULANO

M RATO

RATO

RUA DOS. SALITRE

AVENIDA DA LIBERDADE

AVENIDA

M

RUA SARAIVA DE CARVA

AVENIDA ALVARES CABRAL

RUA DA ESCOLA POLITÉCNICA

English Church
and Cemetery

Jardim
Botánico

R. DE S. JORGE

RUA D. SEQUEIRA

RUA D. ESTRELA

Jardim da
Estrela

R. DE S. BERNARDO

RUA DE S. BENTO

R. DE IMPRENSA NACIONAL

R. DA CONC. DA GLÓRIA

ESTRELA

RUA DE S. MAÇAL

RUA DE D. PEDRO V

RUA S. AMARO

S. AMARO

Estrela
Basílica

AVENIDA INFANTE SANTO

RUA DA BETA VISTA

Palácio da
Assembleia
Nacional

RUA DA CRUZ DOS POIAIS

R. EDUARDO COELHO

Church of
São Roque

CALÇADA DA ESTRELA

RUA DA ACAD. DAS CIÊNCIA

RUA DO SÉCULO

RUA DA ROSA

AVENIDA SANTANA À LAPA

RUA DA FRANCESINHA

RUA DA LAPA

RUA B. CARNEIRO

BAIRRO
ALTO

T. D. INGLESINHOS

T. DA
QUEIMADA

RUA DO QUELHAS PASTELEIRO

R. DE POAIS DE
S. BENTO

C. DO COMBRO

RUA DA ATALAIA

RUA DE BARROCA

RUA DE ESPERA

RUA D. O. NOTICIAS

RUA DO NORTE

RUA DAS GÁVEAS

RUA DA MISERICÓRDIA

RUA DE S. DOMINGOS À LAPA

RUA SÃO JOÃO DA MATA

RUA DAS TRINAS

RUA GARCIA DE ORTA

AVENIDA DOM CARLOS I

RUA GAIVOTAS

RUA D. LORETO

LARGO
DO
CHIADO

LAPA

C. D. MARQ D. ABRANTES

RUA DA BOAVISTA

R. D. CHAGAS

RUA ALCERIM

Museu
Nacional
de Arte
Antiga

M

RUA DAS JANELAS VERDES

CALÇ. SANTOS

LARGO DE
SANTOS

RUA INST. INDUSTRIAL

RUA DOM LUÍS I

RUA DE S. PAULO

RUA D. RIBEIRA NOVA

Teatro de
São Carlos

To Belém

AVENIDA VINTE E QUATRO DE JULHO

CAIS DO
SODRÉ

M

RUA D. MARSIN

AVENID

Cais do Sodré
Station

River Tagus

ATLANTIC OCEAN

PORTUGAL

Lisbon

SPAIN

Don't miss

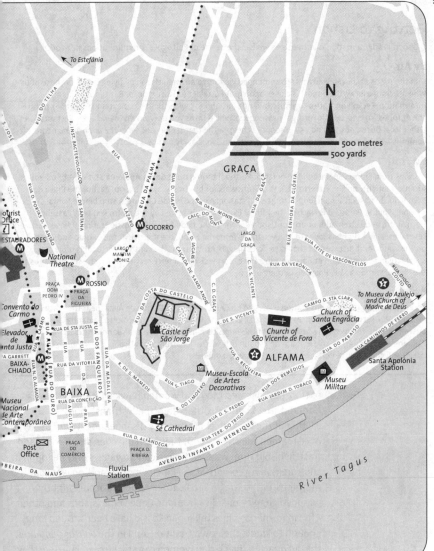

The walls of Lisbon are daubed with political graffiti, the indelible traces of the ferment that followed the 1974 revolution, and pasted with posters advertising concerts. The smell of coffee percolates from cafés whose floors are littered with paper napkins and sugar sachets. In winter, chestnuts are roasted in coal ovens at strategic points and sold in cones of Yellow Pages. Beggars wait on the steps of churches, occasionally heaving themselves up to do the rounds

Getting to Lisbon

Lisbon is an international terminus as well as the centre of Portugal's communications network.

By Air

In the 1940s Sacheverell Sitwell recommended visitors to arrive in Lisbon by flying boat. For those of us who are not so lucky, the airport is close to town, at Portela; **t** (21) 841 3700, or 841 3500 for flight information. Reckon on a 20–25-minute **taxi** ride (around €15 with about €1.50 extra for luggage), or take the **Aerobus** (free to TAP Air Portugal passengers), which takes you downtown to Praça dos Restauradores. Other local **buses**, nos. 44 and 45, do so more cheaply. The **metro** does not serve the airport; the nearest it comes is Areeiro, on the Green Line, three or four bus stops away on nos. 5 or 22.

By Train

Trains from France, Spain, and the north of Portugal terminate at **Santa Apolónia Station** – t 808 208 208 for information – on the waterfront, a 15-minute walk (or bus nos. 9, 17, 35, 49, 90) east of the Praça do Comércio. But Lisbon's main long-distance rail station is now **Gare do Oriente**, a stop before Santa Apolónia, out at Parque das Nações, the former Expo site. It is served by the **metro** Red Line. Passengers from Sintra and Estremadura north of Lisbon decant at the neo-Manueline **Rossio station**, whose tracks are several escalator flights above street level. Trains from the Estoril coast arrive at the **Cais do Sodré station**, on the waterfront just west of the Praça do Comércio. Arrival from the south of Portugal is more spectacular: all trains stop at **Barreiro**, where they connect with a **ferry** service which crosses the Tagus to the **Fluvial station** at the Praça do Comércio.

By Bus

The main long-distance **bus station** is at Arco do Cego, in Avenida Duque de Ávila (near the Praça Duque de Saldanha; served by local buses nos. 1, 20, 21, 22, 27, 31, 36, 38, 40, 44, 45, 49; metro Saldanha). **Regional buses** from the towns on the south bank of the Tagus terminate at Praça de Espanha (next to the Gulbenkian; buses 31, 46; metro Praça de Espanha). If you're departing from Lisbon, allow ½hr to buy a ticket, and check you're in the correct line before you queue.

---

of the outdoor cafés. Men and women hawk lottery tickets on a hundred street corners; others shine pedestrians' shoes.

Other of the walk-on characters are disappearing. *Varinhas* – who once roamed the streets with their piercing cries, short skirts, and fresh fish sold from wooden trays – can nowadays only be found in still-functioning corners of the Ribeira market and, on weekday mornings, in the Rua de São Pedro in Alfama. But the brightly wrapped gaggles of ladies from the Cape Verde islands and other African former colonies milling in Rossio have been around long enough to kindle their own tradition. And in the *bairros populares*, the old quarters, black-clad women can still be seen knitting: they pass the thread behind their necks and appear, at a glance, to have a limitless supply of wool stored beneath their collars. Kittens play on tiled roofs and dogs sniff at handsome 18th-century street fountains. The web of wires above the streets begins to whistle when a tram approaches. Lisbon's trams are mistakenly likened to those of San Francisco, but the latter are cable cars, which are dragged by leads. Built with British equipment during the 1920s, the trams grind their way to parts of the city that are too steep or narrow for buses to negotiate.

Inland, to the north, Lisbon's monumental junctions and polluted palm trees give way to faceless housing developments built since

Getting around Lisbon

By Car

If it were only a matter of cost, Lisbon would be an ideal city to drive in. Parking is ridiculously cheap by the standards of other European cities, except in downtown underground car parks such as the ones in Restauradores and in Chiado, although *lisboetas* are forever complaining about having to pay €1.50 for no less than two hours. But central Lisbon is full of one-way systems to snare the unwary driver, even if a good map such as the **Falkplan** (*see* p.385) should show these clearly. And then there are the other drivers, whose behaviour can shred the nerves of the sensitive. Always be aware that, as elsewhere in the country (only more so), impatient fellow drivers are as likely to overtake you on the inside as on the outside. *See* p.65 for car hire firms' reservations numbers and offices.

By Taxi

If you lose your bearings in Lisbon, fear not: St Anthony is the patron saint of lost things. Maps of Lisbon make the city look deceptively easy to get around: they do not show the hills. Keeping that in mind, the simplest way to move is by taxi. Taxis here are among the cheapest in Europe: pay what you see on the meter, plus a 5–10 per cent tip. The initial fare is €2.35, and few rides in town cost more than €6–12. If it's between 6am and 10pm, the meter should be set to '*tarifa*', unless you're outside the city limits. Swindling taxi drivers are relatively rare, except at the airport, where arriving visitors can buy a voucher valid for a journey downtown at the airport's tourist information desk; you'll pay a little more but avoid unpleasantness.

Getting a taxi to stop downtown is another matter – confusingly, they are free when one of the green lights on the roof is illuminated, but occupied when both are. It's often simpler to find a taxi rank. You can order a taxi on **t** (21) 811 9000 (**Rádio Taxis de Lisboa**) or (21) 793 2756 (**Autocoope**).

By Metro

The metro network, *www.metrolisboa.pt,* is none too extensive, but it's simple to use. Stations are signed 'M'. Tickets cost €0.70; a block of them (purchased from metro stations) works out even cheaper. Avoid rush hour, which is considerably worse than in London.

By Tram

Anyone visiting Lisbon should take at least one tram (*eléctrico*). Each stop is marked by a tin paragem sign on a roadside post or hanging from the tramlines. Enter at the back and exit at the front. Tickets can be purchased on the tram, but it's cheaper to buy a block from the bottom of the Elevador Santa Justa, or from the booth on the north side of the Avenida Fontes Pereira de Melo, near the Praça Marquês de Pombal. One per passenger per tram trip must be punched in the machine behind the driver. Beware pickpockets on board; that outbreak or joviality on the part of the group of local toughs who have just go on may well be a diversion while one slips his hand into your backpack.

By Bus

Buses are often quicker than trams; routes are usually indicated at the stops. Buses accept the same tickets as trams, and the same rules apply.

---

the 1930s. Further out, in the city's outer reaches, shanty towns thrown up by barefoot rural migrants and *retornados* from the colonies in the 1960s and 70s cling on. Local authorities in Lisbon and surrounding areas have been working to rehouse their inhabitants in concrete blocks, but thousands of *lisboetas* still live in the old makeshift warrens, although they now ring to the sound of Cape Verdean *crioulo*.

Despite its lingering problems, Lisbon is undoubtedly a more confident and sophisticated (yet never brash) place than even a decade ago. The benefits of increased trade with Spain and other European countries and the influx of EU subsidies has helped transform the economy – and consumer tastes. Having been forced to make do with picturesque but fusty traditional shops for decades, *lisboetas* have joyfully embraced the world of hypermarkets and mega-malls. Elsewhere, the success of Expo 98 – as much in proving to themselves that they could organize it as in attracting foreign visitors – was a major boost to the city's self-esteem. The site, now called the Parque das Nações, is a major weekend draw for *lisboetas*. More recently, the city entered the world stage again by hosting the 2004 European Football Championships.

History

Lisbon's excellent natural harbour, fertile hinterland, and easily defensible site led the Phoenicians to settle the hill of São Jorge, which they called Alis Ubbo (*c.* 1200 BC). In 205 BC the Romans occupied what came to be known as Olissipo. They were driven out by the northern Barbarians in AD 714, shortly followed by the Visigoths and then the Moors. Dom Afonso Henriques, the first King of Portugal, besieged Lisbon for 17 weeks and drove out the Moors in 1147.

The Siege of Lisbon

The king had enlisted the help of Flemish, Rhinelandish and Anglo-Norman knights, who put in at Porto on their way to the Second Crusade and were lured off course by the promise of booty. Their chronicler, traditionally known as Osbern, records that on the green, upland pastures around Lisbon, 'mares conceived from the wind'. The city was said to contain 60,000 tax-paying families; its great size was attributed to the flowing together of the wickedest men of all nations, as into a cesspool, because there was no proscribed religion. When the siege was under way, the Flemings noticed a posse of Moors creeping out of the city to snatch the half-eaten figs they threw out from their sentry posts. They set snares, and caught three of the infidels. The Anglo-Normans constructed a tower, swathed it with ox hides, and sprinkled it with holy water. Try as they might, the Moors could not set it on fire, and called for a truce. The Crusaders broke the truce by pillaging the city, while the residents departed. The successors' souls were entrusted to the vigorous Gilbert of Hastings, who was chosen as Bishop of Lisbon.

It was Dom Afonso III (1248–79) who first chose Lisbon as his capital. Well sited for the governance of both the north and the south of the country, the city rapidly outstripped Coimbra, Braga, Évora and Silves in size. Its golden age came in the 16th century, when it was a commercial emporium, a hive of merchants, foreigners, and the Inquisition. The maximum population numbered 65,000 in 1527; by 1620 it had swollen to 165,000 and

On the Transience of Saints

St Vincent is the patron saint of Lisbon, but he has gone out of fashion – possibly because he was Spanish. He maintains his place on the emblem of the capital, though. It depicts stylized ravens perching on a barque-in which St Vincent's body was transported to Lisbon, following his arrival (dead) at the cape named after him.

St Vincent's place in the hearts of *lisboetas* has been usurped by St Anthony (called St Anthony of Padua). He was born in Lisbon, opted for life as a missionary but was shipwrecked in Italy, performed a number of miracles, and was canonized the year after his death, in 1232. The *lisboetas* are irrepressibly fond of him, selling little pots of basil, and kindling bonfires during his festival (13–29 June). In the 17th century a regiment entered the name of St Anthony of Lisbon on its membership roll. St Anthony was promoted from private to captain. The regiment's commander sought the saint's promotion to major, stating that 'there is no record of bad behaviour or irregularity committed by him'.

clocked in as the largest city in Iberia, despite the earthquakes of 1531 and 1551, and the yoking of Portugal to Spain under Philip II. King Dom João V organized numerous *festas* in the capital, but the city he had known was to disappear in 1755: two-thirds of the capital was destroyed in the great earthquake.

The Earthquake of 1755

'It began like the rattleing of Coaches, and the things befor me danst up and downe upon the table' wrote Sister Catherine Witham. 'All falling rownd us, and the lime and dust so thick there was no seeing ... We layde under a pair tree, covered over with a Carpett, for Eight days.' In the streets of Lisbon Thomas Jacomb 'saw many coaches, chaises, carts, Horses, Mules, Oxen etc, some entirely some half buried under Ground, many People under the Ruins begging for assistance and none able to get nigh them, many groaning under ground ...' It happened on All Saints' Day, when the churches were bright with candle light; the ensuing fires were almost as destructive as the quake itself (prompting ironic commentary from Voltaire, who places Candide in Lisbon when the catastrophe strikes), and the consequent tidal wave swallowed Lisbon's shipping. The Marquês de Alorna's response to the disaster, 'We must bury the dead and feed the living, and close the ports', is often attributed to Pombal – who rose to the occasion. To quash the danger of plague, corpses were set on barges and sunk at sea. Prices were fixed, taxes suspended, emergency hospitals opened. A four per cent tax was levied to cover the cost of rebuilding.

In the 19th century, after the flight of the royal family to Brazil, Junot presided over Lisbon – for a mere nine months. Following their defeat by Wellington at the battle of Vimeiro, the French were permitted to withdraw. Wellington's successful military strategy towards the end of the Peninsular War hinged on the defence of Lisbon behind the Lines of Torres Vedras. King Dom Carlos and his

Dragon's-tooth Pavements

In the mid-19th century the Governor of the Castelo de São Jorge set prisoners to work on a queasy wave-patterned mosaic pavement for the Rossio. He may have been inspired by publications on Pompeii. At any rate, the idea caught on, and now Lisbon is delightfully ornamented by complicated and witty pavement designs. Each pale limestone or dark grey basalt cube is about 10in (4cm) square – the size of a dragon's tooth – and must be cut by hand. The cubes are pummelled into a bed of sand, from whence they are removed when the sewage pipes need repairing. They get painfully lumpy and uneven if cars drive over them, but they are porous, so they do not interrupt the water cycle. Dragon's-tooth paving prevails in Leiria, Tomar, Caldas da Rainha, parts of Porto and Santarém, and the custom was exported to Brazil, Mozambique and Angola.

eldest son were assassinated in the Praça do Comércio in 1908, and the monarchy was overthrown here in 1910. Spies were rife during the Second World War, and the capital was the scene of the bloodless Revolution of 25 April 1974.

The Baixa

The Baixa is the low-lying centre of Lisbon adjacent to the Tagus. A stream once flowed through the district into the river; its houses were built on stilts to escape frequent flooding – until the neighbourhood was levelled by the earthquake of 1755. Here was Pombal's chance to build a pristine Lisbon: the new streets should be 'forty feet in width, with pavements on either side protected from wheeled traffic by stone pillars, as in London'. He and Eugénio dos Santos, a military engineer, reconstituted the Praça do Comércio as a square open to the river on its south side, and designed a grid pattern of streets stretching 500m inland to the Rossio square and the Praça da Figueira. This has been described as the greatest uniform architectural undertaking of the Age of Enlightenment – but the rationalism of that age has produced a frigid symmetry almost as severe as Pombal himself. All projections and carving were forbidden by law, for reasons of economy and haste. The Baixa was rebuilt for the merchant classes, as the streetnames indicate: Rua da Prata and Rua do Ouro (now the Rua Aurea) were intended for goldsmiths and silversmiths, and the Rua Augusta for cloth-dealers.

Thanks to longstanding rent controls – only gradually being relaxed after driving brand-hungry consumers to out-of-town malls – many of the area's fusty clothes shops remain, along with numerous banks and a huddle of undistinguished restaurants near the Rossio. The central Rua Augusta is reserved for pedestrians. The elegant melon yellow square is periodically used as an outdoor art gallery, or as a venue for council-organized children's games.

The Baixa is the nucleus of the public transport network, so you'll probably end up here sooner or later. Baixa-Chiado metro station serves the area. Buses 39, 40 and 15 may be especially useful, as well as trams 3, 16, 19, 24, 25, 26 and 28.

The Praça do Comércio

The riverfront Praça do Comércio used to be the Terreiro do Paço, which was named after the Ribeira Palace (*paço* meaning court). This stood here from the early 16th century until the earthquake of 1755, enabling the royal family to watch bullfights from their balconies.

A bronze **equestrian statue of Dom José** occupies the centre stage, cast by Machado de Castro (1731–1822). The project took five years to complete, during which time the vacuous king was too ill to have his likeness taken; hence the emphasis is on the helmet rather than the head. It took more than 1,000 people 3½ days to shift the statue into place, with great ceremony. At the front of the pedestal is a bronze medallion depicting Pombal; when the dictator fell from power, the craftsman who had made the medallion was ordered to destroy it. Loath to melt down his work, he bricked it up in a wall of the Arsenal, from which it was retrieved nearly 60 years later.

Manuel Gandra, a geomancer, traces close links between the proportions of the Praça – the monument to Dom José – and the palace and basilica of Mafra, the monument to his father Dom João V. The turrets at the seafront correspond with the turrets at the sides of the palace: accordingly, the equestrian statue occupies the place of the high altar. On 1 February 1908, King Dom Carlos and Crown Prince Luís Filipe were assassinated at the corner of Praça do Comércio and the Rua do Arsenal, near where Lisbon's main post office stands.

West and East of the Praça

Mercado Avenida
24 de Julho
open Mon–Sat, 6–2

The Rua do Arsenal leads westwards to the Cais do Sodré station. Opposite the station is Lisbon's most atmospheric market, the **Mercado Avenida 24 de Julho**. The traders are incredibly

---

Parallel Streets

Until the 18th century, the inhabitants of the Baixa drew their water from what they thought was a well. Now it is covered, like any other pothole, at the junction of the Rua da Prata and the Rua da Conceição, between the Praça do Comércio and the Praça da Figueira. The water was pestilential: exploration of the 'well' revealed a series of subterranean tunnels running parallel to one another. This was long assumed to be Roman baths, but mistakenly so: it is a Roman cryptoporticus, probably dating from the 1st century AD, the intended foundation of the public forum. The 'Termas Romanas' may be visited on just one day of the year, but this is no great loss, as there's nothing to look at.

entertaining. Meanwhile, the first floor is increasingly used for crafts, fashion or antiques fairs.

The Rua da Alfândega runs eastwards from the Praça do Comércio, past the **Church of Conceição Velha**, which was built by Dom Manuel on the site of Lisbon's synagogue. King Manuel and Queen Leonor, widow of Dom João II, are among the dignitaries kneeling at the feet of N.S. da Misericórdia, on the tympanum of its richly carved portal. In the parallel street, the Rua dos Bacalhoeiros, the façade of the **Casa dos Bicos** is studded with little pyramids, a curiosity of early 16th-century architecture, built for a bastard of Afonso de Albuquerque. The house subsequently became a *bacalhau* shop. There are similar examples of the design in Italy and Spain.

The Rua Aurea runs parallel to the Rua da Prata; at its junction with the Rua de Santa Justa stands the incongruous iron **Elevador de Santa Justa**, whose construction is incorrectly attributed to Eiffel. It was built by Raúl Mesnier in 1902. The causeway leading from the top of the *elevador* to Largo do Carmo is closed indefinitely, so this no longer serves as a short-cut to the Bairro Alto; it is just a marvellous vantage point from which to survey the Baixa, and perhaps to sip an overpriced coffee. And you will, of course, need two tickets – one to go up an one to come down.

In and Around the Rossio

In the Rossio itself, a statue of the 16th-century playwright Gil Vicente crowns the façade of the **National Theatre** (1842–6). The building stands on the site of the Paço dos Estaus, home of the Inquisition 1534–1820. (In 1726, Brockwell wrote that an auto da fé was held every three years: the Inquisitor and Court heard Mass; then 'Prisoners, let their Station or Quality be what it will, almost starved, swarming with Vermine, are separately presented and arraign'd at the Bar'. If they failed to repent they were tortured by 'pressing their Thumbs in a Vice, Drawing the Nails from the Fingers, scalping the Crown, etc'. If convicted a third time, 'The prisoner is arrayed in a pitched Vesture with Flames, Devils, Dragons etc. painted on it, great Weights of Iron Chains are linked to his Hands and Feet'. They were chained to an iron chair 10ft (3m) from the fire, and roasted.)

The Rua das Portas de Santo Antão runs to the right of the National Theatre, leading to the Geographical Society's **Museu Etnográfico**. It's a jumble of odd things which caught travellers' eyes, displayed around the upper walkways of a tall lecture theatre. The collection includes door locks and musical instruments from Guinea Bissau; *nkonde* statuettes from the Congo, stuck full of iron nails, with mirrors at their bellies; Angolan chieftains' chairs composed of phalluses; tortoiseshell and banjos from Cabo Verde;

Museu Etnográfico
Rua Portas de Santo Antão 100, t (21) 342 5068; pre-booked guided tours 11am and 3pm, Tues and Thurs; metro Restauradores

and heads shrunk by Brazilian Indians. Historically, one of the most significant exhibits is a stone column retrieved from Angola, with an inscription recording that in 1482 'the very high, very excellent and powerful prince King João second of Portugal sent to have this land discovered and these padrões placed by Diogo Cão, squire of his household'.

The Alfama

 Alfama

Idrisi, the 12th-century Muslim geographer, referred to the Alfama as *al-hamma* (the bath) – but the only remaining public baths are for the birds. The Alfama's steep and higgledy-piggledy streets are built on stone, which preserved them from the devastations of the earthquake: here, just east of the Baixa, are the antique guts of Lisbon. The Alfama is a warren of narrow alleys and uneven staircases awash with laundry, lit from wrought-iron lamp fittings, hymned by caged budgies and the occasional cockerel, clouded by flies, greened by potplants, protected by half-cannon tiled roofs and, sometimes, by plastic tarpaulins strung out to keep the rain or sun off a doorstep. Behind peeling double doors, children bicycle around street-level vestibules. Be wary of pickpockets and camera thieves.

The Sé (Cathedral)

The Sé
Largo da Sé, t (218) 866 752, www.ippar.pt; cathedral open Tues–Sat 9–7, Mon and Sun 9–5; treasury Mon–Sat 10–5; cloister May–Sept, Mon 10–5, Tues–Sat 10–6.30; Oct–April, Mon–Sat 10–5; cathedral free, treasury and cloister adm; tram 28, bus 37

Gilbert of Hastings required a **cathedral**. Three years after his appointment as Lisbon's first bishop, Dom Afonso Henriques ordered one to be built for him, on the ruins of a mosque remains of which have been dug up in the cloisters, just east of what is now the Baixa district. It was designed by Masters Robert and Bernard, the pair who worked on the Sé Velha at Coimbra, in 1150; here they have included two typically Romanesque side towers, and set a rose window in the dignified façade. In 1388 a riotous crowd flung Bishop Martinho Anes from one of these towers, because he was Castilian, and appointed by the Avignonese Pope, Clement VII. The building was damaged and rebuilt after earthquakes in 1337–47 and 1755; now it is heavily restored and rather characterless.

St Anthony passed through the waters of the font: he was baptized in it in 1195. To its left is the chapel of Bartolomeu Joanes, which was built in 1324 and funded by a rich Lisbon merchant. To the left stands Machado de Castro's crib, sculpted in 1766. The organ, a blaster if ever there was one, was added in the 18th century. Chapels lead off the forceful Gothic ambulatory; they contain tombs of João Anes, the first archbishop (d. 1440), and Lopo

Fernandes Pacheco, with a dog at his feet. The ambulatory leads through to the Gothic cloister, whose arches are split in two.

Dorothy Quillinan, Wordsworth's daughter, visited the cathedral in 1845, and in her journal noted 'two dead infants which we saw carelessly laid on a sort of shelf or projection, behind the High Altar. They were dressed neatly ... as if just taken out of the cradle. I insisted upon it that they were wax children. Mr– ... assured me they were dead infants – "angels", as they call them and consider them ... These are the children of poor people who are allowed to leave them for Christian burial without charge.'

Around the Alfama

Santo António da Sé
t (21) 886 9145; open daily 8–12.30 and 3–7, with ¼hr breaks at 12 and 5 for Mass

Opposite the cathedral, the elegant little church of **Santo António da Sé** shelters the room where St Anthony was born in 1195. His birthplace is now an airless chapel, thick with devotion but little else. The church was built in 1728, to the designs of Mateus Vicente, the architect of Lisbon's Estrêla church. It was paid for from the sale of little altars and images of the saint.

One block inland from the cathedral, the meagre and unatmospheric remains of Lisbon's **Roman Theatre** can be seen from the Rua de São Mamede. An inscription records the dedication of the orchestra in the time of Nero.

Museu-Escola de Artes Decorativas
t (21) 888 1991, www.fress.pt; open 10–5; closed Mon; adm; tram 28, bus 37

The Rua Augusto Rosa and Rua do Limoeiro lead uphill from the cathedral to the **Museu-Escola de Artes Decorativas** (Museum of Decorative Arts), which boasts the most comprehensive display of furniture in the country. The collection – which includes embroidered shawls, 18th- and 19th-century Arraiolos rugs, porcelain, glass, and Portuguese silverwork – was assembled by Ricardo Espírito Santo, and installed in a 17th-century *palácio*, which retains its original *azulejos*.

The **Espírito Santo Foundation** was set up in 1953 to foster traditional crafts. Bookbinders, gilders, wood carvers, cabinet makers and others can be visited in the 21 workshops next to the museum. Each produces faithful reproductions using original techniques.

The Castle

The route to the castle is complicated: if you keep going uphill, you'll get there eventually. The **castle of São Jorge** (bus 37) was the nucleus of the city, inhabited by the Phoenicians and subsequently by every conquering race. Dom Afonso Henriques initiated the medley of fortifications when he captured the castle in 1147, and rebuilt the Moorish defences. Over-enthusiastic restoration has sucked the atmosphere from the place, turning it over to gardens with tinkling fountains, crooning peacocks, black swans and turkeys (find a feather and make an earring). Now the main attraction is the panoramic view of Lisbon and the Tagus, although there is a halfway successful Olissiponia multimedia exhibit that includes a vivid virtual recreation of the 1755 earthquake and its effects.

Three sections of bulwarks can be distinguished: the quadrangular fortress, at the highest point of the hill, with 10 square towers; the citadel, within the first band of walls, built on the site of the Roman acropolis and containing the Paço da Alcáçovas, a royal palace until the reign of Dom Manuel and now home to an undistinguished restaurant; and finally a girdle of walls projecting south, towards the Tagus, built for defence against the Barbarians, and which became the main theatre for the Christian assault.

East of the Castle

The original church and monastery of **São Vicente de Fora** (*tram 28*), on a rise above Alfama, were founded by Dom Afonso Henriques outside (*fora*) the city walls; the buildings that stand today were constructed between 1582 and 1627 by Felipe Terzi, possibly assisted by Juan Herrera, architect of the Escorial.

Its Mannerist style is typical of architecture under the Inquisition: the balanced but frigid white limestone façade (with niches for, from left to right, Saints Vincent, Augustus and Sebastian); the grandiose undivided nave focusing attention on the preacher and celebrant. Dom João V commissioned the canopied Baroque altar, which is flanked by eight life-sized wooden sculptures from the Mafra school. In the cloister, late 18th-century *azulejos* depict hunting, rural and court scenes from La Fontaine's *Fables*. These include a rail draped with pocket watches, Dali style. In 1855 the refectory, off the cloister, was selected as the Bragança pantheon: it contains the tombs of most of the kings and queens of Portugal from Dom João IV (d. 1656) and Catherine of Bragança through to Dom Carlos (d. 1908). The coffins used to have glass tops, so the embalmed bodies could spy on the world.

On Tuesday and Saturday mornings, the **Feira da Ladra** (flea market) spreads itself behind the church of São Vicente. It is unlikely to turn up any interesting nuggets, offering mostly doormats, radios, army surplus, empty soda cans, denim and popcorn. Chunky handknit sweaters are a good bet for around €20, or a machete if the weeds are getting bad back home.

Two blocks downhill from the front of the church, the Rua dos Corvos leads eastwards to the church of Santa Engrácia, a lofty and uplifting building in the shape of a Greek cross with rounded arms. Panelled with brown, pink and light and dark grey marble, its balanced design influenced a new wave of Italian Baroque architecture. João Antunes drew up the plans in 1682, after the

Church of Santa Engrácia
open 10–5; closed Mon; buses 12 and 38

13

Lisbon | The Alfama

chancel of the previous church crumbled. It became a synonym for unfinished work: the balustraded cupola was not added until 1966. Then, it became the National Pantheon, harbouring the uniform modern cenotaphs of Camões, Henry the Navigator, and Vasco da Gama among others. *Fado* diva Amália Rodrigues joined them in 2002, after parliament voted to overturn a rule requiring a five-year interval between a person's death and the transfer of their remains to the pantheon. The seatless symmetry yields peculiar echoes, and an elevator goes up to the dome, with views of the port and city.

Casa do Fado e da Guitarra Portuguesa
Largo do Chafariz do Dentro, t (21) 882 3470; open daily 10–1 and 2–6; adm

At the bottom of Alfama, the **Casa do Fado e da Guitarra Portuguesa** is Lisbon's new and very engaging little *fado* museum. Illuminating a uniquely Portuguese art form and well worth a visit, it's a good example of how a well-presented and amusingly illustrated display can bring a topic to life – and it's labelled in English. The museum traces the history of *fado* from 1825 to the present, including a section on *fado* and film, and displays of record sleeves and of clothes worn by *fadistas*. The finale is the recreation of a *fado* bar. The excellent shop sells CDs, cassettes and videos, and there's an opportunity to listen before you buy.

Museu Militar
t (21) 884 2569; open Tues–Sun 10–5; adm; buses 9, 12, 25, 28, 38, 39, 46, 59, 81, 82, 90

Continue a few hundred yards eastwards to the **Museu Militar** the city's oldest museum. The 18th-century building and its later extensions are so coated with paintings as to be almost kitsch. The collection itself occupies 34 rooms – which makes for a great many cannon, swords, guns, shields and maces. Of little appeal to non-specialists.

Xabregas

Xabregas is an eastern suburb whose sole point of interest is the Museu do Azulejo.

The Museu do Azulejo (Tile Museum)

⭐ Museu do Azulejo
Rua da Madre de Deus 4, t (21) 810 0340; open Wed–Sun 10–6, Tues 2–6; closed Mon; adm; buses 17, 42, 104, 105

Anyone who wants to understand the evolution of Portuguese tile design and technique should visit the **Museu do Azulejo** (east of the Alfama, one block inland from the Tagus), which takes non-specialists on an entrancing journey. Examples are arranged chronologically, from the 16th century to the present day. The museum is installed in the attractively refurbished Convent of Madre de Deus.

The collection includes a grotesque rendition of Bacchus, with hairy breasts and a cluster of grapes at his crotch; seven early 19th-century panels illustrating the progress from rags to riches of a hatter called António Joaquim Carneiro; and witty modern tiles of grasshoppers and crabs, with some abstract work. The highlight is a 36m panorama of Lisbon's waterfront, *c.* 1738; many of the buildings no longer exist, including the smoking kilns of factories in the Mocambo district where these very tiles were probably made.

The splendid **church of Madre de Deus** is one of the best places in Lisbon to see rich art in situ, and contains some stunning gilt Baroque woodwork. The convent was founded by Dona Leonor, widow of King Dom João II, in 1509; her symbol, the shrimping net, and her husband's, the pelican, ornament the restored side portal.

Little remains of the original foundation, which was enlarged by King Dom João III, and rebuilt after the 1755 earthquake. This restructuring decapitated the tile-painted sheep that accompany Moses as he is addressed by God, in the main body of the church. The headless flock is part of the Dutch *azulejo* dados, which have more spatial depth and use inkier blue than their Portuguese counterparts. Above the tiles, the walls and ceiling are covered with canvases depicting the life of St Francis, attributed to André Gonçalves (1687–1762); note particularly his semicircular *Coronation of the Virgin*. Sixteenth-century paintings from the original church hang in the chancel. The marble stoup (basin for holy water) in the sacristy is said to have belonged to Dona Leonor herself.

The *coro alto* can be entered from the upper cloister. Gilt woodwork frames paintings by André Gonçalves and other 18th-century artists, covering every inch of the ceiling and walls. Graceful *azulejos* are employed as light-reflectors in the window casements.

The museum has a good little shop, and an attractive cafeteria with splendid fishy and meaty tiles, and tables in a courtyard.

The Bairro Alto and Chiado

Bairro Alto

The **Bairro Alto** was laid out on a grid pattern in the 16th century, but the slope of the streets makes them feel slightly wonky. This was, and to some extent still is, Lisbon's Bohemian quarter; the narrowness of the roads and the height of the peeling, balconied houses that overlook them have held on to a lively streetlife, played out around a hive of restaurants, *tascas, fado* houses and bars with in-house DJs. Almost all cars have now been banished from the area, allowing revellers to be even more carefree in spilling out onto the streets, drinks in hand. In fact, the whole place would be turned over to revelry were it not for successful noise-abatement campaigns by residents that have forced late-night clubs gradually to move to the wide-open spaces of the docks. The Chiado, immediately downhill from the Bairro Alto, is staider. It focuses on the Rua Garrett, where the elegant of Lisbon shop in boutiques and turn-of-the-20th century department stores. In the summer of 1988, a fire began in one such store in the Rua do Carmo. It scarred the face of the Chiado and destroyed a unique part of the city. It was more than a decade before the area was restored to anything like its former status, but the job has been done with restrained style by Portugal's leading architect, Álvaro Siza Vieira. Defying fears that the area had lost out for good to its shopping-centre rivals, it has come to life again, also aided perhaps by the city council's controversial decision to pedestrianize part of Rua Garrett.

The Rua Serpa Pinto runs downhill from the Rua Garrett past Lisbon's fine opera house, the **Teatro de São Carlos** (*tram 28*), which is supposed to have been modelled on San Carlos in Naples. Construction began in 1792; the draped, columned, mirrored royal box flanked by satyrs recalls grand times. A short way down the street, the **Museu do Chiado** displays paintings from the second half of the 19th century, and the early decades of the 20th, with an emphasis on the Romantic era. The Gulbenkian's Centre of Modern Art in Saldanha (see p.373) has a far better collection of modern works.

Museu do Chiado
Rua Serpa Pinto, t (21) 343 2148; open Tues 2–6, Wed–Sun 10–6; closed Mon; adm; metro Baixa-Chiado

The Calçada do Sacramento leads uphill from Rua Garrett to the Largo do Carmo. Here, the grassy nave and vacant arches of the **Convento do Carmo** are Lisbon's most spectacular monument to the great earthquake. The Gothic church perches on the verge of a steep hill, high above the Baixa. It was founded by Dom Nun' Álvares Pereira, the great military leader, in honour of a vow made at the battle of Aljubarrota. The foundations twice gave way, delaying completion until 1423, when the founder himself entered the monastery for the remaining eight years of his life. The church flipped its lid in 1755: the roof collapsed, but the walls, nave arches, and five apses remain intact. Having served as a graveyard, a public refuse pit, and a stable for the neighbouring barracks, the building now houses a muddled **Museu Arqueológico**, with miscellaneous Visigothic pieces, pottery, coins and tombs. Note the stone bust of Dom Afonso Henriques at the back of the chancel, which is believed to be the oldest image of the nation's first king.

Museu Arqueológico
t (21) 346 0473; open Tues–Sun 10–6; closed Mon; adm

The Church of São Roque

The Rua da Oliveira leads uphill to the Largo Trindade Coelho, where the austere façade of the church of São Roque gives no hint of the riches within. The church was built in the late 16th century, following Felipe Terzi's plans; in 1642 the great Jesuit Padre António Vieira – missionary, diplomat and economist – delivered his 40-hour sermon here. The third chapel on the right brims with elegant polychrome *azulejos* dated 1585.

But the **chapel of São João Baptista** (to the left of the high altar) steals the show. It encapsulates all Dom João V's magnificence and folly. The king commissioned it in 1742 from Vanvitelli, who built it in Rome, where it was consecrated by Pope Benedict XIV – in return for a gift of 100,000 *cruzados*. (Traffic between Lisbon and the papal court was not uncommon: the pope had sent a special nuncio to Lisbon bearing consecrated 'nappies' for the Infante Pedro; he was already dead, so they were swathed around the Infante José.) After its consecration the structure was dismantled and shipped to Lisbon, at a total cost of more than £225,000 – making it one of the most precious chapels of its size ever built. For all that, its confection of alabaster, amethyst, diaspore, lapis lazuli, porphyry and several marbles is disappointingly jumbled. The ingredients drown one another. Do look at the magnificent chandelier.

The chapel's fabulous accoutrements are displayed in the **Sacred Art Museum of São Roque**, adjacent to the church. The treasury beggared description (and the people of Portugal): one cope is showered with 33lb (15kg) of gold, and a mitre is carbuncled with Brazilian rubies. There are some lively Italian Baroque gilt candlesticks.

Next door, the *Misericórdia* almshouse is funded by weekly lotteries – hence the bemusing lifesize sculpture of a lottery ticket seller in the middle of the square, with whom the pigeons have their way.

The Jardim Botánico and Around

Rua de S. Pedro do Alcântara curves uphill into Rua D. Pedro V and the Rato district, where the **Jardim Botánico** blooms beside the Academia das Ciências. It is planted on a hillslope, like almost everything else in Lisbon. Though less exotic than the Estufas (*see* p.370), this is one of the few places in the capital where birdsong can be heard in the wild caged birdsong is like piped music. Visitors can get pleasantly lost on the winding paths, among the cacti and goldfish. A second entrance to the Jardim Botánico on Rua da Alegria may or may not be open, depending on the staffing situation.

Jardim Botánico
t (21) 396 8180; open winter Mon–Fri 9.30–6, Sat–Sun 10–6; summer Mon–Fri 9.30–8, Sat–Sun 10–8; adm; bus 58; metro Rato

Fundação Medeiros e Almeida

Just to the north of the Jardim Botánico, along Rua de São Mamede, left down Rodrigo de Fonseca then first right, you'll find one of Lisbon's most impressive private museums – the **Fundação Medeiros e Almeida**. António Medeiros e Almeida was for 50 years a passionate collector of furniture, tapestry, paintings, sculpture, glass and jewellery, much of it created in France, Italy and England in the eighteenth and nineteenth centuries. He had an eye for beauty and a sizeable budget, and left the whole lot to a

Fundação Medeiros e Almeida
41 Rua Rosa Araújo, t (21) 354 7892; open Mon–Sat 10–6; adm

charitable foundation, displayed in the villa where he and his wife lived 1940–70. It can't compete on the international stage in the way the Gulbenkian collection can; on the other hand there's not much in the collection that's Portuguese, which limits its appeal to foreign visitors. There's also a question of taste: some of the pieces are so ornate as to be overblown. Still, it's an impressive place, and certainly worth visiting if you have ample time. It's labelled in English. The shop sells high-quality reproductions of silver and china.

Opposite the Academia das Ciências, Rua de São Marçal runs steeply downhill, past the **British Institute** (Rua Luís Fernandes 1–3), which occupies what was once the substantial home of Francisco Alves dos Reis, mastermind of the 'Portuguese Bank-note Case'. In 1925, notepaper was obtained from the Bank of Portugal and used to instruct the London firm of Waterlow to print 580,000 500-*escudo* notes – which entered Portugal in the Venezuelan diplomatic bag. The alarm was sounded when duplicate serial numbers surfaced; Messrs Waterlow were sued for the outstanding sum of £610,932.

Museu do Design e da Moda

Just to the east of Bairro Alto is the area of Santa Catarina. In 2009 it will become home to a new museum. In 1999 Lisbon's exceptional Design Museum opened in the Belém Cultural Center and was considered to be one of the world's leading museums of 20th-century design. Several eminent critics considered its collection to be the best in Europe. It closed in August 2006 but will re-open in a new space in Santa Catarina in mid-2009. It will be renamed the **Design and Fashion Museum** or simply **MuDe** (which also means 'change' in Portuguese), and will include Portuguese businessman Francisco Capelo's fashion collection. The collection is made up of 1,200 couture pieces, including a famous Jean Desses gown that Renee Zellweger wore to the 2001 Oscars and Christian Dior's landmark 1947 New Look.

Design and Fashion Museum
www.mude.pt

The design collection consists of works by some 230 designers representing trends in design from around the world. There are works by design icons such as Philippe Starck, Charles Eames, George Nelson, Arne Jacobsen, Paul Henningsen, Vener Panton, Masanori Umeda, Henning Koppel and Tom Dixon, and includes almost 200 design classics embracing innovative furnishings, glass and jewellery from 1937 to the present. Check the website for the latest information.

São Bento and Estrela

Immediately west of the Bairro Alto is São Bento, the political district. A 10-minute walk downhill from the British Institute, the

Palácio da Assembleia Nacional
Rua São Bento; tram 28; buses 6, 13, 39, 49, 100; open by appointment only

Estrela Basilica
trams 25, 28; bus 9

Palácio da Assembleia Nacional houses Portugal's parliament. The Prime Minister's official residence is next door to the National Assembly, up the Calçada da Estrela.

The Estrela Basilica

Further uphill is the **Estrela Basilica**, one of the most impressive 18th-century monuments in Lisbon. It was founded by Queen Dona Maria I in thanks for the birth of a son, and the first stone was laid in 1779, under the direction of Mateus Vicente and Reinaldo Manuel, both architects from the Mafra school. The lordly neoclassical façade is well balanced, with twin towers and eight beautiful marble statues; above the church rises a perfectly shaped stone dome. The high, chilly interior dwarfs devotees, who peer through the peculiar light that reflects off multicoloured marbles.

The mausoleum of the foundress is on the left of the high altar, a sombre memorial to the kindly queen who chose as her confessor the Archbishop of Thessalonica (who started his career as a clown, and then became a soldier). She died in Brazil, from whence her corpse was brought six years later. Only the males of the House of Bragança were embalmed: Dona Maria I had been surrounded by aromatic herbs and enclosed in three coffins. When these were opened, to lay the body in its tomb, one of the two presiding princesses fainted from the stench.

North of the Basilica

Opposite the front of the church, the intimate **Jardim da Estrela** provides a pond stocked with giant carp, which frighten people drinking beer at the waterside. A curious carved tree trunk stands at the opposite side of the park, which opens onto the Rua de São Jorge. Across the road are the gates of the crowded **English Cemetery**, laid out in 1717 adjacent to the hospital of the English Factory. (Do not be alarmed by the cemetery's postbox; it is for the vicarage.) Previously, Protestants had to be buried by the water's edge, to avoid profaning Catholic soil. Henry Fielding (1717–54) lived long enough to be spared this indignity; the author of *Tom Jones*, who described Lisbon as 'the nastiest city in the world', is buried among the cypresses and Judas trees, in the second aisle to the left.

The **Amoreiras district**, north of Estrela, was once a bustling factory district, established by the Marquês de Pombal, but is now infamous for the eponymous post-modern shopping centre and residential block (*buses 11, 15, 58, 11, 23, 53*) designed by Tomás Taveira. It appears to be a chrome and glass interpretation of a medieval fortress, totally out of keeping with the rest of the city, but not without a soul. Some people claim it is the most desirable place to live in Lisbon – because then you can't see the building itself. The shopping centre, which was Lisbon's first of its size, is a blend of upmarket boutiques, restaurants and cinemas.

Amoreiras is the destination of the monumental **Aqueduto das Águas Livres**, which gave *lisboetas* their first taste of freely available clean drinking water. Built 1729–48, it was financed by a surcharge on wine, meat and olive oil purchased in the capital. On the last leg of the 12-mile (19km) route, 14 arches bound across Lisbon's Alcântara valley, uninterrupted by the earthquake of 1755. This stretch was open to the public until 1844, the year in which Diogo Alves murdered people by throwing them off it. Group visits may be arranged to see the internal workings of the aqueduct and the imposing Mãe d'Água reservoir on the edge of the restful Jardim das Amoreiras. Opening onto this garden is the **Arpad Szènes-Vieira da Silva Foundation**, a showcase for the paintings of Portuguese modernist Maria Helena Vieira da Silva (*see* p.34) and her Hungarian husband Arpad Szènes. Exiles for artistic as much as political reasons, they were active in the School of Paris in the 1930s and 40s. As well as rotating the 1,500 paintings by the pair through the gallery, the foundation organizes exhibitions of works from their estate, some by very prominent Paris-based international artists.

Jardim das Amoreiras
t (21) 813 5522

Arpad Szènes-Vieira da Silva Foundation
t (21) 388 0044

Lapa

Lapa is Lisbon's diplomatic quarter, where ambassadorial residences rub shoulders with humble dwellings, in the west of central Lisbon overlooking the river.

Museu Nacional de Arte Antiga

Museu Nacional de Arte Antiga
Rua das Janelas Verdes, t (21) 391 2800; open Tues 2–6, Wed–Sun 10–6; closed Mon; adm, free Sun till 2; buses 27, 40, 49

The **Museu Nacional de Arte Antiga** is the most significant and thrilling Portuguese museum. *Antiga* is misleading: the collection covers Portuguese art from the 11th century to the 19th century. It illustrates the nation's relationship with Flanders, Africa, India, China and Japan, and includes European paintings, and applied arts from magnificent ecclesiastical silverwork to 18th-century furnishings.

The museum's entrance in the Jardim 9 de Abril forms part of its new wing, which was attached to the 17th-century Palace of the Counts of Alvor and the haunted chapel of the razed Convent of Santo Alberto. A small cafeteria issues reasonably priced hot food, salads, cakes and coffee, which can be eaten in the shady garden.

Portugal in the World

When the first Portuguese landed in Tanegashima, in 1543, the Japanese called them 'Namban-jin', barbarians from the south. The name stuck, and now applies to all the Japanese plastic arts created during nearly a century of contact with Portugal. Japanese artists were bemused by the exotic Portuguese, and painted them in detail for the home market. The arrival of the missionaries is pictured in two beautifully composed **namban screens**: in each, the Portuguese have bulbous noses – their hosts had never seen such large appendages. Nor had they seen buttons, so every button is detailed. The Portuguese brought Persian horses for the *shoguns*, and dealt in Indian goods, hence the artists imagined (wildly inaccurate) Indian architecture. In one screen, all the priests are Jesuits; the other screen was painted 15 years later, by which time other orders had arrived in Japan.

In India the Portuguese found both skilled craftsmen and abundant raw materials, especially wood and ivory. They took advantage of both from 1498 onwards. One of the most prolific products of this cultural marriage is the many-drawered **Indo-Portuguese chest**, or *contador*, which was based on a European model; but the legs offered Indian craftsmen free rein. **Ivory casks** depict Indian gods beside European hunting scenes. **Embroidered colchas**, used both for wall hangings and as covers for beds, show a broader cultural salad. They are illustrated with European classical mythology and biblical references, as well as hunting scenes. African craftsmen were exploited more selectively – the museum contains a small display of their works in ivory from the little island of Sherbro, off Sierra Leone, from Benin and from Mombasa.

Lisbon was the first market in Europe for the **porcelains** of China, which were shipped by junk to Macau, then westwards. Chinese porcelain was made for three markets: for the imperial family, for domestic use, or for export. Some of the exports are displayed; many of the platters were intended for the Middle East, since Muslims ate communally from large dishes, while the Chinese ate from small, individual bowls. Chinese porcelain had evolved from the blue and white Ming dynasty ware to polychromed designs by the early 18th century, when Portugal began importing it in such quantities as to stunt the home industry. When Pombal forbade the importation of European porcelains into Portugal in 1767, the Portuguese tried to make polychromed faïence copies of Chinese export porcelain tureens and animal-head containers. They created handsome small vases in various sizes. This was the first Portuguese work to come near to matching the grace of Chinese porcelain.

Portuguese Painting

The *Panels of São Vicente de Fora* are of unparalleled significance: they offer a portrait of the generation of the Discoveries. Painted by Nuno Gonçalves 1467–70, the six panels depict 60 uncompromising individuals who were determined to know the world.

The panels were found just over 60 years ago in the defunct church of São Vicente, dismantled and coated with filth – a tiny square has been left uncleaned, at the bottom of the left-hand panel, on the white robe of a Cistercian monk of Alcobaça – so we do not know their intended order. Fishermen are pictured in the panel next to that of the monks; the two right-hand panels show representatives of the army backed by members of the Jewish community. In the centre two panels, St Vincent receives the homage of various dignitaries, backed by an assembly, all painted with a disregard for depth.

Dom Jorge da Costa, Archbishop of Lisbon 1460–1500, is included in the centre right-hand panel. In the centre left-hand panel, the saint is flanked by Henry the Navigator and the widowed Duchess of Bragança, who wears a white headdress. Before the saint kneel Dom Afonso V, in profile, and a lady, possibly Queen Leonor, who had died in 1455. The face in the top left corner of this panel is believed to be the painter's.

Nuno Gonçalves may have learnt his technique from Jan van Eyck, who visited Portugal in 1428 in the suite of Philip the Good, Duke of Burgundy. But there are notable differences from Flemish work: he uses yellow where others use gold; there are no distracting details of the interior. Certainly Gonçalves can stand comparison with the foremost painters of his age.

Of the Luso-Flemish school, note particularly the work of **Frei Carlos**, a Flemish monk who lived in the Alentejo, and was staggered by the quality of light there. Look at his *Annunciation* from an angle, to see what he does with volume in space. The anonymous early 16th-century *Inferno* was a daring work to hang in a convent: Hell is a common kitchen, where the chief devil is a feathered Brazilian Indian.

European Art

European paintings are arranged chronologically rather than thematically, so it is possible to see the evolution of struggles with perspective and space, and of telling a story in cartoon or triptych form. Paintings were required to fit formal categories; when Patinir explored a countryside, he had to justify the subject by tacking on the figure of *St Jerome*, hung in Room 4. Patinir was doing for external space what Dürer was doing for mental space: his *St Jerome* – hung next to the Patinir – was painted in 1521.

Hieronymous Bosch's *Temptations of St Anthony* takes the biscuit. St Anthony's life spanned the late 3rd and early 4th centuries; much of it was spent in pious meditation in the Egyptian desert. Bosch set him in a kaleidoscope of the Middle Ages, where sinners are punished through excess: the libidinous couple are tied together, the greedy man is being fed gold coins. St Anthony is portrayed four times, but never once looks at the horrifying scenes around him: the saint was strong and pious enough to struggle against exposure to these evils. The artist was admired by contemporaries for his piety and perception at a time when the foundations of society were being shaken by Erasmus, Copernicus, Columbus and, following Bosch's death in 1516, by Luther. Our own uncertain future makes Bosch's apocalyptic vision terrifyingly pertinent.

Small, bright Room 7 offers a change of pace. It includes rare examples of Portugal's coarse early attempts to imitate Chinese porcelain: the Chinese emperor decapitated anyone attempting to reveal its secret. (Europeans guessed at its ingredients in vain, hazarding crushed oyster shells, long-buried dung, snails, or a paste of crushed shellfish and eggs buried for a century.)

Genre painting is emerging by Room 8: one panel relishes still life but resolutely titles itself *The Meeting of Jesus and Mary and Martha*.

French Silverware

The world's largest, finest and most varied collection of 18th-century French silverware is gathered here. These works of breathtaking craftsmanship and imagination were made fashionable by the court at Versailles, where monarchs dined in public for eight hours every day. In the 50 years after 1724, the Louvre workshop of Thomas Germain and his son François-Thomas produced an estimated 3,000 pieces of gold and silverware for the sovereigns and nobility of Portugal.

Much was destroyed by the earthquake of 1755, leaving Dom José I to re-equip the royal tables: kettles spout swans and dragons, mustard pots are oyster shells, and silver toothbrushes stand beside the discreet silver box in which a lady kept her beauty spots. The huge centrepiece illustrates the differences in the work of Germain father and son: Thomas Germain crafted the body in a more classical style than the fantastic lid created by his son. In 1985, the 16 silver-gilt figurines, designed by Cousinet, promenaded at the table of Queen Elizabeth and the Duke of Edinburgh, linked, as their maker intended, by garlands of fresh flowers held between their outstretched arms.

Puppet Museum
Rua da Esperança 146,
t *(213) 942 810; open*
Wed–Sun 10–1 and 2–6

Museu da Marioneta

A 10-minute walk from the Museu da Arte Antiga, in Madragoa, the **Puppet Museum** has splendid quarters in the former Convento

Lisbon | Lapa: Museu da Marioneta

13

das Bernardas. About half the puppets are Portuguese; all are very well displayed, and offer an interesting insight into villagers' views of the world.

The museum is intimate, but not cute: puppets have mocked politicians since the 18th century, when puppet operas became fashionable. Puppet plays were banned under Salazar. Each of the puppets takes two months to create; they eventually emerge, say, as Apollo, whose hair is woodshavings, or Dulcineia, whose head is faceless. There are regular shows for children and occasionally the museum's owner puts on a puppet opera, with a cast of 12–20. Puppets from Thailand, Burma, Indonesia and Japan are also on display. The paraphernalia of performance includes a tempest machine.

Saldanha

Saldanha is the district north of the Praça Marquês de Pombal and west of the Praça Duque de Saldanha.

The Estufas

Estufa Fria
t (21) 388 2278; open winter 9–4.30; summer 9–5.30; adm; buses 2, 12; metro Parque

In the early 1930s, a gardener noticed that plants grew particularly well in the disused limestone quarry that became the **Estufa Fria**, a botanic garden in the Parque Eduardo VII. Originally conceived as a sort of green cathedral, the ferns, fuchsias and what Dr Seuss would call um-pum-pullas are protected by a canopy of matted wooden slats; a giant hothouse proper was added (the Estufa Quente), to house a collection of orchids offered to the city. These rub petals with giant poinsettias, assorted cacti and pineapple plants.

Birds are caged beside the upper walkways, including parakeets, pheasants and Japanese ducks. The Estufas are well worth a stroll for anyone in need of respite from the city streets.

The Calouste Gulbenkian Museum

24 Calouste Gulbenkian Museum
45 Avenida de Berna, t (21) 782 3000, www.gulbenkian.pt; open daily 10–5; adm; buses 16, 26, 30, 31, 41, 46, 56; metro S. Sebastião, Praça de Espanha

The Avenida António Augusto Aguiar runs along the eastern side of the Parque Eduardo VII, leading to the Praça da Espanha and the Parque de Palhavã, in which stands the **Calouste Gulbenkian Museum**. The cafeteria in the basement of the Gulbenkian is good, but the one in the Centre of Modern Art is even nicer: it serves among the best salads in Lisbon, but there's always a queue.

Gulbenkian and his Foundation

Calouste Gulbenkian has become the fairy godfather of Portugal's cultural welfare. The Armenian magnate's fortune took on stratospheric proportions just before † ... he negotiated a five per cent stake in the ... fields of Iraq. He lived in Portugal from 19 ... the age of 86; he bequeathed his collecti... Occidental art to his adopted country, ar ... a foundation, the purpose of which was ... educational, scientific'.

The foundation now has assets of mor... ... dollars, making it the largest private charitable institution outside the United States; half as much again has been disbursed in grants and scholarships. These include underwriting Portugal's travelling libraries, endowing a museum of modern Portuguese art, building schools, science laboratories, medical clinics and hospitals, funding low-cost housing, orphanages, and centres for the disabled. Since the early 1960s, many members of the Foundation's own orchestra, choir and ballet have studied abroad.

Gulbenkian had taken British nationality. For a time he intended to bequeath his collection to the British nation; one of the reasons he changed his mind was that Britain declared him a 'technical enemy' during the Second World War (for continuing his rôle as honorary economic counsellor at the Iranian embassy in Paris, after the Vichy regime had been established). Gulbenkian's tact and discretion secured his most spectacular coup: the purchase of works of art from the Hermitage, 1928–30, when the government of the USSR was desperate for foreign currency. He referred to his urge for collecting as 'a disease', but wanted only 'to possess the finest specimens' – if a painting had been damaged or repainted too many times, he was not interested. Gulbenkian believed that a work of art 'must give joy'. He loved paintings 'filled with character and a certain mystery', and with 'a high level of feeling'.

The Museum

The purpose-built Gulbenkian Museum was opened in 1969; leafy views of the Palhavã Park make breathing spaces amid the collection. The museum is intimate and thoughtfully laid out. Everything it contains is worth looking at, and its size makes this possible. Ideally the museum should be visited on two occasions, one for the Oriental and Classical art (covering Egyptian, Greco-Roman, Mesopotamian, Oriental Islamic, Armenian and Far-Eastern art), and one for European art (covering medieval ivories, illuminated manuscripts, Renaissance works and 18th- and 19th-century sculpture, painting, silver and decorative arts). The gift shop is limited but subsidized, enabling it to sell the cheapest postcards and posters in Lisbon. A series of free printed guides in English thoroughly elucidates each section of the museum.

Egyptian, Greco-Roman and Mesopotamian Art

The small collection of Egyptian art is arranged chronologically, to illustrate its evolution from the Old Kingdom to the Roman era. Note the alabaster bowl (no.1), of magnificent proportions and the simplest of designs, which is sublime but was intended merely for measuring grain – among the gods, since it was found in a funerary chamber. Egyptian robes cling to peoples' bodies because their skin was coated with creams to protect it from the severe climate: a flat, ivory spoon (no.9) was used to remove these creams from their pots, and was then floated on water to prevent the ointments from melting.

Around the corner, Gulbenkian's coin collection is unforgettable: he wrote to a dealer that he wanted it 'to reflect Hellenic art when it was at the summit of its beauty and expression'. It leads to a small arrangement of Mesopotamian art, of which the centre-piece is a low relief of *Spring* (no.86) sprinkling sacred water on the fields.

Oriental Islamic Art

Gulbenkian paid particular attention to Oriental Islamic art: glass, ceramics, fabrics and illuminated manuscripts of the 12th–18th centuries are given plenty of space, and yet are able to interact with one another. They are linked by the density of their colours, the delicacy of their design, and a tendency towards symmetry. There are some interesting cross-currents, such as the way in which carpet design was influenced by those of bookbindings and silk brocades, or ceramic design by that of architectural tiles. A mosque lamp (no.324) hung in Damascus or Cairo in the 14th century: chains were attached to the six handles. The upper part of the lamp is inscribed with a verse from the Koran describing God as the light of the heavens and the earth.

Oriental Art

One of the most forceful pieces of Oriental Islamic art is displayed in the gallery next door: a superbly proportioned 15th-century jade jug (no.282), from Persia or Samarkand. Jade was believed to split on contact with poison, so a jug such as this came in handy for the wary ruler. Elsewhere in the gallery of Oriental art, cabinets are filled with bright but unlovely Chinese porcelain (the wig stand, no.385, is a curiosity), and with Japanese lacquerware. Every surface required 200 applications of lacquer, each of which took 100 hours to dry. It was ruined if dust settled on the wet lacquer, so many workshops were by the sea, where there is less dust.

Early European Art

The section of European art kicks off with several exquisite medieval ivories, which tell stories to illiterates and were designed for travelling. The paintings are arranged in chronological order, where possible by schools. Of the early paintings, note van der Weyden's stubbly *St Joseph* (no.897), the fragment of an altarpiece (another section of which is in London's National Gallery), and Diereck Bouts's wordless *Annunciation* (no.895). Domenico Ghirlandaio's *Young Woman* (no.979) is one of the earliest frontal portraits of the Italian Renaissance. Bugiardini, a friend of Michaelangelo, blends the sweet and the sour aspects of the face of a Young Woman.

Rembrandt's son Titus posed as *Alexander the Great* (no.966); the subject is sometimes described as Pallas Athena, but would seem too dolorous to be a goddess. His *Portrait of an Old Man* (no.967) shows a dignified greybeard steeped in sadness and bewilderment. You can almost hear the silk russle in Rubens's *Portrait of Hélène Fourment*, his sensual second wife. A couple of years before it was painted, van Dyck had been in Italy, where he painted a *Portrait of a Man*.

Three huge tapestry panels from the series *Children Playing* (nos.1005–7) offer a break from the paintings. The panels were woven in silk, wool and silver and gold thread: more than 200 colours were required to reproduce the tones of Giulio Romano's paintings of cherubs. The little fellows get up to all sorts of tricks, including the tormenting of frogs.

18th- and 19th-century Art

French paintings and sculpture of the 18th century are displayed near the decorative arts of the same period. One writing table (no.687) came from the apartments of Queen Marie-Antoinette – look at the craftsmanship and the way in which the materials are fused – and a silk hanging (no.1027) was intended to cover her walls at Versailles. Other apartments at Versailles have provided the Gulbenkian with the rolltop desk (no.688) by Riesener, who was possibly the greatest furniture maker of the 18th century. The museum houses a breathtaking collection of French gold- and silverwork of that age – some of the craftsmen are also represented in Lisbon's Museu de Arte Antiga.

French 18th-century portraiture is best served by La Tour's masterwork, the *Portrait of Duval de l'Épinoy* (no.913). Pastels do not allow the artist to correct his work – hence Duval's head was reworked on an upper sheet of paper. Houdon's smooth marble *Diana* (no.609) was sold to Catherine the Great of Russia. It depicts the naked goddess running.

English portraits and landscapes of the 18th and 19th centuries include works by Gainsborough, Romney and Lawrence. Turner's *Quillebœuf, Mouth of the Seine* (no.976) is charged with swirling, elemental electricity. One room is devoted to luminous works by Guardi (nos.985–1003), and another to 19th-century French sculpture. Gulbenkian was a fan of naturalism – represented by the works of Corot (nos. 929–935) and Daubigny (nos.936–940), among others. The collector had a standing contract with René Lalique, the man who put decoration back into French jewellery design, with his delicate and imaginative Art Nouveau creations.

José de Azeredo Perdigão Centre of Modern Art

José de Azeredo
Perdigão Centre of
Modern Art
*open Tues 2–6,
Wed–Sun 10–6;
closed Mon; adm*

Linked to the main Gulbenkian Museum by a sculpture garden, the **José de Azeredo Perdigão Centre of Modern Art** is far and away the most important repository of modern and contemporary Portuguese art, with a rotating display tending towards the contemporary. Leading 20th-century Portuguese painters represented in the permanent collection include **Amadeo de Sousa-Cardoso** (1887–1918; *see* 'Amarante', p.199), who was constantly changing his style, but tied them all together in his final speedy and fragmented works, and his friend **Eduard Viana**, who collaborated with him on the review *Orpheu* – as did all the Modernists. **Almada Negreiros**, another Modernist, painted simplified human figures and attempted to foster a Portuguese national identity – which endeared him to Salazar. The dictator wanted a distinct Portuguese style of painting, architecture and sculpture. Expressionist painters such as **Mário Eloy** and **Carlos Botelho** did their best to sidestep this interference, the former painting nature and the latter painting Lisbon. **Vieira da Silva** introduced abstraction to the capital; her style owes much to *azulejos*. In the mid-1940s, the dictatorship prompted artists to paint subjects which would draw attention to the plight of the populace. **Vespeira**, **Júlio Pomar** and **Rogério Ribeiro** painted workers and peasants to such effect that the secret police withdrew a number of works from the General Exhibition at the Lisbon Society of Fine Arts in 1947.

One -ism gave birth to another: disenchanted Neo-Realists became Surrealists – **Vespeira** and **Fernando de Azevedo** revelled in this apolitical form of revolutionary art. They lived in a regulated society and hoped their work would undermine its rationalism. Both turned to abstraction in the late 1950s.

D'Assumpção and **Vieira da Silva** became renowned for their abstract works; just as the movement was catching on, Pop Art appeared. The 1970s witnessed the exploration of light and time through acrylics and photography. **Paula Rego** is one of the most respected contemporary Portuguese artists: her paintings are sinister and disturbing, harking back to a childhood world of domination. Of younger artists represented in the collection, **Julião Sarmento** is more abstract, with minimalist sketches on a whitewashed canvas, and **José Pedro Croft**'s conceptual art uses basic props such as artfully positioned chairs, while **Rui Chafes** is known for monumental sculptures in iron or stone.

Sete Ríos

Sete Ríos occupies the northwestern corner of Lisbon.

Palácio dos Marquêses de Fronteira

Fronteira Palace
Largo de São Domingos de Benfica 1;
t (21) 778 2023; guided tours to house and garden June–Sept Mon–Sat 10.30am, 11am, 11.30am, noon, Oct–May Mon–Sat 11am, noon; closed Sun; adm

The Fronteira Palace was built to be lived in, and has been filled with rich pickings over the centuries. It is one of the most enjoyable and stimulating attractions in the whole of Lisbon, with mind-boggling *azulejos* and a superb collection of modern Portuguese art.

The first marquis, a general, was active in the War of Restoration. In 1671–2, he built an Italianate hunting lodge 1 hour and 10 minutes' horse-ride north of the Rossio. A new wing was added after the earthquake of 1755, and several loggias were enclosed. The Marquês does not want crowds trekking through his home, which is why access is so restricted and complicated.

The Gardens

The gardens have retained their 17th-century layout, including a formal garden of 365 manicured box trees, quartered to indicate the four seasons. Delightfully bumptious *azulejo* panels personify the months of the year, the signs of the zodiac, and all the planets known at the time, up to Saturn. To one side is an oblong tank, flanked by steps which lead to a walkway above. Reflected in the water are 14 panels of plumed horsemen, influenced by the paintings of Velásquez.

The Palace

Visitors to the Palace are shown six rooms, which evolved under the hands of generations of artists. In the Battle Room, tiles of c.1670 depict all the major battles of the War of Restoration (when the Portuguese ended 60 years of Spanish domination). They are clumsy but whimsical: cannons and muskets emit little green plumes of smoke; the forces labelled 'Englezes' mark a phalanx of English troops who ran out of ammunition and used their guns as clubs. The inky Delft panels in the dining room – with finely textured horses' tails – were among the first imported into Portugal.

The Delft (dining) room opens onto the Gallery of the Arts terrace, sided with fantastic *azulejo* panels of 1670, depicting personifications of the arts, interspersed with mythological figures. Astronomia is the celestial lady whose breasts are the sun and moon. Apollo is pictured with the flayed skin of Marcius, who dared to defy the god in a music contest. These odd bedfellows overlook Fronteira's Romantic garden, and beyond it to the remains of Monsanto wood. The chapel at the end of the terrace was built in 1584, predating the house; tradition has it that St Francis Xavier said his last Mass here before embarking for India. It is beautifully decorated with shells and the fragments of Ming china broken after King Dom Pedro II and his lackeys supped off it.

The Marquês' collection of modern Portuguese art – which includes work by the Marquesa – is worth a visit in its own right. An old kitchen is devoted to work by João Cutileiro, the Évora sculptor of contorted flesh-coloured ladies. Be sure the tap is turned on to bathe the figure sitting in the sink. No other museum dares display Cutileiro's other penchant: sculpted phalluses.

North Lisbon

The Avenida de Berna runs eastwards from the Gulbenkian Museum. It bisects the Avenida da República (which stretches north from the Praça de Duque Saldanha), passing the Moorish-style **Campo Pequeno bullring**, closed for several years for construction work and re-opened in 2006. This is built of bricks the colour of dried blood, with cupolas at each axis. It once sat nearly 8,500 spectators, some of them on stone benches, which would gather lichen were they given half a chance. It now houses a shopping mall.

Campo Pequeno bullring
buses 1, 17b, 21, 27, 32, 36, 38, 47, 54; metro Campo Pequeno

The Avenida da República runs northwards into Campo Grande. At the northwest corner of the Jardim do Campo Grande, the **Museu da Cidade** (City Museum) puts Lisbon in its historical context, using a variety of media.

Museu da Cidade
t (217) 513 200; open 10–1 and 2–6; closed Mon; adm; buses 1, 3, 7, 7a, 17b, 33, 36, 36a, 46a, 47, 50; metro Campo Grande

The museum is installed in the sober 18th-century Palácio Pimenta, whose most endearing feature is the witty 'cut-out' *azulejos* of hares, swans, fish and other animals hung upside down on the kitchen walls. Upstairs the functions of rooms are illustrated by their *azulejo* dado. Visitors are greeted by two fabulous long-necked, fruit-topped modern ladies sculpted by **Jorge Barradas**. The collection includes a huge maquette representing the city before the 1755 earthquake, and Dirk Stoop's (1610–86) painting of the Praça do Comércio as it used to be – with merchants weighing their goods around the central fountain, and charlatans bamboozling gullible *lisboetas*. Almada Negreiros's famous portrait of Fernando Pessoa shows the poet with a copy of *Orpheu*, the modernists' journal.

Museu do Traje e da Moda
Largo Júlio Castilho, t (21) 759 0318, www.museudotraje-ipmuseus.pt; open 10–6; closed Mon; adm; buses 1, 7, 7a, 17b, 36

Museu Nacional do Traje e da Moda

Continuing north, the village of Lumiar has been swallowed by the capital's sprawl. In the Largo Júlio de Castilho, the **Museu do**

Traje e da Moda (Museum of Clothing and Fashion) presents temporary exhibitions of aspects of lay dress and fashion, at all social levels, from medieval times to the present. Society has dreamt up some strange and revealing images for us over the ages, which are interesting in themselves, as well as enlivening the study of painting. The museum's photocopied 'Short history of the civil costume in Portugal ...' includes snippets of information about male and female hairstyles, chips about jewellery, and patches about shoes (all of which were cloaked by foreign influences).

Quinta do Monteiro-Mor
open 10–5 daily

The display is woven into the 18th- and 19th-century Quinta do Monteiro-Mor, which stands in a wonderfully peaceful, mature terraced park. In 1793 this was referred to as one of the three most beautiful gardens in Lisbon; a climatic freak gives it a particularly dense and varied vegetation.

Museu Nacional do Teatro
t (21) 757 2547; open 10–6; closed Mon; adm

The Museu Nacional do Teatro (Theatre Museum), stands within the grounds. It has a more specialized appeal, featuring costume and backdrop designs, photographs of actors and actresses in performance, and wild, winged, episcopal costumes by Almada Negreiros, in bright appliqué.

Convento de Odivelas

The Avenida Padre Cruz continues northwards past the Museu do Traje, feeding onto the 250–2 road. Just 1km outside Lisbon stands

Convento de Odivelas
Largo Dom Dinis, Odivelas, t (21) 933 7107; pre-booked guided tours Mon–Fri 10–11.30 and 2–5.30

the Convento de Odivelas, founded by Dom Dinis 1295–1305. It was badly damaged by the earthquake of 1755, but the Gothic apse and two side chapels remain. The founder's tomb is here; built during the king's lifetime, it set a fashion for funerary architecture. The flanking sculptures have been decapitated.

Queen Philippa of Lancaster, wife of Dom João I, died here in 1415. Before expiring, she called for three swords with scabbards and guards of gold, pearls and cut stones, to give to her three sons. She showed little fear – small wonder: the chronicler Azurara describes her as 'a woman most acceptable to God'. She was buried at Batalha, during the night, as the heat was excessive.

In the 18th century, the convent was renowned for its poetry recitals. Guests were then invited to drinks, accompanied by glacé pumpkin and lemon peel, meringues, little squares of quince jelly, and *toucinho do céu* (bacon from heaven). Perhaps it was over one such pudding that King Dom João V was introduced to the captivating Dona Magdalena, who bore him a son, Dom Gaspar, the future Archbishop of Braga. But another nun, Madre Paula, caught the king's attention (at the age of 17) and held it for at least 10 years. Their son, Dom José, became Grand Inquisitor. (In his later years, the king resorted to aphrodisiacs, and his last mistress, a French actress called Petronilla, was dismissed for the sake of his health.)

The convent is now a private school so visits, which are guided by the caretaker, must be booked in advance; phone and ask for the school board secretary (*secretária da direcção*).

Northeast Lisbon: The Parque das Nações

To reach the site, catch a metro or regional train to the impressive new Oriente station, which feels like the belly of a giant insect, or take bus 25A which leaves from the Praça do Comércio.

In 1998 Lisbon successfully hosted **Expo 98**, a world exhibition to crown the second millennium. It's hard to underestimate the effect it had on Portuguese people's image of their country: here was Portugal, slick, cutting edge and on the world stage – which ushered in a new confidence. Around 150 acres (60ha) of the city's riverfront was renovated for the exhibition, and the site still draws crowds, particularly at weekends. It's a pleasant place to wander, with lots of sculpture and art, cable cars to the sail-shaped **Torre Vasco da Gama** (with a viewing platform at 340ft/104m; *adm*; see 'Where to Eat', p.398), and jet skis in the harbour. It has also been transformed into a business centre, with high-rise offices. The huge **Pavilhão Atlântico arena** is used for concerts – see the local press or the tourist office for details.

The principal remaining attraction is Europe's largest **Oceanarium**. Five tanks are home to 10,000 creatures repatriated from the Antarctic, North Atlantic, Pacific and Indian Oceans, with the huge central tank representing the Open Ocean. It's a wonderful place to eyeball strange creatures. Do hobnob with the otters, nicknamed Amália, after the diva, and Eusébio, after the footballer. Note the moon jellyfish, which are used for stress therapy in Japan.

Oceanarium
Avenue Dom João II, Parque das Nações, t (218) 919 333, www.oceanario.pt; open April–Oct 10–7, Nov–Mar 10–6; adm

Belém

'Belém' means 'Bethlehem': if there is a star over the district, it guides hordes of tourists to the water's edge, 4 miles (6km) west of the city centre. Commuter traffic and rattling trains shatter the calm of Belém's suburban villas. Belém is built on the white stone that was quarried to build the Jerónimos monastery.

Tram 15 runs to Belém, as do buses 14, 27, 28, 29, 43, 49 and 51.

History

Throughout the night of 7 July 1497, Vasco da Gama and his captains kept vigil in the Church of Our Lady of Belém. The following morning, they carried tapers to the riverside, and there made a general Confession. They were absolved of their sins, lest they die on the journey. Almost exactly two years later, da Gama returned to Belém having discovered a sea route to India. A contemporary described da Gama as 'a discrete man, of good understanding and great courage'. Sailing in four naos, which were larger and heavier than caravels, he and his crew of not more than 170 men moored at the Cape Verde Islands (off Senegal), the last land they were to see for 62 days. They ate raisins, salt, biscuits, honey and dried beans – but scurvy struck: on the return journey 'all our people again suffered from their gums, which grew over their teeth, so that they could not eat. Their legs also swelled, and other parts of the body, and these swellings spread until the sufferer died.'

At Calicut, the courtiers scorned the copper rings, red berets and hawks' bells which had delighted the Africans. They refused to deliver these tacky gifts to the Zamorin. A Moor at the Zamorin's court spoke a little Castilian, and communicated the potentate's first message to his visitor: 'May the Devil take thee! What brought you hither?'

'We came in search of Christians and spices,' da Gama replied.

Jerónimos Monastery

Jerónimos Monastery
t (21) 362 0034;
open winter daily 10–5;
summer daily 10–6.30;
adm

The **Jerónimos Monastery** (across a little park from the riverside Avenida da India) is the most thrilling and significant building in Portugal. The purest example of Portugal's own Manueline style of architecture has a vital energy and tension, and its treatment of space is breathtaking.

History

In 1460, Henry the Navigator founded a hermitage on this site; friars of the Order of Christ assisted seafarers until 1496, when Dom Manuel gazumped his forebear with plans for a modest Jeronymite monastery. When da Gama returned to Belém in 1499, the king thankfully granted his new foundation the 'pepper penny', a five per cent tax on all the spices and precious stones coming from India, and on the gold brought from Guinea. These revenues were deposited with the Medicis' agent in Lisbon. Dom Manuel turned his attention from Batalha Abbey to Belém, employing as his master of works Diogo Boitac, who had flexed his muscles on the church of Jesus at Setúbal. Between 1502 and 1517, Boitac completed the general structure of the buildings, following the tenets of the late European Gothic style. For the decoration, these doctrines were integrated with Manueline ornamentation, which employed ropes, cables, and armillary spheres.

In 1517 João de Castilho replaced Boitac, bringing a new awareness of Renaissance forms. In the doors, the pillars of the nave, and part of the cloister, he and his collaborators harmonized pure classicism with Iberian exuberance – but the new king, Dom João III, became preoccupied with the Convent of Christ at Tomar, and João de Castilho was removed thence. Most of the building was completed in the first quarter of the century. Diogo de Torralva was appointed as master of works in the middle of the century, and worked on the chancel, the choir, and parts of the cloister. Jerónimo de Ruão, son of the sculptor João de Ruão, added some finishing touches to the chancel and the transepts' chapels, 1571–2.

By 1739, the rents received by the monastery had dried to a mere trickle; so severe was the shortage of funds that the monks resorted to selling *pásteis de nata* (custard tarts). It may have been these that appeased the earthquake of 1755, for the buildings were left virtually undamaged. From 1807, part of the building was occupied by the army. When the monasteries were dissolved in 1834, the monastic buildings were occupied by an orphanage for 700 boys. The complex was insensitively 'reconstituted' in the mid-19th century, when the cupola was added.

The Monastery

Facing the river, João de Castilho's elegant, harmonious **south portal** bears more than a trace of Flemish realism – at the top of the portal, even the Virgin's broad hat and ample skirt echo those of a Belgian burgher's wife. Henry the Navigator is represented by a bearded figure between the doors.

Chanterène's **west portal** is stunted by its modern covering. This was his first commission in Portugal; he experimented with ornament, but had not attained the mighty powers that were to come. Dom Manuel and his second wife Dona Maria are portrayed either side of the door, accompanied by their respective patron saints. Above them are niches occupied by the four Evangelists, and buttresses depicting the Apostles.

The navigators provided Manueline architecture with a fund of decorative motifs, and also a concept of space. They had lived with the horizon, and the definition of space in the soaring, ivory-coloured **interior** is more impressive than anywhere else in Portugal.

The nave and aisles are of the same height, united by fanlike vaulting which is supported by polygonal columns decorated with flat classical objects – medallions, skulls, three-headed snakes and harpies, and, on one column, signs of the zodiac. An astonishing unsupported star vault is suspended above the wide transept; after seeing that, the later, classical apse, with its stupendous gilt tabernacle, comes as a mild shock. In the transepts elephants support the tombs of Dom Sebastian and Dom Henrique, the Cardinal-King.

The two-storeyed **cloister** is entered through the giftshop. The cloister's fantastical lower level was decorated by João de Castilho, contemporary with the church. Its wild galaxy of human and animal faces peep through the vegetable ornament bound by ropes and anchors. Strange creatures are here, especially a sort of distorted snail. The upper level, completed in 1544, is more sober. A door leads to the upper choir, with superb choir stalls carved from Brazilian wood c. 1560, their sides ornamented by tortured souls in low relief.

Museums

Museu da Marinha (Marine Museum)

Museu da Marinha
*t (21) 362 0019;
open Tues–Sun 10–6;
closed Mon; adm*

At the west end of the monastery, the **Museu da Marinha**'s naval uniforms and models of ships do little to bring to life Portugal's astonishing naval history. The highlights are a celestial globe c. 1700, an early 16th-century map of the coast of Brazil, and the cabin and quarters of the yacht made for Dom Manuel II (1908–10), complete with silver radiators, roulette table and piano. (It was rumoured and later verified that the king had drawn more money from the public treasury than the official accounts showed – his apologists pointed out that the royal allowance had not risen since the late 19th century.)

Museu Nacional de Etnologia

Museu de Etnologia
t (21) 304 1160; open Tues 2–6, Wed–Sun 10–6; closed Mon; adm

The Rua dos Jerónimos runs along the eastern side of the monastery. A gentle 10-minute uphill walk leads to the excellent **Museu de Etnologia**. The presentation is exemplary, and its several simultaneous temporary exhibitions – which run the gamut from African masks through European carnival traditions to traditional agricultural equipment – will broaden anyone's horizons.

Museu Nacional dos Coches (Coach Museum)

In 1726 Dom João V purchased a *quinta* in Belém, slightly east of the monastery. Shortly afterwards he annexed it to another, which served as a royal palace and is now the official residence of the President of the Republic. The burnt-pink building is closed to the

Coach Museum
t (21) 361 0850;
open Tues–Sun 10–6;
closed Mon; adm

public, but, just to the south, the royal riding school now houses the **Coach Museum**, in the Rua de Belém. It was built by the Italian architect Jacomo Azzolini for Dom José in Louis XVI style, and hosted various courtly tournaments 1787–1810.

The collection is one of the finest in the world – rivalling those of Versailles and Madrid – though it is incomplete, since Dom João VI took some particularly fine examples with him when he fled to Brazil in 1807. Coaches were not mere vehicles, they were part of the royal razzle-dazzle, propaganda on wheels – and there was plenty of time for such ostentation to make its mark: it took five or six days to get to Porto. For all that, the museum misses the snort of horses, and the sheer number of coaches dulls the excitement. The most thrilling are those Baroque confections laden with gilt sculpture, at the back of the hall, where mermen ride lions borne by cherubs. The three carriages employed by the Marquês de Fontes on his 1716 embassy to Pope Clement XI glitter with statuary, glorifying Portugal's maritime enterprises and the thrust given to the arts and sciences by Dom João V.

Coaches never recovered from Pombal's austerity measures in the second half of the 18th century: he limited the use of rich fabrics and rich metals in an attempt to avoid imports – and to exalt the king's carriage. It was this period that produced the most curious chaise, a sort of giant gas mask on wheels.

Various spurs and stirrups are displayed in the gallery upstairs. The wooden gentleman with a wraparound moustache is the *estafermo*, literally a 'scarecrow' or 'dullard', but nicknamed 'pain-in-the-arse'. Riders tested their dexterity by attempting to touch him with a lance. If they were too slow, he rotated, whip in hand, and lashed them.

The Torre de Belém

Torre de Belém
open June–Sept
10–6.30, Oct–May 10–5;
adm

Returning to the waterfront, the bold and elegant **Torre de Belém** squats at the downstream, or western, side of the district. This is the closest Portugal gets to a national monument, and the finest example of Manueline architecture with Moorish trimmings. Its five-storey tower and projecting bastion were planned by Francisco de Arruda as a lookout post and a base for cannons, to exclude corsairs from the Tagus. When it was built, 1515–21, the tower was surrounded by water; the Tagus nearly lapped the doorstep of the Jerónimos monastery. But the river bank has crept southwards, and now the tower stands beside the shore.

The striking exterior decoration is at its most fanciful in the sentry posts' melon domes, which are based on a design popular in Marrakech. The dome of the northwestern sentry box is supported by a rhinoceros (symbolizing Africa, as elephants symbolized Asia). Moorish balconies and finely carved balustrades ornament the upper storeys, and the crenellations are cross-bearing shields of the Order of Christ. The same cross was echoed in red and white on the sails of the discoverers' ships.

The projecting bastion takes the form of a cloister, below which were the damp store-rooms used as dungeons until the time of Dom Miguel. The cloister is topped by a thrilling terrace, which formed the second line of fire. It feels like an enchanted cake (that smells of the sea). Visitors can climb the tower to get good views of Belém and the river.

At the Waterfront

Museu Nacional de Arte Popular
t (21) 301 1282; open Tues–Sun 10–12.30 and 2–5; closed Mon and hols

On the opposite side of the dock beside the Torre, the **Museu Nacional de Arte Popular** is too large and arid a setting for its display of folksy paraphernalia. It serves as a good introduction to the sausage-dog doorknockers, black pots, baskets, wooden-soled shoes, fire grates, carved horns for pepper, cork jars and cowbells of the various regions of Portugal.

Monument to the Discoveries
t (21) 303 1950; open July and Aug Tues–Sun 9–7; Sept–June Tues–Sun 9–5; closed Mon; adm

In 1960, the 500th anniversary of the death of Prince Henry the Navigator was marked by the construction of the **Monument to the Discoveries**, opposite the monastery and next to the Museu de Arte Popular. The monument resembles the prow of a ship. Henry the Navigator is sculpted at the prow, backed by Camões and others, whose stylized hairdos are respectfully avoided by the seagulls. From the top of the monument, you can hear traffic humming across the **Ponte 25 de Abril**, which clocks in at 3,325ft (1,013m), making it the longest suspension bridge in Europe when built. At its completion in 1966, it was named 'The Salazar Bridge'. Now it commemorates the date of the Revolution, and most of the bridges in Portugal seem to have followed suit.

Ajuda

On a hill overlooking the Tagus, the western district of Ajuda is connected to Belém by wide, gently sloping streets. Ajuda is serviced by tram 18 and buses 14, 27, 29, 32, 40 and 42. No.14 runs from the Coach Museum in Belém. The broad Calçada da Ajuda

Ajuda Palace
t (21) 363 7095; open
Mon–Tues, Thu–Sun
10–5; closed Wed; adm

leads inland from the Coach Museum to the **Ajuda Palace** which dominates a hill high above the Tagus (a 20-minute walk uphill from Belém). Construction began in 1802, on the site of a previous royal palace destroyed by fire: behind the classical façade of white pedra lioz stretch interminable rooms stuffed with rich, and for the most part tasteless, 19th-century furnishings acquired by Dona Maria II and her artist husband Dom Ferdinand, who escaped when they could to the Pena Palace at Sintra. It's difficult to see the wood for the trees, but keep an eye open for the Louis XV and XVI commodes, the Gobelins tapestries, assorted stools, writing desks and sideboards, and the silver by Germain. The delightful parquet is different in every room. The Banqueting Room can accommodate 160 guests, and occasionally still does.

Slightly downhill, the Rua do Jardim Botánico leads westwards to the small **church of Memória**, founded by Dom José in 1760, on the site of the attempt to assassinate him two years previously. As the king returned home from an amorous engagement, his carriage was ambushed twice, but not halted. The king received an arquebus shot in the arm, and unknowingly avoided a third trap by ordering his coachman to drive directly to the royal surgeon. The regicide plot proved useful to Pombal. He pinned the blame both on the Jesuits and on the families of the Duke of Aveiro and the Marquis of Tāvora, who were punished with excruciating savagery. Pombal's tomb was transferred to the church's carved marble interior in 1923. Look for the wooden arm pierced by shots, which was Dom José's votive offering.

Across the River

The Cristo Rei Statue

The statue of Christ the King stands, with robed arms outstretched, on a hill opposite Lisbon. It was modelled on Rio de Janeiro's Christ, and inaugurated in 1959, in honour of a promise made by the Portuguese bishops if the country were preserved from the Second World War. An elevator whizzes visitors up the structure, which contains a gift shop and offers heady views of Lisbon. To get to the statue, take one of the frequent ferries from the Praça do Comércio's Terminal Fluvial to Cacilhas – a brief ride – and catch bus 101 or a taxi from the station next to the ferry dock.

Costa da Caparica and the Setúbal Peninsula

See **Estremadura and the Ribatejo**, 'South of Lisbon', p.323.

(i) **Lisbon >**

National tourist board office: Praça dos Restauradores, **t** *(21) 346 3643,* *www.visitportugal.com*

National tourist board counter at airport: **t** *(21) 849 4323*

Local tourist board: represented at Restauradores office, but have own Welcome Center at Rua do Arsenal 15, **t** *(21) 031 2700,* *www.visitlisboa.com*

Tourist Information/ Services in Lisbon

At the **local tourist board**'s Welcome Center you can buy a **Lisboa Card** for one, two or three days, giving unlimited use of public transport and free or reduced entry to many of the city's museums and other sights. **Falkplan** produce an invaluable map of Lisbon, which can be purchased from various newsagents. It marks every street (with a useful index), most monuments and public transport routes.

Bring flat shoes, as the streets of Lisbon are cobbled and hilly. Comfortable shoes will help you escape from the dope dealers who approach foreigners in the Rossio square and the Praça do Comércio. At night, be wary in the bar-lined streets set back from Cais do Sodré – you're unlikely to be in grave danger, but you might come across a brawl.

Banks

Banks are all well represented in the Baixa and around Rossio, where the remaining exchange offices cling on despite the adoption of the Euro in the homelands of most visitors to Lisbon. The main Baixa branch of **Caixa Geral de Depósitos**, Rua Áurea (Rua do Ouro) 49, **t** (21) 340 5000, also has a money-changing machine.

Internet Access

There are a number of web cafés dotted around town, for example downstairs at the **Taborda** theatre, Rua Costa do Castelo 75, **t** (21) 888 1718 (*open Tues–Sun 2pm–midnight*); at the **Chapitô** complex at no. 7 on the same road, **t** (21) 888 1718. Downtown, there's web access at the tourist board's **Lisboa Welcome Center**, Rua do Arsenal 15, **t** (21) 031 2800 (*open daily 9–8*). The cheapest options are **Portugal Telecom's** bustling outlets on the northwestern corner of Rossio and on the ground floor of Avenida Fontes Pereira de Melo 32 (*open Mon–Fri 9–7*). Expect to pay about €3 per hour, with a half-hour minimum charge. Many hotels also offer

internet access for guests, but at a (sometimes shocking) price.

Other Services

Lisbon has a number of other services you'd be hard pushed to find in smaller Portuguese towns; the exception is laundrettes, of which there is only one downtown, **Lava Neve**, Rua da Alegria 37–39, **t** (21) 346 6195. Dry cleaners are easier to find; one of the many is **5 à Sec** at Rua dos Correeiros 105–107, in the Baixa, and there is another underground in Marquês de Pombal metro station.

Sports and Activities in Lisbon

If your hotel doesn't have a gym or a pool – the one at the **Aparthotel VIP Eden** (*see* p.387) is especially spectacularly situated – you may be able to pay through the nose to use the facilities of the nearest five-star hotel on a one-off basis.

Swimming Pools

There is the cheaper option of using a public pool. Swimming pools in town tend to be less crowded in the summer as *lisboetas* prefer the beach, but, bizarrely, many public ones are closed for the whole of August. The two mentioned below are among the few that do not.

Ateneu Comercial de Lisboa, Rua das Portas de Santo Antão 110, **t** (21) 343 0947. Once-elegant, now decadent private club where you can pay for one or 10 visits. The 25m pool is on the top floor, under a glass dome, but that somehow doesn't feel like the luxury it should be. *Open to non-members Mon–Fri 8–2, 3–8 and 9–10; Sat 1.30–7.*
Piscina da Penha de França, Calçada do Poço dos Mouros 2, **t** (21) 812 5000. Indoor heated municipal pool. *Open Mon–Fri 12.30–9.30; Sat–Sun 10–5.*

Gyms

A handful of private gyms offer day passes or prices for a single activity.
Barriga Killer, Rua Cintura do Porto, Armazém J, **t** (21) 395 6423. On the river side of the railway beyond Cais

do Sodré station, this was Lisbon's first truly modern gym, offering aerobics, weights and cardio training, plus sauna and Turkish bath. *Open Mon–Fri 8am–10pm, Sat 11–4, Sun 11–3.* **Health Club Soleil**, Shop 104, Amoreiras Shopping Center, Avenida Engenheiro Duarte Pacheco 2, **t** (21) 383 2908. Somewhat shabby gym that's nevertheless one of the few places in town that has squash courts, and it is handily located.

Tennis

Tennis is a popular sport in Portugal – could it possibly have anything to do with hours of sunshine? One of the most pleasant settings to play is the **Jamor Tenis Club**, **t** (21) 414 6041, in the leafy lee of the national football stadium at Cruz Quebrada, about a 15-minute drive out of Lisbon. It has 31 clay courts, several of them covered, and six fast ones; you can't book at this municipally run facility, but even at weekends if you turn up before 11 you should easily get on. The Estoril Open is played here.

Festivals in Lisbon

Lisbon gets its knees up in June with the **Festas dos Santos Populares**, a Christianized version of the summer solstice: the **Feast of St Anthony** (12–13 June) decks the Alfama with bunting, grilled sardines and basil, all of which is washed down with plenty of wine; the **Feast of St John** (23–24 June) kindles bonfires in some streets and songs in the air; and the **Feast of St Peter** (28–29 June) brings it all to a close.

Shopping in Lisbon

One of the very enjoyable things about Lisbon shops is seeing how specialized they can be, harking back to the days before petrol stations sold eggs and banks sold electricity. Just off the Praça da Figueira, **Soares & Rebelo** sells seeds, and in the Rua do Carmo 28 **Luvaria Ulisses** sells gloves. **7 Quintas**, **t** (21) 031 2605 (*open Mon–Sat 9–7*), is an excellent

delicatessen on the first floor of the Ribeira market selling top-quality Portuguese honey, dried figs, pine nuts, cheese, *chouriço*, wine and particularly olive oil, some of which comes from single *quintas*.

If you're in search of a wedding present, **Vasco Costa Conceição**, Rua Dom Luís I 36, at the corner of Avenida de Dom Carlos I, **t** (21) 396 5282 (*open Mon–Sat 10–7*), is a contemporary furniture and household accessories emporium, complete with mock croc mirror frames and water hyacinth reed chairs. Although most of the wares are imported, you can fork out on beautifully designed Portuguese cutlery by **Cutipol**, crystal by **Atlantis**, porcelain by **Vista Alegre**, or by **Spal** for daily use, some very striking tin bowls, and crystal-and-silver bowls by **Topázio**.

Goldsmiths and silversmiths sell the fruits of their craftsmanship in the Baixa, as they have for hundreds of years, so trot along if you fancy a *caravela* for your mantelpiece. **Cerâmica Constância**, Rua de S. Domingos à Lapa 8C, **t** (21) 396 3951 (uphill from the side entrance of the Museu de Arte Antiga), design and retail *azulejos*; they can copy photographs, at a price. For individual *azulejo* items, such as coasters and tablemats, head for **Sant'Ana**, Rua do Alecrim 95, **t** (21) 342 2537, off Largo do Chiado. There are witty *azulejos* for sale in the **Rua Academia das Ciências** (in the Bairro Alto), as well as Portalegre tapestries (*see* p.408). **Vista Alegre**, the fine porcelain manufacturers, have two outlets in the Bairro Alto: Rua Ivens 54, **t** (21) 342 8612, and Largo do Chiado 18, **t** (21) 346 1401.

For English-language **books**, try **Livraria Britanica**, Rua de São Marçal 83, **t** (21) 347 6141, opposite the British Institute, or **Livraria Buchholz**, Rua Duque de Palmela 4, **t** (21) 317 0580, near the Praça Marquês de Pombal. You'll find also many bookshops in the Chiado, including Portugal's oldest, **Bertrand**, Rua Garrett 73–75, **t** (21) 342 1941, founded in 1732.

Where to Stay in Lisbon

Rossio and Baixa

★★★★★**Hotel Avenida Palace**, Rua 1 de Dezembro 123, **t** (21) 321 8100, *www.hotel-avenida-palace.pt* (€€€). The delightful Hotel Avenida Palace combines old-world opulence with a location right at the heart of the action. It's well-tended and well-used, and rightly so, striking just the right balance between tradition and modernity following a US$7 million refurbishment in 1998. The chandeliers in the salon sparkle appealingly, and the splendid staircase simply has to be walked down. All external windows are double glazed, though the vibration of traffic lessens on the upper floors. There aren't many double beds – they'll push together two singles. Ask for a room overlooking the Restauradores. Sensibly there's no restaurant – there are many nearby. Parking is available or can be arranged.

★★★★**Hotel Mundial**, Rua D. Duarte 4, **t** (21) 884 2000, *www.hotel-mundial.pt* (€€€). Two minutes from Rossio, the Mundial really pulls in the tour groups. The bedrooms are comfortable but neutral; those at the back are quieter, with views up to the Castelo de São Jorge. The restaurant offers an amazing view of Pombal's Lisbon, with a limited choice of good food, such as the beefsteak cocotte. The restaurant staff are attentive, as they are throughout the hotel.

★★★**Hotel Métropole**, Praça D. Pedro IV 30, **t** (21) 321 9030, *www.almeida hotels.com* (€€€). Under the same management as the Palace Hotel in Buçaco, Hotel Métropole is a civilized place with spacious, comfortable rooms in an excellent central location. Double-glazing reduces but doesn't eradicate the hum of the traffic.

★★★**Hotel Lisboa Tejo**, Rua dos Condes de Monsanto 2, **t** (21) 886 6182/4/7/8, *www.evidenciahotels.com* (€€€). Tastefully renovated, hyper-designed and rather filmic, the location just

behind the Praça da Figueira is great but the interior decoration tries a little too hard to achieve a contemporary look. It's almost very good, but tips over the top. Wooden floors, marble sink-surrounds and air-conditioning.

★★★★**Aparthotel VIP Eden**, Praça dos Restauradores 24, **t** (21) 321 6600, *www.viphotels.com* (€€). A converted Art Deco theatre smack in the centre of the city – the real selling point is the small rooftop swimming pool with fabulous views and a sun deck for beautiful people. The slightly bland, blonde studios and one-bedroom apartments are equipped with sofa beds, to sleep two and four respectively. There are three rooms for disabled people and check-in time is 3pm.

★★★★**Residencial Insulana**, Rua da Assunção, 52, **t** (21) 342 3131 or 342 7625, *www.insula.cjb.net* (€€). Residencial Insulana feels like somewhere in the provinces. It's rather brown, but decent.

Pensão Aljubarrota, Rua da Assunção 53, **t** (21) 346 0112, *p_aljubarrota @hotmail.com* (€). Fourth-floor *pensão* that's small, friendly and a bit worn, with a well-travelled clientele. Some rooms have a shower in the corner; cheaper rooms don't. Shared toilets.

★★★**Residencial Duas Nações**, Rua da Vitória 41, **t** (21) 346 0710 (€). A popular place with a fine reputation and efficient management. Cheaper rooms share a bathroom.

Grande Pensão Residencial Alcobia, Rua Poç do Borratém 15, **t** (21) 884 4150 (€). Almost next door, this place is is quirky, friendly, well-run, somewhat dilapidated and surprisingly pleasant because of it.

Residencial Praça da Figueira, Travessa Nova de São Domingos 9 (3rd floor), **t** (21) 342 6757, *www.rrcoelho@clix.pt* (€). Entered from a road behind the Praça, this very respectable third-floor walk-up offers air-conditioned rooms with great views and not too much noise. Recently revamped rooms have a shower in the corner, but none have their own toilets.

Pensão Santo Tirso, Praça D. Pedro IV 18 (3rd and 4th floors), **t** (21) 347 0428 or 347 0163 (€). It's a steep climb up three flights of stairs to Pensão Santo Tirso. Rooms have good views, but the downside is the noise of traffic. Shower in the corner of the room, plasticky furniture, shared toilets.

Avenida da Liberdade

⭐ Hotel Britania >

⭐ Residencial Florescente >>

Hotel Britania, Rua Rodrigues Sampaio 17, **t** (21) 315 5016, *www.heritage.pt* (€€€€€). Hotel Britania is small and yet substantial. Designed in the 40s by modernist architect Casiano Branco, it has just 30 rooms, and will not accept groups larger than 10, which gives it an unusual intimacy. The fittings are wonderful and the rooms are spacious and comfortable. Staff are exceptionally committed, efficient and friendly.

★★★**Hotel Altis**, Rua Castilho 11, Avenida da Liberdade, **t** (21) 310 6000, *www.altishotels.com* (€€€€). A large corporate-style but comfortable hotel. It has an excellent restaurant with great views that serves traditional grills. There's also a health club with heated pool.

★★★★★**Hotel Tivoli**, Avenida da Liberdade 185, **t** (21) 319 8900 or 319 8950,*www.lisboahoteltivoli.com* (€€€). At the edge of the Rato district, on Lisbon's main boulevard, the plush and overstuffed Hotel Tivoli surrounds a swimming pool on three sides. Guests can use the solarium and tennis court. The good top-floor restaurant offers views of Lisbon, and grilled steak or chops.

★★★★**Tivoli Jardim**, Rua Júlio César Machado 7, **t** (21) 353 9971, *www.tivoli jardim.com* (€€€). Just off the Avenida da Liberdade, the Tivoli Jardim has access to the swimming pool and tennis court of its five-star sister, next door (*see* entry above). Staff are abundant. Renovated in 2008. Single rooms overlook the gardens, and the parking lot overlooks the restaurant, which could spoil an entrecôte sautéed with mushrooms.

 Pensão Alegria Residencial >>

★★★**Hotel Jorge V**, Rua Mouzinho da Silveira 3, **t** (21) 356 2525, *www.hotel jorgev.com* (€€€). Between the Praça Marquês de Pombal and the Jardim Botánico, there's something oddly appealing about the worn carpets and old fittings of this nicely sized hotel.

★★★**NH Liberdade**, Avenida da Liberdade 180B, **t** (21) 351 4060, *www.nh-hotels.com* (€€). Slick and stylish hotel, typical of the NH chain, with excellent facilities, including Wi-Fi, rooftop bar and swimming pool.

Residencial Florescente, Rua Portas Santo Antão 99, **t** (21) 346 3517, *www.residencialflorescente.com* (€). Opposite the Coliseu in an attractive pedestrian street, Residencial Florescente is a very appealing place. Public spaces are pleasant, rooms are very decent, maids are uniformed and it's well run.

Pensão Portuense, Rua Portas Santo Antão 151, **t** (21) 346 4197, *www.pensao portuense.com* (€). Further up the road, Pensão Portuense is decent, but the rooms are strangely arranged.

Pensão Residencial 13 da Sorte, Rua do Salitre 13, **t** (21) 353 9746, *www.trezeda sorte.no.sapo.pt* (€). A bargain at the price, with attractive rooms and a great central location with rooms overlooking the Avenida.

★★★★**Residência Roma**, Travessa da Gló 22a, **t** (21) 346 0557/8/9, *res.roma @mail.telepac.pt* (€). Clean, decent and outmoded Residência Roma is a good option for families staying for four days or longer, because apartments with kitchenettes are available for the same price as double rooms.

★★**Hotel Suiço Atlântico**, Rua da Glória 3–19, **t** (21) 346 1713, *suissoatlantico@ grupofbarata.com* (€). Hotel Suiço Atlântico has seen better days. It's good value if there are three or four of you travelling together and you're not too fussed by the general smell of medicated toilet paper.

Pensão Alegria Residencial, Praça da Alegria 12, **t** (21) 322 0670, *www.alegria net.com* (€). Pensão Alegria Residencial is well worth anyone's consideration. It occupies a town house of 1865 in a mature garden square, with blooming window boxes and pleasant rooms with wooden floors and large windows.

Pensão Pérola da Baixa, Rua da Glória 10, **t (21) 346 2875 (€). Second-floor walk-up Pensão Pérola da Baixa is a bit of a squash, but otherwise OK. There's a shower in the corner of each room, but only three have toilets. There's a resident stripy cat.

Marquês de Pombal

★ The Ritz Four Seasons >

*****The Ritz Four Seasons, Rua Rodrigo da Fonseca 88, **t** (21) 381 1400, *www.fourseasons.com* (€€€€€). A great hotel by any standards. Built in the 1950s, it offers a particular kind of elegance: the spaces are generous and splendid, and if you look hard enough you're bound to see ladies of a certain age buffing their bouffants into shape before emerging from the shadows. Rooms have balconies overlooking the park, perfect for watching the sunrise at dawn. The hotel is justifiably famous for its service, and as ever the distinction is in the detail: the ice placed in the ice bucket in one's room every evening, the butler's tray discreetly positioned near the entrance, from which the liveried doorman issues joggers with a map, bottled water and flannels. The staff smile naturally. With the opening of the new indoor pool and spa, the facilities are complete. The dining room tends to be business-y at lunchtime, when a dainty and beautiful buffet is served for around €40. Evenings are more mistress-y; as well as the à la carte menu, a fixed-price dinner is available for around €40, or €50 with wine. At weekends there's jazz in the bar.

*****Tiara Park, Rua Castilho 149, **t** (21) 381 8700, *www.tiara-hotels.com* (€€€€€). Formerly the Meridien Hotel, now taken over by the prestigious Tiara chain, this luxury hotel is reliably plush throughout, with good-size modern rooms, fitness rooms, sauna, tennis courts and access to the nearby Club VII swimming pool complex. The *Le Ganesh* bar sports Indian-style

décor, while the *L'Appart* restaurant dishes up traditional cuisine with a contemporary twist.

*****Sheraton Lisboa Hotel, Rua Latino Coelho 1, **t** (21) 312 0000, *www.sheraton.com/lisboa* (€€€€). The views from the upper rooms and restaurant of the Sheraton Lisboa Hotel are quite breathtaking, and there's a first-floor outdoor pool and gym. The rooms have been recently remodelled and are spacious and luxurious with gleaming marble bathrooms. The hotel also has superb facilities for business travellers with a fully equipped business centre and Wi-Fi.

****Hotel Real Palácio, Rua Tomás Ribeiro, **t** (21) 319 9500, *www.hoteis real.com* (€€€). The Hotel Real Palácio possibly attempts to be more opulent than is wise for a hotel of these slightly limited proportions. There's more marble on show than in a Versace store, and very nice it is too if you like that sort of thing, but the room rates demand somewhere memorable for more than the quality of its breakfast buffet.

****Hotel Real Parque, Avenida Luis Bívar 67, **t** (21) 319 9000, *www.hoteis real.com* (€€€). The older sister of the Real Palácio, Hotel Real Parque is close enough to share staff. There are less glitz and more tour groups, with a very high a turnover of guests. They generally leave with no complaints: everything is absolutely adequate.

****Hotel Marquês de Pombal, Avenida da Liberdade 243, **t** (21) 319 7900, *www.hotel-marquesde pombal.pt* (€€€). If you're looking for somewhere contemporary with the facilities of a large hotel, this is a good choice. Don't be put off by the bland lobby; rooms are cool, easy on the eye, slightly Art Deco and well equipped. There's a health centre and a garage, and a metro station nearby.

***Hotel Miraparque, Avenida Sidonio Pais 12, **t** (21) 352 4286, *www.miraparque.com* (€€€). Overlooking the Parque Eduardo VII, this pleasant hotel dates back to the 1950s although thankfully the décor

⭐ **Lisboa Regency Chiado >>**

does not! Rooms are pleasant if simply furnished and the restaurant serves solidly reliable local dishes in a pleasant wood-panelled dining room.

★★★**Hotel Eduardo VII**, Avenida Fontes Pereira de Melo 5, **t** (21) 356 8822, *hoteleduardovii@mail.telepac.pt* (€€€). On a branch road off the Praça Marquês de Pombal, this solid Best Western hotel stands beside the park of the same name. It frequently receives the epithet 'very adequate'. The restaurant's view of the city is panoramic but not boggling, with rich food.

★★★**Residencial Astória**, Rua Braamcamp 10b, **t** (21) 386 1317, *www.evidenciahoteis.com* (€€). Recently modernized Art Deco guest house.

★★★**Hotel Dom Carlos**, Av. Duque de Loulé 121, **t** (21) 353 9070, *main@domcarloshoteis.com* (€€). Efficient, sober, lamplit and wood-panelled. Trees screen the hotel from the main road, muffling it.

★★★**Comfort Inn Embaixador**, Av. Duque de Loulé 73, **t** (21) 351 3350 (€€). Down the road from the Dom Carlos, one of a plethora of business hotels in this area, the Embaixador is OK but nothing special.

★★★**Residência Horizonte**, Avenida António Augusto de Aguiar 42, **t** (21) 353 9526, *www.hotelhorizonte.com* (€). Hot, clean and functional, arranged around a stair well, northeast of the Praça Marquês de Pombal.

★★**Residência Mar dos Açores**, Rua Bernadim Ribeiro 14, **t** (21) 357 7085 (€). Look for the striking green-tiled exterior, this friendly place has homey, well-furnished rooms and a better-than-most buffet (continental) breakfast.

Estefânia

★★★**Residencial S. Pedro**, Rua Pascoal de Melo 130, **t** (21) 357 8765, *yaltahoteis@netcabo.pt* (€). Named after one of Lisbon's largest hospitals, this popular, nondescript *residencial* is clean but tacky.

★★★**Residencial Luena**, Rua Pascoal de Melo 9, **t** (21) 355 8246 (€). Clean and decent, though fairly basic.

Bairro Alto and Chiado

★★★★**Lisboa Regency Chiado**, Rua Nova do Almada, 114, **t** (21) 325 6100, reservations **t** (21) 325 6200, *www.regency-hotels-resorts.com* (€€€€). Rising from the ashes of the fire that ripped through the Chiado in 1988, it took eleven years for the Hotel Lisboa Regency Chiado to materialize, under the eye of architect Alvaro Siza Vieira. The result is an unusual and very attractive hotel in what must be the city's prime location, excellent for restaurants, shopping, transport and generally wandering about. Hardly surprising, then, that it appeals to an effortlessly chic clientele. The interior decorator has drawn on the principles of feng shui to banish the spirit of the fire and create harmony. The place does feel quite different for it – there's an appealing sort of fizz in the air. The corridors' hexagon-patterned carpet continues into bedrooms, furniture is oversized, doors are black, and the more expensive rooms have terraces with terrific views. There are a few parking spaces available. The bar is open to non-residents, but even more of a draw is breakfast at €12.50 per head. How do they get the cheese and the pomegranates perfectly ripe?

⭐ **Pensão Londres >>**

★★**Pensão Londres**, Rua Dom Pedro V, 53, **t** (21) 346 2203, *www.pensao londres.com* (€€). A large converted town house with ceiling mouldings, near the Port Wine Institute. It's friendly and efficiently run, and most rooms are light and airy.

Casa de São Mamede, Rua Escola Politecnica 159, **t** (21) 396 2166, *www.saomamede.web.pt* (€€). This elegant 18th-century former magistrates' house has been tastefully renovated and maintains a palatable old-world feel. The rooms have original tiles and antiques.

Pensão Estrela de Ouro, Largo Trindade Coelho 6–3, **t** (21) 346 5110 (€). Nicely placed on the edge of the Bairro Alto, and being raised three storeys above the traffic means it isn't too noisy – though it's a long walk up. Bedrooms are light and wooden-floored, but the communal bathrooms are very pokey.

Pensão Globo, Rua da Teixeira 37, **t** (21) 346 2279, *www.pensaoglobo.com* (€). In unusually good nick. The location is good for eating and drinking, but bring earplugs. Some rooms are extremely squashed. Shared toilets.

Living Lounge, Rua São Nicolau 41, **t** (21) 346 2060, *www.livinglounge hostel.com* (€). Opened by four local artists, this is the best hostel in town. Each room and dorm is individually designed with colourful murals and furniture, while the kitchen has exposed beams and great facilities. Free Wi-Fi is an added perk.

Lapa

Lapa Palace >

*****Lapa Palace**, Rua do Pau de Bandeira 4, **t** (21) 394 9494, *www.lapa-palace.com* (€€€€€). Standing next to the British Ambassador's Residence, Orient-Express Hotels' Lapa Palace is the only hotel to rival the Ritz, and in summer it's the one to plump for. The appeal lies in the magnificent mature 10-acre (4ha) garden and landscaped pool that give the place the feel of a resort, and for that reason there are a fair number of children about. The core of the hotel is a late-19th-century *palácio*, with 21 rooms in slightly boudoir-ish antique style, to which has been added a large wing. All sorts of luxury extras are available, if you can tear yourself away from the pop-up TV at the foot of your bed. Shame about the lobby, which would go down well in Dubai. The head chef was transferred from the Hotel Cipriani in Venice, and the hotel requires that at least half the kitchen staff are Italian.

Solar dos
Mouros >>

****York House**, Rua das Janelas Verdes 32, **t** (21) 396 2435, *www.york houselisboa.com* (€€€€€). Poor old York House has been overhauled, enlarged and to some extent wrecked. Now maids sit on the stairs, whistling, because there's not much work for them. This former convent used to be

a delightful place, and the courtyard and its palm tree still are. Rooms come in new or old style, the former hyper-simple and spare, the latter antique. But the corridors are oppressive and the whole place feels rather creepy.

As Janelas Verdes, Rua das Janelas Verdes 47, **t** (21) 396 8143, *www. heritage.pt* (€€€€). Two town houses have been knocked together to create As Janelas Verdes, an appealing little hotel with very good service, excellent views of the river from the top-floor, wood-panelled library and a little garden draped with bougainvillaea. It's rather over interior-decorated in a sort of created-yesterday-to-look-as-if-this-is-how-it's-always-been way, and rooms are a tiny bit boxy, but these are quibbles. Breakfast is an extra €12.50 per person.

Alfama

Solar do Castelo, Rua das Cozinhas 2, **t** (21) 887 0909, *www.heritage.pt* (€€€€€). Within the castle walls, Solar Do Castelo is a stylish fourteen-roomed hotel occupying a mansion built in 1765 on the site of the Alcáçova Palace kitchens. It provides a clever combination of new and old. Just don't expect views.

Solar dos Mouros, Rua do Milagre de Santo António 6, **t** (21) 885 4940, *www.solardosmouros.com* (€€€€€–€€€€). Fabulous Solar dos Mouros offers twelve unique rooms decorated in contemporary style by owner/painter Luis Lemos. It feels more like a home than a hotel; there's a lot of good art about, and he has a fine eye for colour and design. All rooms have wooden floors and a fine view; one lacks air-conditioning.

****Hotel Olissippo Castelo**, Rua da Costa do Castelo 112–126, **t** (21) 882 0190, *www.olissippohotels.com* (€€€€). On the edge of the Alfama and just below the castle walls, Hotel Olissippo is an interesting small hotel with a good sense of design, occupying a house built in 1899. It has quickly become popular, the attraction being the views.

****Albergaria Senhora do Monte, Calçada do Monte 39, **t** (21) 886 6002 (€€). Perched on Lisbon's highest hill in the Graça district, inland from the Castelo, this hotel offers attractive rooms whose main delights are the broad, dizzy views of Lisbon. Guests without cars will depend on tram no.28, unless they enjoy steep climbs.

Sé Guest House, Rua de S. João da Praça 97, **t** (21) 886 4400 (€€). Opposite a corner of the cathedral, the justifiably popular Sé Guest House is a first-floor apartment that feels like a home – family photographs, rugs on floorboards, big windows. The only drawback is that none of the rooms have bathrooms; given that you're paying quite handsomely, you'll need to weigh up how much of a problem that is.

Pensão São João da Praça, Rua de S. João da Praça 97, **t** (21) 886 2591 (€). Upstairs, Pensão São João da Praça is a similar set-up but without the personal touch. And if you're staying on the third floor, there are a lot of stairs. Hence it's half the price for a double room – but if you're on your own, you'd do better to stay downstairs.

(★) **Pensão Ninho das Águias >**

***Pensão Ninho das Águias, Rua da Costa do Castelo 74, **t** (21) 885 4070 (€). The 'eagle's nest' really does feels as though it's perched on the top of the world. The plain, simple bedrooms offer vast, exhilarating views of Lisbon. The place is weird. A mad staircase spirals upwards from the lobby, with its stuffed eagle, and there are birdcages on the patio. Without a car, there is a long walk down to the centre of town.

Belém

*****Pestana Palace, Rua Jau 54, Alto do Santo Amaro, **t** (21) 361 5607, *www.pestana.com* (€€€€€). It took 11 years to win planning permission to redevelop the decaying Palácio Valle Flôr and build two new wings, on a hill east of Belém. It's plush, luxurious and replete with indoor and outdoor pools, a health club and a chapel. The jewel of a garden is open to the public. The restaurant has a reputation for fine Portuguese food.

Jerónimos 8, Rua dos Jerónimos 8, **t** (21) 360 0900, *www.design hotels.com/jeronimos8* (€€€€). Close to the monastery this stylish hotel has a zen minimalist feel with its red and white Bussaco Wine Bar, lashings of white linen and paintwork in the rooms and avant garde design throughout.

Eating Out in Lisbon

Lisboetas need no excuse for eating out; they do it frequently and unhurriedly. The capital caters to all sorts, offering sardines grilled in the street outside a glorified cupboard, or glittering banquets. *Fado* houses are often quite decent restaurants, too; they're dotted around town and listed separately at the end of the chapter.

Baixa

The Baixa's pedestrianized streets are home to many restaurants. You'll soon get the picture: notice board with menu in four languages, waiter keen to usher you to one of the outdoor tables as you walk past. There's a bit of bustle at lunchtime, but after the shops and offices have closed the restaurants are left to the tourists.

Terreiro do Paço, Praça do Comércio, **t** (21) 031 2850 (€€€€). Touted by *Condé Nast Traveller* magazine as one of the world's top 50 restaurants. Local celebrity chef Vitor Sobral creates exquisite dishes that are a modern rendition of traditional Portuguese cuisine. *Closed Sat and Sun lunch*.

Gambrinus, Rua das Portas de Santo Antão 25, **t** (21) 342 1466 (€€€). The smartest of the many restaurants on the rather touristy road that leads leads north from the northeastern corner of Rossio. Gambrinus feels American; the service is excellent, and guests can indulge in large quantities of shellfish.

Casa do Alentejo, Rua das Portas de Santo Antão 58, **t** (21) 346 9231 (€). For somewhere much more earthy, try further up the road. Housed in a splendid old building, with ferns, gilt-mirrored ballroom, chandeliers and *azulejo* tiles depicting scenes from Camões' novels, this semi-private 'club' (anyone can walk in) caters mostly for Alentejans and their friends resident in Lisbon. Upstairs a basic kitchen produces large quantities of adequate Alentejan food, and all ages stand round the counter drinking beer.

Bonjardim, Travessa de Santo Antão 11–12, **t** (21) 342 7424 (€). In an alley off the Rua das Portas de Santo Antão, this place otherwise known as 'the king of chickens' is one of the best budget options in the area.

★ Arco do Castelo >>

Megavega, Rua dos Sapateiros 113, **t** (21) 346 8063 (€). Dine on inexpensive healthy dishes in scrubbed pine surroundings at this centrally located restaurant. The menu includes vegan choices and a choice of hot or cold dishes and some innovative salads (a rarity in this city!). *Closed Sun.*

Alfama

★ Restô do Chapito >

Restô do Chapito, Rua da Costa do Castelo 7, **t** (21) 886 7334 (€€). Two-floor eatery of the Chapitô circus-school/theatre complex, a wonderful place which functions as a terrace tapas bar with great views down to the river, and a slightly offbeat, not-quite-hitting-the-mark restaurant with faux giraffe-skin cushion covers. The circus school has performances 10am–2am from September to June. It's hard to be anything other than happy when you're here. Patrons tend to be young-ish, but there's quite a good mix of ages. *Closed Mon; dinner only Tues–Fri 7.30pm–2am; Sat and Sun 10am–2am.*

Casa do Leão, Castelo de S. Jorge (€€). Within the castle walls, the Casa do Leão offers a slightly outré menu beneath an arcaded, sand-blasted ceiling, with a fireplace that makes for a cosy atmosphere in winter. Lunch is served on the terrace, beneath wizened olive trees and the gaze of passers-by. There's also a café within the castle walls that closes at 8pm.

Lautasco, Beco do Azinhal 7, **t** (21) 886 0173 (€€). Off the Rua de São Pedro, offering a chance to eat outdoors in a small, shaded residential courtyard, beneath tall windows, birdcages, wrought-iron balconies, roof weeds, and ubiquitous laundry. The food is

nothing special; braised rabbit is the most adventurous of the dishes.

Viagem de Sabores, Rua de S. João da Praça 103, **t** (21) 887 0189 (€€). Below and behind the cathedral, Viagem de Sabores is a softly lit, mellow place with a stone floor, high ceilings and an invitation to linger. The kitchen is fully visible; in it are prepared a combination of Portuguese and Turkish dishes. Try the stuffed chicken breast. *Open for dinner only. Closed second half of August.*

Arco do Castelo, Rua Chão da Feira 25, **t** (21) 887 6598 (€€–€). Tiny bistro-style Arco do Castelo specializes in Goan dishes. They're very tasty, too. Try the chicken with cinnamon and coconut, or the prawn curry. *Closed Sun.*

A Tasquinha, Largo do Condador Mor (€€–€). Just below the castle, provides a pleasant terrace on which to dine. It's fairly standard fare – but with standards high, that's a bonus. *Closed Sun.*

Pois Café, Rua São João da Praça, **t** (21) 886 2497 (€). Run by two Austrian women who fell in love with Lisbon while travelling, this is a wonderfully relaxing place to hang out, with comfortable chairs, books, newspapers and a healthy selection of snacks, meals and freshly squeezed juices. *Closed Sun.*

Farol de Santa Luzia, L. Santa Luzia 5, **t** (21) 886 3884 (€). Opposite the Miradouro and uphill from the cathedral, Farol de Santa Luzia is striplit and overly bright, which is a pity because the food is good. *Closed Sun.*

Cantinho do Aziz, Rua de S. Lourenço 8, **t** (21) 887 6472 (€). The music of Mozambique and the football on TV coincide in this tiny place between the castle and the Baixa. The standard of hygiene does not inspire confidence, but the food is good and spicy. Small children wander about.

Bairro Alto and Chiado

The Bairro Alto is Lisbon's kitchen, with the highest concentration of restaurants, and a mellow atmosphere to aid digestion. Fancy restaurants focus on the Chiado.

Tavares, Rua da Misericórdia 37, **t** (21) 342 1112 (€€€). Just off the upper end of the Rua Garrett, is described by a 1913 Baedeker guide as 'tastefully fitted up in the modern style', and it retains those pre-war heavy gilt mirrors and stucco. The menu is peppered with continental dishes. Meats may be served with wine-based sauces, though *bacalhau* with potatoes and onions makes an appearance. Note, however, that some readers have complained that the standard is unreliable. *Closed Sat.*

Pap'açorda, Rua da Atalaia 57–59, **t** (21) 346 4811 (€€€). Pumped-up Spaniards wearing Zara drink champagne at the bar in Pap'açorda, a famous restaurant now rather up itself. Directed by the same expert chef who oversees Bica do Sapato. *Closed Sun and Mon.*

Olivier, Rua do Alecrim 23, **t** (21) 342 2916 (€€€). A small, intimate restaurant in this brand new location where you can kickstart your appetite with the delicious nine-tapas starter. Other dishes include octopus *carpaccio* and duck in a deliciously sticky port sauce.

Rosa da Rua, Rua da Rosa 265, **t** (21) 343 2195 (€€). A stylish restaurant with a minimalist stone and metal interior. Serves tasty and unusual dishes such as fried pork with chestnuts and steak with a peanut butter sauce.

Cervejaria da Trindade, Rua Nova de Trindade 200, **t** (21) 321 9316 (€€). Established in 1836, the Cervejaria da Trindade is something of a landmark, although less for its food than for its *azulejo* wall panels depicting the elements and the seasons. Be careful where you sit, as there is a lot of through traffic.

⭐ Bota Alta >   Bota Alta, Travessa da Queimada 37, **t** (21) 342 7959 (€€). Unless you go early you'll have to queue for a table at this cheerful and unpretentious little bistro-style at the corner of the Rua da Atalaia. Varied clientele, succulent dishes. *Closed Sun all day and Sat lunch.*

Ali-a-Papa, Rua da Atalaia 95, **t** (21) 347 4143, *reservations* 914 024 178 (€€). Ali-a-Papa serves Moroccan cous-cous in an intimate, feminine setting. Meat dishes are fine, vegetarian are poor, and the service is a let-down.

Stravaganza, Rua do Grémio Lusitano 18–26, **t** (21) 346 8868, *stravaganza@ restaunet.pt* (€€). For good Italian food in a clean-lined, modern setting, try Stravaganza. There are tables outside, and vegetarians are catered for. *Open noon–2am; closed Sun.*

Sinal Vermelho, Rua das Gáveas 89, **t** (21) 346 1252 or 343 1281 (€€). There's something Parisian about Sinal Vermelho – it's rather smart, the food is good and the waiters are more professional than many. *Closed Sun.*

Lisboa à Noite, Rua das Gáveas 69, **t** (21) 346 8557 or 346 2603 (€€). Don't be put off by the name ('Lisbon at night'). It's a fairly sophisticated, modern place decorated on a black-and-orange theme with an almost exclusively Portuguese clientele. *Closed Sun.*

Império dos Sentidos, Rua da Atalaia 35–37, **t** (21) 343 1822, *www.imperiodos sentidos.pt* (€€). Império dos Sentidos makes a rather sexy assault on the senses – candles, chimes, flowers, dragon's tooth floor. Most of the tables are for two, and the food is modern Italian (what else?). The menu announces 'Use of mobile phones during meals affects dangerously the boiling of the spaghetti.' *Reservations necessary. Closed Mon.*

Cravo & Canela, Rua de Barroca 70, **t** (21) 343 1858 (€€). Recently re-opened, Cravo & Canela is dimly lit and well turned out. Wine glasses are huge, plates are square, and there's an attractive bar in case you've forgotten to make a reservation.

Tasco do Manel, Rua de Barroca 24, **t** (21) 346 3813 (€€). Don't expect privacy at Tasca do Manel, just good kid and suckling pig. There are tables outside, but they're a bit of an afterthought. *Closed Sun.*

Cocheira Alentejana, Travessa do Poço da Cidade, 19, **t** (21) 346 4868 (€€). It's nice to see Alentejan cooking getting a look in at Cocheira Alentejana, where the walls are decorated with tools for working on the land. There's a slightly restless feel to the place, perhaps because patrons are sometimes obliged to share tables with strangers. Steaks are very good, chips less so. *Closed Sat lunchtime, Sun.*

Calcuta, Rua do Norte 17–19, **t** (21) 342 8295 (€€). Lisbon is home to this reliably good Indian restaurant. There's no flock wallpaper in sight, just varnished wood. The menu is limited and there's not much competition, so they can get away with not being brilliant.

★ **Alfaia** >>

Fidalgo, Rua da Barroca 27, **t** (21) 342 2900 (€€). Dating from 1972, Fidalgo is an institution in these parts, dishes include traditional *bacalhau* and some more unusual choices, like wild boar medallions. Small and busy, get here early to grab a table. *Closed Sun.*

Snob, Rua do Século 178, **t** (21) 346 3723 (€€). A sound choice with a broad menu, particularly renowned for its steaks. The atmosphere is clubby with a dining room lined with bottles. *Closed at lunchtime.*

El Gordo I, Rua de São Boaventura 16, **t** (21) 342 4266 (€). An attractive tapas bar with a midnight-blue, starry ceiling, lanterns and a few hams hanging above the bar. *Closed Wed.*

★ **Casa do Algarve** >>

El Gordo II, Travessa Fiéis de Deus 28, **t** (21) 342 6372 (€). El Gordo II offers an opportunity to eat outdoors – on a series of low stairs. Diners are young and the menu tends towards tapas. Dim lanterns hang indoors and swing to reggae. *Closed Mon except Aug–Sept.*

★ **A Primavera do Jerónimo** >

A Primavera do Jerónimo, Travessa da Espera 34, **t** (21) 342 0477 (€). A charming little place: the dishes of the day are listed on a post-it note in the window, and wandering musicians come and stand in the door. The kitchen is in a corner of the room, behind glass. Josephine Baker once ate here and they have the black-and-white photo to prove it.

Baralto, Rua Diário de Notícas 31, **t** (21) 342 6739 (€). A tiny, cosy, appealing little bistro with a menu of international and Portuguese specialities. *Closed Sun.*

Põe-te na Bicha, Travessa da Água da Flor 36, **t** (21) 342 5924 (€). The set menu at Põe-te na Bicha offers good value for €14. Gay-friendly without being exclusive.

O Barrigas, Travessa da Queimada 31, **t** (21) 347 1220 (€). Tables are packed close together at this restaurant, which is popular with the French, possibly because meat is served very rare. T-shirts obligatory. *Closed Thurs.*

Alfaia, Travessa da Queimada 24, **t** (21) 346 1232 (€). A gleeful place with *azulejos*, ridiculous paper vines hanging from the ceiling, and generous helpings of good food.

Stasha, Rua das Gáveas 29-33, **t** (21) 343 1131 (€). Stasha has an earthy, Brazilian feel, though not because of anything on the very broad menu. There's a dragon's-tooth floor, and ochre walls. It gets going rather late. *Closed Mon.*

Adega das Mercês, Travessa das Mercês 2, **t** (21) 342 4492 (€). Adega das Mercês attracts a middle-aged, cigar-smoking Portuguese clientele. There's not a lot of atmosphere, but the food is good, particularly when cooked on the charcoal grill.

Casa do Algarve, Largo Academia de Belas Artes 14, **t** 91 994 7966 (€). Popular with students from the *academia* opposite, Casa do Algarve is a wonderful little café/restaurant with fabulous views. Go for a beer. *Closed Tues and Wed evenings and Sat and Sun lunchtime.*

Rato

Comida de Santo, Calçada do Eng. Miguel Pais 39, **t** (21) 396 3339 (€€€). Downhill from the Science Academy, a fun Brazilian restaurant particularly suited to small groups. Brightly painted jungle birds and leaves flit across the wallpanels, washed by mellow music. The exquisite *moquequa* dishes are stewed in coconut milk and palm oil.

Mezzaluna, Rua Artilharia 16, **t** (21) 387 9944 (€€€). Said by many to be Lisbon's best Italian restaurant – the chef does particularly wonderful things with vegetables – Mezzaluna is a good choice if you've had enough of of hearty Portuguese fare. At lunchtime it's full of besuited executives; evenings are more mixed – and romantic.

Casa da Comida, Travessa das Amoreiras 1, **t** (21) 342 8295 (€€€). One of the most elegant restaurants in Lisbon with a pretty patio for al fresco dining and a menu of delicious local dishes like *faisoa à convento de Alcântara* (stewed pheasant marinated in port wine).

São Bento and Estrela

★ **Tasquinha D'Adelaide** >

Tasquinha D'Adelaide, Rua do Patrocinio 70–74, **t** (21) 396 2239 (€€€). Well off the tourist trail, Tasquinha D'Adelaide has all the attributes of an excellent neighbourhood restaurant: small, unpretentious, welcoming – most diners are regulars and are greeted with a kiss – and committed to the loving preparation and respectful consumption of great food and wine. The menu has a slightly French feel to it. Do save room for dessert – and maybe walk down the road to A Paródia bar afterwards (*see* p.400). *Booking essential. Closed Sun.*

★ **Alcântara Café** >>

Cantinho da Paz, Rua da Paz a S. Bento 4, **t** (21) 396 9698 (€€). Near the National Assembly, this long-established Indian restaurant serves a range of subtle Goan curries. It's small and a bit squashed, with a varied clientele. The prawn curry is particularly good, the fish curry nutty and hot, and the chicken curry just plain hot.

Lapa

Sua Excelência, Rua do Conde 34, **t** (21) 390 3614 (€€€). Two blocks inland from the entrance of the Museu de Arte Antiga and bears the stamp of its manager: intimate, conversational, and protracted. He is a perfectionist who recites the menu – without prices – in the appropriate language. He minces his way through: 'We take a little rabbit. We chop it up ...' The softly lit restaurant is best suited to an evening excursion. The said rabbit is delicious, as is the creamed *bacalhau*. Dessert is a choice of cakes. *Closed Wed in winter and Sat in summer.*

Saldanha

A Góndola, Avenida de Berna 64, **t** (21) 377 0426 (€€€). Opposite the Gulbenkian Museum, A Gondola offers a rare opportunity to dine outdoors without being gawked at. Patrons eat their good Italian food beneath a mature trellis, or in the smart and sober interior. *Closed Sat evening and Sun.*

Estefânia

Primeiro de Maio, Rua Francisco Sanches 71, **t** (21) 382 2971 (€€). In a road parallel to the Avenida Almirante Reis, near the Arroios metro station, this place appeals to respectable *lisboetas* in search of good, hearty food in no-frills surroundings. Try the clams and pork speciality. *Closed Wed.*

Alcântara

Alcântara Café, Rua Maria Luisa Holstein 15, **t** (21) 363 7176 (€€€). Still effortlessly stylish over a decade after opening in a former warehouse, this restaurant attracts a varied clientele who adore its reliably good Portuguese and international dishes and service that's both impeccable and warm.

BBC, Pavilião Poente, Avenida Brasilia, **t** (21) 362 4232 (€€€). One of Lisbon's most fashionable restaurants, and with a fabulous view of the river, BBC turns into a disco for well-heeled not-so-young *lisboetas* after midnight. Owned by hunky TV presenter and actor Paulo Pires, which explains the groups of young women arriving in the hope of catching sight of him. Midway between Alcântara and Belém.

Espaço Lisboa, Rua da Cozinha Económica 16, **t** (21) 361 0212 (€€€). Impressive if slightly twee mock-up of a Lisbon patio by the designer of the Alcântara Café. The food – mainly excellently prepared Portuguese staples – is pretty good, too.

Kais, Rua Cintura do Porto Armazém, **t** (21) 393 2930 (€€€). Opened in 2003 by the owners of long-established nightclub Kapital (*see* p.400) in a former tram-shed on the dockside, Kais has delusions of grandeur, but, as far as the essentials go, its feet are pretty much on the ground: excellent though unadventurous international food and reliably good service. *Closed Sun.*

Belém

Most people wanting to eat in Belém head for the **Rua Vieira Portuense**, where a row of restaurants offer tables outside at the edge of the park. There's an art to selecting which one of them is busy enough to imply good food, but not so busy that you'll have to wait for hours. Alternatively, you could eat in the Centro Cultural, where the chef at in-house restaurant **A Commenda** has earned a fine reputation.

⭐ **O Caseiro >**

O Caseiro, Rua de Belém 35, **t** (21) 363 8803 (€€€). Between the monastery and the coach museum, O Caseiro is intimate, fun and tasty. Banknotes turn brown on the brick arches which support a beamed ceiling hung with gourds, melons and onions. Loaves of bread dangle from a plough pinned to the wall. *Porco à Alentejana* and simply cooked fresh fish are the house specialities.

A Commenda, Centro Cultural de Belém, Praça do Império, **t** (21) 364 8561 (€€€). Elegant and modern, with quick-witted service and a buffet lunch on Sundays. *Closed Sun eve*.

Cais de Belém, Rua Vieira Portuense 64, **t** (21) 362 1537 (€€). Cais de Belém aspires to grand things, attracting an older Portuguese clientele. *Closed Wed*.

Nune's Real Marisqueira, Rua Bartolomeu Dias 120, **t** (21) 301 9899 (€€). One of the city's best-loved seafood restaurants where tanks of fish await your selection.

Picanha, Rua Vieira Portuense 78, **t** (21) 365 8300 (€). Part of a popular Brazilian chain, offering all-you-can-eat meat or fish for around €13. The food is nicely presented, too.

O Rafael, Rua de Belém 106, **t** (21) 363 7420 (€). Along the road, O Rafael is a modest bistro.

Santa Apolónia

Bica do Sapato, Avenida Infante Dom Henrique, Armazém B, **t** (21) 881 0320 (€€€). One of the trendiest restaurants in Lisbon, as well as one of the most expensive, Bica do Sapato has fabulous food but wildly varying service. Like the Lux nightclub next door, part owned by John Malkovich

and Lisbon nightlife pioneer Manuel Reis.

Deli Delux, Avenida Infanta D. Henrique, Armazém B, Loja 8, **t** (21) 886 2070, *www.delidelux.pt* (€€). The first deli in Lisbon to combine a gourmet shop with a cafeteria. Located next to Bica do Sapato, the menu includes salads, sandwiches, cheese and charcuterie platters and homemade desserts and wines by the glass. At weekends a brunch is available.

Casanova, Cais da Pedra, Armazém B, Loja 7, **t** (21) 887 7532 (€). The best wood-fired pizzas in Lisbon, with great attention paid to fresh ingredients. No reservations, so be prepared to queue, but turnover is quick, especially in summer when the riverside terrace is in use. *Closed Mon*.

Cacilhas

A couple of restaurants in Cacilhas, across the Tagus, offer stunning panoramic views of the city, but they have become rather expensive and touristy. Take a ferry from the Praça do Comércio.

Atira Te Ao Rio, Cais do Ginjal 69-70, **t** (21) 275 1380 (€€). A Brazilian restaurant (name translates as "throw yourself into the river"!). But don't consider that before dining on the excellent Brazilian fare here. The sea views from the terrace are superb.

Ponto Final, Cais do Ginjal 72, **t** (21) 276 0743 (€€). Right at the end of the quay (hence the name) enjoy more good views from here. The cuisine remains firmly in traditional Portuguese mode with an emphasis on excellent seafood dishes.

Parque das Nações

Many of the restaurants on the Expo 98 site have been demolished to make way for offices, but it shouldn't be difficult to find somewhere to eat; if you're stuck just head back to the shopping centre and pick up a bite there. If you'd like a substantial meal, walk towards the southern end of the park.

Nobre, Edifício Nau – Marina Expo, **t** (21) 893 1600 (€€€). Between the two halves of the marina are two restaurants under the same management within a white scaffolding superstructure. On the upper floor, Nobre occupies a wooden-floored glassy white space, serving fine seafood.

Restaurante Panorâmico, Torre Vasco da Gama, **t** (21) 893 9550 (€€€). Two-thirds the way up the Torre Vasco da Gama, Restaurante Panorâmico is notable for its huge views. The food is good, particularly the fish, but it doesn't quite reach the same heights.

Origens, Alameda dos Oceanos, Lote 2A, **t** (21) 894 6166 (€€€). Seriously organic restaurant with meat, fish and vegetarian choices.

Marina, Edifício Nau – Marina Expo, **t** (21) 895 6169 (€€). On the lower floor is this good tapas restaurant with shaded tables on the deck outside. *Open Mon–Sat 12–12, Sun 12–6.*

Vegetarian Restaurants

Lisbon contains a higher concentration of vegetarian restaurants than the rest of the country – which is not saying much. As Portugal is very big on macrobiotics, most vegetarian restaurants are advertised as the former, but all provide vegetarian options on their menus.

⭐ **Os Tibetanos** >

Os Tibetanos, Rua do Salitre 117 (Metro Avenida), **t** (21) 314 2038 (€), is the best option for vegetarians in Lisbon. A stripped-pine haven of tranquillity, featuring regrettably small portions of weird and very wonderful vegetarian food. The daily menu is the best value. Definitely soul food. *Closed Sun.*

Celeiro, Rua 1 de Dezembro 65, off Rossio, **t** (21) 030 6030 (€). A self-service restaurant reminiscent of a school canteen, situated below a health food supermarket. It's best to get there early as by 1pm the queue snakes up the stairs, through the shop and out into the street. The wholesome food comes in huge portions. *Open lunchtimes only; closed Sun.*

Centro Macrobiótico Vegetariano, Rua Mouzinho da Silveira 25, **t** (21) 342 2463 (€). Has the great advantage of having a courtyard in which to eat large portions of healthy, though not always very tasty food. It stops serving food at 8pm. *Closed Sun.*

Espiral, Praça Ilha do Faial 14A, off Largo de Dona Estefânia, **t** (21) 355 3990 (€). Part of Lisbon's 'alternative centre', comprising a health food shop, a bookshop and this large, basement restaurant which displays art for sale on the walls, a noticeboard detailing all sorts of green activities and live music most weekends. The atmosphere is warm and there are Chinese, fish and vegetarian dishes on the menu.

Tao, Rua dos Douradores 10, **t** (21) 885 0046 (€). A well-priced vegetarian option that only uses organic ingredients. There is a choice of dining rooms – one with chairs, the other more bohemian with cushions on the floor.

Instituto Kushi, Avenida Barbosa du Bocage 88 (€). Lurks behind a macrobiotic shop and offers standard vegetarian fare in large portions. The staff are noticeably helpful.

Restaurante do Sol, Calçada do Duque 25, **t** (21) 347 1944 (€). Up many steps behind Rossio train station. Peeling white walls and long red-clothed tables characterize this simple self-service restaurant that serves excellent fresh juices and wholesome though rather bland food.

Yin-Yang, Rua dos Correeiros 14, 1st floor, **t** (21) 342 6551 (€). Set in the heart of the Baixa district, this self-service restaurant is a no-frills affair, dishing up huge amounts of delicious vegetarian and macrobiotic food to a varied lunchtime crowd. The fresh juices are also good. Attached is the obligatory healthfood shop and a noticeboard gives information on meditation and yoga classes.

Cafés

Lisbon's once-grand coffeehouses are a little seedy, which somehow makes them all the more enjoyable.

Café A Brasileira, Rua Garrett 120, **t** (21) 346 9541. At the heart of the Chiado, A Brasileira is a Lisbon landmark: its outdoor tables are a great place to watch the fashionable world go by – as the painter Almada Negreiros and the poet Fernando Pessoa were well aware. To mark the centenary of the latter's birth, a lifesized bronze sculpture of him was seated at an outdoor table.

Pavilhão Chinés >

Café Nicola, Rossio 24/25, **t** (21) 346 0579. Down in Rossio, this place also has literary ties: a series of wall paintings depict the life of the poet Bocage (*see* 'Bocage', p.326).

Pastelaria Suiça, Rossio 96, **t** (21) 342 8092. Opposite Café Nicola, tourists and *lisboetas* alike queue for outdoor tables on Rossio or round the back, on Praça da Figueira.

Versailles, Avenida da República 15A, **t** (21) 354 6340. Ladies sip coffee in this grandest of the city's *pastelarias*, with its chandeliers, wall mirrors and fake marble columns.

Antiga Confeitaria de Belém, Rua de Belém 84–92, **t** (21) 363 7423. On Sundays, flocks of *lisboetas* join tourists in the city's museum district to stock up with the best *pasteis de nata* in the city, made according to a much-vaunted secret recipe. First established in 1837, this enterprise shifts thousands of custard tarts a day, to take out or to eat in a bustling warren plastered with pretty old *azulejos*.

Bars in Lisbon

Each year Lisbon's nightlife becomes more vigorous, with the Bairro Alto producing most of the noise. This is the best area of Lisbon to wander through on a Friday or Saturday night. Scores of bars play music from bossa nova and fado to trip hop and jazz, and there is usually no entry charge, so you can meander from one to another. There are three good bars at the crossing of Travessa da Espera and Rua de Barroca, for example – take your pick, or try them all. This being a residential district, you'll have to go further afield for all-night clubs.

Bairro Alto

Bartis >

Bartis, Rua Diário de Notícias 95/97, **t** (21) 342 4795. Right in the thick of the Bairro Alto, this mellow, happy little jazz bar serves a mainly older crowd with beer and Portuguese liqueurs. A good place for a late snack, including excellent chicken toasties.

Clube da Esquina, **t** (21) 342 7149. A popular place serving head-spinning

cocktails where you can also boogy to a good mixture of sounds, courtesy of the resident DJ.

Pavilhão Chinês, Rua Dom Pedro V 89, **t** (21) 342 4729. Slightly uphill, this is a fantastic bar entirely walled with cabinets of fans, sheet music, cigarette holders, china objets d'art and a jumble of other curiosities. Admire them from chinoiserie tub chairs. *Open Mon–Fri 2pm–2am, Sat 6pm–2am, Sun 9pm–2am.*

Portas Largas, Rua da Atalaia 105, **t** (21) 346 6379. This irrepressible bar can't help but spilling into the street as the evening wears on, and it feels rather like a non-stop street party (which merges with the queue for Bota Alta restaurant and hopeful punters at the door of club Frágil). The later it gets, the merrier the place is.

Suave, Rua Diário de Notíças 6. Welcoming informal atmosphere attracting a fashionable laidback crowd with its edgy artwork and congenial service.

Solar do Vinho do Porto (Port Wine Institute), Rua de S. Pedro de Alcântara 45, **t** (21) 342 3307. On the edge of the Bairro Alto overlooking the Praça dos Restauradores, this is a pleasant but snooty lamplit bar, flanked by stone walls and tapestries. Like its sister institute in Porto, it claims to sell 166 non-vintage ports by the glass, though the selection dwindles on closer enquiry. The house once belonged to Ludwig, architect of Mafra, but he has left no traces. No instruction is available. *Open 10am–midnight except Sun and holidays.*

A Tasca, Travessa da Queimada, 13–15, **t** (21) 343 3431, *bartequila@yahoo.com*. The most lethal of places: a modern tequila bar with tequila slammers for €3.

Alfama

Bar Das Imagens, Calçada Marquês de Tancos 1–1B, **t** (21) 888 4636, *bardasimagens@mail.telepac.pt*. A steep climb up from the Baixa, this terrace bar provides fine views and a DJ. *Open Wed–Sat 4pm–2am, Sun 3–9; closed Tues and Wed, Jan and Feb.*

Miradouro da Graça, Largo da Graça. More of a destination in its own right, and untroubled by passing traffic, the terrace bar Miradouro da Graça is right where its name says it is: in front of the Graça church. Drinks are served from two booths 10am–2am, under umbrella pines.

Caxin, Rua da Costa do Castelo 22, t 91 876 1732. If the sight of hookahs helps you unwind, Moroccan bar Caxin is a good place for it. If you don't want alcohol, settle for tea on a low stool. The atmosphere can get very smoky (and heavy) later on.

Galloping Hogan's, Rua dos Bacalhoeiros, 4a–4c, t (21) 886 9860, *www.gallopinghogans.com*. Three doors to the right of the Casa dos Bicos, Galloping Hogan tries the hardest of the city's Irish pubs, being kitted out with pickings from a neo-gothic church. Live music every night from around the world.

Taborda, Rua da Costa do Castelo 75, t (21) 798 8159. Taborda has a long, thin bar with a relaxed atmosphere that feels rather like Brighton. There's live music, a huge picture window offering relatively mediocre views – in this city where one gets so spoilt – and an under-used outdoor terrace.

Estrela

⭐ A Paródia >

A Paródia, Rua do Patrocinio 26b, t (21) 396 4724. A superb little bar in the style of an opium den, from the creator of the Pavilhão Chinês. Expect dim lights, beaded lampshades, a collection of matchboxes stuck to the wall, black-and-white Victorian nudie photographs and the sense that one is afloat outside the vagaries of day and night. Occasional live piano music.

Entertainment and Nightlife in Lisbon

Lisbon has long been one of the best places in Europe to hear **African music**, often for free. Also keep an eye out for visiting **Brazilian singers** such as Caetano Veloso, Maria Bethânia, Milton Nascimento and Ney Matogrosso. The big venues for **rock concerts** are the Atlantic pavilion at the Parque das Nações, the downtown Coliseu, and the Aula Magna, at the University. Among longer-established **Portuguese bands** are Rádio Macau, Xutos e Pontapes, GNR, and Madredeus. Pedro Abrunhosa is more funky, while Mariza's punky image has done wonders for *fado*. There are some good rap acts, led by Da Weasel.

The Gulbenkian Foundation underwrites most **classical music** concerts, so it's a good idea to pick up a programme of events from the museum. They are not well advertised, particularly the 60-odd concerts that run from October to May.

Good **jazz** can be heard at the Cultural Centre in Belém, which also has free concerts 7–9pm weekdays (except in August) in its Bar Terraço (*open weekdays 12.30–9, weekends 12.30–7*), which provides very acceptable, cheap food and great river views from the terrace.

B.Leza, Largo Conde Barão 50–2, t (21) 396 3735. In the Santos area, not far from Kapital, B.Leza is one of the best places to hear live African music. A mixed crowd drink and dance to Dany Silva and other performers from the Cape Verde Islands, a former Portuguese colony whose rhythms blend those of Africa and Latin America.

Enclave, Rua do Sol o Rato 71A, t (21) 388 8738. A restaurant and club owned by Cape Verdean singer Tito Paris, whose band serenades diners until midnight before decamping downstairs where there's space to dance.

Frágil, Rua da Atalaia 128, t (21) 346 9578. Long the fashion leader in the Bairro Alto scene, with the most forbidding door policy, Frágil still has regular facelifts and a changing programme of DJs.

Hot Clube de Portugal, Praça da Alegria 39, t (21) 346 7369, *www.hcp.pt*. Just west of the Avenida da Liberdade, this is one of the capital's foremost jazz venues, a sweaty cellar with good live bands on Friday and Saturday evenings, at around 11.30pm. *Open Thurs–Sat 10pm–2am.*

Kapital, Avenida 24 de Julho 68, opposite Santos station. This is the place to be seen for those moneyed nightlifers who are more worried about seeing and being seen than about being at the cutting edge: the music is a mixture of mainstream dance and old Portuguese and international rock standards.

Kremlin, Rua das Escadinhas da Praia 5, **t** (21) 395 7101. A lot hipper and attracting a younger, more varied crowd than its sister Kapital, but some abrupt changes of decoration and musical policy in recent years have given it a somewhat directionless feel.

⭐ **Lux >**

Lux, Avenida Infante D. Henrique, Armazém A, Cais da Pedra, **t** (21) 882 0890/8, *www.luxfragil.com*. If you only go to one nightclub in Lisbon, go to Lux, the three-level dockside wonder. Yes it's famous, but it's not intimidating. Go late, drink, dance and wish everyone could have so much fun.

Fado in Lisbon

Fado restaurants are frequently more expensive than the quality of food would warrant; you are paying the singers' wages, after all. But many places allow you to come in after dinner for a drink, usually with a minimum or cover charge.

Don't talk or clink cutlery during songs, or you may get indignantly hushed, at least in the more authentic places where management and patrons care passionately about *fado*. *Fado vadio* ('vagabond fado') places, where audience and performers are interchangeable, are multiplying; they're authentic all right, but the quality of the singing is rarely impressive.

Alfama

⭐ **Taverna do Embuçado >**

Taverna do Embuçado, Beco dos Curtumes 10, **t** (21) 886 5088 (€€€). Difficult to find but worth it when you do: enter an alleyway from the Travessa do Terreiro do Trigo and shoo the pigeons away. Inside you'll find candles, arches, leather dining chairs, very good food and singers who know their stuff. Best choice for a night out.

Dinner from 8pm, fado from 9.30. Reservations recommended.

Parreirinha de Alfama, Beco do Espírito Santo 1, **t** (21) 886 8209 (€€). Photographs of dolorous *fadistas* fill the walls above the tile dado and coach lamps cast a gentle light on the renditions at this long-established *fado* house.

Marquês da Sé, Largo Marquês. Lavradio 1, **t** (21) 888 0234 (€€). In a side street below and behind the cathedral, this candlelit restaurant occupies a series of elegant stone vaults. For a *fado* joint it's unusually smart and unusually popular with an upmarket Portuguese clientele. Fish is the speciality, and the monkfish is very good. *Fado at 9.30pm. Dinner only, from 8pm.*

Clube de Fado, Rua São João da Praça 92/4, **t** (21) 888 2694 or 885 2704, *www.clube-de-fado.com* (€€). Also in the Sé area, Clube de Fado offers five or six singers from 9.30pm. Diners enjoy *filet mignon* beneath a vaulted ceiling, with white walls and a varnished stone floor. Most patrons are tourists who don't dress for the occasion. *Dinner only, from 8.30pm; bar opens at 7.30pm.*

Bairro Alto

Café Luso, Travessa da Queimada 10, **t** (21) 342 2281 (€€€). Housed in the arched brown cellars of the 17th-century Palace of São Roque near the church of the same name in the Bairro Alto, Café Luso has been belting out *fado* since the 1930s, and still has the feel of the 50s. It's popular, it's candlelit, and it's as pricey as it comes. *Dinner from 8pm; fado and folk dancing 9–10.30; fado 11pm–2am.*

O Forcado, Rua da Rosa 219, **t** (21) 346 8579 (€€€). Offers a reasonably genuine atmosphere, although purists accuse it of being touristy. A series of bullfight posters line the white walls above a tile dado. Dinner is available. Fado *9.30pm–3am.*

Adega Machado, Rua do Norte 91, **t** (21) 322 4640 (€€€). Clap-along-with-the-music place where the *fado* is too smooth and pleasant to be genuine. Oil lamps burn on tables served by smiley waitresses in frilled folkloric dresses. Fado *and folkloric dances 9.30pm–3am.*

Adega Mesquita, Rua Diário de Notícas 107, **t**. (21) 321 9280, *www.adegamesquita.com* (€€). Touristy but provides a high standard of *fado* singing and folk dancing in a suitably rustic atmosphere complete with mounted bull's head on the wall.

⭐ Tasca do Chico >

Tasca do Chico, Rua Diário de Notíças 39, **t** (21) 343 1040. (€). Two nights a week, 'Chico's bar' spills out onto the street, as all and sundry sing their hearts out for a mixed audience of locals and tourists. Fado *Mon and Wed 8pm–1am.*

Lapa

Senhor Vinho, Rua do Meio à Lapa 18, **t** (21) 397 7456 (€€€). In posh Lapa, this classic, welcoming *fado* house is recommended for those in search of the genuine article.

The Alentejo

The Alentejo stretches across just under a third of continental Portugal, to the south of the River Tagus and the province of Ribatejo – 'alem Tejo' means 'beyond the Tagus'. The climate is fiery – in summer, temperatures rise to an average of 93°F (34°C) in Évora, and a stultifying 104°F (40°C) in Beja. The unproductive land supports just 12 per cent of Portugal's population.

The appeal of the Alentejo lies in its austere beauty, in its strong, pure colours and its vast, arid space. The red earth is planted with wheat fields which sprout green in spring and mellow into a summertime gold, beneath the peculiarly clear blue sky. Brilliant, whitewashed settlements punctuate the plains, offering a profile of oblong chimneys wide enough to hoist and smoke a pig in. The horizon is interrupted by grain silos like giant test-tube racks.

14
Don't miss

⭐ 'Sintra of the Alentejo'
Castelo de Vide p.412

⭐ Enchanting village
Marvão p.414

⭐ Renaissance city
Évora p.428

⭐ Medieval streets with a view
Monsaraz p.440

⭐ Explore the riverbank
Mértola p.450

See map overleaf

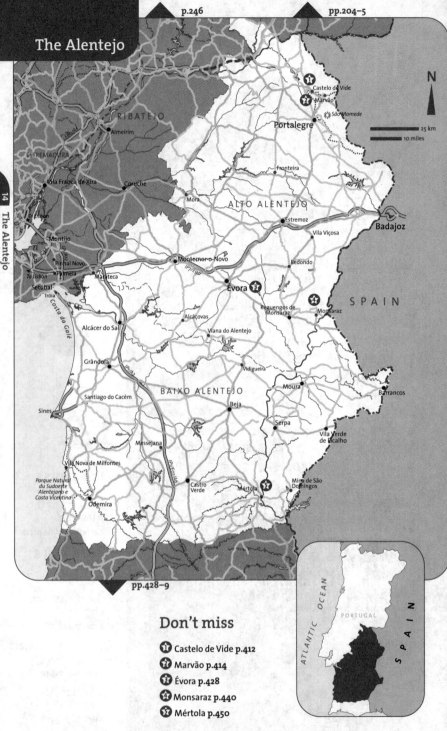

p.246
pp.204–5

The Alentejo

N

25 km
10 miles

14
The Alentejo

RIBATEJO

Almeirim

Castelo de Vide
Marvão
São Mamede
Portalegre

ESTREMADURA

Vila Franca de Xira
Coruche
Mora

Fronteira

ALTO ALENTEJO

To Lisbon

Montijo
Pinhal Novo
To Lisbon
Palmela
Setúbal
Tróia

Montemor-o-Novo
Mazateca

IP7/E90

Estremoz
Vila Viçosa
Badajoz

Redondo

Évora

Costa da Galé

Alcácovas

Alcácer do Sal

Viana do Alentejo

Reguengos de
Monsaraz
Monsaraz

SPAIN

Grândola

Vidigueira

Moura

Barrancos

Sines

Santiago do Cacém

BAIXO ALENTEJO

Beja

Serpa

Messejana

Vila Verde
de Ficalho

Vila Nova de Milfontes

Parque Natural
du Sudoeste
Alentejano e
Costa Vicentina

Castro
Verde

Mértola

Mina de São
Domingos

Odemira

pp.428–9

Don't miss

⭐ Castelo de Vide p.412
⭐ Marvão p.414
⭐ Évora p.428
⭐ Monsaraz p.440
⭐ Mértola p.450

ATLANTIC OCEAN

PORTUGAL

SPAIN

Getting around The Alentejo

Distances are comparatively large, and travel can be monotonous. **Roads** between settlements tend to be straight and level. The **railway network** is limited: Portalegre and Elvas are on the main branch line from Lisbon; the former has bus connections to Estremoz and Évora. Baixo Alentejo gets a raw deal from the railway network, which focuses on Beja. The express **bus** network has few links between Alto Alentejo and Baixo Alentejo, so it's worth considering taking relatively long-distance local buses.

The Alentejans are some of the friendliest of the friendly, though stubborn. They are the butt of a rash of jokes. How many Alentejans does it take to milk a cow? Five. One to hold the udders and four to lift the cow up and down. Their folk choirs are renowned throughout Portugal, but to the unfamiliar they sound rather grim. It's difficult to make out the words – perhaps they are singing about water, which is of great concern (hence the elaborate, centrally located fountains). People fear drought – the Constituições of the See of Évora, published in 1534, impose penalties on the practice of carrying images to water in time of drought and threatening them with immersion if they do not bring rain. Women wear black felt hats like trilbies, and pack lunches in cork thermoses for themselves and their menfolk. In winter they wrap themselves in striped rugs of undyed wool. Portugal's gypsies congregate in the Alentejo, and George Borrow noted the *banditti* who infested the region in 1835: they 'dance and sing, eat fricasseed rabbits and olives, and drink the muddy but strong wine of the Alemtejo'. Peculiar beliefs spice the province: if you have warts, cross your hands and rub them against the ribs of a deceived husband without his knowing.

History

The history of the Alentejo has been shaped by landholding and irrigation. The soil is thin and dry, transport costs are high, and there are few mountains or rivers: hence the Romans introduced huge farms known as *latifúndias* some time between 202 BC and 139 BC. They built 18 dams in the south of Portugal, irrigating fields of wheat planted among olive trees, where pigs grazed when the land lay fallow. Wine production was concentrated on the river valleys and along the main road from Lisbon to Beja via Évora.

The Moors made few changes to the pattern of landholding – though pig breeding declined, given the Koranic injunction. Merchants and representatives of the caliph invested their wealth in land, so in the Alentejo, towns grew into concentrations of absentee landlords.

When the Alentejo was conquered from the Moors, vast tracts of land were doled out to the military orders, though the king retained all important cities and towns. Urban Muslims were compelled to reside outside the town walls, and rural Muslims

The Economy and the Land

Most workers are employed on *latifúndias*; often the more permanent labourers are housed in hilltop homesteads called *montes*. Silviculture offers an alternative to wheat: Baixo Alentejo has been colonized by copses of silvery eucalyptus, planted for pulp and harvested after four years. They are almost as thirsty as the rice that grows at Alcácer do Sal. Plums flourish at Elvas, and the oranges of Vila Viçosa are superb. Alentejan cork-oaks drop acorns, which are hoovered by black pigs. Sheep and goats roam the scrub. The west-coast port of Sines alone has broken out of the traditional economy: it receives heavy cargoes from the Mediterranean and the Americas, and is a base for heavy industry including petroleum refining, petrochemicals, the extraction of iron from its ore, and naval repairs.

Cork and Olives

The plains of wheat around Évora and Beja yield to fields peppercorned with cork-oak or olive trees, both of which are short, small-leafed and gnarled. Portugal is the world's largest producer of cork. The bark, up to 4in (10cm) thick, is cut from the trees every nine years: the trunk and branches are ringed in 6–10ft (2–3m) sections with a light axe, and then cut straight down one side. If the weather is too dry, the cork shatters into many pieces; if the weather is too wet and cold, the tree dies of shock. The flayed trunks are a shrieking salmon pink, which blackens with time. Cork oaks are protected by Portuguese law, and cannot be cut down without permission; otherwise, penalties are stiff and may involve a stint behind bars. Olive trees are shaken until they yield their crop as well as their dignity; mechanized shakers are now edging their way in, requiring a new strain of less tenacious trees.

These days the cork industry, supporting around 20,000 livelihoods, is under threat from screw-caps and plastic 'corks' which are becoming widely popular among wine-makers, retailers and consumers. In turn this places Portugal's wildlife habitats, which support a wide variety of rare species of animals, birds and insects (*see* 'Parque Natural da Serra de São Mamede', p.411), under a ponderous future. Portuguese environmentalists fear that cork forests may one day be replaced by faster-growing cash crops such as pine and eucalyptus.

were milked by heavy taxes – between a third and a half of Muslim town dwellers fled to southern Spain. Dom Sancho I (1185–1211) tried to offset this depopulation by encouraging emigration from Flanders.

From the 14th century, the maritime trade offered rich rewards to speculators, and Alentejan agriculture suffered from lack of investment. The seaports and the cities enthralled villeins, who continued to leave the land. Portugal began importing wheat in the early 16th century. It was not until chemical fertilizers were introduced in 1884 that heathland was brought under new cultivation. Salazar was keen to increase wheat production, but his schemes of 1929 and 1958 met with little success.

The landless rural workers of the Alentejo were the sinews of civilian support for the Revolution of 1974. In July 1975, a law called for the expropriation of properties with more than the equivalent of 1,250 acres (500ha) of dry land or 125 acres (50ha) of irrigated land. (Two years later, the limit was raised by 40 per cent.) In October 1975 *latifúndias* around Beja were occupied by workers. Roughly 900 cooperatives were established; most of them have been dismantled or fallen apart, and landowners are buying back their land.

Wines of the Alentejo

Portugal's most recently Demarcated Region, in the east of the Alentejo, incorporates the towns of Reguengos de Monsaraz, Redondo, Borba and Vidigueira, producing very drinkable, full-bodied, mouth-filling red wines, all of which are matured in cement *depósitos* (except for J.M. da Fonseca's Tinto Velho, from Reguengos, where the lightly crushed grapes ferment in clay pots which are continually sprayed with cold water to keep them cool: the wine is then stored in oak casks to mature and soften for up to two years). The reds approach a powerful 13.5%, while the whites, which are less successful, reach 12.5%.

What to Eat

Alentejan pigs are nourished on the acorns which litter the land, so the gastronomy of the province revolves around their particularly flavourful meat. The favourite local dish is the unusual but rich and tasty *porco a Alentejana*: cubes of pork are marinated, fried and boiled, before being mixed with cockles, and lightly coated with a sauce of tomato concentrate, oil, onions and parsely. *Açorda a Alentejana* is a simpler dish, made of eggs poached in watery bread, with coriander and garlic. The pine-kernel sweets of the western Alentejo are well worth a try. The ewe's-milk cheese of Serpa, served 'fresh' with salt and pepper, is a good idea for a picnic, and if you're planning on doing some of your own cooking, do use the excellent Elvas olive oil.

Alto Alentejo

The Upper Alentejo offers greater scenic diversity than the Lower Alentejo, as well as a greater choice of accommodation for travellers, and a firmer artistic footing.

Portalegre

The capital of Alto Alentejo and its 13,000 souls crown a hill at the southwestern edge of the Serra de São Mamede, 109km southeast of Tomar (Ribatejo) and 80km south of Castelo Branco (Beira Baixa).

It was fortified by the Infante Afonso Sanches after his father's death in 1279, and became the subject of a feud with his brother Dom Dinis, who besieged Portalegre for five months in 1299. They settled their quarrel by exchanging Portalegre and Marvão for Sintra and Ourém. Portalegre was briefly occupied by the Spanish in 1704 during the Spanish War of Succession, just when the silk-weaving industry had supplanted the woollen industry and had begun to bring wealth to the town.

This wealth is manifest in a clutch of 18th-century *palácios*, with wrought-iron railings and armorial blazons. The chimneys of cork factories rise on the edge of town – but more impressive is the sycamore in the Rossio Square, whose outer branches have a perimeter of 250ft (76m), making it one of the largest on the Peninsula. The Rossio Square is at the base of Portalegre's hill, and shoppers flow between there and the upper part of town, which is dominated by the cathedral. Sometimes there are so many shoppers that Portalegre feels like a market town without a market.

Getting to Portalegre

Trains make the hour-long ride from Elvas to Portalegre three times a day. From Lisbon, there are four rail connections a day, changing at Entroncamento or Abrantes, or both (total 3½hrs).

The four daily **buses** from Lisbon take 4¼hrs to arrive, and Portalegre is the centre of the local bus network, with semi-frequent connections from Elvas, Estremoz, Castelo de Vide and Marvão.

Tapestries

Museu da
Tapeçaria Guy
Fino
*Rua da Figueira 9,
t (245) 307 980; open
Thurs–Tues 9.30–1 and
2.30–6; adm*

Portalegre's tapestries have achieved world renown and the best place to see them is the **Museu da Tapeçaria Guy Fino**. The tapestries are extraordinarily detailed, tightly woven, vibrantly coloured woollen reproductions of paintings. A slide is made of a specially commissioned or extant painting, and then projected onto graph paper. On this, each colour is painstakingly numbered, and matched with one of 8,000 coloured wools to produce 250,000 knots per square metre. This well-designed museum illustrates this process and displays a great collection, including works by Almada Negreiros, Costa Pinheiro and Le Corbusier. Unfortunately none of the labels or tours are offered in English.

The Church and Convent of São Bernardo

Across the Parque Miguel Bombarda, the Avenida George Robinson leads to the church and convent of São Bernardo (also called N.S. da Conceição). This is now a training school for the Infantry, who will allow visitors to look at the church if they ask nicely. Founded in 1518 by Dom Jorge de Melo, Bishop of Guarda, the church's portico is sided with grand *azulejos*, dated 1739, picturing the baptism of Christ and other scenes. Within the church is the founder's tomb, which he commissioned *c.* 1540, some eight years before his death. Chanterène's work at the base of the tomb is very delicate; the rest seems too heavy to be the work of the master himself. The effigy of this conceited bishop is clothed in pontifical robes, and the Virgin Mary waits to welcome him to Heaven. All this from a man with at least two children, one of them by a nun in the convent! The history of the convent is carved into the back of some stalls in the *coro alto*. It stops suddenly in 1779, when Pombal closed the institution.

Elsewhere Outside the Town Walls

José Régio
Museum
*t (245) 203 625; open
9.30–12.30 and 2–6;
closed Mon and hols;
adm*

At the opposite end of the Avenida George Robinson, continue in the same direction through a tangle of streets to the Praça da República, off which stands the **José Régio Museum**. He was a poet, teacher and obsessive collector, who died in 1969. His home displays nearly 60 naive images of Christ by unschooled craftsmen, firedogs and pestles and mortars used for culinary, pharmaceutical and magical purposes. There is a 'typical' 17th-century kitchen, and

a bedroom designed for meditation. An 18th-century *palácio* fronts the Praça da República, just outside the town walls.

The Cathedral Square

Castle
open Tues–Sat 10–12 and 2–5, Sun 10–12; adm

The remains of the 13th-century **castle** are uninteresting.

Flanked by pinnacled towers, the **cathedral** was founded by the first Bishop of Portalegre, a Spaniard, in 1556 and overhauled in 1795. The only remarkable feature is the quantity of paintings in the side chapels – the best are in the fourth chapel on your left approaching the altar, and in the 16th-century high altar retable.

Municipal Museum
t (245) 330 616; open 9.30–12.30 and 2–6, Sat 9.30–11.30 and 3–6.30; closed Wed and hols; adm

The **Municipal Museum** is next to the cathedral, housed in a 16th-century seminary rebuilt in the 18th century. It contains one of the oddest collections in Portugal – hundreds of images of St Anthony, from the Middle Ages to a contemporary lottery ticket. Also displayed are Baroque polychrome figures, including *Our Lady of Pain*, with seven silver daggers stuck in her breast. The proceeds from the sale of innumerable sweets, made by the nuns of Santa Clara, paid for the ornate silver and ebony tabernacle. Also downstairs are lots of bloody Christs, chalices, and ivories carved in Bahia. Upstairs there are outstanding collections of fans, silver snuffboxes, and Chinese porcelain cups. Near the last of these are two uncomfortable chairs, identified from paintings as having belonged to the Marquês de Pombal.

(i) **Portalegre >**
Regional tourist office: Estrada de Santana 25, t (245) 300 770, www.rtsm.pt

Smaller local office: Rua Guilherme Gomes Fernandes 22, t (245) 307 445; open Mon–Fri 10-1 and 2-6

Tourist Information/Services in Portalegre

The **local tourist office** can suggest walking routes in the nearby national park. The **bus station, t** (245) 330 723, is on the Castelo Branco road. The **railway station, t** 808 208 208, is 12km south of town, with connecting buses from the main bus station.

Where to Stay in Portalegre

★★★**Estalagem Quinta da Saúde**, Quinta da Saúde, **t** (245) 202 324 (€€). Three km northeast of town, on the road to the Serra de São Mamede, this provides rooms in bungalows, with basic glazed-wood furniture. The windows are small, with wooden shutters and without much of a view. There is a restaurant (*see* below) and pool.

★★★**Hotel Dom João III**, Avenida da Liberdade, **t** (245) 330 192 (€). This hotel is in the lower part of town, opposite the northeastern corner of the municipal garden, which is composed of large, empty spaces. Characterless – though comfortable – rooms with vestibules.

★★★**Residencial Mansão Alto Alentejo**, Rua 19 de Junho 59, **t** (245) 202 290 (€). In the road that faces the front of the cathedral. Clean and simple, with painted furniture. The small windows make it slightly airless.

★★**Pensão Nova**, Rua 31 de Janeiro 28–30, **t** (245) 330 812 (€). The rooms are pretty. The reception desk also serves the nearby **Pensão São Pedro** (€), which offers small but decent

wallpapered rooms, in an extension of the family home.

Pousada
Pousada Flor da Rosa, Crato, **t** (245) 997 210, www.pousadas.pt (L3 HD). Located some 20km west of town, this extraordinary *pousada* is worth the detour. Located in a renovated medieval castle that has loads of atmosphere (and ghosts!) as well as lovely gardens and a pool.

Turismo de Habitação
Quinta das Varandas, in the Serra de São Mamede Nature Park, **t** (245) 208 883 or 969 096 978 (€€). Part of the oldest estate in this region, the house is well maintained and undauntingly comfortable. The grounds are particularly inviting, with fountains and ponds in the Italian Romantic style.

Solar das Avencas, Parque Miguel Bombarda No.11, **t** (245) 201 028 (€€). Several rooms are available in the eighteenth-century Solar das Avencas. It's a memorable place with antiques that aren't too heavy, an enclosed garden and a reading room. One of the rooms is splendid, and breakfast is vast. The owners speak French and have a tendency to poke you.

Eating Out in Portalegre

Estalagem Quinta da Saúde, Quinta da Saúde, **t** (245) 202 324 (€€€). The restaurant at the *estalagem* (*see* above) is one of the best places to eat in or around Portalegre. It's very pleasantly decorated in the style of a grand mountain lodge, with an open fire. A board of cured meats is produced as an appetizer. For dessert, try the *touçinho-do-ceu*, a deliciously light eggy cake.

O Abrigo, Rua de Elvas 74, near the cathedral square, **t** (245) 331 658 (€). Child-friendly, and has a very pleasant atmosphere, with a cork ceiling and lampshades. Try the *lulas de caldeirada* (squid stew). The Nisa cheese is very good too. *Closed Tues.*

O Cortiço, Rua Dom Nuno Álvares Pereira 17–21, **t** (245) 202 176 (€). Opposite the bus station, and much more popular with the locals. The walls are lined with cork, and the food is good and solid. This is a wise choice for a filling meal if you're on a tight budget. *Open 9am–12am.*

Casa Capote, Rua 19 de Junho 56, **t** (245) 201 748 (€). A good little place. *Closed Sun.*

Around Portalegre

Parque Natural da Serra de São Mamede

ⓘ Parque Natural da Serra de São Mamede
Park Headquarters: Rua General Conde Jorge de Avilez 22, Portalegre, t (245) 203 631

Centro de Interpretação: Rua de Santo Amaro 27, Castelo de Vide, t (245) 905 299; open Mon–Fri 9.30–12.45 and 2–5.45; for information in English on walking in the park

Portalegre is a good starting point for exploring the Serra de São Mamede, a 120 square mile (320 square km) nature park, covering the 25-mile (40km) long mountain range which skirts the Spanish frontier (from Castelo de Vide southwards to Esperança). It's one of Europe's richest wildlife habitats, and supports both common and important rare species of wildlife. Forests of sweet chestnut, oak, and acres of cork-oak trees support an ornithologist's paradise: more than half of Portugal's birds nest here. Bring binoculars for remarkable sights of brightly-coloured hoopoes and bee-eaters; birds of prey including vultures, eagles and harriers; songbirds; and the well-documented white storks, which nest precariously on village rooftops. One of the largest colonies of bats in Europe is found here, as well as butterflies, lizards, snakes, toads, otters, and larger beasts such as deer, boar, mongoose and the genet, a curious cat-like creature that originates from Africa, with a spotted coat, striped tail and long face. You'll be lucky if you see the Iberian lynx – sadly it is almost extinct in Portugal. Many of the rare bird species are at risk from threats faced by the cork oak forests (*see* 'Cork and Olives', p.406).

Alter do Chão

ⓘ Alter do Chão
Palácio do Álamo, t (245) 610 004; open Mon–Fri 10–2

In the mid-18th century, Dom João V chose to locate his stud farm at Alter do Chão, on a plain 33km southeast of Portalegre and 46km north of Estremoz. Andalucian horses were imported, eventually producing the unique Lusitanian breed. The operatic **castle** stands in the Praça da República, an irregular pentagon built by Dom Pedro in 1359. The courtyard is full of orange and cypress trees, ivy and pigeons. Opposite the castle, the **Misericórdia**'s weather vane is a plump, skipping rat. Across the Praça da República marble columns support the twin cupolas of a **Renaissance fountain** dated 1556, constructed for the Duque de Bragança, D. Teodósio I, and displaying the family's and village's heraldry.

Pillories

It's not a fountain or an ornamental garden that stands at the centre of most towns and some villages in Portugal. Right next to the town hall, time after time, there you have it, the pillory: an elegant stone column to which criminals were shackled and whipped. Alternatively, the villain was incarcerated in a cage atop the pillory. Pillories can be very attractive. They were built from the 13th century to the 18th century, and their detail varies according to current artistic tastes: they can be twisted, patterned with stone dots, or ornamented with armillary spheres. Still, the deterrent aspect of pillories doesn't seem to justify their prominence: they symbolize something bigger – municipal liberties. The early kings and great lords of Portugal granted charters to boroughs, indicating their freedoms, guarantees, taxes, punishments and fines. Judicial power was vested in the *alcaide* (castellan) and was administered at the pillory. So pillories came to be associated with decentralized government and local control.

Castelo de Vide

① Castelo
de Vide

When a young couple eloped at the beginning of the 13th century, they galloped off to colonize a rocky mount which Dom Afonso II had given them. They called the place Terra de Vide (Land of the Vine), which changed to **Castelo de Vide** when the castle was built. Dom Afonso walled the town in 1280, sparking a conflict with his brother King Dom Dinis. Castelo de Vide is an appealing little place; it's much more interesting – though less spectacular – than Marvão, because it has more life, and there's a great choice of accommodation. Its dazzlingly white ancient cottages huddle around the castle, plunge down a hill slope and course up again in six parallel streets off the pillory square. So much dizzy plummeting has earned it the nickname 'Sintra of the Alentejo'. Castelo de Vide's higgledy-piggledy *Judiaria*, the Jewish 'ghetto', has remained intact.

Around the Town

The leafy **Praça Dom Pedro V**, at the centre of the lower town, offers a good view of the castle, and is surrounded by handsome houses including the **Torre Palácio**, where the statesman Mouzinho da Silva was born in 1780. The church of Santa Maria da Sevesa backs onto the Praça; at the front of the church, the downhill road leads to a little square in which stands the charmingly worn and uneven **Fonte da Vila**. This 16th-century marble lozenge shelters beneath a columned tabernacle, and once constituted the social centre of the town. The water is delicious, and medicinal for diabetes, and kidney and bone complaints.

Synagogue
*on the corner of Rua
da Juniaria and Rua da
Fonte; open daily
9–5.30*

An alley rises steeply towards Portugal's oldest synagogue, lined with modest 16th- and 17th-century houses. Each of these has two doorways, one for entry and one for commercial transactions. Some are plain, others are ornamented by stone studs. The excellent view of the town from the top of the alley stretches beyond, to Marvão's rocky hilltop. From the outside, the **synagogue**

Getting to Castelo de Vide

From each of Elvas and Portalegre, only one **train** daily is feasible: leaving at 5.20pm and 4.12pm respectively, both connecting with the 7.02pm from Torre das Vargens (2½hrs total).

Approximately five local **buses** run daily from Portalegre. From Marvão, you must change at Portagem. There are two express buses a day from Lisbon.

looks like any other house. The plain interior contains a tabernacle with round hollows for sacred oil and a shelf for sacred scriptures. The floor of a room immediately below the place of worship has been hollowed to a depth of about 10ft (3m); it was once lined with cork and used for storing cereals. There may have been a tunnel from the synagogue or a house nearby, which emerged outside the castle walls: an escape route at the time of the Inquisition.

The Afonsine Ordinances of 1446 ruled that Portuguese Jews must live in districts set apart for them in cities, into which they were literally locked early each evening. They had their own courts and their own judges, though they were still ultimately responsible to the king; they had to wear a distinctive costume, and Jewish men were forbidden to enter alone the house of an unmarried Christian woman.

In and Around the Judiaria

The Judiaria is a tangled mass of tiny streets at the rear of the synagogue, nestling under lichenous terracotta roofs, with minuscule windows and bulging sides. Masses of plants are potted – with gross irony – in tins which held pig lard, and Friday is laundry and bath day, to be clean for church on Sunday.

Castle
*open daily May–Sept
9–7; Oct–April 9–5*

The **castle** completed in 1365, is none too inspiring since the keep was mutilated by an explosion in 1705. Its most interesting feature is a 40ft (12m) tall brick cylinder, popularly believed to be a funerary chamber. No skeletons have been found, however, and it was probably a store-room for munitions, or a lookout post with impressive views of the Serra de São Paulo. In 1630 the household servants of Castelo de Vide contributed funds to build the small **church of Senhora da Alegria** (Our Lady of Joy) within the castle walls, entirely tiled with polychrome *azulejos*.

In the late 17th century the little church of **Senhora da Penha** was built 3km south of town, near some donkey tracks which appeared in the granite when a shepherd invoked the Virgin Mary and she arrived riding the animal.

Services in Castelo do Vide

Buses stop near the fountain by the **post office**, at Rua de Olivença.

The **railway station, t** (245) 901 663 or 905 228, is 4km northeast of town.

Internet Access

Artitudo, Rua Mouzinho da Silveira 14, **t** (245) 908 085. Web access, café, gallery and bookshop (*open daily noon–2am*).

14

The Alentejo | Castelo de Vide

(i) **Castelo de Vide >**

Rua de Bartolomeu Álvares da Santa 81, t (245) 901 361, cm.castvide@mail.tele pac.pt; open July–Aug daily 9–12.30 and 2–7, Sept–June until 5.30

(★) **Residencial Casa do Parque >**

Where to Stay in Castelo de Vide

★★★Hotel Sol e Serra, Estrada de São Vicente, **t** (245) 901 301 (€€). Pleasant, spacious, friendly and nicely situated, with a kidney-shaped pool, and views of the wooded hill slope opposite.

Albergaria El-Rei Dom Miguel, Rua Bartolemeu Álvares da Santa 19, **t** (245) 919 191 (€). Small, pretty guesthouse in the centre of town. Has attractively decorated rooms with period furniture and sparkling, modern bathrooms.

★★★Residencial Casa do Parque, 37 Avenida da Aramanha, **t** (245) 901 250 (€). At the upper side of the municipal garden, this offers good value. Rooms are pleasant, spic-and-span, double-glazed, and some of them have views of the little park and the hills beyond. There's a small outdoor pool, as well as a good, friendly restaurant (€). *Reservations recommended.*

Residencial Isabelinha, Largo do Paço Novo, **t** (245) 901 896 (€). Run by the same people as the Casa do Parque, and strikes a more modern note by featuring air-conditioned, rather functional rooms, complete with television.

Turismo de Habitação
Casa Amarela, Praça D. Pedro V 11, **t** (245) 901 250, *victor-guimaraes@mail.pt* (€€€). With its splendid granite casements overlooking the town's main square, eighteenth-century Casa Amarela looks very promising. It offers rooms

under the *Turismo de Habitaçao* scheme – so the reception desk comes as a surprise, as the scheme is for homes not hotels. Indeed, the house seems to have been done up with visitors in mind, but it's probably all the more comfortable for it and it has been tastefully done. And there's some amazing yellow marble in the bathrooms.

Eating Out in Castelo de Vide

Marino's, Rua Volta do Penedo, **t** (245) 901 408 (€€€). On the edge of the main square, has a nice view of the hill slope – and is undeservedly empty. Serves Italian and local dishes. *Closed Sun and Mon lunch, and 20 Dec–15 Jan.*

O Alentejano, Largo Mártires da República, **t** (245) 901 355 (€€). At the top of a delightful little fountained square.

Dom Pedro V, Praça Dom Pedro V, **t** (245) 901 236 (€), is a popular, cave-like place with staff who are eager to please. Try the *migas*, cooked with potatoes as it was in the 19th century. Don't be put off by the neon sign, or the approach past the toilets.

Os Amigos, Rua Bartolomeu Álvares da Santa, **t** (245) 901 781 (€). Sit outside and watch the world go by, and eat snails at dusk.

Café

Café Central, Rua Bartomeu Álvares da Santa, **t** (245) 901 183. In the evening ladies eat pastries here.

Marvão

 Marvão

Marvão is a medieval walled village of 1,000 souls in the Serra de Marvão, built on a steep rock escarpment at an altitude of 2,820ft (860m). It overlooks a barren scene of rough beauty: to the north, south and east stretch endless, almost volcanic, hummocky rock outcrops; to the west lie dark and dusty reds and greens.

The village is enchanted – a muddle of narrow cobbled streets, with very white dwellings built around unexpected shoulders of rock and wide flagstone steps. Granite window casements are

Getting to Marvão

By **road**, Marvão is 19km northeast of Portalegre, 12km southeast of Castelo de Vide.

The **railway station** is 9km north of town, near the Spanish border. There is one direct **train** a day from Lisbon (3hrs); for Elvas and Portalegre you must change at Torre das Vargens (one feasible connection, total 2hrs).

Buses are also infrequent. Theoretically, two run daily from Portalegre, making a day trip possible, but the service is erratic, so it is best to check.

mottled with lichen, house numbers are stencilled above the doorways. Plant pots are made from the bark of cork trees. Swallows dip in and out of the village, and kites fly above. Marvão appears to have sidestepped several centuries – though it's now on the tourist trail, and is popular with Spanish day trippers.

History

The Romans knew Marvão as Herminio Minor, since when its location has made it a tough nut to crack. In 715 the Christian Visigoths inhabiting the mount were slaughtered by the Moors, who resettled the place two generations later, under the order of the Lord of Coimbra, Emir Maruan (meaning pleasant or mild), after whom it was named. Dom Sancho II granted it a municipal franchise in 1226, determining that one-third of the men of the borough were to garrison the castle; the rest were to participate in the annual raiding parties into enemy territory.

What to See

At the northern tip of Marvão, the rugged **castle** (always accessible) seems to grow out of the natural rock. Walls swirl upwards, ever less penetrable. Dom Dinis ordered the construction of the keep c. 1300, incorporating a tinkling cistern within the walls, which held half a year's supply of water. Villagers used to play handball on its roof, peace permitting. There are spectacular views from here, south and west towards the Serra de São Mamede, and east to the Spanish frontier. The **Núcleo Museológico Militar** (Military Museum), at one end of the castle, has a display on the town and castle's history (in Portuguese), and examples of 17th- and 18th-century weaponry.

Núcleo Museológico Militar
open Tues–Sun 10–1, and 1.30–5; adm

The closest building to the castle is the church of Santa Maria, which houses the good little **Museu Municipal**. Its most interesting section covers popular medicines and prayers. There are also mannequins in traditional dress, Palaeolithic remains, some cannon cleaners about 10ft (3m) long, and Dom Manuel's charter.

Museu Municipal
open daily 9–12.30 and 2–5.30; adm

About 300 yards down Marvão's access road, the **Convento de Nossa Senhora da Estrela** (Our Lady of the Star) takes its name from an image of the Virgin which was found by shepherds guided by a shooting star. The sculpture had been buried by frightened Christian Visigoths as they fled the Moors, and it is popularly believed to protect Marvão from unfriendly armies. The Franciscan convent was founded in 1448, but revamped by the Bishop of Portalegre in 1772; now it houses the *Misericórdia* hospital. The key to the church is kept opposite the church door, straight through from the entrance to the convent. The side chapel contains a splendid marble altarpiece, and the 18th-century *azulejos* in the sacristy have been mis-mounted into a strange collage.

(i) Marvão >
*Largo de Santa Maria,
t (245) 993 886; open
daily Sept–June
9–12.30 and 2–5.30,
July–Aug until 6*

⊛ Pensão D.
Dinis >>

Tourist Information/ Services in Marvão

The **tourist office** have details of houses available to let, as well as walking information. The **bus stop** is just outside the town walls, near Portas de Ródão, one of Marvão's four village gates.

Sports and Activities in Marvão

Clube de Golfe de Marvão, Quinta do Prado, São Salvador da Aramenha (off the EN246 road), **t** (245) 993 755. Eighteen-hole golf course, with a restaurant and bar in the clubhouse.

Where to Stay and Eat in Marvão

★★★★**Albergaria El Rei Dom Manuel**, Largo do Terreiro, **t** (245) 909 150 (€€€). This small guesthouse has plenty of charm with attractively furnished, albeit small, rooms with terracotta tile floors and superb views. The management are young, enthusiastic and friendly. Some English is spoken.

Casa da Árvore, Largo de Camões, **t** (245) 993 854 (€€). A middle-class home with five rooms available to guests. It's bright, fetching and somehow impersonal. There are great views from the terrace.

Casa das Portas de Ródão, Largo da Silveirinha 1, **t** (245) 992 160, or **t** 938 589 157 (€€). Just inside the entrance to the village is a detached three-bedroomed house available to

let, all nicely done but a bit of a squeeze for four people.

Pensão D. Dinis, Rua Dr. Matos Magalhães, **t** (245) 993 957 (€). Near the castle, a simple, friendly place in an old house with great views, offering good value. Book Room 15, which has its own terrace from which to survey the world. Some rooms have air-conditioning. The place has a bar nearby, which serves light meals indoors or on the shady terrace.

Pousada
Pousada de Santa Maria, Rua 24 de Janeiro 7, **t** (245) 993 201/2, *www.pousadas.pt* (L1 C). Combines civilized living with local furniture and hospitality. There are several reception rooms with log fires, and nicely detailed décor. The nine cosy bedrooms have parquet floors and wonderful views of the bleak rocky hills and plains around Marvão. The dining room is wrapped around the sitting room, taking full advantage of the view. The service is attentive and the menu features local specialities. However, it faces hefty competition from far less expensive rivals.

Varanda do Alentejo, Praça do Pelourinho 1, **t** (245) 993 272 (€). A popular local eatery where you can enjoy daily specials such as pork and clams. Eat al fresco on the attractive terrace if weather permits. Some rooms (€) are also available.

Casa do Povo, Rua de Cima, **t** (245) 993 160 (€). A restaurant that is popular with Spanish day-trippers, but manages not to be too touristy. Meals are available on the terrace-with-a-view, or upstairs in the restaurant proper.

Estremoz

The walled market town of Estremoz ('shtreh-*mozh*') climbs up a hillslope, 57km south of Portalegre and 44km northeast of Évora, rising above the undulating plains. Groves of holm oaks and cork oaks, orchards and vineyards thrive in the fertile, well-watered countryside, which includes extensive deposits of pure white marble in its limestone base.

The town blazon is composed of stars (*estrelas*) and a lupin tree (*tremoceiro*), the two elements said to lie behind the name 'Estremoz'. The old fortified hilltop settlement centres on the castle keep. From there, stepped streets lined with low, whitewashed houses run down to the modern heart, the huge, sandy Rossio Marquês de Pombal. Some houses are numbered with stencils, below which women stand and gossip at their two-tiered 'stable' doors, or scrub their marble doorsteps. There are some great places to stay and eat, and it's pretty good for wandering too. Unlike Évora, Estremoz has escaped creeping gentrification, and it's an easy two-hour drive from Lisbon airport.

History

Three kings – Sancho II, Afonso III and Dinis – built the castle, whose plain keep is known as the Tower of the Three Crowns. Dom Dinis came to Estremoz in 1281 to negotiate for the hand of Princess Isabel of Aragon, subsequently constructing a palace to put her in. Their wedding celebration mortified conservatives when, for the first time in court history, male and female courtiers danced together.

Its strategic location and royal palace boosted the military and political importance of Estremoz, which became one of the key castles in the Alentejo. Dom Pedro I lived here until his death in 1367, and in 1380 Dom Fernando inhabited the tower, shortly before his wife Leonor Teles installed her lover, the Count of Andeiro, in the siesta room. Vaubanesque fortifications were erected at the end of the 17th century. During the Civil War, the town was staunchly Miguelite, its most grizzly moment coming in July 1833, three days after the liberal victory in Lisbon, when 39 liberal prisoners, including a child of six, were butchered with an axe on the castle's staircase landing.

The Castle Keep

Estremoz is dominated by the sober marble Torre das Três Coroas (Tower of the Three Crowns) of 1258. It rises 90ft (27m) above the hilltop, offering huge views – on a clear day you can see Portalegre, Évora and even Palmela – and dizzy glimpses through holes for pouring boiling lead and olive oil. Most of the castle and palace

Getting to Estremoz

Estremoz station was closed in 1990. This means that each of the two infrequent **train** routes from Lisbon requires two changes: from Lisbon's Terreiro do Pato, change at Barreiro after ½hr, take a train to Évora (2¼hrs) and change there for the bus to Estremoz (1¼hr). Alternatively, depart Lisbon's Santa Apolónia (early morning), change at Entroncamento after 1½hrs, and catch a train for Portalegre (2¼hrs), from where a bus runs to Estremoz (1½hrs).

Express **buses** run infrequently from Lisbon (3hrs), via Setúbal (2¼hrs), and Coimbra. There are more frequent services from Elvas and Arraiolos (each ¾hr), and local Belos buses run frequently from Évora.

were destroyed by an explosion in the gunpowder room, in 1698. Dom João V restored the latter as a depository for his collection of 40,000 weapons, which were stolen by the French in 1808. The palace is now a *pousada*.

The Sainted Queen Isabel

The **Capela de Rainha Santa** (*to enter, ask at the Museu Municipal*) occupies the little room in the castle where the sainted queen expired in 1336. Queen Isabel was killed by the journey from Compostela to Estremoz via Coimbra – 11 years after the death of her husband, Dom Dinis – having given away most of her income to the poor. She had kept herself and her ladies constantly at work embroidering and weaving, breaking from their routine on Fridays in Lent to wash the feet of 12 poor men, 'the most leprous they could find', according to the chronicler Ruy de Pina.

Dona Isabel was an able peacemaker, mediating between Dom Dinis and his legitimate son Prince Dom Afonso, who became obsessed with the idea that his father would grant the succession to one of his seven bastard half-brothers. It was Dona Luísa de Gusmão, widow of Dom João IV, who founded the chapel in 1659, a time when Dona Isabel's aptitudes as a peacemaker were sorely missed. Now it is lined with 18th-century *azulejos* depicting scenes from the life of the queen, including the conversion of bread into roses: suspicious that his wife was ferreting away her bread for the poor, Dom Dinis asked the queen to drop her skirt. The bread she had been carrying in it was transformed into roses, and Dom Dinis couldn't find a crumb.

Around the Castle Square

In the square at the foot of the keep, the **Igreja Matriz de Santa Maria** was commissioned by Dom Sebastian in the second half of the 16th century. It's usually kept locked, though the building is used for radio broadcasting – try midday on Sunday. The unusual interior is square but for the chancel, with irregularly spaced columns, elegant marble pulpits, and faded frescoes.

The **Museu Municipal** occupies an early 17th-century almshouse on the south side of the castle square. Its collection of decorative

Museu Municipal
*t (268) 339 200;
open May–Sept
Tues–Sun 9–12.30 and
3–6.30, Oct–April
Tues–Sun 9–12.30 and
2–5.30; adm*

Estremoz pottery figures illustrates the humour and consistent style of this peasant art, depicting barbers, milkmen, musicians and the like. There's a nice figure of Spring, dressed in a tutu and wearing a tiara of petals and an arc of flowers. Upstairs, there are carved horns, rustic furniture, an Alentejan kitchen and some guns. Ask at the museum for the key to its annexe in the former communal granary, hung with modern pictures of variable quality. Next to this is the **Gallery of the Audience Hall**, a Gothic loggia which is all that remains of the 13th-century establishment, except for the keep. The blazon of Estremoz is embedded on the gallery's wall.

It's worth walking round to the quiet, grassy southwestern side of the upper part of town, where the medieval defensive walls run parallel with the 17th-century walls.

The Lower Town

In the lower part of town, the **Câmara Municipal** (Town Hall) fronts the Rossio Square, occupying a convent founded in 1698; visitors are welcome to look at the excellent *azulejos* of hunting scenes which line its broad staircase. On the east side of the Rossio, facing the castle, the two-roomed **Museu Rural** is full of curiosities, including bamboo sheaths worn on the fingers of one hand to prevent them being chopped by the scythe held in the other, and large carved horns which stored fieldworkers' cheese and olives. The **church of São Francisco** stands adjacent to the north side of the Rossio. The Gothic structure dates back to 1213, but the only noteworthy fixtures are a 17th-century tree of Jesse and the tomb of Vasco Esteves Gato, installed in 1401.

Museu Rural
open Mon–Sat 9.30–12 and 2–5.30; adm

The **Museu da Alfaia Agrícola** (Museum of Agriculture) stands in the Rua Serpa Pinto, which leads off from the *Lago*. Filled with machines, yokes, ploughs and saddles, it is of little interest to the non-specialist.

Museu da Alfaia Agrícola
t (268) 339 200; open Tues–Fri 8.30–12.30 and 2–4, Sat–Sun 2–5

There are **marble quarries** at the junction with the Elvas road. From here, the marble is sent to factories nearby to be broken down, and then on to Sintra to be fashioned and polished.

The Saturday Market in the Rossio Square

The Estremoz market is typical of Alto Alentejo. Vendors arrive in the early light carrying leeks, turnips, maybe a rabbit in a basket, blossom picked from a bush. They lay their goods on hessian mats and sit quietly beside them. Some sell oranges sorted into seven sizes, others crates of hard little cheeses, like white ice-hockey pucks. The men stand together outside the Café Alentejano, pivoting on their heels, dispensing firm, single handshakes, raising a felt hat or a cap. And then, at about midday, everything unsold is packed away, and taken home again.

(i) Estremoz >
*Largo da República
26 (in a little square off
the Rossio Marquês de
Pombal), t (268) 334
010; open daily
9.30–12.30 and 2–6*

(★) Páteo dos
Solares >

(★) Pensão Café
Alentejano >>

(★) Pousada
Raínha Santa
Isabel >>

(★) Hotel
Convento de
São Paulo >

Services in Estremoz

The **post office** is at Rua 5 de Outubro, and offers internet access (*open Mon–Fri 9–6*). The **bus station** is by the old train station, east of the Rossio.

Where to Stay in Estremoz

★★★★★Páteo dos Solares, Rua Brito Capelo, t (268) 338 400, *www.pateo solares.com* (€€€€). As you enter, you're faced with a marble font filled with violets, and that set the scene: this 41-bedroom eighteenth-century manor is extremely attractive, unusual and very well designed. Colours are neutral, and there's a feeling of calm and contentment. Choose room 208 and lie in the bath overlooking the outdoor pool and the hills beyond. The restaurant (€€) is characteristically appealing and very sensibly recommends a wine to go with each entrée.

★★★★Hotel Convento de São Paulo, 15km south of Estremoz at Aldeia da Serra, Redondo, t (266) 989 160, *www.hotelconventospaulo.com* (€€€€). Occupies a vast and magnificent monastery founded in 1182; the present building dates from 1796 and is most remarkable for the 54,000 blue-and-white *azulejos* that line every corridor, cloister and chapel. The place is fabulously quiet and possessed of the cleanest air imaginable; the views of the plains are equally impressive. With just 32 rooms, the hotel is never going to feel crowded; indeed, however thick the cherry-red carpet in the corridors, it retains an aura of sobriety. This is worth bearing in mind if you come here on honeymoon: lying in bed in the grandest room you're confronted with a ceiling fresco of God the Father. The service is excellent and the staff fairly relaxed. The restaurant (€€€) is dedicated to the serious pursuit of gastronomy, and is not overpriced, although the tables are a little too close together. Try the lamb roasted in olive oil.

★★Residencial Mateus, Rua do Almeida 39–41, t (268) 322 226 (€). Offers honest rooms in the old quarter.

★★Residencial Carvalho, 27 Largo da República, t (268) 339 370 (€). Next to the tourist office. Windows don't always open, so the ants can't get out, but the water is nice and hot and the furniture decent. It's a good place: grandiose, but somehow it carries it off.

Residencial Miguel José, Travessa de Levada 8, t (268) 322 326 (€). Near the post office. It has dark corridors, and solid rooms, with flowers, bits of lace and patterned bedside rugs.

Pensão Café Alentejano, Rossio Marquês de Pombal, t (268) 337 300 (€). The rooms are very good value, with locally painted furniture, high ceilings and air-conditioning. The first-floor restaurant is a happy place with good food and a relish of life. A hoot.

Pousada
Pousada Raínha Santa Isabel, t (268) 332 075, *www.pousadas.pt* (L2 H). Installed in the former royal palace, this is the most splendid and regal of the country's *pousadas*. In the entrance hall, charming wooden Baroque figures hold snakes for inspection. Don't take the elevator unless you have to – the wide marble staircase and its tile dado are a great treat. Many of the 23 bedrooms have canopied beds, and distant views. It's a very friendly place, with efficient service. Eat pork and clams in the baronial restaurant, which is fragmented by pillars and arches, and lit by chandeliers, or have a light meal beside the luxurious little swimming pool. *Reservations necessary.*

Turismo de Habitação
Herdade da Barbosa, between Sotileira and São Bento do Cortiço, t (268) 234 510 (€€). Ten kilometres north of Estremoz, this place offers five rooms under the Agro Tourism scheme. It's nothing fancy, but it offers an opportunity to get close to the land, for the cork harvest in June or July, for fishing for black bass in the lake 500 yards away in August, or the hazelnut and walnut harvest in September or October, and so on through the year. The bedrooms are

charming, chickens wander about the place, and there's a small pool. Dinner can be provided at two days' notice.

Monte Dos Pensamentos, t (268) 333 166 (€). Three kilometres out of Estremoz on the Lisbon road, turn right before the service station to find this very pretty country villa. It has four large rooms, each decorated with splendid beds, marble fireplaces, antique screens, Arraiolos carpets and colourful plates. Indeed, plates run riot on all the walls but the effect is cheery – they lift the heaviness of the dining room and complement the airiness of the sitting room. *Minimum stay of two nights.*

Eating Out in Estremoz

São Rosas > São Rosas, Largo D. Dinis 11, **t** (268) 333 345 (€€€). Next to the keep is that unusual thing, an elegant, rustic

family-run restaurant with staff who know what they're doing, a fine wine list and excellent food. It's not worth coming to Estremoz specially to dine here, but it's certainly part of the package that makes the town so appealing. Take your time and enjoy it. There's a set menu for €19.50. *Closed Mon.*

Águias d'Ouro, in the Rossio, **t** (268) 337 030 (€€). Diners sit on cuboid chairs and eat dishes such as *peito de vitela* (calf's heart), served by rather incongruous black-tied waiters.

Adega do Isaias, Rua do Almeida 21, **t** (268) 322 318 (€€). A rustic cellar *tasca*, with wooden tables and terracotta wine jugs. Grilled meats are the speciality; recommended for more casual eating.

Café

D Tea, Rua 31 de Janeiro 30, no tel. A trendy café serving tasty snacks.

Around Estremoz

Borba

Borba is a small town nestled into the northern slopes of the diminutive Serra de Borba, and serves as a base for marble quarrying at Monte Claros, producing stone of a quality to rival that of Tuscany. Indeed, Portugal's marble exports rank second in the world. The marble has brought modest wealth, though there are no longer opportunities for striking it rich overnight – until the 18th century, emeralds were found in the neighbourhood. In Borba, everything within reason is made of marble – doorsteps, cornerstones, stairs, fireplaces, the municipal crazy paving, even the urinals at the bus station.

The late 16th-century **church of São Bartolomeu** is the only building of note; all its treasures are marble, canopied by a splendid vaulted Renaissance-style ceiling. The **Fonte das Bicas** is a stylish triangular-shaped fountain carved in the white marble of Montes Claros in 1781, bearing Dona Maria's royal blazon. Among the date palms behind the fountain, two brightly painted railway carriages now house a cramped but curious bar.

Vila Viçosa

Four km southeast of Borba, the tidy, white little town of Vila Viçosa stands on a plain at the base of the eastern slopes of the

Getting to areas Around Estremoz

There are six express **buses** a day to Borba from Lisbon (3hrs) and lots of local ones from Estremoz. Local buses run from Estremoz or from Évora (1hr), and two expresses a day from Lisbon (3¾hrs).

Serra de Borba. The grid-patterned streets are lined with orange trees, whose fruits unload themselves unceremoniously onto the pavements. Most of the medieval houses which surrounded Dom Dinis' castle of 1270 were torn down in 1663, to make way for defences against the Spanish, who besieged the town two years later. The roads around Vila Viçosa pass meadows and eucalyptus woods, cacti and elegant white egrets.

History

Vila Viçosa is belittled by the massive palace of the Dukes of Bragança. Dom Jaime, the melancholic fourth duke, began the aggrandizement of Vila Viçosa; in 1501 he set in train 101 years of construction on the palace. It brought him little joy: suspicious of an affair, he stabbed to death his duchess and her page in front of the whole household. Happier events were celebrated with bullfights in the Terreiro do Paço, close enough for the ladies of the palace to smell blood, with comedies, masques and fireworks, with Italian acrobats on stilts, with dancing to the music of trumpets, kettle-drums and woodwind instruments called shawms. One room of the palace is still called the *Sala da Cabra-cega* (the room of blind man's buff). An Italian cardinal visiting Portugal in 1571 reported trumpets sounded every time His Grace lifted his cup to take a drink of water.

In 1580 Philip II of Spain trampled on the ducal claim to the throne. Portuguese resentment burst 60 years later, and virtually forced João IV, the eighth duke, to cease composing music, dismount his beloved hunter and take the throne. This marked the beginning of the decline of the palace, which was stripped to furnish the Paço da Ribeira in Lisbon. Subsequent dukes ruled Portugal until 1908, occasionally coming here to hunt in the *tapada*. Dom Carlos left Vila Viçosa one morning in February and was shot dead that afternoon in Lisbon. His successor Dom Manuel II frequented this palace until he was toppled by the Revolution of 1910.

Paço Ducal
*Terreiro do Paço,
t (268) 980 659,
www.fcbraganca.pt/
paco/fcb.htm; open
April–Sept Tues
2.30–5.30, Wed–Fri 10–1
and 2.30–5.30, Sat and
Sun 9.30–1 and 2.30–6;
Oct–Mar Tues 2–5,
Wed–Sun 9.30–1 and
2–5; Treasury: open
Oct–May Tues–Fri;
closed Mon and hols;
all guided tours in
Portuguese; adm; entry
to the Armoury, Coach
Museum, Chinese
Porcelain Collection
and Treasury are by
separate ticket*

Paço Ducal

On the northwestern edge of town, the road from Borba passes the large square Terreiro do Paço, which fronts the plain and very, very long marble façade of the **Paço Ducal** (Ducal Palace). The entrance is in the middle of the edifice.

Within, most of the furniture is dull and dates from the late 19th century: the notable pieces were removed to Lisbon, where they were destroyed in the earthquake of 1755, or to Brazil, in the train of Dom João VI. The ceiling of the **Sala dos Duques** is covered with paintings of the dukes, including some that may be by Quillard, a pupil of Watteau. One exceptional tapestry is the portrayal of Alexander the Great in the **Sala de Hercules**, worked with rich tones in Brussels in the 16th or 17th century.

The private apartments are more revealing; they are kept as they were when Dom Carlos and his wife Marie-Amélie left for Lisbon. His uniforms hang in his cupboard, her knick-knacks cover her dressing table. They took sufficient pleasure in their food to equip the kitchen with 4,850lb (2,200kg) of copper pots and pans.

A simple cloister of 1505 leads through to the **Armoury**, which has a good collection of armour and *epées*. The stables have been converted into a **Coach Museum**, housing interminable lines of the things.

Around the Terreiro do Paço

The **Convento das Chagas** stands at right angles to the palace. Founded in 1530 by Dona Joana de Mendonta, the second wife of Dom Jaime, it contains the tombs of the duchesses, and has been converted into a *pousada* (*see* 'Where to Stay', p.424). Since 1677, the tombs of the dukes have been supported by stone lions behind the sober façade of the church of the **Mosteiro dos Agostinhos**, opposite the palace in the Terreiro do Paço. If it's closed, ask at the guard's lodge through a gate to the left.

The fourth side of the Terreiro borders the **Tapada** (Chase), which is surrounded by a wall some 11 miles (18km) long, but no longer reverberates with the snorts of deer and wild boar. The stags' antlers have furnished the ducal dining room. (Dom João, the eighth duke and future king, had a penchant for more exotic animals. He sent the pope a rhinoceros for his birthday, but the unhappy creature broke a hole in the side of the ship that was carrying it, sinking the vessel and drowning itself with most of the crew.)

A little way along the main road leading north from the Terreiro stands the **Porta dos Nós** (Gate of Knots), an inelegant example of Manueline whimsy, like the entrance to a dude ranch.

Castelo/
Museu de Caça e
Arqueologia
t (268) 980 659,
www.fcbraganca.pt/pac
o/fcb.htm; open
April–Sept Tues
2.30–5.30, Wed–Fri 10–1
and 2.30–5.30, Sat and
Sun 9.30–1 and 2.30–6,
Oct–Mar Tues 2–5,
Wed–Sun 9.30–1 and
2–5; adm

The Castelo

In the other direction, the Avenida Duque de Bragança runs uphill from the Terreiro past the walled **castle**. Inside, the **Museu de Caça e Arqueologia** (Museum of Hunting and Archaeology) displays hunting trophies, some of which date from the days of the Bragança dukes. The castle walls enclose a tiny, picturesque settlement, with charming wrought-iron streetlamp fittings and the church of **Nossa Senhora da Conceição**. Its 15th-century structure was altered in 1572 and in 1870, when the façade and single tower were revamped. The chapel to the right of the chancel contains *azulejos* by Policarpo de Oliveira Bernardes (1695–1776), whose design is much weaker than his father's work on the Lóios chapel in Évora.

The Avenida Bento de Jesus runs from the castle to the Praça da República, at the end of which stands the beautifully symmetrical 17th-century **church of São Bartholomeu** which is of no special interest – though the sacristan will be happy to show you the bell-tower. He keeps half a bottle of port there.

ⓘ Vila Viçosa >
Praça da República 34, t (268) 881 101, www.cm-vilavicosa.pt

ⓘ Borba >>
Rua do Convento das Servas in the câmara municipal *(town hall), t (268) 894 113*

Services in Vila Viçosa

The **bus station** is in the Rua André Gomes Pereira: to get to the Praça da República, walk along the Rua Dr António José d'Almeida, almost opposite the bus station, and to get from there to the Terreiro do Paço, continue along the Rua Florbela Espança.

Wineries in Borba

The local *adegas* produce red Borba and white maduro wines. The following are not particularly tourist-oriented, but you may pick up some bargains.
Adega Cooperativa de Borba, Largo Gago Coutinho e Sacadura Cabral 25, Borba, t (268) 891 665. *Open Mon–Sat 9–7.*
Sovibor, Rua de São Bartolomeu 48, Borba, t (268) 894 210. *Open Mon–Fri 9–12.30 and 2–4.30.*

Where to Stay and Eat

Vila Viçosa

Senora Maria de Conceição Paiseão, Rua Dr Couto Jardim 7, t (268) 980 168 (€). Charming rooms, with Alentejan painted furniture.
Framar, Praça da República 35, t (268) 980 158 (€). Sells marble pestles and mortars at street level. The restaurant above is deep and wide, with a parquet floor, and is enlivened by a large mural painted on wood. The *ensopado de cabrito a Alentejana* (kid stew) is not bad. *Closed Mon.*
Restaurante Restauração, Praça da República 22/24, t (268) 881 271 (€). A decent menu. *Closed Mon.*
Os Cucos, Mata Municipal, t (268) 980 806 (€). Dine from a fish and meat menu, in the municipal gardens, near the market.

Pousada
Pousada Dom João IV, t (268) 980 742, *www.pousadas.pt* (L2 H). A *pousada*, housed in the handsomely tiled and painted Renaissance buildings of the former Convento das Chagas de Cristo. The cloisters, nuns' cells, retreats and oratories add character, and the restaurant will satisfy those seeking well-cooked local specialities. It also has a peaceful quadrangle, and a large swimming pool.

Turismo de Habitação
Casa de Peixinhos, Estrada do Paúl, t (268) 980 472 (€€€). Part of a farm estate, situated about 500 yards from Vila Viçosa. The 17th-century *casa* has a mercifully cool setting, in a grove of orange trees. The eight rooms are grandly furnished, with marble scattered throughout.

Borba

Turismo de Habitação
Casa de Borba, Rua da Cruz 5 (near the post office), Borba, t (268) 894 528, *www.casadeborba.com* (€€). Located in the centre of the village, a resplendent 18th-century mansion with an elaborate marble staircase. Each of the five rooms has a bathroom, and the whole place is decorated with antiques, paintings and more marble. A games room, lounge and swimming pool are also on offer.

Évora Monte

Turismo de Habitação
Monte da Fazenda, Évora Monte, t (268) 959 172 (€€–€). A dazzling white and blue exterior masks a mellow interior which is simply and elegantly furnished with pale, wooden furniture and white lace bedspreads. The house offers three apartments each with its own entrance, two rooms and a swimming pool. Available for rent on a weekly basis.

Elvas

Elvas is a busy hilltop frontier town of 15,000 souls, 12km west of the Spanish border and 42km east of Estremoz, close to the southward curve of the River Guadiana.

Within its star-shaped fortifications, Elvas is charming, cobbled, and constantly aware that it is a frontier town. The modern settlement outside the town walls is dull and Elvas' monuments are unlikely to detain visitors for too long: of the many churches, one is outstanding (N.S. da Consolação).

Elvas is famous for its candied plums, which are more or less gooey from year to year. Cheap accommodation is scarce, and the town's restaurants are uninspiring.

History

Its strategic importance earned Elvas the sobriquet '*chave do reyno*' (key to the kingdom). It was recaptured from the Moors in 1230. In 1659 the Spanish were besieging Elvas; an epidemic had left the garrison with just 1,000 men. But with the help of fog and a relief army from Estremoz the Spanish were forced to abandon their encampment and 15,000 muskets. Already the strongest fortress in the country, Elvas spawned complementary works: four forts in the 17th century and the massive Forte de N.S. da Graça, in the later 18th century. Wellington used Elvas as a base prior to the bloody sieges of Badajoz in 1811 and 1812.

The Old Cathedral and Around

Take the road uphill from the *pousada*, through the **Porta de Oliventa** of 1685. The third turning to the right leads to the **Museu de António Tomáz Pires** installed in a Jesuit college, whose redeeming feature is a room full of *artesanato*, with firedogs, stamps for impressing owners' marks on loaves of bread in the communal bakery, carved horns, and a local speciality – handcut paper doilies.

The Rua de Oliventa continues uphill to the Praça da República, at the upper end of which gapes the squat and sober **Igreja de Nossa Senhora da Assunção**, the former cathedral surmounted by a weathervane which is either a devil or a cherub holding a mace and enlivened by porcine gargoyles. Francisco de Arruda designed the building *c.* 1517, but it suffered renovation in the 17th and 18th centuries.

Behind the cathedral stands the fantastic octagonal **Igreja de N.S. da Consolação** which is thrilling within. Diogo de Torralva prepared a rough draft for its design in 1543, basing its shape on that of a nearby Templars' hermitage that had been destroyed three years previously. The ornamentation and proportions are

Museu de António Tomáz Pires
*Largo do Colégio,
t (268) 622 402; open
Tues–Fri 9–12 and 2–5;
adm*

Igreja de Nossa Senhora da Assunção
*open Mon–Fri;
closed hols*

Igreja de N.S. da Consolação
*open Tues–Sun
9.30–12.30 and
2.30–5.30*

Getting to Elvas

Trains from Lisbon are infrequent (4½hrs, change at Entroncamento and/or Abrantes), as are trains from Marvão-Beira (2¾hrs), via Castelo de Vide (2½hrs); change at Torre das Vargens from both. There are three direct trains a day from Portalegre. Rede Expressos **buses** run fairly frequently from Lisbon (3½hrs), Évora (1¾hrs) and Estremoz (¾hr).

exceptionally beautiful. Marble pillars support the cupola, which is decorated with blue and yellow *azulejos* of 1659 right up to the lantern, as are the walls and ceiling. Note the emblem of the Dominican order.

Pass under the arch behind the **pillory** (*see* p.412), turn left at the Alcáçova church and right at the T-junction, and you'll arrive at the delightful **Rua das Beatas**, in which little dwellings bulge irregularly, and plants flourish. The castle is at the end of this road.

The Castelo and the Town Walls

Castelo
open daily 9.30–1 and 2.30–5.30; adm

Based on Romano-Moorish foundations, the **castelo** was remodelled both by Dom Dinis and Dom João II, who commissioned the tower. The inside feels charmingly lived-in, with catapult balls ringing the flowerbed. The structure incorporates the 700-year-old governor's residence, which now displays an atmospheric 'typical' Alentejan kitchen and a bedroom complete with drinking gourds. The most interesting route back to the centre of town is via the little roads which run along the town walls.

Outside the Town Walls

Passing through the town gate, the multistorey **Aqueduto da Amoreira** stands to the right. The aqueduct was built between 1529 and 1622 and paid for by the country's first royal water tax. The town's blazon, a plumed warrior on horseback carrying a standard, is etched on a panel on the aqueduct. It commemorates Gil Anes, who trotted over to Badajoz in 1438 and stole its standard. The Spaniards chased him back to Elvas, caught him and deep-fried him in a cauldron of oil. As he died, he cried in earnest, 'The man dies but his fame endures.'

Senhor Jesus da Piedade
open 10–12 and 2.30–6.30

An extraordinary museum of *ex votos* is attached to the unusually named church of **Senhor Jesus da Piedade**, a 10- or 15-minute walk to the southwest of town – the custom of naming Jesus with an attribute in the same way as the Virgin may be unique to Portugal. There are five rooms full of over 6,000 *ex-voto* offerings, old and new – paintings, embroidery, photographs, wax images and, most movingly, crutches. The town's September festivities coincide with an annual pilgrimage to the church dating back around 200 years.

ⓘ **Elvas** >

*Praça da República,
t (268) 622 236; open
May–Sept Mon–Fri 9–6,
Sat–Sun 10–12.30 and
2–5.30, Oct–April daily
until 5.30*

Services in Elvas

The **bus stop** and ticket office,
t (268) 622 875, is in Praça 25 de Abril.
A shuttle bus service runs to and from
the **railway station**, t (268) 622 816,
4km down the Campo Maior road.

Festivals in Elvas

The **Festas do Senhor da Piedade**
and the **Feira de São Mateús** take
place in late September. The fair is
mostly agricultural, but there are
bullfights, riding competitions,
displays of folk dancing, and
handicrafts on sale. The first and last
days of the fair coincide with religious
processions.

Where to Stay in Elvas

★★★★★**Estalagem Quinta de Santo
António**, Estrada de Barbacena, t (268)
636 460, *www.qsa.com.pt* (€€).
Provides upmarket-rustic
accommodation set in 2,000 acres
(800ha) of land, including an 18th-
century garden, a cistern surrounded
by Baroque statues, tennis courts, a
swimming pool and a plethora of
palms and fountains.

★★★**Hotel D. Luís**, Avenida de Badajoz,
t (268) 636 710, *www.hoteldluis-
elvas.com* (€€). Near the aqueduct,
offering well-furnished bedrooms. Has
a bar that serves light meals and
snacks.

António Mocisso e Garcia Coelho, Rua
Aires Varela 15, t (268) 622 126 (€).
Modern and spread over two
locations. Rooms have bathrooms and
air-conditioning, but they are small.

★★**Residencial Luzo-Espanhola**, Rua
Rui de Melo, t (268) 623 092 (€). One
of the cheapest places in town.

Pousada
Pousada de Santa Luzia, Avenida de
Badajoz, t (268) 637 470/2,
www.pousadas.pt (L1 C). Outside the

town walls, at the junction of the
continuation of Estrada Nacional 4
and the road to Ajuda, is a 1940s
building with attractively coordinated
bedrooms, featuring Alentejan
furniture and trellised tiles in the
bathrooms. The annexe is full of
antiques. The striplit L-shaped dining
room (€€€–€€) is a very popular place
with the locals; fish dishes are a
speciality, including the shellfish stew
cooked in a *cataplana*.

Eating Out in Elvas

El Cristo, Parque da Piedade, t (268)
623 512 (€€). Next to the church of
Senhor Jesus da Piedade, a 10-minute
walk from town. More popular for its
seafood than its ambience, being
large, striplit, and sited in an annexe.
The food is good. Much of it is priced
by the kilo: you can reckon on 14oz
(400g) per portion.

O Aqueduto, Avenida da Piedade,
t (268) 623 676 (€€). Just down from
the Capela de Nossa Senhora da
Nazaré, offering reasonably good
seafood specialities. The floors are
crazy-paved with chips of stone, the
tablecloths a verdant green, and the
lighting not unpleasantly bright. The
choice of dishes includes *costeletas de
cabrito panadas* (breaded lamb
chops).

A Coluna, Rua do Cabrito 11, t (268) 623
728 (€€–€). Good-value set menus,
surrounded by walls of *azulejos*.

Canal 7, Rua dos Sapateiros 16A,
t (268) 623 593 (€). Opposite the
tourist office is possibly the best
budget restaurant in Elvas, unfailingly
packed with a varied but lively crowd.
The food is very good, with a take-
away option.

There is also a café/restaurant in
the **Centro Artístico Elvense**, t (268)
622 711 (€). On Praça da República next
to the bus station, serving an
excessively good *arroz de marisco*.

Évora

 Évora

Some 150km east of Lisbon and 77km north of Beja, **Évora** is one of the joys of Portugal, delightful both to sightseers and to wanderers. Memorable, unspoilt though somewhat gentrified, it occupies the gentle slopes of a wide hill on the Alentejan plain, surrounded by olive groves, wheat fields and vineyards. Its 45,000 souls rank it as one of the country's largest cities; but just 15,000 live within the encircling walls, so it feels like a town. It is this inner town that has been declared a World Heritage site by UNESCO. Walking its clean, cobbled streets you come across arches and arcades, whitewashed *palácios* and Renaissance fountains, which together give Évora a wholeness in spite of the range of its monuments.

Houses stretch under the arches of the aqueduct, and it is around here that life is played out. Artisans tap out their trades, making pine coat-hangers or tables; old ladies tend a couple of cratefuls of fruit or vegetables. In winter, children keep themselves warm with fleecy sheepskin jerkins, whereas old men seem to prefer faded, habit-like capes.

History

Évora's history is as fertile as the title Pliny the Elder gave it – Ebora Cerealis. It was a political centre of Roman Iberia, and its townspeople have been able to claim Roman lineage since *c.* 61 BC, when Julius Caesar sent a group of his countrymen to mingle among the natives. Évora may have been the headquarters of Quintus Sertorius, who was sent to govern Hispania and bit the hand of his imperial master when he attempted to make the province independent, around 80 BC. (Sertorius had a pet albino fawn, which he swathed with gold necklaces and earrings, and taught to nuzzle his ear as if it were whispering to him. He ordered that good news should be delivered to him secretly, so he could pretend that the doe had brought it to him from the goddess Diana.)

The Visigoths came, and then the Moors, who stayed from 711 to 1165. In the 12th century, Idrisi, the Arab geographer, described Évora as a large, walled town with a great mosque and a castle, surrounded by singularly fertile countryside rich in wheat, fruit and vegetables. The Moors were expelled by Gerald the Fearless, an ingenious outlaw who drove lances into the outer wall of the city to form a staircase, which he mounted by night. Dom Afonso Henriques made Gerald castellan of the town, and he is depicted on the town's blazon, accompanied by two disembodied heads.

In 1166 Dom Afonso Henriques issued Évora with its first charter, in Latin, stating that every man who had a house, a yoke of oxen,

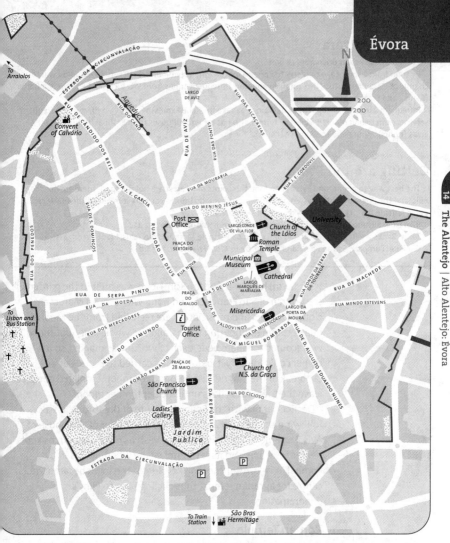

40 sheep, an ass and two beds was obliged to keep a horse and turn it out for military service. When there was a brawl among villagers, wounds were to be taxed, and those who caused them fined according to a fixed penalty.

The Renaissance and After

Évora flourished from the 14th century to the 16th century, enjoying the regal attentions of the locally based House of Avis. The *Cortes* were summoned here, and great artists duly followed. Together they produced a wealth of noble palaces and artworks, and in 1559 Cardinal Henrique founded a university. In 1490, Évora hosted the splendid celebrations for the marriage of Afonso, son of Dom João II, to Infante Isabel of Castile. For this, a wooden hall

Getting to Évora

Évora is an easy 1½hr **drive** from Lisbon.

By **train** from Lisbon, take the ferry to Barreiro for the infrequent indirect rail service requiring you to change at Casa Branca too (3hrs total). In addition, infrequent trains from Vila Viçosa take 1¾hrs, via Borba (1½hrs), and Estremoz (1¼hrs).

Infrequent **buses** from Reguengos de Monsaraz take 1hr. Rede Expressos and Eva both run very frequent services from Lisbon (1½hrs), while the former also has infrequent buses from Setúbal (1¾hrs), Beja (1¼hrs), Elvas (1¾hrs), Moura and the Algarve (1½hrs).

Getting around Évora

The best way to get around Évora is **on foot**: the points of interest are not far apart, there are no steep hills, and the one-way traffic system is maddening. If you do bring a car, park it in one of the many **car parks** outside the city walls – they're all well signposted.

Bike Hire: Silvano Manuel Cágado, Rua Cândido dos Reis 66, **t** (266) 702 424.

Taxis: Ranks are in Praça do Giraldo and Largo da Porta de Moura. **Rádio Taxis, t** (266) 734 734/5.

Car Hire: Europcar, Estrada de Viana lote 10. *Open Mon–Fri 9.30–1, 3–7, Sat 9.30–1.*

150ft (44m) high and 600ft (180m) long was built in the garden of the Church of São Francisco, and hung with striped Moroccan cloths. Dancers and musicians were recruited from the Moorish quarters of neighbouring towns, and the whole neighbourhood was scoured for spare beds, each of which was marked, so its owner could identify it, before being carried to Évora. But an outbreak of the plague, just before the jamboree, obliged guests to leave the town for 15 days until the September moon.

Decline set in with the Spanish seizure of the throne in 1580, following the death of Dom Henrique, last ruler of the House of Avis. The limelight left Évora's limewash as future monarchs kept nearer to Lisbon, and its Jesuit university was duly closed by Pombal in 1759. After the 1974 Revolution the town became the centre for agrarian reform, thus circling back to Pliny's denomination.

Roman Temple

Portugal's best-preserved Roman monument stands at the highest point in Évora. The temple dates from the late 2nd or early 3rd century AD, its granite Corinthian columns topped with Estremoz marble. Although it is popularly known as the Temple of Diana, scholars now think that the sanctuary may have been dedicated to the god Jupiter. Perhaps his indignation at the slight resulted in the building's conversion into the municipal slaughterhouse, until 1870.

Church of the Lóios

t (266) 704 714; open Tues–Sun 10–12.30 and 2–6; admission to the church, which is privately owned, is included in the price of the ticket for the museum at the Palácio dos Ducques de Cadaval

The Church of the Lóios

The **church of the Lóios** (St John the Evangelist), to one side of the Roman Temple, features the country's most captivating employment of *azulejos* – it would be a great pity to leave Évora without seeing this stunning church. Built on the site of the Moorish castle, the monastic church was founded by Rodrigo Afonso de Melo, Count of Oliventa, in 1485, for the Canons Secular of St John the Evangelist, who were nicknamed 'Lóios'. Entered through a Flamboyant Gothic portal, the single nave serves as the pantheon of the de Melo family, whose Gothic and Renaissance tombs include that of Dom Francisco, in the transept, attributed to Chanterène. He tutored the sons of Dom João III.

One's attention is captured, however by the very beautiful *azulejos* which subtly complement the internal architecture, with trompe-l'œil tiles mirroring high windows. The main panels show scenes from the life of St Lorenzo Guistiniani, patriarch of Venice. Created in 1711, they are the master work of António de Oliveira Bernardes, who presided over the greatest period of Portuguese tile production, and they pre-date his work in Barcelos and Viana do Castelo.

Around the Roman Temple

Downhill in the same road, the two tall towers and courtyard of the **Palácio dos Ducques de Cadaval** incorporate the small **Salas de Exposição do Palácio**. A finely painted *Virgem do Leite* (milk), from the workshop of Frei Carlos, is stared at by portraits of grim-looking ecclesiastics, whose faces are all the same. There are also two Flemish bronzes and an equestrian portrait of the third duke by Quillard, a pupil of Watteau, c. 1730.

Salas de Exposição do Palácio
open Tues–Sun 10–12.30 and 2–5; adm

In the street behind the Lóios and the palace, the **university** is rather disappointing. Arranged around a two-storeyed classical cloister, it was founded in 1559 by Cardinal Henrique, the future regent, to satisfy the Jesuits' wish for a university they could control, as Coimbra had successfully resisted their influence. But the new foundation never achieved its rival's size or breadth of studies. The corridors are lined with Baroque *azulejos* and all the doors are numbered, which saves visitors from getting lost.

University
Largo dos Colegiais, t (266) 740 800; open Mon–Fri 8am–9pm, Sat 8–1

Museu de Évora

Opposite the Roman Temple, the Archbishop's Palace, reconstructed in the late 17th century, now houses Évora's **Municipal Museum**, with important collections including sculpture and 15th- to 16th-century Flemish and Portuguese paintings.

Municipal Museum
t (266) 702 604; open Tues–Sun 9.30–12.30 and 2–5.30; adm

Two tombs are outstanding: one can almost feel the softness of the pillows supporting Fernando Cogominho's effigy, or the warmth of the dog at his feet – a faithful friend since 1364. The simple, classical cenotaph of Bishop Dom Afonso de Portugal is one of Nicolas Chanterène's most elegant works, included among several pieces by him in the museum. The Frenchman was married in Évora, and here he established a school of sculpture, through which he was able to introduce the sculptural aspects of the Italian Renaissance to Portugal.

Upstairs, note the delicate triptych of the Passion enamelled on copper in Limoges in 1539. Primitive paintings by 16th-century Flemish and Portuguese artists working in Portugal are juxtaposed. Both groups relish colour, but on the whole the Flemish Frei Carlos and Francisco Henriques have a greater depth of feeling and grasp of perspective than Gregório Lopes, Garcia Fernandes or the Master of Sardoal.

The museum's star attractions are the 13 panels of *The Life of the Virgin*, which formed the altarpiece of the cathedral until Ludwig redesigned its apse. The panels were painted by anonymous members of the Bruges School, working under one master, c. 1500. They were created in Portugal – there is a typically Portuguese plate in the *Nascimento da Virgem* (the Birth of the Virgin) – with the probable exception of the one larger panel, though Italian Renaissance buildings are used in the background. Saints Ana and Joaquim, the parents of the Virgin, are pictured with a cartoon-like castle, and she is pregnant at her marriage (*casamento*).

The Cathedral (Sé)

Cathedral
t (266) 759 330; open daily 9–12 and 2–5; Sacred Art Museum and cloister open Tues–Sun 9–12 and 2–5; adm

Behind the museum, the **cathedral** seems half-fortress, half-church. Its irregular façade is closest akin to that of the Sé Velha in Coimbra, a good example of the transition from the Romanesque to Gothic styles. According to the chronicler André de Resende, it was begun by the second bishop in 1186, on the site of a mosque, 20 years after the Moors were initially expelled from Évora. Perhaps it served as a mosque again when the Moors retook the town 1192–1211. Construction probably continued through the 13th century.

The bearded gentlemen flanking the portal are the Apostles, standing on ledges of human figures and fantastical animals. These fine medieval Portuguese sculptures were probably commissioned between 1322 and 1340. They all look similar, except St Peter and St Paul, who are the progeny of Telo Garcia of Lisbon.

The interior is very brown; the obtrusive white mortar binding the stonework gives it an oddly Victorian feel. The chandeliers hang on giant rosaries. Because they were considered insufficiently dignified for an archiepiscopal see, Ludwig, the Italian-trained architect of the Convent of Mafra, rebuilt the chancel and high altar in 1718, including a lovely sculpture of the crucified Christ. Ludwig is buried here.

The Cloister and Sacred Art Museum

Tickets down to the cloister and up to the Sacred Art Museum are sold just inside the entrance portal. The stunning Gothic cloister of c. 1323 is pierced by open circles with almost Moorish designs.

Sculptures of the Evangelists stand at the corners of the quadrangle, but the most moving sculpture panels the tomb of the 14th-century Bishop Pedro, whose long head is supported by angels.

A terrace above the cathedral's west entrance leads to the museum. Filled with a manageable number of reliquaries and embroidered vestments, it features a late 13th-century French Madonna whose seated ivory body parts to reveal scenes from her life. Introspection indeed. Near her is a 16th-century weathervane, looking more like a witch than an angel.

Central Évora

Walking down the steps by the cathedral, and continuing in the same direction, the **Largo da Porta da Moura** (Moor's Gate) is a pleasant place to come upon. It is arranged around a Renaissance orb-fountain whose walls are rippled, presumably by centuries of buttocks. Behind them the Cordovil House sports a hybrid Manueline-*mudéjar* porch. The beautiful modern building at the upper end of the square comprises the Courts of Justice.

The Rua 5 de Outubro, opposite the cathedral, leads down to the **Praça do Giraldo** and its 15th-century fountain, shaped like a *cataplana*. This is a focus for low-commotion timepassing.

The Rua da República runs downhill from the Praça, from which a road to the left opens on to the strange late Renaissance façade of **Igreja da N.S. da Graça**, which was worked in part by Diogo de Arruda, and is topped by four disgruntled giants in the process of standing up. The nave has fallen down not once, not twice, but three times.

The Church of São Francisco

Church of São Francisco

Capela dos Ossos open daily 9–1 and 2.30–6; adm

The Rua da República continues downhill past the back of the Gothic **church of São Francisco**, reconstructed 1460–1501 (Praça 1 de Maio). Gargoyles spew moss down its plastered sides. The church is entered through a gigantic, dizzying porch. As in the cathedral, the mortar is eye-catching. The single nave is daringly high and wide, while the chancel is a jumble of styles including a beautiful 18th-century neoclassical altar. The church hosts Évora's freakiest monument, the **Capela dos Ossos** (Chapel of Bones), on ground level. Half-close your eyes and the walls seem built of flint: the macabre truth is more disturbing. For the walls are composed of over 5,000 monks' bones. Femurs, tibias, skulls, all are arranged rather neatly, but the effect is horrid. And the decaying skeleton strung on one wall is repellent. A notice at the entrance proclaims *'Nós ossos, que aqui estamos, Pelos vossos esperamos'* – 'We bones here are waiting for your bones'. Less threateningly, the chapel's three founding fathers are commemorated with an epitaph of 1629. Note the plaits of hair near the entrance desk, offered as *ex votos*.

Southern Évora

The **Museu de Artesanato** (Handicrafts Museum), opposite the church of São Francisco, includes items for sale. A quick look will suffice for the painted pots and furniture, miniature farm implements, wood- and cork-work, and goat- and cow-bells.

Further downhill along the Rua da República, a public garden contains a rather uninteresting copy of the **Ladies' Gallery** of the Palace of Don Manuel. On this site Vasco da Gama was given the commission which led to his discovery of the sea route to India. Next to it are some fake Gothic ruins, assembled in 1863 from the remains of the former bishop's palace.

From the 17th-century town walls the odd **São Bras Hermitage** of 1482 is visible, buttressed by plastered cylinders, and crenellated. There's nothing particularly significant inside the building.

Northern Évora

On the opposite side of town, not far from the aqueduct, the interesting **Convento do Calvário** was founded in 1570 for an offshoot of the Franciscan Order. Knock on the door facing the centre of town, just off the Rua de Cândido dos Reis. The two-storey cloister has a lived-in feel to it, partly because of the caged budgies.

The church has some good but ill-lit paintings of the life of Mary, attributed to Simpo Rodrigues, and some good but flaking frescoes. The gilt woodwork is quite magnificent, producing a markedly tabernacular effect.

The Environs of Évora

The **Cartuxa** (Charterhouse) is just outside the Porto da Lagoa. The soaring 17th-century façade is wonderful, but the rest of the church is closed to visitors. Although it was founded in 1274, the **monastery of São Bento de Castris**, 3km further on, is unremarkable, except for a single 18th-century *azulejo* panel in the church, forming part of the life of St Bernard. It pictures a pregnant lady with a dog in her womb.

ⓘ **Évora** ›
Praça do Giraldo 73,
t *(266) 702 671,*
cmevoradida@mail.
evora.net; open
May–Sept Mon–Fri 9–7,
Sat–Sun 9.30–12.30 and
2–5.30, Oct–April daily
9.30–12.30 and 2–5.30

Tourist Information/ Services in Évora

The **tourist office** is a short walk uphill from the **bus station**, off Avenida de São Sebastião, **t** (266) 769 410. The **railway station**, **t** (266) 702 125, is less than 1km southeast of town: walk straight ahead and up the Rua da República to get to the Praça do Giraldo. The main **post office** is in the Rua de Oliventa (*open Mon–Fri 9–6.30, Sat 9–12*), uphill from the Praça do Sertório.

Lavandaria Olimpica, Largo dos Mercadores 6, **t** (266) 705 293 (*open Mon–Fri 9–1 and 3.30–7, Sat 9–1*), will wash your clothes.

Sports and Activities in Évora

Wine Tours

Rota dos Vinhos do Alentejo, Praça Joaquim António de Aguiar 20–21, Apartado 2146, t (266) 746 498, *www.vinhosdoalentejo.pt*. Details of wine routes (*rota dos vinhos*), and *adegas* open to visitors for wine-tasting.

Outdoor Activities

Desafio Sul, Rua Francisco de Holanda 48, t (266) 758 431/2. Walking tours, canoeing, archery, mountain-biking and climbing.

Sightseeing Tours

Turaventur, Rua João de Deus 21, t (266) 743 134, *www.turaventur.com*. Hearty tours on foot, mountain bike or by jeep; visits to *adegas*, local megalithic and architectural sites.

Mendes & Murteira, in the Barafunda shop, Rua 31 de Janeiro 15A, t (266) 739 240, *www.evora-mm.pt*. Cultural tours, tailored to your requirements.

Puppet Shows

It's worth asking at the tourist office if there is a performance of the Bonecos de Santo Aleixo. These stringed puppets about 1ft (30cm) tall are manipulated from above, following models created in the mid-19th century by a villager called Nepamoceno. The satirical performances are accompanied by much stamping, singing and shrilling – hilarious whether or not you understand the language.

Where to Stay in Évora

Very Expensive (€€€€)

★★★★M'ar de Ar, Travessa da Palmeira 4–6, t (266) 739 300, *www.mardear hotels.com*. Recently taken over (formerly the Hotel da Cartuxa), this hotel oozes luxury with grandiose columns in the public areas and sophisticated décor in the rooms. The facilities include a palm-fringed outdoor pool. Unusually for Évora, it's large and not old. The restaurant (€€) is good, but it would be a pity not to venture into town.

Expensive (€€€)

★★★★Albergaria do Calvário, Travessa dos Lagares 3, t (266) 745 930, *www.albergariadocalvario.com*. Occupies a building formerly used for the production of olive oil, arranged around a central courtyard, with only five of the 25 rooms looking outwards. It all looks attractive, but rooms are a little stark, and pricey for what you get. Possibly the only hotel in the country to provide guests with kettles. Some rooms have showers rather than baths. The associated restaurant is five minutes away.

Moderate (€€)

★★★★Residencial Riviera, Rua 5 de Outubro 49, t (266) 737 210. In the street between the cathedral and the Praça do Giraldo. Recently delightfully revamped.

★★★Estalagem Monte das Flores, 4km southwest of Évora, on the road to Alcáçovas, t (266) 749 680, *montflor @clix.pt*. A farm's stables and servants' quarters have been converted into an inn that attracts young and beautiful Portuguese, keen on horse-riding. That is the main appeal. When not in the saddle, you may sit on musty-looking armchairs in the dauntingly large sitting room or on ponyskin wallseats in the bar. Bedrooms are furnished with flowery Alentejan furniture. Pork and steak dishes are popular in the dining room.

★★★Évora Hotel, Quinta do Cruzeiro, Apartado 93, t (266) 748 800/5, *www.evora-hotel.com*. Resort hotel 1.5km out of town. Inside it's surprisingly pleasant, with indoor and outdoor pools, helpful staff and youthful guests, though it could be accused of having aspirations higher than its station. The food is quite good but not well served.

★★Albergaria Vitória, Rua Diana de Lis 5, t (266) 707 174, *www.albergaria vitoria.pt*. Situated southeast of the town walls is a comfortable modern

⭐ Pousada
dos Lóios >>

set-up, where the uniformed staff work efficiently and seem to enjoy doing so. Rooms have balconies.

★★Hotel Santa Clara, Travessa da Milheira 19, **t** (266) 704 141/2, *www.hotelsantaclara.pt*. Centrally located, near the Convento Santa Clara, the simple rooms all have bathrooms and mod cons. A terrace allows views over the roofs of the city. Basic but fine.

Inexpensive (€)

★★★Residencial Diana, Rua Diogo Cão 2, **t** (266) 702 008 or 743 113, *residencialdiana@mail.telepac.pt*. Located off the road running between the cathedral and the Praça do Giraldo is this comfortable and well-established *residencial* in a solidly built house, with high ceilings, and strong furniture. There's a friendly, chatty atmosphere, especially at breakfast.

★★★Residencial Giraldo, Rua dos Mercadores 27, **t** (266) 705 833. In one of the parallel streets running downhill from the Praça do Giraldo, with high ceilings, plenty of wooden furniture and properly hot water, but it is dingy in parts.

★★Pensão Policarpo, Rua da Freiria de Baixo 16, **t** (266) 702 424, *www.pensaopolicarpo.com*. In the 16th century, the Count of Lousã built himself a town house, which is now this *pensão* – down the steps by the cathedral, turn left and go past the Misericórdia church. Three generations of the Policarpo family have run it. The place is atmospheric, with granite columns and open-air corridors, but a bit of a maze. It has now become somewhat dog-eared, though the bright and flowery Alentejan painted furniture – and the charm – are still there. The breakfast room is barnlike and lovely. Parking is available, and some of the staff speak English.

Casa dos Teles, Rua Romão Ramalho 27, **t** (266) 702 453. A pleasant, homey place. There are just four rooms, sharing two bathrooms, so perfect for a large family or friends.

Pousada

Pousada dos Lóios, Largo Conde de Vila Flor, **t** (266) 730 070 (L2 H). Next to the Roman temple is a wonderful and memorable place to stay, occupying the old Lóios monastery, which first offered hospitality to travellers in 1491. Guests pass through the two-storeyed cloister (note the double-horseshoe Manueline doorway) to snug bedrooms scattered with Arraiolos rugs. Beware morning church bells, but take advantage of the attractive swimming pool. Dine in the vaulted cloister or in the grand hall under iron chandeliers. The food does justice to the setting, and non-residents are made welcome. You might sample the *migas a Alentejana* (fried pork with bread).

Turismo de Habitação

There are many houses under this scheme in and around Évora; the tourist office can provide full details, but the pick of the bunch are highlighted below.

Monte da Serralheira, **t** (266) 741 286 (€€). Dutch-owned farmhouse about 3km from Évora. There are horses to get dusty on and a lake to cool off in. Three apartments sleep four, and two sleep two. Each has its own entrance and terrace; prices are per day or week.

Casa de S. Tiago, Largo Alexandre Herculano 2, **t** (266) 702 686, *www.casa-stiago.com* (€€). 16th-century town house dating from the reign of King Manuel I. The rooms display a happy mixture of the simple and the grand, while always feeling comfortable.

Quinta da Espada, Estrada de Arraiolos, 3km along the Arraiolos road, **t** (266) 734 549 (€€). The name means 'The Sword Estate' – legend has it that Gerald the Fearless, who liberated Évora from the Moors, hid his sword here. Perhaps it is still lurking somewhere in the beautiful grounds, which are distinguished by an aqueduct. Still, the house looks like a typical Alentejan farmhouse, albeit very prettily furnished.

Casa de San Pedro, Quinta de San Pedro, **t** (266) 707 731 (€€). Stands in a cool park with family portraits of 19th-century ladies and heirloom-style furnishings. This is not always too relaxing, but the reception is friendly enough.

Quinta da Nora, Estrada dos Canaviais, 3km from Évora, **t** (266) 709 810 (€€). Charming farmhouse with beautiful grounds, a swimming pool and a working vineyard. The six rooms harbour lovely, heavy furniture and beamed, sloping ceilings. The lounge has its own panel of dazzling *azujelos* and Arraiolos rugs. Ridiculously good value.

Quinta do Xarrama, 2nd Bairro do Frei Aleixo, **t** (266) 700 405, *qxarrama@clix.pt* (€€). From the centre of town, take the Estremoz/Espanha road and turn right after the Intermarche. This farmhouse has five individual rooms with genteel décor. All have bath-rooms, and there's a terrace and a pool. Activities such as wine- and cheese-tasting, biking, walking and jeep-drives are offered; meals are available.

Casa Santos Murteira, Rua de S. Pedro 68–70, Alcáçovas, **t** (266) 948 220, *www.casasantosmurteira.com* (€€). An elegant village house with handsome, tasteful interiors, including antique furnishings in the bedrooms. Relax under a creeper-strewn trellis, float in the pool or just hang around in a hammock under the trees. *Meals on request.*

Eating Out in Évora

⭐ Cozinha de S. Humberto >

Expensive (€€€)
Cozinha de S. Humberto, Rua da Moeda 39, **t** (266) 704 251. St Humberto is the patron saint of hunting, and in one of the parallel streets which run downhill from the Praça do Giraldo is an atmospheric place to celebrate him. The 300–400-year-old building is decorated with glass, plates and kettles. The *calducho* is good, but the desserts aren't riveting. *Closed Thurs.*

⭐ O Fialho >

O Fialho, Travessa das Mascarenhas 16, **t** (266) 703 079. Near the theatre, it has received a lot of hype, and has a good reputation for regional cooking. It's decorated as a tavern, with lots of

⭐ Jardim do Paço >>

local pottery and bizarre deer-foot coatpegs. Chairs are leather with bosses, and a huge display of fruit rests under the wood-beamed ceiling. Pork, lamb and game in season are specialities of the large menu; there is also a very good wine list. *Reservations recommended.*

O Grémio, Rua Alcárcova de Cima 10, **t** (266) 742 931. Built into the city wall, this place is venerable, and popular with locals and tourists alike. *Closed Wed.*

Moderate (€€)
Guíao, Rua da República 81, **t** (266) 703 071. Located just off the town's bustling main square, this popular restaurant has an attractive tiled interior and is noted for its excellent fish dishes, including grilled squid.

Luar de Janeiro, Travessa do Janeiro 13, **t** (266) 749 114. Smart in a way that's particular to Portugal. Smoked hams hang from the ceiling. This restaurant takes its wine seriously, and the food is very good too. *Closed Thurs.*

O Aqueduto, Rua do Cano 13A, **t** (266) 706 373, near the aqueduct, glows with a warm yellow light, and has a nice feel to it. It is well run, with plenty of black-tied waiters serving good-quality regional dishes. Shrimps are displayed on a table, bay leaves are stored in tall pots over the earth-coloured floor, and down a couple of steps six huge vessels dwarf the tables they surround. The choice includes *migas com carne de porco* (pork with breadcrumbs). *Closed Mon.*

Mr Pickwick, Rua Alcárcova de Cima 3, **t** (266) 706 999. Blatantly geared to tourists but a good choice for fussy families. Menu includes international choices such as crêpes, chicken vol-au-vents, lamb chops and omelettes, as well as traditional dishes such as *cataplana Alentejana* and pork with clams.

Repas, Praça 1 de Maio 19, **t** (266) 708 540. Superb location right on the square with reasonable, if not excellent, food. Come here for the atmosphere and views.

Jardim do Paço, **t** (266) 744 300. Next to the Lóios church. Anyone should consider a meal which offers a nicely presented all-you-can-eat buffet lunch or supper including drinks and puddings for €17.50, which you can eat at tables in the large and delightful courtyard, a wonderful setting, to the accompaniment of canned opera.

Inexpensive (€)

⭐ O Sobreiro >

O Sobreiro, Rua do Torres 8, t (266) 709 325, near the Calvário Convent off the Rua Cândido dos Reis, comes as a great relief – there is not a bow-tie in sight. The interior setting is plain and rustic, with wooden farm equipment on the walls, and bread-bowls made of cork complete with bark. It fills quickly and empties early, but the service is constantly efficient. Most of the locals choose *cozido a Portuguesa*: assorted boiled meats do not make a pretty dish, but it's tasty. *Closed Mon.*

⭐ Cozinha da Graciete >

Cozinha da Graciete, Travessa Afonso Trigo, t (266) 742 020. Among Évora's restaurants the simplicity here is a breath of fresh air: it serves very good food with no pretensions. Despite the distance from the sea, the *arroz de mariscos* is worth trying. *Closed Sun evening and Mon.*

Taberna Típica Quarta-Feira, Rua do Inverno 16, t (266) 707 530. Popular with locals, most of them elderly and male. The manager's big personality fills the small space. *Closed Sun.*

O Tunel, Rua Alcárcova Baixa 59, t (266) 706 649. A simple place serving generous inexpensive portions of local, well prepared dishes.

Café

Café Arcada/Cervejaria Lusitana, Praça do Giraldo 10. Big and bow-tied, but it still does what most cafés do, with tables placed outside at which you can sit and watch the old men as they gather around the fountain in the evening.

Bars and Nightclubs in Évora

Bar 'A Oficina', Rua da Moeda 27, t (266) 707 312. Friendly place attracting all ages; jazz and blues music. *Open Mon–Sat 9pm–2am.*

Disco Kalmaria, Rua de Valdevinos, t (266) 707 505. Central nightclub.

Around Évora

Arraiolos

Set among low hills, beneath the circular walls of a castle, the village of Arraiolos is famous for its **carpetmaking** – consisting of a simple woollen cross-stitch in magically beautiful patterns.

The hilltop castle was built by Dom Dinis in 1310, and the great soldier Nun' Álvares Pereira lived here at various times during 1415–23. Only the circular walls now remain intact; they give the feeling of a giant animal pen. The whitewashed conical buttresses of the 16th-century **Convento dos Lóios**, now a *pousada*, stand 500 yards to the north of town, surrounded by birdsong. The monastery was given to the Brothers of St John the Evangelist in 1526, and contains tiles dated 1700.

Anta do Zambujeiro

One of the largest **dolmens** in Europe looms 12km from Évora. It's difficult to find, and is more important for its history than its

Getting to areas Around Évora

atmosphere. Drive 10km southwest of the city, to Valverde, turn right at the Convento de Bom Jesus and then right at the T-junction. The road becomes a track. Fork left. The track splits into four: take the second from the left. Drive through a stream and fork right. After 100 yards you will see a corrugated-iron shelter.

In this place 5,000 years ago, the dead were buried together in the foetal position. The roofless chamber of their tomb is approached by a 46ft (14m) long corridor of granite blocks propped at unlikely angles, and is walled with obelisks of at least twice human height. Late Neolithic clansmen transported the stone from 1km away, and covered the whole with earth. Personal possessions such as jewellery and chipped stone instruments were buried nearby. Shepherds build fires in the tomb to keep themselves warm at night.

Viana do Alentejo

Some 29km south of Évora, an astonishing fortified **Gothic church** blends with Viana do Alentejo's crenellated **Castelo** walls. This produces an extraordinary tiered effect, from the church, to its flying buttresses, to the walls that defended it. These are cornered with massive cylindrical towers, which are miniatured in the church's own pepper-pot pinnacles. Inside the church are octagonal pillars with a fine rhythm, ringed with seaweed and rope. The church is attributed to Diogo de Arruda, and dates from the late 15th century or early 16th century.

Arraiolos Carpets

The tradition started at the local monastery in the 17th century, when canvas or linen was embroidered with local wool. By the third quarter of that century, the carpets were being exported to other parts of the country. In 1787 William Beckford noted that at Arraiolos 'I laid a stock of carpets for my journey, of strange grotesque patterns and glaring colours, the produce of a manufactory in this town which employs about 300 persons ... my carpets are of essential service in protecting my feet from the damp brick floors. I have spread them round my bed and they make a flaming exotic appearance.' The patterns were inspired by various sources – Portugal's Moorish heritage, the carpets of Herat and Isfahan brought back by the discoverers, legendary tales of Persian exoticism, and, from the beginning of the 19th century, Aubusson carpets, all of which were sprinkled with a little popular imagination. The carpets have various assets: durability, colours that are slow to blanch, and the possibility of repair in the case of, say, a cigarette burn.

A number of workshops in Arraiolos produce carpets, all of which have their own showrooms. It's cheaper to buy them here than anywhere else; half of the price goes to the hunched sewers. Cushion covers are a cheaper alternative.

Where to Stay and Eat Around Évora

ⓘ **Arraiolos >**
Praça Lima Brito,
t (266) 490 240,
www.cm-arraiolos.pt

ⓘ **Viana do Alentejo >>**
Praça da República,
t (266) 953 106

Arraiolos

Accommodation is best outside Arraiolos, and the same goes for dining; in the town itself there's little choice.

Monte da Estalagem, Venda do Duque, t (266) 467 273, *www.monteda estalagem.com* (€€). About 4km off the road towards Évora Monte from Vimieiro, 30km from Évora. A comfortable farmhouse with bright, colourful décor.

Pousada
Pousada Nossa Senhora da Assunção, Apartado 61, t (266) 419 340,

www.pousadas.pt (L3 HD). Housed in the restored monastery, blending the traditional with the modern. Pool and tennis court.

Viana do Alentejo

Casa de Viana do Alentejo (Turismo Rural), Rua Cãndido dos Reis, t (266) 953 500, *jorge@casadeviana.com* (€€). Situated near the *castelo*, a typically Alentejan house with unfussy décor that complements original features. It has five double rooms with bathrooms, an open fire in the lounge, and a roof terrace with views of the church. Meals and bike hire are available.

Monsaraz and its Megaliths

Monsaraz

✪ Monsaraz

The walled hilltop village of **Monsaraz** has held off centuries of development – its medieval streets retain a peculiar magic, despite the tour buses. The four parallel cobbled streets of Monsaraz offer massive views of the plains of the Alentejo, peppercorned with olive and cork trees. The low, bulging houses are whitewashed or built of chaotic grey slate, with mellow terracotta roofs and terracotta jugs used as gargoyles, and whimsical iron dachshund doorknockers. Bitches with distended teats sprawl in the shade, and women wearing black trilby hats sit outdoors and crochet.

Monsaraz was taken from the Moors in 1167 and in the same year was given to the Templars. The joy of the place comes in absorbing the village and its life – there are a couple of churches, but with the exception of a damaged 14th-century marble tomb in the **Igreja Matriz** they contain little of interest. Next door, the **Museu de Arte Sacra** displays a small collection of vestments, books and 14th-century figurines. Note the former law court's 15th-century fresco depicting 'The Good and Bad Judge'; the latter has a devil on his shoulder and is accepting a bribe. At the other end of town, the **castle** forms part of a chain of fortresses built by Dom Dinis in the 14th century. Part of it has been converted into a bullring. Vertical lines scratched into the inner side of the village's entrance gate were used for measuring material on market days.

Igreja Matriz
open daily 9–1 and 2–6

Museu de Arte Sacra
Largo Dom Nuno Álvares Pereira, t (266) 503 315; open daily 9–6

Megaliths

The Alentejo was a centre of megalithic culture between 4000 and 2000 BC, and the area between Reguengos de Monsaraz, 36km

Getting to Monsaraz and its Megaliths

Infrequent **trains** from Lisbon terminate at Évora, where there is one connecting bus daily to Reguengos de Monsaraz, 1hr away. The bus returns after only two hours, making a day trip a real rush, but just about feasible. Express **buses** run once or twice a day from Lisbon to Reguengos de Monsaraz (3hrs) and Évora (½hr). From Évora, local buses run the same route once daily. There are two daily buses from Reguengos de Monsaraz to Monsaraz itself, making a day trip from Évora just possible, but allowing very little time once you've arrived.

southeast of Évora, and Monsaraz, 16km further east, preserves some good examples of menhirs (tombs with large flat stones laid on upright ones) and a cromlech (a circle of upright stones), which can all be visited on a circular tour around the two towns. (The name '*reguengos*' denotes what was once a royal estate, yielding to the crown a fifth to a quarter of the produce of the soil.) The tourist office in Évora produces a glossy booklet detailing the megaliths and their locations.

Some 8km east of Reguengos de Monsaraz, just past S. Pedro do Corval, and about 50m to the left of the road, stands **Lovers' Rock**. It's a natural-standing knobbed fertility stone, just shorter than the trees around it. On Easter Monday, hopeful local single ladies roll up their left sleeves and pelt the rock with fist-sized stones. If a missile stays atop, a baby is due within a year. The base of the rock is littered with disappointments.

Off the road from Telheiro (where there is a whitewashed fountain dated 1422) to Outeiro, a menhir is visible across the fields, about 18ft (5.5m) high. Local farmers found the **Menhir da Bulhôa** lying flat and chopped off a third of it to make an olive-oil press. Decorated with faint zigzag patterns and stars, it is considered too oval and tapering to be a credible phallus, and was probably erected in memory of a chief, or as a geographical marker.

Five km from Monsaraz, on the road to Xeres de Baixo, the **Cromlech do Xerez** stands 300 yards to the right. Fifty stubby menhirs are arranged in a square, with a great big phallic one in the middle. The splendid central member of the group weighs 7 tonnes. Probably a place for ritual prayer and meeting, it's best seen when the sun is low, casting long shadows from the clusters of natural shrub-studded boulders in the surrounding ploughland. Fertility in an agro-pastoral economy was related not only to people, but also to the land and flocks.

14

The Alentejo | Alto Alentejo: Monsaraz and its Megaliths

ⓘ **Monsaraz** >
Praça Dom Nuno Álvares, t (266) 557 136; open Sept–June daily 10–1 and 2–6, July–Aug until 7

Shopping in Monsaraz

Fabrica Alentejana de Lanificios, Rua dos Mendes 79, t (266) 502 179. Just inside the village walls, a great source of tasteful gifts produced locally, particularly scarves and blankets, run by the excellent Mizette.

Where to Stay in Monsaraz

Monsaraz
Many villagers have converted their cottages into accommodation; ask for details at the tourist office.

Estalagem de Monsaraz >

Casa Dom Nuno >

Pensão Donna Antónia >

Santiago >

****Estalagem de Monsaraz**, Largo de S. Bartolomeu, t (266) 557 112, *www.estalagemdemonsaraz.com* (€€). A cosy place that benefits from a great location just outside the village walls – allowing space for a terraced garden, a little pool, and breakfast outdoors – and a charming and experienced manager; the combination makes for a happy stay. All bedrooms have views, but only two have huge views, and one of the suites has a fantastic little crow's-nest terrace. If you want to come for the weekend, book at least two weeks in advance.

Casa do Embaixador, Largo D. Nuno Álvares Pereira 2, t (266) 557 432 (€€). Two suites and one room available, all appealing and tasteful, though there's not much room to unpack.

Casa Dom Nuno, Rua do Castelo 6, t (266) 557 146 (€€). Near the church square is a surprisingly large old house, artistically and comfortably decorated, with stone floors, wooden ceilings and Renaissance doorways. Some of the six rooms offer fantastic views from their fat beds with handmade bedcovers, which makes them particularly appealing. Rooms are big and airy, with painted furniture. A collection of keys hangs on the wall of the galleried sitting room like musical notes. There are very nice modern bathrooms, and a small bar – it's good value.

Pensão Donna Antónia, Rua Direita 15, t (266) 557 142 (€€–€). Very nice place with an internal courtyard and air-conditioning. The suite has a huge terrace.

Casa Paroquial Santo Condestável, Rua Direita 4, t (266) 557 181 (€). A sober place with a stone ceiling, stone floors and a slightly baronial feel. One room has a view.

Reguengos de Monsaraz

****Hotel Província**, Apartado 54, Reguengos de Monsaraz, t (266) 508 070, *www.hotel-provincia.com* (€€). A smart hole-up; very relaxed and spacious, the Província aims to oblige and therefore offers everything the modern tourist might ask for: a swimming pool with accompanying cocktail bar, a reading room with bar, gym, wine cellar, Palm Tree Patio,

vegetable garden and children's area. The décor is inevitably slightly sanitized but not unattractive, with themed rooms, and the many spots for guests to lounge are pleasantly arranged with basket seating or comfy sofas. Its restaurant, **Santiago** (€€€), offers a fine choice of Alentejan cuisine, from *migas* to *gazpacho*.

Turismo de Habitação

Horta da Moura, Apartado 64, 7200 Reguengos de Monsaraz, t (266) 550 100 (€€). Impressive converted farmhouse set in extensive grounds and featuring rough white walls, beamed ceilings and terracotta floors. It provides a luxurious base for exploring the River Guadiana – by bicycle, on horseback or even by horse-drawn carriage. The many other facilities include tennis. The mellow dining room serves a variety of well-cooked regional specialities.

Monte Alerta, Telheiro (2.5km from Monsaraz), t (266) 550 150, *www.montealerta.pt* (€€). Very pretty blue-and-white painted *quinta*, comfortably furnished to feel quite homey, with beautiful gardens and a pool.

Casa de Terena, Rua Direita 45, Terena, south of Alhandroal, t (268) 459 132, *www.casedeterena.com* (€€). Restored 18th-century building, in the heart of an ancient, unspoilt village, and just metres from the medieval castle. All rooms have ensuite bathrooms, the characterful interior is filled with all manner of antiques, and visitors are given a very warm welcome.

Eating Out in Monsaraz

Casa do Forno, Travessa da Sanabrosa, t (266) 557 190 (€€). Near the main square; simple but good regional dishes, including *borrego assado* (roasted lamb). *Closed Tues.*

Santiago, Rua de Santiago 3, t (266) 557 188 (€). Any meal eaten on the outdoor terrace will be memorable – not for the food, which is good enough, but for the fantastic views. None of the village's other restaurants can compete.

Lumumba, Rua Direita 12, t (266) 557 121 (€). *Closed Mon.*

Baixo Alentejo

The Lower Alentejo lacks the dramatic hills of the upper part of the province, but offers an unspoilt coastline. A harsh, slow life unfolds in the remote settlements, with limited accommodation for travellers and few monuments of note. Beja is the principal town of the province, which is at its most beautiful along the banks of the River Guadiana.

Beja

Some 78km south of Évora and 175km north of Faro, Beja occupies the highest point of the plain which separates the catchment areas of the Rivers Sado and Guadiana. The principal town of the Lower Alentejo is prosperous, purposeful and pedestrian in its new parts, and pleasantly lackadaisical in its old parts. Here

Baixo Alentejo

Getting to Beja

Beja offers some transport connections with the south of Portugal. By **train** from Lisbon's Terreiro do Pato, take a **ferry** to Barreiro (½hr), connecting with the 1¾hr infrequent train service to Beja. Trains run infrequently from the Algarve; from Faro, change at Funcheiro (total 3¼hrs).

Rede Expressos **buses** from Lisbon take 3¼hrs. Serpa is a mere ½hr away, Mertola ¾hr and Moura 1¼hrs.

shoemenders work in holes-in-the-walls, old people in low houses wait and watch at their street-level windows, and the streets are paved with dragons' teeth and egg-shaped cobbles. Beja's main appeal today is as a useful stopover point in the corn lands.

History

Beja was named Pax Julia to commemorate the peace between Julius Caesar and the Lusitanians. It was a commercial centre made up of freemen and foreigners, who practised a variety of Eastern religions: inscriptions have been found dedicated to Cybele, Isis, Serapis and even Mithras. Of the brilliant Muslim court that followed, few traces remain – only the tiles that wall the Convento. In the mid-15th century, Afonso V made Beja a duchy. In June 1808 several of Junot's soldiers were killed in a riot in Beja. Junot ordered reprisals; 1,200 Bejans were killed, and the French commander reported: 'Beja no longer exists, its criminal inhabitants have been put to the sword and their houses pillaged and burned.' Beja still exists, but its charms are limited.

The Castelo and Around

Castelo
Largo do Libador,
t (284) 311 800;
open Tues–Sun
1 May–31 Oct 10–6,
1 Nov–30 April 9–4;
Torre de Menagem:
adm

The **castelo** yet another of Dom Dinis' fortifications, stands on the edge of medieval Beja. Its courtyard buildings now house a military museum. The building's 130ft (40m) high **Torre de Menagem** allows the luxury of three Gothic windows, and very big views.

To one side of the castle is the church of **São Tiago**, which has good pillars of 18th-century *azulejos*. To the other side, the **Igreja de Santo Amaro** houses the **Museu Visigótico** (Museum of Visigothic Archaeology), with artefacts mostly from the 7th–8th centuries well displayed among the whitewashed arches of the church.

Museu Visigótico
Largo de Santo
Amaro, t (284) 323 351;
open Tues–Sun; joint
adm with Museu
Regional

Downhill from the castle, on the Lisbon road, stands the **Hermitage of Santo André,** founded in the reign of Dom Sancho I to commemorate the capture of Beja from the Moors in 1162. The 13th-century Convento de São Francisco, adjacent to the public garden, is undergoing an extended harvest festival – as a supermarket.

Museu Regional
Largo da Conceiçõ,
t (284) 323 351; open
Tues–Sun 9.30–12.15
and 2–5.15; joint adm
with Museu Visigótico

The Convento de N.S. da Conceição

The **convento de N.S. da Conceição** houses the **Museu Regional**. In the 17th century this was the home of that deserted and reproachful correspondent, Mariana Alcoforado, authoress of the five *Love Letters of a Portuguese Nun*. Her chevalier quit Beja at the end of the Portuguese war with Spain (1661–8). The originals of her letters to him have never been found, but they were published in French in 1669, and subsequently translated into English: 'I do not know why I write to you. You will only take pity on me, and I don't want your pity. I despise myself when I think of all that I have sacrificed for you. I have lost my reputation...' By the grille where the lovers blew kisses, a flippant curator has displayed Roman ampullae created to hold tears, and a nippled jug for a baby.

The Conventual Building

The conventual building, which was founded in 1459, is a good example of the transition from Gothic to Manueline style; the structure and the ogival arches are Gothic, while the decoration betrays the later influence. The quite extraordinary, exuberant *Sala do Cap'tulo* (the chapter house) is decorated with kitsch painted panels as well as *azulejos*, and the ceiling is remarkable. Each pattern of carpet tiles has a single eccentric, because the Moors who made them believed that only Allah could be perfect.

The Museum

In the museum's collection, three 16th-century paintings are outstanding: *São Vicente*, from the school of the Master of Sardoal; a Flemish *Our Lady of the Milk*, breast feeding; and a Portuguese *Descent from the Cross*. Note too a blue and white Ming bowl decorated with horsemen, the name of its first owner and the date of acquisition. There are two curious tombs. One is a stone half-barrel, built for a vintner. The other is Roman, with a little wolf, stating that now the land will be lighter.

Around the Convent

Church of Santa Maria
open at 12 and 6pm

The **church of Santa Maria** is next to the museum, with a façade like icing sugar. It's built in the so-called Alentejan Gothic style, with many later additions including an enormous tree of Jesse. Its Moorish foundations are still visible around the gargoyled back of the church.

The Environs of Beja

Pisões
Herdade de Algramaça,
t (266) 769 800; open
Tues 1.30–5.30, Wed–Fri
9–12 and 1.30–5.30,
Sat–Sun 9–12 and
1.30–5; closed Mon,
1 Jan, Easter Sun, 1 May,
25 Dec; adm

Ten km southwest of Beja a rough track leads to the ruined Roman villa of **Pisões** which was inhabited from the 1st to the 4th centuries. There's nothing much to see above ground level: below lie geometric mosaics that blend browns and greens, and occasionally launch into flora and fauna. The villa has a very small peristyle, which gave onto a rectangular basin more than 150ft (45m) long.

(i) Beja >
*Rua do Capitão J.F. de
Sousa 25, just outside
the medieval town
walls, t (284) 311 913,
www.cm-beja.pt; open
June–Oct Mon–Sat 9–7;
Nov–May 10–1 and 2–6*

Tourist Information/ Services in Beja

Both the **tourist office** and the **town hall** (*câmara municipal*) offer free bike use; a deposit of some sort of identification is required.

The **bus terminus**, t (284) 313 620, is in the southeast of town (walk down the street flanking the odd modern Casa da Cultura), while the **railway station**, t 808 208 208, is to the northeast, 0.5km from the town centre.

Where to Stay in Beja

Moderate (€€)

★★★**Hotel Francis**, Praça Fernando Lopes Graça, t (284) 315 500, www.*hotel-francis*.com. Near the bus station, looks a bit grim but is perfectly adequate inside. Staff are helpful and friendly, and there's a gym (*closed Sun*).

★★★★**Residencial Cristina**, Rua de Mértola 71, t (284) 323 035. Around the corner from the beginning of the road to the Algarve. Quite reasonable, with air-conditioning and no distinguishing features.

★★★★**Pensão Residencial Santa Barbara**, Rua de Mértola 56, t (284) 312 280, www.*residencialsantabarbara.pt*. Provides clean, satisfactory rooms, with stand-up balconies and telephones. Central.

★★★**Residencial Coelho**, 15 Praça da República, t (284) 324 031. In a nice little square with six trees, near the Misericórdia, but really pretty basic. Rooms come with showers rather than baths.

★★★**Residencial Bejense**, Rua do Capitão J.F. de Sousa 57 (near the tourist office), t (284) 311 570 . Excellent place: friendly, well-run and good value. Three family photos in the corridor and other details give it a personal touch, and the small bar gives it a bit of a life of its own.

Inexpensive (€)

★★**Hospederia Rocha**, Largo Dom Nuno Álvares Pereira 12, opposite the *pousada* (uphill from the post office), t (284) 324 271, www.*hospederia-rocha*.com. If budgeting is your

(★) Residencial
Bejense >

priority, this is the cheapest place in town. Faded and characterful, it is furnished with a jumble of old furniture, and high ceilings. Some parking is available.

Pousada

Pousada de São Francisco, Largo Dom Nuno Álvares Pereira, t (284) 313 580, www.*pousadas.pt* (L2 H). Occupies a former monastery right in the centre of town. From the outside it looks like the town hall, but within there's no mistaking its provenance: there's a beautiful Gothic chapel and a glassed cloister. Bedrooms are nicely furnished, with vaulted ceilings and terracotta floor tiles, and there's a square pool and giant chess set in the garden. So far, so good. The problem is that some of the spaces are so vast as to seem like a railway station, and there's something indefinably oppressive about the place.

Eating Out in Beja

Os Infantes, Rua dos Infantes 14, t (284) 322 789 (€€). In the road opposite the entrance to the museum is a rather smart little place serving fine, traditional Alentejan food – such as *migas* with pork – under a low vaulted ceiling. The service is relatively snappy.

Dom Dinis, Rua Dom Dinis 11, t (284) 325 937 (€). Opposite the castle's keep, serving meaty regional specialities from a grill in the corner of the front dining room. It doesn't quite know whether it's trying to be upmarket, but the food is good.

O Alentejano, Largo dos Duques de Beja 6–7, t (284) 323 849 (€). In the square next to the museum, it's full of locals in old leather jackets, sitting under the fake wood ceiling and enjoying their meat, rice and potatoes. Portions are large and prices reasonable. *Open Sat–Thurs*.

Luís da Rocha, 63 Rua Capitão João Francisco de Sousa, t (284) 323 179 (€). Along the street from the tourist office, Luís da Rocha is good, with friendly service, and popular. Unusually for Beja, there are several fish dishes on the menu, but the speciality is *cabrito a pastora* (boiled kid). Also try the chops.

Getting to Moura

Moura is a 1¼hr **bus** ride from Beja.

Moura

Moura is a small town surrounded by oak and olive groves, some 5km from the Guadiana and 58km northeast of Beja. Moura's upper town is a place of mansions, and definitely worth a wander. Otherwise, it is distinguished only by being a bit more Moorish than most, featuring a Moorish quarter, and a coat of arms depicting a Moorish girl dead at the bottom of a tower. This is the unfortunate Salúquiyya, daughter of a Moorish lord, engaged to a neighbouring Moorish mayor. Legend says she opened the gates of the town to her beloved on her wedding day, as any decent girl would, and got more than she'd bargained for. Christians had ambushed her lover and his party, killed them and put on their clothes. Once in the town, the Christians stormed the castle. The remorseful bride flung herself from a tower, to join her beloved in eternal *amour*. Portuguese legends are full of *Mouras encantadas*, enchanted Moorish princesses, who sometimes have a snake's tail in place of their lower limbs. In fact, Moura was taken from the Moors in 1165 by Gerald the Fearless.

In the 13th century, Moura's dwelling space overflowed the castle walls to form the **Mouraria**, the Moorish quarter (look out for the signs saying 'Poç Árabe'), the archetype of other whitewashed Alentejan settlements.

The tourist office has the key to the spacious **Igreja Matriz**. It's a fine example of the transition from Gothic to Manueline, with a Manueline portal of twisted columns pimpled with balls, and armillary spheres flanking the national blazon. The inferior Sevillian tiles within are dated 1651.

14

The Alentejo | Baixo Alentejo: Moura

ⓘ Moura >
Largo de Santa Clara,
t (285) 251 375,
www.cm-moura.pt;
open Mon–Fri 9–1 and
2–5, Sat–Sun 10–1 and
2.30–5.30

Where to Stay in Moura

★★**Hotel de Moura**, Praça Gago Coutinho 1, **t** (285) 251 090, *www.hoteldemoura.com* (€€). The tile-fronted hotel was once grand, and is now pleasantly faded, with flat iron balconies, very high and elaborate ceilings and a rear courtyard.

★★★**Residencial Alentejana**, Largo José Maria dos Santos 40, **t** (285) 250 080, *www.residencialalentejana.com.pt* (€). Large rooms that manage to retain a certain charm. Friendly and clean.

Residencial Italiana, Rua da Vitória 8, **t** (285) 254 239 (€). Clean rooms in need of an airing.

Eating Out in Moura

O Trilho, Rua 5 de Outubro 5, **t** (285) 254 261 (€€–€). Popular with locals. *Open lunch and dinner Tues–Sun.*

O Túnel, Rua dos Ourives 13, **t** (285) 253 384 (€). Attractive little place with a tunnelled ceiling and several brick arches. The food is surprisingly good, though at lunchtime the waiters are overstretched. Specialities include grilled or barbecued meats. *Closed Sun.*

Getting to Serpa

The nearest **train** station is at Beja, from where there are connecting buses (½hr), which continue to Moura (½hr). There are a couple of Rede Expressos **buses** daily from Lisbon (4hrs) and Beja (½hr).

Serpa

The peaceful little town of Serpa is located where the plains give way to smooth, undulating hills, 28km southeast of Beja. There's something quintessentially Portuguese about the place – its 8,000 souls appear to live a life untainted by anything other than the Moors, 750 years ago. Kids stare at visitors, who seem to be invisible to the old people ruminating beside 2,000-year-old olive trees. Serpa boasts Portugal's Whitest Street, cobbled and quiet, and also some of the country's finest ewes'-milk cheese.

The western approach to Serpa is very striking – the plain, flat façade of the Solar of the Counts of Ficalho is built into the town walls, supplied by a slender aqueduct and chain pump, beside the conical late 13th-century **Portas de Beja** (Gates of Beja).

The Castle Hillock

Within the town walls, a wide staircase near the tourist office leads up to the castle hillock, which was first inhabited by the Celts in the 4th century BC. Gnarled olive trees camouflage equally gnarled time-passers on the cobbled terrace fronting the clock tower and the Gothic **Igreja Matriz**.

Castle
*open Tues–Sun
9–12.30 and 2–5.30*

Beside the church, a dislocated chunk of wall perches dramatically above the entrance to the **castle**. It has been there since 1707, when part of Dom Dinis' fortification was blown up by the Spanish Duke of Ossuna during the War of Spanish Succession.

**Museu de
Arqueologia**
*t (284) 540 100;
opening hours as castle;
currently closed for
renovation, telephone
for further information*

Elsewhere, the crenellated castle walls are intact, offering beautiful views of the wide-open country. The small **Museu de Arqueologia** displays prehistoric remains including the tools of daily life employed by *homo erectus*, and a seated life-size rendition of the Last Supper in plaster of Paris.

In and Around the Walled Town

The great pleasure of Serpa is wandering the irregular streets of the walled town, around the Rua da Figueira (fig tree) and the Rua da Parreira (trellis). Housed in the old municipal market, the **Museu Etnográfico**, off the Largo do Corro backs on to the eastern side of the town walls. It displays the tools of cobblers, carpenters and blacksmiths. There's a press for pork tripe, a huge Sheffield bellows and a swineherd's costume, complete with Mexican-style saddle bag and a pig-whip.

**Museu
Etnográfico**
*t (284) 540 120;
open Tues–Sun 9–12.30
and 2–5.30; closed New
Year hols, 1 May, 25
April, 25 Dec and
municipal hols*

Returning to the Largo do Corro, the Rua A.C. Calisto becomes the Rua do Calvário. Turn right into the Alameda do Correia da Serra for the compact **Botanic Gardens**, fronted by a Roman road lined with olive trees planted by the Romans themselves. The garden is a good place to watch life go by.

The **Pulo do Lobo waterfall** ('Wolf's Leap') can be reached by following the road from Mértola to Beja and turning right after about 3km. The waterfall tumbles in singular scenery – the river has cut a profound gorge through the valley which itself is made up of strange and rather creepy rock formations. A powerful and primeval place.

① Serpa ›
Largo Dom Jorge de Melo 2/3, **t** *(284) 544 727; open 9–6*

Tourist Information/ Services in Serpa

The **bus station** is located in the new part of the town. To get to the **tourist office**, walk along the Rua Soldado and turn right into the Rua dos Cavalos. The tourist office is at the bottom of the steps to the citadel.

Where to Stay in Serpa

Estalagem de São Gens, Alto de São Gens, **t** (284) 540 420, *www.estalagem sgens.com* (€€). It's on a mount of olives, 2km south of town, and the cool and pleasant modern building is well designed to exploit the views of endless, chequered yellow and brown plains. There's a swimming pool, and a fairly elegant dining room featuring a rustic menu. The roast leg of pork is very good, while an à la carte choice might be stewed hare in white rice or partridge with nuts. Pastries are homemade.

Casa da Muralha, Rua das Portas de Beja 43, **t** (284) 543 150, *www.casada muralha.com* (€€). A good option is this Turismo Rural property, nestled in the castle walls. Elegant rooms with bathrooms, and a charming bougainvillea-filled garden.

Pensão Residencial Beatriz, Largo de Salvador 10, **t** (284) 544 423, *www. residencialbeatriz.com* (€). Occupying a corner slot next to the supermarket, this *pensão* offers spacious, clean, air-conditioned rooms, complete with bathroom and TV. Comfortable, if rather plain.

Residencial Serpínia, Rua Serpa Pinto 34, **t** (284) 544 055, *www.residencial serpinia.com* (€). On the edge of town as you enter it from Moura is a decent place without much character, but acceptable if you need a bed.

Casa de Hóspedes Virgínia, Rua do Rossio 75, **t** (284) 549 145 (€). Clean, with a variety of rooms; some are OK, some are rather mean, with small windows.

Pensão O Casarão, Rua do Calvário 15, **t** (284) 549 295 (€). Alternatively, across the square and round the corner to its right, there are very cheap rooms available.

Turismo de Habitação

Monte da Diabróoria, Beringel (EN121), **t** (284) 998 177, *www.diabroria.com* (€€). A huddle of picturesque farm buildings close to a game reserve. Inside, the rooms are rustic and characterful, with animal skins splayed out on the floors, and roaring fires.

Eating Out in Serpa

Alentejano, Praça da República 8, **t** (284) 544 335 (€). In the main square, it has brick arches, a blue ceiling, and an almost Italianate feel to its first-floor restaurant. *Open 12–3 and 7–10.30. Closed Mon.*

Cervejaria Lebrinha, Rua do Calvário 6–8, **t** (284) 549 311 (€). Near the Botanic Garden, this place has superb draught beer, and offers a menu that includes *camarão grelhado* (grilled shrimp) and *bacalhau a casa* (house-style cod), plus stews and other meat dishes. *Open 11am–2am. Closed Tues.*

Restaurante O Zé, Praça da República 10, **t** (284) 549 246 (€). Provides tables in the main square. It's simple, but features good *gazpacho* and local cheese. *Open 11–3.30 and 5.30–midnight. Closed Sun.*

Molhó Bico, Rua Quente 1, **t** (284) 549 264 (€). Friendly local place serving well-cooked veal steak and other specialities. *Open 10.30am–2am. Closed Wed.*

Mértola

 Mértola

The delightfully slow little town of **Mértola** creeps up the steep bank of the curvaceous River Guadiana, at its confluence with the River Oeiras, 50km south of Serpa and 58km north of Castro Marim. The gritty soil around Mértola hampers agriculture, but the habitat is suitable to partridges, rabbits, hares, foxes, wolves and wild boars. The subsoil is rich in manganese, copper and lead, but they're expensive to extract, and the deposits at São Domingos are almost exhausted. Nowadays the town hall is the only significant employer; most visible wealth comes from contraband, usually televisions bought duty-free in Ceuta in Morocco, and taken to Spain.

Modern Mértola is ugly and nondescript, but tiers of tiny low houses crowd between the river and the castle ruins. The Guadiana is narrow enough for fishermen to shout across on a Sunday afternoon, as they mend their nets. Well off the tourist trail, Mértola is a great base from which to explore the beautiful banks of the Guadiana. Downstream, the river is serene and happy, smooth enough to mirror its own green banks. Turtles peep out at visitors, storks rap undeterred, and snakes serpent themselves away in terror.

History

The Phoenicians sailed up the Guadiana and founded a settlement here, which became an important commercial centre for themselves and the Carthaginians. The Romans made Mirtilis grand, because it occupied a key defensive point on their road from Beja to Castro Marim; it minted coin between 189 and 170 BC. The Moors called it Mirtolah, and built walls around it in the 12th century. These failed to prevent Dom Sancho II conquering the town in 1238. He handed it to the Order of Sant'Iago, to settle and defend.

Around the Town

At the uppermost point of town, the decaying **castle** (*always accessible*) dates from 1292. The walls offer the best view of the town; try to spot the endangered lesser kestrel, which is being encouraged to breed in this region. Just downhill, an 11th-century

Igreja Matriz
open Tues–Sun, hours vary

mosque was converted into the **Igreja Matriz** without substantially altering the structure. The pineapple-top merlons are typically *mudéjar*, but the cylindrical towers that buttress the church are native. A belltower now performs the *muezzin*'s function, and, within the church, an altar stands in front of the *mihrab*, the niche which indicates the direction of Mecca. The square church has five naves, with 13th-century Gothic vaulting.

Further downhill, the câmara municipal has recently discovered its Roman foundations. These have been adapted into a well-

Getting to Mértola

Express **buses** run once a day from Lisbon (4¼hrs), via Beja (¾hr), or, in the other direction, from Vila Real de Santo António (1½hrs). There are a couple more buses just to Beja. If you are travelling on a Sunday, the ticket office is only open until 10am so be sure to get up early enough – the inspectors are highly unsympathetic and won't let tourists on the bus without a pre-paid ticket.

designed **Núcleo Romano** (Largo Luís de Camões), with various Roman artefacts and sculptures. Also note the **Núcleo Visigótico** and the **Núcleo Islâmico**, in the south of the old town, with a very good collection of 11th-13th-century ceramics, jewellery and coins. Nearby, the **Museu de Arte Sacra** (Largo de Misericórdia), includes three retables which show Dom Sancho II's battle with the Moors.

To the north of the old town is the **Museu Paleocristão** (Rossio do Carmo), with wonderfully carved funerary stones.

The district of Mértola hosts a flock of **black vultures**. The species is in danger of extinction, and the Mértola birds are now dependent upon the munificence of the municipality.

Convento de São Francisco
t (286) 612 119, www.conventomertola. com; open Fri, Sat and Sun 10–6; adm; guided tours in Portuguese, English and Dutch

A bridge crosses the Rio Oeiras just south of Mértola. Walking across this, you come to the **Convento de São Francisco** planted with kumquats and herbs and now inhabited by a Dutch family, who have remodelled it into an odd confection of art gallery-cum-nature reserve. Walk through the convent to get to the path by the river, where you may see nesting storks. Accommodation is also available.

Mina de São Domingos

Seventeen km east of Mértola lie the old copper mines, **Mina de São Domingos**. Known to the Romans, they were rediscovered in 1857 and worked by a British firm and some 7,000 dependants, who worked and lived under hard conditions, until about 1960. Then the mines closed and the population was decimated. Now it's something of a ghost town, an ideal setting for a Tarkovsky film. São Domingo was once illustrious enough to be the first town in Portugal to have telephones, trains and electricity. More importantly to the Portugese, it was the first town that allowed foreign players in its football team: two Englishmen played for the town in the 1920s.

Parque Natural do Vale Guadiana

Park Headquarters
Centro Polivalente de Divulgação da Casa do Lanternim, Rua D. Sancho II 15, Mértola, t (286) 610 090, www.icn.pt

The Rio Guadiana is surrounded by the 230 square miles (600 sq km) of the **Parque Natural do Vale Guadiana**. Mainly uninhabited and rich in flora and fauna, it is a habitat for many rare and endangered species such as the black stork (which can be most easily seen in Mértola), the horned viper, azure-winged magpie, red kite, Bonelli's eagle and the Iberian toad. The **Park Headquarters** has little information in English, but may be helpful for accommodation.

(i) **Mértola >**
*Largo Vasco de Gama
(in the old part of town,
on the road up to the
cathedral), **t** (286) 612
573; open Oct–May
daily 9–12.30 and
2–5.30, June–Sept daily
10–1 and 3–7*

(★) **Casa das
Janelas Verdes >**

(★) **O Migas >>**

Tourist Information/
Services in Mértola

All Mértola's **museums** have the same opening hours: *Oct–May Tues–Sun 9–12.30 and 2–5.30, June–Sept Tues–Sun 10–1 and 3–7*. The **bus station** is in the new town, near the main road to Beja.

Where to Stay
in Mértola

Casa das Janelas Verdes, Rua Dr Manuel Francisco Gomes 38, **t** (286) 612 145 (€). A rustic treat, with three rooms available under the Turismo Rural scheme. It's quaint and bourgeois, with crucifixes, budgies and sloping ceilings. Just avoid the room at the back, which is squashed and viewless. There's a superb covered terrace with hundreds of pot plants attached to the walls and views to the river – this is an excellent place to spend a few quiet days reading.

Residencial Beira Rio, Rua Dr Afonso Costa 108, **t** (286) 611 190, *www.beira rio.pt* (€). Just below the town, this is very nice indeed, with spruce, air-conditioned rooms, many with a view of the river and some with a balcony from which to listen to the goat bells. It's a shame the few buildings on the opposite river bank aren't more attractive. The garden is full of sweet-smelling orange trees.

Pensão San Remo, Avenida Aureliano Mira Fernandes, **t** (286) 612 132 (€). In the square opposite the bus depot, it is decent but a bit soulless. The reception desk is at the restaurant of the same name, opposite. The back rooms have neither view nor sunshine, though this keeps them cool. The constant and forceful supply of hot water will be a treat for budget travellers who are coming from other parts of the Baixo Alentejo.

Eating Out in Mértola

Cegonha Branca, Avenida Aureliano Mira Fernandes 2C, **t** (286) 611 066 (€€). In winter, try *lampreia* (lamprey), which is an eel-like fish, cooked with rice in its own blood (more appetizing than it sounds).

Restaurante Alengarve, Avenida Aureliano Mira Fernandes 20, **t** (286) 612 210 (€). A better one of several modest affairs, in the square opposite the bus station. Good-value dishes are pork and chick pea or rabbit stews.

O Migas, next to the municipal market building, **t** (286) 612 811 (€). This is really all you need: a small, fun, friendly place with great food. Try the *migas*.

Alcácer do Sal

The route south from Lisbon passes through the attractive town of Alcácer do Sal, which wells up from the Sado river and its flooded rice paddies and salt marshes. The Phoenicians established themselves here in the second half of the 7th century BC, discarding those amphorae and striped painted pots that excited subsequent archaeologists. It was the capital of the Moorish province of Al-kasr (*al-kasr* is the Arabic for 'castle') and, before 1500, it produced some

Getting to Alcácer do Sal

By **road**, the town of Alcácer do Sal is 94km south of Lisbon.

Where to Stay in Alcácer do Sal

(i) Alcácer do Sal >
Rua da República,
t (265) 610 070

Pousada
Pousada Dom Alfonso II, t (265) 613 070, *www.pousadas.pt* (L3 HD).

Situated in the town's Moorish castle, the *pousada* has been sympathetically modernized inside to provide some open, bright spaces. The crenellated castle walls run alongside the two outdoor pools.

of the purest salt (hence the 'do sal') in Europe, assisted by a tiny seaweed present in the Tagus and Sado estuaries, which retained the impurities. From the days of the Moors until the 19th century, this was the chief market town for the Alentejo's cereal crops.

Today the main reason for stopping here is to see the majestic **storks**, which build basket nests on church roofs, particularly up by the ruined Moorish castle. The **castle**, nowadays a *pousada* (*see* 'Where to Stay', above), incorporates the late 12th-century **church of Santa Maria**, whose well-proportioned interior features the Capela do Santissimo, in which babies and angels romp among plants and birds on yellow, blue and green 17th-century *azulejos*.

Below the castle, the classical-style **church of Santo António** (*open daily*) was founded in 1524 and topped by a dome of semi-transparent jasper. Inside is a marble Chapel of the 11,000 Virgins. Closer to the river, the former Igreja do Espírito Santo now serves as a small **Museu Arqueológico** with local finds.

Museu Arqueológico
Praça Pedro Nunes,
t (265) 610 070;
open daily

Santiago do Cacém

Some 97km south of Setúbal, the airy town of Santiago do Cacém sweeps across the amphitheatre formed by two hills, in the middle of the hummocky, fertile Serra de Grândola. The squat windmills of the neighbourhood now stand defunct, except for one with kite-like sails.

Legend tells how the town received its name: a blood-curdling leader fled the eastern Mediterranean and armed a squadron of troops. She led them inland from Sines and on St James' Day (*Dia de Santiago*) cut off the head of the town's Muslim ruler, who was called Kassen. Hence Santiago de Kassen. The historians are more sober: the knights of São Tiago (St James) captured the town from the Moors in 1186, only to be driven out by the Caliph Yakub five years later. Things were finally settled in 1217, when the fierce Bishop of Lisbon retook Santiago, with the help of the Templars and the knights of São Tiago.

The landscape of the Serra de Grândola is pretty and friendly rather than dramatic, offering good opportunities for walkers. The

Getting to Santiago do Cacém

Santiago's train station was closed in 1990, making connections awkward. Take the **ferry** from Lisbon's Terreiro do Paço, change **trains** at Barreiro and, after 2hrs, at Ermidas-Sado, from where there are connecting **buses** to Santiago. Services from all stations in the Algarve are similarly infrequent. Semi-frequent Rede Expressos **buses** from Lisbon take 2¼hrs, some via Setúbal (1½hrs), with infrequent buses in the other direction from Vila Nova de Milfontes (1¼hrs). The same company runs several buses daily from main towns in the Algarve, and two from Beja.

old part of town around the castle is decaying, with the exception of several symmetrical *palácios*; the new part is overshadowed by a block of flats built like a battleship. Gypsy horse carts lollop through, with terriers like mascots, and mirrored harnesses.

Santiago is useful as a base for visiting the sand beach at the Lagoa de Santo André, half an hour away by bus or car.

On a hill to the north of the town, pervaded by a great peace and sense of the past, stand the ruins of Roman **Miróbriga**, signposted from the N121. To get to these, go about 1km up the Lisbon road, where there's a signposted turning, sharp right. Turn left off this after a 10-minute walk. The fenced site occupies several gentle green hillslopes, crossed by paths lined with cypress trees.

Miróbriga
t (269) 825 148; open Tues–Sun 9–12 and 2–5.30; closed hols; adm, free adm Sun before 2pm

Miróbriga probably started life as a Celtic *castro* in the Iron Age, around the 4th century BC. Coins unearthed here indicate that by the 2nd or 1st century BC the settlement was trading with towns in southern Spain. On the highest point stands a temple of Aesculapius, with a temple of Venus; below them a shed protects the market. A path leads down to the baths, complete with gymnasium and massage room and the circus with seating for 25,000. There's enough space to get pleasantly lost and drift about conjuring up 1st- and 2nd-century Romans – you may even stumble across the housing sector, which remains undiscovered. Excavations are still in progress.

ⓘ **Santiago do Cacém >**
Largo do Mercado,
t (269) 826 696,
www.cm-santiago-do-cacem.pt

Services in Santiago do Cacém

The **bus station** is near the centre of town in the Praça M. Albuquerque.

Where to Stay in Santiago do Cacém

★★★★**Albergaria Dom Nuno**, Avenida Dom Nuno Álvares Pereira 88, **t** (269)

823 325, *www.albdnuno.com* (€€). In the straight, modern street at the bottom of the municipal park. Large, neutral and clean, with a kitchen-like restaurant.

★★★**Pensão Residencial Gabriel**, Rua Prof. Egas Moniz 24/26, **t** (269) 822 245, *luisgabnunes@netvisao.pt* (€). A short walk from the bus station (in the direction of the old part of town), this is pleasantly furnished, comfortable and adequate.

Eating Out in Santiago do Cacém

Charming, friendly country restaurant. The house specialities include *bacalhau* in cream sauce. *Closed Mon.*

Restaurante O Gourmet, Rua Machado dos Santos 8, **t** (269) 822 659 (€).

Museu Municipal
Largo do Município,
t (269) 827 375,
www.cm-santiago-do-
cacem.pt/cultura/
museu.htm;
open Tues–Fri 10–12
and 2–5, Sat–Sun 2–5;
closed Mon and hols

Back in town, the excellent **Museu Municipal** displays a selection of knick-knacks from the site. The museum is housed in a late 19th-century prison, operational until the Revolution of 1974. The traditional kitchen displays a *barreleiro,* a hollowed cork log: boiling water was poured over a muslin cloth containing wood ash and sweet-smelling herbs, to produce suitably alkaline water for washing. Also in the kitchen are a cork baby cage, complete with bell, a collection of birds' nests, and a paddle for punishing urchins.

On a hilltop above the town, the extensively restored 620ft (190m) Moorish **castle walls** offer panoramic views of the Serra de Grândola. The walls encircle the cemetery of the 13th-century **Igreja Matriz**, with attendant white marble tombs, cypress trees, and a compost heap of decaying flowers.

The Alentejo Coast

The coast of the Alentejo, which stretches south from the estuary of the River Sado near Tróia (see p.324) to the border with the Algarve just south of Zambujeira, offers the country's best opportunities for low-key beachlife away from the crowds. The grey rock cliffs of the coastline are punctuated by sandy coves and bays, which offer meagre shelter from the wind and waves of the Atlantic ocean, and do very little to warm the chilly water, which is noticeably cooler than that in the eastern Algarve. The Alentejo coast attracts those Portuguese who are in on the secret (although the word is becoming more widespread), and a mixed bag of world travellers and surfers.

There is little infrastructure – the remoter spots are literally off the beaten track. Elsewhere, accommodation is basic, with one or two exceptions, and getting about is difficult without your own transport.

Lagoa de Santo André

Twelve kilometres northwest of Santiago do Cacém, half an hour by road, a strip of sand separates a lagoon from the sea. The **beach** is large and flat, headed by a collection of fish restaurants arranged around a pleasant, reedy little bay. If you're swimming in the ocean, be particularly careful of the undertow.

Getting to The Alentejo Coast

If you're dependent on public transport, there are two access points to the coast: at Santiago do Cacém, from which there are semi-frequent **buses** to the Lagoa de Santo André; and at Odemira, from which there are semi-frequent buses to Vila Nova de Milfontes. Vila Nova de Milfontes can also be reached by the thrice daily (more often at weekends) express bus from Lisbon (3¾hrs) and Santiago do Cacém (1¼hrs).

Sines

Twenty kilometres southwest of Santiago de Cacém, the Cabo de Sines is a giant industrial pimple on the coastline. As you approach, the smell of pine trees gives way to an industrial stink, emitted by the refinery's tubular monsters. The seawater here is polluted.

Sines' Museum/ House of Vasco de Gama
Castelo de Sines, t (269) 632 237; open Tues–Sun 10–1 and 2–5

Beyond the industrial areas, the **old town** is slightly less charmless. The medieval **castle** was reputedly the birthplace of Vasco da Gama in 1469. In 2008 the **Sines' Museum** and the **House of Vasco de Gama** were opened in the castle. The museum will feature temporary exhibitions, the first one showing the archaeological riches of the municipality. The House of Vasco de Gama, located in the main tower, tells the story of de Gama's life. The **Museu Arqueológico** has some interesting pieces of jewellery, thought to be Phoenician, that were found in the locality.

Museu Arqueológico
Rua Francisco Luís Lopes 38, t (269) 632 330; open Mon–Sat 10–12.45 and 2–4.45; closed Sun and hols

Porto Covo

The soil alternates between deep red, light red and white on the approach to Porto Covo, a laid-back little place with the sea at the end of its straight main street, 6km off the Sines–Odemira road. The whitewashed village cottages, with their traditional blue trim, are particularly pretty. There used to be no problem camping in the caves around the several small **beach coves** – being careful of the tides – but now that the campsite has opened, the police tell people they're not allowed there or in the woods.

Ilha do Pessegueiro (Peach Tree Island)

Approached from a turning off the Porto Covo–Milfontes route, a tiny settlement huddles together opposite a barren little island about half a mile offshore, the main focus of the settlement being the campsite. Sometimes fishermen can be persuaded to ferry visitors to the island, which is topped by a ruined castle built by Dom Pedro II towards the end of the 17th century, to stave off pirates. There's no public transport, and no peach trees – the island is quite windswept.

Vila Nova de Milfontes

The coast road passes through a barren wilderness between Porto Covo and Vila Nova de Milfontes, an undeveloped and very pretty port town at the mouth of the estuary of the Rio Mira. The skyline is low and the street plan pleasantly muddled. This is the most popular resort in the Alentejo, so the few rooms soon get fully booked. If you choose to swim in the estuary rather than the ocean, watch out for the terrifically strong current.

Odemira

Nestling in hilly land 20km inland on the River Mira, Odemira is more or less unspoilt by tourism. The town is a useful junction for visiting beaches; its white houses with blue trim are traditional to the region.

A well-preserved and still-working Alentejan **windmill** stands on the outskirts of the town and shows traditional wheat- and corn-grinding in action. At the **pottery workshop**, visitors can watch earthenware and other handicrafts being produced (contact the tourist office for more details).

ⓘ **Vila Nova de Milfontes >**
*Rua António Mantes,
t (283) 996 599; open
daily 10–1 and 2–6*

 Castelo de Milfontes >>

Services in Vila Nova de Milfontes

Buses stop on the main road into the town from Lisbon and Odemira, Rua Custódio Bras Pacheco.

Where to Stay and Eat on The Alentejo Coast

Lagoa de Santo André

Os Dois Galos, Deixa-o-Resto, **t** (269) 746 234, *www.osdoisgalos.com* (€€). A welcoming hotel with seven rooms, a restaurant, lounge/bar, swimming pool and shop. 4km from the beach.

Hotel Rural Monte da Leziria, Estrada Municipal, Vila Nova de Santo André, **t** (269) 084 935, *www.monteda leziria.com* (€€). This 28-room hotel is surrounded by pine trees. Has a bar, garden and terrace. You will need a car to get to the nearest restaurants.

Parque de Campismo Lagoa de Santo André, **t** (269) 708 550 (€). Located right on the north side of the lagoon, 2km from Santo André, with plenty of shade from small trees. Facilities include hot showers, washing machines, a restaurant, bar and a shop. *Open 14 Jan–13 Nov.*

Porto Covo

Parque de Campismo da Porto Covo, Estrada Municipal 554, **t** (269) 905 136 (€). Pretty, shady and breezy campsite

near the sea, with all amenities; offers pinky-orange painted apartments as an alternative to a pitch.

Ilha do Pessegueiro (Peach Tree Island)

Parque de Campismo da Ilha Pessegueiro, Estrada da Ilha, **t** (269) 905 178, *www.ilhapessegueiro camping.com* (€). Offers apartment accommodation (€€), and good facilities.

Vila Nova de Milfontes

Castelo de Milfontes, Avenida Marginal, **t** (283) 998 231 (€€€€). Castle Milfontes was built in 1652 during the reign of João IV, to defend the river from attacks. It's a wonderful place to stay; the interior is furnished with a suit of armour, animal horns on the stone walls, oil paintings, and a single long dining table at which all guests dine. The food is said to be excellent. All rooms have fantastic sea views, although the better rooms are in the tower. There's a wonderful terrace where you can sit looking straight out over the sea. Picnic lunches are available on request.

Pensão Casa dos Arcos, Rua dos Carris, **t** (283) 996 264 (€€–€). Built and furnished in a modern style. A basic place to lay your head.

Moinho da Asneira, Quinta do Rio Mira, **t** (283) 996 182, *www.moinhoda asneira.com* (€). A country estate overlooking the River Mira, with rooms available in the main house or adjacent cottages.

★★★★Residencial Mil-Réis, Largo do Rossio 2, **t** (283) 998 233 (€). Uninteresting, but not bad.

★★★Residencial Eira da Pedra, Rua das Pensões, **t** (283) 998 675 (€). The unprepossessing exterior and rather lurid reception area belie comfortable rooms which are rather good value; some come with a sea view and may be rented by the week.

Marisqueira Dumas Mil, off Avenida Marginal, **t** (283) 997 104 (€€). Reputable fish restaurant, serving *caldeirada* (seafood stew) and other specialities.

Restaurante O Pescador (also known as **O Moura**), Rua da Praça 18, **t** (283) 996 338 (€€). Another good place to eat fish: try the monkfish, or *caldeirada*.

A Fateixa, Largo do Cais, **t** (283) 996 415 (€). So relaxed that the chef might forget to cook your food, but the place has an 'authentic' feel, because it's situated right next to the quay, and the sight of lobster pots induces a belief in the freshness of the food. There are a couple of tables to sit at outside.

Odemira

Quinta do Moinho de Vento, **t** (283) 990 040, *www.quintado moinhodevento.com* (€€). Pretty, modern apartments to rent. Interiors are spacious, though basic, with all mod cons.

Pousada

Pousada Santa Clara, Santa Clara-a-Velha, **t** (283) 882 250, *www.pousadas .pt* (L1 N). Located near the Barragem de Santa Clara, in a peaceful spot, this *pousada* has a comfortable, modern atmosphere, with an open fire in the lounge, a pool and great views of the reservoir from the terraces and pool area. A choice of activities – water sports, bike rides, tennis and fishing – is on offer.

ⓘ **Odemira >>**
Praça de República,
t (283) 320 900,
turismodemira@
hotmail.com

The Algarve

The Algarve is a great amphitheatre facing the sea: the landscape changes from the thickly wooded Serra de Monchique (2,960ft/902m) and the rounded, cultivated hills of the Serra do Caldeirão (1,890ft/577m), to a zone of crests running parallel to the coast, cut by the valleys of rivers flowing down from the hills. Here are the orchards of the Algarve – the almonds, the carobs, the olives, and the figs which the Romans lauded and which, in the 17th century, were dried and exported to Flanders and the Levant.

15

Don't miss

⭐ **Spirit of exploration**
Sagres **p.516**

⭐ **Spa in the hills**
Caldas de Monchique **p.504**

⭐ **12th-century Moorish capital**
Silves **p.496**

⭐ **Charming town by the beach**
Tavira **p.474**

⭐ **Swim in warm, clear water**
Praia do Beliche **p.464**

See map overleaf

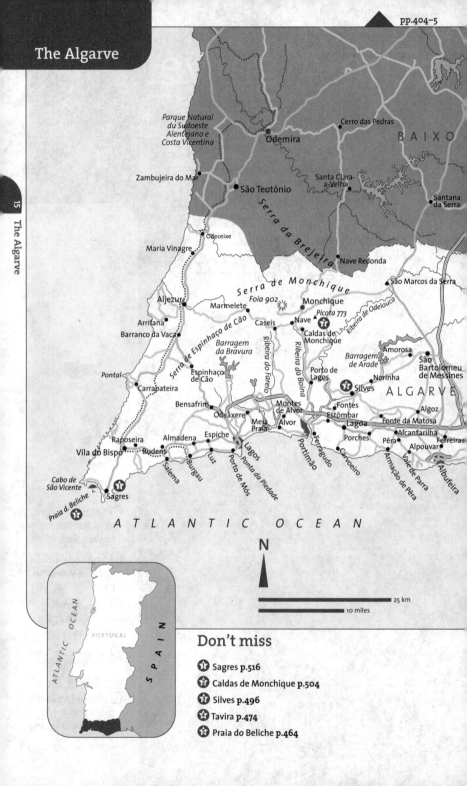

The Algarve

BAIXO

Parque Natural du Sudoeste Alentejano e Costa Vicentina

Cerro das Pedras

Odemira

Zambujeira do Mar

Santa Clara-a-Velha

Santana da Serra

São Teotónio

Serra da Brejeira

Odeceixe

Maria Vinagre

Nave Redonda

São Marcos da Serra

Serra de Monchique

Aljezur

Marmelete

Foia 902

Monchique

Picota 773

Ribeira de Odelouca

Arrifana

Caseis

Nave

Barranco da Vaca

Caldas de Monchique

Amorosa

Serra de Espinhaço de Cão

Barragem da Bravura

Ribeira do Farelo

Ribeira da Boina

Porto de Lagos

Barragem de Arade

São Bartolomeu de Messines

Pontal

Espinhaço de Cão

Norinha

ALGARVE

Carrapateira

Silves

Bensafrim

Montes de Alvor

Fontes

Algoz

Odeaxere

Estômbar

Fonte da Matosa

Raposeira

Almadena

Espiche

Meia Praia

Alvor

Lagoa

Alcantarilha

Porches

Pêra

Alpouvar

Ferreiras

Vila do Bispo

Budens

Luz

Lagos

Portimão

Ferragudo

Carvoeiro

Vale de Parra

Albufeira

Salema

Burgau

Porto de Mós

Ponta da Piedade

Armação de Pêra

Cabo de São Vicente

Sagres

Praia d. Beliche

ATLANTIC OCEAN

N

25 km

10 miles

ATLANTIC OCEAN

PORTUGAL

SPAIN

Don't miss

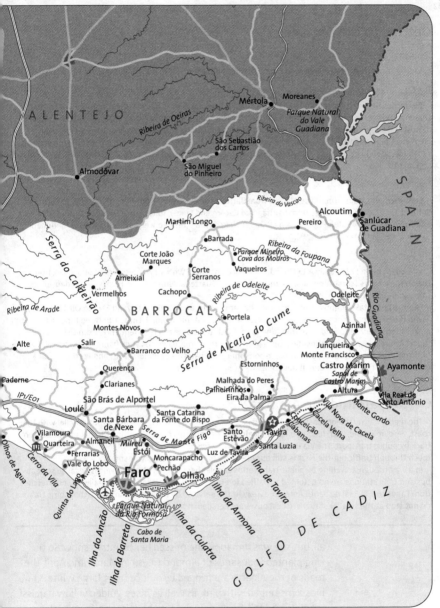

The Algarve is also laden with orange trees (though fresh orange juice is almost impossible to buy). The almond trees' pale pink blossom clouds the province from the middle of January to the end of February, above a mantle of bright yellow Bermuda buttercups. (A legendary Moorish king married a legendary Scandinavian beauty and brought her to his capital at Silves. He offered her his

Getting to the Algarve

By Air

Most visitors to the Algarve fly into Faro's international airport, turn nut-brown, and fly out again.

By Car

Car ferries between Ayamonte in Spain and Vila Real de Santo António operate infrequently, now that there is a bridge/border crossing (open constantly). The 'Via da Infante' toll-free motorway runs from here almost the length of the Algarve to northeast of Lagos, enabling through travellers to avoid the old N125 east–west highway, which is usually clogged with local traffic. (The Via do Infante is eventually to continue north to Lisbon.) The A2 motorway from Lisbon to the Algarve gives a journey time to Faro (a distance of 315km) of 2½hrs.

By Train

Semi-frequent trains run to the Algarve from Barreiro (take the ferry from Lisbon's Terreiro do Paço), via Setúbal, Ermidas-Sado (change from Santiago do Cacém and Sines), Tunes (3hrs; change at Tunes for Silves and Lagos, 1¼hrs), Albufeira (4hrs), Faro (4½hrs), Olhão, Tavira (5hrs), Conceição, Cacela, Castro Marim and Vila Real de Santo António (5¾hrs).

By Bus

EVA buses run a twice-daily Alta Qualidade service, complete with stewardess, drinks and video, from Lisbon to Ferreiras (4hrs), Albufeira, Vilamoura (4½hrs), Quarteira, Almancil and Faro (5hrs). Various other companies offer the same service.

Express buses take slightly longer to cover the same route, and continue beyond Faro to Olhão (5½hrs), Tavira (6hrs), Cacela, Monte Gordo and Vila Real de Santo António (6½hrs). These run three times daily, with an additional service to Faro from mid-June to mid-October. Buses run less frequently from Lisbon to Lagos. A single Express bus runs the length of the country from Chaves to Lagos (17hrs), via Vila Real (15½hrs), Viseu (13hrs), Coimbra (11½hrs), Lisbon (6hrs), Setúbal (5hrs), Albufeira (1hr) and Portimão (½hr). EVA buses are the main Algarvian bus company.

Getting around the Algarve

The region has no major coast road offering picturesque views; the N125 highway runs parallel with the coast, 2–10km inland, with feeder roads branching off from it. This makes it difficult to get off the beaten track by public transport. The Via do Infante motorway a few more kilometres inland has siphoned off much through traffic but the N125 is still busy, because of increased car ownership.

In a way, though, travelling by public transport is simpler here than in other provinces because staff at bus and train stations are accustomed to baffled foreigners, and make allowances. A railway line stretches from Lagos to Vila Real de Santo António, a 4–4½hr trip serviced by frequent trains: note that some trains do not stop at the smaller stations. (Local buses are detailed in the text.)

---

all, but she was unhappy: she missed her country's snow. So the king planted thousands of almond trees.) In March and April, the roads of the Algarve are fringed by quince trees' large white blossoms tinged with pink, as well as irises, golden yellow narcissi, jonquils, and tall, freely branched asphodels whose white flowers are veined with red.

The coastal zone separates into two areas: the **sotavento**, east of Faro, with sand dunes, salt lagoons, and a broken spit of sand sheltering the coast; and the **barlavento**, to the west of Portimão, a more humid area of mainly rocky coast, with cliffs up to 260ft (80m) high, whose sandy bays and coves are separated by weird grottoes and peculiar rock outcrops, exposed to the Atlantic winds.

The Wines of the Algarve

Vines flourished in the south of Portugal under the Moors, who left the making and selling of wine to Christian Mozarabs. Today, the Algarve is a Demarcated Region, but the wines are undistinguished. All but three per cent are reds, with a hefty 13 per cent alcohol content, stemming from the grapes' very high sugar content. It's certainly worth trying the Algarvian dry white apéritif wine, matured in wood and similar to an amontillado, as well as the fiery but flavourful *medronho* distilled from arbutus berries in the Monchique hills.

What to Eat

Superb fresh fish is the joy of Algarvian cooking, with an emphasis on sardines (*sardinhas*) and tuna (*atum*), both of which are quite unlike the tinned varieties. Cockles (*amêijoas*) are popular, cooked with smoked pork sausage, cured ham, tomatoes and onions in a *cataplana* (sealed wok). Several different fish can be used to make *xerém*, a kind of maize mash. Inland, you may find hare and partridge served during the hunting season. Algarvian *gaspacho* differs from its Spanish cousin in that the ingredients are diced rather than puréed, leaving the soup pleasantly crunchy. The marzipan sweets of the Algarve, shaped like fruits and filled with sugared egg yolk, may have Moorish origins, since they resemble those sold in North Africa. Figs and almonds are variously combined to make other delicious sweets and desserts. The Moors introduced citrus fruits to the Peninsula: the oranges of the Algarve are succulent, juicy navels.

The two are divided by an area of reddish sandy cliffs wooded with pines. The Mediterranean climate brings mild winters and long, warm summers – an equilibrium assisted by the hills, which shelter the province from the northerly winds that blow cold in winter and very hot in summer. The annual rainfall at the coast is just 400–500mm.

Tourism is not the Algarve's only moneyspinner. Fishing is a buoyant source of revenue, as well as brick factories with brick chimneys, and hothouse tomatoes, strawberries, and avocados for export. Inland, dry stone walls pen sheep with pendulous undocked tails, a breed which originated in west Africa, whose coarse wool is used for stuffing mattresses and weaving into heavy blankets. The shepherds wear ex-army swallowtail caps, surplus from the African wars.

Adventurous and independent travellers can take heart: there is not too much development west of Lagos, east of Faro, or inland. Lonely beaches backed by tiny whitewashed settlements do exist, though access is sometimes a problem – but hurry, lest the developers beat you there. Inland, there are some lovely walks in the hills, detailed in the Algarve tourist office's commonsensical *Guide to Walks*.

The rapid development of the Algarve has put great strains on the water supply: it's best not to drink tapwater in the summer, when water levels are running low. This sometimes leads to the supply being cut off for a few hours in the early evening, and usually reconnected just when you're resigned to being salt-encrusted overnight.

Best Beaches

See pages 466–7 for a map showing the locations of these beaches.

Faro and the Eastern Coast

Praia Faro offers the choice of cool Atlantic or warm lagoon waters, but is jam-packed in high season. **Ilha da Armona** has warm shallow waters and long sands. **Ilha de Tavira** is a huge sandbar beach, with activities and crowds near the ferry and campsite. **Praia Verde** is the most unspoilt stretch of beach east of Tavira.

Around Albufeira

Praia da Falésia is an immaculately groomed long golden sweep. It is reached across a footbridge spanning an inlet of the sea and picturesque meadows and dunes. **Praia da Albufeira** is a longish beach solid with bodies in the summer. To the left is **Fisherman's Beach**, peppered with vivid fishing boats and a varied set of restaurants ranged along the coastline. To the west a conical rock pierces the sky; a path cut into the cliffs enables you to walk round the headland, through caves and wide chambers above tunnels in which the sea sighs.

Armação de Pêra

Praia da Cova Redonda is where children build castles on a large, curving beach above which tower sandstone cliffs. **Praia da Senhora da Rocha** is a lovely beach set against overhanging sea-scarred cliffs and bisected at low tide by giant rocks. The western part is preferable, and good for diving. **Praia da Marinha** is scattered with rock bridges and free-standing shelves rising out of the sea; its image adorns many a holiday brochure. It attracts a young sexy crowd of travellers, and tends to be busy all year round. **Praia da Benagil** is reached by a long flight of stairs leading down to a small cove dotted with bright fishing boats. **Praia do Carvalho** is fittingly known as Smuggler's Cove; the overhanging cliffs have formed grottoes and walkways which now harbour mischievous children.

From Alvor to Salema

Praia do João de Arens is quite secluded, the rocks forming caves and grottoes; the steep climb down from the cliffs doesn't deter many people. **Praia de Três Irmãos** is a small cove always thronged by a large number of families. **Praia Dona Ana** is a much-photographed cove-beach that is often too small for the summer crowds. Tour boats from Lagos stitch their way among the caves. **Praia do Camilo** is even smaller, though just as pretty, with strange rock formations rising out of the warm green water.

Praias do Canavial and **Porto de Mós** are small stretches of body-dotted sand which are marginally quieter than the other beaches in Lagos and very popular with young Portuguese. **Praia do Burgau** is backed partly by the Burgau Beach Bar, partly by sharply sloping cliffs. The smooth, clear water is ideal for children. **Praia da Salema** is popular with travellers as well as English and German families. There are grass-hat umbrellas on the beach and the water is turquoise. Head to the right of the beach and the colourful fishing boats. **Praia da Boca do Rio**, a couple of km east of Salema, has easy access. It's good for diving when the water is calm; there is the wreck of a French ship some 300 yards off-shore. When the waves are up, surfers take over.

Around Sagres

Praia da Martinhal is beloved of windsurfing groupies. **Praia da Mareta** is the southernmost beach east of Sagres Point. Waves break against rocks on which people bask like lizards. It is popular with young families. **Praia do Tonel** is sandy and the waves powerful – an ideal combination for surfing and hanging out. To the right you can clamber over the rocks to reach a lovely small beach. **Praia do Beliche** 🏵 is a beautiful secret, with imposing cliffs that have formed many caves and coves. The water here is the warmest, clearest and calmest and there is good shelter from the wind, though the numerous steps down may not suit everyone.

Around Vila do Bispo

Praias do Castelejo and **Cordoama** are two of the most stunning beaches in the Algarve. The beaches stretch for miles, and large waves throw a constant film of spray on to the stark slate cliffs. **Praia da Barriga** is small and quiet, reached by a dust track winding through wooded hills. The cliffs are low, forming curious shapes.

Praias do Mirouço, **Murração** and **Amado** – jade waters lap black cliffs stacked high into the sky, while lower-strata rock extends out into the sea. All these beaches are deserted and hard to reach. **Praia do**

Bordeira is backed by shifting dunes, rather than cliffs, which fall away on either side of the curving bay. Behind the beach a stream becomes an estuary, which frequently metamorphoses into a lagoon nurturing young fish, and is the feeding ground for many birds such as the white stork. The beach has easy access and is calm and quiet: ideal for children.

Around Aljezur and Odeceixe

Praia do Monte Clérigo is a nice family beach you can drive right up to. **Praia da Amoreira** is a lovely long beach near a stream, flanked on the left by gentle grass-topped cliffs and backed by scrub-heavy dunes. The crouching slate cliffs to the right are marvellous to explore, especially when the tide is low. This is a fun beach for children as there are many small caves and shallow pools in the rocks.

Praia de Odeceixe lies a beautiful 4km walk west of the village and is reached by a good road that runs alongside the river and farmland. The river cuts through the beach to empty itself into the sea; the water's warmer for swimming at this point. Black cliffs rise out of sand blackened by powdered slate, and rose quartz runs through the rocks like the luminous trail of a celestial snail.

History

Drawn by the mineral wealth of the Peninsula, the Phoenicians settled in Spain c. 1364 BC, founding the city of Ossonoba (possibly on the site now occupied by Faro) as an important base for their trade in marble and amber, but little now remains of their civilization.

The blood and customs of the Algarve have been much more forcibly influenced by the Moors, who occupied the region from the early 8th century to the mid-13th century, though they too left few material remains. Their legacy is of roof terraces, inner patios, slim chimneys patterned like sugar cellars, through which smoke percolates, and bucket wheels for raising water. The people of the Algarve have darker complexions than their northern counterparts, and also tend to be more garrulous and agitated.

The conquest of the Algarve, undertaken by Dom Sancho I, remained incomplete until Dom Afonso III's military successes of 1249. In the 12th and 13th centuries, Christians labelled that part of the country which remained in Moorish hands 'Algarve'. For the Moors themselves, the province of al-Gharb encompassed the western part of the Peninsula as well as the coast of North Africa at Ceuta, Tangiers and Fez. Thus when Tangier surrendered to Dom Afonso V, he styled himself 'King of Portugal and the Algarves, both on this side and beyond the sea'.

Tourism

The Portuguese are fond of saying that 'The Algarve is not Portugal'. This used to be true because the southern province was Moorish; today it is German, Scandinavian, British and French. The 52-mile (85km) stretch of coast between Faro and Lagos is jam-packed with high-rise hotels, apartment blocks, villa complexes, shopping centres and water parks – and more are on the way. Concrete mixer trucks throw up clouds of dust along roads lined

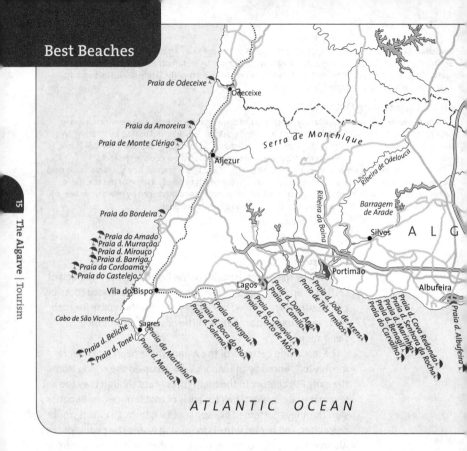

with rubble, supplying building sites bustling under the midday sun and the midnight floodlights.

When Faro airport opened in the early 1960s, the Algarve was something of a secret. The Salazar government kept such planning applications as there were under tight control, until the Revolution of 1974 toppled both the government and the controls. Tourism would bring employment to a poor region, so opportunist local councils adopted a more laissez-faire approach. Building did not really take off until the mid-1980s, when Spanish hoteliers upped their prices, and British tour operators looked for new pastures.

In 1964 the Algarve offered 1,000 tourist beds; by 1988 this had reached 58,500 and by 1990 the figure was 70,200, accounting for just under half the tourist beds in the entire country. Visitor numbers told a similar story, with 7.9 million out of a total of 16.5 million visitors to Portugal from abroad holidaying in the Algarve. By the turn of the millennium, things were deemed to have gone too far: growth in visitor numbers to the Algarve has now slowed down, and restrictions have been imposed to control development in areas where there is concern for the quality of Portuguese tourism.

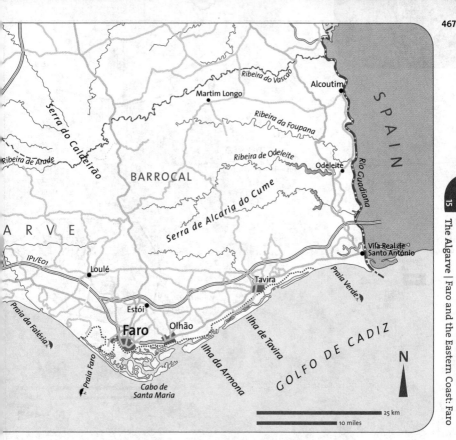

Faro and the Eastern Coast

Faro

Faro, capital of the Algarve, is built around an attractive harbour at the edge of a wide lagoon, 9km from the beach. Just under 300km from Lisbon and 53km from the Spanish border, it's a pleasant town studded with squares where you can linger under shady carob and oleander trees, or sit under the palms of Jardim Manuel Bivar and watch the sun glinting on the harbour. It's a gentle place with white, shambling houses, interesting monuments and designer shops along pedestrianized streets, where people sip coffee and shoot the breeze. Faro feels different from the coastal resorts because it is home to businesses and industries; smart locals rub shoulders with sunburnt tourists while the university students bring a bit of fizz to the place.

History

Dom Afonso III captured Faro from the Moors in 1249 and rebuilt the town walls. Elizabeth I's favourite, the Earl of Essex, was an

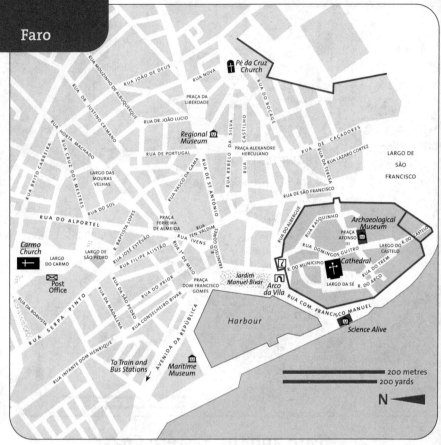

early visitor. In 1596, after sacking and burning Cadiz, he landed at Faro beach with Sir Walter Raleigh and 3,000 troops. Portugal was ruled by England's enemy Philip II of Spain and was therefore a fair target. Essex installed himself in the bishop's palace, from which he removed 200 gilt black leather volumes and presented them to Sir Thomas Bodley, who had recently founded a library at Oxford. Then he set Faro on fire and departed. Parts of the city were destroyed by earthquakes in 1722 and 1755.

The Old Town

The old part of town rests behind fortified walls. Enter through the 18th-century Italianate **Arco da Vila**, a gate with a niche for St Thomas Aquinas, who was invoked to save the city from a plague in the 17th century.

Pretty, cobbled Rua do Município opens on to a square edged with orange trees, in which stands the Renaissance **cathedral (Sé)**. It has appropriated the tower of its Gothic predecessor and the building has a wide nave flanked by 18th-century *azulejos*, and a wild, dovecote-like Baroque reliquary. The quirky chinoiserie organ was

Cathedral (Sé)
*open Mon–Sat 10–5
for visitors, 6 for masses*

Getting around Faro

Six kilometres out of town, **Faro airport, t** (289) 808 800, copes with over 5 million passengers each year. Bus nos. 14 and 16 take 20 minutes into town and cost around €1. A taxi to the centre of town will cost about €10 – agree on the price first if the meter is not being used. From the **railway station**, walk down the Avenida da República, past the **bus station**, to get to the harbour. Buses 16 and 17 leave every half-hour from opposite the tourist office to Faro beach.

painted in 1751. Just outside the side entrance, note the remains of a **capela dos ossos** (Bone Chapel), a taster for the main event at the Carmo Church (*see* below). Take the 68 narrow winding steps to the top of the tower for a wonderful view over the Old Town rooftops and the lagoon. Watch the international and domestic flights from the nearby airport from the top of the old Bishop's Palace and the Arco da Vila, where two pairs of storks have nested.

Archaeological Museum
Praça Afonso III,
t (289) 897 400,
www.cm-faro.pt; open
Mon–Fri 10–6.30, Sat
10–1; closed Sun and
hols; adm

Behind the cathedral, the Convento de Nossa Senhora da Assunção now houses the **Archaeological Museum** whose illuminating collection was retrieved locally. Part of it is displayed in the stunning two-storey cloister of 1543. The two 1st-century busts of Hadrian and Agrippina, wife of Emperor Claudius, were discovered at nearby Milreu (*see* p.484) while the excellent 3rd-century Neptune mosaic was found close to the railway station. A cabinet near the mosaic displays Roman *lachrymae*, tiny vessels intended to hold tears.

Ciência Viva
Rua Commandante
Francisco Manuel,
t (289) 890 920,
www.cienciaviva.pt;
open mid-Sept–June
Tues–Fri 10–5, weekends
and hols 3–7, July–mid-
Sept Tues–Sun and hols
4–11pm; adm

It is worth taking some time to explore the lovely quiet cobbled streets of the Old Town. Tucked away in a peaceful corner is the **Galeria do Trem**, which periodically stages exhibitions of Portuguese art. Pick up a copy of *Agenda* from the tourist office for opening times.

Outside the Old Town

On the edge of the marina **Ciência Viva** (Science Alive) is a lively hands-on centre. Aimed more at locals than foreign visitors (most captions and explanatory notes are in Portuguese only), its friendly staff are happy to help. In the evenings star-gazers can visit their observatory.

Maritime Museum
Rua da Comunidade
Lusiada, t (289) 894
990; open Mon–Fri
2.30–4.30; closed Sat
and Sun

Two of Faro's other museums are worth a visit. On the dock past the Hotel Eva, the **Maritime Museum** contains models of fishing boats from the past and present, labelled in English. Algarvian handicrafts, rural photos and reconstructions of interiors are on display at the **Regional Museum**.

Regional Museum
Praça da Liberdade 2,
t (289) 827 610; open
summer Tues–Fri
9.30–5.30, Mon and Sat
2–5.30; winter Tues–Fri
10–6, Mon and Sat
2.30–6; adm

Tower blocks loom behind the **Carmo Church** in the Largo do Carmo, wrecking the effect of its grand façade of 1713. Lovesick angels support the richly gilded retable; to the right, a door leads to the macabre **Capela dos Ossos** (Bone Chapel). The walls of this simple and ghoulish chamber are entirely lined with some 1,250 skulls and other monks' bones, extracted from graves around the church in 1816.

Capela dos Ossos
open Mon–Fri 10–1
and 3–5, Sat 10–1; adm

(i) **Faro >**
8 Rua da Misericórdia next to the Arco da Vila, t (289) 803 604; open summer 9.30am–7pm

⭑ **Residencial Adelaide >>**

⭑ **Hotel Eva >**

Tourist Information and Services in Faro

For information on **buses**, **t** (289) 899 760; for details of **trains**, **t** (289) 826 472.

The **post office** is in the Largo do Carmo.

The daily **market** is in the Largo Mercado off the Rua Dr Justino Crimano. The region's **main hospital** can be reached on **t** (289) 891 100 at Rua Leão Peredo.

Sports and Activities in Faro

There are no championship golf courses in the immediate vicinity but the **Colina Verde** course, Hotel Apartamentos Golfe Colina Verde Sitio da Maragota, Moncarapacho, **t** (289) 790 110, *www.golfcolinaverde.com*, is a par-3 course with full-size greens that is ideal for holiday golfers.

Where to Stay in Faro

Expensive (€€€)
★★★★Hotel Eva, Avenida da República, **t** (289) 803 354, *www.tdhotels.pt*. It may not be the city's most modern hotel, but it has the best views of the harbour, the old town and the lagoon, and the breezy rooftop swimming pool (for guests only) is a knockout. The spacious rooms have large balconies, and the service is generally well-meaning.

★★★★Hotel Faro, Praça Dom Francisco Gomes 2, **t** (289) 830 830, *www.hotelfaro.pt*. It's surprising to find a hotel as slavishly styled as this one built above a shopping centre in the centre of town. Windows are big, carpets are white, and furnishings favour looks over comfort. The fourth-floor terrace bar is rather cool and well worth a visit.

Moderate (€€)
★★★Residencial Algarve, Rua Infante Dom Henrique 52, **t** (289) 895 700, *www.residencialalgarve.com*. Rebuilt in 1999 in the exact architectural style of the late 19th-century original, it's light and bright, with a nice breakfast area; rooms have cable TV, air-conditioning and baths.

Inexpensive (€)
Most of the cheaper places to stay are to be found in or around the Rua Conselheiro Bivar, which is off Praça Dom Francisco Gomes, or its extension, Rua Infante Dom Henrique.

★★★Residencial Madalena, Rua Conselheiro Bivar 109, **t** (289) 805 806. Very central, clean and popular.

★★Residencial Samé, Rua do Bocage 66, **t** (289) 824 375. Just outside the Old Town, clean but otherwise dull. All rooms have TV and air-conditioning.

Residencial Dandy, Rua Filipe Alistão 62, **t** (289) 824 791. Simply furnished pleasant rooms with high ceilings and small balconies.

Pensão São Filipe, Rua Infante Dom Henrique 52, **t** (289) 824 182. There's something rather appealing about this place, largely to do with the nice landlady who also cleans. She has cheap taste, though.

Residencial Adelaide, Rua Cruz dos Mestres 9, **t** (289) 802 383. For a bit of real Portugal, this distinctive and very friendly place has decent large rooms to let. Laundry service is available. Adelaide is a colourful and chirpy landlady.

If all else fails (as it may well do in high season), there is a **youth hostel**, **t** (289) 801 970, on the Rua do Matadouro, which is near the police station.

Camping
Faro's **campsite** is on the sand spit, **t** (289) 817 876.

Eating Out in Faro

Moderate (€€)
O Aldeão, Largo de São Pedro, **t** (289) 823 339. An elegant restaurant overlooking the lovely Igreja de São Pedro church. Dishes from the Alentejo and Algarve are prepared with minute attention to detail.

Adega Dois Irmãos, Lago do Terreiro do Bispo, **t** (289) 823 337. In the centre of town, just off the pedestrianized streets, it has been going strong since

1926 with perhaps the best fish and seafood in town.

⭐ **Mesa dos Mouros** >

Mesa dos Mouros, Largo da Sé, **t** (289) 878 873. In the Old Town the best place to eat is the classy Mesa dos Mouros which occupies a sturdy ancient stone house and a classy terrace right by the cathedral. Stylish and modern, it's a good place for fish and *tapas*.

⭐ **Tasca O Chalaver** >>

Cantinho da Ronha, Rua do Bocage 55, **t** (289) 813 872. Well off the tourist trail, serving great food and jam-packed at lunch time.

Vasco da Gama, Rua Vasco da Gama 49a, **t** (289) 821 666. Pick your own fresh fish from the tank.

⭐ **Sol e Jardim** >

Sol e Jardim, Lago do Terreiro do Bispo, **t** (289) 820 030. For a more informal meal try this fun place occupying a large internal courtyard draped with flags and covered with a trellis. The grilled fish is good. *Closed Sun in winter*.

Adega Nortenha, Praça Ferreira de Almeida 25, **t** (289) 982 2709. A good value traditional restaurant with a small terrace for al fresco dining. Popular dishes include tuna steak and roast lamb with garlic.

A Taska, Rua do Alportel 38, **t** (289) 824 739. A joy of a restaurant. Locals sit at solid wooden tables, selecting large portions of excellent food from a small and very traditional menu. Try *xarém com conquilhas*, a sort of thick maize broth cooked with garlic, herbs, sausages and cockles presented in a deep clay pot and easily enough for two.

Moderate–Inexpensive (€€–€)
Adega Nova, Rua Francisco Barreto 24, **t** (289) 813 433. There is local bonhomie aplenty and good helpings of good-quality no-nonsense food in a beer-hall atmosphere.

Inexpensive (€)
Gengibre Canela, Rua de Mota 10, **t** (289) 822 424. A rare vegetarian restaurant in these parts, serving innovative and tasty dishes.

⭐ **Adega Rocha** >

Adega Rocha, Rua da Misericórdia 51. Just outside the Old Town walls, is a thoroughly local experience. Sit down at a table and a plate of whatever is on the barbecue will be promptly plonked down in front of you. Typically it's a plate of mixed fish with the usual potatoes and salad accompaniment.

Tasca O Chalaver, Rua Infante Dom Henrique 120, **t** (289) 822 455. Another place for a memorable local meal. You choose your dinner from a large fish-and-meat-covered slab, then it is transferred to a huge open grill which smokes away under a black hood. The white walls are soot-marked, and covered by gnarled vines which squiggle across the sloping, corrugated-iron ceiling.

Café Aliança, Rua Francisco Gomes 7, **t** (289) 801 621. Right on the seafront is a venerable Faro institution. This old rambling place serves everything from full meals to a cup of coffee. It's atmospheric when full but rather depressing and down-at-heel in the cold light of day with just a few customers spread around.

Cafés

The best place for a coffee break while doing the shopping is at the famous cafe **Gardy** on Rua de Santo António. **Cidade Velha**, just the other side of the cathedral in the Old Town, is a pleasant little snack bar, which also sprawls out onto the cobbled pavement. **Taverna do Sé**, just behind the cathedral, is worth seeking out for its mellow atmosphere (jazz or classical music often wafts through its windows).

Entertainment and Nightlife in Faro

For bars, make your way to the Rua do Prior and the Rua Conselheiro Bivar, which run parallel to the Avenida da República. There's a good choice, including the laid-back **Kingburger Bar**, Rua do Prior 40, which stays open until the early hours. **Ovelha Negra** is more modern, but it's not intimidating. Trip Hop can be wonderful in the right setting. Nautical-but-nice **Âncora Bar** feels more grown up than most, with a coffered ceiling.

Getting to and around Olhão

Frequent **buses and trains** take 15mins from Faro. For bus information, ring **t** (289) 702 157. Inexpensive **ferries to the islands** depart from the quay, a short walk from the tourist office. Buy your ticket at the kiosk before boarding. Ferries make the 15min trip to **Ilha da Armona** every 60 or 90 minutes June–Sept. (They run three times daily in May and Oct, and twice daily at other times.) Ferries to the **Ilha da Culatra** depart seven times daily June–Sept, and four times daily for the rest of the year.

Olhão

Eight kilometres east of Faro, the appealing little fishing town of Olhão is sheltered from the open sea by a series of offshore islands, which comprise part of the Rio Formosa Estuary and nature reserve. There's some very attractive architecture about if you look above street level, and an appealing park along the waterfront. Old men sell dried octopus and crabs from chipped little trestle tables. Ferries run from Olhão to the two flat islands of Armona and Culatra, hidden from view, which are fringed with uncrowded white-sand beaches.

Olhão's cubic houses with their flat roofs and external staircases were inspired by trade with North Africa, and brought a modest fame – they owe nothing to the Moors, as the town was founded in the 16th century. Its moment of glory came in 1811, when two local fishermen sailed to Rio de Janeiro in a caique without navigational charts, to tell the fugitive King Dom João VI that Napoleon's troops had left Portugal. As a reward the king granted Olhão the status of a town.

Ria Formosa Nature Reserve

The reserve was established to protect the rich variety of water birds – especially various herons – and marine life that finds a home on the sand islets between Faro and Manta Rota. Even if you haven't brought your binoculars there's a good source of information about the district's wildlife a kilometre east of Olhão

ⓘ Olhão >
Largo Sebastião Martins Mestre (walk up Rua Olhanense and it is on left), **t** *(289) 713 936; open Mon–Fri 9–12 and 2.30–5, Sat 9–12, June–Sept daily 9.30–7*

Tourist Information and Services in Olhão

Olhão's **huge fish and shellfish market** (*Mon–Fri*) occupies two large halls overlooking the harbour with silver domes at each corner. On *Saturdays* there is also a general **open-air market** outside.

What to See in Olhão

Olhão celebrates the fertility of the sea by staging a large **seafood festival** in August. The streets are awash with masticating crowds, jostling each other around long trestle tables.

The town is decaying sleepily; all the action happens at the restaurant-edged waterfront. At the centre of town stand two churches roofed with terracotta. An angel with a bell skirt serves as a weathervane for the **Igreja Matriz**, built in 1698. At the rear of the church, the **Capela dos Aflitos** (Chapel of the Suffering) is always open, for the wives of fishermen to pray during storms. To see what the seagulls see, climb to the top of the church tower (*usually open Tues–Sun 9.30–12 and 3–6, or try knocking on the adjacent door for the key*).

Where to Stay in Olhão

★★★**Pensão Bela Vista**, Rua Dr Teófilo Braga 65–67, **t** (289) 702 538 (€). The great selling point is its sunny terrace. Rooms must be reserved in advance, despite the fact that they and their windows open onto a courtyard, making the place a bit of a goldfish bowl.

★★**Pensão Boémia**, 20 Rua da Cerca, near Largo da Liberdade, **t** (289) 721 122 (€). There is an element of *La Cage aux Folles* about this place, which offers a friendly welcome in the town's little back streets. Four of the 15 rooms have terraces.

Pensão Bicuar, Rua Vasco da Gama 5, **t** (289) 714 816, *www.pension-bicuar.net* (€). Delightful small guesthouse with comfortable attractive rooms and the use of a kitchen for guests.

Olhão's **campsite** is 3km east at Marim, **t** (289) 700 300. For accommodation on Ilha da Armona, try either the **campsite**, **t** (289) 324 455, or **Orbitur**, **t** (289) 714 173, who have inexpensive bungalows.

Eating Out in Olhão

Restaurants are elbow to elbow on Avenida do 5 Outobro, opposite the harbour, offering very fresh fish.

A Bote, Avenida 5 de Outubro 122, **t** (289) 721 183 (€€). Located near the bustling market, this typical restaurant is famed locally for its superbly prepared grilled meat and seafood dishes. *Closed Sun*.

Faz Gostos, Av da República 148, **t** (289) 701 900 (€€). Enjoy innovative, French-inspired dishes such as lobster bisque with a puff pastry crust and monkfish flambéed in a champagne sauce. Another speciality is a locally inspired dish – duck breasts with figs, grapes and a port wine reduction.

Restaurant St Antoine, Ilha da Armona, **t** (289) 706 549 (€€). One to try on the islands, where Didier and Ilse bring a touch of Belgian cooking to Algarve fish dishes.

Ria Formosa, Avenida 5 de Outubro 14, **t** (289) 714 215 (€€–€). Another fish option, this time with a view of the sea and distant beaches, is in the gardens just before the fish market (coming from Faro direction).

Vai e Volta, Largo do Grémio (€). Occupying the corner of a peeling square, everything is grilled over charcoal outside and second helpings are always on offer.

For delicious *bolos* and marzipan sweets created by genial bakers, visit the **Pastelaria e Confeitaria Contreiras e Almeida** on pedestrianized Rua Dr João Lúcio, which fills with a sweet-scented cloud. The **Pastelaria Luís Palermo** serves as a community meeting point nicely off the tourist trail.

Quinta do Marim Reserva Natural da Ria Formosa
t (289) 704 134; open weekdays 9–12.30 and 2–5

Visitor Centre
open 9–5.30

at **Quinta do Marim Reserva Natural da Ria Formosa**. Within its 160 acres (60ha) is a thoughtful numbered visitor trail of well-marked paths with excellent signs in English, showing examples of various eco-systems and calling in at bird hides and a fascinating mill powered by the tides. The trail takes around two hours to cover, if you go slowly. There's also a slightly bedraggled **Visitor Centre**.

The region's most curious creature is the famed **Portuguese water dog**, which is a sort of large unkempt poodle with webbed feet. Algarvians claim that these dogs can be trained to dive several metres to chase shoals of fish into nets and, more plausibly, that they retrieve drifting tackle and nets. You can see them in kennels along the trail.

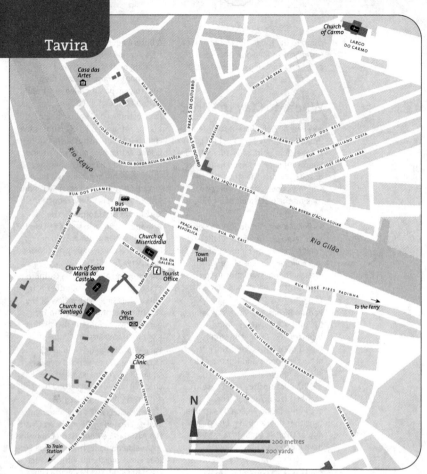

Tavira

Thirty kilometres northeast of Faro and 23km southwest of Vila Real de Santo António, the most beautiful town in the Algarve has hardly been affected by its moderate flow of visitors; the only tide to sweep through it is that of the Gilão River, whose banks are lined with both grand and humble houses, and which is crossed by a bridge originally built by the Romans.

★ Tavira

Founded by the Turduli c. 2000 BC or by the Greeks c. 400 BC, Tavira's fortune was based on tuna fishing. Shoals of the fish used to be harpooned off Faro from the end of April to the end of June, as they swam eastwards to spawn in the Mediterranean, and off Tavira, when the fish returned westwards, thinner, in July and August. Tuna are now only found on the high seas, but the Tavirans have retained a taste for the firm grey meat.

Tavira's gentle hillslopes, castle battlements and 25 churches create a lovely roofline of peaked and weathered terracotta. There are wonderful beaches nearby.

Getting to Tavira

Frequent **buses and trains** run from Faro (both ¾hr). The **bus terminus** is on Rua dos Pelames, **t** (281) 322 546, from which you turn left and walk two minutes to reach the tourist office, while the **railway station** is 1km away, along the Rua da Liberdade.

Around the Town

Tavira's ruined castle walls still top the town and give spectacular views. Immediately below, the **churches of Santa Maria and Santiago** are a beautiful, Moorish ensemble, heralded by Santa Maria's cockerel weathervane.

The **Misericórdia**, near the tourist office, has an attractive Renaissance portal, built between 1541 and 1551, with Saints Peter and Paul at its corners. There is a fine pair of 18th-century bench seats in the **Carmo church** (cross the river and go through the Largo de São Braz; collect its huge key from no.22 opposite).

Tavira has in recent years become a centre for local artists and writers. There are regular exhibitions of local art at **Galeria Municipal**, part of the town hall on Praça da República, the **Casa das Artes** on Rua João Vaz Corte Real and the beautifully converted **Palácio da Galeria** on Calçada da Galeria.

15 The Algarve | Faro and the Eastern Coast: Tavira

ⓘ Tavira ›
Rua de Galeria 9,
t (281) 322 511;
open Tues–Thurs 9.30–7,
Fri–Mon 9.30–1
and 2–5.30

⭐ Hotel Villa
Galé Albacora ››

Tourist Information and Services in Tavira

The old market hall by the river, the **Ribeira Market**, is now home to shops and restaurants.

The **post office** is a two-minute walk up the Rua da Liberdade. Tavira's **SOS clinic**, **t** (281) 381 750, where English is spoken, is on Avenida Dr Mateus Teixeira de Azevedo. The **Caixa Geral bank** on Rua José Pires Padinha opposite the garden has an **automatic exchange machine**, though facilities can become stretched on summer weekends.

Activities in Tavira

Walking

Guided walking tours of the town are on offer daily from the prosaically named **Historical Itineraries of Tavira** for a small charge. Either ask at the helpful tourist office or **t** (281) 321 946 for details.

Golf

Since the turn of the millennium, Tavira has acquired three 18-hole courses. **Benamor Golf**, Quinta de Benamor, Conceiçao de Tavira, **t** (281) 320 880 *www.golfbenamor.com*, requires precision and features some memorably tricky holes. **Quinta da Ria**, Cacela Velha, **t** (281) 950 580, *www.quintadariagolf.com*, is specially peaceful, bordering the nature reserve. **Quinta de Cima**, part of the same development, provides a good challenge to golfers of all standards.

Multi-activity

Numerous operators offer horse-riding and cycling; some take in the Parque Natural de Ria Formosa. **Alcatia Domus**, **t** 966 381 001, organizes both activities, plus river trips, canoeing and other outdoor pursuits.

Where to Stay in Tavira

★★★★Hotel Vila Galé Albacora, Quatro Águas, **t** (281) 380 800, *www.vila gale.pt* (€€€€). A short drive out of town is a unique development and one of the most interesting large hotels in the Algarve. It occupies a former tuna fishing village in the Ria Formosa National Park, with the best rooms looking across the river to the Ilha de Tavira; the hotel runs six boats

⭐ **Residencial Lagôas** >>

⭐ **Convento de Santo António** >>

⭐ **Hotel Porta Nova** >

⭐ **Quinta do Caracol** >>

⭐ **Residencial Marés** >

a day to the beach there. With its chapel, museum and grid pattern, the place has a sense of history; it is low-rise but not overlooked and the staff are very friendly. The focus of most action is a shamrock-shaped pool, with good facilities. There are two restaurants: the main one is pretty standard and the fancy one is deserted. Mosquitoes are a problem – you'll be issued with two forms of insect repellent.

★★★★**Hotel Vila Galé Tavira**, Rua 4 de Outubro, **t** (281) 329 900, *www.vilagale.pt* (€€€€). Despite the North African theme of the interior decoration, this hotel never really feels unique and is not nearly as nice as its sister hotel just out of town. Opened in 2002, it is built around a courtyard with a pool, which some rooms overlook. All rooms have terraces and every night there is live entertainment in the bar.

★★★★**Hotel Porta Nova**, Rua António Pinheiro, **t** (281) 324 215, *www.hotel portanova.com* (€€€). Apart from August, when the prices hike up, offers very good value for money, particularly in June and September. It may be located in one of Tavira's duller areas, but there are very good views from the upper floors, and four-star facilities including pools and health club.

★★★**Eurotel**, Quinta das Oliveiras, **t** (281) 325 041, *www.eurotel-hotels.it/portogallo-e.htm* (€€). A couple of kilometres east of Tavira, is the Eurotel, with its adjoining villa complex of Quinta das Oliveiras. There are plenty of facilities and lovely grounds inhabited by geese, but the place is often booked up early by package-tour operators.

★★**Residencial Marés**, Rua José Pires Padinha 134–40, **t** (281) 325 815, *www.residencialmares.com* (€€). The best *pensão/residencial* in Tavira is just along the front past the converted market. It's extremely comfortable, with river views.

★★**Residencial Princesa do Gilão**, Rua Borda d'Água de Aguiar 10–12, **t** (281) 325 171 (€). Spruce, and overlooks the river, with very good views towards the main part of town.

★★**Residencial Lagôas**, Rua Almirante Cândido dos Reis 24, **t** (281) 322 252 (€). The best cheap place to stay is across the river from the Praça da República – turn right off the Praça Dr António Padinha. Small and clean, it is arranged around two levels of rooftops. There are communal fridges, and laundry facilities on one of the roofs, which make a great place to look at the stars with a bottle of wine or two. The wonderfully good-humoured landlady Maria jokes in several languages, and runs the excellent **Bica** restaurant downstairs (*see* 'Eating Out').

★**Residencial Castelo**, Rua da Liberdade 4, **t** (281) 323 942 (€). A warren of rooms, with self-catering options.

Turismo de Habitação
Convento de Santo António, 56 Rua de S. António, **t** (281) 321 573 (€€€). Behind the army barracks is a 17th-century monastery, lovingly converted and filled with antiques. It's been in the family of the charming Isabel for two centuries. The six bedrooms retain the peaceful aura of monks' cells. If luxury is more your line, opt for the suite. The watchtower overlooks the salt marshes, and the circular swimming pool is flanked by an ancient bucket-mill well. Guests are free to eat or linger in the central courtyard. Excellent value for the warmest of welcomes.

Quinta do Caracol, São Pedro, **t** (281) 322 475, *www.quintadocaracol.com* (€€€). On the landward side of the railway station is a wonderful 200-year-old converted farmhouse, whitewashed and draped with bougainvillea. Each of the seven homey apartments (one for two persons; the rest for four to five) includes a basic kitchenette and a shower room; some overlook the raised circular pool, once used for washing laundry, now painted and intended for wallowing. Other facilities include a hard tennis court and a bar frequented by the resident owners and their family.

Casa Camaleōn, Sitio do Valongo, **t** (281) 370 887, *www.casa camaleon.net* (€€). Six kilometres east of Tavira, along the road to Vila Real, turn inland for 1.5 km following signs for Cumeada to get to a villa under the Turismo Rural scheme. A peaceful place in a style Elle Decoration would love: beautiful colours used sparingly, ceiling fans, furniture when it's necessary, a shaded patio and quarried stone. There's neither pool nor dinner, but if that's not a problem this is a very good choice for a holiday away from the resorts.

Quinta da Fonte do Bispo, 270 Estrada Nacional Santa Catarina, **t** (281) 971 484, *www.qtfontebispo.com* (€€). Lying some 11km northwest of Tavira on the road to São Brás, this converted farmhouse lounges in 15 acres (6ha) of wooded land, which includes a swimming pool and tennis courts. The six self-catering apartments are stone-floored and wood-beamed, with a bedroom, kitchenette and a sitting room with sofa beds. An equally rustic bar and breakfast room opens on to a flower-draped patio. The new owners also organize regular jazz concerts, wine tastings and similar.

Tourist Villages

Both **Pedras d'el Rei**, Santa Luzia, 3km west of Tavira, **t** (281) 325 354 (€€), and **Pedras d'el Rainha**, Cabanas, 5km east of Tavira, **t** (281) 320 182 (€€), are well designed and close to undeveloped beaches. Villas overlook shared lawns, so the sites feel spacious and private, while the interiors are simply furnished in cool local materials. Both villages incorporate a swimming pool, restaurant, post and telephone facilities, babysitter and a well-stocked supermarket, which sells firewood for chilly winter evenings. The beach is a short walk away. Villas range in size from 2 to 10 beds.

Eating Out in Tavira

In Tavira itself there are lots of places to eat along the riverfront.

Quatro Águas, Quatro Águas, **t** (281) 325 329 (€€). On the harbour where the ferry departs for the Ilha is a cool, elegant restaurant with a fish tank of beady-eyed crustaceans.

Taska Abstrakto, Rua António Cabreira (€€). If you've got time on your hands,

try this delightfully Bohemian little place dishing up fabulous Portuguese food, prepared by a French chef and served by a beguiling French lady with an eye patch. Call in a day ahead to request the *cataplana*. *Open evenings only.*

O Patio Restaurante, Rua António Cabreira 30, **t** (281) 323 008 (€€). Atmospheric, very tastefully decorated, with a rooftop terrace and service that will make you guffaw. *Closed Sun.*

Imperial, 22 Rua José Pires Padinha, **t** (281) 322 234 (€€). A little closer to the centre of town, Imperial is always bustling and is renowned for its fish. *Closed Wed.*

O Caneção, 162 Rua José Pires Padinha, **t** (281) 325 260 (€€). If *cataplana* is your thing, you will get the widest possible selection further along the quayside. Here they modestly boast of producing the world's best. What is for sure is that they wok up some unusual varieties, including lamb. *Closed Thurs.*

Aquasul, Rua Dr Augusto da Silva Carvalho 11–13 (€). Cosy restaurant on the north side of the river with sassy staff. It's the place to go if your stomach is rebelling against fresh fish; good pizzas and starters provide variety.

Carmina, Rua José Pires Padinha 96, **t** (281) 322 236 (€). For a good cheap fish meal aim for the down-to-earth Carmina. It's festooned with fishing paraphernalia, full of salty old sea dogs and right opposite the fish auction. *Closed Sun.*

Avenida, Avenida Dr Mateus Teixeira de Azevedo, **t** (281) 321 113 (€). Ordinary-looking place with good *arroz de marisco*. *Closed Tues.*

Bica, Rua Almirante Cândido dos Reis 24, **t** (281) 322 252 (€). Very plain but serves a range of beautifully prepared food including the most delicious fresh tuna steaks, cooked with onions in butter. The massive portions are very good value and the house wine is very drinkable.

Vela 2, Rua Poço do Bispo, **t** (281) 323 661 (€). This fun place is Benfica-crazy and serves good grilled fish, too.

⭐ Carmina >>

⭐ Bica >>

 ⭐ Taska Abstrakto >

Entertainment and Nightlife in Tavira

A metallic hangar on the outskirts of town houses Tavira's best disco, **UBI**, a popular venue which hosts different party nights. Follow Rua Almirante Cândido dos Reis to the edge of town; the disco is in a large warehouse on the right. It's open from 11pm to very late. You can get there earlier and get in the mood at its **Bubi Bar** (open nightly in summer, Fri and Sat in winter).

Competition comes from the **Refi Café**, Rua Gonçalo Velho (south of the river almost on the front, to the left of the Roman Bridge). In summer it opens from 9pm until 3am, playing drum 'n' bass, acid jazz, jungle and other dance beats; in winter it reverts to being more of a music bar, with weekend-only and occasional events.

There are a number of fairly desultory bars in the Rua Poeta Emiliano Costa; try **Dom Manuel**. **Arco Bar**, Rua Almirante Cândido dos Reis 67, it is popular with a gay and straight crowd. The atmosphere is mellow.

The **Cine-Teatro António Pinheiro**, Largo Marcelino Franco, screens both arthouse films and blockbusters.

East of Tavira

Cabanas

A short walk from Conceição, 5km east of Tavira, Cabanas is a simple fishing village sheltered from the sea by a sandbank, with many restaurants on its promenade. Squelch out to the sandspit at low tide, when the locals are digging for shellfish with trowels, and when fossils can be found on the beach at the end of the coast road. The beach is popular with families, but not exclusively so. The mainland sandy beach is backed by grassy dunes and a ruined fort.

Cacela Velha

If anywhere in the Algarve deserves the epithet 'unspoilt', it's the hamlet of Cacela Velha, on the coast 3km east of Cabanas. Surrounded by ploughed fields, the settlement clusters around a whitewashed church and a little 18th-century fortress perched atop a cliff.

Most of the mainland beach has been colonized by silvery bushes, but there are sheltered spots among them where you can sunbathe and picnic, or you could try to persuade someone to row you over to the sand spit that shelters Cacela from the sea (at low tide you can even walk across). This is a great place to watch the sun go down to the sound of tinkling goat bells.

Monte Gordo

A little farther on, 4km west of Vila Real de Santo António, the rather joyless modern resort of Monte Gordo has little to recommend it. Grid-patterned streets of no-frills houses with gardens are being elbowed out by lofty hotels and large restaurants, which vie for space overlooking the very wide white beach that is popular with the British and Dutch.

Vila Real de Santo António

At the eastern tip of the Algarve, the frontier town and tuna-processing port of Vila Real de Santo António vegetates at the mouth of the River Guadiana. A bridge crosses to Ayamonte in Spain.

When Dom José ascended to the throne in 1750, the Portuguese bank of the Guadiana was deserted south of Castro Marim. The Marquês de Pombal ordered the town to be built in five months in 1774, on the site of a settlement flushed away by a tidal wave *c.* 1600. This was to be the headquarters of the pilchard- and tuna-fishing industry; to ensure the success of his venture, Pombal ordered Monte Gordo to be burnt flat. The layout resembles that adopted by Pombal in the reconstruction of Lisbon (wide streets cut into squares) but has none of Lisbon's elegance.

Since the construction of the road bridge, Vila Real has lost most of its ferry traffic and suffered a commercial decline. Recently however, the town seems to have spruced itself up, most noticeably in the conversion of the splendid old Moorish-style market building, topped by bright yellow domes to become the **Centro Cultural**, with regular exhibitions of art and music and the **Manuel Cabanas Museum** with its remarkable collection of woodcut art. You'll find it just off the main square along the pedestrianized Rua Téofilo Braga.

Manuel Cabanas Museum
t (281) 580 045; open daily 10–5

The main square, **Praça Marquês de Pombal**, is furnished with a church, an obelisk, dragons' tooth paving and a border of trimmed orange trees – a pleasant place for a drink at one of the many cafés.

ⓘ Monte Gordo >
on the beachfront just before the casino, t (281) 544 495; open summer 9.30–7; shorter hours in winter

Services in Monte Gordo

Bicycles may be hired at Rua Pedro Álvares Cabral 23, near the pharmacy.

Sports and Activities in Monte Gordo

There are a few **water sports** operators on the beach in Monte Gordo.

Boat Trips

The gently winding Guadiana, smooth and banked with rich greenery, is navigable as far as Mértola (*see* p.450). Boat trips up the River Guadiana from Monte Gordo are run by **Riosul**, Rua Tristão Vaz Teixeira 15, t (281) 510 200, *www.riosul travel.com*. They also do Jeep safaris alongside the river or you can combine the two into a 'Super Safari'. You can also book a trip with **Turismar** in Monte Gordo, t (281) 513 504; they depart Vila Real most days in high season at 9.30am, going upstream as far as Alcoutim (*see* p.482).

Where to Stay East of Tavira

Around Cacela Velha

Cantinho da Ria Formosa Residencial Rural, Ribeiro de Junco, 8900-057 Vila Nova de Cacela, t (281) 951 837/699, *www.cantinhoriaformosa.com* (€€). Just west of Cacela Velha is a simple blue-and-white farmhouse with views to the golf course and horses to rent.

Monte Gordo

★★★★**Hotel Casablanca**, Praceta Casablanca, t (281) 511 444, *www.casablancain.pt* (€€). Set back from the beach and is equipped with small indoor and outdoor swimming pools, a poolside snack bar and a walled sun area. Bedrooms are both cool and attractive.
Hotel Baia, Rua Diogo Cão, t (281) 510 500, *www.hotelbaia.net* (€€). Clean and functional.

(i) **Vila Real de Santo António** >

Centro Cultural, Rua Téofilio Braga, t (281) 542 100; open daily 10–5

★★**Pensão Monte Gordo**, Avenida Infante Dom Henrique, **t** (281) 542 125 (€). Modern and favoured for its spot on the seafront.

Vila Real de Santo António

★★★**Hotel Guadiana**, Avenida da República, **t** (281) 511 482, *www.hotelguadiana.com.pt* (€€). Hotel in the grand style with several national flags flapping outside and a sweeping staircase within. The large air-conditioned rooms are good value, tastefully furnished and modern, with a television in every room.

Villa Marquês, Rua Dr José Barão 61, **t** (281) 530 420 (€). A friendly place with bright rooms, plus a rooftop terrace with sweeping views.

Youth hostel, 40 Rua Dr Sousa Martins, **t** (281) 544 565 (€). A cheap option is the town's modern youth hostel.

Camping

There is a **campsite** 2km inland from Vila Nova at Caliço, **t** (281) 951 195.

Monte Gordo's **campsite** is on the road to Vila Real, **t** (281) 542 588.

Eating Out East of Tavira

Around Cacela Velha

 O Costa >

O Costa , Fábrica, **t** (281) 952 297 (€€). For a wonderful meal off the tourist trail, this is about as good as it gets. It's on the beachfront, overlooking moored motorboats and sky-blue water, under a leafy trellis – the perfect setting for a grilled tuna steak. You won't be alone: the locals fill the place, although there is a menu in English.

A Camponesa >

A Camponesa , off the main road, Vila Nova de Cacela, **t** (281) 951 351 (€€).

The sole reason for going to Vila Nova de Cacela, 2km further east, is to eat huge portions of wonderfully fresh grilled fish at low prices here. The surroundings are about as simple as you can get: concrete floor, corrugated-iron roof, formica tables, paper placemats, and no walls. It's a popular restaurant full of people delighted to have found The Real Thing.

Casa Velha, Cacela Velha, **t** (281) 952 297 (€). A good place to sit outside after watching the sun go down.

Monte Gordo

Copacabana, Avenida Infante Dom Henrique, **t** (281) 541 536 (€€€). Serves reliable Portuguese and Italian food on a fragrant terrace surrounded by flowers.

Maharaja Patiala Tandoori, Rua Goncalo Velho, **t** (281) 543 206 (€€–€). Choose from around 100 dishes from Northern India including starters, tandoori specials, curry dishes, balti dishes and vegetarian and vegan choices. Don't miss the mango lassi!

O Tapas, Rua Pedro Vaz Caminha 24, **t** (281) 541 847 (€€–€). Still packs in the locals and serves them large portions of good fish and seafood. *Closed Mon.*

Vila Real de Santo António

Caves do Guadiana, 90 Avenida da República, **t** (281) 544 498 (€€). Renowned for its superlative seafood. *Closed Thurs.*

Nightlife

The **casino** on Avenida Infante Dom Henrique, Monte Gordo, **t** (281) 512 224, opens at 6pm and will invite you to roll the dice till 4am. Remember to take your passport.

Up the River Guadiana and Inland

This is the Algarve that tourists haven't yet discovered. The stunningly beautiful River Guadiana winds its way from the Serra do Caldeirão, through fertile, cultivated valleys lined with wild arum lilies and explosions of orange-topped cacti. The landscape has changed little down the ages; neither have some of the farming methods. The Barrocal locals are positively jaunty, but they bear the burden of poverty.

If the Guadiana's still, clean waters sound appealing, you may be able to charter a boat at Vilamoura and sail the river. If you're not a sailor, the best way to explore this area is by car. A sturdy vehicle is best suited to negotiating some of the secondary roads. Buses are infrequent, so it's common to see pairs of women laden with baskets of herbs hitching by the roadside. Few speak English, so you may need to communicate with smiles and gestures. Spring is the most glorious time to visit; amid the cork oaks, pines and eucalyptus, rock roses bloom from a multicoloured carpet of wild flowers.

Castro Marim

Sheep wade through the marshes 4km north of Vila Real de Santo António, and emerge with dirty underbellies. Their shepherds hail from Castro Marim, a little town which is more impressive from a distance than close to. It is set in the lee of a hill topped by a semi-circular **Castelo**, built by Dom João IV on foundations laid by Dom Afonso III in the 13th century. Dom João IV was also responsible for the construction of the **Fortress of São Sebastião** on a hill opposite. Inside the Castelo there is an unimpressive little **archaeological museum** and the 14th-century **Igreja de Santiago**, which is distinguished solely by its association with Henry the Navigator (see p.517), who worshipped here when he visited Castro Marim. Dom Dinis granted Castro Marim to the Order of Christ, recently founded to replace the disgraced Knights Templar. The town served as their headquarters until their removal to Tomar in 1334.

Castro Marim's other feature of interest is the **Reserva do Sapal** nature reserve, whose headquarters are in the former fortress, and who publish maps of a marshy 4½-mile (7km) walk past fenland and commercial salt pans. Keep an eye out for waterbirds such as the flamingo and avocet picking their long-legged way through the shallow-water feeding grounds.

North of Castro Marim

A rewarding drive 40km north to Alcoutim takes in beautiful countryside and passes through the tiny villages of **Monte Francisco**, **Junqueira** and **Azinhal**. If Castro Marim is small and sleepy, these villages are tiny and comatose. **Odeleite** is a small settlement on the river, built in a gully so the houses are piled on top of one another. Red and pink bougainvillaea cascades down the white house fronts, and low stone walls crumble slowly.

Castelo
open daily 10–6, winter until 5

Archaeological museum
open daily 10–1 and 3–6, winter until 5; adm

Reserva do Sapal
open daily dawn to dusk

(i) **Castro Marim >**
Rua José Alves Moreira,
t *(281) 531 232*

(i) **Alcoutim >**
*Praça da República
(just up the road from
the church),* **t** *(281) 546
179; officially open
9.30–5.30*

Tourist Information in Castro Marim/Alcoutim

Castro Marim's **tourist office** may be able to help you find accommodation in private houses.

If you want to stay in Alcoutim early in the year, to see the spring flowers, ask around for a room or enquire at the often shut **tourist office**.

Sports and Activities in Castro Marim/Alcoutim

Castro Marim Golfe, Sitio de Lavajinho, **t** (281) 510 330, *www.castromarimgolfe.com*. The Atlantic Course is an 18-hole golf course laid out on attractive rolling terrain.

Jeep safaris and boat trips up the Guadiana depart from Vila Real de Santo António and Monte Gordo (*see* p.479). The tourist office staff in Alcoutim can also give you details of daily boat trips on the river. The boat winds south to Foz de Odeleite, or cruises north to Mértola

and sometimes Spain. The journeys in either direction are hazily beautiful.

Where to Stay and Eat in Castro Marim/Alcoutim

Accommodation is scarce, but it may be possible to find a room in someone's house in one of the larger villages such as Cachopo or Barranco do Velho.

Estalagem do Guadiana, Alcoutim, **t** (281) 540 120, *www.grupof barata.com* (€€). Family-friendly place near the river with decent little rooms and a nice swimming pool. Service in the restaurant is somewhat inefficient.

O Soeiro, Alcoutim, **t** (281) 546 241 (€). This plain restaurant with a terrace near the quay doubles as a *pensão* in summer.

One of the Algarve's best **youth hostels**, **t** (281) 546 004, is just out of Alcoutim. It is set in a lovely position overlooking the river, and bicycles and canoes can be rented here.

Alcoutim

The village of Alcoutim rests on the bank of the River Guadiana, mirrored across the water by the Spanish village of Sanlúcar de Guadiana, close enough to hear the braying of a Spanish donkey and the chiming of Spanish church bells, one hour ahead of Portugal's. The Spanish side looks more prosperous – it will cost you a €1 boat fare to verify this.

Castle
open daily 9–5.30

One corner of the otherwise plain 14th-century ruined **castle** , at the highest point in the village, is planted with daisies and set with trestle tables; it makes a lovely place to picnic, overlooking a poultry yard and the river. The castle is also home to a small archaeological museum tracing the history of other castles on this site.

Archaeological museum
*open Tues–Sat
9–12.30 and 2–5.30;
adm*

A 17th-century low relief of John the Baptist is set into the corner of the **Igreja Matriz** by the river.

Inland from Alcoutim to the Barrocal

The Barrocal region, named after the limestone that underlies most of the northeastern Algarve, makes up about a quarter of the province, but is sparsely populated and little visited. It is bounded by Alcoutim and Ameixial in the north, and by Castro Marim and São Brás de Alportel in the south. Very little happens in between to dilute rural life, far removed from the busy, bright and beer-soaked resorts of Albufeira or Quarteira. The limestone mountains of the Serra do Caldeirão reach just half the height of Monchique's peaks, but their inhabitants are locked in a stronger time warp. Small white hamlets are scattered irregularly in the valleys, surrounded by sloping farmland which defies the use of tractors or other modern machinery. Crops are planted and harvested by hand, by men and women with deeply lined faces.

The N124 road between **Alcoutim** and the small village of **Cachopo** passes through some stunning countryside. Continuing from Alcoutim, turn south just before you reach Martim Longo onto the 506 to Vaqueiros to visit the ancient copper mine, also known as the **Parque Mineiro Cova dos Mouros**, located in the Foupana Ecological Park. The site dates back to a Chalcolithic settlement around 2300 BC, of which there's a reconstruction. A self-guided tour, with good captions in English, covers the surface workings, including the crumbling miners' accommodation and shafts, run by the British from the mid-19th century until the mine closed in the 1930s.

Parque Mineiro Cova dos Mouros
t *(289) 999 229, minacovamouros.site pac.pt; open Mar–Oct 10.30–6, Nov–mid-Dec 10.30–4.30; closed mid-Dec to late Jan*

A few kilometres southwest of Martim Longo, just past **Barrada**, feast on the view of the Foupana River as it weaves through brown hills dappled with trees and squat bushes, and striped with terraced crops. the best way to enjoy the view is to walk the 10km to **Corte Serrano**.

The road from the tiny snoozing village of Cachopo to Tavira is one of the most scenic in the Algarve. For the first couple of kilometres it runs along a mountain ridge with a sheer drop on either side, plunging into deep valleys and rising on to rounded slopes thick with pine.

Salir

Straggling down the hill beneath its castle ruins 14km north of Loulé, Salir is much vaunted as a quintessential unspoilt village. It lives up to this label, composed as it is of crumbling whitewashed bricks amid citrus, almond and fig trees. Brazenly bright-coloured climbing flowers seem to bind the low cottages together. In mid-afternoon, as you wind through the steep streets, only the sounds of daytime soap operas filter through the open doors and their beaded curtains. At the top of the village, inside the scant remains of the castle walls, the locals have made simple dwellings for themselves; the middle altitude fosters greener countryside and the views are particularly splendid here.

Inland from Faro

Estói

The Algarve's only *palácio* is decaying 9km north of Faro at **Estói** (*sporadic opening hours*). The late 18th-century building is closed to the public, but the fanciful façade and garden, mashing together styles from the neoclassical to Art Nouveau, can be viewed, if you are lucky. There are talks of the palace being converted into a luxury *pousada*.

Milreu

Roman ruins
*Rua de Faro;
open Tues–Sat 9–12.30
and 2–5.30*

A short drive west lie the **Roman ruins** at Milreu, once a patrician's villa. Little is left standing, and the site lacks atmosphere, but there are some witty fish mosaics in the baths next to the residential area. The temple consecrated to water deities dates from the 4th century. A useful English-language guide is on sale at the entrance.

Moncarapacho

Ten kilometres east of Estói lies á quiet sunny village arranged around the well-cared-for Gothic **Church of Santo Cristo**. Outside, the sculptural decoration of the clean Renaissance portal depicts Jesus bound and flanked by his captors. Inside the pillars and underside of the arches were once painted with an intricate flower design in red and black, which is fading fast. A stone's throw away, the small **parish museum** houses the whimsical collection of sacred art assembled by the local priest, now in his late eighties. Check out the 42-piece 18th-century Neapolitan nativity scene, rescued from a Faro convent.

Parish museum
*Rua de Santo Cristo,
t (289) 792 362; open
Mon, Wed and Fri 11–3*

Loulé

Twenty kilometres northwest of Estói is the Algarve's largest inland town, which is set in countryside alive with orange and lemon groves. Loulé is aesthetically undistinguished; its main attraction is as a market town and handicraft centre, with craft workers often busy in their open workshops. The artisans, many of Moorish origin, have been practising basket weaving, lacemaking, pottery and copper work since Loulé's recapture from the Moors in 1249.

Loulé's **market**, on Praça da República, is a curious building with an arabesque dome topped by the crescent moon of the Muslims. It bubbles with trade every morning, reaching a peak of activity on Saturdays. A weekly **country market** also visits the town on Saturday mornings, drawing an assortment of bargain-hungry tourists who flood Loulé. The market is wise to its powers of attraction and finding a genuine bargain is rare.

Getting to Estói and Loulé

Frequent **buses** run from Faro to Estói (15mins) and to Loulé (30mins). The **bus station** in Loulé is located on Rua Dr F. da Silva, which is off Avenida José da Costa Mealha.

Municipal Museum

*Rua Dom Paio Peres Correia, **t** (289) 400 642; open Mon–Sat 9–5.30*

The **Municipal Museum** is incorporated in what remains of the Moorish **castle** with a small but well displayed archaeological collection.

Loulé's most outlandish building perches on a hilltop some 2km west of town, visible from the town centre. The pure white dome of the Nossa Senhora da Piedade church looks like a UFO, or transport for an angel born without wings. In front stands the tiny 16th-century **Chapel of Nossa Senhora da Piedade**, crumbling quietly. On a little table by the altar there appears to be an accumulation of stray human bits. Don't be alarmed: these wax *ex votos* are an odd but touching feature of many churches. The limbs, heads, chests, breasts, stomachs, hands, babies and pigs are intended to attract divine cures. They are often heaped on altars in a promiscuous jumble, or hung from strings.

(i) **Loulé >**

*Avenida 25 de Abril, **t** (289) 463 900; open summer 9.30–5.30; winter, closes for lunch*

Services in Loulé

The **post office** is on Rua Dom Paio Peres Correia.

Festivals in Loulé

Loulé takes its festivals a good deal more seriously than the rest of the Algarve, which is generally half-hearted in its pre-Lent celebrations. The **carnival** in Loulé features a colourful procession of charming kids' floats and the usual Rio look-alikes, and is well worth a look.

The **Easter** festival of the Sovereign Mother is a more solemn occasion: on Easter Sunday, a 16th-century image of the Virgin is carried into the town from a nearby shrine and returned through crowd-lined streets two weeks later.

Shopping in Loulé

In Loulé, you can watch potters at work in the small shop signed 'Artesanaria Pottery' on Rua das Bicas Velhas. Round the corner at 19 Rua Dom Paio Peres Correia, just before the castle, is the more pricey **Casa Louart**, where you can have ceramics hand-painted to your own specifications. **Casa O Arco** on Rua dos

Almadas (underneath an arch off Praça Dom Afonso III) has some appealing plates, pottery and hand-painted *azulejos*.

Rua da Barbaça, behind the castle, is full of craft workshops: **Caldeiraria Louletana** sells all manner of things copper. Its speciality, a large hand-beaten *cataplana*, will last for ever. A few doors away, **Correaria Louletana** specializes in equestrian leatherware.

Sports and Activities in Loulé

The countryside around this area is ideal to explore on horseback, and **Quinta do Azinheiro** at Aldeia de Tôr, which is located some 8km north of Loulé, **t** (289) 415 991, has a large stable of fine horses for hire at reasonable rates.

Where to Stay Inland from Faro

★★★★**Estalagem Monte do Casal**, Cerro do Lobo, **t** (289) 991 503, *www.montedocasal.pt* (€€€). From Estói take the road towards Moncarapacho to get to this pleasantly converted tranquil 18th-century farmhouse, set in lush, fragrant grounds with a rustic restaurant, spa and well-shaded pool. This haven of tranquility is no secret, so make your reservations early. The restaurant (€€€) serves carefully prepared regional food, proffered by polite staff.

★★★**Loulé Jardim Hotel**, Largo Manuel de Arriga, Loulé, **t** (289) 413 094, *www.loulejardimhotel.com* (€€). This understated place is the town's only hotel. It occupies the corner of a lovely square fanned by the hazy purple blooms of jacaranda trees. Modern and well-designed, the rooms are built around a small and sunny quadrangle. Abundant plants and flowery sofas enhance the cool fresh feeling of the public rooms.

Pousada

Pousada de São Brás, **t** (289) 842 305, central reservations **t** (218) 442 001, *www.pousadas.pt* (L1 C). Two kilometres north of São Brás de Alportel, 16km north of Faro, a grassy driveway curves up a gentle hill to the low-key *pousada*. The main reason for coming here is peace and quiet; rooms are a reasonable size and pleasantly decorated in an elegant and tasteful modern-meets-traditional style. They are air-conditioned, though there is no television or radio. Grounds include a swimming pool and a tennis court. However, the food is disappointing and the atmosphere in the dining room is over-formal.

Eating Out in Loulé

Bica Velha, Martim Moniz 17, behind the castle (€€€). Loulé's best-known and most acclaimed restaurant, serving first-class regional food. Note that it is only open in the evenings (*Mon–Sat*).

A Muralha, Martim Moniz 41, **t** (289) 412 629 (€€). Set in a lovely bougainvillea-decked rustic garden, this *churrasqueira* includes among its specialities *cataplanas*, *feijoada de mariscos* (beans and shellfish) and of course grilled fish and *espetada* (kebabs).

Os Tibetanos, Rua Almeida Garrett 8, **t** (289) 462 067 (€). Excellent vegetarian restaurant with more salad choice than you can shake a carrot stick at, plus vegan choices.

La Baguette, Avenida 25 de Abril 2, no tel. It's all in the name – excellent baguette sandwiches with a tasty range of fillings.

A more interesting dining experience, if you have your own transport, is to be had at one of the many excellent rustic restaurants just outside Loulé. The following are favourites with locals and ex-pats (all are family-owned and have unpredictable hours, so be sure to book ahead):

O Paixanito, on the Querença road, **t** (289) 412 775 (€€€).

A Carruagem, on the road to Quarteira, **t** (289) 412 775 (€€).

Moinho do Ti Casa, on the road to Querença, **t** (289) 438 108 (€€).

From Almancil to Albufeira

The most intensively developed stretch of the coast takes its holiday trade seriously. Unfavourable publicity beset the Algarve in the 1980s, reflecting badly on rapidly expanding resorts such as Albufeira. Things are more pleasant than reports suggest: the hotels are tall, but the water is calm and clean. East of Albufeira at Falésia the coastline changes from dune-backed golden expanses of sand to precarious burnt-orange cliffs peppered with fantastic rock formations overhanging the sand and shallow water. These long beaches lure those who prefer to relax in the sun, crowds drawing crowds; more active sorts will be attracted by the watersports and golf courses. But, although people flock to the popular strands, lurking among the cliffs there are still quiet coves.

Almancil

Almancil is a dusty traffic-choked feeder town for the major golfing resorts nearby, and sprawls between two horribly busy main roads. Just between the two roads, however, tucked away in its own little hamlet, is the much-visited **Church of São Lourenço**. It is covered with astonishingly beautiful *azulejos* depicting the life of the saint, dated 1730 and signed by Policarpo de Oliveira Bernardes. The tiles have been designed to complement the architectural features of the church, and the best examples are found in the trompe-l'œil cupola.

The **Centro Cultural de São Lourenço** which occupies a terrace of 200-year-old houses down the street from the church is one of the Algarve's hidden gems. It hosts the work of local artists, but the real treat is the delightful sculpture garden, which is full of witty surprises. Young children in particular will enjoy the giant insects and animals ingeniously fashioned from scrap metal.

Further downhill, almost right alongside the thundering EN125, **A Tralha Antiguidades** is worth a look if your idea of souvenirs inclines more towards antique telescopes and Louis XIV chairs than hideous pottery cockerels. They have bigger branches in Albufeira and Portimão.

Vale do Lobo and Quinta do Lago

Vale do Lobo and Quinta do Lago are what the brochures call 'Sportugal' – purpose-built luxury resorts that are dedicated primarily to golf and tennis. Serious money bankrolls these resorts, keeping the roads wide, the bushes trimmed and the vast villas hidden behind pines and careful landscaping. Shops are cosmopolitan chic, discos spangly and many-tiered, and pricey restaurants provide food from countries around the world. Golf buggies ferry expensively coiffured women across the fairways.

Quarteira

Quarteira, on the coast just east of Vilamoura, 6km from the east–west highway, is a jungle of apartment-hotels overlooking a very long, sandy stretch of beach. The beach stretches all the way to Faro, whence frequent buses make the 30-minute journey. However, for all its aesthetic failings Quarteira, unlike its posh neighbour Vilamoura, still has a Portuguese heart. You'll find it near the fish market where grizzled old salts mill around and where a clutch of small, cheap fish restaurants offer excellent value.

Church of São Lourenço
admission by guided tour only, except during services, Mon 2.30–6, Tues–Sat 10–1, 2.30–6, closes at 5 in winter

Centro Cultural de São Lourenço
t (289) 395 475; open Tues–Sun 10–7

Quarteira is famous for its **Gypsy Market**, the largest in the Algarve, drawing coachloads from far and near. If you are in town on a Wednesday morning – and it is amusing for the hullabaloo and crowds, if not the merchandise – then you can't miss it, just across the dual carriageway.

On the main EN125 between Almancil and the Vilamoura turn-off is the smallest of the Algarve's three main waterparks, **Atlantic Park**.

Atlantic Park
t 800 204 767;
open April–Sept

Sports/Activities From Almancil to Albufeira

Golf

Some of the continent's best championship golf courses are to be found here.

San Lorenzo, t (289) 396 522, *www.san lorenzogolfcourse.com*. Consistently ranked in Europe's top five.

Quinta do Lago, t (289) 390 700, *www.quintagolf.com*. Its main (South) course has hosted the Portuguese Open eight times, and its North course (formerly known as the Ria Formosa course), is laid out in a similar style to its prestigious sister.

Pinheiros Altos, t (289) 359 910, *www.pinheirosaltos.com*. Also in Quinta do Lago, but quite independent and excellent.

Vale do Lobo, Almancil, **t** (289) 353 465, *www.valedolobo.com*. Another famous name attracting big hitters, with two 18-hole courses, the Ocean and the Royal, the latter featuring probably golf's most photographed shot, with a long carry over the ochre cliffs.

Tennis

Vale do Lobo Tennis Centre, Vale do Lobo, **t** (289) 396 991, *www.valedo lobo.com/sports/tennis-academy* is large and very well equipped.

Barrington's, Vale do Lobo, **t** (289) 396 622. Offers tennis, state-of-the-art gyms and other sports activities.

Water Sports

Many firms offer water sports packages through upmarket hotels.

Horse-riding

Paraíso dos Cavalos, Almancil, **t** (289) 394 189. One of the best known.

Where to Stay From Almancil to Albufeira

Quinta do Lago

★★★★★**Hotel Quinta do Lago, t** (289) 350 350, *www.quintadolagohotel.com* (€€€€). Surrounds itself with 1,700 acres (700ha) of pine forests and has its own private beach. The Quinta do Lago golf course is adjacent and there is a health club, watersports and tennis facilities.

Vale do Lobo

★★★★★**Dona Filipa-San Lorenzo Golf Resort, t** (289) 357 200, *www.dona filipahotel.com* (€€€€). Vale do Lobo's flagship hotel, with beautifully furnished and superbly equipped rooms, an award-winning children's club (in high season) and access to San Lorenzo golf course (*see* above).

Quarteira

Quinta dos Rochas, t (289) 393 165, *www.geocities.com/quintadosrochas* (€€€). Two km out of Quarteira on the way to Almancil. It is quietly situated, with cool rooms furnished with solid wood furniture, an outdoor swimming pool and friendly staff.

Camping

In Quarteira, there is a **campsite** 5 minutes from the beach, 1km east from the centre, **t** (289) 302 821, with good facilities.

Eating Out From Almancil to Albufeira

Several first-class international restaurants serving well-heeled golfers' appetites can be found in and around Almancil.

Julia's 1, Praia Garrão, **t** (289) 396 512 (€€€–€€), or **Julia's 2** (also known as **Barca Velha**), Vale do Lobo, **t** (289) 393 939 (€€€–€€). For top-quality beachside drinks and dining. Choose seafood and the African rice.

Nightlife From Almancil to Albufeira

The **Gecko Club**, on the Praça at Vale do Lobo, is the new place to be seen in these parts. Styled à la Gaudí, the action starts with sundowners on its beach sun deck and spills in to the early morning with dance tunes spun by hip DJs, and occasional live music.

Vilamoura

Roughly 22km northwest of Faro, and next to Quarteira beach, Vilamoura is the largest tourist development in the whole of Portugal. Although it is over 30 years old, building is still in progress – but that's not uncommon in the Algarve. High-rise hotels vie with one another for air space, though there is no heart to the settlement. Confusing collections of signs point to sports centres, golf courses and holiday villages, and it can take a little time to find your way to the **marina**, which is the main attraction of this resort, with anchorage for 1,000 yachts. It is flanked by luxury hotels and restaurants from which you can watch the rich as they hop off their boats and straight into the **casino** (*see* p.490).

Cerro da Vila Museum
t (289) 312 153; open daily 10–1 and 3–8; adm

Keep an eye out for poorly signposted steps leading to the **Cerro da Vila Museum** where Roman ruins add a touch of history to this ultra-modern resort. A small but smart, well-captioned museum has been built to house the finds.

The **Roma Golf Park** next door is an entertaining little crazy-golf course picking up the Roman theme.

Tourist Information in Vilamoura

There is no permanent **tourist office** here, but in summer a booth is erected on a corner of the marina.

Sports and Activities in Vilamoura

Golf

Oceanico Golf Resort, *www.oceanicogolf.com*, comprises five championship courses. The **Old Course** is most experienced golfers' favourite and the most prestigious, laid out in classic English style; the **Millennium** is a shortish, open course; the **Pinhal** stands in a pine forest and the average golfer will find it more forgiving than the Old Course; the tricky **Laguna** is set among the dunes with many water hazards, so it's a real test of golfing skill; the Victoria Clube de Golf is the longest course in Portugal, designed by Arnold Palmer and opened in 2004.

Vila Sol, Morgadinhos, Alto do Semino, Vilamoura, **t** (289) 300 505, *www.vilasol.pt*. This course has hosted the Portuguese Open and with its 27 holes offers various challenging permutations to golfers of all handicap levels.

Tennis

Tennis players will find over a dozen courts at swanky **Vilamouratenis**, t (289) 310 160.

Horse-riding

Horse-riding schools are plentiful. Try **Cegonha**, t (289) 302 577, www.cegonhacountryclub.com.

Water Sports

Any of the several kiosks at the far corner of the marina should be able to satisfy your water sport whims. They also offer barbecue cruises and grotto tours.

Shopping in Vilamoura

The Marina features many of the well-known European and US high-street retail names, but if you're looking for local stuff at very reasonable prices try **Casa Caravela** near the Marinotel. It's good for gifts, particularly tableware and ceramics.

Where to Stay in Vilamoura

★★★★★**Tivoli Marinotel**, t (289) 303 303, www.tivolimarinotel.com (€€€€€). This sumptuously neutral hotel offers state-of-the-art 1990s design. It is equipped with all the trimmings plus fabulous views of the marina and the sea.

Eating Out in Vilamoura

Akavit, t (289) 380 712 (€€€). Enjoy the nautical décor while sampling some of the best food in the Marina. It puts a modern European spin on old Portuguese favourites and offers several Swedish specials too.

Normandia, t (289) 313 686 (€€). More than a hint of Gallic flavour pervades Normandia, which boasts over 80 different types of beer and 40 whiskies. Their stock in trade is crêpes, but the spécialité de la maison is French-style grilled chicken.

Nightlife in Vilamoura

Casino de Vilamoura, behind the Marinotel, t (289) 310 000. Where the yachties go to be seen in the small hours. As well as gaming, it stages spectacular floor shows and includes the **Blackjack Disco Club**, which opens nightly from June through September and Thursday to Sunday from October through May.

Kadoc, www.kadoc.pt, on the Estrada de Vilamoura between Vilamoura and Albufeira, close to the EN125. One of the Algarve's longest-established clubs, pumping out high-volume Euro-thump to a young crowd. If you're over 30 and fancy a dance, but have no taste for techno, try Kadoc's more mellow club-within-a-club, **Kadoclube** (open Fri and Sat nights).

Vilamoura Jazz Club, Praça do Cinema, t (289) 316 272. A quieter after-dark option, with live jazz most nights from 10.30pm.

Albufeira

Some 39km northwest of Faro and 50km east of Lagos, the pretty, hilly seaside village of Albufeira has become Portugal's most popular package resort. Part of the settlement was submerged by a tidal wave following the earthquake of 1755; nowadays, in the summer months, Albufeira is submerged by a different kind of tidal wave – one that takes longer to subside. The whitewashed pedestrian streets seethe with sun-lovers, who are supplied with cheap beer and saucy postcards. Touts in the main square sell time-share apartments.

Getting to Albufeira

Frequent **trains** and RN **buses** run from Faro (1hr) and from Lagos (1¼hrs), stopping at each stage along the way. The Lisbon train stops here, too, and there are more than a dozen express buses from the capital (3½hrs). Daily buses come from many towns in the north and centre of Portugal as well.

Albufeira's **old town** to the west of this spreading resort still has a distinctive character, even if every other building is a restaurant or bar. The east is completely suburban, with hotels and apartments filling in every inch of space. It reaches its nadir in Montechoro, an unappealing strip of burger joints and English-style pubs.

Just to prove that Albufeira is not entirely the culture-free zone that a cursory glance might suggest, a smart **Museum of Archaeology** has opened a few steps uphill from the Sol e Mar hotel, on the Praça da República.

Museum of Archaeology
open Tues–Sun
10.30–5 Oct–May and
2.30–8 June–Sept

There are also free guided walks around Old Albufeira from February to June. Ask at the Albufeira tourist office for details.

(i) **Albufeira >**
Rua 5 de Outubro
(on the way to the
beach tunnel),
t (289) 585 279,
www.cm-albufeira.pt

Tourist Information/ Services in Albufeira

The **post office** is next door to the tourist office.

It's a five-minute walk from the **bus station**, t (289) 589 755, to the centre of town; to get to the tourist office, walk along the Avenida da Liberdade, turn right at the tip of the gardened Largo Eng. Duarte Pacheco, then turn left into the Rua 5 de Outubro. The **train station**, t (289) 571 616, is 6km north of town at Ferreiras, with connecting buses marked *Estação*.

There are two **medical centres** in Albufeira, dealing with the usual sun- and drink-related ailments: one on Areia de São João to the east of the old town, t (289) 587 326; the other, **Clioura**, has a doctor on call 24 hours, t (289) 587 000.

Shopping in Albufeira

Albufeira is chock-a-block with tourist tat, and it can be hilarious looking at the illuminated stalls which line the streets in the centre on warm summer evenings. For rugs, shawls and other handicrafts head for the **Santa Casa da Misericórdia** on Rua 5 de Outubro. Profits support orphaned, disabled or elderly locals. Just off the same street, almost opposite the tourist office on Rua João de Deus, is the dusty **A Tralha Antiguidades**, a fascinating collection of Portuguese and Algarvian antiquities, most of them far too large to fit in your suitcase. Shops selling multi-cultural ethnic art and jewellery, mostly from North Africa, are common here, as in much of the Algarve. **Tribu**, at No.13, on the lower part of Montechoro's hideous Avenida Sá Carneiro ('The Strip'), stands out from the dross surrounding it.

The most civilized place to buy your booze is **Garrafeira Soares** in the square. It has an excellent selection at keen prices and a tapas bar upstairs where you can taste a wide range of wines, ports, *aguardentes* and Portuguese liqueurs. For second-hand English-language **books**, try Julie's, Rua Igreja Nova 6. The daily **market** sells the usual fish, fruit and veg every morning except Mondays on Rua do Mercado. The **gypsy market** comes to the north of the town, by the municipal market, on the first and third Tuesday of the month.

Sports and Activities in Albufeira

Salgados Golf Club, Vale do Rabelho, Albufeira, **t** (289) 583 030, *www.portugalgolfe.com/courses/salgados.htm*. Albufeira's only 18-hole, links-style golf course is near Galé beach. It has more water hazards than any other course in the Algarve.

Sheraton Algarve Pine Cliffs, Praia da Falésia, Albufeira, **t** (289) 500 113, *www.luxurycollection.com*, and the **Balaia Golf Village**, Balaia, Albufeira, **t** (289) 570 442, *www.balaiagolfvillage.com*, are challenging par-3, nine-hole holiday golf courses.

Montechoro Hotel, **t** (289) 588 486, *www.hotelmontechoro.pt*. This landmark hotel is a good one-stop sporting activities shop. It has numerous tennis courts, and its beach club organizes water sports, including diving.

Where to Stay in Albufeira

Note that most of Albufeira's cheaper accommodation is located in and around Rua Cândido dos Reis and Rua São Gonçalo de Lagos, which is fine if you want to party, but less conducive to an early night, i.e. any time before 4am.

★★★Hotel Rocamar, Largo Jacinto d'Ayet, **t** (289) 540 280, *www.rocamarbeachhotel.com* (€€€). Along the road from the Church of Sant'Ana, it provides standard, airy rooms, with private balconies overlooking the beach.

★★★Vila São Vicente, Largo Jacinto d'Ayet, **t** (289) 583 700, *www.saovicente-hotel.com* (€€€). A bit more of an uphill walk from the beach than will be welcome to some, but still very centrally located, this is a very civilized place; it is an attractive and solid building with 30 rooms and excellent sea views.

★★Residencial Vila Bela, Rua Coronel Águas 32–34, **t** (289) 515 535 (€€). Still on the quieter west side, this hotel is attractively layered and beflowered, with bright rooms and balconies overlooking the small swimming pool.

★★Residencial Vila Recife, Rua Miguel Bombarda 12, **t** (289) 583 740, *monicabarret@gmail.com* (€€). Really a villa, with a very nice hotel wing and great views of the town. With its own pool, it offers good value, and a hint of Club 18–30 high jinks.

★★Pensão Maritim, Praia do São Rafael, west of Albufeira, **t** (289) 591 005 (€€). Nice rooms. The friendly owner welcomes independent travellers and provides local information. The third-floor restaurant offers good views to the beach. A minibus runs guests into Albufeira or you can walk there over the cliffs in about 30 minutes.

Pensão Dianamar Residencial, Rua Latino Coelho 36, **t** (289) 587 801, *www.dianamar.com* (€). A delightful Scandinavian-run pension with pretty rooms and a lovely roof terrace. Some rooms have balconies and sea views.

★★★Residencial Vila Branca, Rua do Ténis, **t** (289) 586 804 (€). Just inland of the Largo Jacinto d'Ayet, provides very smart rooms with air-conditioning and TV, and a nicely furnished bar, all overseen by the friendly receptionist. Breakfast is provided. *Closed Nov–Mar*.

★★★Residencial Frentomar, Rua Latino Coelho, **t** (289) 512 005 (€). West of the Old Town is a modern, quiet option. Its sea-view rooms overlook the whole of Albufeira's beachfront. Rooms are fairly basic (no air-conditioning or TV) but bright and airy, and there is a TV room and a snooker room.

★★★Pensão Silva, Travessa André Rebelo, **t** (289) 512 669 (€). Down an alley opposite the tourist office, offering six pleasant rooms in an old building with flaking ceilings.

Camping

A **campsite** is located about 1.5km north of Albufeira at Alpouvar, **t** (289) 587 629, *www.campingalbufeira.net*. It's very well equipped, boasting the highest grading of four stars, with restaurant and snack bar, a swimming pool and tennis courts.

Eating Out in Albufeira

A Ruina, Largo Cais Herculano, **t** (289) 512 094 (€€€). Overlooking the beach, near the fish market, is this fun place to eat delicious seafood. The lower part is more atmospheric: it features dripping candles, turtle shells, stone-studded walls, tree-trunk tables and the menu on a blackboard. Some diners choose to sit in a cordoned-off area right on the beach.

O Dias, Praça Miguel Bombarda 2, **t** (289) 515 246 (€€€). West of the old town on the clifftop, you can sit on the sunny balcony and watch your meal sizzle on the grill and your compatriots sizzle on the beach.

Cabaz da Praia, Praça Miguel Bombarda 7, **t** (289) 512 137 (€€€), West of the old town on the clifftop, this is a romantic treat. The name means beach basket, but this is no mere picnic. The chef and owner are French, and the food is a superb marriage of Gallic and Portuguese cuisine. *Closed Thurs and lunchtime Sat.*

Atrium, Rua 5 de Outubro 20, **t** (289) 515 755 (€€). A short walk away on the other side of the hill, this occupies the glitzy ballroom of an old theatre. The food isn't great, but there are regular performances of *fado* and folk music.

A Taberna do Pescador, Travessa Cais Herculano, **t** (289) 589 196 (€€). A sprawling seafood restaurant with pavement seating and a great choice of catch of the day dishes, which are mainly served grilled.

Tasca do Viegas, Rua Cais Herculano 2, **t** (289) 514 087 (€€). For good local food, with less emphasis on fish. Their *arroz de tamboril* (monkfish rice) is delicious and reasonably priced for two people to share.

Casa da Fonte, Rua João de Deus 7, **t** (289) 514 578 (€€). The main attraction here is the secluded open-air patio, where you can dine beneath lemon trees and grape vines. There's a nice bar, too. *Closed Mon.*

O Penedo, Rua Latino Coelho, **t** (289) 587 429 (€). On the clifftop, by the Residencial Frentomar. The beautiful little terrace takes advantage of the curve of the cliff to offer unbeatable views along the beach. The food is interesting and tasty, the prices are very reasonable given the location, and the staff are friendly, young and cosmopolitan. Good for vegetarians.

Entertainment and Nightlife in Albufeira

After dark head for **Rua Cândido dos Reis** and **Rua São Gonçalo de Lagos**, which are composed almost entirely of late-night bars and restaurants. Walk down here in the height of summer and every few steps offers a fresh assault on the senses: one thumping tune drowns out another as people dance on your feet and neon dazzles your vision. One block back from Fisherman's Beach, 'Music Street' is home to Albufeira town's main disco, **7½**, which features live bands as well as canned sounds, and the grungey delights of **Snoopy's Bar**. Beer-fuelled fun lasts until about 4, then everyone goes to **Kiss** disco on Areia de São João until 7am.

If you like Kiss you'll enjoy **Liberto's** (they are under the same management). It has an open-air terrace where you can take a breather from the wild goings-on. Or try **Locomia** right on the beach at Santa Eulália. Here you can hear the latest hip-hop, house or salsa sounds from sultry South America. Guest DJs from all over the world drop in.

For less ear-splitting sounds head along the clifftop west to **Bizarro's**, a bar where the Woodstock generation will feel right at home. The charming long-haired laid-back owner has been here for 30 years and has regular live acoustic music. The perfect place to sip a *caiparinha* cocktail and watch the sun set.

From Albufeira to Alvor

The beaches between Albufeira and Alvor are long enough to allow plenty of opportunities to escape from the crowds, if you are prepared to stride out beyond the recumbent bodies. If you feel a tad oppressed by the large-scale development, head for a deserted clifftop and contemplate the gentle foam-fringed waves and elementally inspired rock formations.

Resorts such as **Armação de Pêra** and **Carvoeiro** are geared towards self-catering and package tourists and have little to offer the independent traveller. However, larger towns such as **Portimão** have a heartbeat independent of the tourist trade.

Armação de Pêra

Eight kilometres west of Albufeira the high-rises of Armação de Pêra jostle each other for air. The vestiges of the old village, including an 18th-century fortress with a small chapel overlooking the fisherman's beach, lie towards the east of the resort, but the narrow streets have been swamped by new buildings.

Porches

Four kilometres northwest of Armação de Pêra, the village of Porches has somehow managed to stay aloof from the surrounding resorts, and its heart, around the church, remains tranquil.

Alcantarilha

A sleepy village about 9km west of Albufeira and 3km inland from Armação de Pêra, Alcantarilha consists of a maze of steep narrow streets. The local **church** is remarkable not only for the Manueline coils around its front portal but for its small **Capela dos Ossos** side chamber set with over a thousand skulls and femurs of past parishioners. It is eerily cool, with a crucifix hanging in the middle. From the sublime to the ridiculous, on the N125 between Alcantarilha and Lagoa looms the waterslide park **The Big One** which is big on thrills though smaller than Slide and Splash near Lagoa (*see* p.495).

The Big One
*t 800 204 014 or
t (282) 322 827;
open May–Sept*

ⓘ **Armação
de Pêra**
on the front, t *(282)
312 145; open Mon–Sat
9.30–12.30 and 2–5*

Shopping From Albufeira to Alvor

Porches is famous for its pottery and produces beautifully crafted, hand-painted ceramics. Visit **Olaria Pequena** (*open Mon–Sat 10–1 and 3–6*) on the N125 opposite the sign to Porches, a small blue-edged cottage selling prettily painted ceramics and pots. A few yards west across the road is the much bigger **Olaria de Porches** (*open daily 9–9*). It stocks a huge range of pottery and ceramics from tiny bowls to large hand-painted *azulejo* panels.

Sports/Activities From Albufeira to Alvor

Very well signposted just outside Carvoeiro, **Pestana Golf Club**, t (282) 340 900, *www.pestana.pt*, offers two beautifully designed 18-hole courses, Gramacho and Pinta. The Gramacho has been extended, from a 'double 9' to a conventional 18-hole course. A couple of kilometres east of Carvoeiro is **Vale de Milho**, t (282) 358 502, a compact 9-hole course ideal for holiday golfers. Tennis players will appreciate the **Rocha Brava Tennis Club**, near Carvoeiro, t (282) 358 856, *www.rochabrava.com*.

(★) O Leão de Porches >>

Where to Stay From Albufeira to Alvor

★★★★**Hotel Garbe**, Armação de Pêra, t (282) 315 187, *www.hotelgarbe.com* (€€€€). The grand old lady of the resort, the Garbe caters almost exclusively to package tourists but its bedrooms, public areas and facilities are of a high standard and it enjoys the perfect beachside location.

Vila Horizonte, Estrada do Farol 1260, Carvoeiro, t (282) 356 047, *www.vila horizonte.com* (€€). Delightful hotel with attractive and comfortable rooms that overlook pretty gardens, the pool or the sea. Go for the latter if you can.

Camping

There are two three-star **campsites**, one located just outside Armação de Pêra on the road to Alcantarilha, t (282) 312 260, and the other at Canelas, about 1km from Alcantarilha, t (282) 312 612.

Eating Out From Albufeira to Alvor

O Leão de Porches, Porches, t (281) 381 384 (€€€). This splendid French-inspired restaurant occupies a 17th-century farmhouse in the centre of the village near the church. The menu is delicious – try the rabbit braised in the oven with red wine, mushrooms, onions and herbs. *Book ahead. Closed Wed and Jan.*

Casa d'Italia, Armação de Pêra, t (282) 314 761 (€€€). Just above the Praia da Nossa Senhora da Rocha, tucked away around the corner from the Viking Hotel, this quiet, friendly little *hacienda*-style Italian restaurant is a real find, with a beautiful, small round pool and grassy garden for a post-prandial loll.

Serol, Rua Portas do Mar 2, Armação de Pêra, t (282) 312 146 (€€). On the same street is one of the town's most highly regarded fish restaurants. It's nothing special to look at but the crowds of locals and Portuguese holidaymakers speak for themselves. *Closed Wed.*

Zé Leiteiro, Rua Portas do Mar, Armação de Pêra, t (282) 314 551 (€). On a road leading up from Armação's beach is a simple and bustling restaurant with long green tables outside and long checked tables inside. Choose the fish of the day.

Zoomarine
t (289) 560 300,
www.zoomarine.com;
open daily from 10am;
adm

Slide and Splash
t (282) 341 685;
open daily, Easter–Oct,
from 10am; adm

About 4km east of Alcantarilha, on the N125 near Guia, is **Zoomarine**, a Florida-inspired marine life theme park where various sea creatures perform diverse manoeuvres. There are funfair rides and a collection of brightly arrayed parrots. Puzzling.

On the road to Lagoa stands the biggest and best of the region's waterslide parks, **Slide and Splash**, clearly signposted, containing the usual spaghetti network of giant slides.

Carvoeiro

Carvoeiro (about 23 km west of Albufeira) lost most of its charm years ago, though the ghost of the original village can be seen cutting into the cliffs. There is a plague of supermarkets for self-catering package-tour holidaymakers in apartments and a confusion of bars and restaurants which spill tables on to the streets. In high season it is jammed solid with cars and tourists.

Silves

 Silves

Situated among gentle hills beside the River Arade, 8km inland from Lagoa and 26km northwest of Albufeira, **Silves** was the 30,000-strong capital of the Moorish province of al-Gharb from the mid-11th century to the mid-13th century. By the 16th century, the river had silted up, the political and commercial heavies had moved on and the population dwindled to just 140. Subsequent earthquakes have destroyed much of the character of the place – the only living monuments to the Moors are the orange and almond groves that surround the town, which is now home to 10,000 people. Since losing its political importance, Silves has been happy to vegetate quietly beside the trickle called the river, though lately it has been enjoying something of a quiet tourist-led renaissance.

History

Idrisi, the 12th-century Arab chronicler and geographer, remarked on the 'fine appearance' of Xelb (Silves), a port with 'attractive buildings and well-furnished bazaars', praising the purity of the Yemenite Arabs' language and pronunciation, as well as the region's 'delicate, appetizing and delicious' figs.

For all its opulence, Silves had a troubled history. Soon after the Moors had installed themselves, the city was captured by al-Mu'tadid, of Seville, who planted flowers in the skulls of his decapitated enemies to decorate his palace gardens. Returning to Moorish control, Silves was besieged by Dom Sancho I in 1189. The king had flagged down lusty English crusaders on their way to Jerusalem, promising booty. After a month's bitter siege the Moorish forces filed out of the stronghold bearing nothing but their clothes – which the Crusaders removed, to the disgust of the king. The allies occupied the city, and spent most of that night torturing the remaining inhabitants into revealing the location of their hidden treasure.

Two years later the Caliph of Morocco recaptured Silves, along with the rest of Portugal south of the Tagus except Évora. The Moors were finally driven out in 1242, during the reign of Dom Afonso III.

What to See

Cathedral
*open Mon–Sat
8.30–6.30*

The earth-red **cathedral** was built of Algarvian sandstone in 1189, and reconstructed after the Reconquest of 1242. It was the seat of the Algarve's bishopric until 1580, when that honour was

Getting to Silves

transferred to Faro. The Gothic parts of the cathedral have been altered, and although the building is a peaceful place, few interesting architectural features remain. Note the curious gargoyles on the exterior of the apse. Dom João II's coffin was buried here in 1495, having been lined with quicklime to speed the decay of the body. Four years later, it was disinterred: the quicklime had destroyed the shroud and almost burnt through the wooden coffin, but the body was incorrupt. Truly, a miracle. The splinters of the coffin were set aside as holy relics, and the king, placed in a new coffin, was translated to Batalha in central Portugal. Several fine tombs have remained here, including one decorated with a coiled serpent.

Castle
open daily 9–7, until 8pm in Aug; adm

Uphill from the cathedral, it's exciting to walk along the top of the thick, rust-coloured curtain walls of the **castle**, built by the Moors on Roman foundations, and restored *c.* 1835. The defences encircle a grove of lemon trees and hibiscus, planted above a Roman copper mine later used for storing grain.

Archaeological Museum
open Mon-Sat 9–6; adm

The **Archaeological Museum**, Rua das Portas de Loulé, is around the corner from the castle. Built around a large Moorish cistern that once held a year's supply of water, its collection of ancient rocks and broken plates are occasionally glanced at by lines of schoolchildren dragging their feet.

Fábrica do Inglês
t (282) 440 440, www.fabrica-do-ingles.com; complex open Tues–Sun 9am–midnight; cork museum open 9.30–12.45 and 2–6.15; adm

Down by the river, in the lower part of town, the **Fábrica do Inglês** is a major leisure complex created in 1999 from a 19th-century English-owned cork factory (hence its name). It features Aquavision, billed as 'the greatest multimedia show in the Iberian peninsula', a show called Castle of Dreams, a cork museum (only worth seeing on a guided tour when some of the old machinery is demonstrated), six different catering outlets, ranging from high-class seafood to tea rooms, a children's playground, and 'Cybernetic Fountains'. The latter come to life on summer nights in a water and laser show with live entertainment and 'street parties'. It's an impressive and attractive place with obvious potential, though during the day and on quiet nights the complex has the sad atmosphere of a white elephant.

Continue past the Fábrica, on the road to Messines, to see the **Cruz de Portugal**, an ornate 16th-century, 3m high, white limestone cross. One side depicts *Christ Crucified*, the other the *Descent from the Cross*.

For beautiful views over Silves and the surrounding countryside, take the road to Messines and turn right after the petrol station. Turn right again if you feel like a hot 3km walk through the orange groves. A ruined mill sits atop a small hill, offering an uplifting panorama over the terraced and cultivated surroundings.

(i) **Silves >**
Rua 25 de Abril, t (282) 442 255; open weekdays 9.30–7, weekends 9–12.30 and 2.30–5

Kiosk: Praça do Municipio in front of the old town hall

Services in Silves

The **post office** is on Rua Samora Barros. The daily **market** is off Rua Francisco Pablos and the **gypsy market** comes to Silves on the third Monday of each month. Silves' **health centre** can be reached on **t** (282) 440 020.

Festivals in Silves

A two-week **beer festival** is held in July at the Fábrica do Inglês. The **Feira da Laranja** is an orange festival held for five days every spring. The dates change every year; consult tourist office.

Shopping in Silves

Estúdio Destra is housed in a lovely 16th-century building near the castle and is the studio of Kate Swift, a descendant of Frank Swift, who did much to revive the traditional ceramics industry in the Algarve. Pieces range from individual tiles and small ceramics to wall-sized panels. On the front, by the river, **Fantasia** is an Aladdin's Cave of merchandise, leather, rugs, carpets and lots of lamps, all from North Africa.

Where to Stay and Eat in Silves

★★★Hotel Colina dos Mouros, Pocinho Santo, **t** (282) 440 420, *www.eurosun. com/colimou.htm* (€€). This is the only hotel in town. Its 57 rooms have great views, some of the castle. They are simply furnished but fairly comfortable, with air-conditioning and satellite televison, and there is an outdoor swimming pool.

Quinta do Rio, Sitio São Estevão, **t** (282) 445 528 (€). Signposted from the Messines road is this beautifully situated *quinta* in an orangery in the hills. It has been restored by the charming Italian management, who will arrange excursions and horse-riding.

Vila Sodré, Rua da Cruz de Portugal, **t** (282) 443 441 (€). Take the road towards Messines, not far past the Cruz de Portugal. It has attractive rooms overlooking orange trees. Senhor Silvino gallantly tries to provide 'quality tourism'.

Residencial Ponte Romana, Horta Cruz, **t** (282) 443 275 (€). Glows in burnt-red sandstone by the river. Inside, a marble staircase leads to very airy rooms, some with a view over the river. There is a popular restaurant (€€), serving good, if standard, Portuguese food in a yard strewn with typical farm bits.

Rui, Rua Comendador Vilarinho 27, **t** (282) 442 682 (€€€). Oysters bubble in their tank at the well-known Rui, which serves fish and shellfish priced by the kilo in no-nonsense surroundings. *Closed Tues off season.*

Café Inglês, **t** (282) 442 585 (€€). Beautifully located on the castle steps, this part-English-owned café offers tables out front, inside a traditional old house, or in its lovely courtyard garden. They serve good international-Portuguese cooking and homemade cakes. Live music Sunday afternoons. *Closed Sat.*

Bistro O Cais, Rua José Estevão, **t** (282) 448 098 (€€). A cosy restaurant on the waterfront, which is becoming increasingly popular with the local resident expatriates. The dishes are contemporary and tasty, including a pork satay in a creamy peanut sauce.

Casa Velha, Praça do Municipio, t (282) 445 491 (€). Basic old-fashioned traditional Portuguese dining room.

Cafe Rosa, Praça do Municipio (€). You can munch a sandwich in the historic foyer of the old town hall which is completely covered with blue and white *azulejos*.

Around Silves

Alte, situated 28km northeast of Silves, is a flowery little village that is still touchingly proud of its second placing in a national 'picturesque village' contest. That was in 1938 and Alte is still cannily accustomed to passing tourists, though no less pretty for it. It's also well known for its folk-dance groups, who come into their own in the May Day festivities which culminate in a procession to the village stream in celebration of water.

The **parish church** dates from the 15th century and has a fine Manueline portal. An elderly guide runs through his patter in French and German, pointing out the 16th-century *azulejos*, the gilt *talha dourada* altar and the European saints depicted in the aisles. The church has a peaceful, shady yard; carob trees fan the benches. At the bottom of the village the stream provides a popular picnicking spot.

Portimão

Seventeen km east of Lagos and 28km west of Albufeira, Portimão fumes on the western bank of the River Arade, a couple of kilometres from the coast. An impressive new bridge straddles the river, the twin of the bridge over the Guadiana (*see* p.479). This built-up town with a population of 36,000 is a major port and sardine-canning centre. It has little to recommend it for an overnight stay, though a visit to its famous fish and sardine restaurants is almost mandatory, and a brisk walk around the town is worthwhile.

Standing at the mouth of the River Arade, Portimão was settled by the Carthaginians and maintained by the Romans. The town has mushroomed since the 1920s, when the Arade silted up and Portimão became a busy port and fishing centre.

The 14th-century **Igreja Matriz** stands at the highest part of the town. The original portal remains, 19th-century *azulejos* line the walls and an impressive *talha dourada* altar glints with several layers of gilding. From the church make your way along Rua Dr Ernest Cabrito heading towards the quayside. Pause awhile at **Largo 1 de Dezembro**, a lovely square with solid benches covered in panels of *azulejos* depicting significant events in Portuguese history.

Getting to and around Portimão

Frequent **trains** from Faro take one to two hours. Frequent trains from Lagos take half an hour. There are frequent EVA and Rede express **buses** from Lisbon (4hrs) and myriad regional services. Frequent EVA buses take an hour to travel from Albufeira, 30mins from Lagos and about 2hrs from Faro. An express bus that runs the length of the coast from Vila Real to Lagos stops at Portimão, taking about 3hrs from Vila Real, 2hrs 20mins from Tavira and 1½hrs from Faro.

Continue along Rua Judice Biker to the garden squares by the water and the famous '**sardine dock**'. A rash of seafood restaurants clusters round the harbour by the old bridge, serving the sardines demanded by tourists.

(i) **Portimão >**
*on the waterfront,
Cais Comércio et
Turismo,* **t** *(282) 470 732,
www.cm-portimao.pt;
open daily 10–6, later in
summer*

Services in Portimão

The **train station** is to the north of the town on Largo Ferra Prado, from where it's about a 15-minute walk straight down to the pedestrianized shopping street, Rua do Comércio. **Buses, t** (282) 418 120, come and go from two streets parallel to one another: Avenida Afonso Henriques and Avenida Guarané, a short walk east of the sardine doçk.

For **medical assistance** use the Clínica da Rocha in Praia da Rocha, **t** (282) 414 500. The most central **post office** is on the main square in front of the harbour, Rua Serpa Pinto. Nearby is the **British Consulate**, at Largo Francisco A Mauricio 7, near Largo da Barca, **t** (282) 417 800.

Shopping in Portimão

There is a good number of leather and shoe shops (mostly around Rua Santa Isabel). **O Aquário** is a popular place, with branches at Rua Vasco da Gama, Praça da República and Rua Direita, selling crystal, porcelain, copper items and souvenirs/gifts. On Rua Judice Biker, opposite Largo 1 de Dezembro, is a branch of **A Tralha Antiguidades** with an intriguing collection of antiques.

A five-minute walk from the centre, along Av. São João de Deus, will take you to the busy fish, fruit and vegetable **market**. The huge **gypsy market** materializes on the first and third Monday of each month.

Sports and Activities in Portimão

Fishing and boat trips along the coast or up the river to Silves depart from the quayside. If you want to pit your wits against a shark, try **Cepemar Algarve's Big Game Fishing Centre**, **t** (282) 425 866, which has a good safety reputation.

The famous **Penina Championship Course**, Montes de Alvor, **t** (282) 420 200, *www.lemeridien-penina.com*, is one of the finest golf courses in Portugal, host to the Portuguese Open on eight occasions – a real test of skill for low-handicap players. Adjacent, the 9-hole **Resort Course** is somewhat less forgiving. A relative newcomer to the golf circuit is the **Morgado do Reguengo Course**, Estrada Portimão-Monchique, **t** (282) 402 150, *www.morgado doreguengo.com*. It is one of the region's longest courses and has big ambitions, eventually to include two 5-star hotels in its grounds.

Where to Stay in Portimão

★★★**Residencial O Pátio**, Rua Dr João Vitorino Mealha 3, **t** (282) 424 288 (€). Bursts with character, thanks mostly to the cheerful hand-painted Alentejan furniture. Try for a room that opens on to the patio and roof garden, or one that has 17th-century decorated tiles. The cheaper rooms have showers instead of baths.

**Residencial Arabi, Praça Manuel Teixeira Gomes 13, t (282) 460 250 (€). Overlooks the square and the harbour beyond. The wide marble staircase is graced with plants and pictures with a Moorish theme. The rooms are pleasant enough, but those overlooking the square can be noisy.

Camping

Portimão's **campsite** is some 4km out of town on the Monchique road, t (282) 491 012.

Eating Out in Portimão

You can have a cheap sardine feast at any one of half a dozen basic establishments at the sardine dock. Happy diners fill long wooden tables along the quayside, supplied by smoky barbecues with a constant stream of sardines and other fish. In character and quality they are all much the same, although the first in the line,

Taverna do Maré, and the last, **Casa Bica**, are particularly to be recommended.

If you want to set your sights and your budget higher, head through the arches to the vivid Largo da Barca and Rua Vasco Pires (immediately off the square), where the garrulous clientele is mainly Portuguese and the square is filled with the smell of fish sizzling on the charcoal grills. Long tables and benches line the square; deep pink flowers tumble down the walls. These are counted among some of the Algarve's best fish restaurants. All of the following are excellent and have similar wide-ranging fish- and seafood-based menus:

Dona Barca, Largo da Barca, t (282) 484 189 (€€€–€€).

Forte & Feio, Largo da Barca, t (282) 418 894 (€€€–€€).

O Barril, Rua Vasco Pires, t (282) 413 257 (€€€–€€).

Around Portimão

Portimão sprawls a couple of kilometres towards the mouth of the River Arade, which is guarded by the **Fortaleza de Santa Catarina**. The courtyard of the fortress is open (*free*) and is worth a trip for its great views. Below it the marina has a range of stores, restaurants and bars. The fortress that can be seen on the opposite side of the river is privately owned.

Praia da Rocha

Praia da Rocha, at the river mouth, is a huge, beautiful sandy beach backed by tall cliffs in earthy shades. It must have been idyllic, once. Now it is packed with monster hotels and crowded with bodies, bars and restaurants. It's only worth visiting if you're interested in early designs for tourist developments, as this was one of the first on the coast.

Ferragudo

On the eastern bank of the River Arade, Ferragudo stands opposite Portimão like an echo from the past. The village has retained much of its charm, at least around the riverfront, where there's a buoyant morning market. Fishing nets drape the pavement and beaded curtains stir in the open doorways of flaking, whitewashed houses. The settlement straggles uphill, but

ⓘ Praia
da Rocha ›
*on main beach strip,
Avenida Tomás
Cabreira, t (282) 419 132;
open daily 10–6,
summer much later;
winter closed for lunch*

Festival in Praia da Rocha

September brings a treat for unsuspecting tourists when the **Algarve Folk Music and Dance Festival** draws traditionally dressed groups from all over Portugal, with a competition ending on the beach at Praia da Rocha.

Where to Stay and Eat in Praia da Rocha

★★★★Hotel Oriental, Avenida Tomás Cabreira, **t** (282) 480 800, *www.tdhotels.pt* (€€€€). An exotic, Xanadu-type affair with many minarets, set in lovely grounds with 85 luxurious rooms.

Albergaria Vila Lido, Avenida Tomás Cabreira, **t** (282) 424 127 (€€€). At the quiet end of the resort towards the Fortaleza de Santa Catarina. This too has a nice old-world air, though it is very smart, very Portuguese and with all mod cons.

★★Residencial Toca, Rua Engenheiro Francisco Bivar, **t** (282) 418 904 (€). A well-priced, friendly place with good-sized rooms, some with balconies. Parking is an extra perk.

The Penguin Terrace (O Teraço de Pinguim), on the steps leading down to the beach (€). A delightful laid-back place with a great beach view, inventive twists on old Portuguese favourites plus excellent salads.

Casalinho, just below the Penguin Terrace, right on the beach (€). Highly rated by the locals for its fish and other Portuguese specials. Be flash and go for one of its flambées. *No booking.*

Scorpius, Rua Bartolemeu Dias (€). Inexpensive and excellent seafood and traditional cuisine, popular with the locals (always a good sign!).

Nightlife in Praia da Rocha

Praia da Rocha is very lively at night, with a **casino**, **t** (282) 415 001, based at the Hotel Algarve on Avenida Tomás Cabreira, that puts on the usual floorshows.

it's best not to stray too far from the bridge as modern development soon takes over. The main beach, **Praia Grande**, is quite large and within the Arade's breakwaters, but the view of skyscrapers at Portimão and Praia da Rocha is a turn-off. A couple of smaller beaches nearer the point are nicer.

Alvor

Alvor was known to the Romans as *Portus Hannibalis*, before the Moors named it *Albur*. Alvor was captured and recaptured several times during the 12th century, until in 1250 the Moors were finally driven out. In 1495 it gained fame – of a kind – when Dom João II died here after catching a chill in Monchique.

The wetlands of **Alvor Estuary** are a rich breeding and feeding ground for water birds. Environmentalists campaigned for many years for the area to be declared a nature reserve in order to impose a tighter control on rampaging development. In 2006 the area was finally designated a Natura 2000 site, but further action and protection is needed to protect its natural heritage.

Getting to Alvor

Frequent **buses** make the short journey from Portimão to Alvor; it takes about 15 minutes.

In the old part of town the narrow streets, of almost unsullied whiteness, lead up a low hill to the yellow-bordered 16th-century **Igreja Matriz**. Its fascinating Manueline portal is carved in reddish stone; the concentric arches depict sea flowers, dragons, lions and musicians, all wrapped by a giant octopus tentacle. Inside are some fine *azulejos*.

(i) **Alvor >**

at top of hill leading down to the main street on Rua Dr Afonso Costa, t (282) 457 540; open 9.30–12.30 and 2–5, summer until 7

Sports and Activities in Alvor

Five kilometres west of Portimão at Montes de Alvor lies the famous **Penina Golf Club** (*see* p.500). The 18-hole **Alto Golf** course, Quinta do Alto do Poço, Alvor, **t** (282) 460 870, *www.altoclub.com*, forms part of the Alto Club tourist development but is open to all. It has a lovely site overlooking the sea and is suitable for golfers of any reasonable standard.

The **Centro de Hipico Vale de Ferro** at Mexilhoeira Grande, a few kilometres north of Alvor, **t** (282) 968 444, *www.valedeferro.com*, is one of the Algarve's best known horse-riding schools.

Where to Stay in Alvor

★★★★★**Hotel Alvor Praia**, **t** (282) 400 900, *www.pestana.com* (€€€€). Overlooking the Três Irmãos beach, this is more attractive than some of the surrounding places, being only six floors high. It has all the facilities you'd expect, plus a range of accompanying sporting activities. *Book well ahead.*

★★★★★**Le Meridien Penina**, on the main EN125 between Alvor and Lagos **t** (282) 420 200, *www.lemeridien peninaview.com* (€€€€). Set in a large estate which incorporates three golf courses, including the famous Penina (*see* p.500) this is heaven for both golfers and their widows seeking a luxurious retreat. Superb rooms, all five-star facilities, private beach club and an excellent children's club.

Camping

Alvor's campsite is on the outskirts of the village, **t** (282) 458 002.

Eating Out in Alvor

Alvor is well stocked with good fish restaurants, mostly on or just off the main street, Rua Dr Frederico R. Mendes, which plunges straight down to the harbour.

Hellman's, **t** (282) 458 208 (€€). Directly behind and overlooking Os Pescadores (*see* below). It puts a modern international spin on local fare as well as offering several of its own inventive dishes. The views from its top terrace are superb. *Open evenings only.*

Vagabondo, Rua Dr Frederico R. Mendes, **t** (282) 458 726 (€€). Under the same management as Hellman's, and offers the same blend of friendly lively young staff and innovative modern cooking, with a patio of orange and almond trees on which to sprawl. *Open evenings only.*

Os Pescadores (€). At the very bottom down by the river quay, serving good, honest food in a pleasant setting. Plastic chairs are arranged under umbrellas, from which diners watch their fresh fish being grilled.

Tasca Morais, Rua Dr António José de Almeida, **t** (282) 459 392 (€). For a traditional Portuguese restaurant, set in a one-storey house at the top of the hill, make your way here. The food is simple – go for the *cataplana* – and the service is friendly. *Evenings only; closed Wed.*

Medronho

If you thought moonshine was something that happened when the sun went down, you're in for a shock. The Algarve's distinctive firewater is distilled from arbutus berries and can be purchased from shops under a variety of labels, but the best stuff is home-made. It's also illegal, but that doesn't seem to prevent most households in the mountains keeping a little hidden away somewhere.

The Serra de Monchique

Beginning 23km inland from Portimão, the breathtaking Monchique hills form a barrier between the Algarve and the Alentejo. The highest points are at Foia (2,960ft/902m) and Picota (2,535ft/773m), sufficient to shelter the Algarve from northerly winds and trap the rain blown inland from the coast, giving the western end of the range the highest rainfall in the Algarve, mostly between the end of November and the beginning of May. Steep streams bubble out of the schist, making it easier to irrigate terraced plots of land. There are several places on the road to Foia from where, on a clear day, you can see the whole of the west coast as well as a large chunk of the south coast.

The hills are thickly wooded with eucalyptus, cork oaks like cheerleaders' pom-poms, and every shade of pine tree. The roads are flanked by yellow-flowered mimosa. Peonies and pale purple rhododendrons bloom before the end of April, while small arbutus trees flourish throughout the range – keep an eye out for their large, dark green, toothed leaves, and globular, warty, red fruits. Better still, try the flavourful *medronho* brandy distilled from the berries (*see* above). It's not the brandy but the flat light that makes the hills appear to be superimposed on one another.

Caldas de Monchique (Monchique Spa)

★ **Monchique Spa**
for details of treatments,
t (282) 910 910

Most of Portugal's spas feel like sanatoria; the **Monchique Spa** is different, largely thanks to the recognition that it isn't only sick people who want to use it. From 9am to 1pm it is only open to people with doctors' prescriptions, but from 3pm to 7pm it caters for people who want to be pampered, including anti-stress and anti-cellulite treatments, hydro-massage baths, jet-spray and vichy showers, skin cleansing, mud packs and so on.

Monchique

The road winds 7km north from Caldas de Monchique, climbing 650ft (200m) to Monchique, a little town of 10,000 souls. The views of the coastal plain are fabulous, as are the camellia trees. The lush countryside and its climate, always slightly cooler than the coast thanks to its elevation, is perfect for trekking (*see* 'Sports and Activities', p.505).

The cheerful lower central square, **Largo dos Chorões**, has a fountain and a clever modern twist on the traditional Algarvian *nora*, or well. Among a jumble of unsightly modern houses, a cobbled street leads up from the main square to the **Igreja Matriz**, which has an odd Manueline portal from which five carved knots radiate. Above the town are the flower-clad ruins of the Franciscan monastery of **Nossa Senhora do Destêrro**, founded in 1632 by Dom Pero da Silva, later Viceroy of India.

From Monchique to Aljezur

West of Monchique, the road climbs past stacks of logs, and eucalyptus trees. Recalcitrant cows are led along the road, which suddenly enters a land of heather and scrub. The exhilarating peak of the range is **Foia**, 8km from Monchique and forested with innumerable broadcasting aerials.

Climbing up to the **Picota peak** makes a wilder and more interesting walk than Foia, through farms and chestnut coppices.

The 30km journey west to Aljezur is a beautiful drive, passing the fragrant and flower-filled villages of Nave, Caseis and Marmelete before weaving through pine-covered hillsides.

Shopping in The Serra de Monchique

Monchique is the best place to buy the **wooden folding chairs** found in hotels and homes around the country. This simple design was brought to Portugal by the Romans and is considered evidence of a Roman presence in Monchique. José Leonardo Salvador, the 'Monchique Chair Man', makes them from alder wood. He is something of a local celebrity, having starred in a BBC documentary. His shop, **Casa Dos Arcos**, Estrada Velha, **t** (282) 912 692, displays his work beautifully. You'll find the 'Chair Man' just outside the centre of Monchique on the road out towards Lisbon. Just out of town on the other side, coming in from the coast, you will see the **Casa Zebra**, which also produces and sells wooden folding chairs.

The best place for **ceramics** is the **Cerâmica Artesanal** in the delightful 19th-century Casa da Nogueira on Rua do Corro, at the back of the parish church. All pieces are handmade and hand-painted on the premises.

At the kite shop **Papagaios** on Rua Caminho do Convento, you can buy unusual **kites** to fly on the beach.

Sports/Activities in The Serra de Monchique

Experienced **walkers** might like to pick up a copy of the *Trilhos de Bio-Park Network Monchique* map which, in Ordnance Survey-like detail, covers some 200 miles (300km) of trails in and around the Serra de Monchique. Another invaluable aid is the walking tours guide book *Algarve* by Sunflower Landscapes. You can buy it in Britain or locally.

If you would prefer to take a guided tour, ask at the Monchique tourist office for local guides, call **Albergaria Bica Boa**, **t** (282) 912 271, or **Alternativ Tour**, **t** (282) 913 204 or 965 004 337, *www.alternativ tour.com*, a local enterprise which conducts walking (and also cycling) tours in English and other languages. Another English walking group is the **Algarve Walkers**, **t** (282) 449 098. **Wandern auf den Picota** (Walks on the Picota), **t** (282) 911 041, is the best known of the German-speaking groups operating in this area.

The mountains of Monchique are also ideal for exploring on **horseback**. Ask for details at the tourist office.

Where to Stay and Eat in The Serra de Monchique

Caldas de Monchique

With the redevelopment of Caldas de Monchique comes a choice of brand-new accommodation, all managed by the Spa; to book any of the three described below, **t** (282) 910 910, *www.monchiquetermas.com*. There are also a number of well-presented apartments available accommodating two to four people (€€€–€€). If you are staying at any of these places the Spa can arrange walking tours in English. The only drawback is the lack of parking, which can prove to be a headache.

★★★**Hotel Termal** (€€€). Very much a part of the Spa complex, modern and boxy from without, comfortable and functional within, but its other excellent options would make an attractive base for anyone looking for a different slant on the Algarve.

(★) Estalagem Dom João II >

★★★★**Estalagem Dom João II** (€€€). Part of the Spa complex. Very attractively decorated 19th-century building with Arraiolos rugs on wooden floors and good-quality reproduction furniture.

★★★**Pensão Central** (€€€). Part of the Spa complex. A pension only in name, it is like its sister, the Estalagem (*see* above).

★★★★**Albergaria do Lageado**, t (282) 912 616 (€). Just off the central square is this small, compact and pretty place, which offers basic but very pleasant bedrooms in the summer season only; its charm begins with the trellised patio off the dining room, from which a path leads up through a rock garden to a lovely family-sized swimming pool (*open to non-residents*). Guests lie on deckchairs surrounded on three sides by tree-covered slopes and birdsong. The restaurant serves simple dishes.

Restaurante 1692, t (282) 912 687 (€€). a good restaurant in the square, which uses locally sourced products whenever possible, with a bar in a former stable. Don't leave without tasting the fig ice cream.

Monchique

Residencial Miradouro da Serra, Rua dos Combatentes do Ultramar, t (282) 912 163 (€). Near the main square in Monchique. The rooms are clean and tastefully decorated.

A Charrette, Rua Samora Gil 30–34, t (282) 912 142 (€€–€). A very Portuguese affair, unfussily bare with lots of chatter and a limited but tasty menu.

Restaurante Central, Rua da Igreja 5, t (282) 913 160 (€). A Monchique

(i) Monchique >
*Largo dos Chorões,
t (282) 911 189; open
Mon–Fri 10–4.30, Sat
10–12; closed Sun*

institution, with every available surface pasted with letters and messages from countless visitors. It's fun but you'll get better food elsewhere.

Around Monchique

The road to Foia abounds with excellent restaurants and places to stay.

★★★★**Estalagem Abrigo da Montanha**, Estrada da Foia, t (282) 912 131, *www.abrigodamontanha.com* (€€). Friendly mountain inn built of granite, with childishly jolly décor, tiny balconies and vast views. There's a small pool with a view and a windy deck, off-street parking and a little-used restaurant.

Jardim das Oliveiras, t (282) 912 700 (€€). A little west of Monchique is this delightful place on a terrace in an olive grove. If you want to stay the night there are three cosy rooms, all with woodburning stoves and local antiques. The restaurant (€€) serves typical mountain cooking – local sausage, suckling pig, game and specials such as loin of pork stuffed with fig.

★★★★**Albergaria Bica Boa**, Estrada de Lisboa, t (282) 912 360 (€€). Located just south of Monchique, offering pleasant rooms and a mix of Irish and Portuguese cooking.

Restaurant Dona Filipa, Quinta de São Bento, Estrada da Foia, some 5km from Monchique, t (282) 912 143 (€€€). It was once a holiday home of the Portuguese Royal Family – presumably a minor branch. The fixed-price menu, €30, changes daily; by contrast the setting is pleasantly antique and timeless. Try the wild boar with chestnuts if you get the chance, preferably on a winter's evening when the dining room really comes into its own. *Reservations recommended.*

The Monchique area is famous for its chicken *piripiri*. Two good places to try it are:

Restaurant Paraiso de Montanha, Saramagal, t (282) 912 150 (€€). The restaurant is set on a wide terrace with breathtaking views. *Closed Thurs.*

Agua da Sola, Alcaria do Banho, t (282) 912 618, (€). This is in one of the first places west of Monchique.

From Lagos to Sagres

West of the Bay of Lagos, development diminishes: Lagos is the only sizeable resort on this section of the coast. With its amber rocks rising out of transparent green waters, lively harbour activity, glitzy marina, funky nightlife and smattering of culture, it's also the most attractive resort west of Faro. Its coastline – the cliffs and their weird outcrops – are best appreciated from the sea, especially around Ponta da Piedade.

The small resorts west of Lagos offer much quieter beaches. In most cases, the original fishing villages have been swamped, but in the village of Salema the locals still pursue a traditional lifestyle. Construction has concentrated on villas and apartment complexes, so no high-rise hotels violate the horizon; brightly coloured fishing boats resting on the sands provide obstacle courses for little children. These low-key resorts are especially popular with English families but a number of young travellers break their monopoly

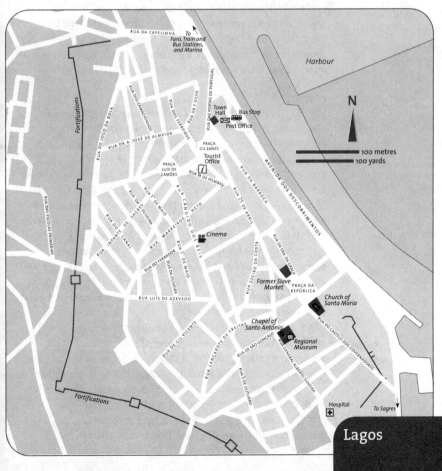

Lagos

every year, making the nightlife interesting. The farther west you go, the more the balance shifts in favour of the travellers.

The coast west of Lagos is particularly suited to scuba-diving and snorkelling, with calm and very clear waters harbouring shipwrecks and octopuses roaming the rock crevices and vivid watery gardens.

Lagos

The Baía de Lagos is one of the widest bays of the Portuguese coast, sheltered on the west by the Ponta da Piedade promontory, and on the east by the Ponta dos Três Irmãos. The harbour town of Lagos commands the bay, on the hilly western bank of the estuary of the River Bensafrim.

Lagos is the principal resort of the western Algarve, particularly popular with Germans and English, attracting a more varied and sexy crowd than Albufeira. The vertical rock cliffs of the coast are pocked with grottoes, which can be explored by boat; the marina at Lagos has a wide variety of colourful craft. Yet there's still room for the locals to lead their lives without too much interruption. They shop in the market opposite the harbour and let their dogs pick at bones in the narrow, winding streets.

History

The Lusitanian settlement of *Lacobriga* was destroyed by an earthquake, making way for its resettlement by the Carthaginians in 350 BC. When Sertorius took *Lacobriga* from the Romans in 76 BC, it grew into a flourishing town. Many of the early voyages to explore the coast of Guinea set sail from this port – spawning the rope- and sail-making industries – after Gil Eanes sailed around Cape Bojador in 1434 and found the imprints of the feet of men and camels. Lançarote returned with a report on elephants, whose 'flesh will suffice to satisfy 500 men, and [the Guineans] find it very good'. Lançarote also returned with 235 Moorish slaves, prompting Europe's first slave market. The chronicler Azurara, who ordinarily writes dispassionately, seems genuinely moved: 'What heart, even the hardest, would not be moved by a sentiment of pity on seeing such a flock?'

The last Mediterranean crusade departed from Lagos in 1578, under the command of the ascetic, obstinate 25-year-old king Dom Sebastian, ending in disaster at Alcácer-Quivir. Before he left, the king made the town capital of the Algarve, a title it retained until 1755, when Tavira and finally Faro took over. Lagos has survived many battles in its past, including an attack from Sir Francis Drake in 1587, whom the tourist office brochure once passionately described as 'that English pirate'. This has obviously been

Getting to Lagos

Under normal traffic conditions it takes just 45 minutes to **drive** from Faro airport to Lagos city centre. Frequent **trains** make numerous stops on their way from Vila Real de Santo António (4hrs), including Tavira (3hrs), Faro (2¼hrs), and Albufeira (1¼hrs). From Lisbon, take the ferry to Barreiro, and catch a train to Tunes. Change at Tunes for Lagos (5¼hrs rail travel). EVA and Rede Expressos **buses** arrive from Lisbon (4½hrs), and from Vila Real de Santo António (4hrs), via Tavira (3½hrs), Faro (2¼hrs), and Albufeira (1¼hrs), among others.

invaluable training: Lagos withstands its annual invasion from northern Europe with good humour and little loss of integrity.

Around Town

The sculpture of Dom Sebastian in the Praça Gil Eanes portrays him as a spaceman, which is sculptor João Cutileiro's way of updating the myth of Sebastianism, the messianic cult fostered by the Spanish domination of 1580–1640, which hoped for a return of the saviour to restore his people to greatness and prosperity, a cult which lingers even today.

The Rua da Barroca runs parallel with the river into the Rua da Senhora da Graça. Portugal's only **slave market** was held where this opens into the Praça da República, under the arches of the Custom House, now converted into a small art gallery. There should be a memorial, but there isn't – just a plaque. In the 19th century, Portugal was the first colonial power to abolish slavery.

From the corner of the Praça take the Rua de São Gonçalo to the **Chapel of Santo António**. Access is only permitted via the Municipal Museum, which mixes oddities, works of art, and ethnography. Pickled freak animal foetuses, colonial hair picks, and a funky pair of 19th-century sunglasses vie for attention with a fantastical 17th-century embroidered altarcloth, the 16th-century vestments used at Dom Sebastian's last Mass in Portugal (on Meia Praia beach), and Lagos' charter of 1504. Rural displays include a selection of Algarvian chimneys. You don't have to be Santa Claus to get a kick out of the Algarve's chimneys, which were introduced into the whole country from the south. Their pretty latticed flues hark back to Moorish times; the white oblong structures puff out lace-like smoke. Don't miss the chapel, with ebullient gilt woodwork carved by an unknown sculptor *c.* 1715.

The **statue of Henry the Navigator** on the Praça da República, facing the Avenida dos Descobrimentos, is a reminder that the prince and patron of the Great Discoverers (*see* p.517) had a palace nearby, but it was lost in the earthquake of 1755. Across the road, however, is an ancient survivor, the **Forte da Ponta da Bandeira**, built in the 17th century. It has little historic importance but houses a small exhibition and restaurant, and is worth visiting for its views alone.

Municipal Museum
t (282) 762 301; open 9.30–12.30 and 2–5; closed Mon and hols; adm

Forte da Ponta da Bandeira
Tues–Sat 10–1 and 2–6, Sun 10–1; adm

15

The Algarve | From Lagos to Sagres: Lagos

Lagos Zoo
*Sitio do Medronhal,
Barão, t (282) 688 236,
www.zoolagos.com;
open May–Sept 10–7,
Oct–April 10–5; last
adm 1hr before closing*

ⓘ **Lagos >**
*Largo Marquês de
Pombal, t (282) 763
031; open daily
May–Sept 9.30–1 and
2–5.30; closed Oct–Apr
Sat and Sun*

Around Lagos

Just outside town **Lagos Zoo** is popular with both tourists and locals. This attractive little place is home to wallabies, lemurs, several species of monkey and exotic birds including several varieties of toucan.

Services in Lagos

The **post office** is on the Praça Gil Eanes.

The **bus station**, t (282) 762 944, is on the harbour front. The best bus stop for the town centre is on the Avenida dos Descobrimentos.

The **train station**, t (282) 762 987, is just across the river; take the footbridge, turn left and you're just a few metres from the centre of town.

The **hospital** is on Rua do Castelo dos Governadores, t (282) 763 034, or, better still, seek the sevices of MediLagos, by the Motel Marsol on the ring road due north of the old city wall, t (282) 760 181.

Shopping in Lagos

The lively main **market** (*open Mon–Sat 9–1*) occupies two floors, with fish on the ground floor. It faces the harbour, almost on the corner of Rua das Portas de Portugal. By the bus station, located on the Avenida dos Descobrimentos, an orderly **Saturday morning market** unfolds on patches of hessian – you'll find the usual fruit and vegetables, with rabbits, chickens and the odd fish thrown in. There's a **gypsy market** on the first Saturday of each month.

Lagos has two treats for **antiques** lovers. On the main street, Rua 25 de Abril, **Casa do Papagaio** is a Lagos institution with its delightful junk-shop-cum-museum atmosphere and resident *papagaio* (parrot). Much more refined is the **Casa da Barroca**, on the oft-overlooked Rua da Barroca, which runs parallel to 25 de Abril. Near Papagaio on Rua 25 de Abril, the trendy **Olaria Nova** is a welcome change from the usual tired old tourist ceramics and souvenirs, with some unusual modern pottery plus top quality jewellery, clothing and accessories.

Sports and Activities in Lagos

Boat Trips

The *Bom Dia, wwwbomdia.info*, is a two-mast sailing boat which offers **trips round the grottoes**. Tickets can be bought at the marina or by the river. If you're interested in **deep-sea** and **big-game fishing**, the *Espadarte do Sul* is a bluewater fishing boat with a friendly crew and good equipment, t (282) 767 252. Prospective catches include tuna, blue marlin and many species of shark.

Golf

Palmares Golf, Meia Praia, t (282) 790 500, *www.palmaresgolf.com*, is one of the Algarve's prettiest 18-hole courses, with gorgeous views to sea and hills. The outward 9 is a classic links course.

Quinta da Boavista Golf, t (282) 782 151, *www.boavistagolf.com*. Immediately west of town, and well signposted, this is a spectacular 18-hole course, also with great views.

Horse-riding

Just west of Lagos, **Tiffany's**, Vale Grifo, Almádena, t (282) 697 395, *www.teamtiffanys.com*, is one of the best and longest-established horse-riding schools in the vicinity.

Water Sports

There is a **water sports** centre at the town end of Meia Praia which teaches windsurfing as well as hiring out boards, jet bikes and waterskis.

The long-established Anglo-German Luz Bay diving club, which made its name at Praia da Luz, now operates out of Porto de Mós as **Blue Ocean Divers**, t (282) 782 718.

Where to Stay in Lagos

Very Expensive (€€€€)
★★★★**Hotel Tivoli Lagos**, Rua António Crisógono dos Santos, t (282) 769 967,

www.algarvetivolilagos.com. Occupies a series of nine linked buildings, which makes it easy to get lost. What was a rather lovely hotel has become jaded. However, the gardens are attractive, there is an indoor and outdoor pool and gym. The hotel provides frequent transport to its Duna Beach club at Meia Praia Beach, with a pool and supervision on the beach.

Expensive (€€€)

★★★★**Albergaria Marina Rio**, Avenida dos Descobrimentos, opposite the marina, **t** (282) 769 859, *www.marinario.com*. Very well kitted out (including a pool), efficiently run, and some rooms have good views over the harbour and marina. However, it's mostly devoted to German block-bookings.

Moderate (€€)

Vila Mós. Twenty minutes' walk away from Lagos is a high-quality development with 74 tastefully furnished apartments overlooking Porto de Mós beach, with indoor/outdoor pools, health club and buffet breakfast in the restaurant. It's good value.

★★**Pensão Lagosmar**, Rua Dr Faria da Silva 13, **t** (282) 763 523. It's clean and friendly in a quieter part of town. Rooms have terraces.

Inexpensive (€)

★★★**Pensão Mar Azul**, Rua 25 de Abril 13, **t** (282) 769 143, *www.pensao marazul.com*. Offering value in the centre of town, the Mar Azul is very pleasant and well maintained. Most of the rooms have private bathrooms.

★★★**Pensão Rubi-Mar**, Rua da Barroca 70, **t** (282) 763 165. Pleasant rooms and in a central location.

★**Pensão Sol e Sol**, Rua Lançarote de Freitas 22, **t** (282) 761 290. Basic but well located and rooms have their own bathrooms.

There are **very cheap** rooms to be had in people's houses; ask at the tourist office or hang around the bus stop and wait for touts.

★ Pensão Mar Azul >

★ O Escondidinho >>

Camping

A lively **campsite** called **Trinidade**, **t** (282) 763 893, sprawls on the Ponta da Piedade road. It attracts a young party crowd. The other campsite is 1.5km from Lagos towards Porto de Mós, called **Imulagos**, **t** (282) 760 031.

Eating Out in Lagos

Expensive (€€€)

Dom Sebastião, Rua 25 de Abril 20–22, **t** (282) 762 795. This place is usually humming with activity but the service is still good. It's a split-level tavern with a dragons'-tooth floor, a black-beamed ceiling, leatherbound menus, and very good local fish and seafood. *Reservations recommended. Closed Sun in winter.*

Alpendre, Rua António Barbosa Viana 17, **t** (282) 762 705. Inland from the Praça Gil Eanes, the wood-beamed Alpendre serves very good food, but the leather armchairs dispel intimacy, the menu is too large, and smoochy Muzak plays in the background. Fillets of sole are *flambéed* with vermouth.

O Galeão, Rua da Laranjeira 1, **t** (282) 763 909. Very smart. Go for the *arroz de tamboril*: succulent pieces of firm monkfish cooked with rice, herbs, sausages and tomatoes.

Moderate (€€)

Os Arcos, Rua 25 de Abril, **t** (282) 763 120. Spills out onto the pavement. The service can be curt although the seafood is often excellent.

O Escondidinho ('the hideaway'), Beco do Cemitério, **t** (282) 760 386. Slightly off the tourist trail is a simple fish restaurant, but portions are huge and the atmosphere jovial, verging on boisterous. *Closed Sun.*

O Alberto, Largo Convento Senhora da Glória 27, **t** (282) 769 387. Has an open kitchen where you can watch waiters burning themselves on the hot plates.

No Patio, Rua Lançarote 46, **t** (282) 763 777. This English-owned restaurant has a lovely patio (despite the confusing name, which means "on the patio" in Portuguese!). The menu has a good mix of dishes, including spicy

Mexican-inspired plates, curries and risottos.

Moderate–Inexpensive (€€–€)
Mediterraneo, Rua da Senhora da Graça, **t** (282) 768 476. The tables spill out onto the corner of a pretty little pedestrianized street, or you can squeeze into the attractive cosy interior. Dishes span the world with several vegetarian options though quality is variable. *Closed Sun, Mon, and Dec–Mar.*

Inexpensive (€)
Café Xpreitaqui Nature, Rua Silves Lopes. Close by, this is a good place for non-meat eaters, with excellent quiches, salads, and the best selection of juices, shakes and coffees in town. *Closed Sun.*

Restaurante Piri-Piri, Rua Lima Leitão 15, **t** (282) 763 803. Deservedly popular – sometimes too popular, overtaken by large groups. The generous portions are expertly cooked and served by courteous waiters. Usually the half-portions are enough; try the *peixe espadarte* – grilled swordfish served with an onion and butter sauce.

Adega da Marina, Avenida dos Descobrimentos 35, **t** (282) 764 284. Barn-like dining room with a beamed, vaulted ceiling, long refectory-style tables, fishing nets, anchors, and a swordfish. The garrulous clientele – families with excited kids who can shout as much as they like with impunity – is mostly Portuguese and the high quality of the food matches the atmosphere.

Ritinha, Rua do Canal 25, **t** (282) 763 791. Tucked away at the top of town, small, plain and popular with local families. Has no menu in English.

Bars, Entertainment and Nightlife in Lagos

There is a cacophony of bars. Two of the town's most attractive, **Café do Cais** and **Amuras Bar**, are part of the marina development, reached via a footbridge. At Amuras you can enjoy Latin sounds on a rooftop terrace.

Largest, and the best of the young and trendies, is the family-run **Mullens**, Rua Cândido dos Reis 86, **t** (282) 761 281, with a stone floor and black benches. Mullens doubles as a restaurant (€€) and the food is good. There is a whole bevy of noisy bars at the end of **Rua 25 de Abril. Millenium Jardim** is a civilized bar that also serves pizza. **Bon Vivant** offers Gaudíesque decoration and rooftop terrace.

At the **cinema** on Rua Cândido dos Reis, opposite Mullens, there is a 9.30pm show nightly during which you can drink beer or do pretty much anything you fancy – just so long as you don't put your feet on the seats. *Closed Thurs.*

The **Centro Cultural de Lagos**, Rua Lançarote de Freitas, **t** (282) 763 403, holds art exhibitions and music recitals (including *fado*) for culture vultures.

West of Lagos

Luz

Backed by bare cliffs, Luz is popular with English families, and there is even an English primary school here. Luz was probably idyllic once; the older villas are large, rambling affairs on the cliff above the beach, with 'Private Property' signs everywhere. The resort is Anglo-continental, though there is a little patch of sky above the church that's still Portuguese

Getting to areas West of Lagos

Semi-frequent **buses** run from Lagos to Luz (15mins), Burgau (30mins), Salema (45mins) and Raposeira (1hr), but you may have to walk from the highway.

The handsome 400-year-old **fortaleza**, at the end of the beach promenade, is now a restaurant (*see* p.514) but curious visitors who want to take a peek inside are always welcome (within opening hours).

Praia da Luz is a long stretch of sand with a shelf of large stone slabs to one end of the beach, backed by apartments and a handful of restaurants and bars. The two large, popular complexes which dominate the resort, the Ocean Club and Luz Bay Club, provide plenty of watersports and tennis facilities.

Burgau

Eighteen km west of Lagos, Burgau is small and mostly undeveloped. Its cobbled streets run down to the beach hemmed in by scree, to wonderfully clear water. The fishing community is almost extinct save a few colourful boats.

Salema

Seventeen kilometres east of Sagres and 22km west of Lagos, Salema is a rickety fishing village with a sheltered bay, whose rock cliffs fall to a sweep of smooth sand. Development is noticeable and growing all the time, but there is still a happy mix of locals and beach people. The 2km road from the highway passes through a beautiful ravine banked with wild flowers. At the beach, an alley flanked by low and humble houses leads to the left, while to the right a road rises steeply up the cliff with development groping upwards from here. The locals sit on a bench in the shade and offer rooms in their houses to let. You can reckon on around €50 for two bedrooms and a kitchen.

Raposeira

A small ordinary little village about 11km north of Sagres and 27km west of Lagos, Raposeira has narrow, cobbled streets and a couple of cafés slumber in a sleepy haze. Three kilometres to the east crouches the little white 13th-century **Chapel of Nossa Senhora de Guadalupe**, where Henry the Navigator is supposed to have worshipped.

Two lovely, quiet **beaches** lie some 4–6km south of Raposeira, calling for a hire car or sturdy legs. **Praia da Zavial** is a crescent-shaped bay with sand stretching way back. It's not too big but very picturesque. **Praia da Ingrina** is a tiny cove flanked by rocks creating a deep pool of water. Both beaches have restaurants and their calm waters and easy access make them particularly suitable for children.

From the campsite you can walk to Sagres, a distance of around 4½ miles (7km), without seeing a single house.

Sports and Activities West of Lagos

Up in the hills above Salema 16km west of Lagos, near Budens, the **Parque da Floresta** at Vale do Poço, t (282) 690 054, *www.vigiasa.com*, complex is best known for its 18-hole golf course. It's very hilly, quite challenging and very popular. Many other sports are available on this well-run estate including swimming, archery, bowls, horse-riding, mountain biking, tennis plus gym, sauna and jacuzzi.

(★) Casa Grande >>

Where to Stay West of Lagos

Luz

Apartments comprise most of the accommodation, but there are a couple of other options:
★★★★**Hotel Belavista**, on the road to the beach, t (282) 788 655, *www.belavistadaluz.com* (€€€). Large, sugary-pink, quite plush and very comfortable, with good-sized rooms and smooth service.
★★★★**Hotel Luz Bay**, Rua do Jardim, t (282) 789 640 (€€). A modern hotel with excellent facilities, including two pools, Turkish steam room and tennis courts. Idea for families.

Salema

★★★**Hotel Residencial Salema**, 28 de Janeiro, t (282) 695 328, *www.hotelsalema.com* (€€). A straightforward modern hotel with a fabulous position on the beach. Rooms are plain and tidy and facilities include satellite TV and a more generous buffet breakfast than most.
A Maré, t (282) 695 165, *www.algarve.co.uk* (€€). Also perched high above Salema beach, run by a friendly English couple. The breakfast room is

light and airy and all bedrooms are tastefully decorated with personal touches throughout. The top room has a wonderful view.

Various houses have rooms to let (€): try Rua dos Pescadores to the left of the beach and look for signs stuck in windows.

Burgau

Casa Grande, t (282) 697 416, *www.nexus-pt.com/casagrande* (€€). It's a rambling old place, built in 1912, tatty at the edges but comfy, and with bags of character, mostly injected by Sally, the chatty English owner. She is a great source of information as well as enormous fun. The restaurant (€€€–€€); *open evenings only; closed Sat and Sun*) is a wooden barn with tile-topped tables, extravagant murals and occasional live music. The food – Portuguese-international – includes several vegetarian dishes but quality is variable.
Hotel do Burgau (€€) A more conventional choice. A modern, boxy sort of place with 43 air-conditioned rooms and a small swimming pool.

Camping

Around Luz, there are two campsites, one situated a couple of kilometres north of town at Espiche, t (282) 789 431, and another about 1.5km east of the beach, called **Valverde**, t (282) 789 211, *www.orbitur.pt*.

In a leafy little valley between the coast road and the beach at Salema is a very attractive and well-run campsite, **Quinta dos Carriços t** (282) 695 201, *www.quintadoscarricos.com*, with some simple, tasteful studios and apartments (€) also available. The German management is determined to keep the place quiet, so no music is allowed. There's a mini-supermarket, a restaurant, a bar and,

★ O Celeiro >>

of course, an area reserved for nude campers. It's good value and well worth considering a stay if you don't want glitz.

At Raposeira, there is a campsite near Ingrina, t (282) 639 242.

Eating Out West of Lagos

Luz

Fortaleza da Luz, t (282) 789 926 (€€€). Whether or not you plan to dine, do call in for coffee in the fortress, where the ancient bare brickwork is adorned with shields, weapons and armour. Dinner by candlelight is romantic, and the food is generally very good. The lunchtime menu is lighter, with pizzas and vegetarian dishes included (€€–€), and you can eat outdoors on the *esplanada*, with great coast views. There's live music at Sunday lunchtime.

O Português, Rua da Praia, t (282) 788 804 (€€). At the far end of the beach, set back a block or two. Open-plan kitchen and a warm atmosphere. The food is of a high quality, especially the grilled fish, and the wine list is distinguished. *Closed Thurs.*

Paraiso, on the beach (€). All you'd want from a restaurant on the beach: shaded tables on a wooden deck overlooking sand and turquoise sea, good service, and a menu of grilled fresh fish, salad and French fries.

Burgau

O Celeiro, t (282) 697 144 (€€€–€€). For the best typical Portuguese food, head for this place, on the highway near the village of Almadena, 2km east of Burgau and 10km west of Lagos. It's a busy, rustic restaurant arranged around a wood-burning stove, with copper implements hanging from the walls. The menu adds a flamboyant touch to typical dishes, and the wine list represents most regions in the country. *Book in advance.*

Salema

Atlântico, t (282) 695 142 (€€). At the beachside, it has tables outside and serves delicious fresh tuna in a variety of styles.

Boia, Rua dos Pescadores 101, t (282) 695 382 (€). Beach terrace and a couple of vegetarian dishes. Good breakfasts are served in the bar.

Entertainment and Bars West of Lagos

There's a **cinema** in Luz, at the main commercial centre on the left as you head for the beach. It screens the latest releases on weekends at 10pm. In Salema, there are a couple of **bars** on Rua dos Pescadores.

Sagres and the West Coast

This unspoilt stretch of coast is a haven for the independent traveller, with some good-value accommodation, often in people's houses, no monster hotels, and miles of beautiful, empty beaches. The raw weather and stark scenery deter those who spend their holidays baking; this coast is windswept, keeping the air piercingly fresh and making the heat bearable. The sandstone cliffs of the south coast stage a gloriously vivid ochre finale on the beaches of Sagres before being superseded by a mixture of hard limestone and folded layers of jagged black slate.

The majority of the travellers and foreign settlers along this coast are German, attracted by the relaxed lifestyle. The English don't make it much further than Lagos and its easy delights. But beware – these beaches are a much less suitable location for a family holiday: the undertow can be very strong and a lot of the quieter beaches have no facilities or lifeguards, so great care must always be taken when swimming.

The Vincentina Coast

The area west of Burgau stretching up to the Alentejan town of Odemira forms a protected nature reserve, known as the Vincentina Coast. The government exerts tight planning controls despite heavy lobbying by big firms and pressure from foreign governments.

Among the endangered species represented in this area is the **ospreys**. This area is one of the last refuges in the Mediterranean for this bird. The last of Portugal's **rock doves** inhabit the cliffs around Cape St Vincent, as do pairs of **peregrine falcons**. **Storks** also nest here, eschewing their normal urban habitat. **Otters** like the salt marshes and sometimes the sea, where they catch fish, for example at Praia da Bordeira. All sorts of **amphibians** inhabit the small ponds found in the coastline plateau between October and April, migrating solely to reproduce in these temporary waters. The rarest species in the Iberian Peninsula is the beautiful **lynx**, which can be found in the Monchique and the Espinhaço de Cão ranges and comes down to roam the coast, preferring dunes with lots of scrub.

Sagres

⭐ Sagres

On a barren rock promontory pelted by northwesterly winds, 34km west of Lagos, the unexpected village of **Sagres** harbours the spirit of Portugal's groping exploration down the west African coast: a small peninsula some 300 yards wide juts out from the coast, and on this Henry the Navigator founded his school of navigation.

The wind and the sea are his only true monuments. The insubstantial and sprawling modern village of 3,000 inhabitants appears deceptively large from a distance, disappointing close to. On the road to Sagres, the countryside becomes barer and the sky wider, and the wind picks up the sweet smell of the gum cistus that is so prolific on this part of the coast. The approach heightens the feeling that this is the *Fim do Mundo* (End of the World), as was supposed by the ancients who were convinced that from Sagres Point (the western headland and the most southwesterly point in Europe) one fell into a seething pit of serpents and scaly monsters. Indeed the road ends at Sagres: there is no way to leave here except back the way you came.

The village is laid along three parallel streets. In the square, lined by cafés and a bar, travellers sit outside the Café Conchinha, occasionally playing a guitar as the wind whips up whirlpools of

Getting to Sagres

dust and napkins all around them. Along the headland, fishermen with rods the size of interplanetary receivers lean against the walls at the top of the cliffs catching anchovies, bream and snook. Some locals also scratch a living from scraping barnacles (*perceves*) from the rocks in winter. At the other end of the village the harbour glints bright blue as fishing boats unload their catch from these fertile waters.

History

In 1437, the Infante Dom Henrique, **Henry the Navigator**, son of Dom João I and Philippa of Lancaster, was obliged to leave his younger brother Dom Fernando as a hostage for the return of Ceuta to the Moors. A lesser man than Henry, as his pupil Magellan later remarked, 'would have hidden himself with seven yards of sackcloth and a rosary of oak-apples, to die in the wilds of the Serra de Ossa.'

But Henry found a more useful outlet for his ascetic tastes: he devoted himself – and his revenue as Duke of Viseu, Governor of the Algarve, monopolist of the soap and tuna-fishing industries, and Governor of the Order of Christ – to encouraging and financing the exploration of the west coast of Africa. He built the town on Sagres Point in 1443 for purely altruistic reasons: ships rounding the headland would be surprised by Atlantic storms and shelter in the cliffs, only to lose crews to starvation. So the Vila do Infante was built to provide shipping provisions and spiritual succour, with a couple of churches and a cemetery. Henry then founded a **school of navigation** there, gathering astronomers and astrologers, geographers, cartographers, Jews, sailors and wandering Arabs, who were able to give first-hand accounts of their travels. It was here that the first caravels were built in secret, constructed of Alentejan oak and caulked with pine resin. These revolutionary new designs contributed greatly to Portugal's seafaring prowess.

The infrastructure of trade developed so quickly that, when Cadamosto arrived here in 1454, one of Henry's secretaries showed him 'samples of sugar from Madeira, dragons' blood, and other products'. Such was the volume of trade at Sagres that the apprentice Columbus wrote, 'The Torrid Zone is not uninhabitable, for the Portuguese are sailing to and fro in it every day.'

Prince Henry died in 1460, a few decades short of witnessing Portugal's greatest triumphs: Bartolomeu Dias' successful navigation around the Cape of Good Hope in 1488 and Vasco da

Gama's discovery of the route to India at the turn of the century. Henry also missed Columbus' unexpected visit to Sagres in 1476, when pirates sank the convoy of ships with which he was sailing between Genoa and England. Wounded, he swam to shore.

The entire library of Henry the Navigator was unfortunately destroyed when Sir Francis Drake called in at Sagres and set fire to the place, as he sailed home after burning Cadiz in 1587.

The Fortress (Fortaleza)

The mighty fortress which occupies the rocky plateau was completed in 1793 – not that you'd know it now. Astonishingly, a few years ago the Ministry of Culture agreed to its development and, despite a national campaign for its conservation, covered it with an unsightly layer of now cracking concrete and peeling white paint. Some old buildings (of no historical importance, so it was claimed) were demolished to make way for a **café-restaurant** and an **exhibition block** – both built in an ultra-modern boxy style that won few allies. The exhibition hall is given over to temporary shows, usually art or photography, while interactive displays tell you about the flora, fauna and history of Sagres and the fortress.

The principal ancient surviving buildings are the simple 14th-century **Chapel of Nossa Senhorita da Graça** (*open to the public*), and outside the main area, a squat white buttressed building known as the **Auditorium** (*closed to the public*). It used to be the supplies and ammunition store and its current appearance goes back to its last renovation, in 1793. In the courtyard the most intriguing feature is the huge, flat wind compass, discovered in 1928. Named the **Rosa dos Ventos**, it is believed to date back to Henry the Navigator, though no one knows how it was used. Despite the government's efforts to destroy Sagres' most striking piece of history, a powerful energy still survives here.

From the fortress, walk out to the edge of **Sagres Point** and try not to get swept to America, to its left. The **lighthouse**, which boasts the most powerful lamp in Europe, is sometimes open to the public (*at the whim of the lighthouse keeper, no set times*). If you are allowed up the steps, leave him a small tip. If the cool breeze gives you goosebumps, check out the good-value sweaters sold from stalls lining the approach to the lighthouse.

Tourist Information and Services in Sagres

Turinfo has a vested interest in the advice it offers; for rooms it may be better to make your own arrangements. They usually make the accommodation situation sound desperate, but a quick walk around the square and the town will unearth a plethora of clean and cheap rooms.

The **post office** is on Rua do Mercado, which runs parallel with the main road into Sagres.

ⓘ Sagres >

Official tourist office: Rua Commandant Matoso, t (282) 624 873; open 9.30–12.30 and 2–5.30; closed Sun all year and Mon in winter

Turinfo: Praça da República, t (282) 620 003

⭐ **Vila Velha >>**

Shopping in Sagres

The **market hall** is next door to the post office, selling fruit, vegetables and fish on weekday mornings. The **gypsy market** hits Sagres on the first Friday of each month, occupying a field in front of the post office.

Sports and Activities in Sagres

The clean, very clear waters around Sagres boast 50ft (15m) visibility and water temperatures never less than 60°F (15°C), attracting a variety of fish, octopus and crustaceans in the rocks; the sea bed displays its most impressive foliage in August. The Ilhas do Martinhal **diving school**, t (282) 624 736, at Sagres harbour at the bottom of the steps to the left, offers tuition, equipment hire and the usual services.

The **surfing** here is world renowned. Contact **Clube do Martinhal**, at Mareta beach in Sagres, t (282) 642 333. It also offers other water sports.

Go right down to the harbour front for **boat trips** on the *Estrela-do-Rio* which goes to Cape St Vincent and beyond. If you are lucky you may spot dolphins on the way.

Turinfo (*see* above) hires out bikes and mopeds, and arranges fishing trips and jeep safaris. The **West Coast jeep tour** takes in Cape St Vincent and Vale Santo, and hugs the coastline between Sagres and Bordeira beach along rough tracks which cars find difficult to negotiate.

Where to Stay in Sagres

★★★**Hotel da Baleeira**, Baleeira, t (282) 624 212, *www.memmohotels.com* (€€€). The best thing about this hotel, with its coffin-shaped swimming pool, is its location overlooking the harbour and its wonderful views stretching east to the cliffs of the Algarve. Rooms are spick and span, though package tours block-book.

★★★**ApartHotel Navigator**, Rua Infante Dom Henrique, t (282) 624 354, *www.hotel-navigator.com* (€€). Clean, with polite staff, its small-roomed gadgety apartments are furnished in inoffensive modern style. The building is arranged around a shady pear-shaped swimming pool. Like all the hotels here, sadly, it's being overrun by package-tour operators.

★★★★**Residência Dom Henrique**, Sítio da Mareta, t (282) 620 000 (€€). Fabulous ocean views, on a cliff above the Mareta beach. Some of its clean, simple guest rooms overlook the beach, and you can hear the surf from the conservatory. The little restaurant serves grilled squid.

★★★**Mareta View Hotel**, Beco Dom Henrique, t (282) 620 000 (€€). Boutique bed and breakfast overlooking a sandy beach. There are just 17 rooms, several of which have views and large terraces. A jacuzzi and gazebo are located in the pretty gardens.

There are rooms to let in people's houses (€) – ask Klaus at the Rosa dos Ventos bar (*see* p.520) about **Casa Marreiros**, which has clean, airy rooms and a big communal kitchen.

Pousada

Pousada do Infante, 8650-385 Sagres, t (282) 624 222, central reservations t (218) 442 001, *www.pousadas.pt* (L2 N). Peacefully located on the headland between the fishing harbour and Mareta beach, this is a large, modern villa with fantastic views across the beach to the promontory and its fort. It's worth paying extra for a sea view, the sunsets can be spectacular. The rooms could do with some refurbishment. The restaurant is adequate. A small swimming pool and tennis court help justify the price tag.

Camping

Sagres' **campsite** is about a kilometre inland from the village, t (282) 624 371, *www.orbitur.pt*.

Eating Out in Sagres

Vila Velha, t (282) 624 788 (€€€). On the way to the Pousada do Infante stands Sagres' best restaurant. Dutch Lia painstakingly prepares the traditionally inspired dishes served in huge portions in the rustic dining room. Her affable Portuguese husband supervises the smooth service and brings the fresh fish of the day to your table for inspection. The three vegetarian dishes are very good, as is the house wine. *Evenings only; closed Mon.*

Carlos, t (282) 624 228 (€€€). Opposite the turning for Vila Velha on Rua da Baleeira is a large, sugary-pink and typically Portuguese affair serving reliably good food to visitors and enthusiastic locals alike. The ubiquitous fish soup is superior and the grilled *cherne* (grouper) is very good and very large. If it's on the menu, go for the marvellous *lulas recheadas*, squid stuffed with rice, herbs and pork meat. The house wine is worth a slosh.

Fortaleza do Beliche, t (282) 624 124 (€€€). In a little fort about a third of the way along the road from Sagres to Cape St Vincent. Run by Enatur, the *pousada* people, it's decorated in 'Navigator style', with maps and fake candelabra. The waiters are smartly dressed and courteous; the food is OK, though the menu is unadventurous and overpriced. You can also stay here (€€€) but beware the high turnover. If you do decide to tarry, choose Room 4 with a great sea view.

Bossa Nova, Rua Citie Matoso, **t** (282) 624 566 (€€). Large, airy restaurant with a covered terrace where German hippies happily rub shoulders with children dressed in Marks & Spencer's best. The food is pricey given that it's mainly pasta and pizzas – you pay for the atmosphere – but the vegetarian options are cheaper. Avoid the tropical curry.

Flying Bar Marisqueria, Sítio do Botelha, **t** (282) 624 762 (€). Practise your Portuguese ready for this tourist-free venue. The restaurant is small and plain; you can sit in the bar or outside in the colourful garden. Choose your shellfish from the tank; eat octopus in tomato sauce, three sorts of crabs, clams and cockles cooked with garlic and herbs, or *arroz do mariscos* (seafood rice), which may take some time to prepare (for a minimum of two). A treat every time.

Rosa dos Ventos, on the main square, **t** (282) 624 480 (€). Bar serving a full range of good-value snacks and meals; here, they understand salads in a way most Portuguese don't.

Entertainment and Nightlife

In the evenings a happy mix of international (mainly German) travellers and locals get drunk at Rosa dos Ventos and around 2am stagger off to **Topas** disco, which is great fun. To get there, take the main road to Lagos and take a left signposted for *Topas* and *Flying Bar*. Follow the road to the end, for about 10 minutes, to Topas.

Around Sagres

Cape St Vincent

The invigorating headland on the brink of Europe stands on raw, limestone cliffs, rising 200ft (60m) out of the sea, 6km west of Sagres. There is no settlement to speak of, but the land mass announces itself with one of the most powerful lighthouses in Europe and a ruined monastery.

The landscape is hardy, dominated by gum cistus, rosemary and juniper bushes, but in springtime colourful wild flowers peek through cracks in the rock. On the way from Sagres to the Cape, you'll see the fragile white cistus roses, poppies bearing tissue-thin scarlet blooms, and small purple pimpernels twisting through rock crevices. In the summer, white sea daffodils appear while red and bright pink bougainvillaea climb the walls alongside the deep purple flowers of the clematis. There are at least three plant species named after the Cape and indigenous to this area alone: *Biscutella vincentina*, *Scilla vincentina* and *Centaurea vincentina*.

Many birds of prey stop here on their autumn migration path for a feed and a rest. The easiest to spot are the gannets, casting large shadows as they circle and plunge down to pluck their meal from the waves. Starlings and blue rock thrushes are common, and cooing rock doves can occasionally be seen at sunset.

The Romans called this the *Promontorium Sacrum*; at sundown the sun appeared a hundred times larger than elsewhere, and hissed as if it were being quenched. (A freak of atmospherics continues to magnify some of the sunsets, and occasionally the sun appears to yield a green flash as it vanishes.) In later times, when the body of St Vincent arrived from Valença in a boat guided by ravens, the promontory became a Christian shrine and for centuries boats dipped their sails as they passed. The shrine has gone, but the ravens remain (by legend some of them accompanied St Vincent's body on its removal to Lisbon in 1173).

A later resident was rather more lively: Henry the Navigator lived and died on the site where the lighthouse stands, commuting to his school of navigation at Sagres. In 1693 these seas bore a naval battle between the French and the combined British and Dutch fleets, and it was here that the British fleet under Jervis and Nelson battled the Spanish in 1797. The waters at the Cape seem to carry memories of these battles, especially when they are heard moaning and sighing through the **blowhole** on the headland.

Vila do Bispo

Ten kilometres north of Sagres, on a junction of the west and south coast roads, lies a serene little town with a sunny central square and a lovely white church. Behind the fine Manueline doorway the interior blazes with giltwork, painting and 18th-century blue *azulejos*. Otherwise there's nothing much here except the district town hall and the nearest police station to Sagres.

Carrapateira

This small village lies 23km north of Sagres and is favoured by a few very laid-back German travellers. There are some private rooms for rent in people's houses: ask at the café in the square. The valley to the east of Carrapateira is hazily beautiful: green fields bloom with an abundance of wild flowers and goatherds slumber in the shade of cork trees while the creatures roam. For a lovely walk to Bordeira beach, follow the stream jewelled with waterlilies and diving kingfishers.

Where to Stay and Eat

Vila do Bispo

★★Pensão Mira-Sagres, Rua 1 de Maio, t (282) 639 160 (€). Opposite the church, this is perfectly adequate, despite the strangely musty smell. Alternatively, ask for rooms at **No.18 Praça da República** (€), next to the bank, or at the restaurant on the same side of the square.

Café Correia, next to the post office, opposite the church, t (282) 639 400 (€). The best place to eat is the plain and large Café Correia. Their *caldeirada* (fish stew) is very good. *Closed Sat.*

Carrapateira

⭐ Monte Velho Nature Resort >

Monte Velho Nature Resort, t (282) 973 201, *www.montevelhoresort.com* (€€€). Near Carrapateira, and 4km from Amado beach, this is about as far as you can get from the overdeveloped, mass-market Algarve: when you stand outside the ranch-style building you see 180° of hills and nothing else. The place has an ayurevedic, Greek yoghurt feel, with spice colours, hammocks, wooden ceilings and contagious mellowness. There's no TV or telephone, and it is utterly quiet except for birdsong and the braying of donkeys. There are seven apartments but no self catering facilities: breakfast is provided, and a light Italian-inspired supper can be requested. Otherwise you'll need to eat at the beach or picnic. Monte Velho is owned by the surfer Eric Balsemão, with close and fairly easy access to some of the best surfing – and most beautiful – beaches in the Algarve. *Book months ahead. Minimum stay in July and August is 1 week, otherwise 2 nights.*

Pensão das Dunas, t (282) 973 118 (€). Occupies an attractive old house on the edge of the dunes, with a flower-filled courtyard, an abundance of cats, and tasteful blue-and-white bedrooms. Shared bathrooms.

Arrifana

Ask for rooms at the **Restaurante Fortaleza**.

There is a handful of restaurants, all of which are remarkably similar; **Brisamar** has the best views.

There is a **snack bar** (€) overlooking the beach itself at the bottom of the winding road. Eat a generous portion of prawns on the terrace while admiring the tough beauty of the beach.

Arrifana

This small, lacklustre settlement sits above the beach, 49km north of Sagres and 8km west of Aljezur. At the end of the village the ruins of the *fortaleza* offer magnificent views. The rounded hills of the coastline, green with glistening cistus, drop in sheer slate-grey cliffs to a smooth bay backed by shingle and dotted with small stacks, against which breaking waves foam. A weird cone-shaped rock, the *Pedra da Agulha* (Needle Stone), protrudes from the sea.

From Aljezur to Odeceixe

Aljezur

A very small town 50km north of Sagres, Aljezur straddles a broad river valley. The older part hugs the hillside, while newer houses bake quietly on the other side of the valley through which a small stream trickles. The ruin of an old **Moorish castle** watches over all.

Getting to and around Aljezur and Odeceixe

EVA **buses** run semi-frequently from Lagos to Aljezur (¾hr) and Odeceixe (1½hr). There are two buses a day to Arrifana and Monte Clérigo on Mondays and Thursdays only.

Sandwiched between the foothills of Monchique, the Espinhaço de Cão range and the Atlantic, Aljezur has a forgotten feeling about it, especially palpable at the castle on a hot day. If you are suffering from a headache, make a trip over the river and visit the 18th-century church that houses the skulls of the last two Moors killed in Aljezur: lay your hands on them to be instantly relieved. The views from the castle are splendid: from the top you can see the two parts of the town, divided by a vivid green patchwork of cultivated land. In the distance, the hazy purple hills of Monchique seem to occupy another age, and on the other side soft green hills are dotted with cattle and provide peeks at the sea.

Odeceixe

The road winds 71km from Sagres, descending through eucalyptus woods to offer glimpses of Odeceixe snugly settled in the crook of the surrounding hills. The river that runs alongside marks the boundary with the next province, the Alentejo. The green and well-cultivated land infuses the village with a gentle peacefulness that soothes the soul. In the tiny central square old men sit under the tree to talk, unconcerned by the rainbow-attired travellers slouching past.

Tourist Information in Aljezur

(i) **Aljezur >**
Largo do Mercado,
t (282) 998 229; open
daily 9.30–5.30,
summer until 7; closed
for lunch at weekends;
help with private
rooms and villas

The **post office** and **banks** are on Rua 25 de Abril, the main road in from Lagos.

Shopping in Aljezur

The **market hall** in Aljezur is behind the tourist office and sells fresh fish, fruit and vegetables every weekday morning. The **gypsy market** descends on Aljezur on the third Monday of every month.

Where to Stay and Eat

Aljezur

There are no hotels in Aljezur. The nearest is about 5km southwest of the town in Vale da Telha tourist village, a large-scale development with a campsite, villas and a hotel.

★★Hotel Vale da Telha, **t** (282) 998 180 (€). This modern hotel looks like a row of matchboxes. Long, dark corridors lead to decent-sized bedrooms with small bathrooms and tiny balconies, and it's all very clean.

There is also a **campsite** at Serrão, 3km north of Aljezur on the way to Amoreira beach, **t** (282) 990 200.

Restaurante Ruth on Rua 25 de Abril, **t** (282) 998 534 (€€). Draws locals from miles around to sample its fresh seafood. The snow-haired owner is very friendly and the menu small. Go for the fresh fish of the day, or *perceves* (barnacles) if you can. The *ementa turística* is particularly good value.

Odeceixe

The tourist office at Aljezur can supply you with a list of approved accommodation, though you needn't worry about finding rooms – touts will approach you with offers.

Taberna da Gabão, Rua da Gabão, **t** (282) 998 886 (€€–€). Has a mainly Portuguese clientele clamouring to fill its large, barn-like interior. Good food comes in large portions: try *feijoada com polvo*, a huge helping of beans cooked with octopus, sausage and parsley, served with rice.

Pensão Luar, Rua da Várzea, **t** (282) 974 194 (€). At the bottom of the village on the road to the beach. It's clean, with lovely views over farmland and hills from the front-facing rooms.

Snack-Bar Stop, in the square (€). A good place to sit and watch the action (though action isn't a strong point here): in season this is likely to be provided by the makeshift German hippy commune; out of season, by the locals chasing a diseased dog.

Language

If you have a basic knowledge of Latin and French or Spanish, you should be able to make sense of written Portuguese, which is a Romance language. Pronunciation is another matter: Portuguese is diabolically difficult to speak. Plunge on in. The Portuguese are far too polite to make fun of your attempts, and most people will be delighted that you've made the effort. (Also, they are fond of reminding visitors that Portuguese is the seventh most widely spoken language in the world.) English is not uncommon in the cities and tourist areas, but it's just as alien to the Portuguese as their language is to us; French is a more useful *lingua franca*, since the Portuguese learn it as their second language.

Some anthropologists reckon that the Portuguese made their pronunciation as different as possible from Spanish, to empha-size their own identity. It may take several flagons of local wine before you can get your tongue around the vowels. A single stressed syllable (denoted by an acute accent or a circumflex) tends to swallow up the rest of a word. The tilde (~) is most commonly used as 'ão', which produces a nasal 'ow' as in 'cow'. Consonants tend to be slurred. 'C' is soft before 'e' and 'i', but hard before 'a', 'o', and 'u'. 'ç' is pronounced 's'. 'J' is pronounced like the 's' in 'leisure'. 'G' sounds the same when it comes before 'e' or 'i' – otherwise it is hard, as in 'get'. 'Lh' takes on the sound of 'ly', 'qu' that of 'k'. 'S' is pronounced 'sh' when it comes before a consonant or at the end of a word. 'X' also sounds like 'sh'.

Greetings

good morning *bom dia*
good afternoon or evening *boa tarde*
goodnight *boa noite*
goodbye *adeus*
see you later *até logo*

yes *sim*
no *não*
please *por favor*
thank you *obrigado (when spoken by a man),* *obrigada (when spoken by a woman)*
excuse me *com licença*
I'm sorry *desculpe*

Common Phrases

Please help me *Ajude-me por favor*
Do you speak English? *Fala inglês?*
How much is it? *Quanto custa?*
Where is the toilet? *Onde ficam os lavabos?*
I'm in a hurry *Tenho pressa*
Why? *Porquê?*
Where? *Onde?*
How are you? *Como vai?*
I'm lost *estou perdido*
I don't understand *não compreendo*
What do you call this? *Como se chama isto?*

Asking Directions

Is this right for ...? *Vou bem para?*
Can you direct me to ...? *Pode indicar-me o caminho para ...?*
the railway station *a estação*
round trip *ida e volta*
the centre of the city *o centro da cidade*
bus stop *paragem de autocarro*
taxi rank *ponto de táxi*
police *polícia*
hospital *hospital*
chemist *farmacêutico*
museum *museu*
church *igreja*
beach *praia*

Accommodation

a single room *um quarto simples*
a double room *um quarto de casal*
with private bathroom *com banho*

bring me *traga-me*
a towel *uma toalha*
soap *sabonete*
toilet paper *papel higiénico*

Eating Out

See **Food and Drink**, 'Menu Reader', pp.51–2.

Time

What time is it? *Que horas são?*
when *quando*
do you open?/ do you shut? *abrem?/ fecham?*
When will it be ready? *Quando fica pronto?*
immediately *imediatamente*
yesterday *ontem*
tomorrow *amanhã*
today *hoje*
this afternoon *logo à tarde*
this evening *logo à noite*
one night *uma noite*
one day *um dia*
midday *meio dia*
midnight *meia noite*
now *agora*
later *mais tarde*

Money

Can I have *Pode dar-me*
the bill *a conta*
the receipt *o recibo*
the change *o troco*
Can you change? *Pode trocar?*
Do you take traveller's cheques? *Aceitam traveller's cheques?*
a bank *um banco*
What is the rate of exchange? *Qual é o câmbio*
signature *assinatura*
notes *notas*
coins *moedas*
money *dinheiro*

Post Office

What is the postage? *Quanto é a franquia?*
on this letter *nesta carta*
postcard *bilhete postal*
parcel *volume*
by air mail *por via aérea*
stamps *selos*

Measurements

big *grande*
bigger *maior*
small *pequeno*
smaller *mais pequeno*
long *comprido*
short *curto*
cheap *barato*
expensive *caro*
beautiful *belo*
ugly *feio*

Everyday Purchases

Do you sell ...? *Vendem ...?*
films for this camera *filmes para esta máquina*
newspapers *jornais*
books *livros*
magazines *revistas*
in English *em inglês*
ballpoint pens *esferográficas*

Days of the Week

Sunday *domingo*
Monday *segunda-feira*
Tuesday *terça-feira*
Wednesday *quarta-feira*
Thursday *quinta-feira*
Friday *sexta-feira*
Saturday *sábado*
Holidays *feriados*

Chemist

Have you anything for ...? *O que têm para ...?*
bad sunburn *queimaduras de sol*
colds *constipações*
constipation *prisão de ventre*
diarrhoea *diarreia*
sore feet *pés doridos*

Numbers

one *um*
two *dois*
three *três*
four *quatro*
five *cinco*
six *seis*
seven *sete*
eight *oito*

nine *nove*
ten *dez*
eleven *onze*
twelve *doze*
thirteen *treze*
fourteen *catorze*
fifteen *quinze*
sixteen *dezesseis*
seventeen *dezassete*
eighteen *dexoito*
nineteen *dezanove*
twenty *vinte*
twenty-one *vinte e um*
thirty *trinta*
forty *quarenta*
fifty *cinquenta*
sixty *sessenta*
seventy *setenta*
eighty *oitenta*
ninety *noventa*
one hundred *cem*
one hundred and one *cento e um*
one thousand *mil*

Colours

white *branco*
black *preto*
red *vermelho*
blue *azul*
green *verde*
brown *castanho*
yellow *amarelo*

Architectural Terms

Municipal town hall *Câmara*
Mother Church/parish church *Igreja Matriz*
viewpoint *miradouro*
pillory *pelourinho*
villa/country seat *quinta*
public square *rossio*
cathedral/diocese *sé*
manor house *solar*
keep *torre de menagem*

Rulers of Portugal to 1910

House of Burgundy

1128/39–85	Afonso (Henriques) I
1185–1211	Sancho I
1211–23	Afonso II – Uracca (1220)
1223–48	Sancho II
1248–79	Afonso III
1279–1325	Dinis – Isabel of Aragon (1282)
1325–57	Afonso IV
1357–67	Pedro I – Blanca of Castile (1328) – Constanza of Castile (1336) – Inês de Castro
1367–83	Fernando I – Leonor Teles (1372)

House of Avis

1383–85	João I (Regent) – Philippa of Lancaster (1387)
1385–1433	João I (King)
1433–38	Duarte
1438–81	Afonso V
1481–95	João II – Leonor (1471)
1495–1521	Manuel I – Isabel of Castile (1497) – Maria of Castile (1500) – Leonor of Spain (1518)
1521–57	João III
1557–78	Sebastião (Sebastian)
1578–80	Cardinal Henrique
1580	António, Prior of Crato

House of Hapsburg

1580–98	Philip II of Spain (I of Portugal)
1598–1621	Philip III of Spain (II of Portugal)
1621–40	Philip IV of Spain (III of Portugal)

House of Bragança

1640–56	João IV
1656–67	Afonso VI – Isabel of Savoy (1668)
1667–83	Pedro II (Regent) – Isabel of Savoy (1666) – Maria of Neuberg (1687)
1683–1706	Pedro II (King)
1706–50	João V – Maria-Ana of Austria (1708)
1750–77	José I
1777–92	Maria I – Pedro III (1760)
1792–1816	João VI (Regent) – Carlota Joaquina of Spain (1784)
1816–26	João VI (King)
1826–28	Pedro IV
1828–34	Miguel
1834–53	Maria II (da Glória) – August of Leuchtenberg (1834) – Ferdinand of Saxe-Coburg-Gotha (1836)
1853–55	Ferdinand (Regent)
1855–61	Pedro V
1861–89	Luís – Maria-Pia of Savoy
1889–1908	Carlos
1908–10	Manuel II

Select Bibliography

I feel like a dwarf on the shoulders of giants: I owe a huge debt to many literary sources, which I have not been able to acknowledge in the text. The editions listed are those I have used. The following have been invaluable:

Azevedo, Carlos de, *Churches of Portugal* (Scala Books, 1985).

Bradford, Sarah, *The Story of Port* (Christie's Wine Publications, 1983).

Ellingham, Mark, etc., *The Real Guide: Portugal* (Prentice Hall, 1989).

Farinha, João Carlos (ed.), *Routes to the Landscapes & Habitats of Portugal* (Assírio and Alvim, 2001).

Gallop, Rodney, *Portugal A Book of Folk Ways* (C.U.P., 1961). Popular anthropology.

Gil, Júlio, *The Finest Castles in Portugal* (Verbo, 1986).

King, John, *Portugal* (Lonely Planet, 2003).

Livermore, H.V., *A New History of Portugal* (C.U.P., 1969).

Read, Jan, *The Wines of Portugal* (Faber and Faber, 1987).

Robertson, Ian, *Blue Guide: Portugal* (Ernest Benn, 1984).

Smith, R.C., *The Art of Portugal 1500–1800* (Weidenfeld and Nicholson, 1968). Professorial overview of the arts.

Vieira, Edite, *A Taste of Portugal* (Robert Hale, 1988). Anecdotal cookbook.

Whol, Helmut and Alice, *Portugal* (Scala Books, 1983). Incisive and independent-minded text to accompany glossy photographs.

À Descoberta de Portugal (Seleções do Reader's Digest, 1982). Clipped descriptions of villages, with longer pieces on local quirks.

The Fine Wines of Portugal (Decanter Magazine, 1987).

Guia de Portugal Vols I, II, and III (Biblioteca Nacional de Lisboa, 1924, 1927). Detailed exegesis of everything, everywhere.

Guia de Portugal Vol III (1985), IV i (1985), IV ii (1986), V i (1987), V ii (1988) (Fundação Calouste Gulbenkian). Modern editions of the above series.

Tesuros Artísticos de Portugal (Seleções do Reader's Digest, 1976). Facts about monuments and art.

History

Alarcão, J. de, *Roman Portugal* (Aris and Phillips, 1988).

Boxer, C.R., *The Portuguese Seaborne Empire 1415–1825* (Hutchinson, 1977).

Cheke, Marcus, *Dictator of Portugal: Marquis of Pombal* (Sidgwick and Jackson, 1938).

Cheke, Marcus, *Carlota Joaquina, Queen of Portugal* (Sidgwick and Jackson, 1947).

Crone, G.R., *The Discovery of the East* (Hamish Hamilton, 1972).

Francis, David, *Portugal 1715–1808* (Tamesis, 1985).

Hanson, C., *Economy and Society in Baroque Portugal 1668–1703* (Macmillan, 1981).

Marques, A.H. de Oliveira, *History of Portugal* (2 vols) (Columbia, 1972).

Nowell, Charles, *A History of Portugal* (Van Nostrand, 1952).

Payne, S.G., *History of Spain and Portugal* (University of Wisconsin Press, 1973).

Read, Jan, *The Moors in Spain and Portugal* (Faber and Faber, 1974).

Robinson, Richard, *Contemporary Portugal* (George Allen and Unwin, 1979).

Sanceau, Elaine, *The Perfect Prince* (Livraria Civilização, 1959).

Trend, J.B., *Portugal* (Ernest Benn, 1957).

Ure, John, *Henry the Navigator* (Constable and Co, 1977).

Monographs

Delaforce, Angela, *The Solar de Mateus* (unpublished ms.).

Goffen, Rona, *Museums Discovered: The Calouste Gulbenkian Museum* (Woodbine Books, 1984).

Guides

Baedeker's Portugal (The Automobile Association, 2nd edition).

Ellingham, Mark, etc., *The Rough Guide to Portugal* (R.K.P., 1987) (Penguin, 2002).

Lowndes, Susan, and Bridge, Ann, *The Selective Traveller in Portugal* (Evans, 1949).

Raposo, Francisco Hipólito, *Beira Alta, Estremadura e Ribatejo and O Minho* (Mobil, 1987). Detailed local guides.

Raposo, Francisco Hipólito, *Alto Alentejo* (Mobil, 1986). As above.

Articles in Journals, Periodicals and Newspapers

Amorim, Roby, 'The Welcoming Chimney' (*Atlantis*, November/December 1986).

Bairrada, Eduardo Martins, 'Pavement Artists of Lisbon' (*Atlantis*, January/February 1987).

Barrett, Frank (*The Independent*, 22 July 1989).

Blum, Patrick, and Smith, Diana, 'Financial Times Survey: Portugal' (*Financial Times*, 11 Oct 1989).

D'Orey, Leonor, and Teague, Michael, 'In the King's Service' (*House and Garden*, November 1986).

Jardim, Bela, 'Pillories' (*Atlantis*).

Newby, Eric, 'Insider's Guide to Lisbon' (*The Observer Magazine*).

Smith, Diana (*Financial Times*, 19 September 1987, 7 January 1988).

Miscellaneous

Cabral, Martim (ed.), *Portugal: Business Partners in Europe* (De Montfort, 1986).

Campbell, Roy, *Portugal* (Max Reinhardt, 1957).

Macaulay, Rose, *They Went to Portugal* (Penguin, 1985).

Pina-Cabral, João de, *Sons of Adam, Daughters of Eve* (Clarendon Press, 1986).

Watson, Walter Crum, *Portuguese Architecture* (Archibald Constable, 1908).

Literature

Bell, Aubrey (trs.), *Four Plays of Gil Vicente* (C.U.P., 1920).

Camões, Luis Vaz de, *The Lusiads* (Penguin, 1985).

Garrett, Almeida, *Travels in My Homeland* (Peter Owen/UNESCO, 1987).

Macedo, H. (ed.), *Modern Poetry in Translation 13/14 Portugal* (Modern Poetry in Translation, 1972).

Pessoa, Fernando, *Selected Poems* (Penguin, 1988).

Pires, José Cardoso, *Ballad of Dogs' Beach* (Dent, 1986).

Queiroz, Eça de, *The Maias* (Dent, 1986).

Saramago, José, *Baltasar and Blimunda* (Cape, 1988)

Primary Sources

Alcobaça and Batalha (Centaur Press, 1972).

Azurara, *Chronicle of the Discovery of Guinea.*

Beckford, William, *Recollections of an Excursion to the Monasteries of Lopes, Fernão, The English in Portugal* (Aris and Phillips, 1988).

Further Reading

The classic introduction to the country and its people is **Marion Kaplan**'s *The Portuguese* (Penguin). Although outdated in some respects, it puts its finger on the button again and again.

Paul Buck's *Lisbon – a Cultural and Literary Companion*, in Signal Books' Cities of the Imagination series, is a highly personal, generally well researched meander around the capital.

In *Portugal, a Traveller's Guide* (John Murray 1992), **Ian Robertson** does a similar job for the country as a whole.

For potted history, **David Birmingham**'s *A Concise History of Portugal* (Cambridge University Press, 1993) does the trick, within the limitations of its 190-odd pages of text.

The best English-language survey of recent developments in Portuguese society from a readable academic perspective is *Modern Portugal*, edited by **António Costa Pinto** (The Society for the Promotion of Science and Scholarship, Palo Alto, 1998).

Index

Main page references are in **bold**. Page references to maps are in *italics*.

About the Author

David Evans divided his time between New York and London from the age of 21 months to the age of 21 years, when Portugal seduced him. He's still passionate about the country, and has written about it for newspapers and magazines on both sides of the Atlantic. He studied at Eton and read History at Cambridge, where he learnt to conjure up the past and developed an eye for architraves. His years as a Franciscan friar gave him a love of landscape, his work as a butler taught him to pour a double decanter at arm's length, and a brief stint as a catwalk model showed him that frivolity can be fun. He enjoys walking among trees, drinking martinis, unearthing bargains and following his curiosity, which is as omnivorous as a Portuguese goat. He was ordained in the Church of England in 2005.

Author's Acknowledgements

I could not have undertaken this project, or completed it without the encouragement and support of my aunt and uncle, Susan and John Mayo. In Lisbon, Michael and Rosita Simpson-Orlebar became my fairy godparents: they welcomed me into the Ambassador's residence for several months and surrounded me with kindness. My mother Louise Evans generously lent me a house to write in. I would also like to thank Paula Levey, who offered me the job and saw it through, and Lorna Horsfield, who edited the first edition of this book.

The Portuguese National Tourist Office has been unstintingly generous with time and hospitality. This book would have been impossible without the help of Alberto Marques and Luís Cancela de Abreu. I would also like to thank António Serras Pereira, Pilar Pereira, Álvaro de Sousa, Celestino Domingues, Gabriela Ferreira, João Custódio, Isabel Terenas, Christopher Cramer, Maria Emília Riberio and Alice Martin.

A great many people have shared their enthusiasm and expertise. I am very grateful to: Maria de Lourdes Simões de Carvalho, Eugénio Lisboa, José Maria Montargil, Fernanda dos Santos, Susan Lowndes Marques, Diana Smith, Madalena Cabral, Luís Rebelo, Mark and Ana Hudson, Paula Guimarães, Mafalda Soares da Cunha, Concha Corrêa Botelho, Nono Félix da Costa, Francisco Viegas, Pedro and Lucia Wallenstein, Joanna Clyde, Romeu Pinto da Silva, Joao Barbosa Lisboa, the Conde de Campo Bello, Margaret Aird, Evelyn Hayward, António Madeira, Inês Enes Dias, Gerald Luckhurst, Catherine Mayo, Mark Hewitt, Tanya Garveigh, Rory Macrae, John Delaforce, Angela Delaforce, the Charles Drace-Francis, Janes Fernandes, Maria Deolinda Cerqueira, Manuel Gandra, Fernanda Frazão, Luís Marques da Gama, Salete Salvado, Maria da Graça Teles, Alda Teixeira, Afonso Belarmino, António Capela, Carlos de Matos, Margarida Leite Rio, José Marquês de Fronteira, Alan and Jocelyn Tait, Ruth Briggs, Cristina Gaspar, José Meco, Martins Carneiro, Rosa Costa Gomes, Joao Baptista Martins, César Valença, José Belo dos Santos, and finally Paulo, Isabel, Leonor, Rosa and Armanda.

About the Updater

Based in Andalucía, southern Spain, travel writer **Josephine Quintero** has updated several Cadogan guides, including Spain and Italy titles. She makes frequent trips over the border to explore neighbouring Portugal, which continues to charm her with its unspoiled scenery, rich culture and heritage and the warm hospitality of the people.

6th edition published in 2009

Cadogan Guides is an imprint of
New Holland Publishers (UK) Ltd
London • Cape Town • Sydney • Auckland

New Holland	80 McKenzie Street	Unit 1, 66 Gibbes Street	218 Lake Road
Publishers (UK) Ltd	Cape Town 8001	Chatswood, NSW 2067	Northcote
Garfield House	South Africa	Australia	Auckland
86–88 Edgware Road			New Zealand
London W2 2EA			

cadogan@nhpub.co.uk
www.cadoganguides.com
t +44 (0) 20 7724 7773

Copyright © David J.J. Evans 1990, 1992, 1995, 1998, 2004, 2009
Copyright © New Holland Publishers (UK) Ltd 2009

Cover photographs: Front: © Philippa Lewis; Edifice/Corbis Back: © Michele Falzone/JAI/Corbis
Photo essay photographs: pp.1, 3, 4, 5, 9 top left/top right, 11 bottom, 12 top, 14, 15 © John Miller; p.6 top © lillisphotography/iStockphoto; pg 6 bottom © aladin66/iStockphoto; p.8 © Owen Franken/Corbis; p.9 bottom © Inicio Pires/shutterstock images; p.10 top © Paulo Resende/shutterstock images; p.10 bottom © Rafal Belzowski/iStockphoto; p.11 top © Dariusz Majgier/shutterstock images; p.12 © porcsenglar/iStockphoto; p.13 top © king_tut/iStockphoto; p.13 bottom © Miguel Angelo Silva/iStockphoto; p.16 © Tony Arruza/Corbis.
Maps: © Cadogan Guides, drawn by Maidenhead Cartographic Services Ltd
Cover design: Jason Hopper
Photo essay design: Sarah Gardner
Editor: Clare Hubbard
Proofreading: Elspeth Anderson
Indexing: Isobel McLean

Printed and bound in Italy by Legoprint
A catalogue record for this book is available from the British Library

ISBN: 978-1-86011-419-9

The author and publishers have made every effort to ensure the accuracy of the information in this book at the time of going to press. However, they cannot accept any responsibility for any loss, injury or inconvenience resulting from the use of information contained in this guide.

Please help us to keep this guide up to date. We have done our best to ensure that the information in this guide is correct at the time of going to press, but laws and regulations are constantly changing, and standards and prices fluctuate. We would be delighted to receive any comments.

All rights reserved. No part of this publication may be reproduced, stored in a retrieval system, or transmitted, in any form or by any means, electronic or mechanical, including photocopying and recording, or by any information storage and retrieval system except as may be expressly permitted by the UK 1988 Copyright Design & Patents Act and the USA 1976 Copyright Act or in writing from the publisher. Requests for permission should be addressed to Cadogan Guides, New Holland Publishers, Garfield House, 86–88 Edgware Road, London, W2 2EA, United Kingdom.

Portugal touring atlas

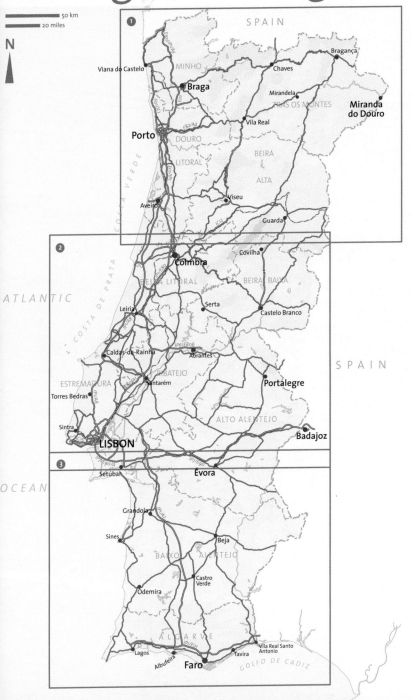

25 km
10 miles

N

Verin

Serra da Coroa
Serra de Montezinho
Rio de Onor
Franca
Parque Natural de Montezinho
Rio Sabor
Varge
Vinhais
jurge
Aguas
Frias
Pedra Bulideira
Castro de
Avelãs
Gimonde
Bragança
Santo
Estêvão
Reboredo
Outeiro
aves
São Julião de
Montenegro
Vilarandelo
Torre de
Dona Chama
Vimioso
Valpaços
Lamas de Podence
Macedo de Cavaleiros
minas
Mirandela
Algóso
TRÁS OS MONTES
Miranda
do Douro
Murça
Sendim
Vila Flor
Mogadouro
Alijo
Sampaio
Serra do Mogadouro
Castelo Branco
Carrazeda
de Ansiães
Rio Sabor
Lagoaça
ão
Torre de Moncorvo
Mata
io João
squeira
Quintana do
Vale do Meão
Nacional
do Reboredo
Rio Douro
Pocinho
Serra do Reboredo
Vila Nova de Foz Coa
Freixo de
Espada a Cinta
Freixe de Numão
Rio Douro
SPAIN
edono
Barca de Alva
em
Rio Côa
Marialva
Figueira de
Castelo Rodrigo
rnancelhe
Castelo Rodrigo
te de Abade
Serra da Marofa
Trancoso
Pinhel
Vila Franca
das Naves
Freches
Almeida
lorico
Beira
Ratoeira
Cavadoude
Vilar Formoso
Linhares
Faia
Guarda
Tejo
Valhelhas
Belmonte
Sabugal

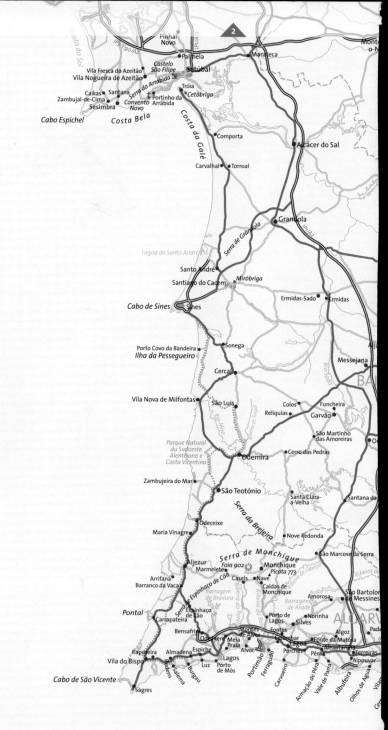

Pinhal
Novo

Palmela

Marateca

Mont
o-N

Castelo
São Filipe

Setúbal

Vila Fresca do Azeitão
Vila Nogueira de Azeitão

Tróia

Cetóbriga

Caixas   Santana
Zambujal-de-Cima
Sesimbra

Convento
Novo

Portinho da
Arrábida

Costa do Sol

Serra do Arrábida

Costa da Galé

Cabo Espichel   *Costa Bela*

Comporta

Alcácer do Sal

Carvalhal   Torroal

Grândola

Lagoa de Santo André

Serra de Grândola

Santo André

Santiago do Cacém

Miróbriga

Ermidas-Sado   Ermidas

Cabo de Sines   Sines

Alj

Porto Covo da Bandeira
Ilha da Pessegueiro

Sonega

Messejana

BA

Cercal

Vila Nova de Milfontas

São Luis

Colos   Funcheira

Reliquias   Garvão

São Martinho
das Amoreiras

O

*Parque Natural
du Sudoeste
Alentejano e
Costa Vicentina*

Odemira

Cerro das Pedras

Zambujeira do Mar

São Teotónio

Santa Clara-
a-Velha

Santana da

Odeceixe

Serra da Brejeira

Maria Vinagre

Nove Redonda

Aljezur   *Serra de Monchique*   São Marcos da Serra

Marmelete   *Foia 902*   Monchique
Picota 773

Arrifana
Barranco da Vaca

Casels   Nave

Caldas de
Monchique

Amorosa   São Bartolom
de Messines

Pontal

Serra de Espinhaço de Cão

*Barragem
de Bravura*

*Barragem
de Arade*

ALGAR

Carrapateira

Espinhaço
de Cão

Porto de
Lagos

Norinha

Silves

Algoz   Pade

Bensafrim

Odiáxere

Montes
de Alvor

Fontes

Estombar

Fonte da Matosa

Rapoteira   Almadena   Espiche

Meia
Praia

Lagoa

Porches

Alcantarilha

Ferreiras

Vila do Bispo

Luz

Alvor

Portimão

Pêra

Alpouvar

Burgau

Lagos
Porto
de Mós

Ferragudo

Canoeiro

Armação de Pêra

Vale de Parra

Albufeira

Olhos de Agua

Vila

Cabo de São Vicente

Sagres

Salema

Serra de Monchique

ATLANTIC OCEAN

2 ▲ ALTO ALENTEJO

São Bente de Castris
ÉVORA
Monte das Flores
Quinta de Valverde
São Miguel de Machede
Redondo
Montoito
Aldeia do Outeiro
Corval
Telheiro
Monsarraz
Reguengos de Monsarraz
Xerez de Baixo
Mourão

Viana do Alentejo

Alvito

Serra de Mendro
Vidigueira
Cuba
Moura
Safara
Barrancos
Santo Aleixo da Restauração

Beringel
Beja
Santa Clara de Louredo
Pisoes
Serpa
Vila Verde de Ficalho
São Brás
Aldeia Nova de São Bento

Trindade

NTEJO

Pule do Lobo
Serra de Serpa

Amendeoira
Algodor
São Marcos da Ataboeira
Corte Gafo de Cima
Serra de Mertola
Mina de São Domingos
Moreanes
Mertola

Ribeira de Oeiras

São Sebastião dos Carros
São Miguel do Pinheiro
nodôvar

Ribeira do Vascão

Alcoutim
Sanlucar de Guadiana
Martim Longo
Pereiro
Barrada
Corte João Marques
Vaqueiros
Parque Mineiro Cova das Mouros
Corte Serranos
Cachopo
Ribeira de Odeleite
Odeleite
aeixial
Vermelhhos
ão
Portela
Serra de Alcaria do Cume
Azinhal
ontes Novos
Barranco do Velho
Junqueira
Monte Francisco
Castro Marim
Querença
Estorninhos
Clarianes
Malhada de Peres
Palheirinhos
Eira da Palma
Santa Catarina da Fonte do Bispo
Conceição
ta Bárbara
exe
Santo Estêvão
Cabanas
mancil
Moncarapacho
Luz de Tavira
rias
Pechão
nta do Lago
FARO
Olhão

Ilha da Armona
Ilha de Tavira
GOLFO DE CADIZ
Ilha da Barreta
Cabo de Santa Marie
Ilha da Culatra

Ayamonte
Vila Real Santo Antonio
Monte Gordo

SPAIN

N

25 km
10 miles

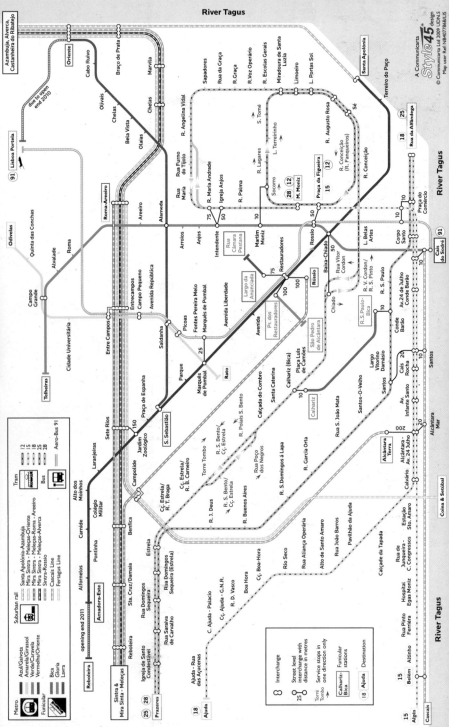